→ # Nicholson's

# London street finder

Designed by Robert Nicholson
and Romek Marber

© Robert Nicholson Publications
Based upon the Ordnance Survey
map with the sanction of the Controller
of H.M. Stationery Office.
Crown copyright reserved

Published and distributed by
Robert Nicholson Publications
16 Neals yard, Shorts gardens
London WC2N 9DP

Index Computer typeset by
Computerprint, London

Printed in England by
Fletcher & Son, Norwich

SBN 90056837 2

**Symbols**

† Church

⊕ Hospital

🚗 Car park

🏛 Historic building

🏘 Small buildings

🎒 Schools

🏟 Sports stadium

⊖ London Underground station

🚂 British Rail station

🚌 Coach station

✈ Air terminal

⇄ British Rail terminal

**PO** Post Office

**Pol** Police station

→ One ways (central area only)

:::::: Footpath

300 ▶
◀ 400 Figure indicating the direction
of street numbering and the
approximate position

Outer area
████████████████ ½ mile
▭▭▭▭▭ ½ km

Large scale  Central area
████████████████████████ ½ mile
▭▭▭▭▭▭ ½ km

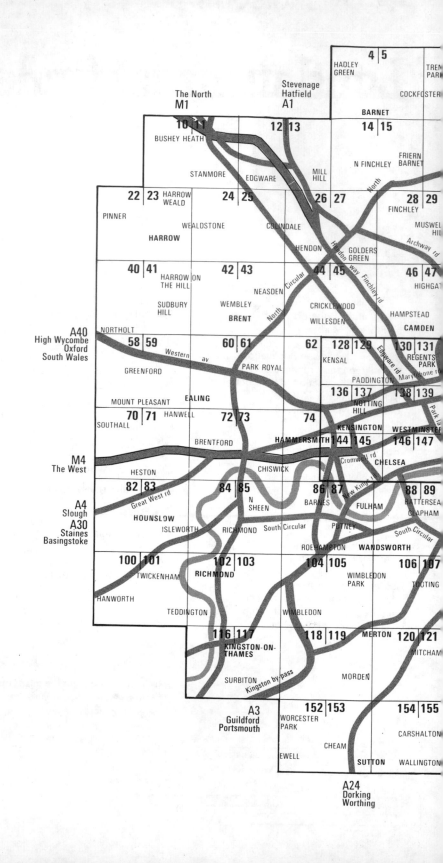

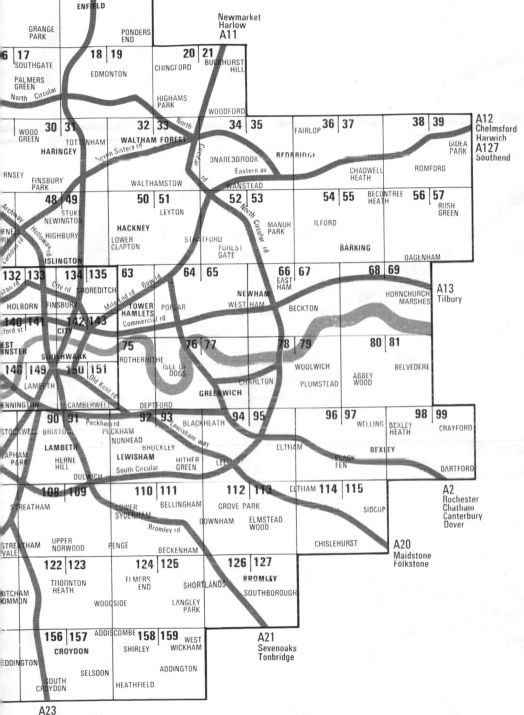

# Maps and routes

This general map, apart from giving map numbers and general orientation, has been designed to show major road routes leading into London.

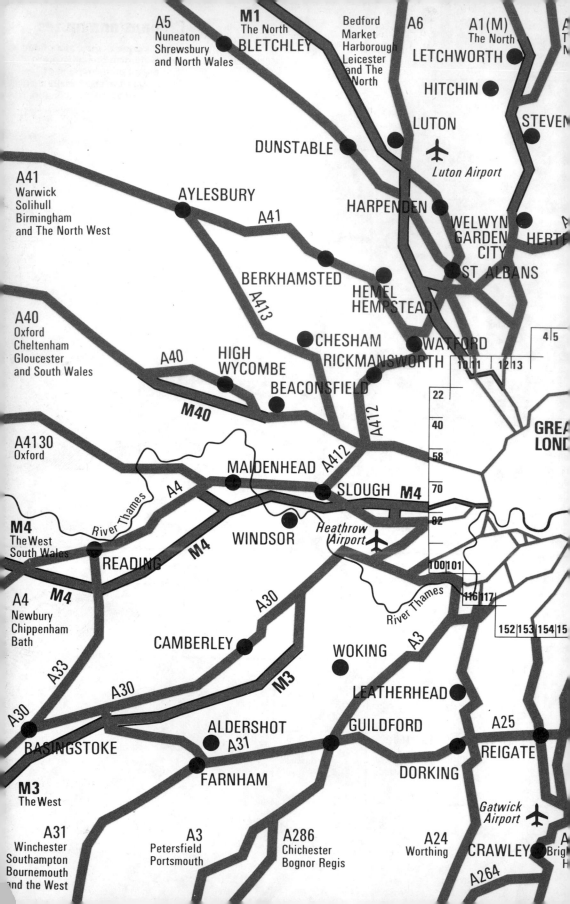

A10
Cambridge
Ely
King's Lynn

A11
Newmarket
Norwich

SAFFRON
WALDON

A604
Cambridge

## Commuter map

This shows the area covered by the London Street Finder in relation to south east England, and gives major routes out of London.

✈ *Stansted Airport*  A120

COLCHESTER

BISHOPS STORTFORD

SAWBRIDGEWORTH

A12
Ipswich
Lowestoft
Great
Yarmouth
Norwich

A133
Clacton
Harwich

WARE

A130

WITHAM

A414

HARLOW

HODDESDON

CHESHUNT

CHELMSFORD

A128

A130

A12

BRENTWOOD

A127

20 21

35 36 37 38 39

Southend
Airport ✈

BASILDON

SOUTHEND

used in
I in
on
t Finder

57

A128

A13

69

81

TILBURY

98 99

GRAVESEND

114 115

A2

126 127

A2

68 159

GILLINGHAM

SITTINGBOURNE

A21

A225

A20

A25

M2
Dover

A25

SEVENOAKS

MAIDSTONE

A20(M)

A20
Hythe
Folkestone
Dover

TONBRIDGE

ASHFORD

EAST
GRINSTEAD

TUNBRIDGE
WELLS

0        5        10
Miles

A22
Uckfield
Eastbourne
Newhaven

A21
Hastings

Kilometres

0      5      10      15

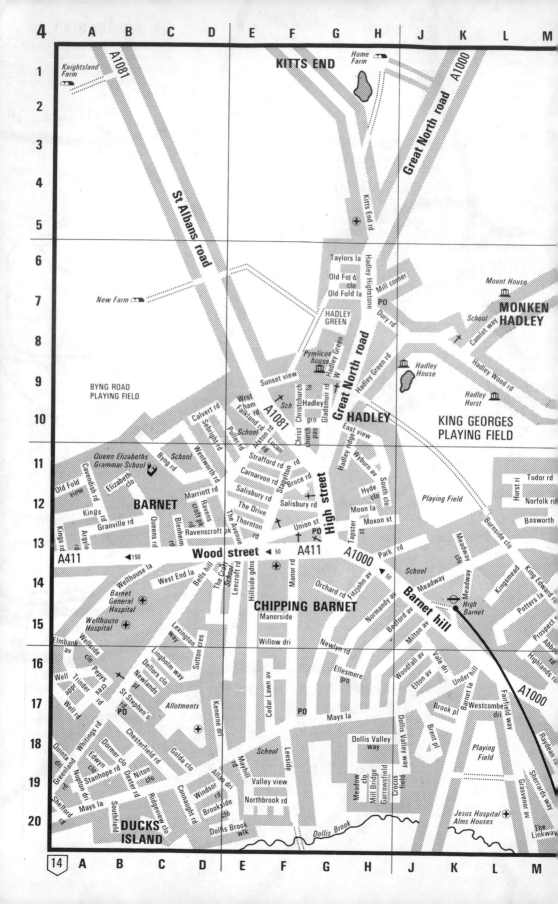

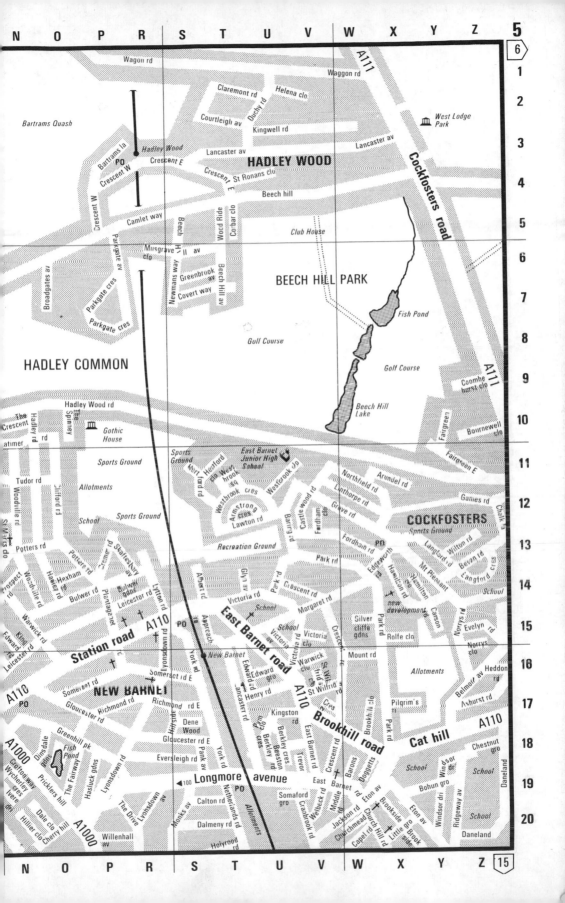

Wagon rd
A111
Waggon rd
Claremont rd
Helena clo
West Lodge
Park
Courtleigh av
Duchy rd
Kingwell rd
Bartrams Quash
Lancaster av
Lancaster av
Bartrams la
Hadley Wood
PO
Crescent E
Crescent W
**HADLEY WOOD**
Cockfosters road
Crescent E
St Ronans clo
Crescent W
Beech hill
Camlet way
Beech
Wood Ride
Corbar clo
Club House
Musgrave
H'll av
clo
Parkgate av
Broadgates av
Newmans way
Greenbrook
av
Covert way
Beech Hill av
**BEECH HILL PARK**
Parkgate cres
Fish Pond
Parkgate cres
Golf Course
A111
Coombe
hurst clo
**HADLEY COMMON**
Golf Course
The
Crescent
Hadley Wood rd
The
Spinney
Beech Hill
Lake
Fairgreen
Bournewell
clo
atimer
rd
rd
Hadley rd
Gothic
House
Fairgreen E
Sports Ground
Sports
Ground
East Barnet
Junior High
School
Arundel rd
Games rd
Tudor rd
Allotments
Hasford
Westbrook
sq
Westbrook cres
Northfield rd
Lynthorpe rd
Chalk la
Woodville rd
Clifford rd
St Mary's clo
School
Sports Ground
Armstrong
cres
Lawton rd
Grove rd
Fordham
clo
**COCKFOSTERS**
Sports Ground
Potters rd
Recreation Ground
Barring rd
Castle wood rd
Fordham rd
PO
Langford rd
Witton rd
Bevan rd
Langford cres
Potters rd
Park rd
Eddyworth
Mt Pleasant
Hexham
Prospect rd
Woodville rd
Hadley rd
Hamilton rd
Carson
School
Park rd
Crescent rd
Bulwer rd
Bulwell
gdns
Leicester rd
Plantagenet
Albert rd
Victoria rd
Margaret rd
new
development
Norrys rd
Evelyn rd
Warwick rd
King
Edward
Lytton rd
Lyndhurst rd
PO
School
School
Victoria
av
Victoria
clo
Silver
cliffs
gdns
Rolfe clo
Norrys
clo
Leicester rd
**Station road**
A110
Approach
York rd
**East Barnet road**
Warwick
rd
Crescent rd
Mount rd
A110
A1000
PO
**NEW BARNET**
Somerset rd
Somerset rd E
New Barnet
Edward
Edward
gro
Lancaster rd
Henry rd
St Wilfrid's
A110
Allotments
Pilgrim's
rl
Belmor av
Heddon
rd
Ashurst rd
A110
Gloucester rd
Richmond rd
Richmond rd E
Dene
Wood
Kingston
rd
Brookhill clo
East Barnet rd
**Brookhill road**
Park rd
**Cat hill**
A110
Greenhill pk
Dene
Dinsdale
gdns
Fish Pond
Gloucester rd E
Pank rd
York rd
Berkley cres
Beeston
Berkley
cres
Trevor
Crescent rd
Barons
School
Windsor
dr
Chestnut
gro
School
Daneland
Grafton way
Wycherley
cres
Ivere
dri
Haslock gdns
Pricklers hill
Eversleigh rd
▲100
**Longmore avenue**
PO
Somaford
gro
East
Barnet
rd
Welbeck rd
Eton av
Bohun gro
School
A1000
The Drive
Lyonsdown
av
The Fairway
Lyonsdown rd
Monks av
Calton rd
Netherlands rd
Cranbrook gro
Mdale
Jackson rd
Brookside
Church Hill gro
Windsor dri
Ridgeway rd
School
Dale clo
Hilter clo Cherry hill
A1000
Willenhall
av
Dalmeny rd
Holyrood rd
Churchmead
Capel rd side
Brook
Little gro
Daneland

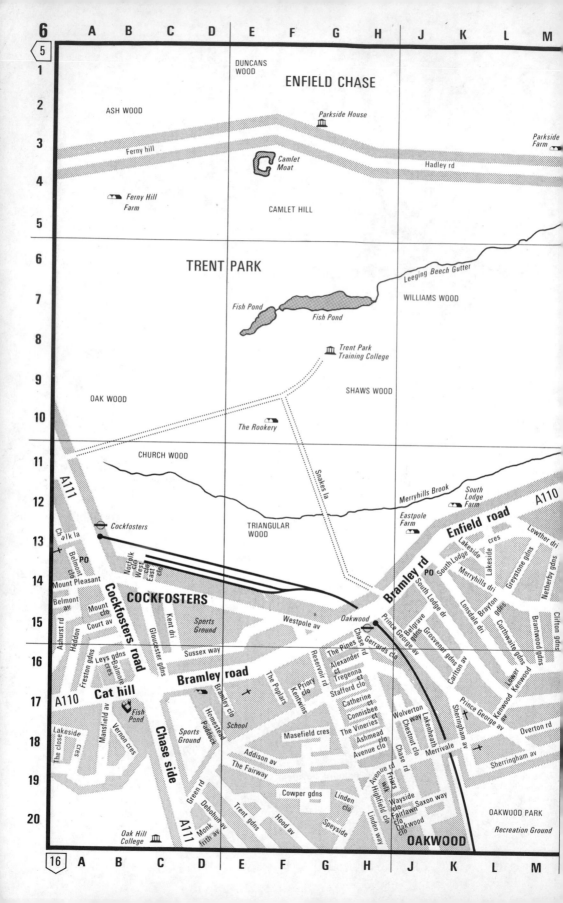

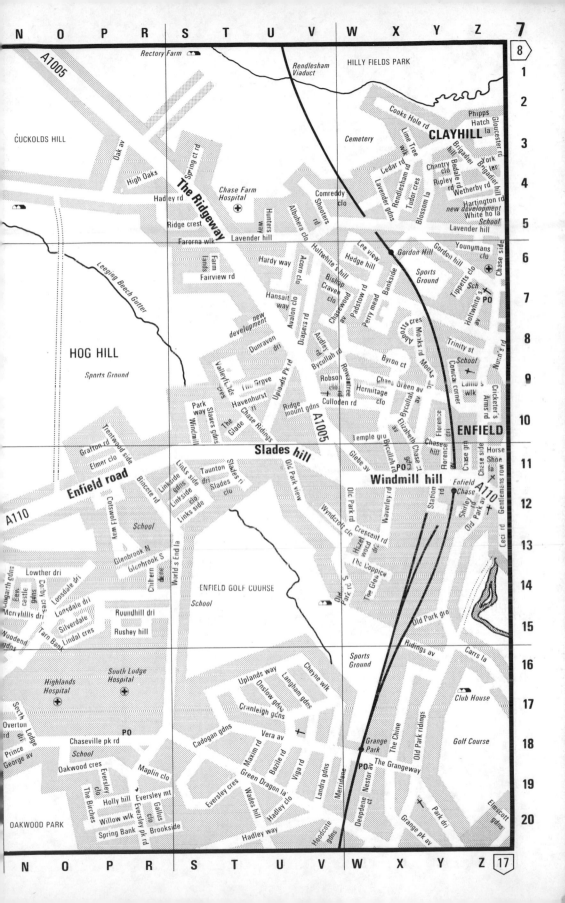

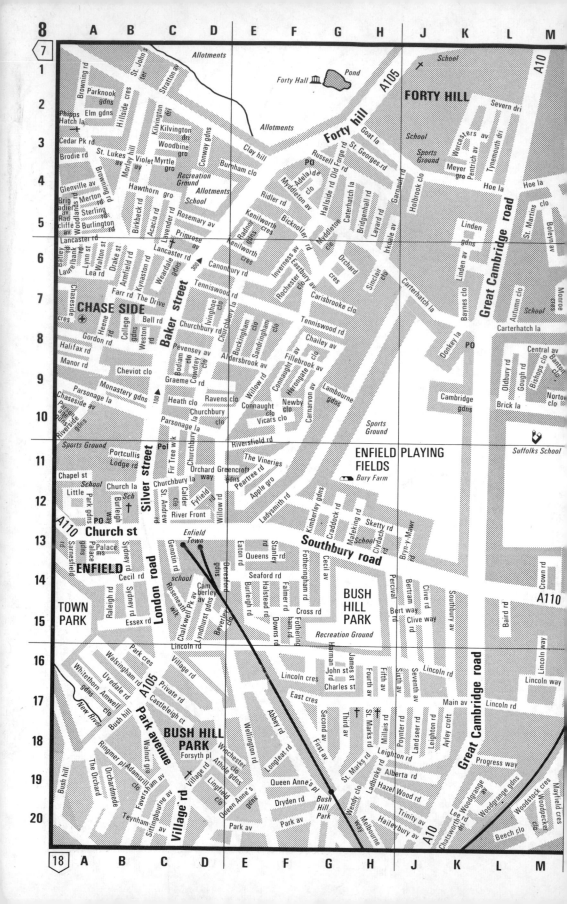

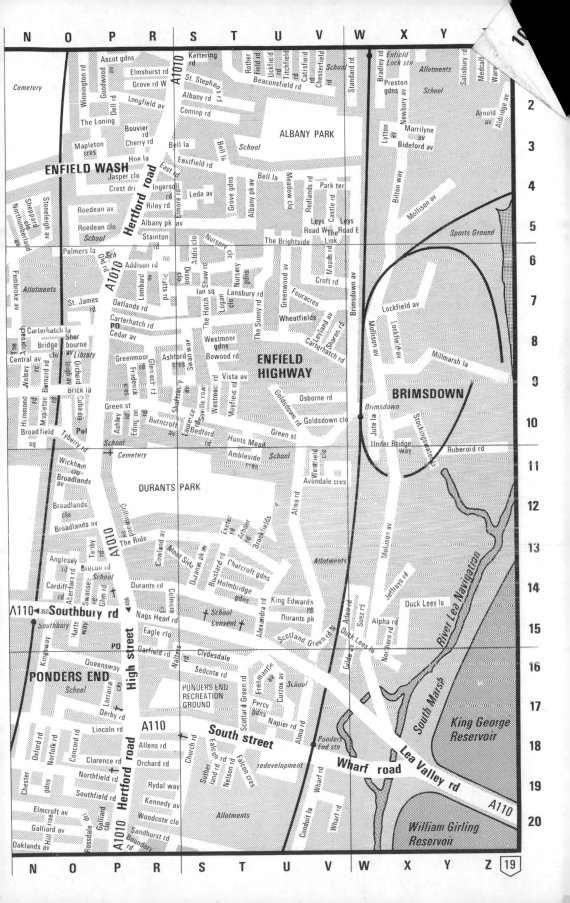

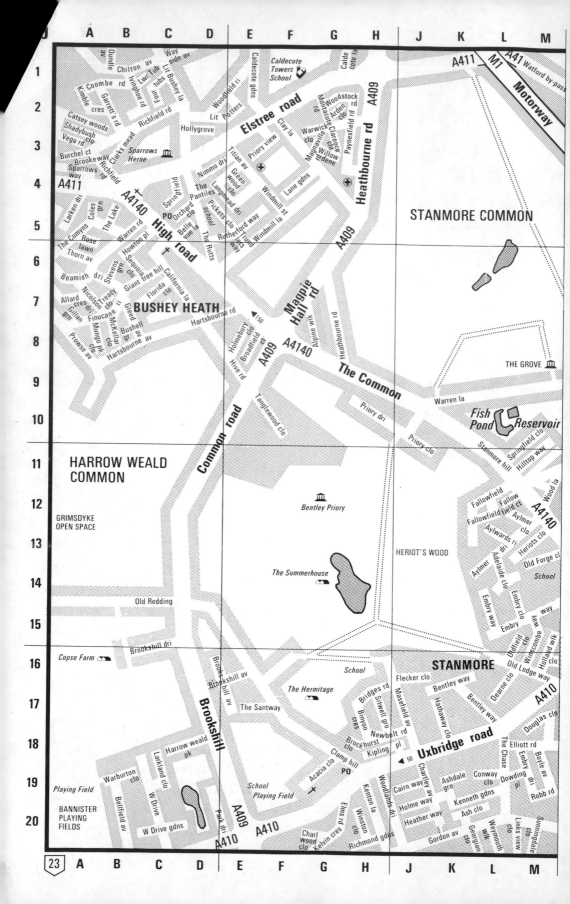

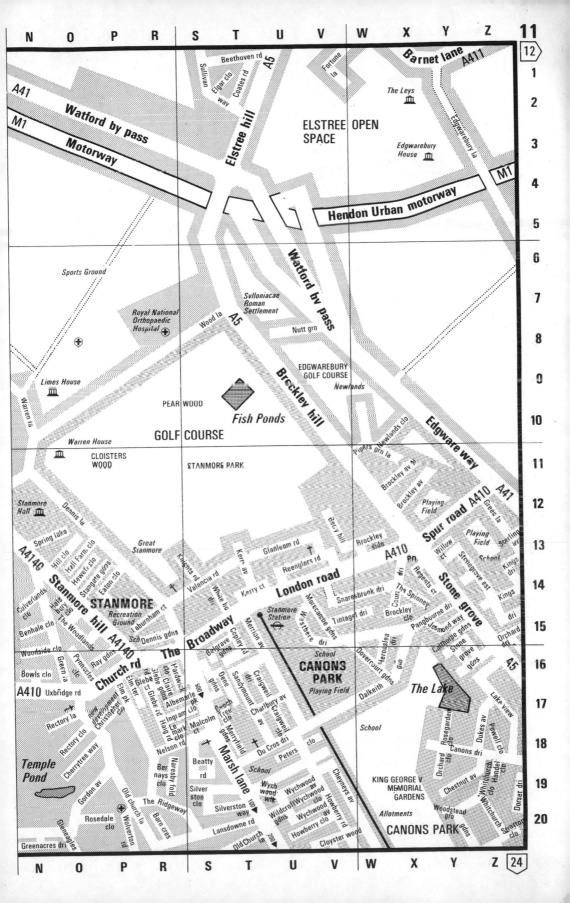

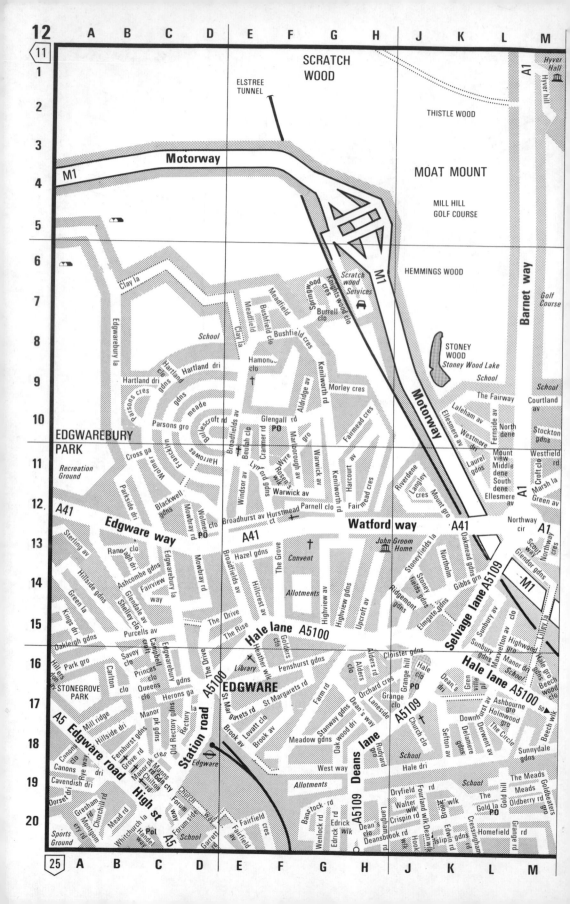

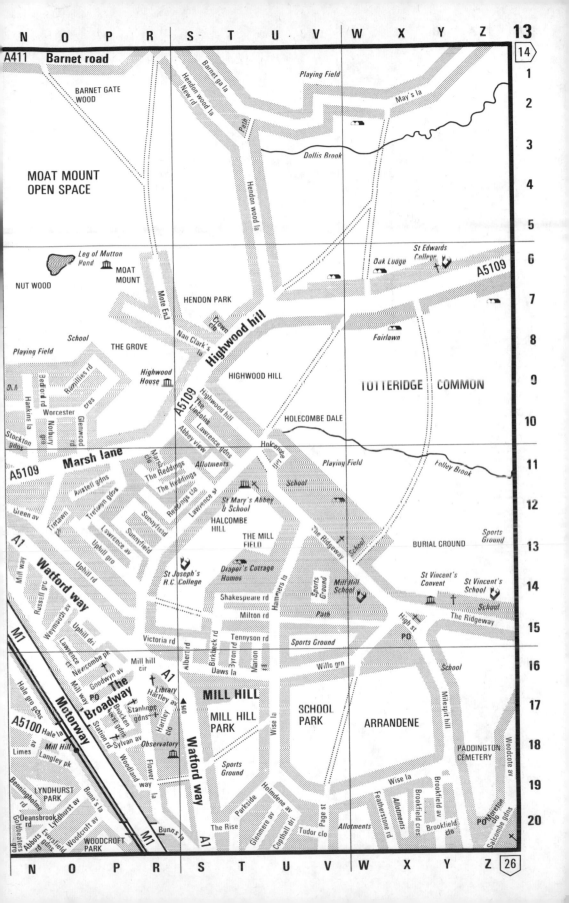

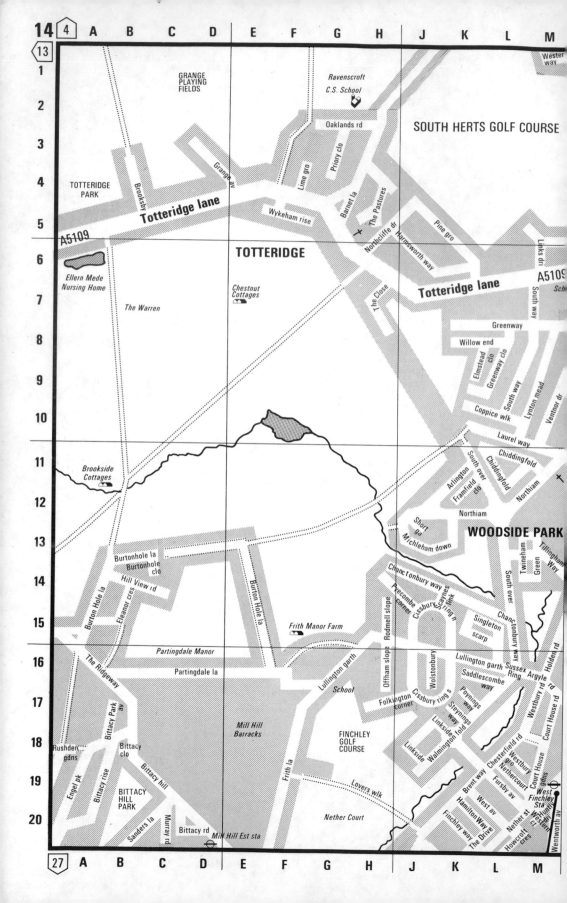

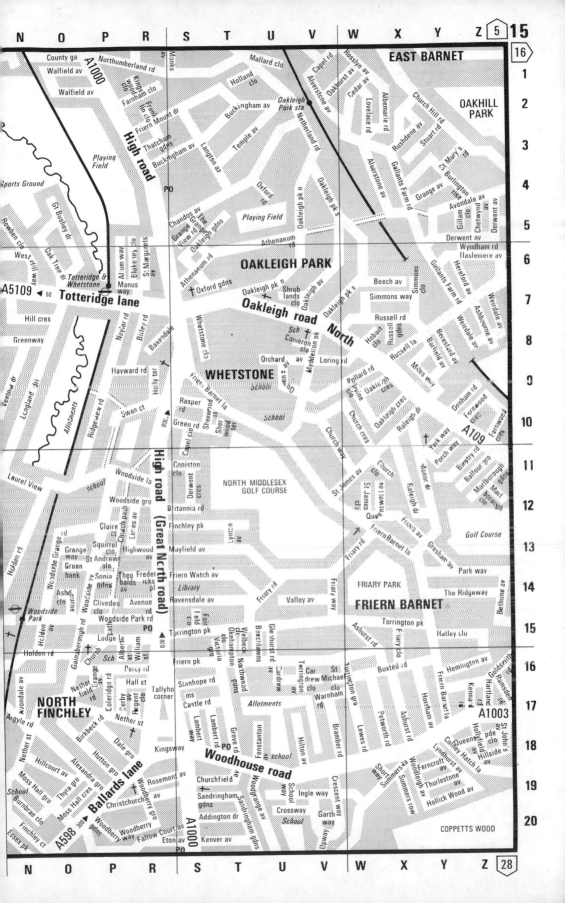

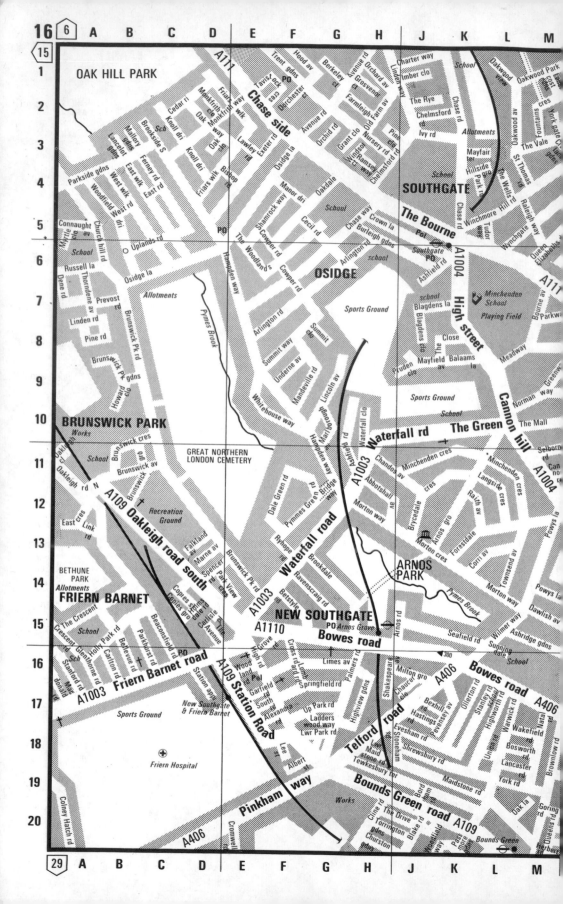

1
2
3
4
5
6
7
8
9
10
11
12
13
14
15
16
17
18
19
20

GROVELANDS PARK

Boating Lake

WINCHMORE HILL

Broadfields
The Alders
Cross ways Park clo
Grange Pk av Bush hill way
Green Dragon la
Devonshire rd
A105 Ridge av
Bridge
Elseidene rd
River Bank
Percy rd

Springbank
Meadow bank
Eversley Pk rd
Houndsden rd
The Spinney
Broadfields av
Cresswell way
Hill crest
Gatward clo
Handsworth gdns
Green Moor Link
Myddelton gdns
Sherbrook gdns
Drayton gdns
way
Firs la

Winchmore Hill rd
The Vale
The Glade
Byland clo
Gladeside
Laurel dri
Paulin dri
Vicars Moor la
Vicars Moor la
Shrubbery gdns
PO
Elm Pk Beaulieu gdns
Firs la

The Sale
Elm Bank
Arthur rd
Park ho
Park ga
Park view
Church hill
Church hill
Stone Hall rd
Hill House clo
Sch
Wades gro
Barber clo
Ringwood
school
Berry clo
Radcliffe rd
River la

Tintern rd
Branscombe gdns
Denleigh gdns
School
Yew Tree
The Green
Winchmore Hill
Green lanes

Green Elizabeth's
Downes
Seaforth gdns
Wilson st
PO
Rose neath
Kings
Station rd
Fords gro
Beverley

SOUTHGATE
The Bourne
A111
Broadwalk
Sports Ground
Mudcroft
Sports Ground
Brackendale
Oaklands
Beechdale
Hillfield pk
Woodland way
Sports Ground
Heppers rd
Hurst ct
Allow rd
Arundel gdns
Fernleigh rd
Haslemere rd
Coombe
Pol
A105 Highfield rd
Cedars av
Carpenter
School
Laburnum gdns
Laburnum gro
School
Hyde Park av
Ivy de Park gdns
Compton rd
Orpington
7 rd
School
Green
library

Bourne hill
St Georges rd
Cranley gdns
Fox la
The Mall
Selborne rd
Timberley rd
Oakfield rd
The Ridgeway
Sports Ground
School
A111
Burford gdns
Caversham av
Westlake
Hoppers rd
College rd
Lytton av
Eaton Pk rd
Avondale
Meadow croft av
Stonard rd
Crestbrook
Oaktree av
Green lanes
River av
Green wood gdns
River av
Woodberry av
Barrowell grn
Barrow clo
Farndale av
Crawford gdns
Ensign dri
Ashgrove
Barrowell grn
The Larches
Sports Ground
The Fairway
Firs croft
Myrtle rd

PALMERS GREEN
Conway rd
Harlech rd
Ullswater rd
Derwent rd
Lakeside rd
Grovelands rd
Cul-Park rd
A105
Devonshire rd
Ushorne
Windsor rd
Park av
PO
Lightcliffe rd
New River cres
Wentworth
Mintern clo
The Rowans
Firs la
Birch
Pem broke rd
The Larches
New Park av
Pembroke rd
Connaught
Hedge lane A111
Waldeck

Hedge lane

A11004
Alderman's hill
PO
Conway rd
Ulleswater rd
Derwent rd
Lakeside rd
Green lanes
Palmers Green & Southgate
Devonshire rd
A105
Fox la
A1004
Lodge dri
The Grove
The Crest
Riverway
School
Hamilton cres
Lynbridge gdns
Doveridge gdns
Cunnaught way
Contaught gdns
Munster gdns
Ulster gdns
Dorchester av
Ashley gdns
Farriday gdns
Kenmore gdns
A406

BROOMFIELD PARK
Broomfield House
Broomfield la
Broomfield
Broomfield la
Elmwood
Balmont av
Hawthorn av
Cranford av
Town Hall
Library
School
Kings Arms Bridge
Ecclesbourne gdns
The Grove
The Rise
Oakthorpe rd
Riverway
Climes av
Arnold av
Law rence av
Wauthier clo
Callard av
North Circular road
200
Mitchell rd
Shillitoe rd
Tile Kiln la
Owen rd
Clappers
Lister gdns
Newlce
Steeple Chesterfield

A406 North Circular road
Elvendon rd
Beech rd
Granville rd
Belsize av
Spencer av
Pymmes
Palmerston rd
Russell rd
Palmerston cres
Elmdale rd
Broomfield av
Pymmes
Regents av
Hereward gdns
Melville gdns
Fairbrook clo
Princes av
Tottenhall
Beale clo
Pasteur gdns
Queens land av
Empire av
Canada av
Tasmania

Cheshire
Park
Mar quis
rd
A105
PO
Lyndhurst rd
Maryland rd
Sidney av
Princes av
Tottenhall rd
School
Melbourne av
Grenoble gdns
Kelvin av
Belsize av
Berkshire gdns
Upsell av
Upsdell av
Norfolk clo
Norfolk av
Wolves la
Green lanes
Fairbrook clo
Grenoble gdns
Sports Ground
Sports Ground
Norfolk av
Norfolk av
Devonshire Hill la
Devonia gdns
Mayfair gdns
Devonshire Hill la

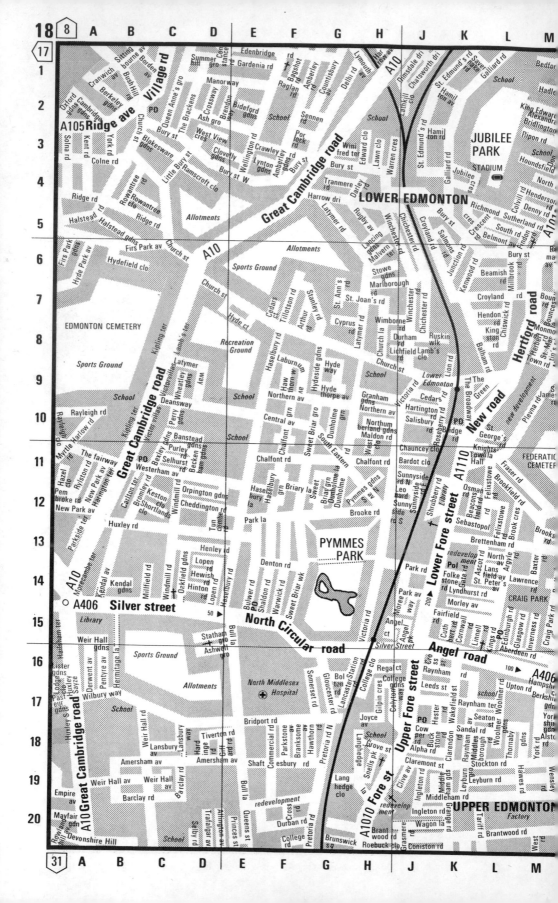

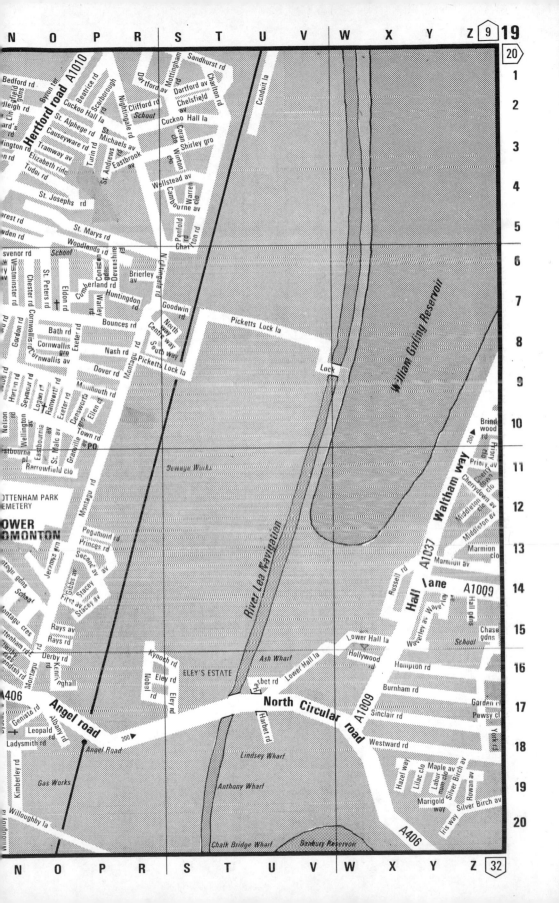

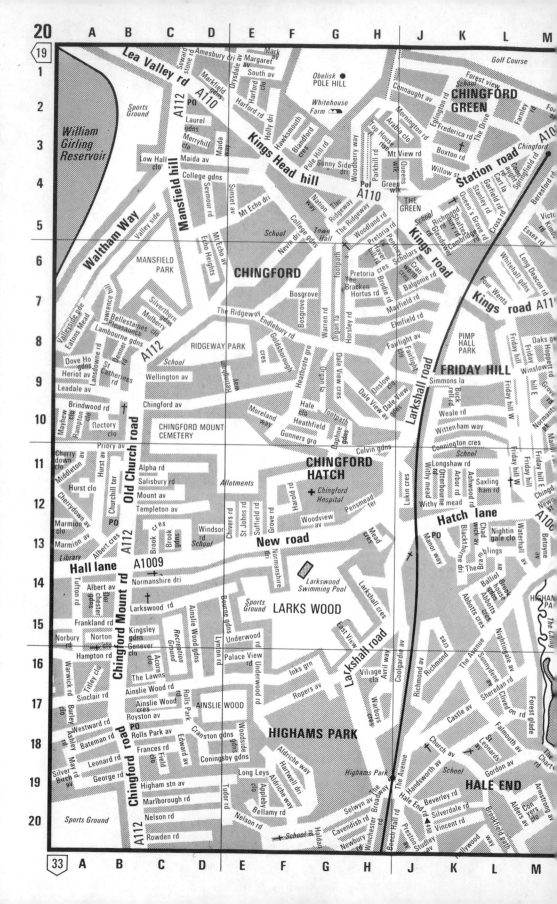

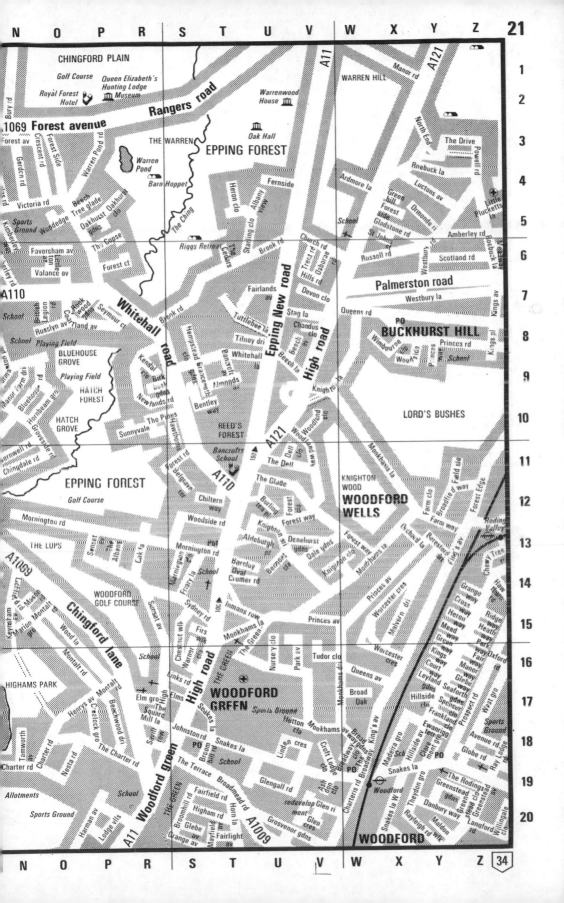

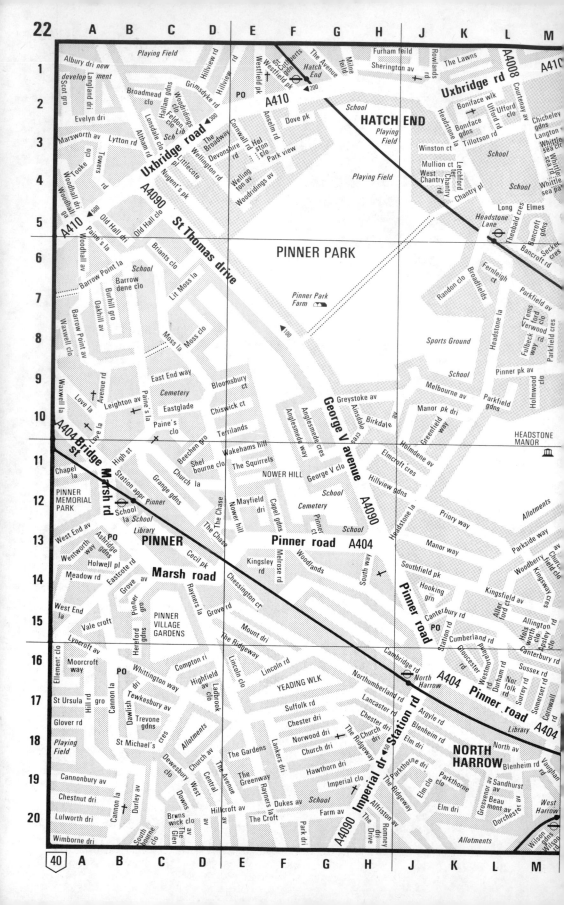

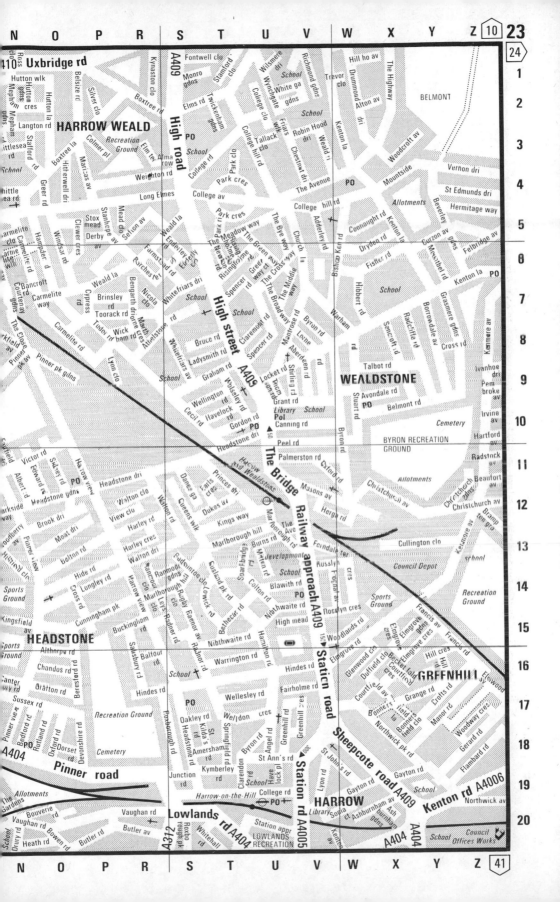

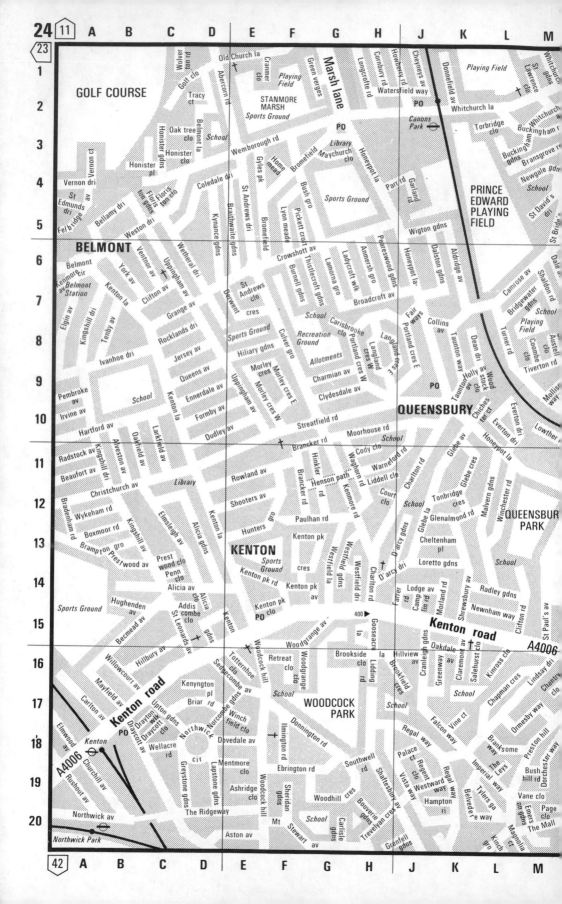

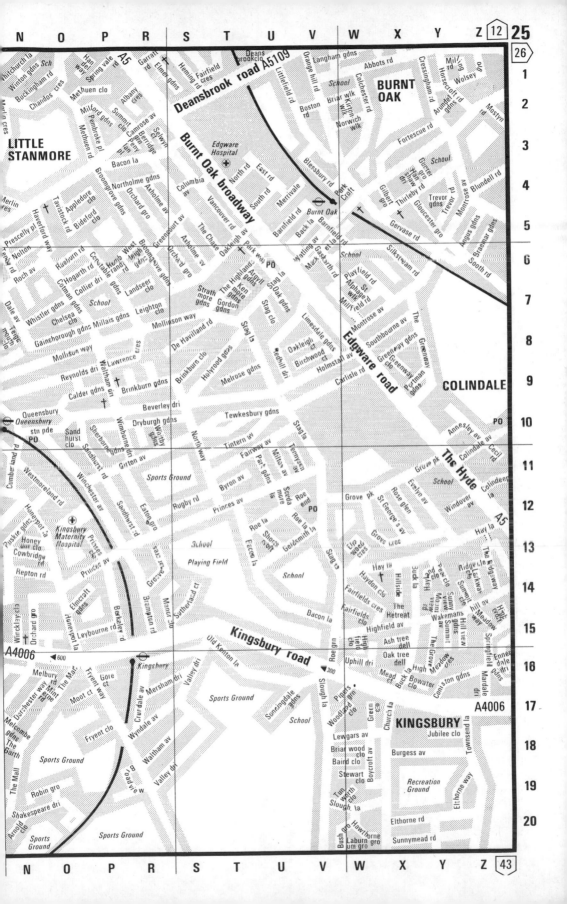

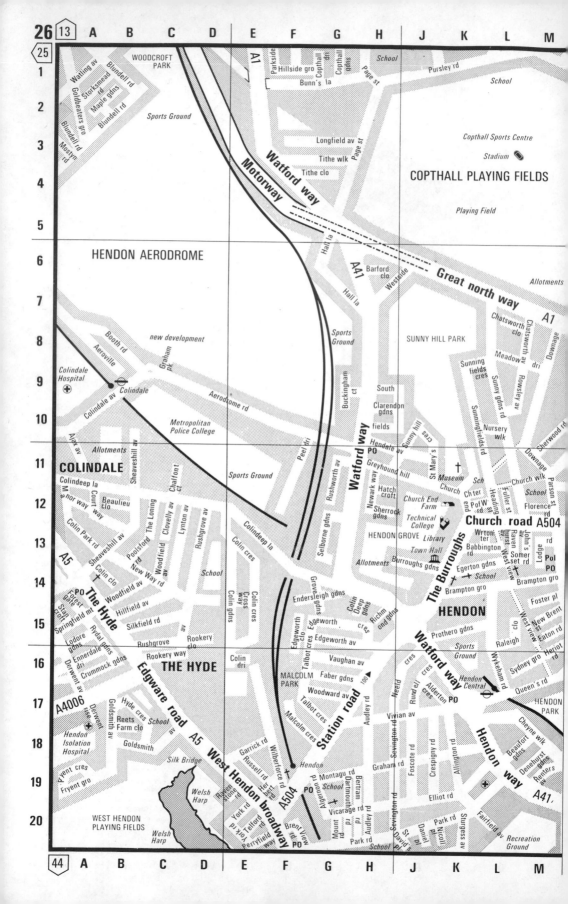

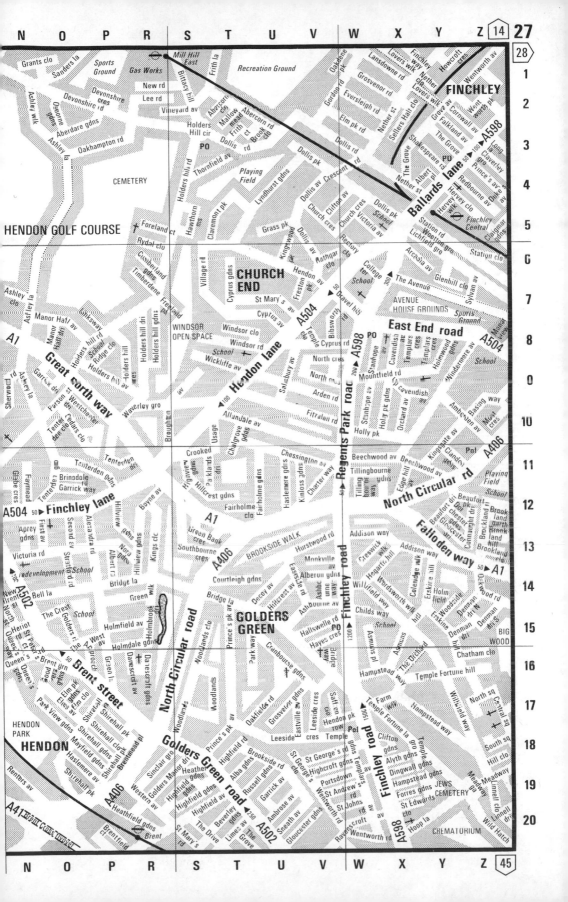

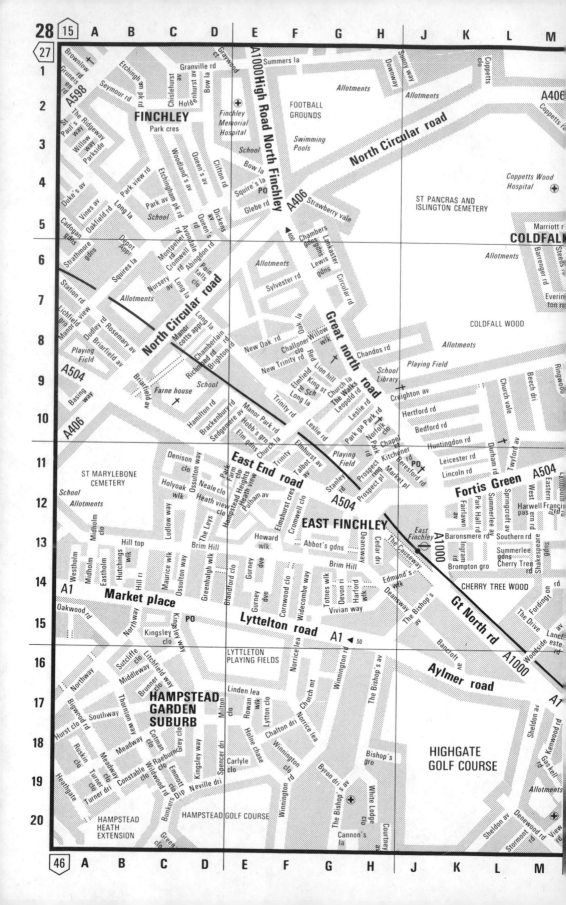

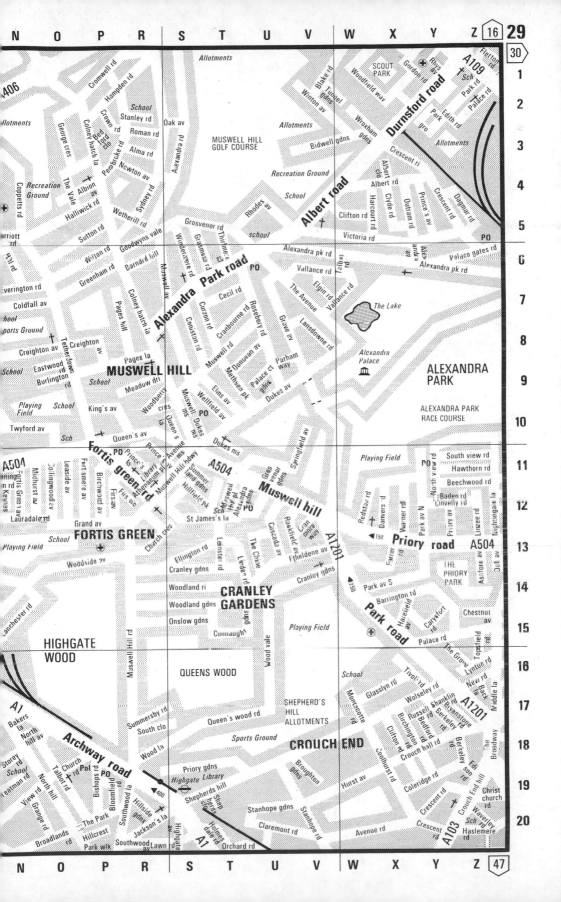

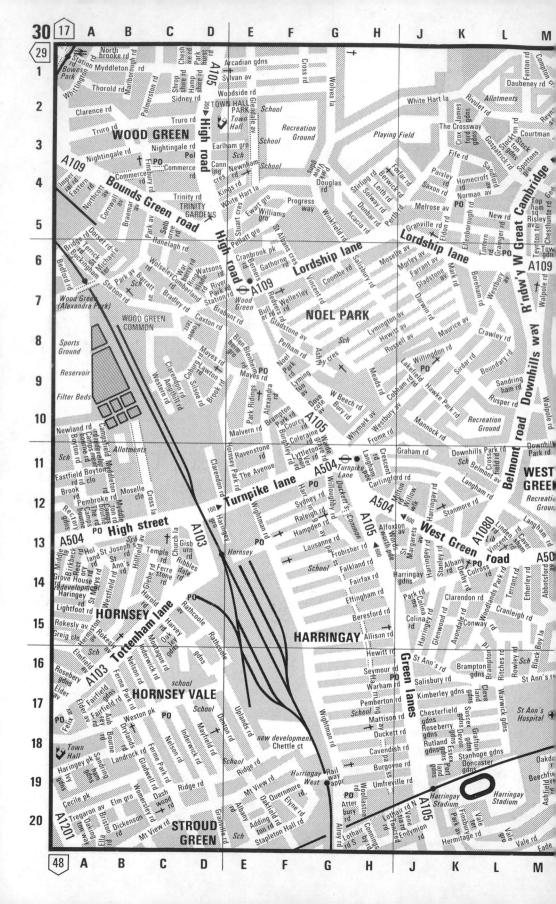

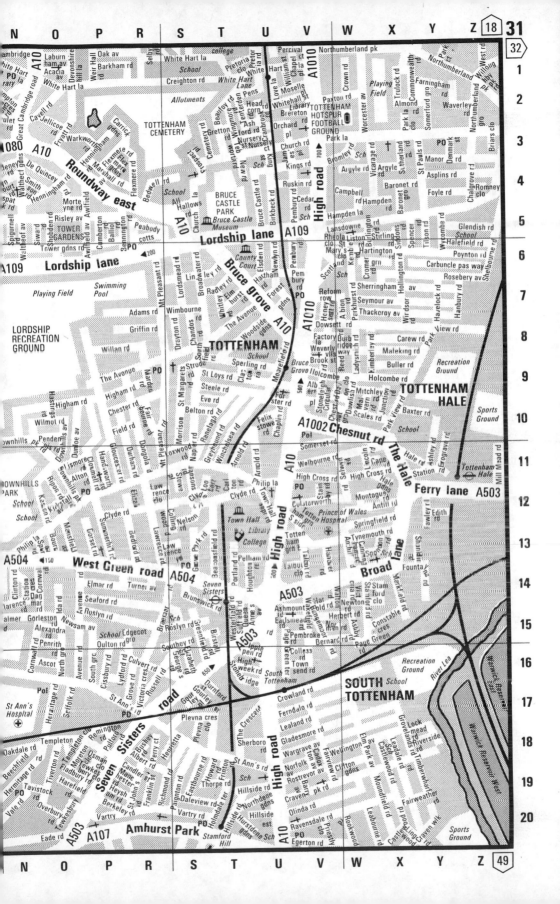

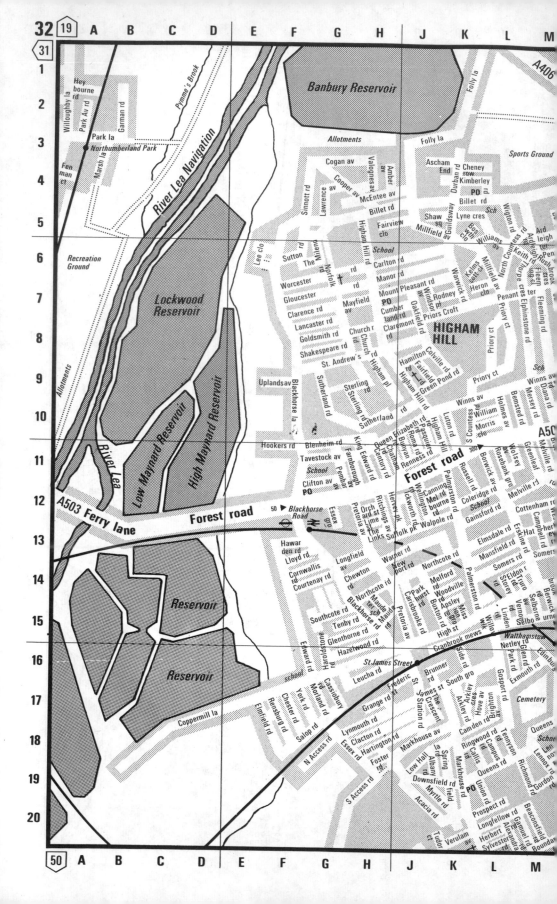

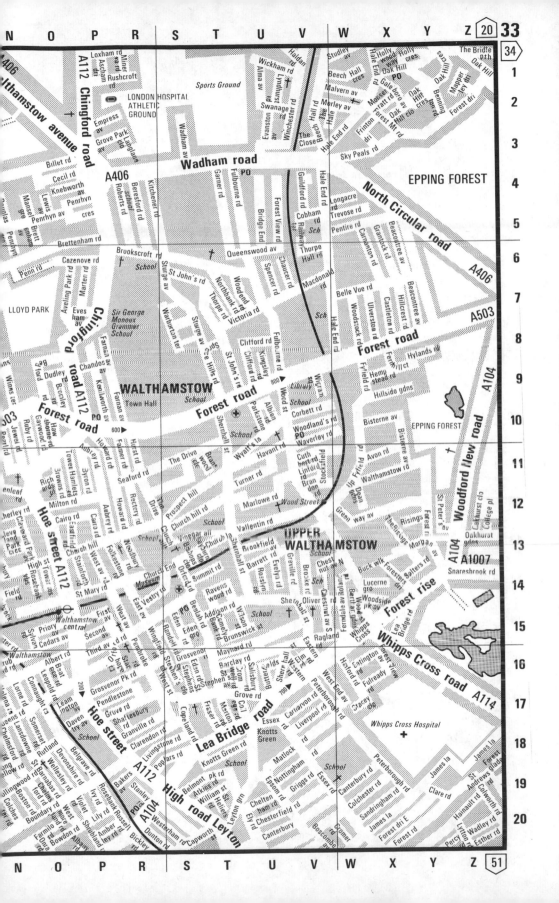

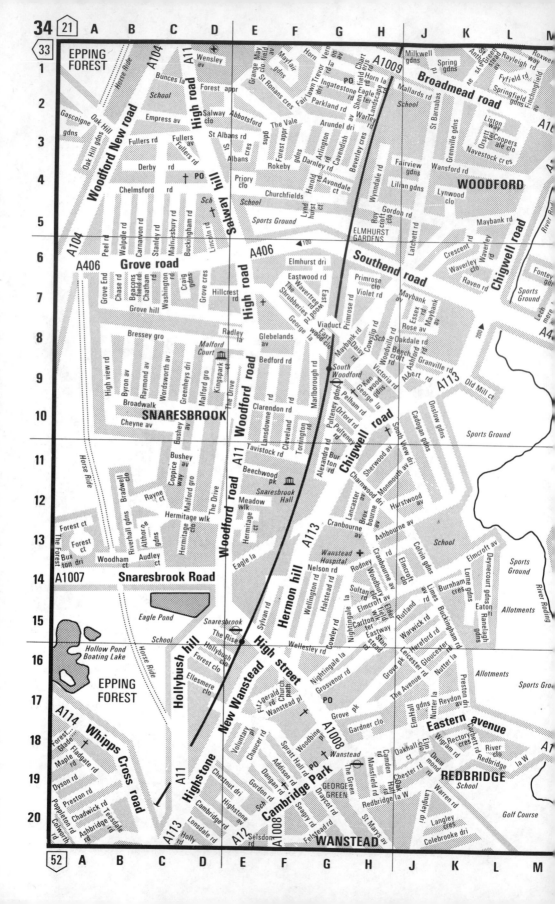

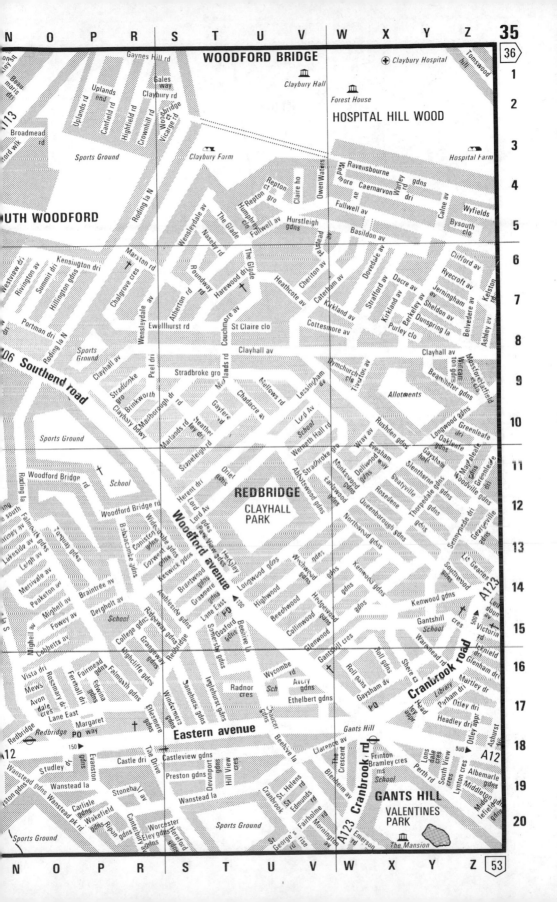

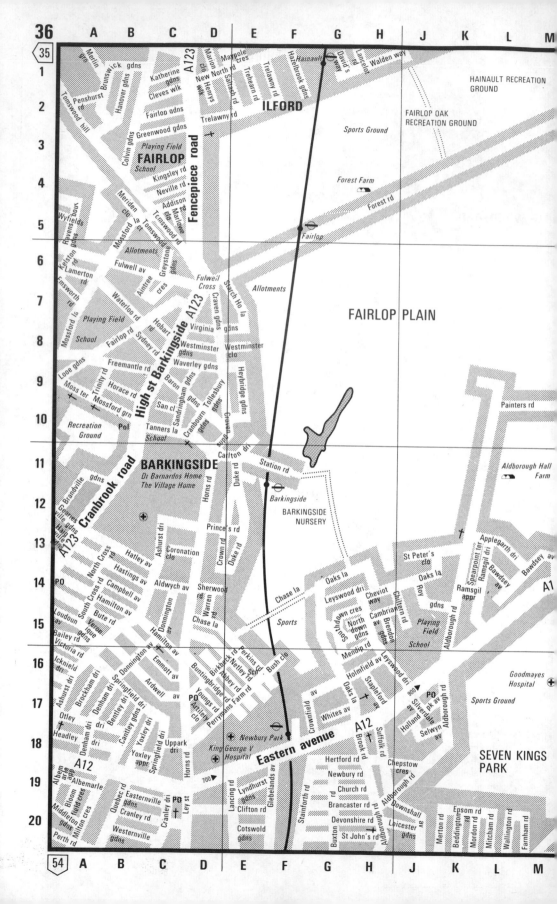

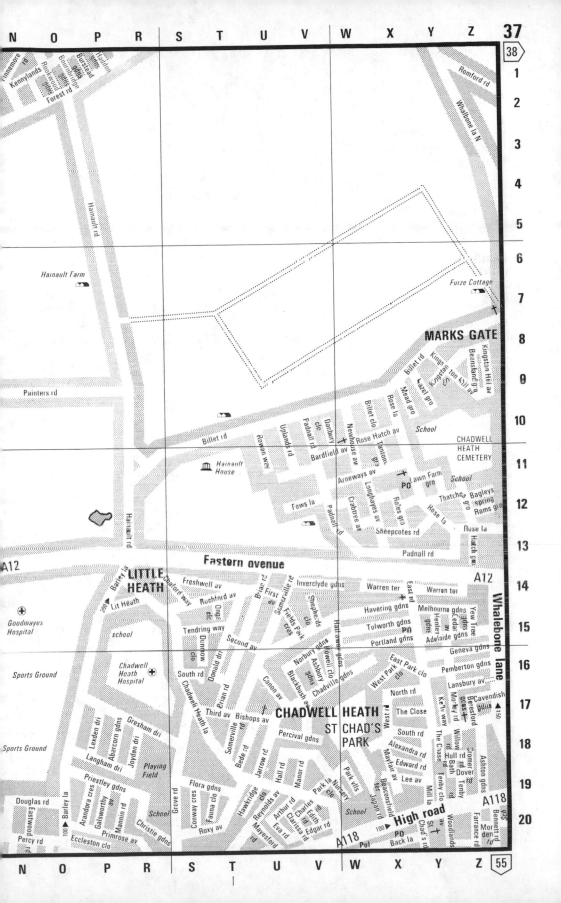

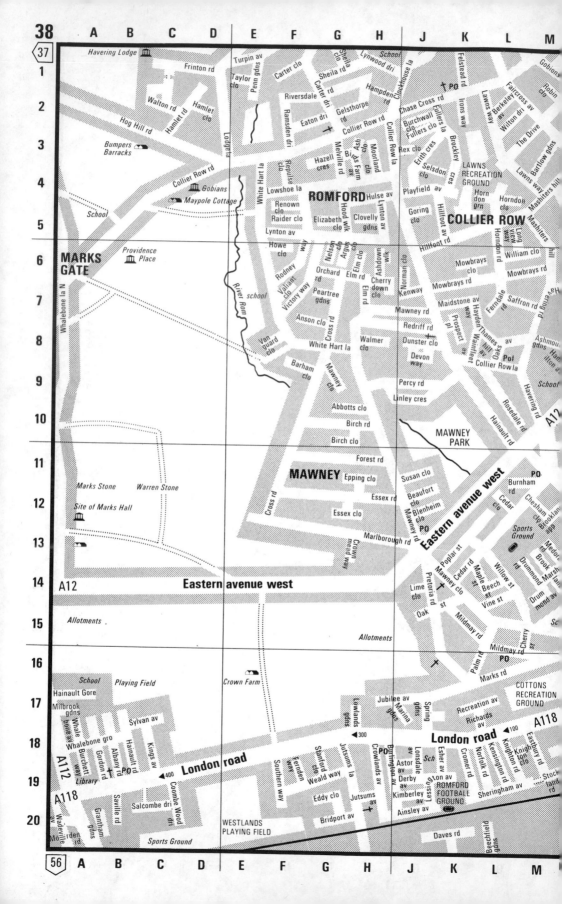

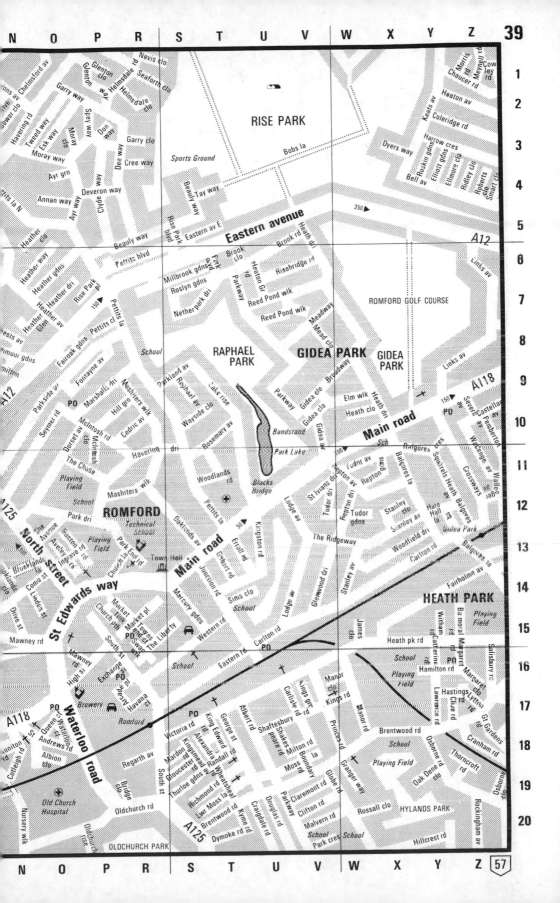

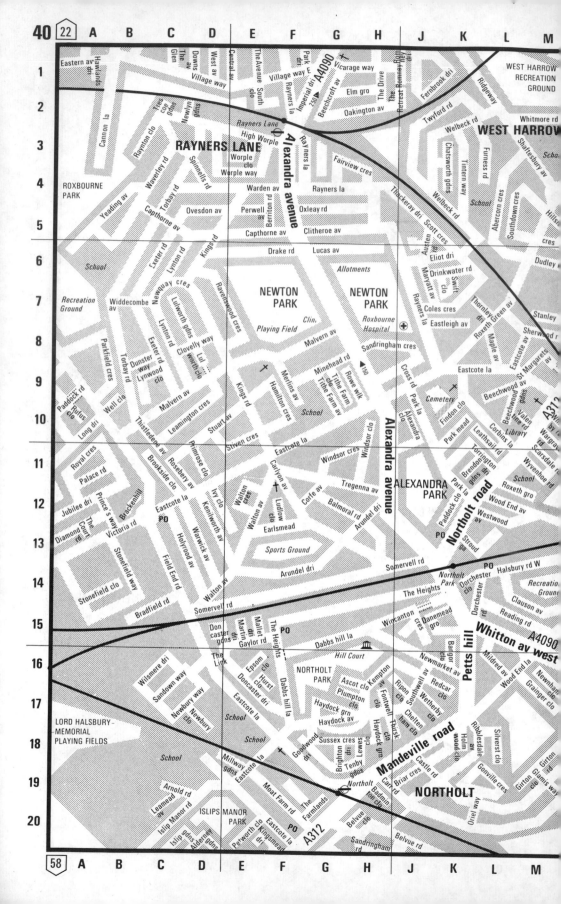

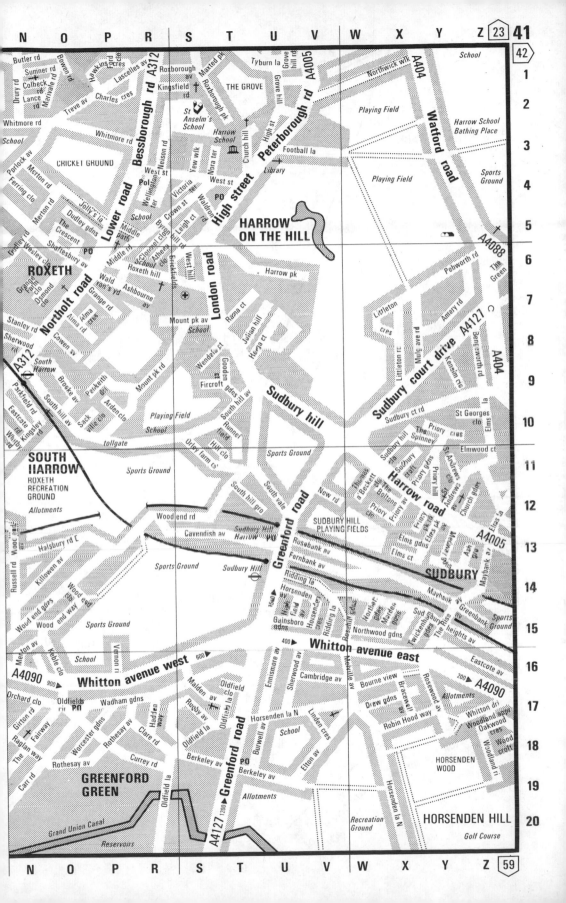

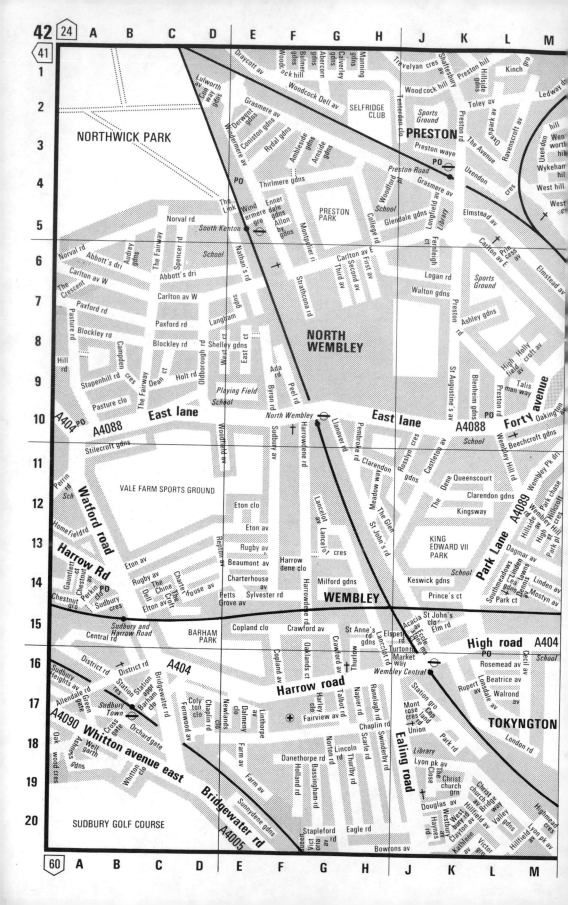

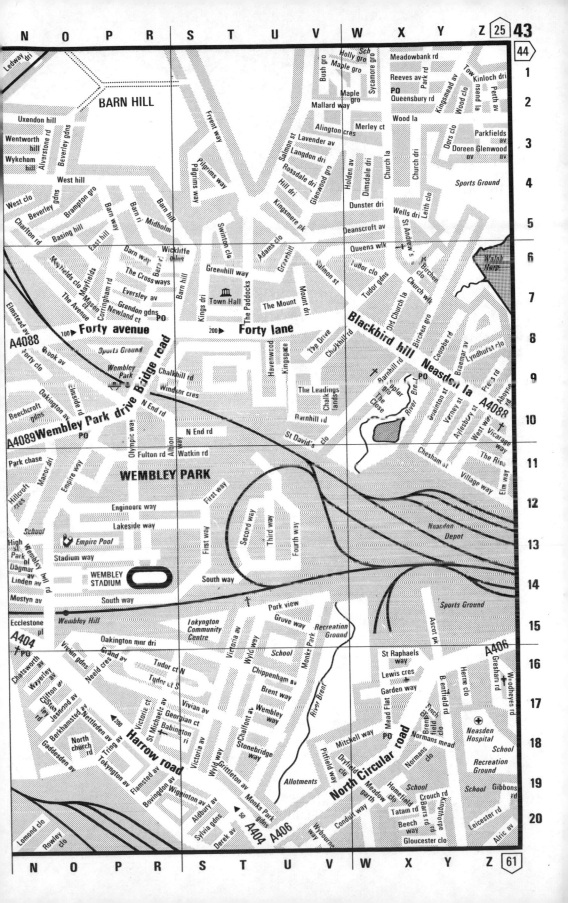

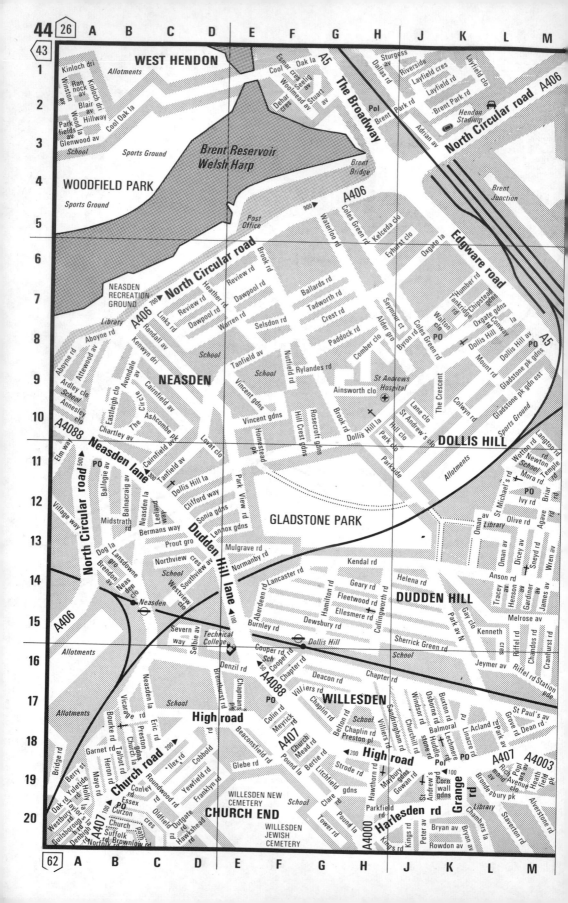

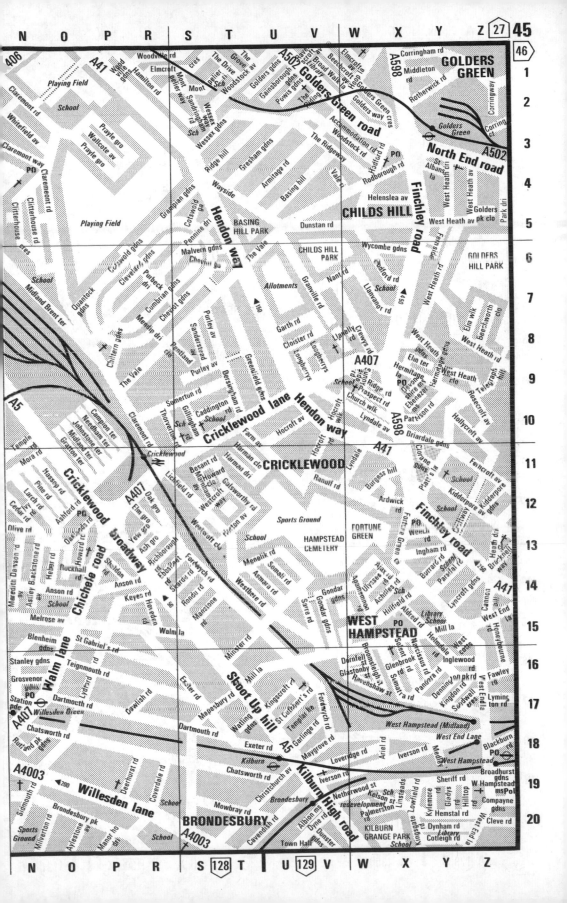

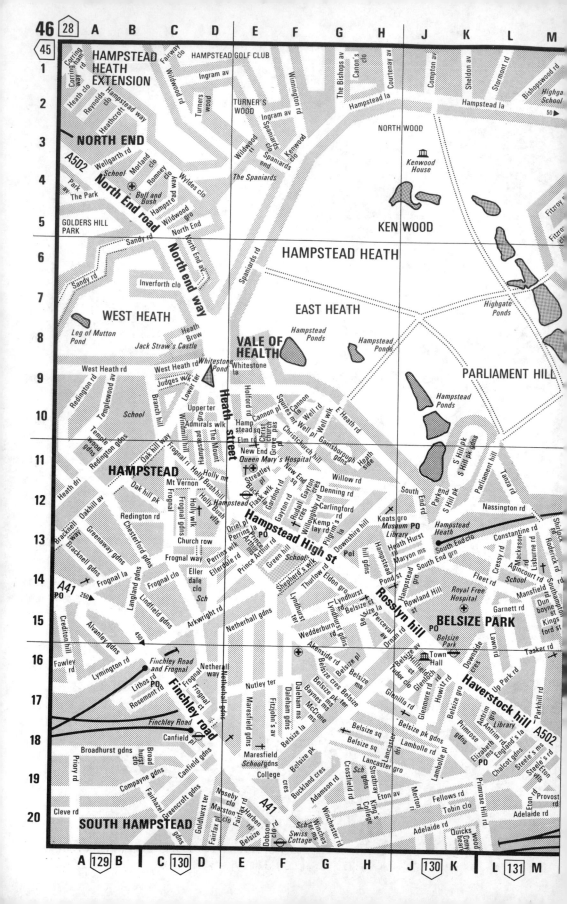

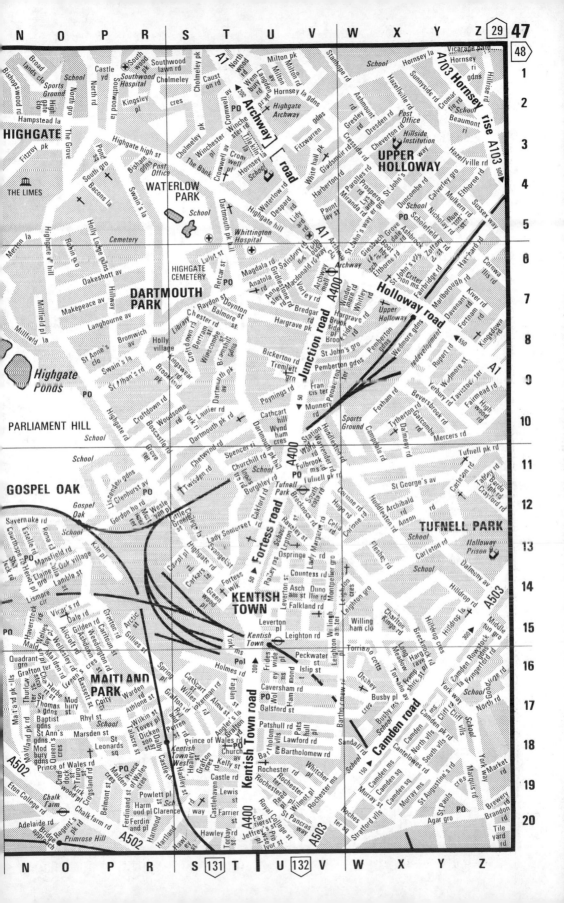

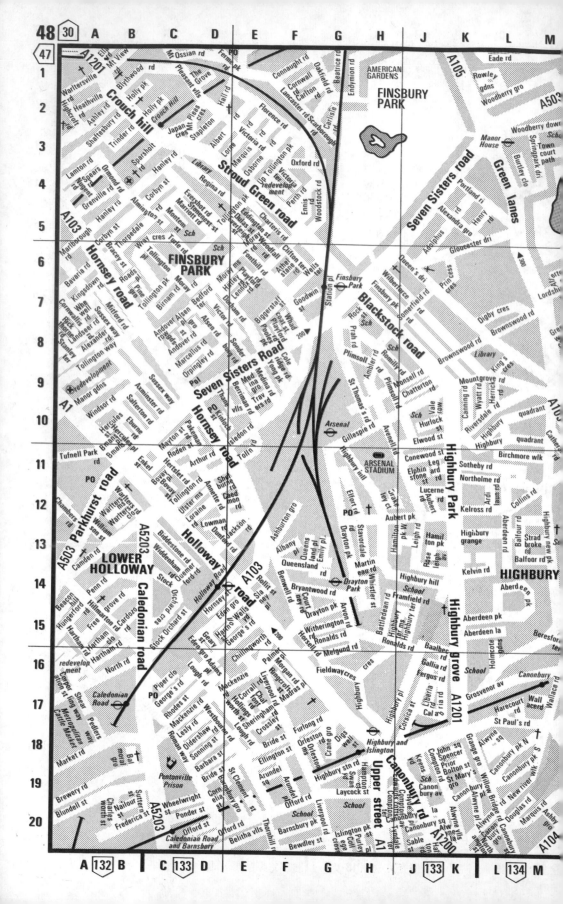

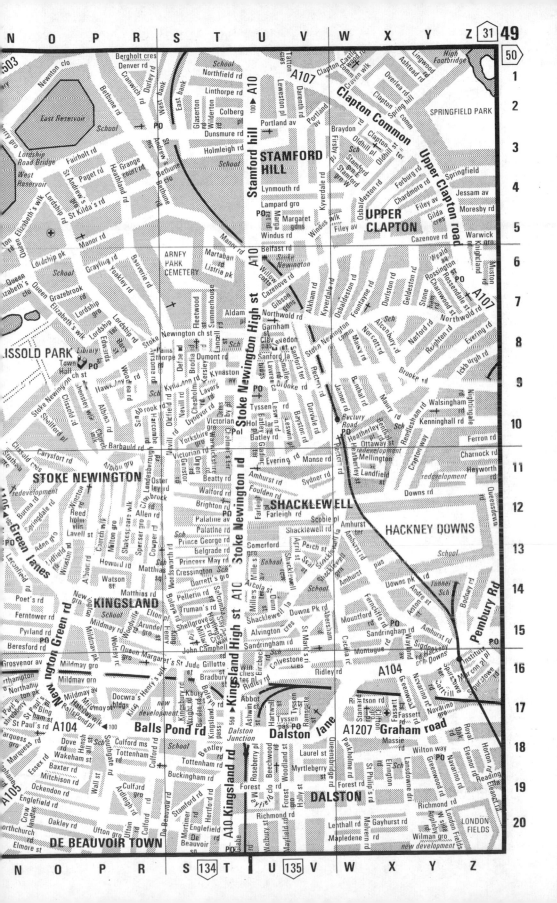

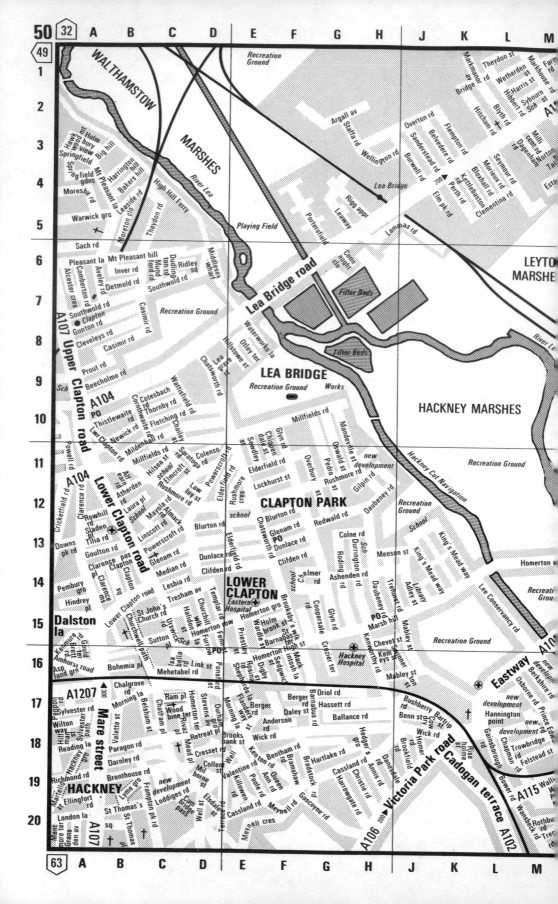

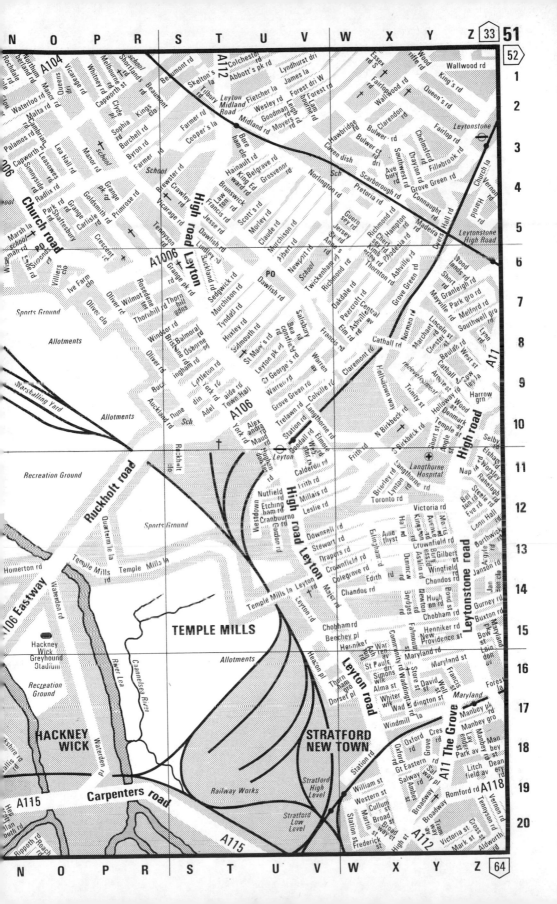

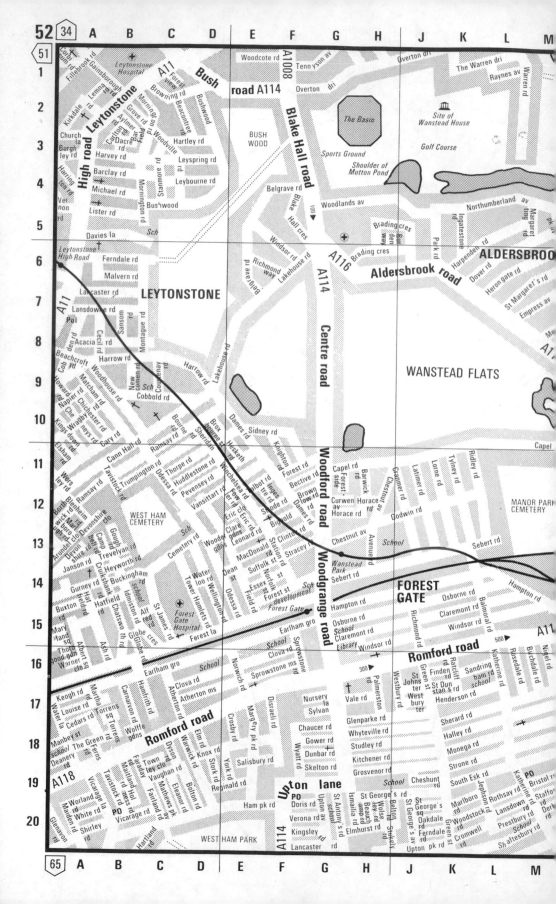

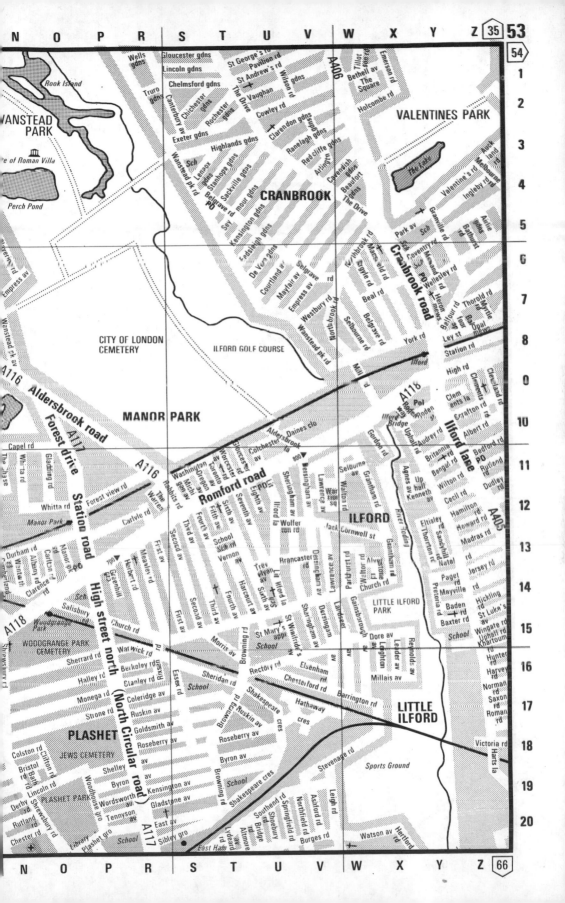

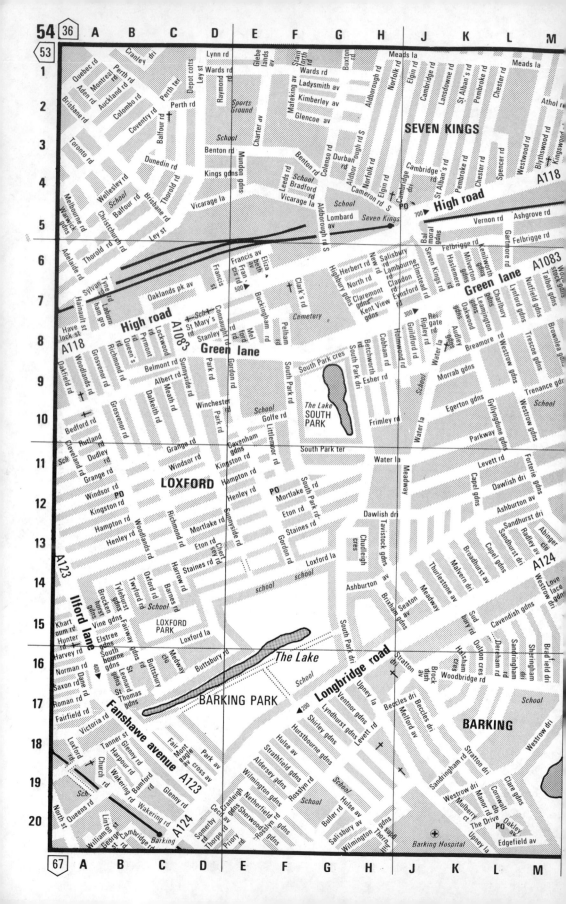

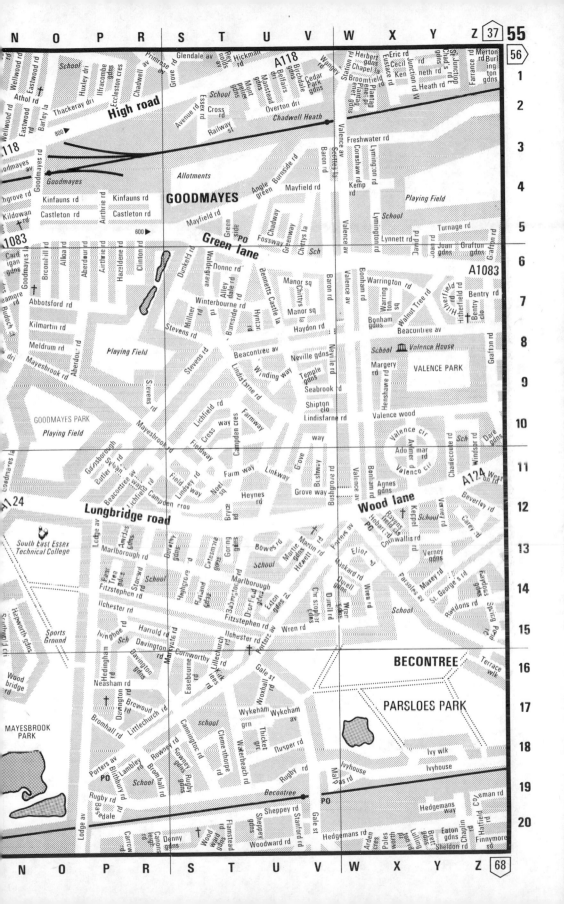

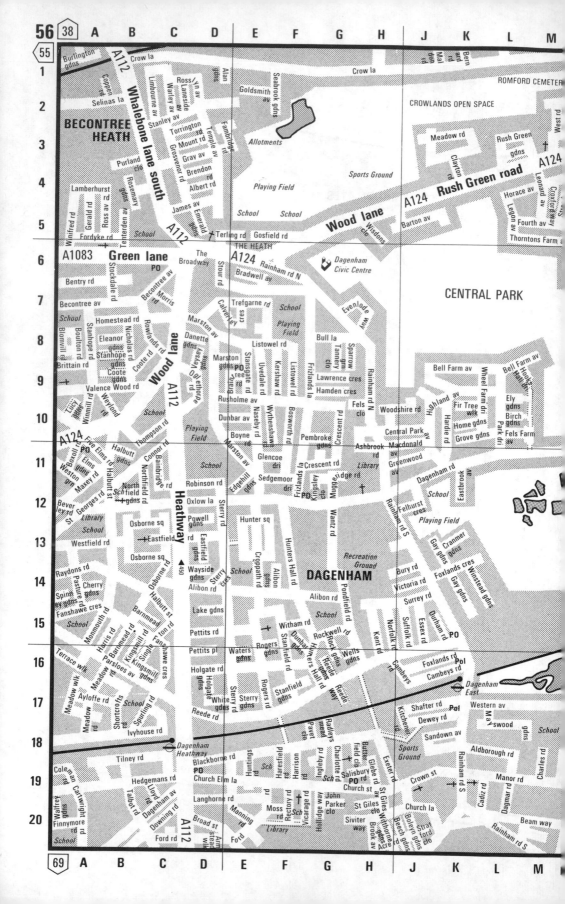

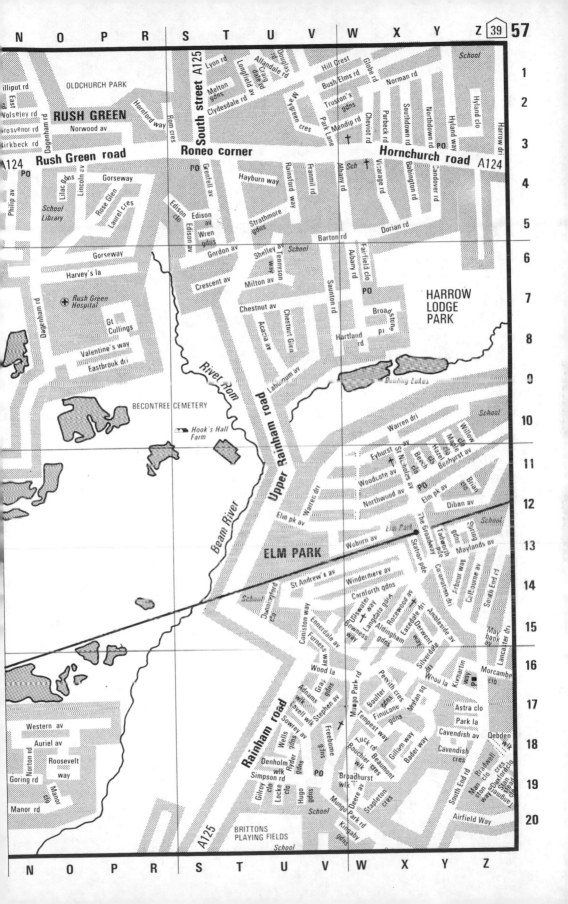

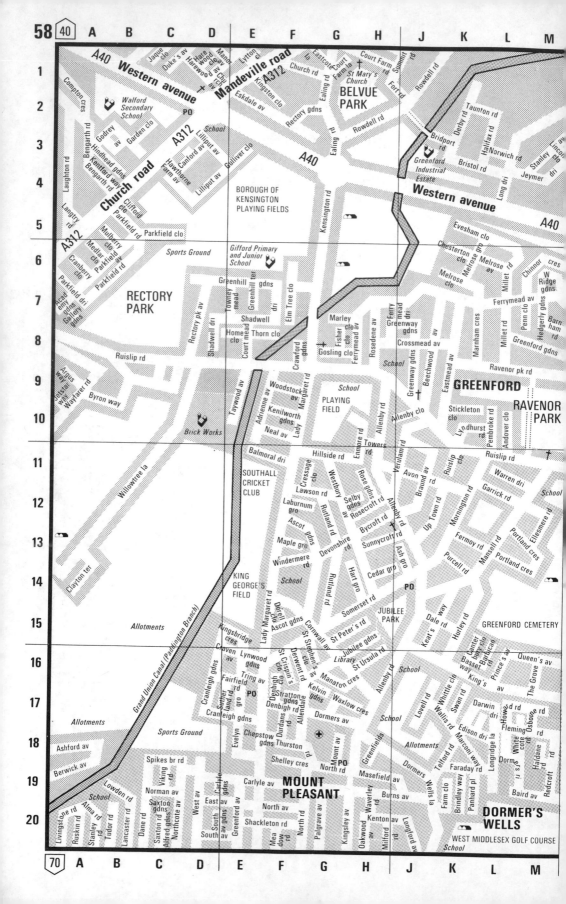

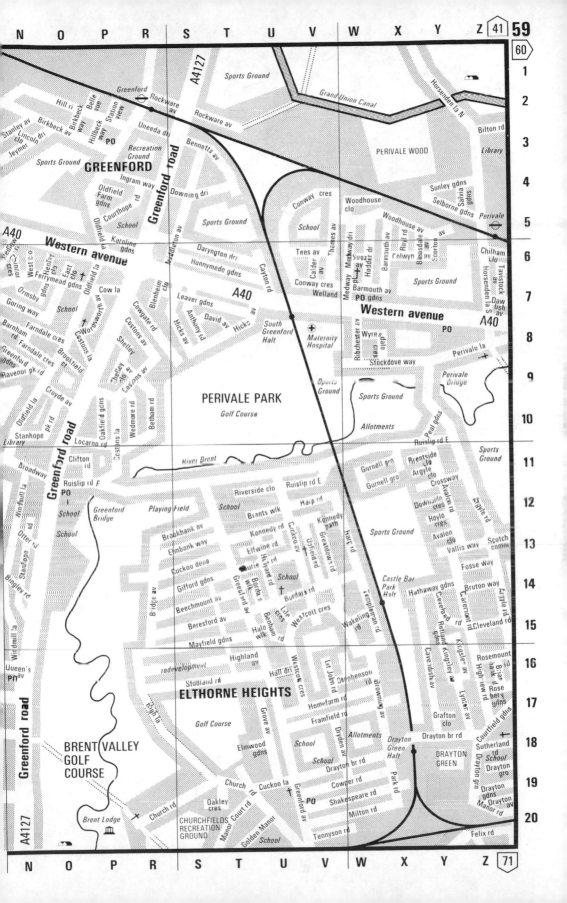

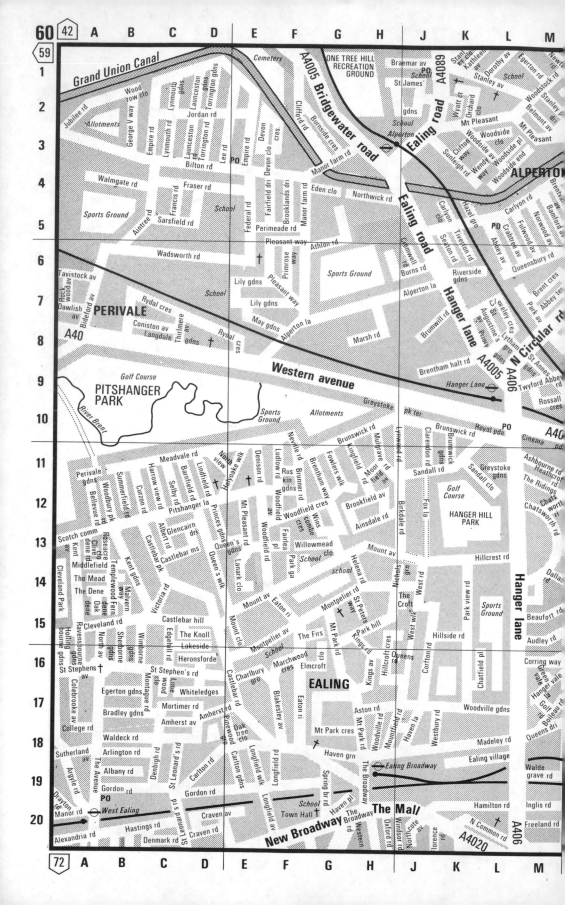

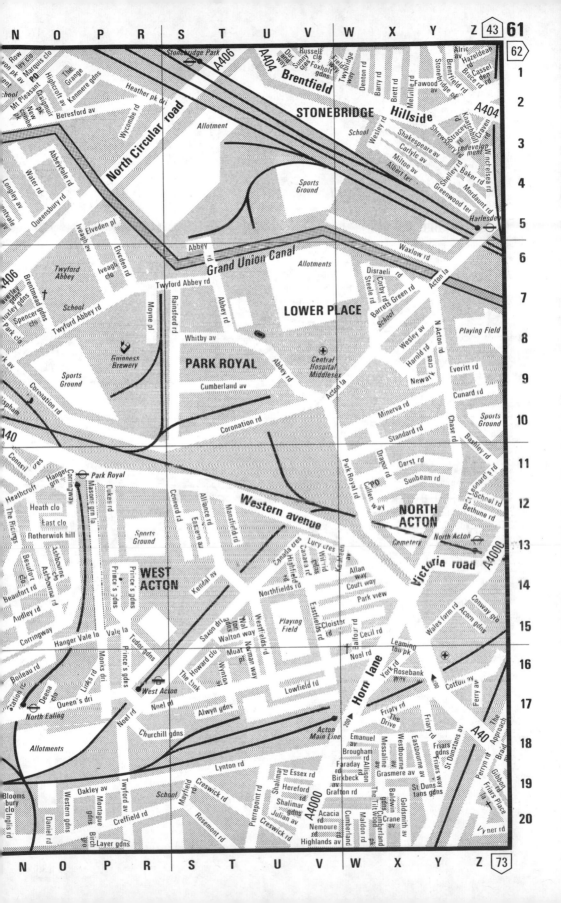

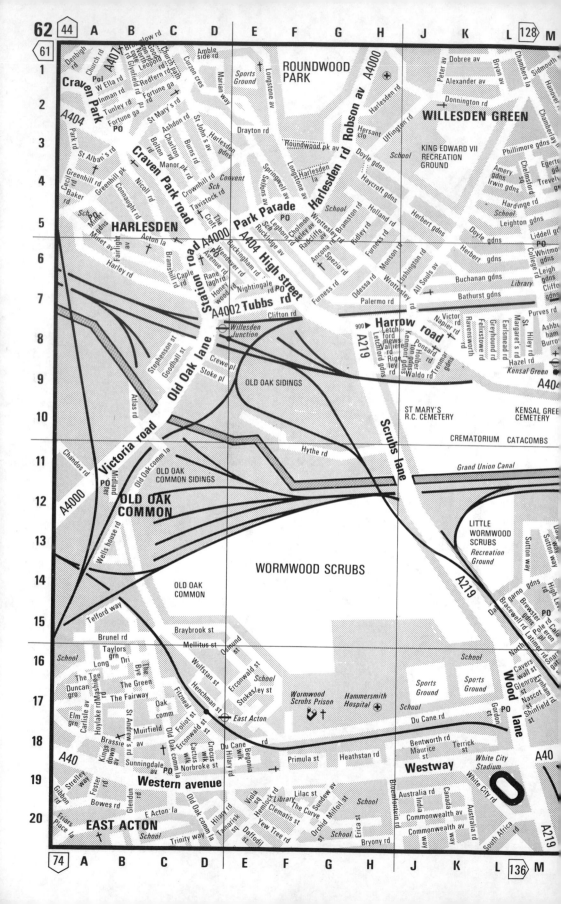

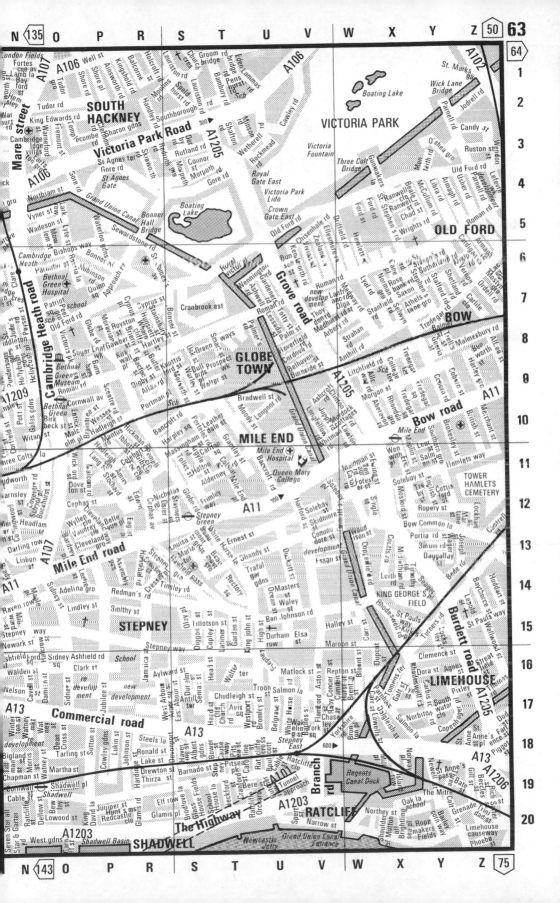

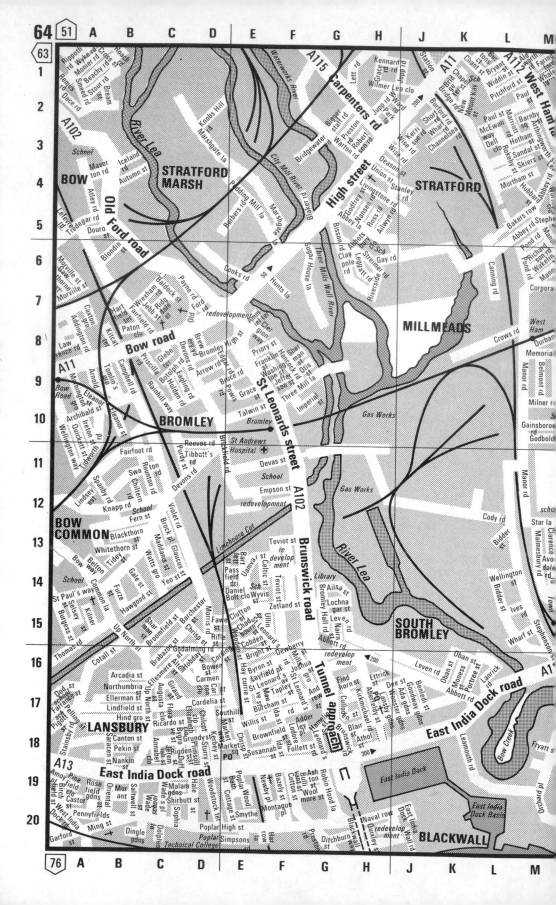

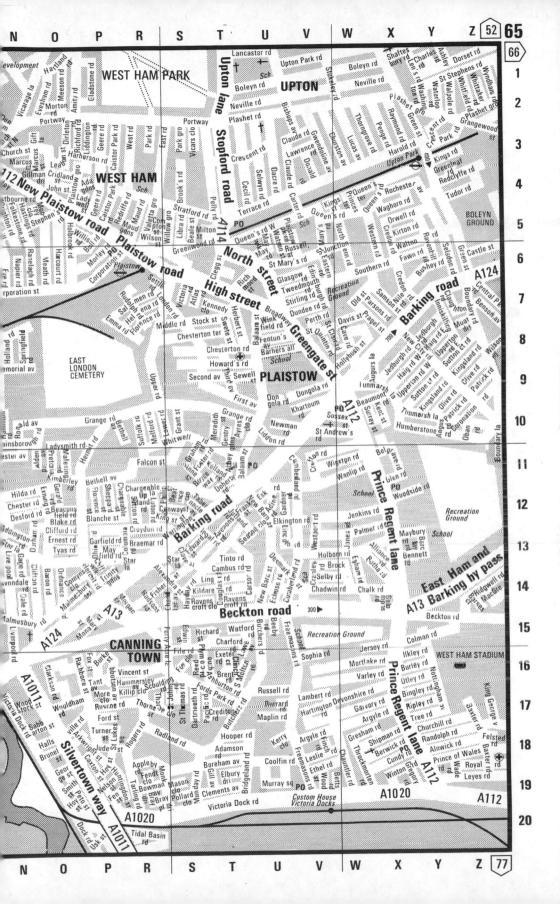

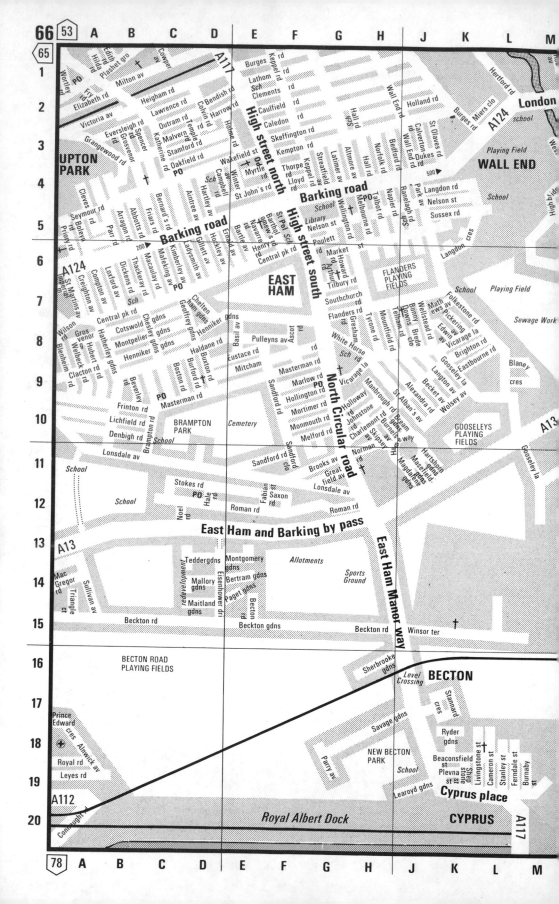

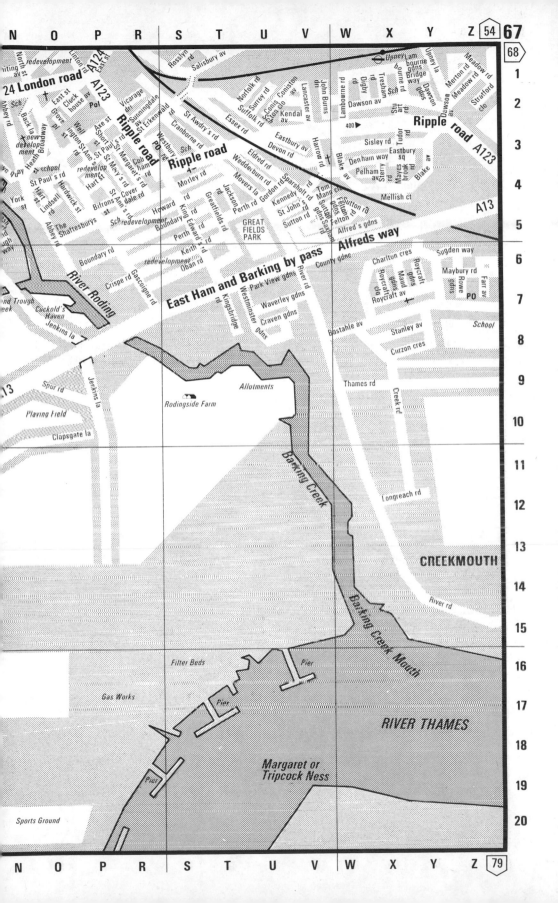

1
2
3
4
5
6
7
8
9
10
11
12
13
14
15
16
17
18
19
20

24 London road
North st
redevelopment
Linton st
A124
East st
Rosslyn
Salisbury av
Upney
Upney la
Lam
bourne
gdns
Bridge
way
Meadow rd
Merton rd
Meadow rd
Stratford
clo

A123
Vicarage
dri
East st
Clock
house av
Pat
Norfolk rd
Surrey rd
Suffolk rd
Cons
Cons clo
Coniston
av
Lancaster av
John Burns
Lambourne rd
Tresham
rd
Digby
Sch
Dawson av

Sunningdale
av
St Eikenwald
St Awdry's rd
Cranborne rd
Essex rd
Kendal
av
Kendal
Eastbury av
Harrow rd
400 ▶
Dawson av
Sch
Topley
Dawson
Ripple road

Grove
Well
ington
Ann's rd
Axe st
Short rd
St Paul's rd
St Margaret's rd
St Mary's rd
Cub
PO
Ripple road
Morley rd
Wedderburn rd
Eldred rd
Devon rd
Sisley rd
Denham way
Pelham
av
Eastbury
sq
Blake av
Steary
Maybrook
Blake
Ripple road A123

new
develop
ment
Heath
Broadway
school
St Paul's rd
Hart st
Hardwick st
Lindsell st
Bifrons rd
Cover dale rd
Howard rd
Jackson rd
Movers la
Perth rd
Kennedy rd
St John's rd
Sutton rd
Tom Mann
Felton
Sutton gdns
Sutton rd
Felton
Alfred's gdns
Mellish ct
A13

York st
The Shaftesburys
Abbey rd
Sch
redevelopment
Boundary rd
King Edward's rd
Greatfields rd
Perth rd
GREAT FIELDS PARK
Sutton rd
Saxham
Alfreds way

Boundary rd
Crispe rd
Gascoigne rd
redevelopment
Keith rd
Oban rd
East Ham and Barking by pass
River rd
County gdns
Charlton cres
Roycraft gdns
Maud gdns
Roycraft clo
Sugden way
Maybury rd
Rowe gdns
Farr av
PO

River Roding
Park View gdns
Kingsbridge rd
Westminster gdns
Waverley gdns
Craven gdns
Roycraft av
Bastable av
Stanley av
Curzon cres
School

nd Trough
eek
Cuckold's Haven
Jenkins la
Spur rd
Jenkins la
Thames rd
Creek rd

A13
Playing Field
Clapsgate la
Allotments
Rodingside Farm

Barking Creek

Longreach rd

CREEKMOUTH

Barking Creek Mouth
River rd

Filter Beds
Pier
Gas Works
Pier
Pier

RIVER THAMES

Pier
Margaret or Tripcock Ness

Sports Ground

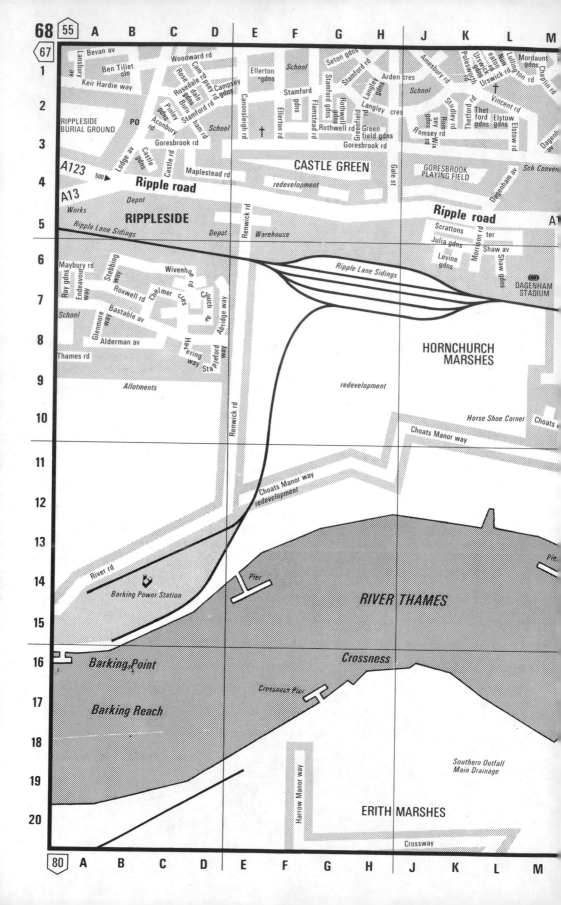

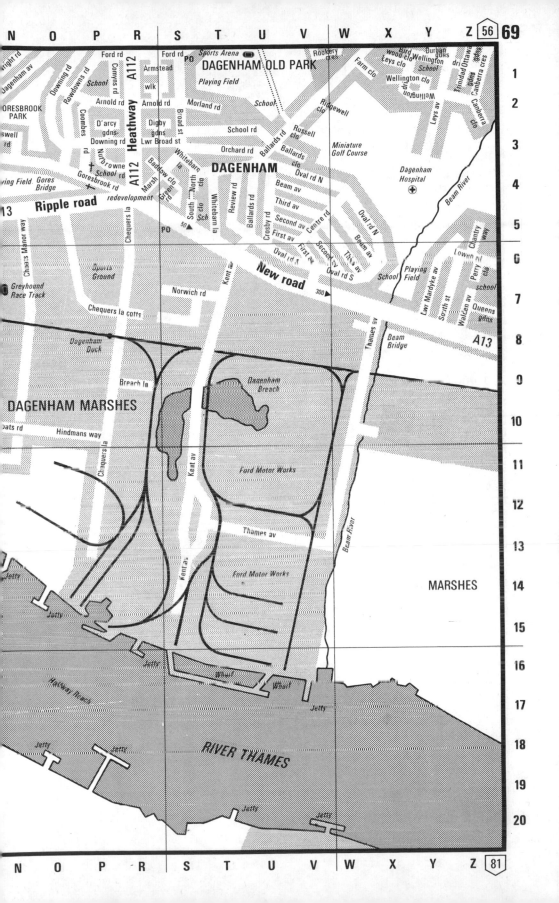

1
2
3
4
5
G
7
8
9
10
11
12
13
14
15
16
17
18
19
20

Wright rd
Jagenham av
GORESBROOK
PARK
swell
rd
13
Ripple road
Cheals Manor way
Greyhound
Race Track
oats rd
DAGENHAM MARSHES
Hindmans way

Downing rd
Rowdowns rd
Coombes
Nurrowne
School rd
Goresbrook rd
Gores
Bridge
ring Field
Sports
Ground
Chequers la cotts
Dagenham
Duck
Breach la
Chequers la

Ford rd
School
Arnold rd
D'arcy
gdns
Downing rd
Chequers la

Convis rd
Armstead
wlk
Arnold rd
Digby
gdns
Lwr Broad st
Badlow
clo
Marsh
Green rd

Ford rd
Sports Arena
PO
Playing Field
Morland rd
Broad st
Whitebars
la
Whitebam la
South
North
South clo Sch
50
PO

DAGENHAM OLD PARK
School rd
Orchard rd
DAGENHAM
Review rd
Ballards rd
Crosby rd
Oval rd S
New road
Norwich rd

Rookery
cres
Farm clo
Ridgewell
Russell
clo
Ballards rd
Ballards
clo
Oval rd N
Beam av
Third av
Second av
First av
First N
Second rd
Oval rd S
300
Kent av

Bird
wood clo
Wellington
School
Wellington clo
Wellington
Leys clo
Miniature
Golf Course
Dagenham
Hospital
Oval rd N
Beam av
This av
School
Playing
Field
Lwr Mardyke av

Durban
gdns Ottawa
Trinidad gdns
Canberra cres
dri
Canberra
clo
Beam River
Lowen cl
Perry
clo
Scroth st
Walden av
Chantry
way
school
Queens
gdns

Thames av
Beam
Bridge
A13
Thames av
Beam River

MARSHES

Dagenham
Breach
Ford Motor Works
Thames av
Ford Motor Works

Jetty
Jetty
Jetty
Jetty
Wharf
Wharf
Jetty
Jetty
Jetty
Halfway Reach
RIVER THAMES
Jetty
Jetty
Jetty

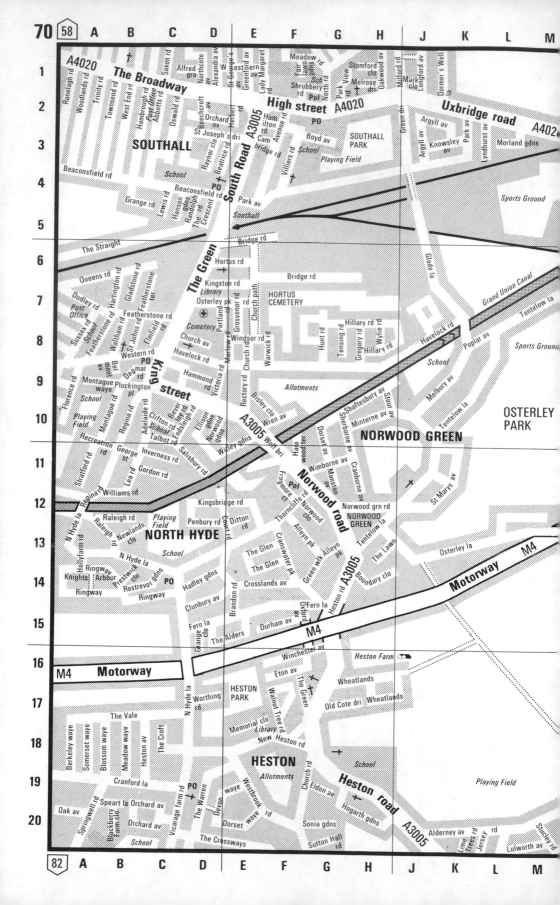

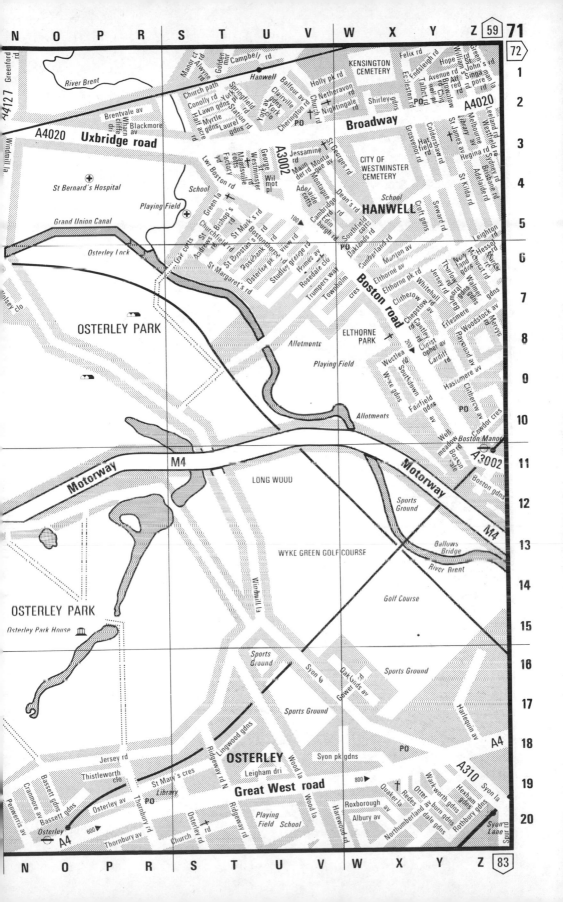

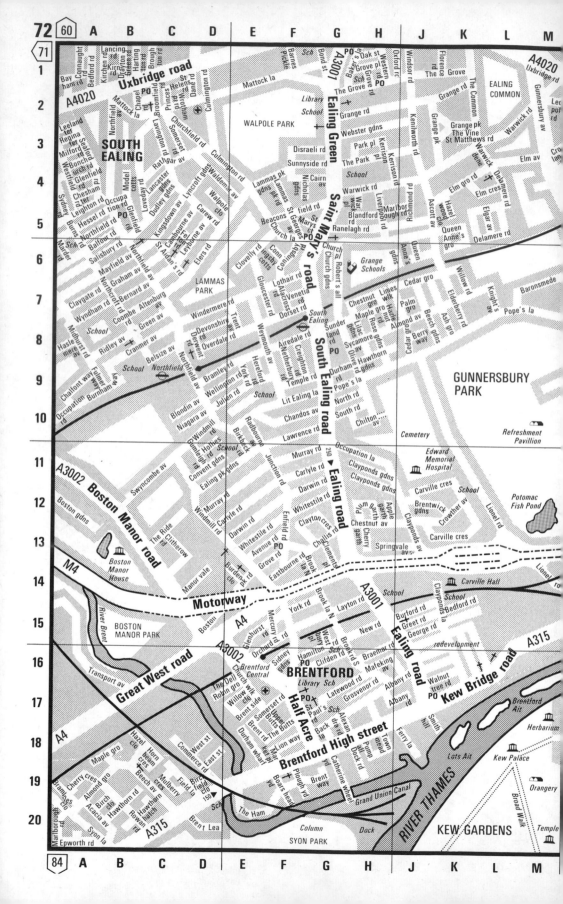

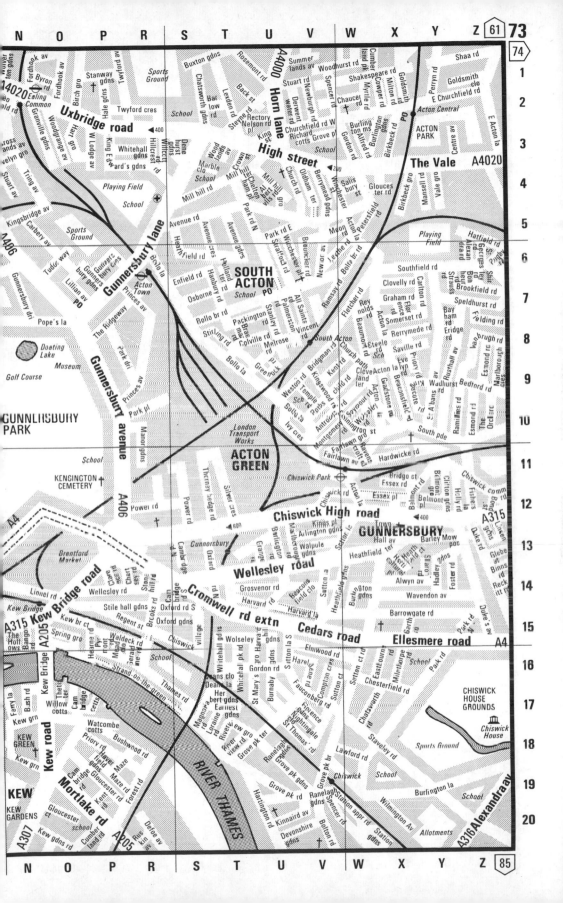

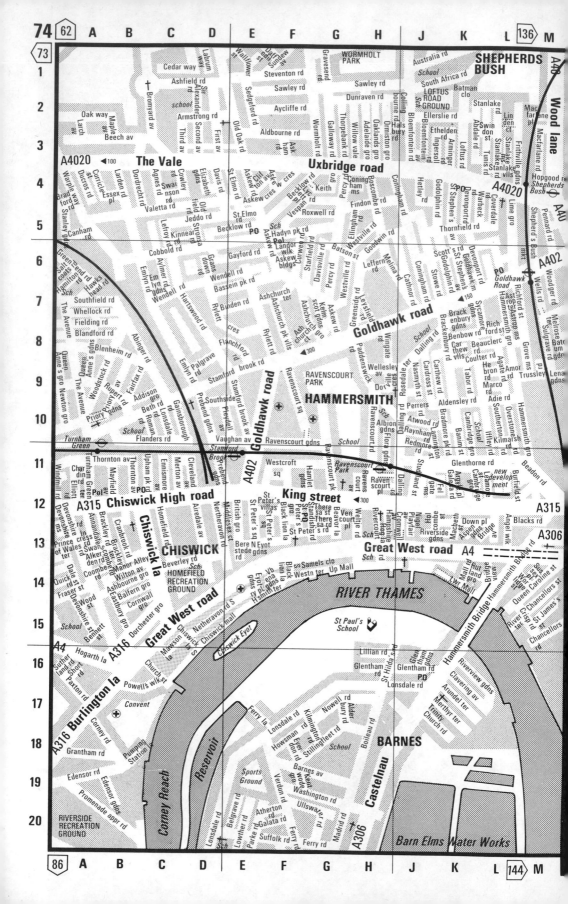

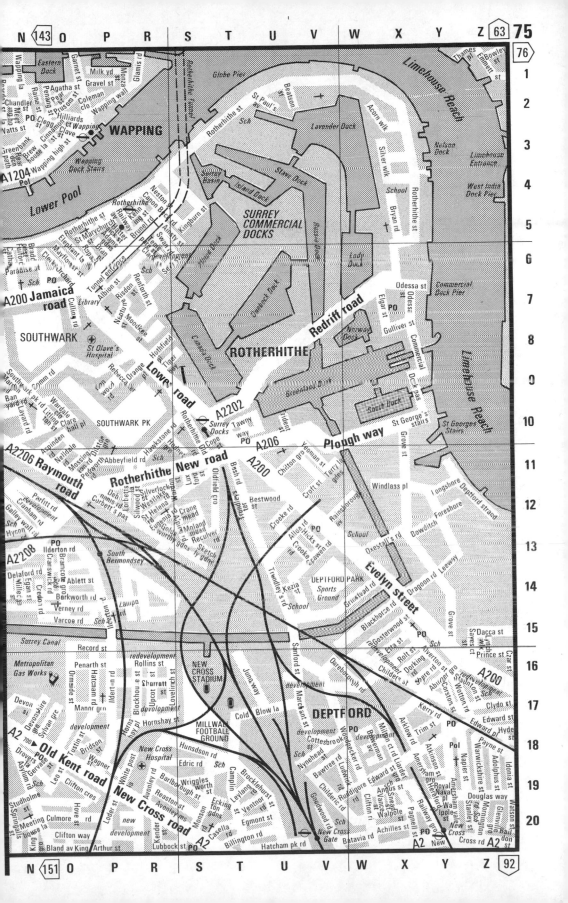

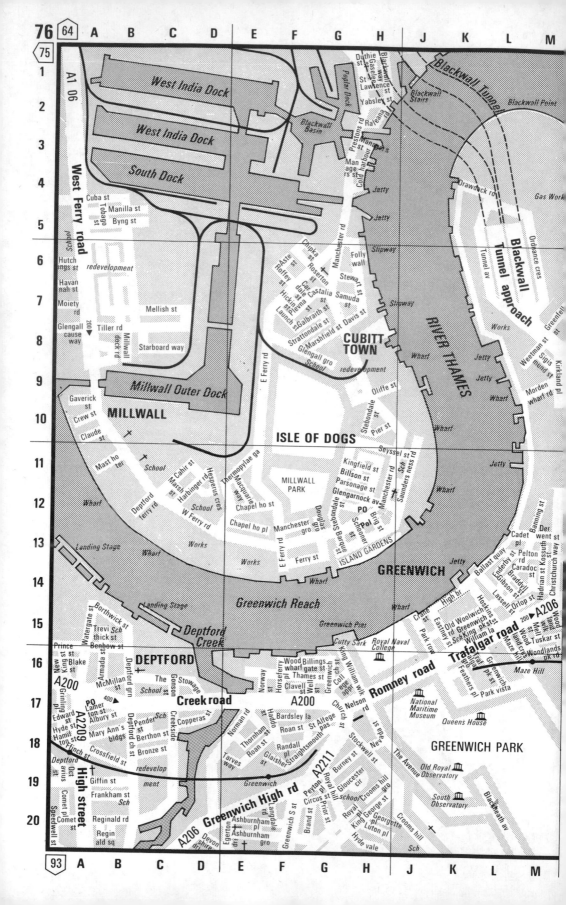

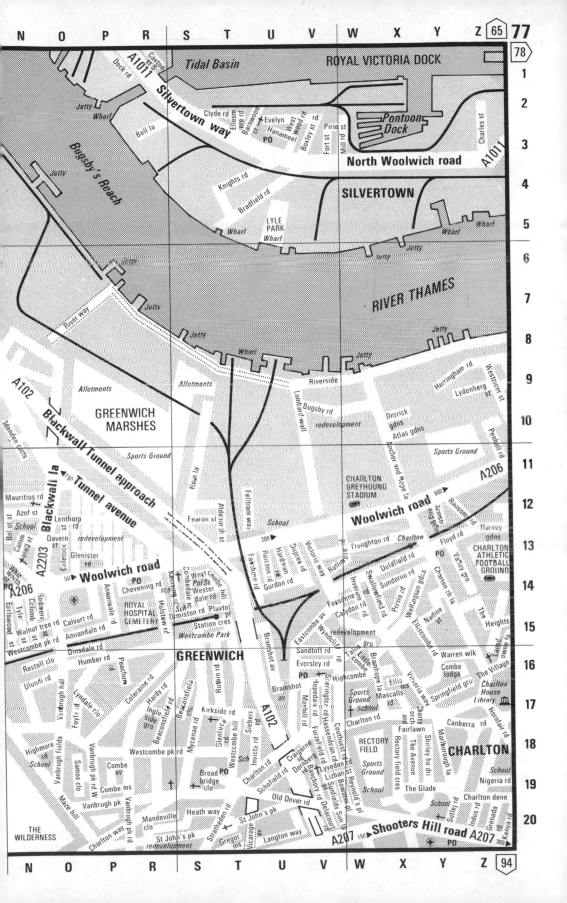

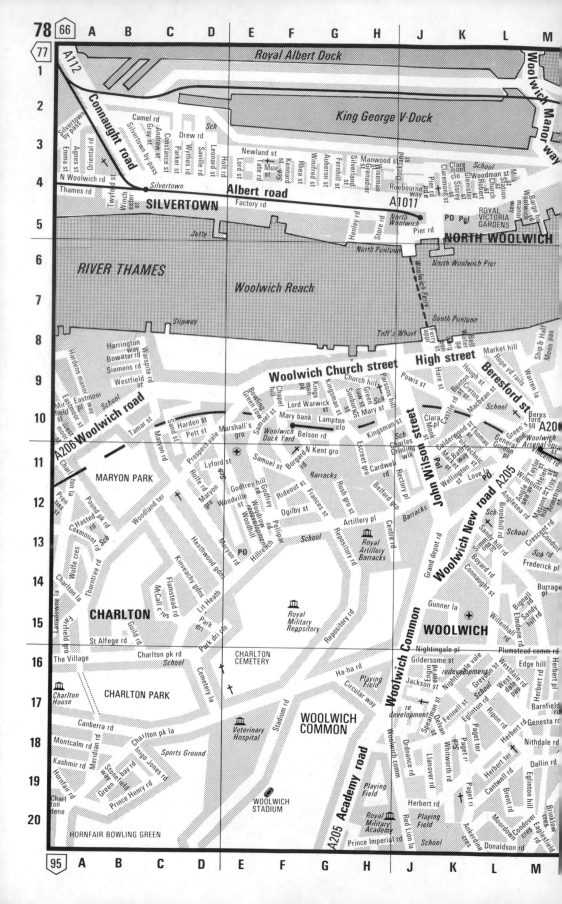

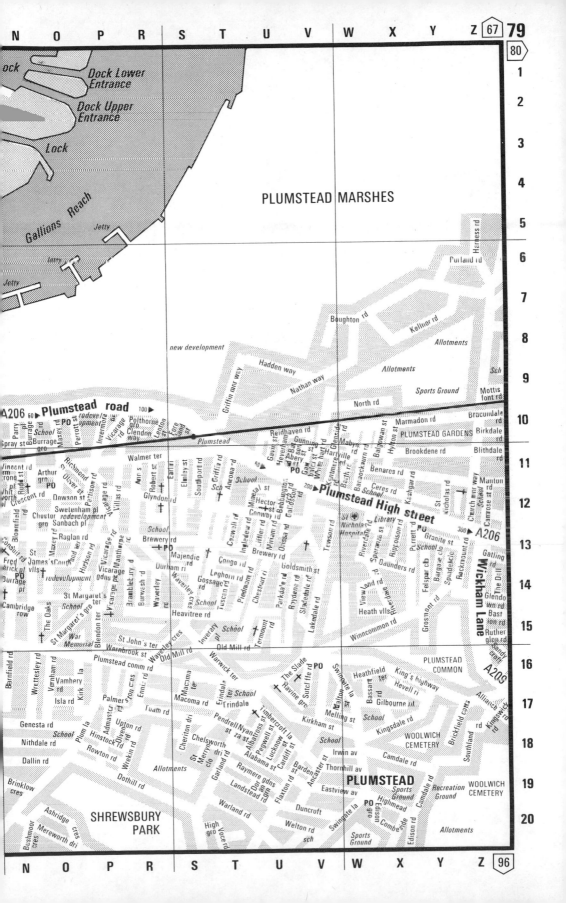

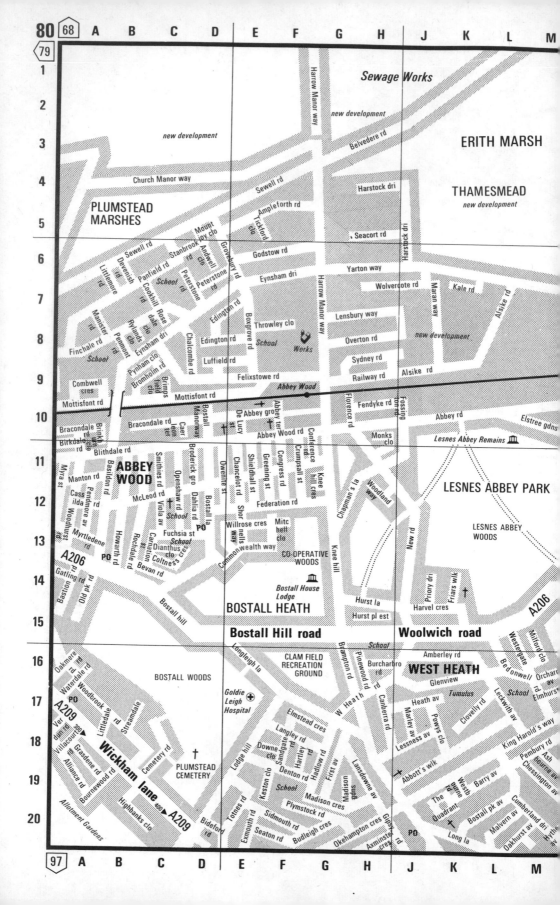

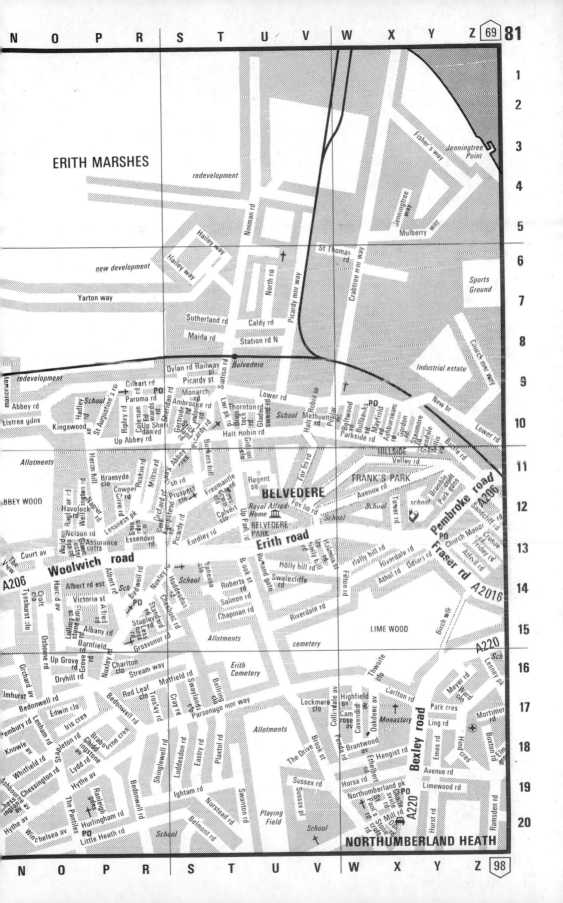

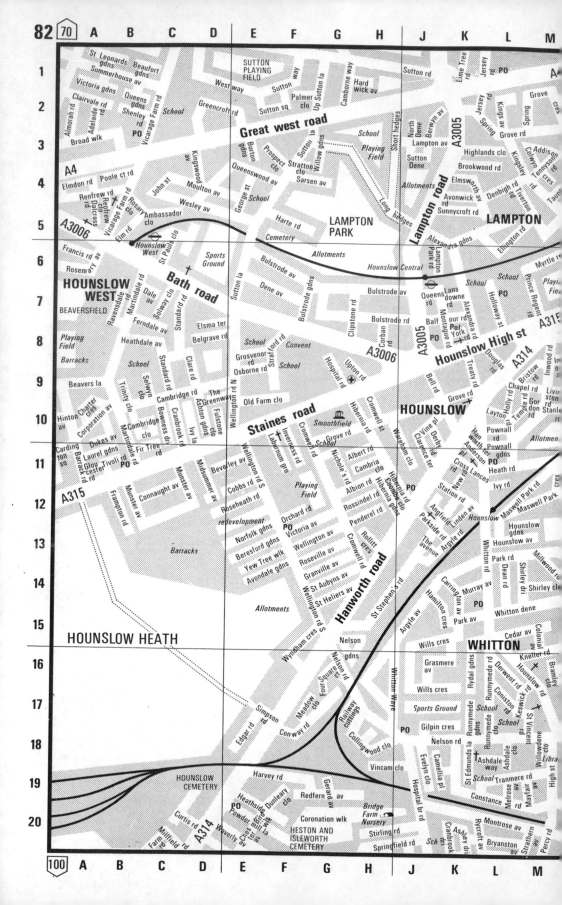

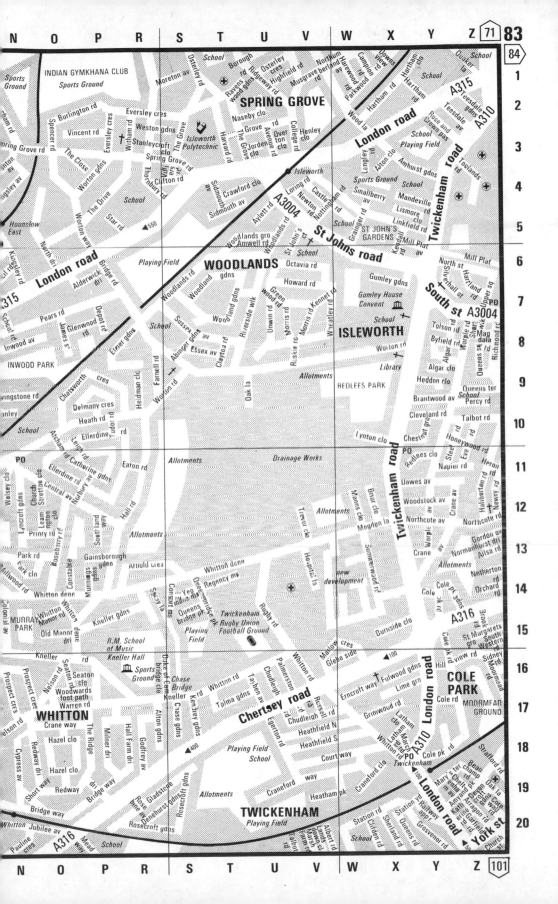

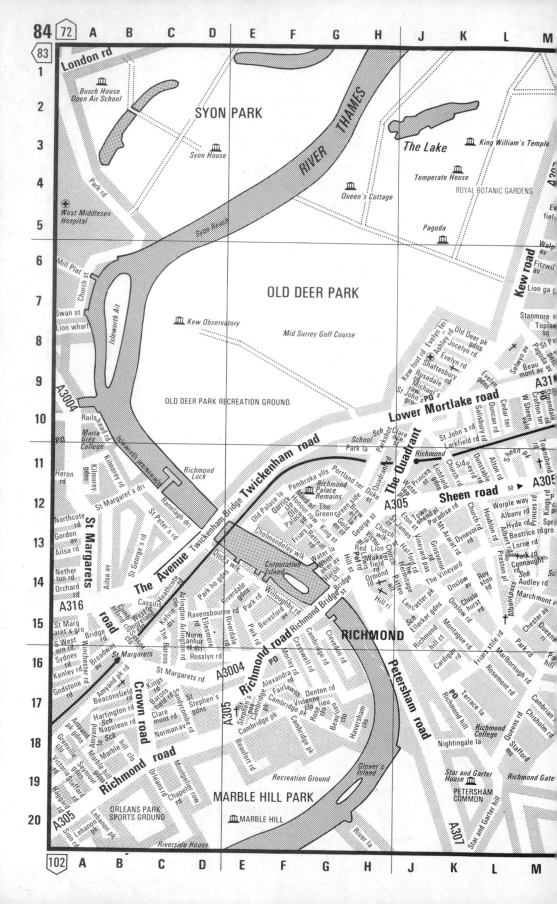

A B C D E F G H J K L M

1
2
3
4
5
6
7
8
9
10
11
12
13
14
15
16
17
18
19
20

London rd

Busch House
Open Air School

SYON PARK

RIVER THAMES

The Lake

King William's Temple

Syon House

Temperate House

ROYAL BOTANIC GARDENS

Park rd

West Middlesex
Hospital

Syon Reach

Queen's Cottage

Pagoda

Ev
fiel

Kew road

Walp
av

Fitzwil
av

Lion ga

Mill Plat

Church st

OLD DEER PARK

Stanmore
Topia
sq

Swan st

Lion wharf

Isleworth Ait

Kew Observatory

Mid Surrey Golf Course

Kew foot rd

Evelyn ter

Old Deer pk
gdns

Ashley rd
Jocelyn rd

Shaftesbury

Evelyn rd

St P

Selwin av

Beau
mont av

Pagoda av

A3004

Rails head rd

OLD DEER PARK RECREATION GROUND

Rosedale
Michael's
row
St John's gro

Evelyn
gdns

Cedar ter

Duncan rd

Salisbury rd

W Sheen

A31

Heron
rd

Matta
Grey
College

Kilmorey rd

Kilmorey
gdns

Isleworth Promenade

Richmond
Lock

Twickenham road

Lower Mortlake road

St John's rd

Richmond

Larkfield rd

The Quadrant

Sch
Clare
shot la

Park la

School
rd

St
Sid

Dunstable
rd

Alton rd

Sheen
rd

Townshend
rd

A305

Northcote
rd

Gordon
av

Ailsa av

St Margaret's rd

St George's rd

St Peter's rd

Ranelagh dri

The Avenue

Twickenham Bridge

Old Palace la

Pembroke vlls

Garrick clo

Cholmondeley wlk

Richmond
Palace
Remains

Portland ter
Duke

The Green

George st

Quadrant

Water la

Princes
st

Lichfield
gdns

Paradise rd

Church rd

Worple way

Albany rd

Hyde la
gro

St Margarets

A316

Nether
ton rd

Orchard
rd

Ailsa av

The
Barons

Cassilis
rd

West

Heathcote

Arlington rd

Park ho gdns

Riverdale
gdns

Duck's wlk

Honour row
Old
Palace

King st
Friars Retreat

Friars la
Whitt
aker av
Heron

George st

Eton st
Victor
rd
Church
Red Lion st
Wakefield
rd

Hermitage

St James

Halford rd

Mt Ararat rd

Grosvenor
rd

The Vineyard

Onslow

Roy
ston
rd

Albert
rd

Preston pl

Beatrice rd

Lorne rd

York
Connaught

Sch
Audley rd

Marchmont

St Marg
aret's gro

S West
ern rd

Sydney
rd

Kenley rd

Godstone rd

Bridge
rd

Winchester rd

Broadway

St Margarets

Crown road

Kelvin rd

Ellesmere
rd

Arlington rd

Norm
anhur
st rd

Rosslyn rd

St Margarets rd

A3004

Richmond road

Ravensbourne rd

Beresford
rd

Park rd

Cambridge rd

Willoughby rd

Clevedon rd

Richmond Bridge

RICHMOND

Ormond

Hill ri

Lancaster pk

Patten alley

Bridge st

Hill st

Onslow rd

Ellerker gdns

Montague rd

Richmond
hill ct

Cardigan rd

Chisle
hurst
rd

Friar's stile rd

Rosemont rd

Marlborough rd

Park rd

Chester av

Queens

Pa
hill

St Stephen's

Alexandra
rd

Fairlawns

Denton rd

Cambridge pk

Rose lieu

Vivienne

Petersham road

Terrace la

Richmond hill

PO

Richmond
College

Nightingale la

Star and Garter
House

PETERSHAM
COMMON

Queens rd

Chisholm rd

Cambrian

Stafford

Richmond
ms

Kings
rd

Barons
field rd

Sandycombe rd

Clare
mont rd

Norman av

A305

St
Stephen's
pas

Cambridge
rd

Cambridge pk

Beaufort rd

Beau

Haversham
clo

Glover's
Island

Amyand

Amyand
pk gdns

Hartington
rd

Napoleon rd

Marble hill clo

Montpelier row

Chapel rd

Recreation Ground

River la

Richmond Gate

Grenville
rd

Seymour
gdns

Victoria

Stafford

Ragan rd

Crown road

Richmond road

Orleans rd

MARBLE HILL PARK

MARBLE HILL

Star and Garter hill

A305

Lebanon pk

ORLEANS PARK
SPORTS GROUND

Syon pk

Riverside House

Riverside rd

A307

A B C D E F G H J K L M

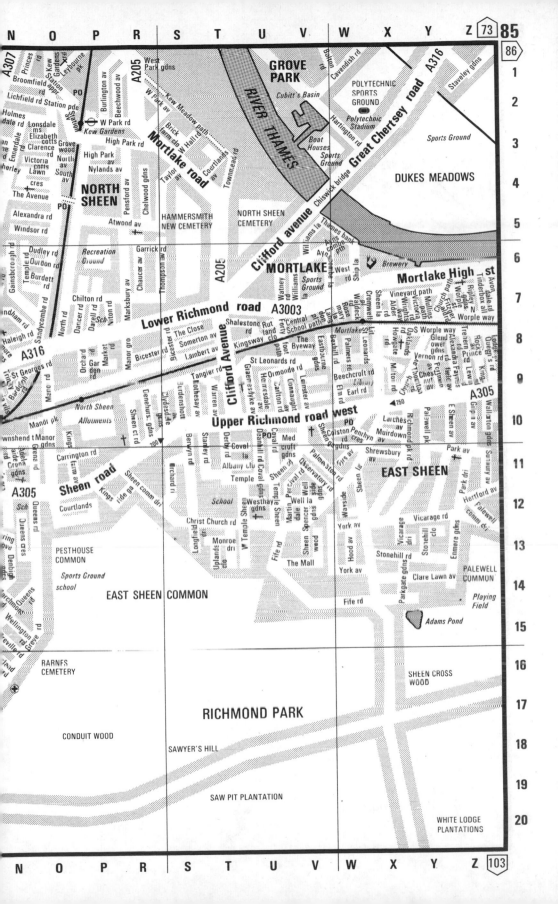

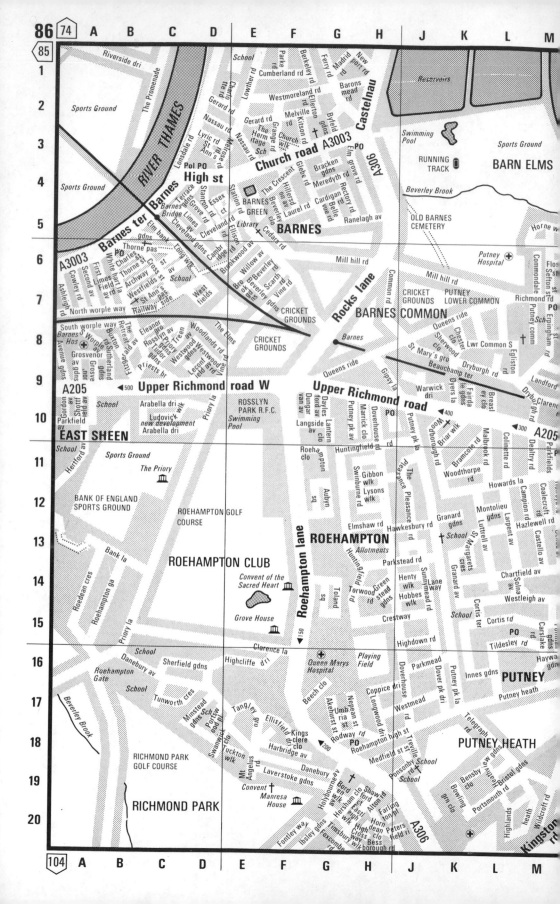

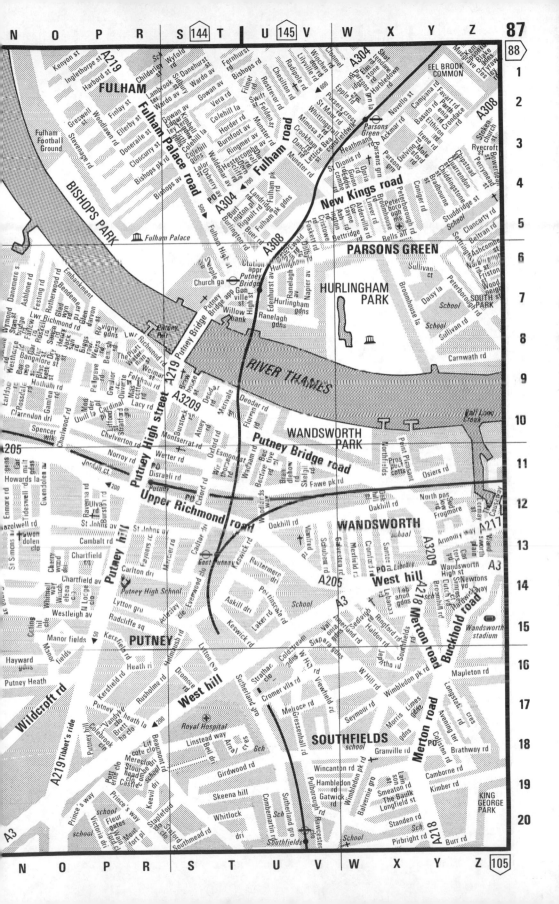

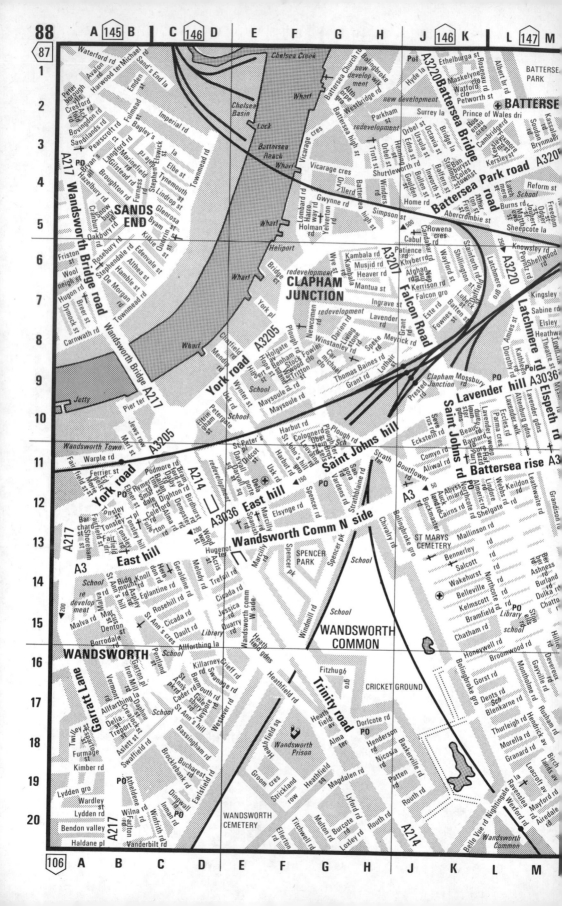

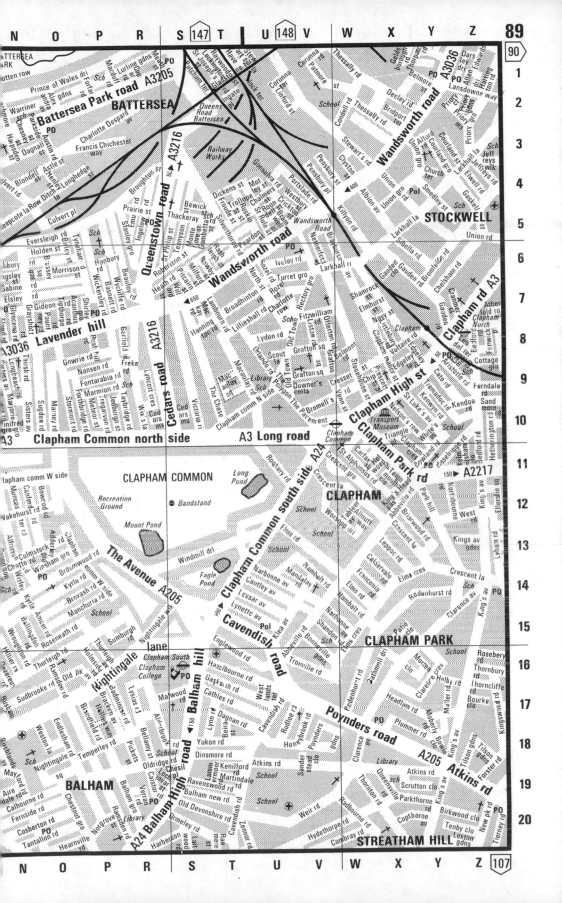

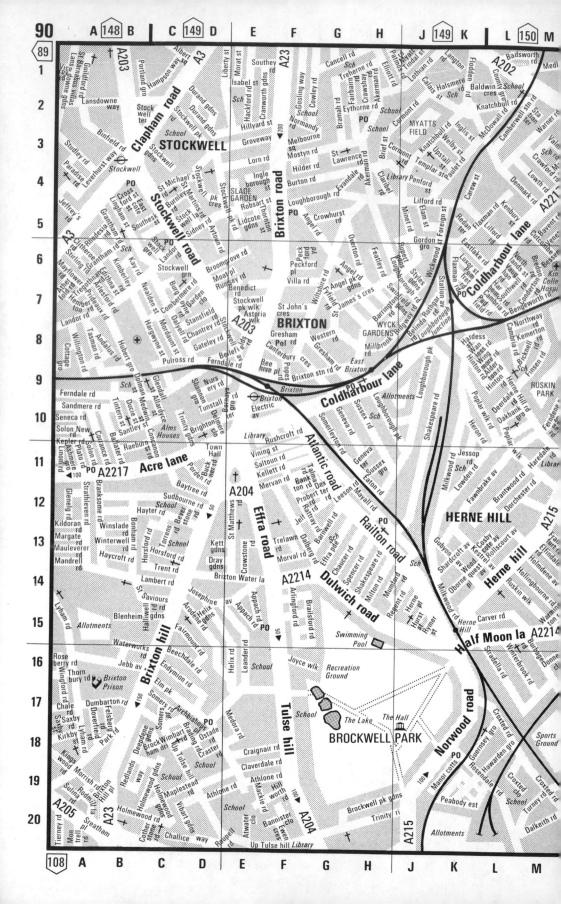

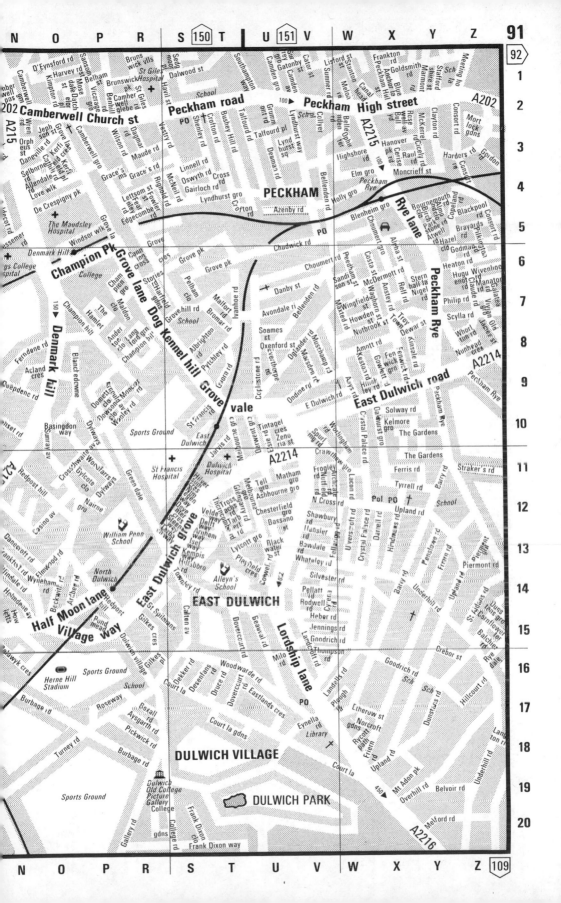

**Camberwell Church st**
**Peckham road**
**Peckham High street**
A202
A215
A2215
**PECKHAM**
Azenby rd
Rye lane
Peckham Rye
**Champion Pk**
**Grove lane**
**Dog Kennel hill**
**Grove**
**vale**
**East Dulwich road**
A2214
**Denmark hill**
A2214
East Dulwich
**East Dulwich grove**
**EAST DULWICH**
**Half Moon lane**
**Village way**
Lordship lane
Herne Hill Stadium
**DULWICH VILLAGE**
**DULWICH PARK**

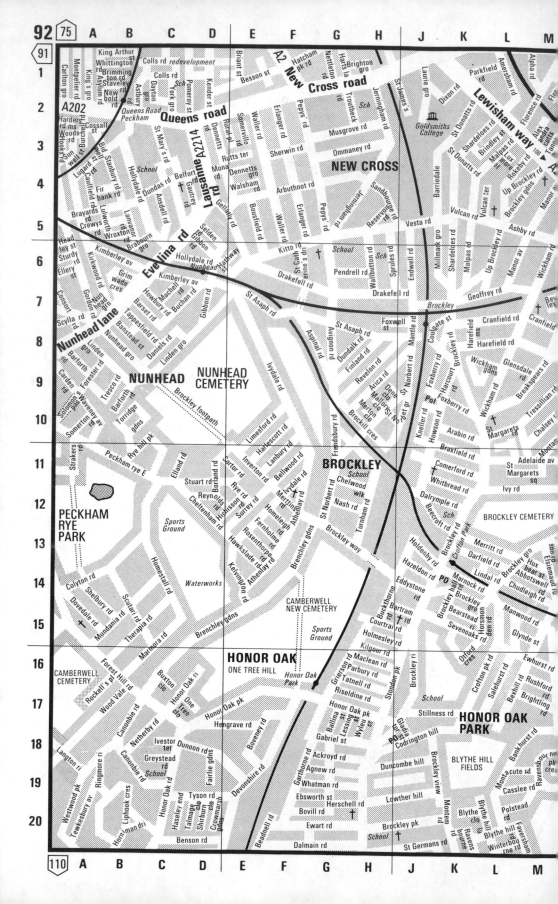

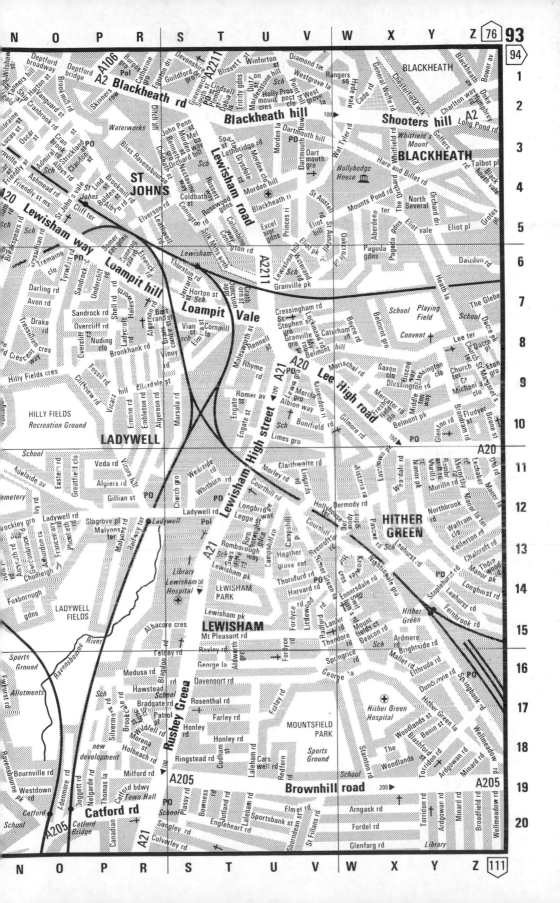

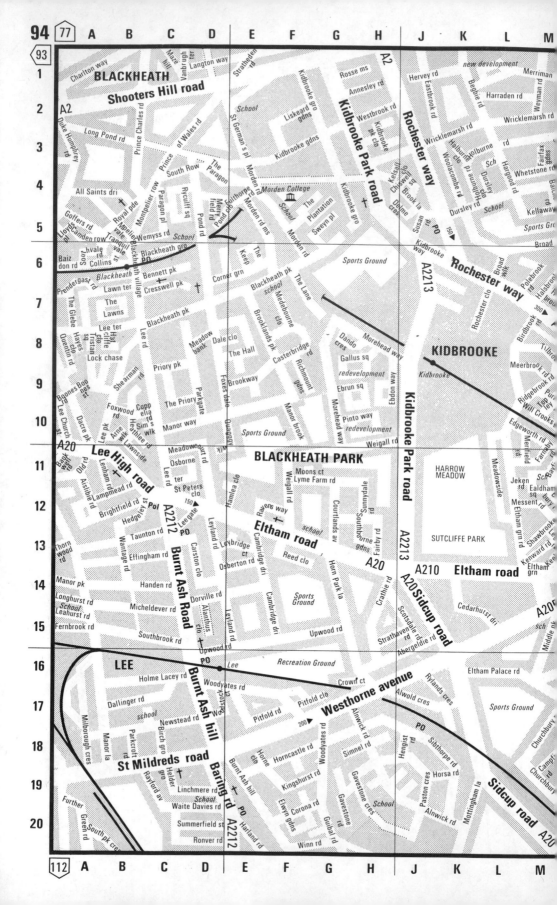

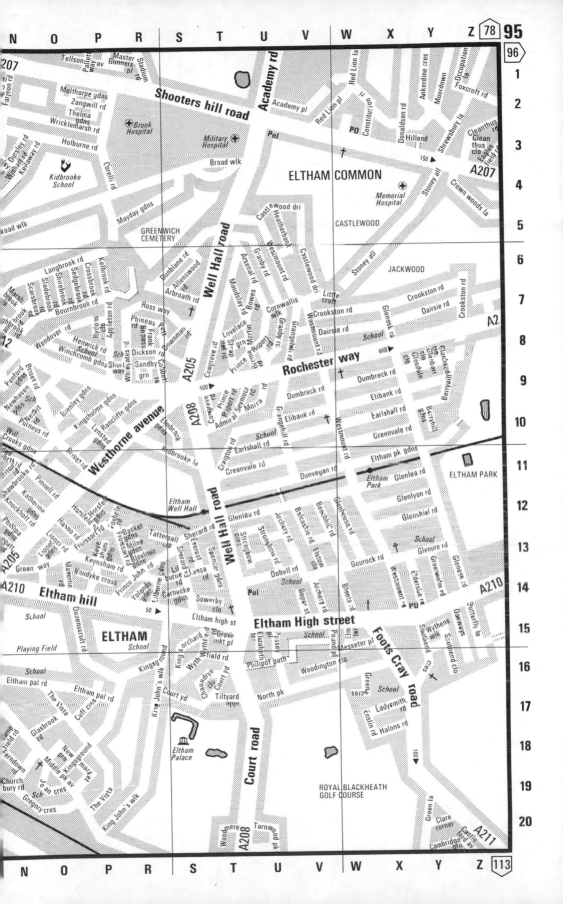

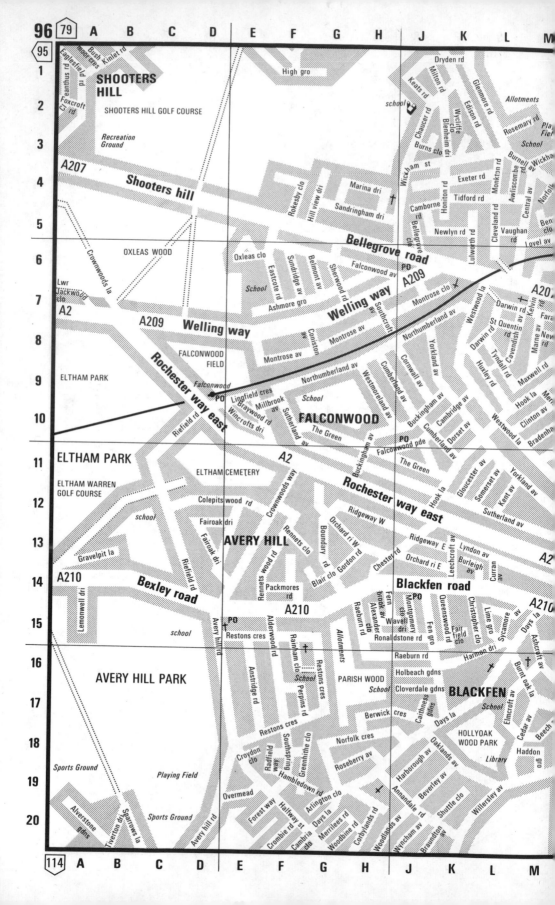

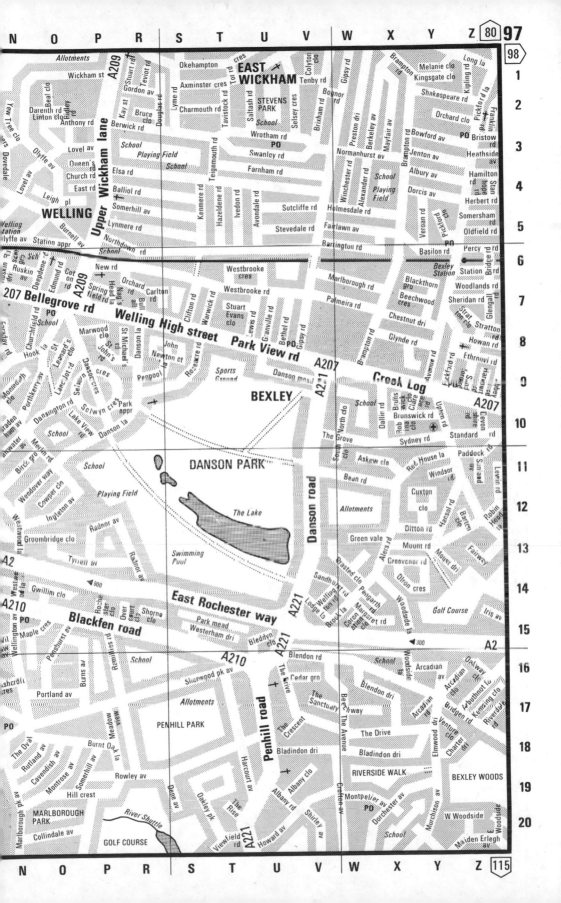

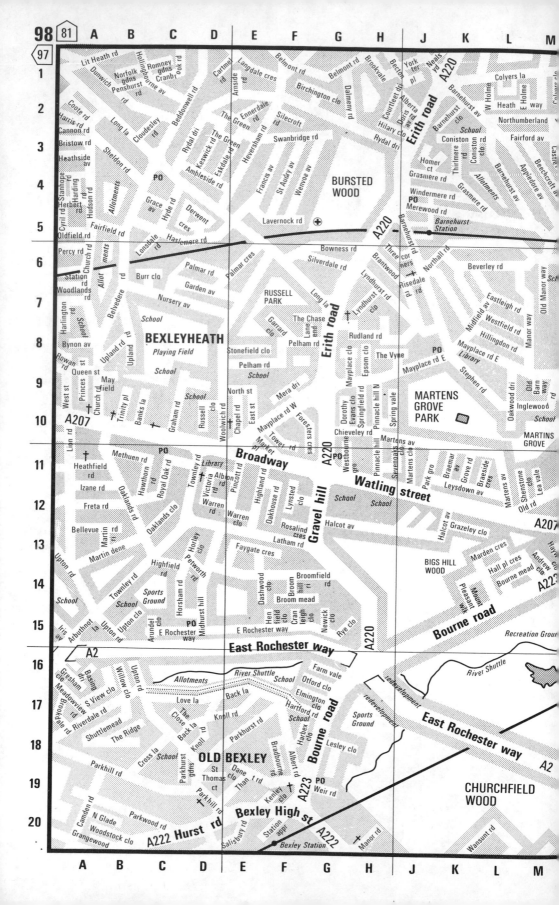

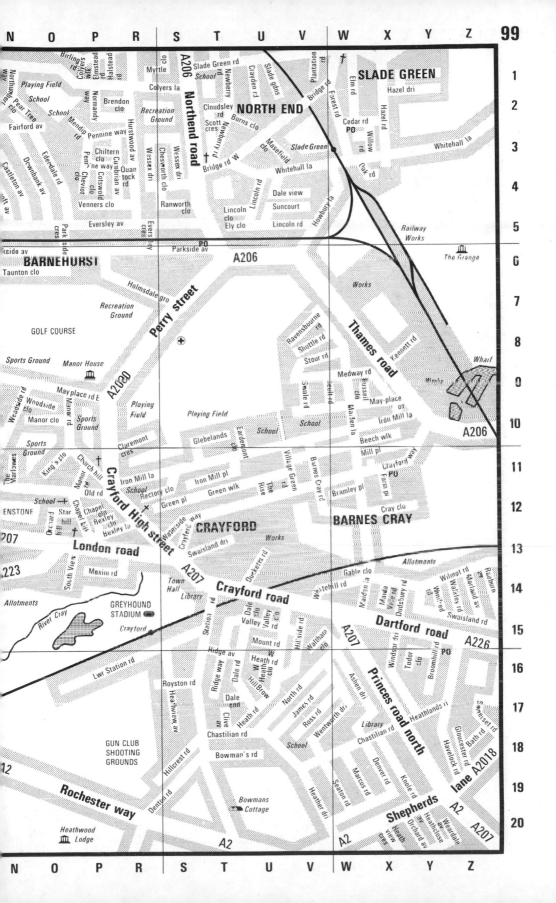

1

2

3

4

5

6

7

8

9

10

11

12

13

14

15

16

17

18

19

20

A206

Slade Green rd

School

Myttle

Colyers la

Birlings rd

Colyers Wlk

Elmstead

Halstead pl

Northumberland way

Pear Tree clo

Playing Field

School

School

Normandy way

Brendon clo

Hurstwood av

Recreation Ground

Newberry

Crayden rd

Slade gdns

Bridge rd

Plantation pl

SLADE GREEN

Elm rd

Hazel dri

Hazel rd

Whitehall la

NORTH END

Cloudsley rd

Scott cres

Burns clo

Newbury rd

Masefield clo

Forest rd

Cedar rd
PO

Willow rd

Oak rd

Fairford av

Mendip rd

Pennine way

Chiltern clo

Penn clo

ne way

Cumbrian av

Cotswold clo

Cheviot clo

Wessex dri

Chesworth clo

Wessex dri

Quantock rd

Bridge rd W

Lincoln rd

Lincoln rd

Dale view

Suncourt

Slade Green

Whitehall la

Castleton av

Downbank av

Edendale rd

Venners clo

Cumbrian av

Ranworth clo

Eversley av

Lincoln clo

Ely clo

Lincoln rd

Howbury la

Railway Works

The Grange

BARNEHURST

Taunton clo

Parkside av

Parkside av
PO

A206

Holmsdale gro

Perry street

Recreation Ground

Works

GOLF COURSE

Sports Ground

Manor House

A2000

May place rd E

Woodside clo

Woodside rd

Manor clo

Manor rd

Sports Ground

Playing Field

Playing Field

Ravensbourne rd

Shuttle rd

Stour rd

Medway rd

Swale rd

Leeth rd

Russell rd

Malden la

Thames road

Kennett rd

Wharf

May-place av

Iron Mill la

A206

Sports Ground

The Marlowes

King's clo

Church hill

Manor rd

Old rd

Claremont cres

Glebelands

Eardemont clo

School

School

Beech wlk

Mill pl

Crayford way
PO

School

ENSTONE

Orchard

Star clo

Chapel hill

Chapel clo

Bexley

Bexley la

Crayford High street

Iron Mill la

Rectory clo

Green pl

Iron Mill pl

Green wlk

Village Green rd

The Rise

Barnes Cray rd

Bramley pl

Cray clo

BARNES CRAY

A207

School

London road

Waterside way

Crayford side way

Swaisland dri

CRAYFORD

Works

A207

Duckets rd

Crayford road

Whitehill rd

Gable clo

Allotments

Maidan la

Marsh dri

Duddsbury rd

Wilmot rd

Morland rd

Walkley rd

Whit rd

Raeburn

Swaisland rd

A223

South View

Maxim rd

Town Hall

Library

Dale rd

Valley rd

Valley rd

Hill side rd

Waltham rd

A207

Dartford road

Windsor dri

Broomhill rd

A226
PO

Allotments

River Cray

GREYHOUND STADIUM

Crayford

Station rd

Mount rd

Ridge av

Dale rd

Dale rd

Hill Brow

Heath clo

North rd

James rd

Ross rd

Wentworth dri

Ashen dri

Heathlands ri

Tudor rd

Havelock rd

A2018

Royston rd

Heathview av

Clive rd

Dale end

Heath rd

School

Marcus rd

Denver rd

Gloucester rd

Bath rd

Lwr Station rd

Hillcrest rd

Chastilian rd

Library

Chastilian rd

Knole rd

Princes road north

Somerset rd

GUN CLUB SHOOTING GROUNDS

Bowman's rd

Seaton rd

Heather dri

lane A2018

Rochester way

Denton rd

Bowmans Cottage

Shepherds

Weardale av

Heath close

Heath view

Orchard av

A2

A207

Heathwood Lodge

A2

A2

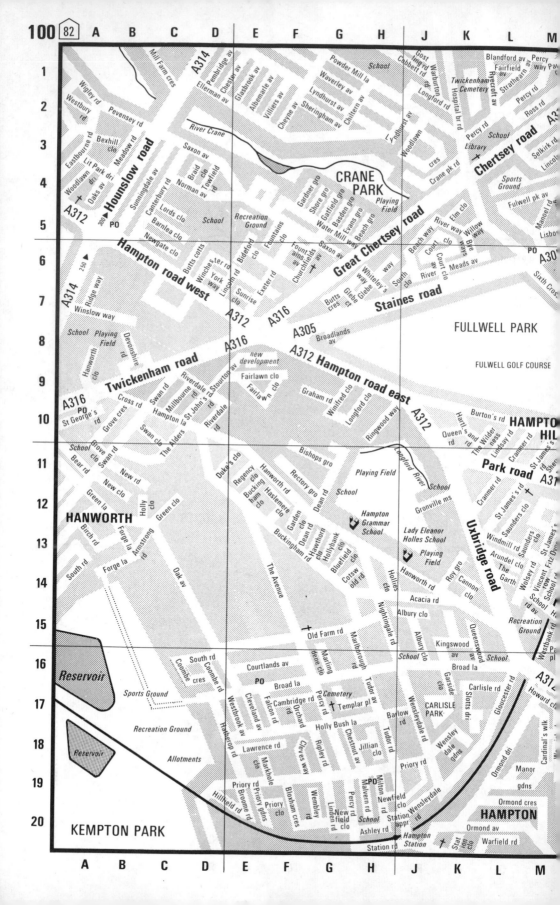

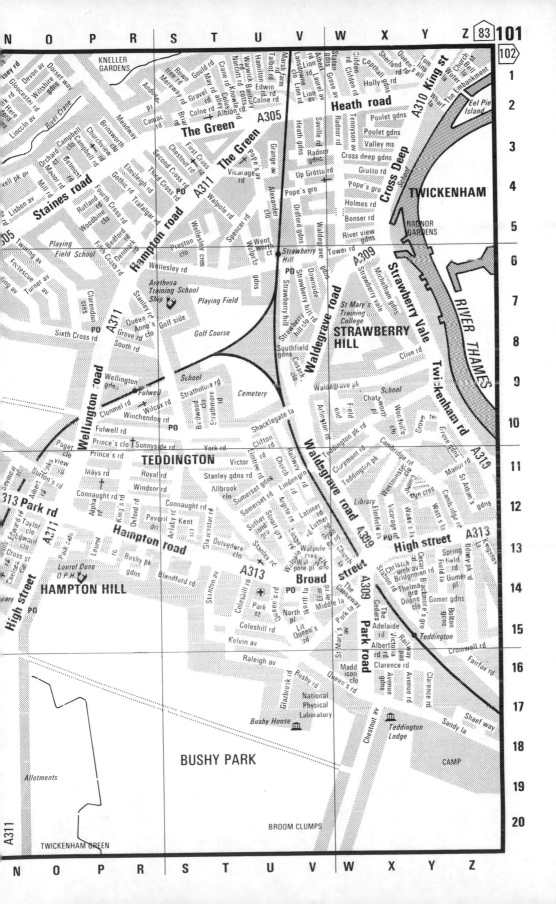

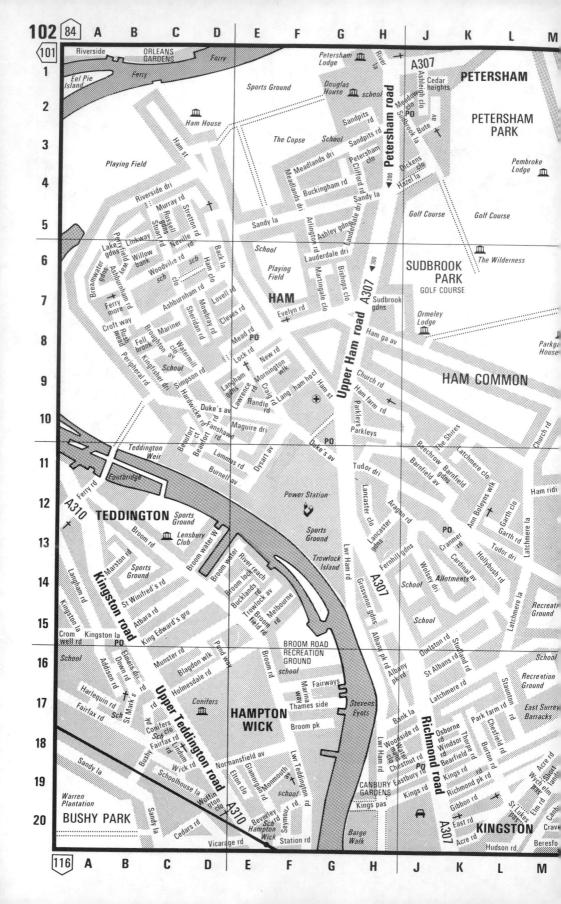

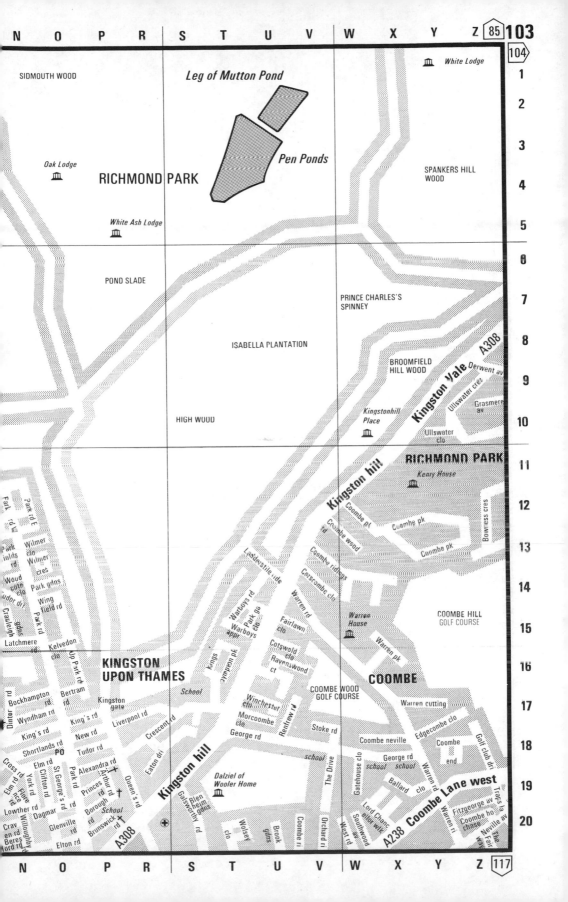

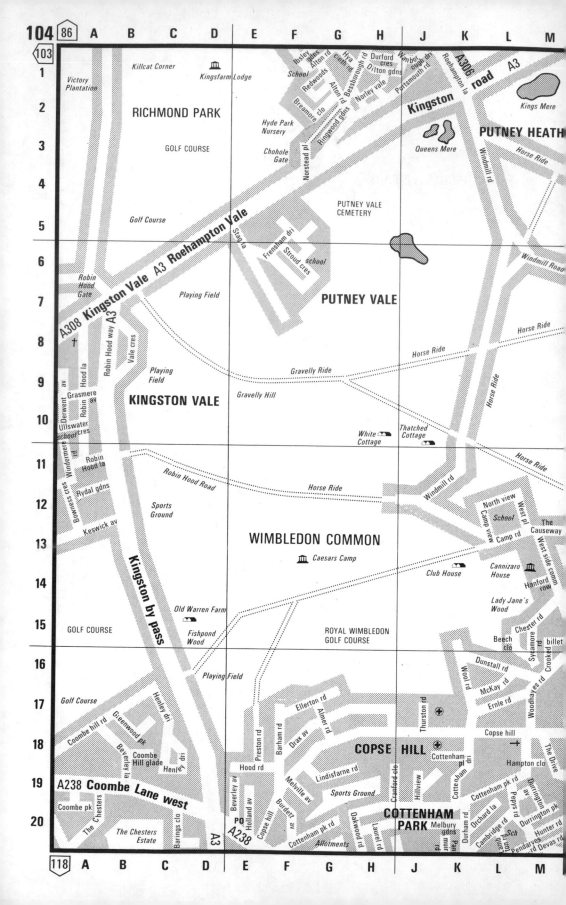

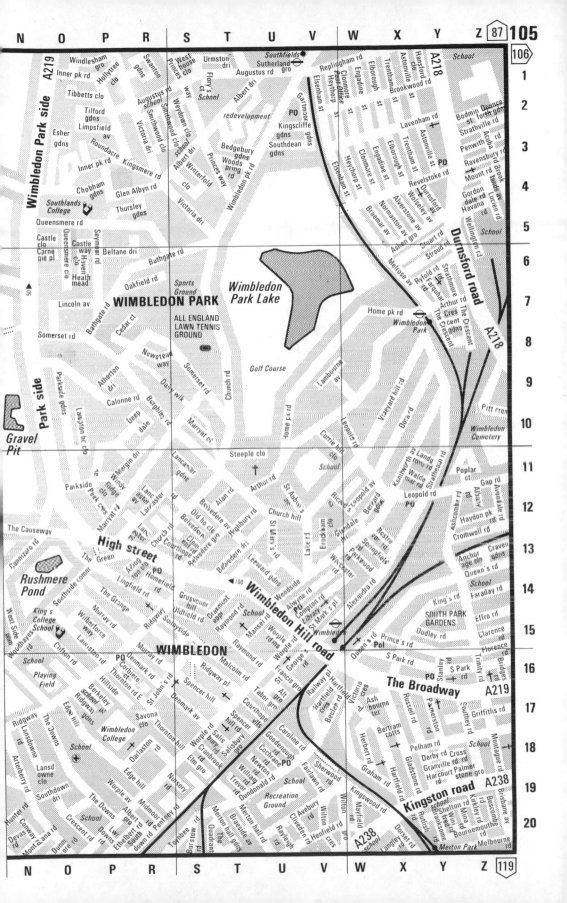

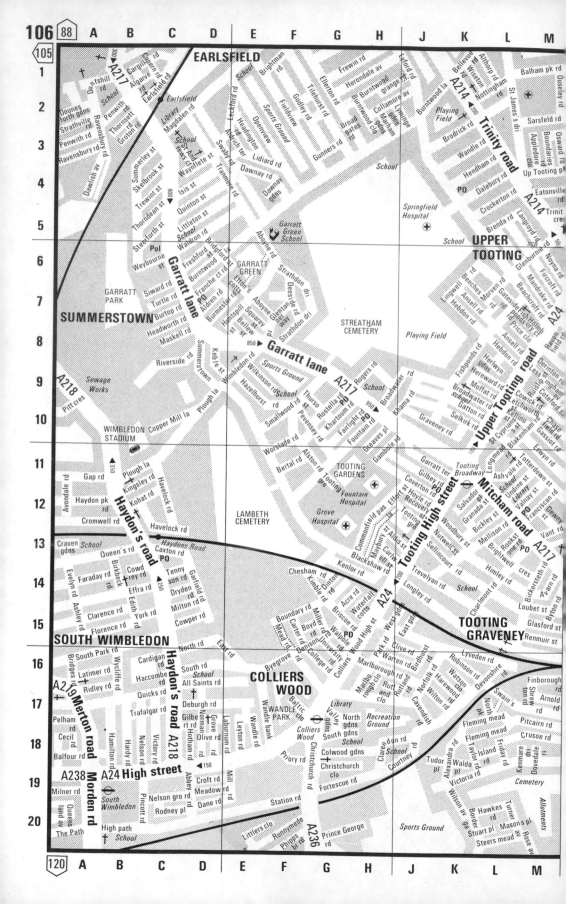

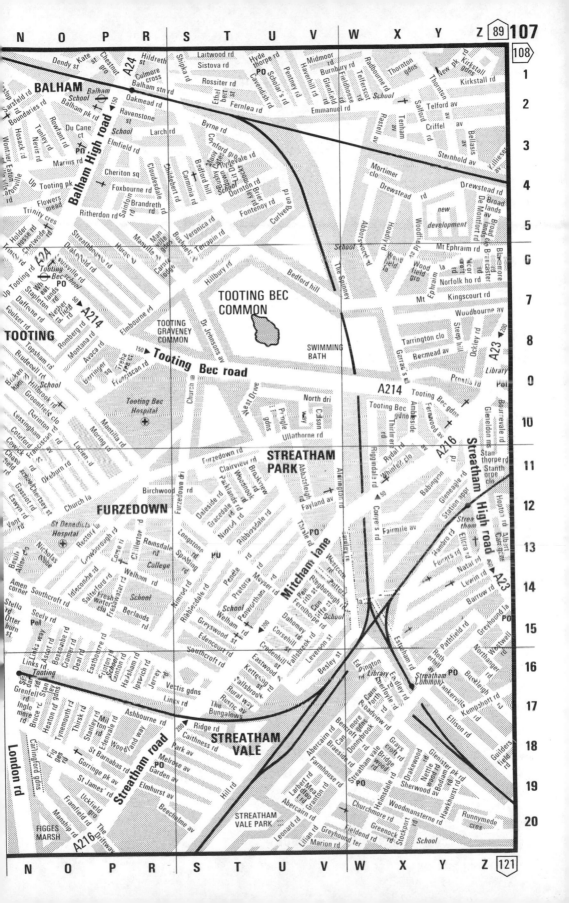

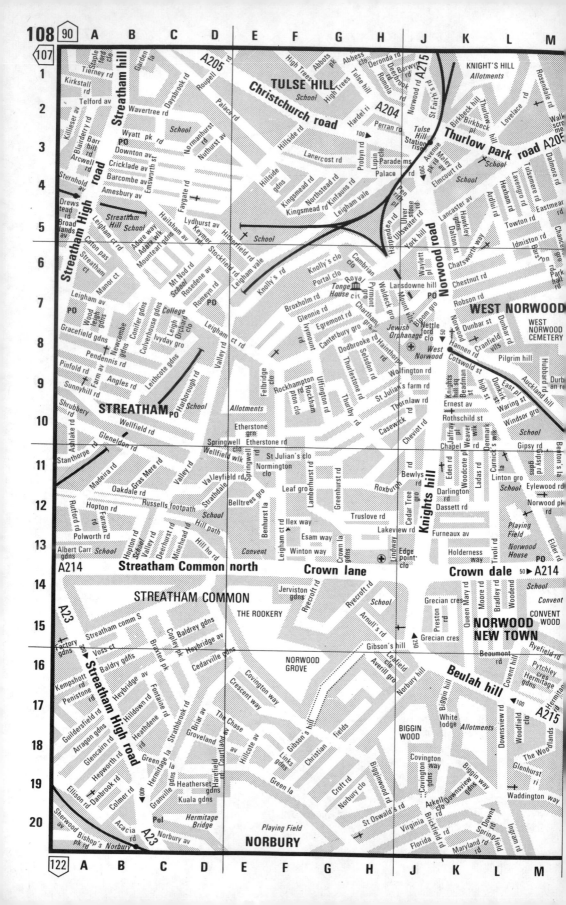

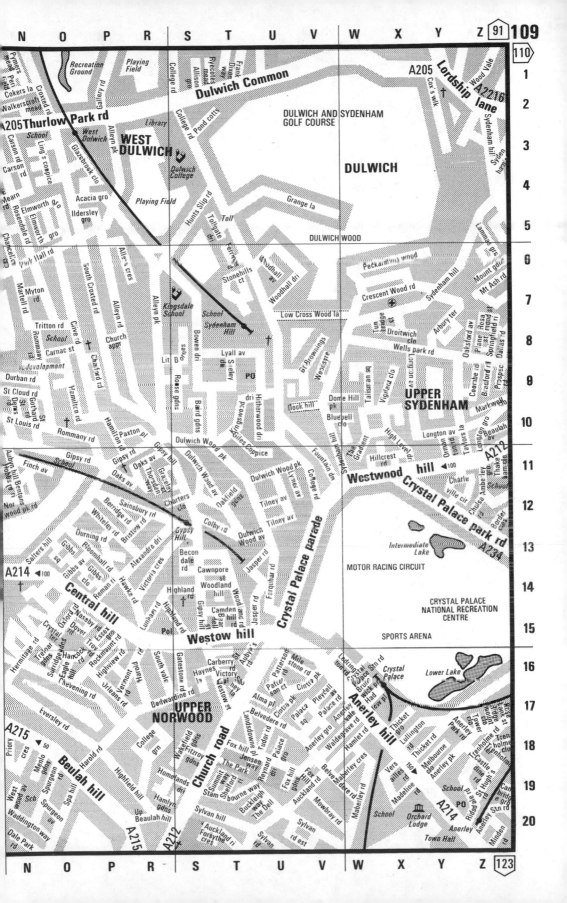

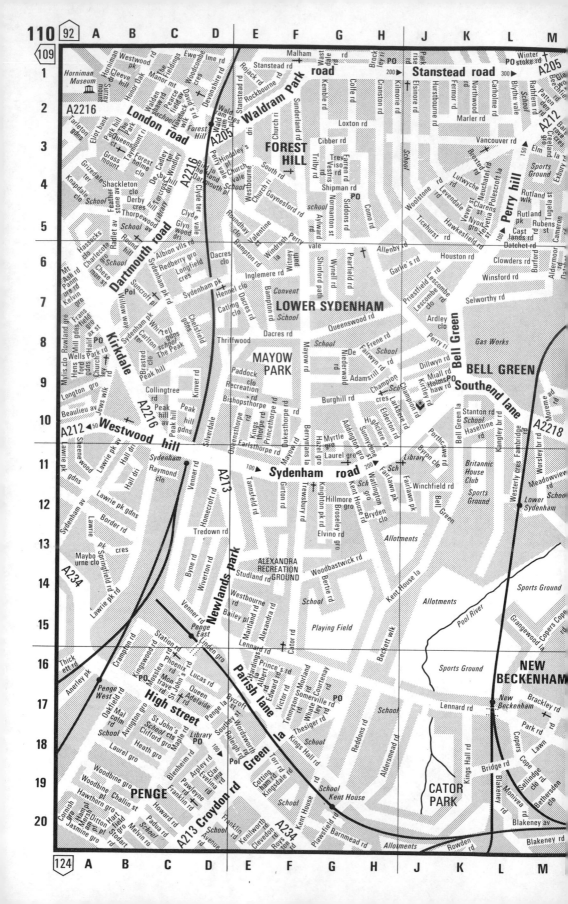

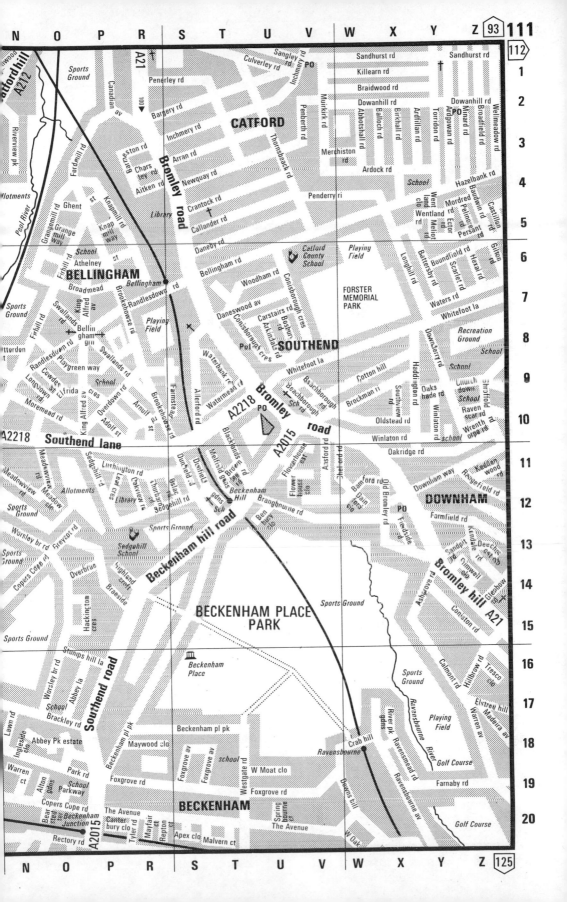

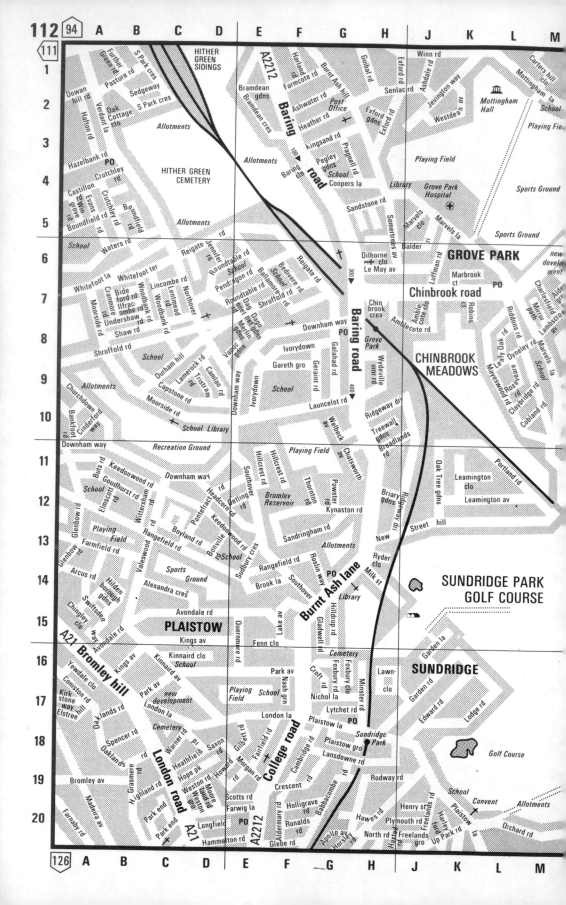

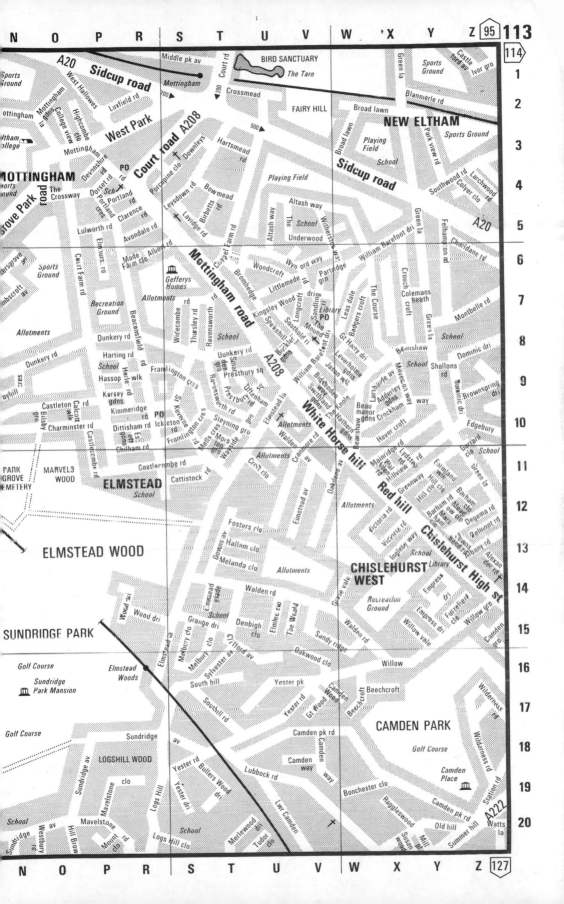

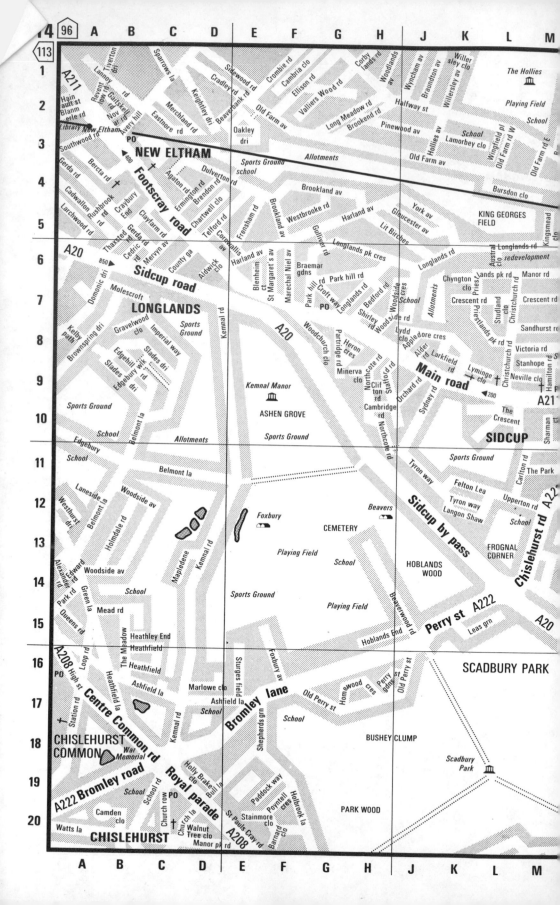

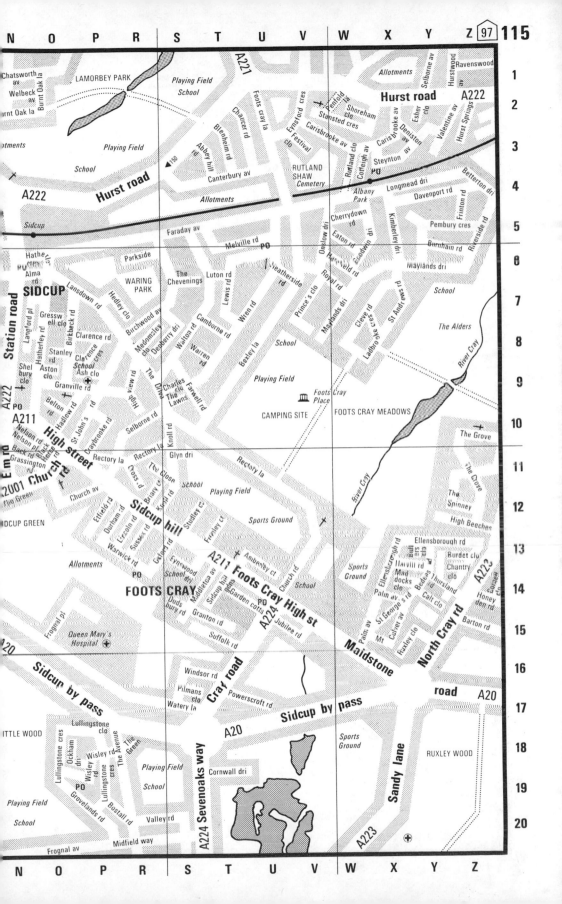

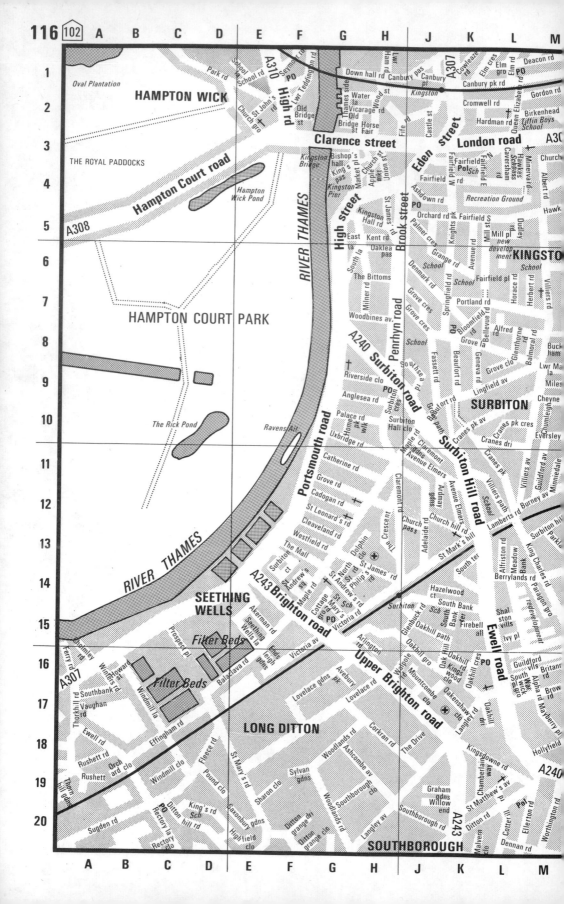

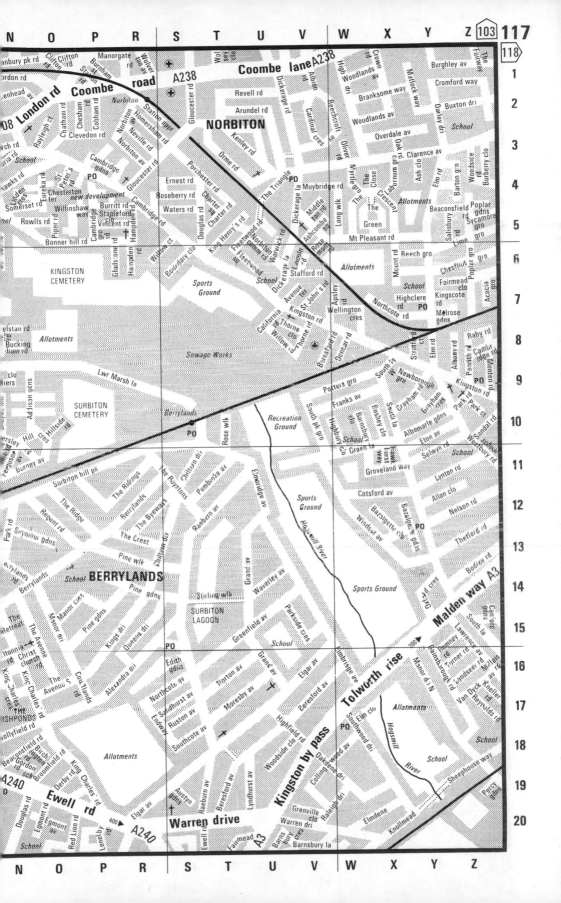

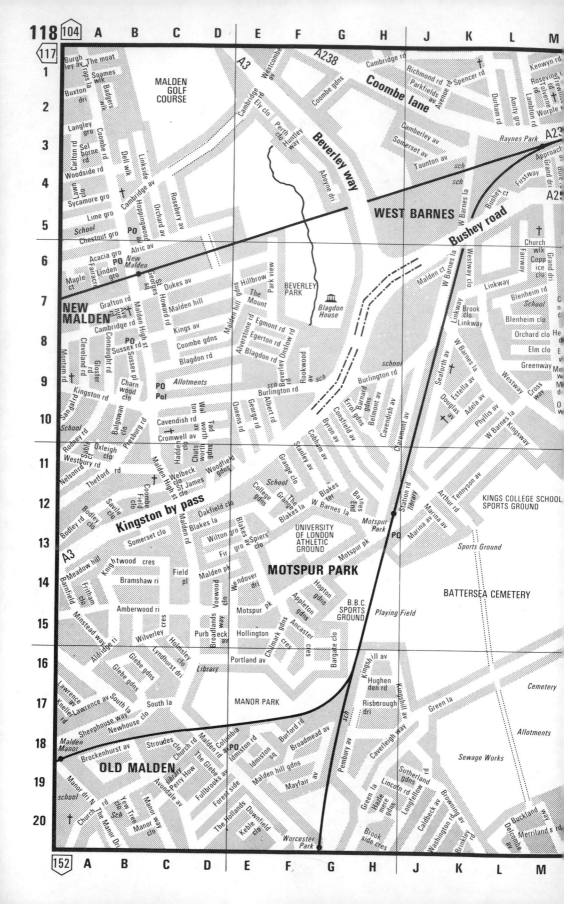

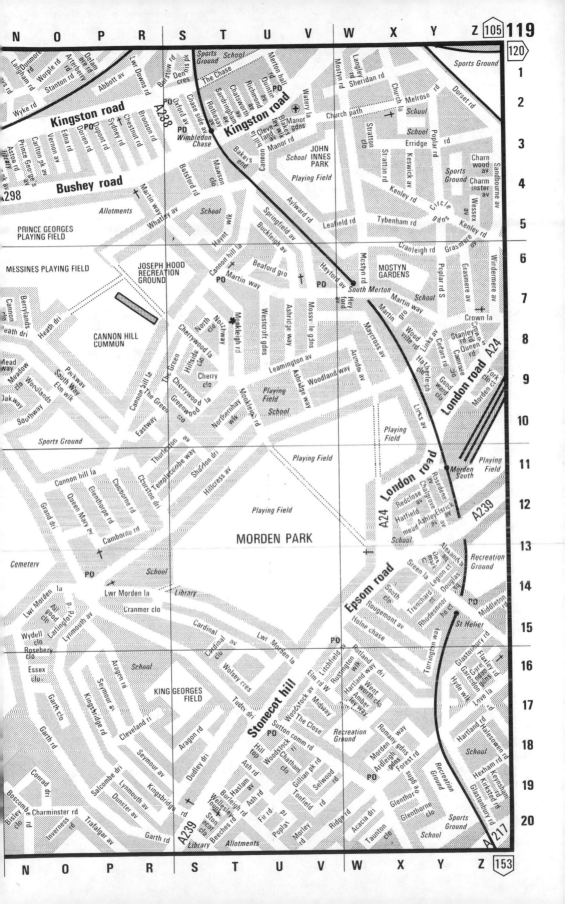

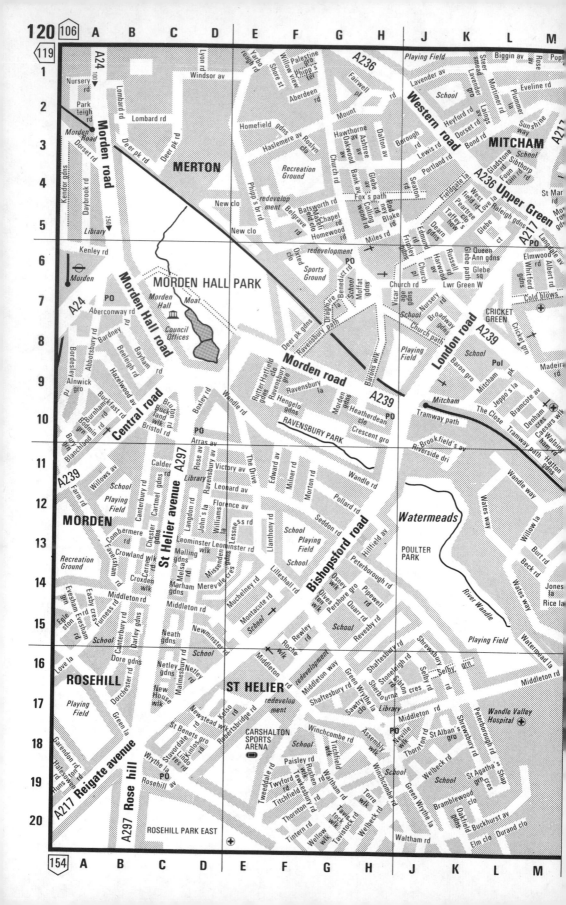

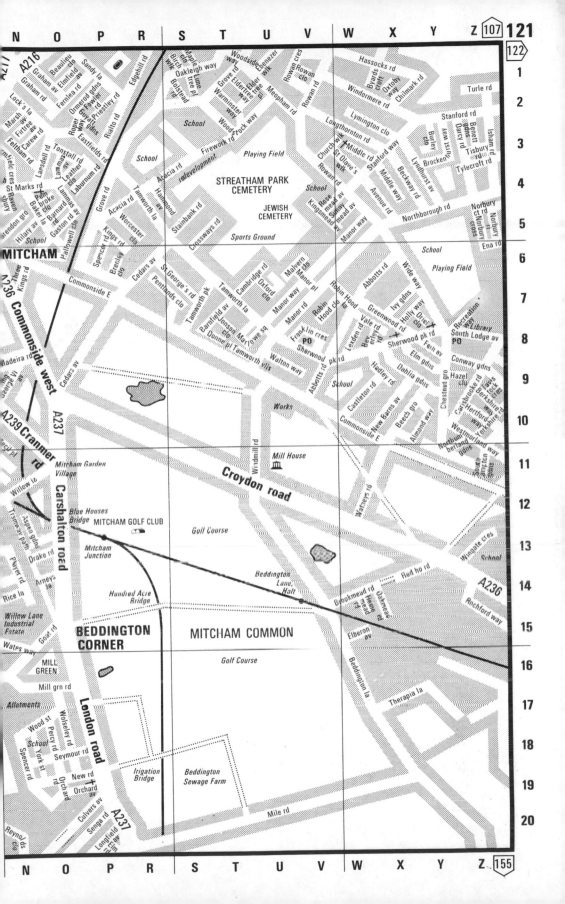

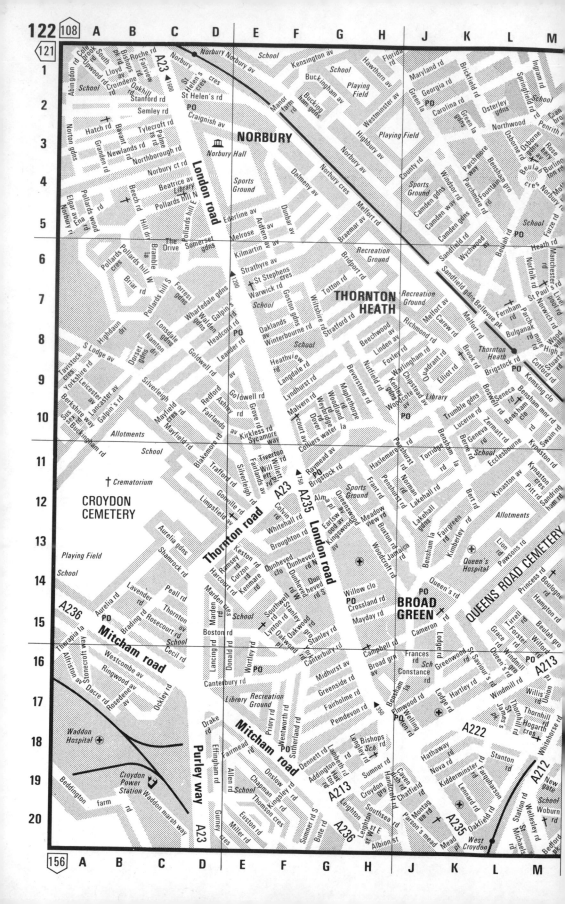

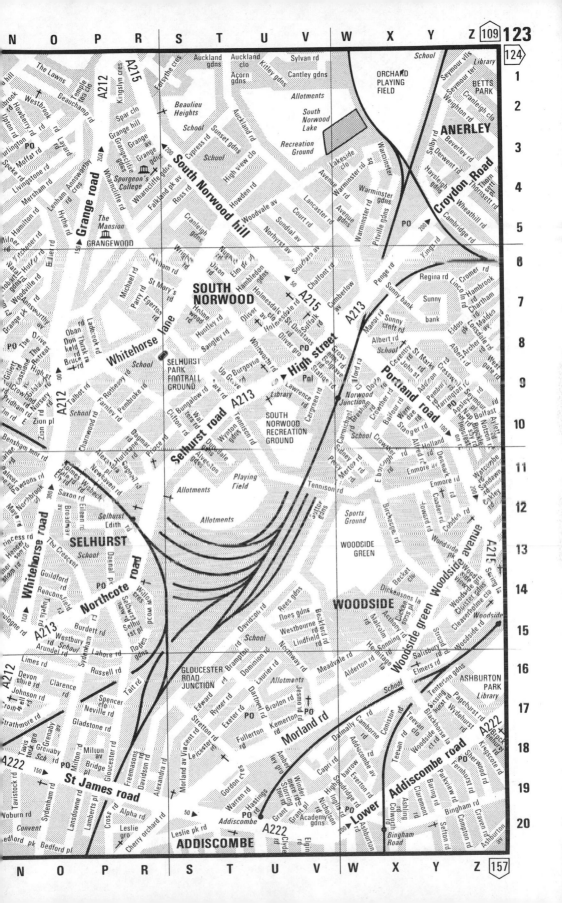

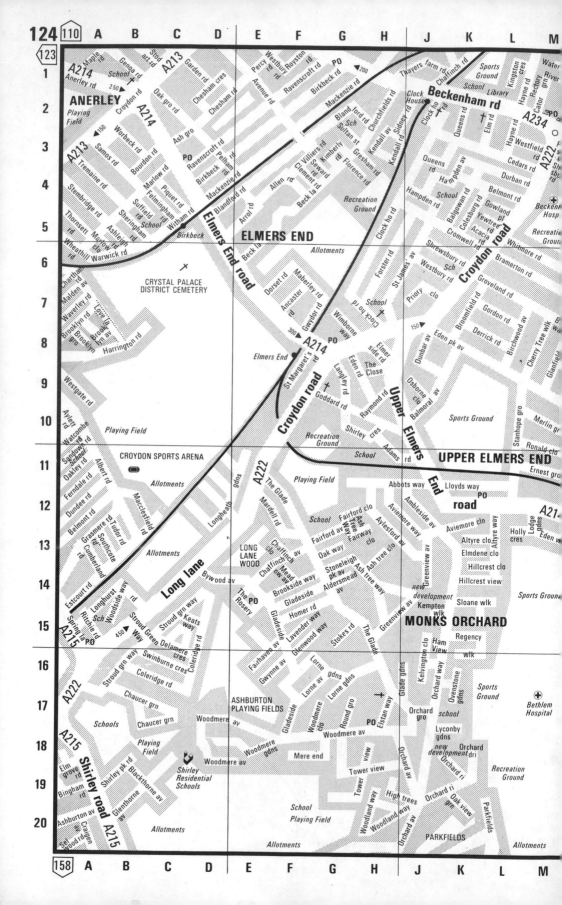

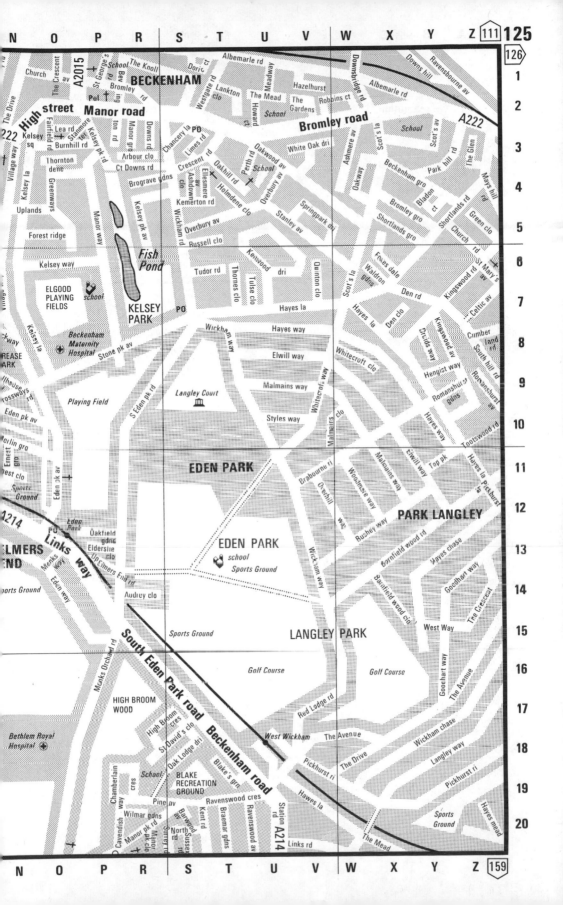

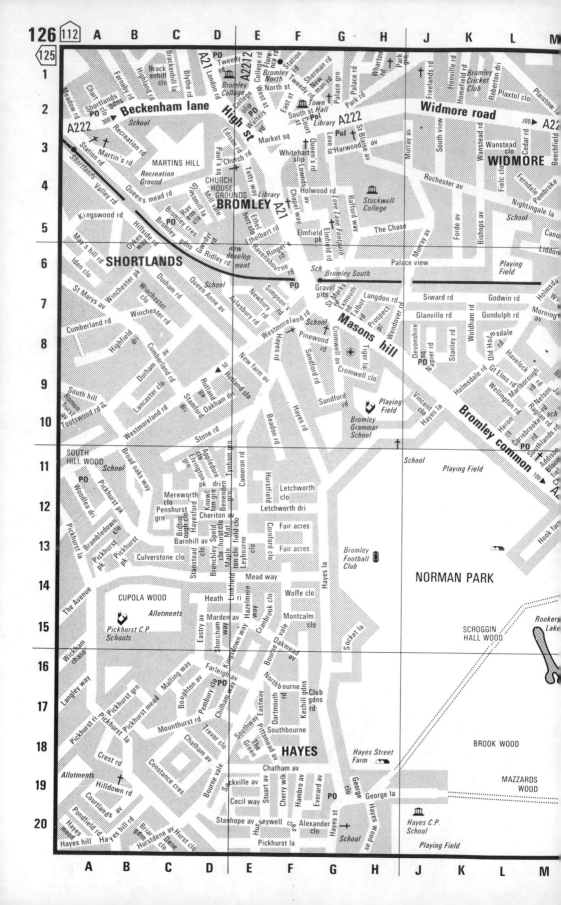

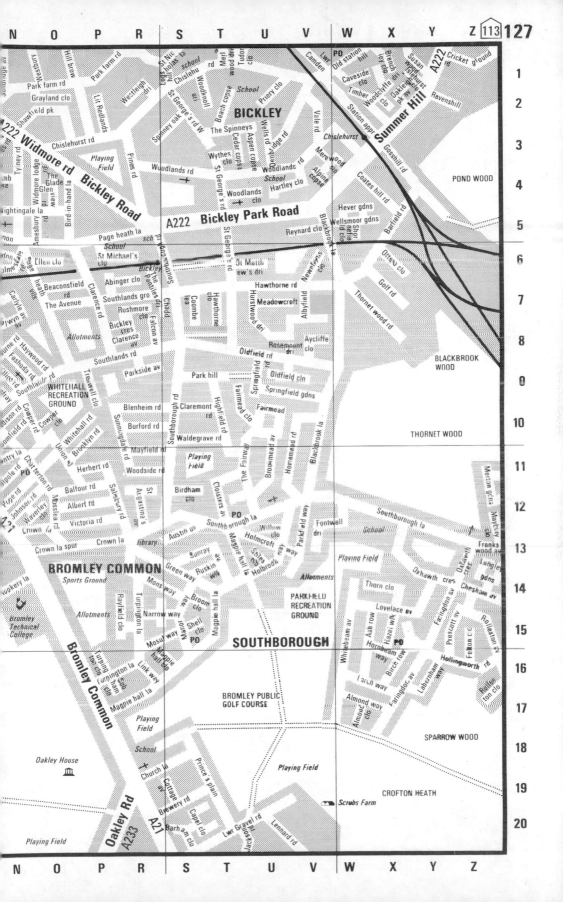

BICKLEY

Widmore rd
Bickley Road

A222 Bickley Park Road

POND WOOD

BLACKBROOK
WOOD

THORNET WOOD

WHITEHALL
RECREATION
GROUND

BROMLEY COMMON

Sports Ground

Bromley
Technical
College

SOUTHBOROUGH

PARKFIELD
RECREATION
GROUND

Bromley Common

BROMLEY PUBLIC
GOLF COURSE

SPARROW WOOD

Oakley House

Oakley Rd

CROFTON HEATH

Scrubs Farm

Playing Field

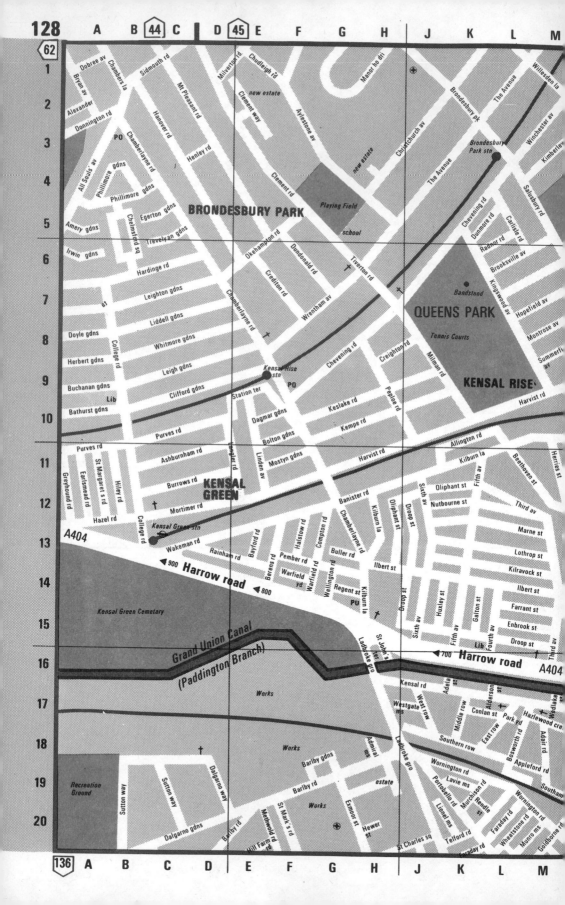

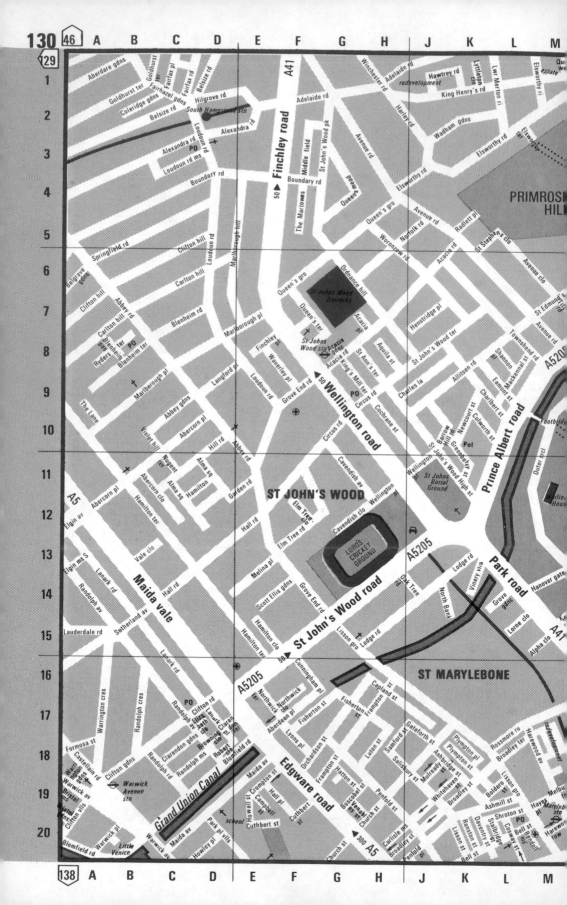

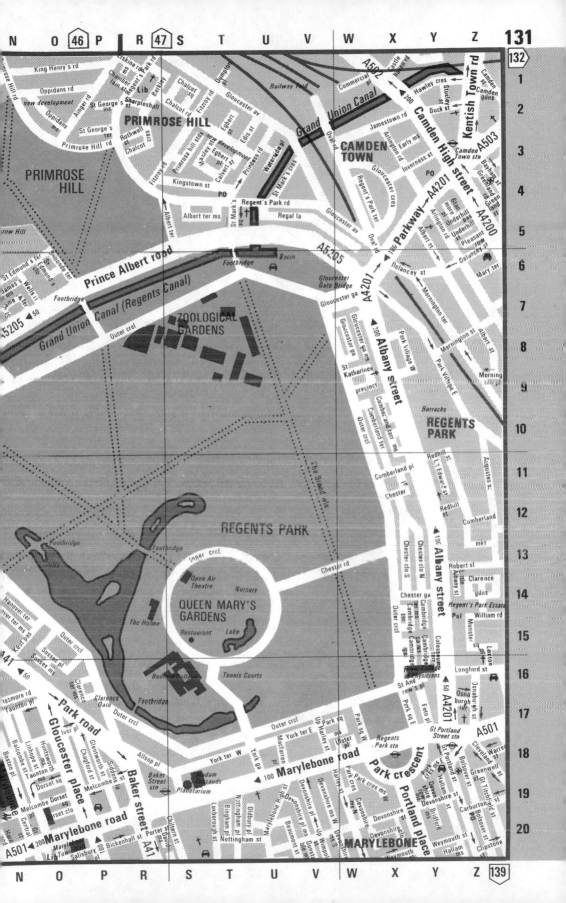

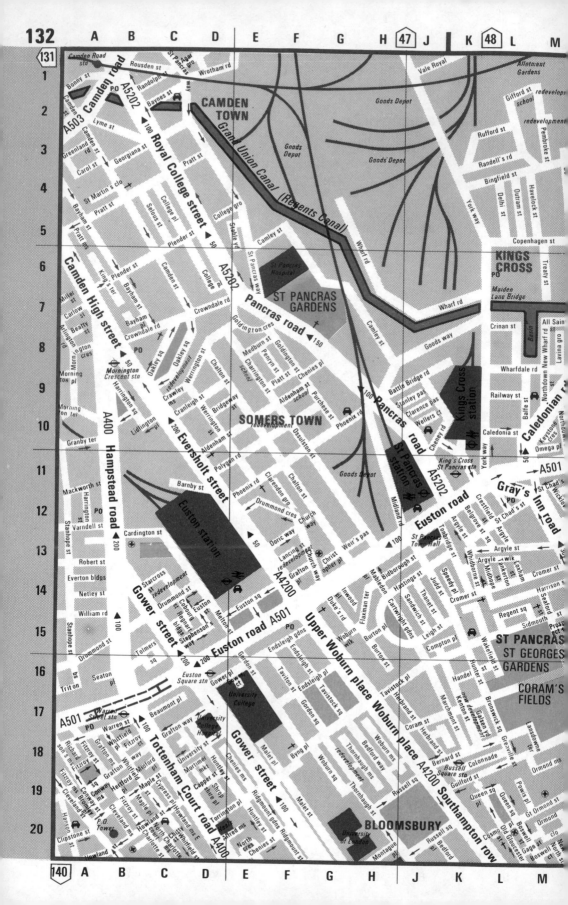

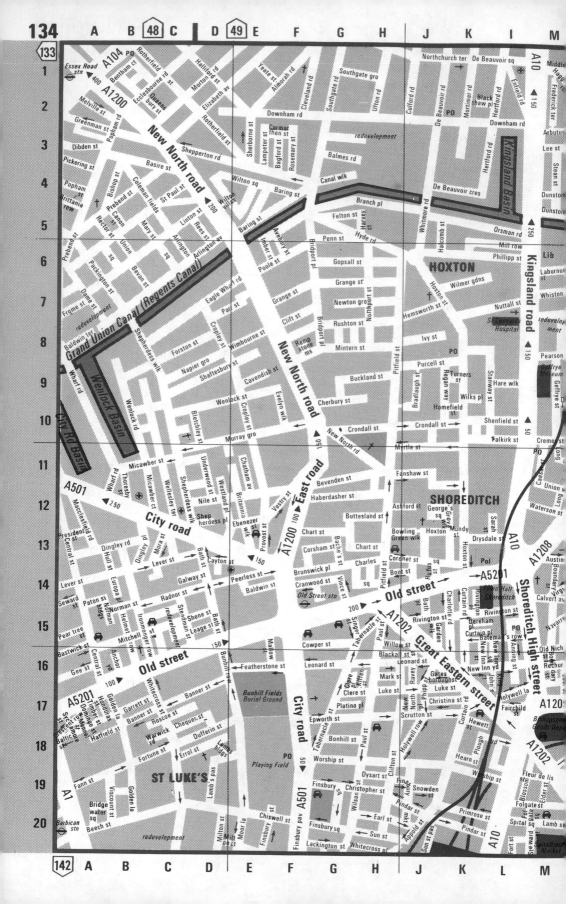

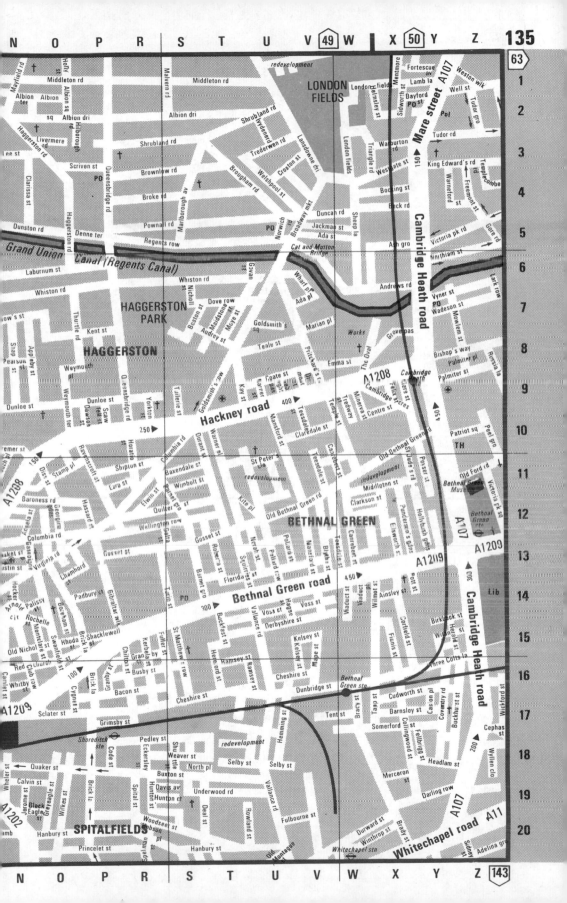

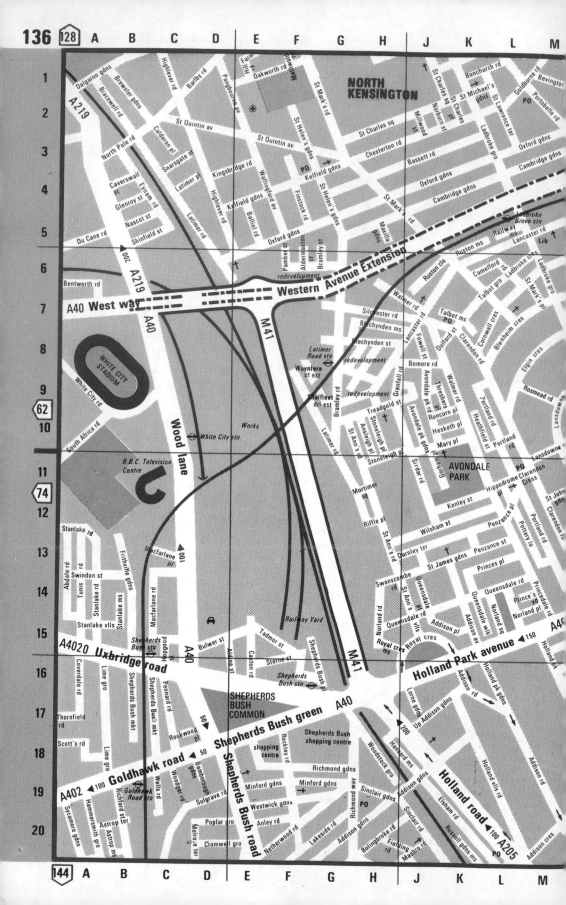

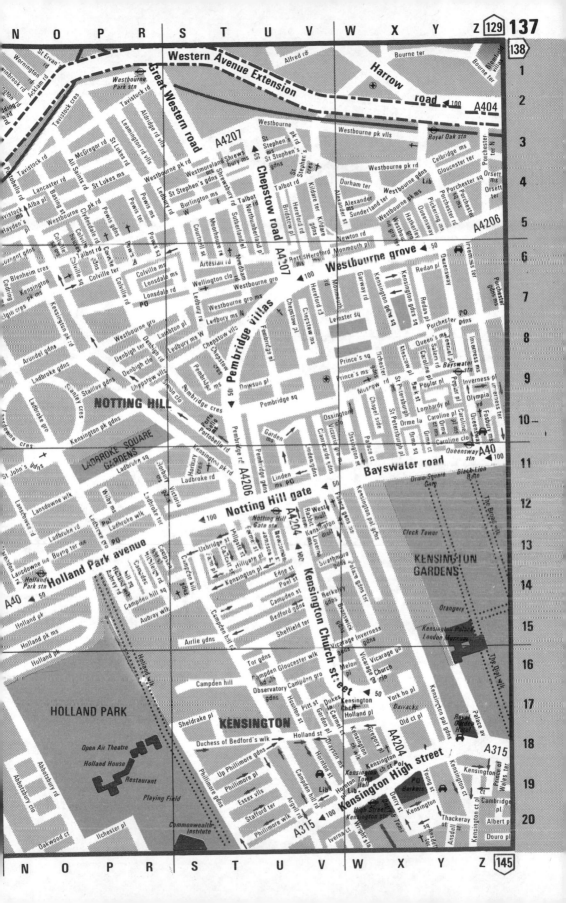

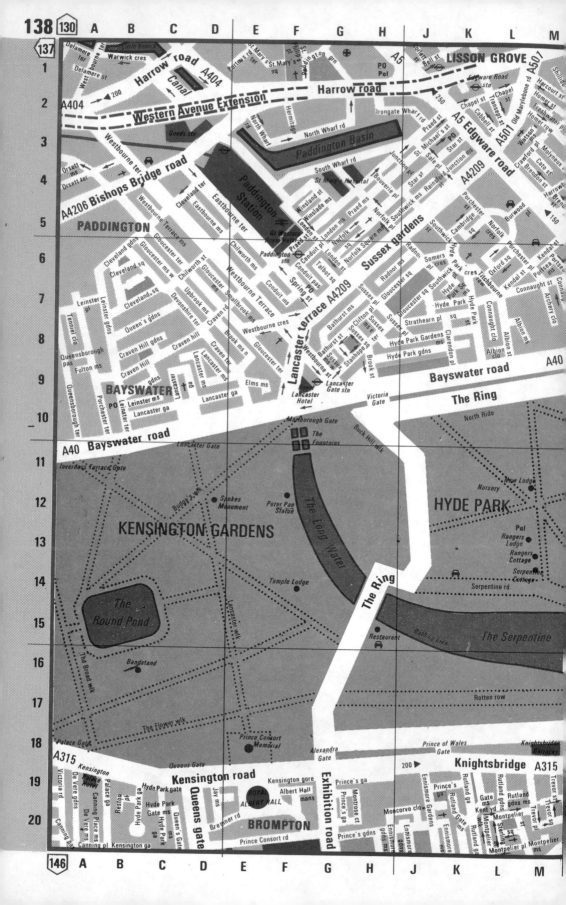

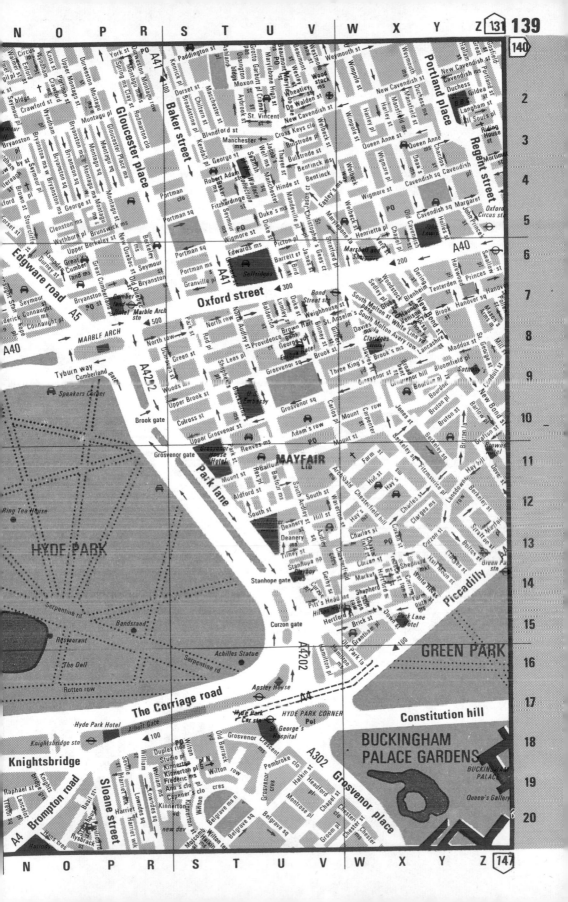

York st   PO  A41  Paddington st
Circus st
Walmer st  Wyndham
gil la  Enford    Durweston st  Montagu pl  Kenrick pl
Upper Montagu st  Montagu sq  Montagu row
Knox st   Ashland  Moxon st
Crawford st   Dorset st  Dessington  Grotto Garbutt pl  Weymouth st
Portman Montagu  Gloucester place  Chiltern st  Aybrook st  St. Vincent  New Cavendish st
Bryanston  Montagu pl   Baker street   Cramer  Oe Walden   Wheatley  Beaumont
Bryanston ms w   Montagu st   Broadstone st  Blandford st  Manchester  Cross Keys clo  New Cavendish st
by st  Montagu  Montagu row  Kendal pl  George st  Thayer st  Bulstrode pl  Duchess
Bryanston  Montagu pl  Gloucester place  Robert Adam  Wallace   Bentinck st  New Cavendish st
Brown st  Bryanston  Montagu sq  st  Collection  Hinde st  Bentinck  Duchess
Seymour  by  George st  Fitzhardinge st  Mandeville pl  Bentinck  Portland place
Clenston ms  Wythburn pl  Brunswick  Duke's ms  Marylebone la  Cavendish sq Margaret
Upper Berkeley st  New Quebec st  Old Quebec  Picton pl  PO  Cavendish sq Cavendish  Holles  Oxford
Edgware road  Seymour  Cumberland ms  Portman sq  Edwards ms  Marshall and  Henrietta pl  Chapel pl  A40  Circus st  John Lewis
Bryanston  Seymour  Portman ms  Barrett st  Statmore  Swallow
Seymour  Granville pl  Selfridges  Bond  Woodstock  Deering  Tenterden  Princes
derick  Connaught  A5  Oxford street  300  Street cla  South Molton  Blenheim  Hanover
A40  Marble Arch  Bayswater  North row  Brown Hart  Ginney st  Davies  South Molton  White Lion st  Brook  Hanover sq
Marble Arch  stn  500  North row  Providence  George yd  Claridges  Lancashire  Maddox st  Mill
Tyburn way  Green st  Leos pl  Brook st  Davies  Brook's ms  Bloomfield pl  Sotheb
Cumberland gate  Shepherd  Grosvenor sq  Three King's yd  Grosvenor hill  Bourdon  New Bond st
Speakers Corner  A4202  Woods ms  US Embassy  Grosvenor sq  Carlos pl  Grosvenor hill  Bruton st  Barlow
Brook gate  Upper Brook st  Adam's row  Mount row  Jones st  Bruton st
Culross st  Balfour  Carpenter  Berkeley sq  Barlow st
Upper Grosvenor st  Reeves ms  MAYFAIR  Mount st  Farm  Hill st  Fitzmaurice pl  Hay Hill  Browns
Grosvenor gate  Grosvenor  Park lane  MAYFAIR  Aldford st  South st  Hill st  Chesterfield hill  Clarges ms  Lansdowne  Berkeley st  Dove st
Ring Tea House  Hotel  Mount st  Balfour  South Audley st  Hay's  Charles st  Curzon st  Bolton
HYDE PARK  Park lane  South st  Hill st  Charles st  PO  Curzon st  Mayfair
Deanery st  Deanery  Tilney st  Stanhope ga  Curzon st  Shepherd  White Horse  Piccadilly
Bandstand  Stanhope gate  Playboy  Derby ga  Market  Hertford  Green Park
Serpentine rd  Club  Pitt's Head ms  Shepherd  stn
Restaurant  Curzon gate  Hill  Brick st  Park Lane  Piccadilly
The Dell  Achilles Statue  A4202  Hamilton  Hertford  Hotel  GREEN PARK
Rotten row  Serpentine rd  Park la  Constitution hill
Apsley House  A4
The Carriage road  Hyde Park  Car stn  HYDE PARK CORNER  Pol  BUCKINGHAM
Hyde Park Hotel  Albert Gate  St. George's  PALACE GARDENS
Knightsbridge stn  100  PO Wilton  Hospital  BUCKINGHAM
Knightsbridge  Duplex pl  Studio pl  Grosvenor  St  PALACE
Raphael st  William  Kinnerton pl  P N  Wilton row  Grosvenor Crescent  A302  Queen's Gallery
Brompton road  Sloane street  Frederic pl  Wilton pl  Pembroke clo  Grosvenor place
A4  Harriet st  Ann's clo  Halkin st  Headfort  Chapel pl  Chester
Hans cres  Kinnerton  Capener's clo  cres  Montrose pl  Chester st  Chester
new dev  Lowndes sq  Kinnerton  Belgrave ms s  Chapel pl  Groom pl
Rysback st  Basil st  Harriet wlk  Belgrave sq  Chester  Chester
Lancelot pl  Harriet sq  Moncomb  Wilton ter  Belgrave pl

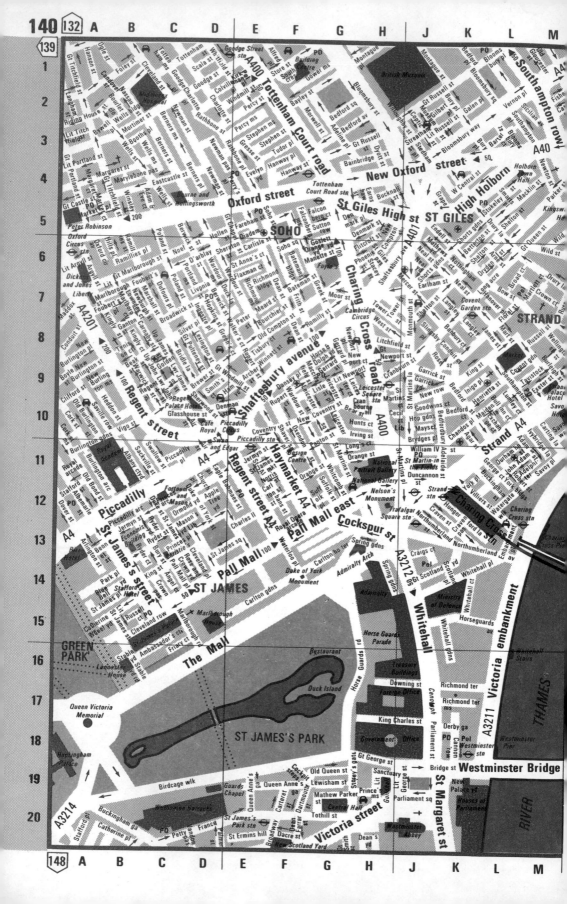

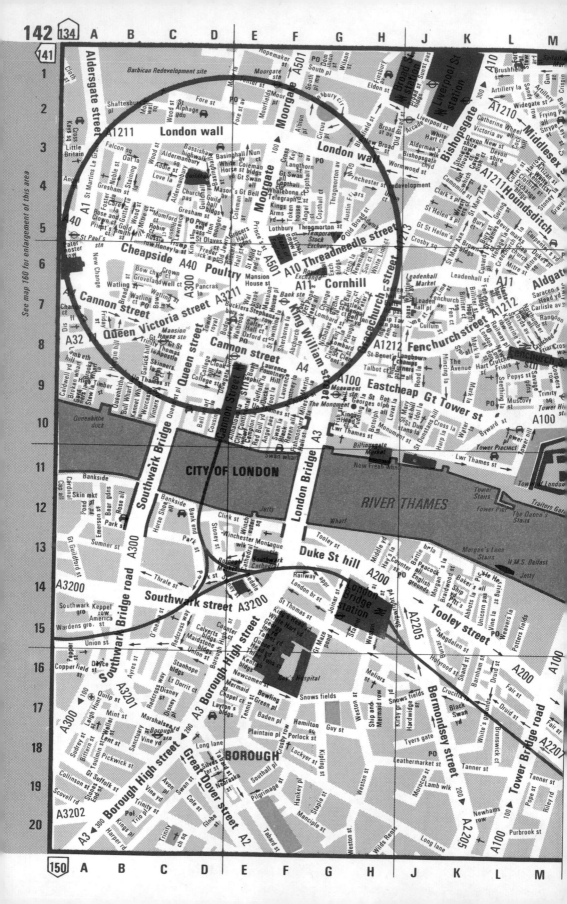

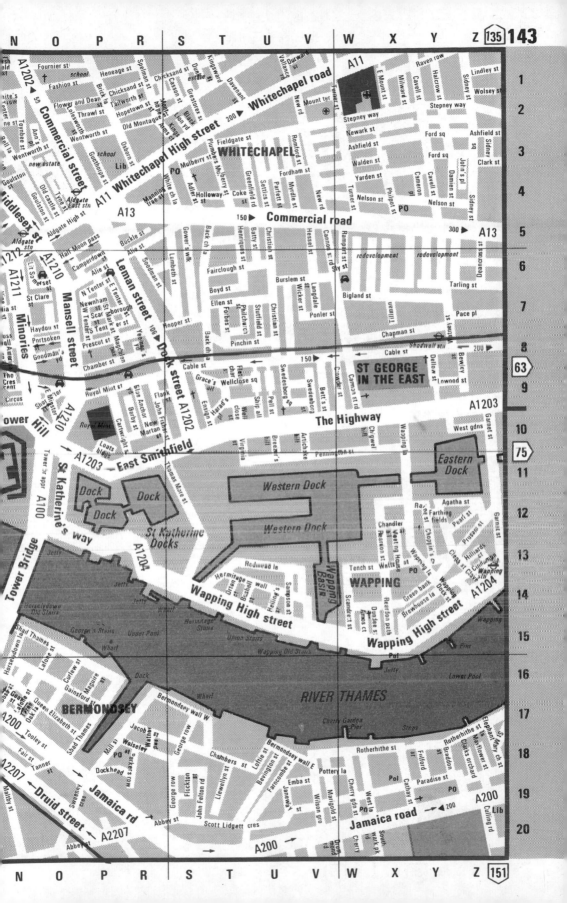

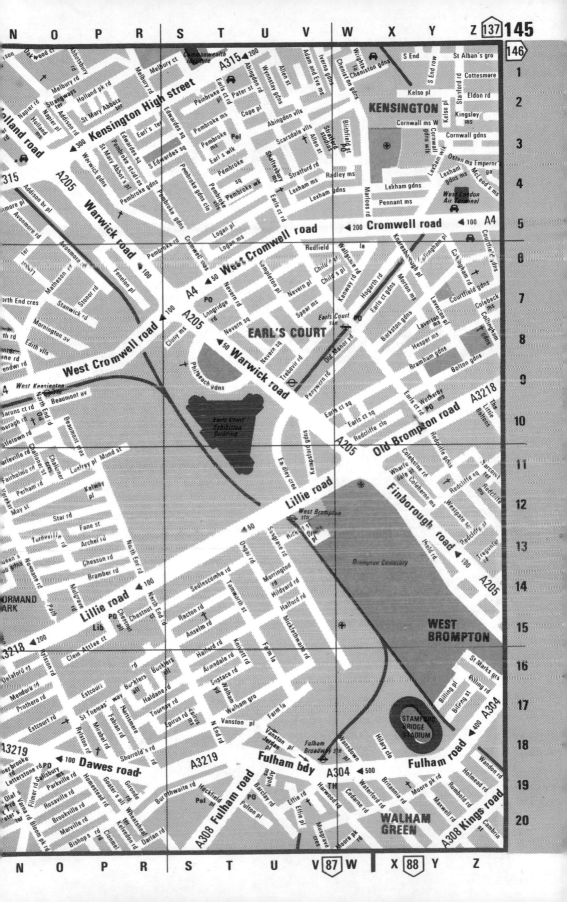

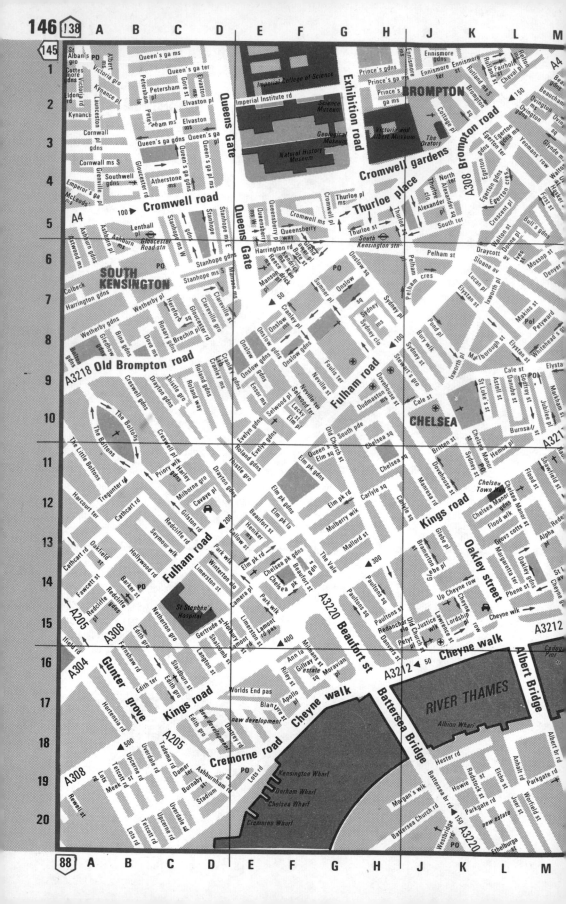

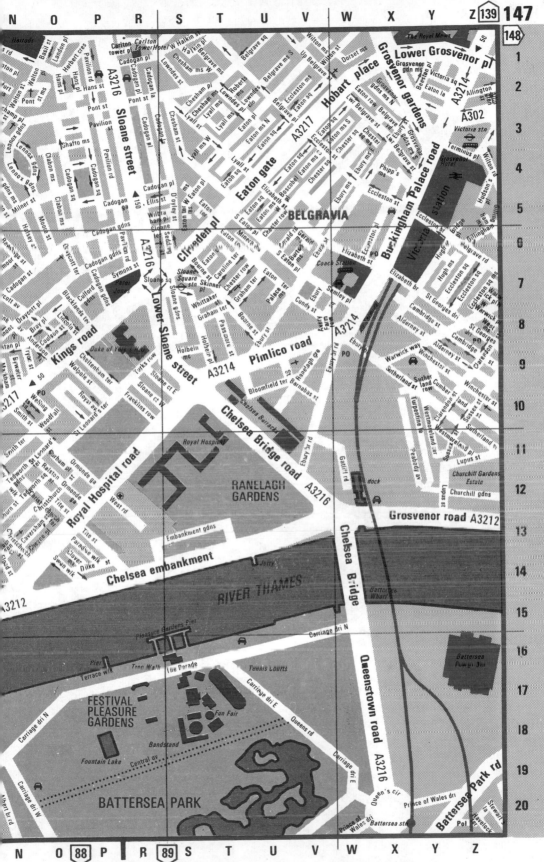

1
2
3
4
5
6
7
8
9
10
11
12
13
14
15
16
17
18
19
20

Harrods  Basil st  Landon pl  Herbert cres  Pavilion rd  Carlton Carlton  Tower pl Tower Hotel W Halkin st  Belgrave  Wilton st  The Royal Mews  50  **Lower Grosvenor pl**

Walton  Hans pl  Cadogan pl  W Halkin st Belgrave  Cheshani ms  Belgrave ms S  Up Belgrave  Wilson st  Dorset ms  Grosvenor gdns m Victoria sq  Beeston st  Eaton la

Pont st ms  Hans rd  Cadogan pl  Lowndes  Robert s  Belgrave ms S  Eccleston  Eaton row Belgrave  Grosvenor gardens  Eaton la  Allington

**A3216**  Hans st  Cadogan la  Lowndes  Chesham ms  Lyall ms W  Lyall st  Belgrave  Eaton ter  Eaton row Belgrave  A3214  A302

Pont st  Pont st  Cadogan pl  Chesham st  Lyall st  Eaton ms N  Eaton sq  Eaton la  W Belgrave  Chester  Grosvenor  Victoria stn

Pavilion rd  **Sloane street**  Cadogan pl  Lyall ms W  Eaton sq  Chester ms  Chester st  W Belgrave  **Buckingham Palace road**  A3214  Hudson s

Shafto ms  **Eaton gate**  Eaton sq  Chester row  Eaton la  **station**  Grosvenor Hotel

**BELGRAVIA**

**RIVER THAMES**

**FESTIVAL PLEASURE GARDENS**

**BATTERSEA PARK**

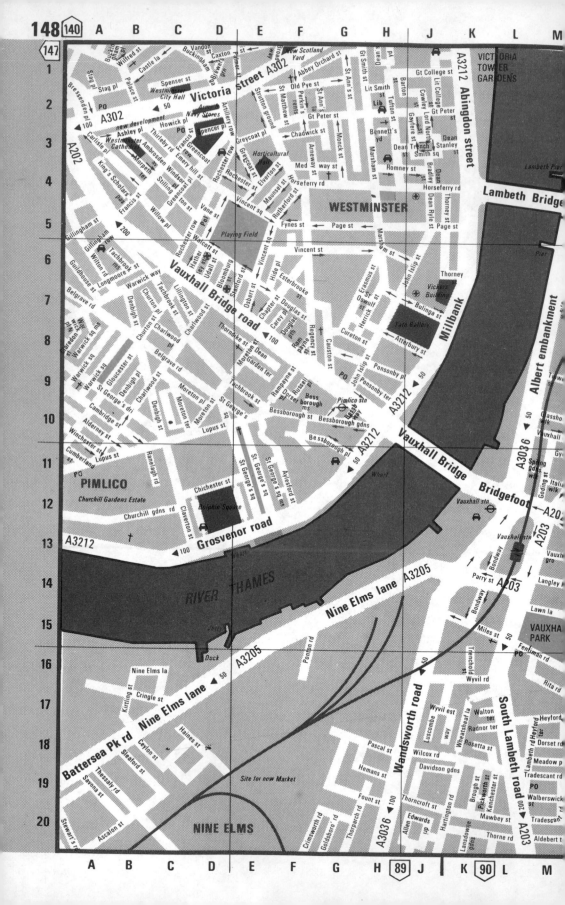

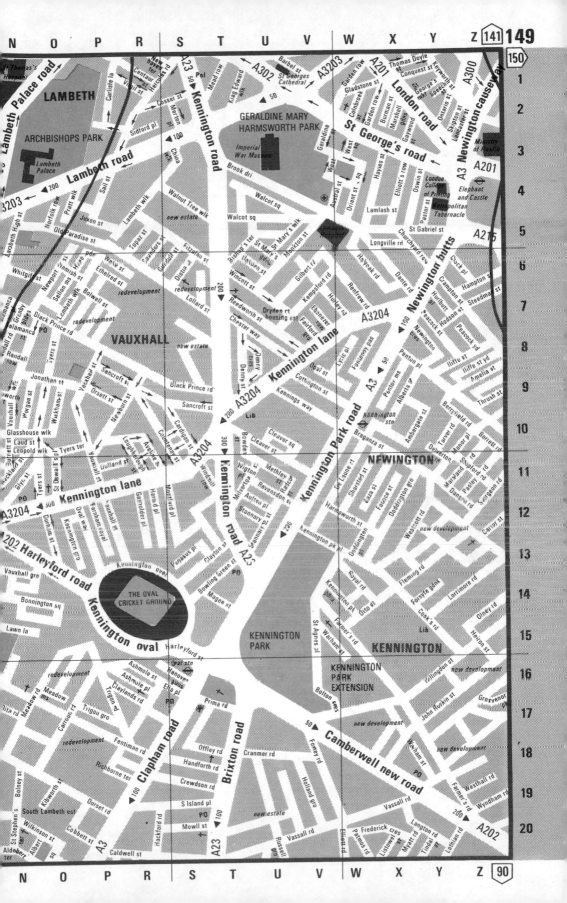

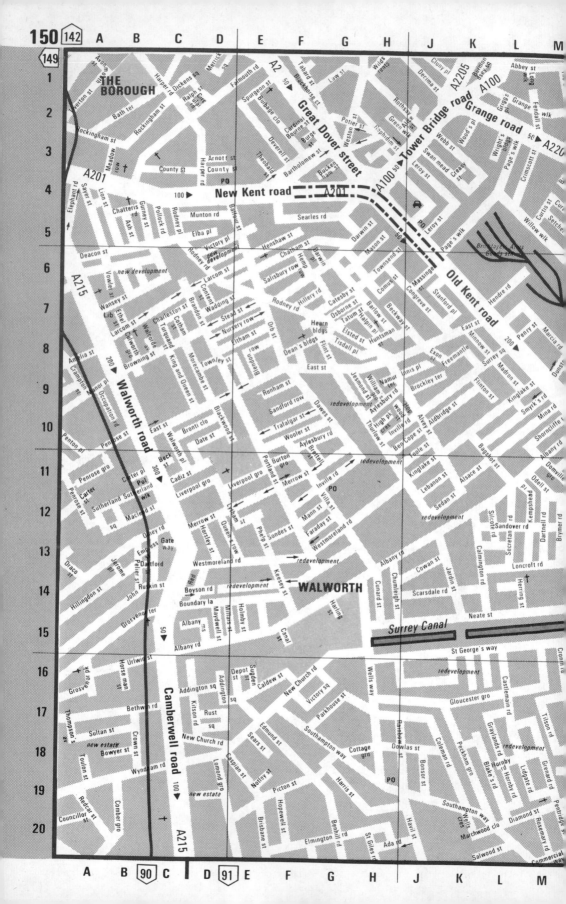

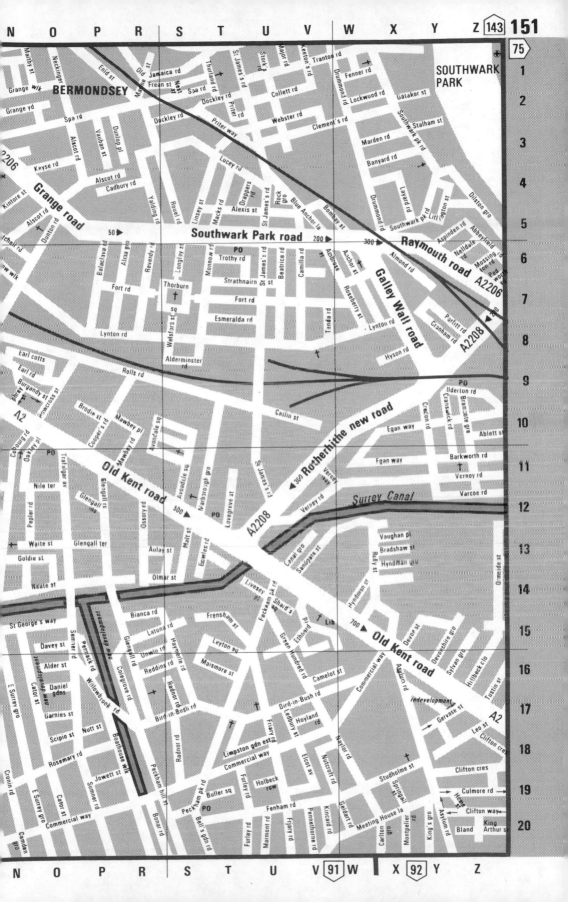

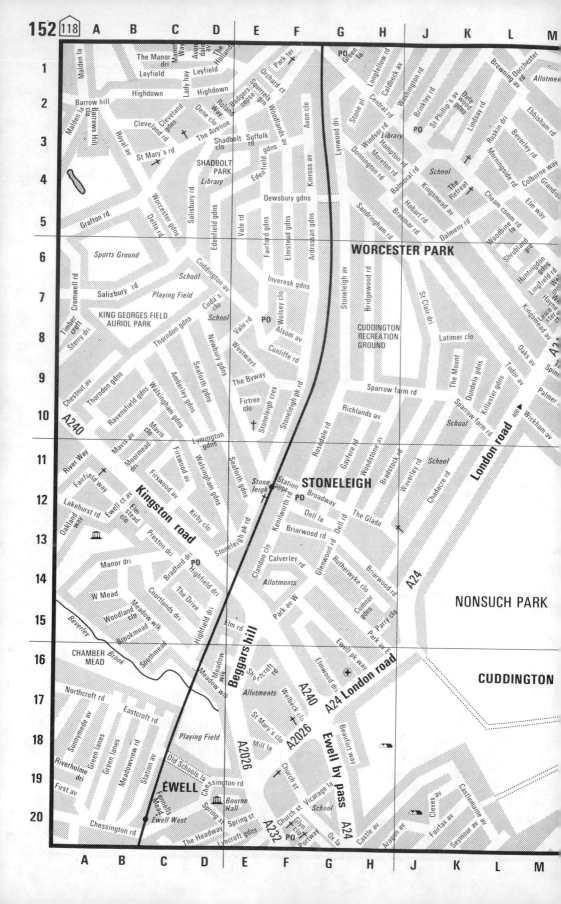

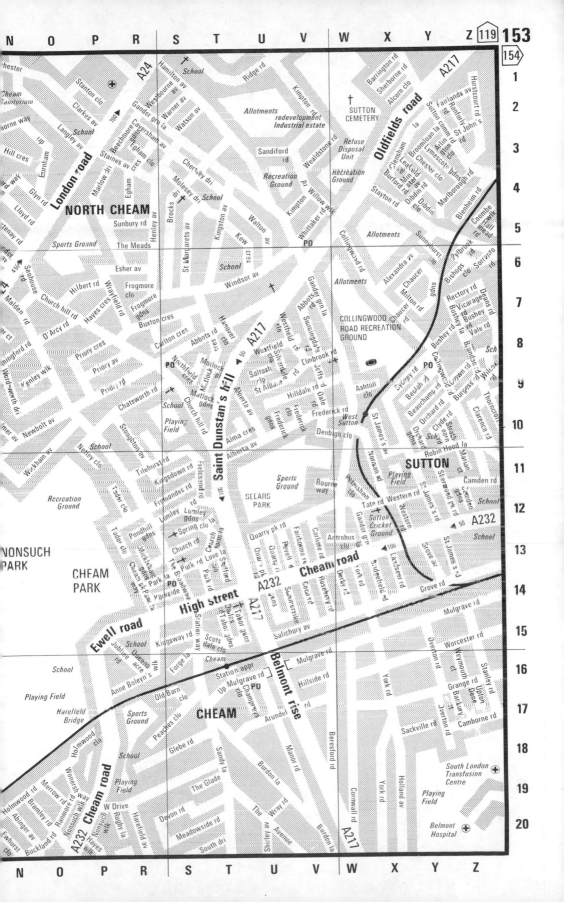

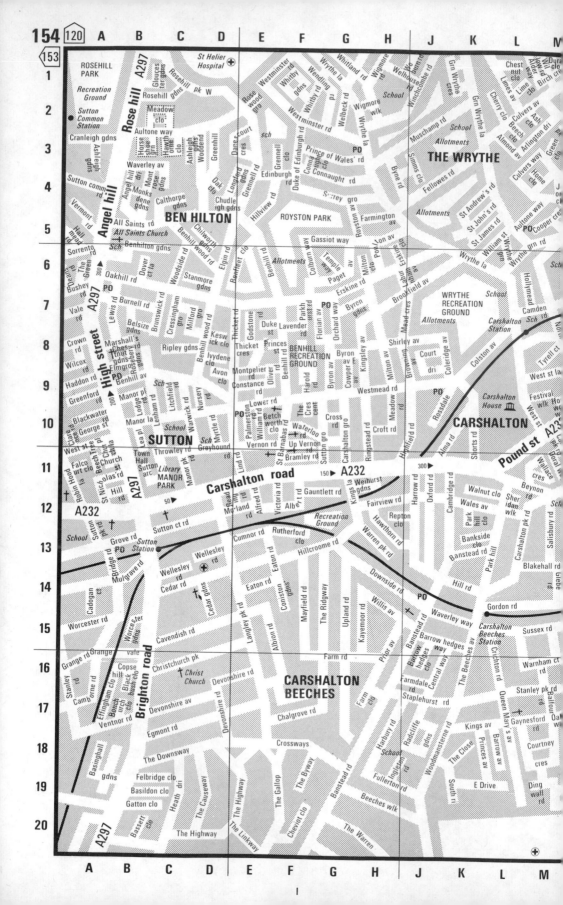

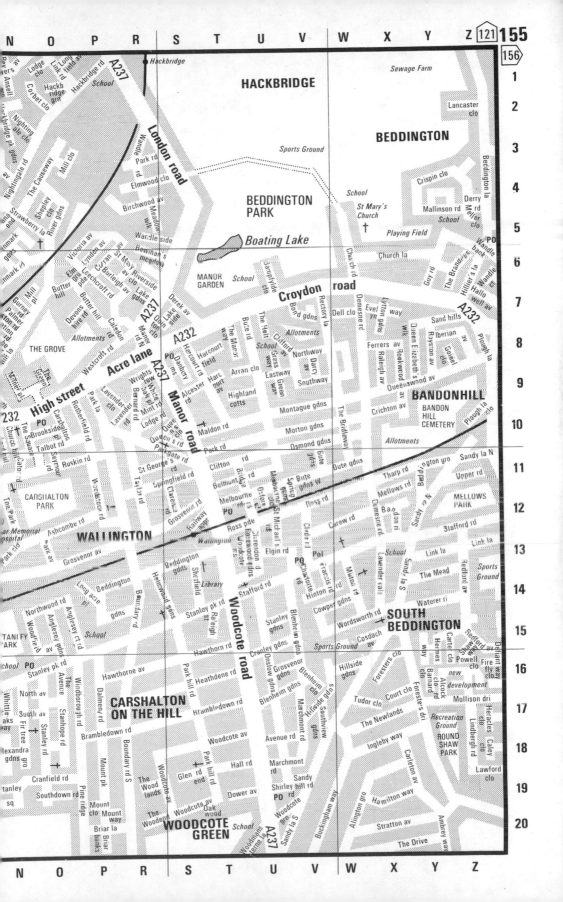

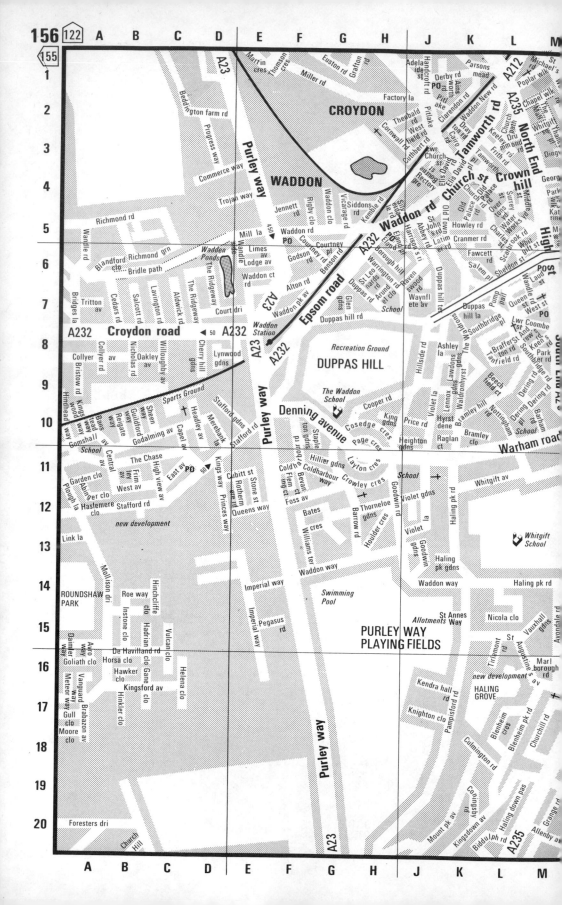

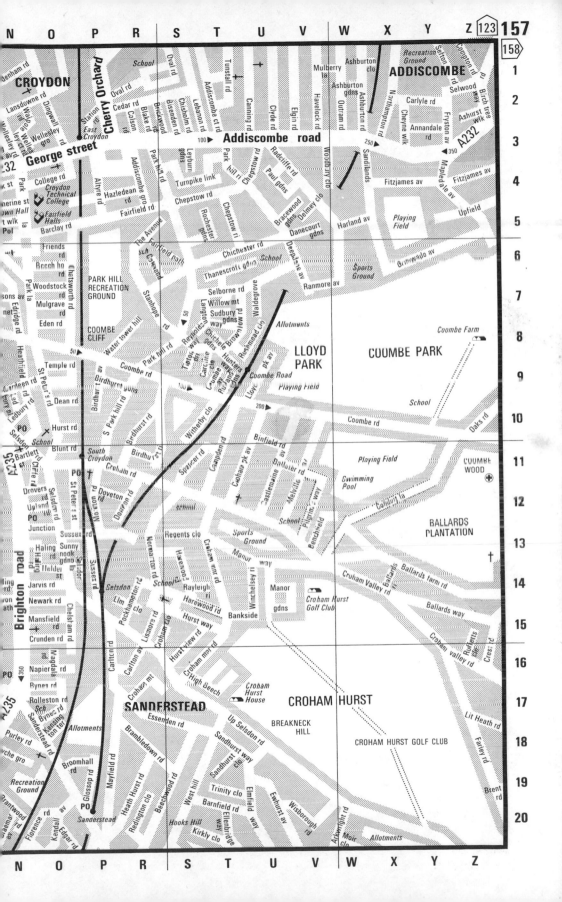

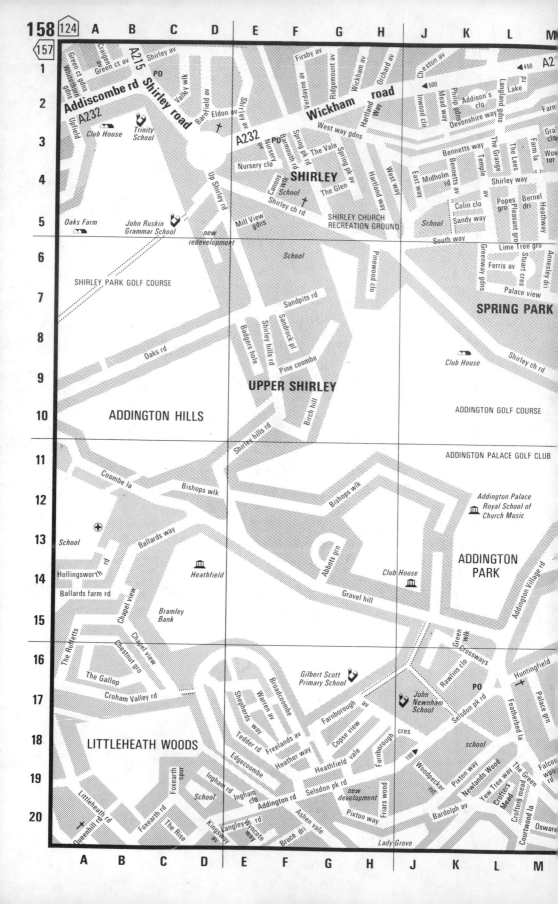

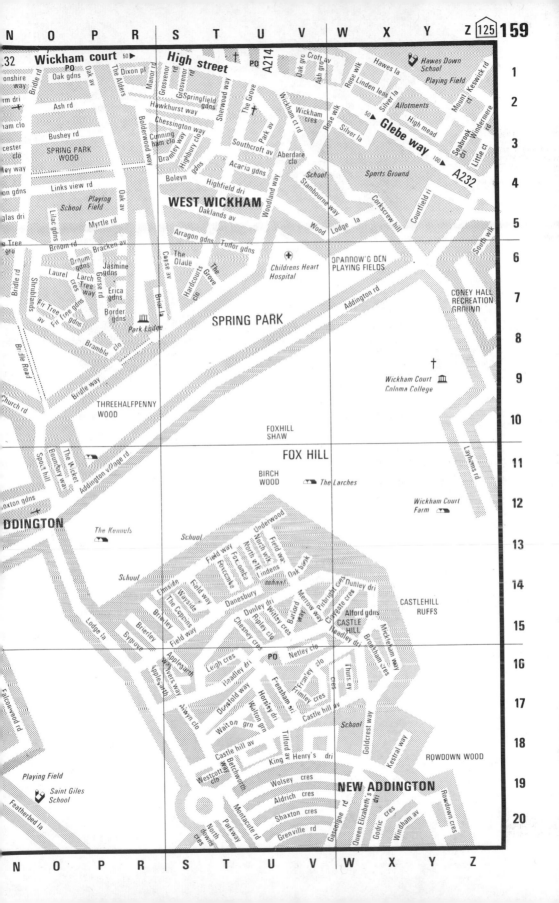

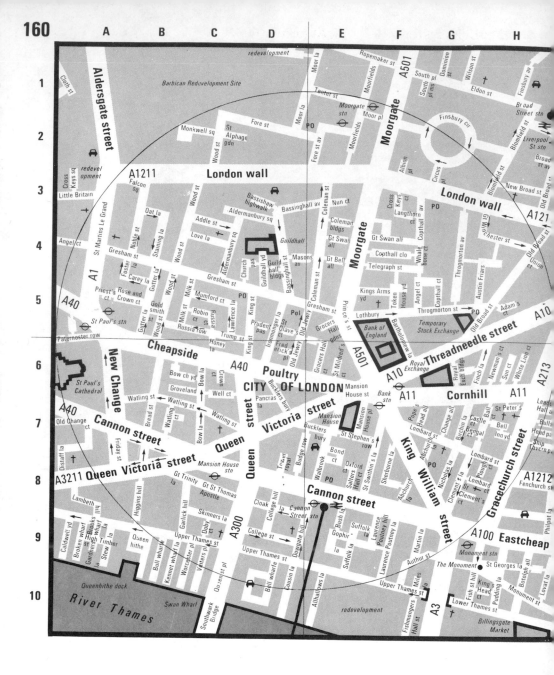

A B C D E F G H

1

2

3

4

5

6

7

8

9

10

Cloth st

Aldersgate street

Barbican Redevelopment Site

redevelopment

Moor la

Ropemaker st

A501

South pl

South pl ms

Dominion st

Wilson st

Finsbury av

Tenter st

Moorgate stn

Moor ct

Moorfields

Eldon st

Broad Street stn

Cross Keys sq

redevel opment

Little Britain

A1211

Falcon sq

Monkwell sq

St Alphage gdn

Wood st

Fore st

Fore st av

PO

Moorgate

Moorfields

Moor pl

Albion st

Finsbury cir

Circus pl

Broad st av

Liverpool St stn

Broad st av

New Broad st

Blomfield st

Blomfield st

Angel ct

St Martins Le Grand

A1

London wall

Wood st

Oat la

Addle st

Love la

Noble st

Staining la

Gresham st

Foster la

Carey la

Gutter la

Church pas

Aldermanbury sq

Bassishaw highwalk

Aldermanbury sq

Guildhall bldgs

Guildhall yd

Guild hall bldgs

Bassinghall av

Coleman st

Nun ct

Gt Swan all

Coleman bldgs

Gt Swan all

Copthall clo

Masons av

Gt Bell all

Telegraph st

Moorgate

Whale bone ct

Copthall ct

Throgmorton av

Austin Friars

London wall

A121

Old Broad st

Union ct

A40

St Paul's stn

Priest's ct

Rose and Crown ct

Gold smith

Gutter la

Wood st

Milk st

Robin ct

Russia row

Mumford ct

Lawrence la

King st

Milk st

Trump st

Honey la

Gresham st

PO

Prudent pas

Ironmonger la

Old Jewy

Pol

Gresham st

Prince's st

Lothbury

Bartholomew la

Kings Arms yd

Token

Throgmorton st

PO

Old Broad st

Temporary Stock Exchange

Adam's ct

A10

Paternoster row

Cheapside

New Change

St Paul's Cathedral

A40

Old Change ct

Bow ch yd

Groveland

Watling st

Bread st

Watling ct

Watling st

Bow la

Crown ct

Well ct

Watling st

Bucklersbury

Pancras la

Queen street

A40

Poultry

CITY OF LONDON

Victoria street

Mansion House st

Bank stn

A10

Royal Exchange

Threadneedle street

A10

Cornhill

A11

Newman's ct

Finch la

Sun ct

White Lion ct

A213

A11

Cannon street

Friday st

Distaff la

Queen Victoria street

Mansion House la

Gt Trinity la

Gt St Thomas Apostle

Mansion House

Bucklersbury

Budge row

Walbrook

Bond ct

St Stephen's row

St Swithin's la

Sherborne la

King William street

Pope's Head al

Change all

Castle ct

Birchin la

Bengal ct

Lombard ct

Abchurch la

Nicholas la

Clement's la

Clement's ct

Lombard st

St Peter's

Ball

Bell Inn yd

Ship Tavern pas

Bull's Head pl

Leade Hall

Gracechurch street

A1212

Fenchurch st

A3211

Lambeth hill

Higgins hill

Caldwell yd

Broken wharf

Gardner's la

High Timber st

Stew la

Queen hithe

Garlick hill

Skinners la

Dobs

Upper Thames st

Upper Thames st

College hill

Cloak la

College st

Cousin la

Dowgate hill

Suffolk la

Cannon Street stn

Bush la

Laurence Pountney la

Laurence Pountney hill

Gophir la

Salters Hall ct

Oxford ct

Suffolk la

Martin la

Authur st

Monument stn

A100 Eastcheap

St Georges la

Botolph all

Philpot la

Swan Wharf

Queenhithe dock

River Thames

Southwark Bridge

Bull wharfe

Kennet wharf la

Worcester la

Vintners pl

Queenhithe pl

A300

Bell wharfe

Allhallows la

Miles la

redevelopment

Upper Thames st

Fishmongers Hall st

The Monument

King's Head ct

Fish st hill

Pudding la

Monument st

Lovat la

A3

Lower Thames st

Billingsgate Market

Cannon street

Stock Exchange

## Alphabetical system

This has been programmed for computer typesetting and is consistent throughout the index in the following order.

Postal districts are in alphabetical order followed by numerical order
High av **NW1**
High av **WC1**
High av **WC2**

Outer districts follow postal districts in alphabetical order
High av **Dgnhm**
High av **Mitch**
High av **Wemb**

## Abbreviations

### Outer districts

Barking **Bark**
Barnet **Barnt**
Beckenham **Becknhm**
Belvedere **Blvdr**
Bexley **Bxly**
Bexley Heath **Bxly Hth**
Boreham Wood **Borhm wd**
Bromley **Brom**
Brentford **Brentf**
Buckhurst Hill **Buck Hl**
Carshalton **Carsh**
Chislehurst **Chisl**
Croydon **Croy**
Dagenham **Dgnhm**
Dartford **Drtfrd**
East Molesey **E. Molesey**
Edgware **Edg**
Enfield **Enf**
Feltham **Felt**
Greenford **Grnfd**
Hampton **Hampt**
Hornchurch **Hornch**
Hounslow **Hounsl**
Ilford **Ilf**
Isleworth **Islwth**
Kingston **Kingst**
Mitcham **Mitch**
Morden **Mrdn**
New Malden **New Mald**
Orpington **Orp**
Pinner **Pinn**
Rainham **Rainhm**
Richmond **Rich**
Romford **Rom**
Ruislip **Ruis**
Southall **S'hall**
South Croydon **S. Croy**
Surbiton **Surb**
Teddington **Tedd**
Thornton Heath **Thntn Hth**
Twickenham **Twick**
Stanmore **Stanm**
Wallington **Wallgtn**
Wembley **Wemb**
West Wickham **W. Wckm**
Woodford Green **Wdfd Grn**
Worcester Park **Worc pk**

### Streets etc

Alley **all**
Approach **appr**
Arcade **arc**
Avenue **av**
Bank **bank**
Boulevard **blvd**
Bridge **br**
Broadway **bdwy**
Buildings **bldgs**
Church **ch**
Churchyard **chyd**
Circle **crcl**
Circus **cir**
Close **clo**
Common **comm**
Cottages **cotts**
Court **ct**
Crescent **cres**
Drive **dri**
East **east**
Embankment **emb**
Estate **est**
Gardens **gdns**
Gate **ga**
Great **gt**
Green **grn**
Grove **gro**
Hill **hill**
House **ho**
Junction **junc**
Lane **la**
Little **lit**
Lower **lwr**
Manor **mnr**
Mansions **mans**
Market **mkt**
Mews **ms**
Mount **mt**
North **north**
Palace **pal**
Parade **p'de**
Park **pk**
Passage **pas**
Path **pth**
Place **pl**
Rise **ri**
Road **rd**
Slope **slope**
South **south**
Square **sq**
Station **sta**
Street **st**
Terrace **ter**
Upper **up**
Villas **villas**
Walk **wlk**
Way **way**
West **west**
Yard **yd**

# A

108 G 1 Abbess clo SW2
151 Z 19 Abbett st SE16
89 V 15 Abbeville rd SW4
60 L 5 Abbey av Wemb
81 S 11 Abbey cres Erith
130 C 9 Abbey Gdn ms NW8
80 E 10 Abbey gro SE2
115 T 3 Abbey Hill rd Sidcp
64 G 5 Abbey la E15
111 O 17 Abbey la Becknhm
129 X 3 Abbey ms NW6
148 F 1 Abbey Orchard st SW1
111 O 17 Abbey Pk estate Becknhm
64 L 5 Abbey rd E15
61 T 7 Abbey rd NW10
61 T 5 Abbey rd NW10
129 Y 4 Abbey rd NW6
130 B 7 Abbey rd NW8
106 D 19 Abbey rd SW19
67 N 2 Abbey rd Bark
81 N 9 Abbey rd Blvdr
80 K 10 Abbey rd Blvdr
97 Z 9 Abbey rd Bxly Hth
156 J 5 Abbey rd Croy
8 F 17 Abbey rd Enf
36 E 16 Abbey rd Ilf
65 T 11 Abbey st E13
143 O 20 Abbey st SE1
150 L 1 Abbey st SE1
80 F 10 Abbey ter SE2
60 M 7 Abbey ter Wemb
13 S 10 Abbey view NW7
80 F 10 Abbey Wood rd SE2
61 O 3 Abbeydale rd Wemb
75 P 11 Abbeyfield rd SE16
151 Z 5 Abbeyfield rd SE16
49 S 17 Abbot st E8
28 G 13 Abbots gdns N2
158 G 13 Abbots grn Croy
142 K 14 Abbots la SE1
108 G 1 Abbots pk SW2
129 W 3 Abbots pl NW6
13 N 20 Abbots rd Edgw
25 W 1 Abbots rd Edgw
124 H 11 Abbots way Becknhm
64 G 5 Abbotsbury clo E15
137 N 19 Abbotsbury clo W14
137 N 18 Abbotsbury rd W14
120 A 8 Abbotsbury rd Mrdn
30 M 14 Abbotsford av N15
34 E 2 Abbotsford gdns Wdfd Grn
55 O 17 Abbotsford rd Ilf
16 H 12 Abbotshall av N14
111 W 3 Abbotshall rd SE6
107 V 11 Abbotsleigh rd SW16
87 N 8 Abbotstone rd SW15
92 M 13 Abbotswell rd SE4
35 U 11 Abbotswood av Ilf
107 W 5 Abbotswood rd SW2
119 P 1 Abbott av SW20
64 K 16 Abbott rd E14
38 G 10 Abbotts clo Rom
20 L 14 Abbotts cres E4
7 X 8 Abbotts cres Enf
42 A 6 Abbotts dri Wemb
51 U 1 Abbotts Pk rd E10
66 B 5 Abbotts rd E6
4 M 16 Abbotts rd Barnt
25 X 1 Abbotts rd Edg
121 X 6 Abbotts rd Mitch
70 C 2 Abbotts rd S'hall
153 V 7 Abbotts rd Sutton
80 J 19 Abbotts wlk Bxly Hth
142 F 8 Abchurch la EC4
136 A 14 Abdale rd W12
74 K 3 Abdale rd W12
63 X 10 Aberavon rd E3
107 V 18 Abercairn rd SW16
120 A 7 Aberconway rd Mrdn
27 T 2 Abercorn clo NW7
130 C 11 Abercorn clo NW8
40 L 4 Abercorn cres Harrow
42 G 1 Abercorn gdns Harrow
37 P 18 Abercorn gdns Rom
130 C 10 Abercorn pl NW8
27 U 2 Abercorn rd NW7
24 D 2 Abercorn rd Stanm
88 K 5 Abercrombie st SW11
159 V 3 Aberdare clo W Wkhm
130 A 1 Aberdare gdns NW6

129 Z 1 Aberdare gdns NW6
27 O 2 Aberdare gdns NW7
9 O 14 Aberdare rd Enf
48 K 15 Aberdeen la N5
48 K 15 Aberdeen pk N5
130 F 17 Aberdeen pl NW8
44 E 14 Aberdeen rd SW4
18 L 15 Aberdeen rd N18
48 L 13 Aberdeen rd N5
120 F 2 Aberdeen rd SW19
157 N 9 Aberdeen rd Croy
23 V 9 Aberdeen rd Harrow
93 X 5 Aberdeen ter SE3
55 P 6 Aberdour rd Ilf
64 H 17 Aberfeldy st E14
107 X 17 Aberfoyle rd SW16
94 J 15 Abergeldie rd SE12
93 Z 11 Abernethy rd SE13
49 V 15 Abersham rd E8
79 U 11 Abery st SE18
28 D 6 Abingdon rd N3
122 A 1 Abingdon rd SW16
145 U 1 Abingdon rd W8
148 K 2 Abingdon st SW1
145 U 2 Abingdon vlls W8
153 N 20 Abinger av Sutton
127 P 6 Abinger clo Brom
54 M 13 Abinger clo Ilf
156 A 12 Abinger clo Wallgtn
83 S 8 Abinger gdns Islwth
75 Y 16 Abinger gro SE8
74 B 8 Abinger rd W4
75 O 14 Ablett st SE 16
118 G 4 Aboyne dri SW20
44 B 8 Aboyne rd NW10
43 Z 9 Aboyne rd NW10
106 E 5 Aboyne rd SW17
68 D 7 Abridge way Bark
88 K 12 Abyssinia rd SW11
31 O 1 Acacia av N17
72 A 20 Acacia av Brentf
57 U 8 Acacia av Hornch
42 J 15 Acacia av Wemb
10 G 19 Acacia clo Harrow
119 W 20 Acacia dri Sutton
130 G 8 Acacia gdns NW8
159 U 4 Acacia gdns W Wkhm
109 P 4 Acacia gro SE21
117 Z 7 Acacia gro New Mald
118 A 6 Acacia gro New Mald
130 G 8 Acacia pl NW8
52 A 8 Acacia rd E11
32 J 19 Acacia rd E17
130 G 8 Acacia rd NW8
30 G 5 Acacia rd N22
108 B 20 Acacia rd SW16
61 V 20 Acacia rd W3
8 C 5 Acacia rd Enf
100 J 14 Acacia rd Hampt
121 R 4 Acacia rd Mitch
123 V 20 Academy gdns Croy
58 A 7 Academy gdns Grnfd
95 U 2 Academy pl SE18
58 G 19 Academy rd SE18
95 U 1 Academy rd SE18
89 O 7 Acanthus rd SW11
45 W 3 Accommodation rd NW11
45 W 14 Achilles clo NW6
75 X 20 Achilles st SE14
88 A 2 Ackfold rd SW6
137 O 1 Acklam rd W10
87 X 3 Ackroyd dri SW6
92 G 18 Ackroyd rd SE23
91 N 8 Acland cres SE5
44 L 17 Acland rd NW2
129 W 1 Acol rd NW6
68 C 3 Aconbury rd Dgnhm
20 C 16 Acorn clo E4
7 V 6 Acorn clo Enf
123 T 1 Acorn gdns SE19
61 Z 15 Acorn gdns W3
75 W 2 Acorn wlk SE16
130 H 8 Acquila st NW8
90 C 11 Acre la SW2
155 R 8 Acre la Wallgtn
106 G 14 Acre rd SW19
56 H 20 Acre rd Dgnhm
102 K 20 Acre rd Kingst
88 D 14 Acris st SW18
61 Z 6 Acton la NW10
73 W 5 Acton la W3
73 W 12 Acton la W4
133 O 13 Acton st WC1
105 Z 3 Acuba rd SW18
150 H 3 Acworth st SE1
64 J 17 Ada gdns E14
65 P 4 Ada gdns E15
135 V 7 Ada pl E2
150 H 20 Ada rd SE5
42 F 9 Ada rd Wemb
135 V 5 Ada st E8

128 M 18 Adair rd W10
140 B 4 Adam & Eve ct W1
145 V 1 Adam & Eve ms W8
140 L 10 Adam st WC2
142 H 5 Adam's ct EC 2
43 U 6 Adams clo NW9
75 P 5 Adams gdns SE16
48 D 16 Adams pl N7
31 R 7 Adams rd N17
124 H 11 Adams rd Becknhm
139 V 10 Adams row W1
65 T 18 Adamson rd E16
46 G 19 Adamson rd NW3
8 B 19 Adamsrill clo Enf
110 H 9 Adamsrill rd SE26
108 B 5 Adare way SW16
108 B 5 Adare wlk SW16
113 X 9 Adderley gdns SE9
89 O 13 Adderley gro SW11
23 V 5 Adderley rd Harrow
64 F 18 Adderley st E14
15 S 20 Addington dr N12
110 G 10 Addington gro SE26
158 K 12 Addington palace Croy
158 L 14 Addington park Croy
65 N 13 Addington rd E16
64 A 8 Addington rd E3
30 E 20 Addington rd N4
122 G 19 Addington rd Croy
158 E 20 Addington rd S Croy
159 W 7 Addington rd W Wkhm
150 D 16 Addington sq SE5
158 M 14 Addington Village rd Croy
159 P 11 Addington Village rd Croy
9 S 6 Addis clo Enf
123 W 18 Addiscombe av Croy
24 D 15 Addiscombe clo Harrow
157 T 2 Addiscombe ct Croy
157 R 4 Addiscombe gro Croy
158 B 2 Addiscombe rd Croy
157 U 3 Addiscombe rd Croy
6 E 18 Addison av N14
136 K 15 Addison av N14
82 M 3 Addison av Hounsl
145 N 4 Addison Br pl W14
136 M 20 Addison cres W14
144 M 1 Addison cres W14
136 F 20 Addison gdns W14
144 F 1 Addison gdns W14
117 N 9 Addison gro Surb
74 B 9 Addison gro W4
136 J 15 Addison pl W11
34 F 19 Addison rd E11
33 T 15 Addison rd E17
123 Y 9 Addison rd SE25
136 M 14 Addison rd W14
127 N 10 Addison rd Brom
126 M 10 Addison rd Brom
9 R 6 Addison rd Enf
36 C 5 Addison rd Ilf
102 A 16 Addison rd Tedd
27 X 13 Addison way NW11
158 K 2 Addisons clo Croy
141 Y 7 Addle hill EC4
142 C 3 Addle st EC2
118 K 10 Adela av New Mald
118 K 9 Adela av New Mald
128 K 17 Adela st W10
92 M 11 Adelaide av SE4
93 N 11 Adelaide av SE4
8 F 4 Adelaide clo Enf
10 K 13 Adelaide clo Stanm
71 V 4 Adelaide cotts W7
37 Y 15 Adelaide gdns Rom
74 H 3 Adelaide gro W12
51 T 9 Adelaide rd E10
47 N 20 Adelaide rd NW3
46 M 20 Adelaide rd NW3
71 Z 4 Adelaide rd W13
82 A 2 Adelaide rd Hounsl
54 A 6 Adelaide rd Ilf
85 N 11 Adelaide rd Rich
70 B 10 Adelaide rd S'hall
116 J 13 Adelaide rd Surb
101 X 15 Adelaide rd Tedd
140 J 11 Adelaide st WC2
156 J 1 Adelaide st Croy
135 Z 20 Adelina gro E1
63 O 14 Adelina gro E1
140 G 3 Adeline pl WC1
140 L 11 Adelphi ter WC2
49 O 13 Aden gro N16
9 V 15 Aden rd Enf
54 A 2 Aden rd Ilf
144 U 16 Adeney rd W6
93 O 19 Adenmore rd SE6

74 L 9 Adie rd W6
144 A 3 Adie rd W6
65 U 12 Adine rd E13
143 S 4 Adler st E1
50 J 14 Adley st E5
79 P 18 Admaston rd SE18
128 H 18 Admiral ms W10
95 T 9 Admiral Seymour rd SE9
93 O 3 Admirals st SE4
46 D 16 Admirals wlk NW3
57 V 17 Adnams wlk Rainh
111 P 10 Adolf st SE6
48 J 5 Adolphus rd N4
75 Z 19 Adolphus st SE8
55 X 11 Adomar rd Dgnhm
44 J 3 Adrian av NW2
58 E 10 Adrienne av S'hall
91 W 9 Adys rd SE15
26 E 9 Aerodrome rd NW9
26 B 8 Aeroville NW9
88 J 6 Afghan rd SW11
45 W 14 Agamemnon rd NW6
47 Y 20 Agar gro NW1
132 D 1 Agar gro NW1
140 K 10 Agar st WC2
74 L 8 Agate rd W6
144 A 3 Agate rd W6
143 Y 12 Agatha st E1
114 C 4 Agaton rd SE9
44 M 12 Agave rd NW2
133 W 15 Agdon st EC1
46 L 13 Agincourt rd NW3
53 X 11 Agnes av Ilf
55 X 11 Agnes gdns Dgnhm
74 C 4 Agnes rd W3
63 Y 16 Agnes st E14
78 A 3 Agnes st E14
92 G 18 Agnew rd SE23
83 Z 13 Ailsa av Twick
84 B 13 Ailsa av Twick
83 Z 13 Ailsa rd Twick
84 A 13 Ailsa rd Twick
64 G 14 Ailsa st E14
64 H 5 Ailwyn rd E15
131 P 2 Ainger rd NW8
22 H 10 Ainsdale cres Pinn
60 H 13 Ainsdale rd W5
38 J 19 Ainsley av Rom
63 N 8 Ainsley st E2
135 W 14 Ainsley st E2
20 C 17 Ainslie Wood cres E4
20 D 15 Ainslie Wood gdns E4
20 C 17 Ainslie Wood rd E4
75 R 5 Ainsty st SE16
44 H 9 Ainsworth clo NW2
63 P 1 Ainsworth rd E9
156 K 1 Ainsworth rd Croy
66 C 5 Aintree av E6
36 B 7 Aintree cres Ilf
60 B 5 Aintree st Grnfd
144 L 18 Aintree st SW6
140 D 10 Air st W1
74 D 12 Airedale av W4
88 M 20 Airedale rd SW12
89 N 19 Airedale rd SW12
72 F 8 Airedale rd W5
57 Z 20 Airfield way Hornch
137 S 15 Airlie gdns W8
53 Z 5 Airlie gdns Ilf
55 P 5 Airthrie rd Ilf
94 A 12 Aislibie rd SE12
111 R 4 Aitken rd SE6
26 A 10 Ajax av NW9
45 W 14 Ajax rd NW6
86 G 17 Akehurst st SW15
46 G 16 Akenside rd NW3
90 H 4 Akerman rd SW19
116 E 15 Akerman rd Surb
79 T 18 Alabama st SE18
72 F 7 Alacross rd W5
56 D 1 Alan gdns Rom
105 T 12 Alan rd SW19
94 D 15 Alanthus clo SE12
141 T 16 Alaska st SE1
138 gdns NW11
137 N 4 Alba pl W11
93 R 15 Albacore cres SE13
85 U 11 Albany clo SW14
97 U 19 Albany clo Bxly
25 R 2 Albany cres Edg
25 Z 4 Albany ct N'wd
140 B 11 Albany Ct yd W1
150 D 15 Albany ms SE17
9 U 2 Albany park rd Enf
84 L 14 Albany pass Rich
9 R 5 Albany Pk av Enf
9 T 4 Albany Pk av Enf
9 T 4 Albany Pk av Enf
102 H 16 Albany Pk rd Kingst
48 F 13 Albany pl N7
33 O 20 Albany rd E10

3 O 13 Albany rd E12
2 J 18 Albany rd E17
0 K 14 Albany rd N15
9 O 18 Albany rd N18
0 E 20 Albany rd N4
0 H 13 Albany rd SE5
5 Z 12 Albany rd SW19
0 B 19 Albany rd W13
1 P 15 Albany rd Blvdr
2 J 17 Albany rd Brentf
7 U 19 Albany rd Bxly
3 Z 13 Albany rd Chisl
9 S 2 Albany rd Enf
7 W 8 Albany rd Hornch
7 Y 8 Albany rd New Mald
4 L 12 Albany rd Rich
8 B 18 Albany rd Rom
1 X 8 Albany st NW1
1 P 13 Albany the Wdfd Grn
1 U 4 Albany view Buck Hl
9 T 18 Albatross st SE18
6 A 19 Albemarle appr Ilf
0 E 2 Albemarle av Twick
5 Z 19 Albemarle gdns Ilf
5 Z 19 Albemarle gdns Ilf
5 X 2 Albemarle pk Stanm
1 R 17 Albemarle rd Barnt
5 X 1 Albemarle rd Becknhm
7 Y 10 Albemarle rd New Mald
0 A 12 Albemarle st W1
3 W 18 Albemarle way EC1
7 V 14 Alberon gdns NW11
4 A Albert av E4
6 M 17 Albert br SW11
8 L 1 Albert Br rd SW11
6 M 18 Albert Br rd SW11
7 N 20 Albert Br rd SW11
8 A 13 Albert Carr gdns SW16
7 Z 12 Albert Carr gdns SW16
9 X 3 Albert clo N22
8 B 13 Albert cres E4
5 T 2 Albert dri SW19
1 N 17 Albert emb SE1
8 M 8 Albert emb SE1
3 S 18 Albert gdns E1
9 P 9 Albert gdns NW6
5 P 20 Albert gro SW20
8 F 19 Albert Hall mans SW7
6 A 1 Albert ms W8
1 U 9 Albert pl N17
7 Y 4 Albert pl N3
7 Z 20 Albert pl W8
1 U 6 Albert rd E10
8 D 4 Albert rd E16
3 O 16 Albert rd E17
4 J 9 Albert rd E4
7 P 13 Albert rd NW4
1 R 18 Albert rd NW6
3 C 16 Albert rd NW7
1 R 18 Albert rd N15
9 V 5 Albert rd N22
8 D 3 Albert rd N4
0 E 16 Albert rd SE20
3 Z 8 Albert rd SE25
8 B 11 Albert rd SE26
3 R 6 Albert rd SE9
0 C 13 Albert rd W5
5 S 14 Albert rd Barnt
1 P 14 Albert rd Blvdr
7 P 12 Albert rd Brom
8 F 18 Albert rd Bxly
6 D 4 Albert rd Dgnhm
1 O 12 Albert rd Hampt
3 N 11 Albert rd Harrow
2 H 11 Albert rd Hounsl
3 Z 10 Albert rd Ilf
4 C 9 Albert rd Ilf
0 M 0 Albert rd Mitch
8 E 10 Albert rd New Mald
4 L 13 Albert rd Rich
9 T 17 Albert rd Rom
4 F 12 Albert rd Sutton
1 X 15 Albert rd Tedd
1 V 1 Albert rd Twick
3 V 20 Albert rd Twick
1 P 14 Albert Rd est Blvdr
2 A 16 Albert sq E 15
9 N 20 Albert sq SW8
0 C 1 Albert sq SW8
1 Z 8 Albert st NW1
6 F 19 Albert st N11
5 P 15 Albert st N12
1 S 4 Albert ter NW1
1 X 4 Albert ter NW10
1 X 4 Albert Ter ms NW1
3 U 4 Albert Vlls rd W3
3 U 10 Alberta av Sutton
8 J 19 Alberta rd Enf

98 J 2 Alberta rd Erith
149 X 9 Alberta st SE17
29 O 4 Albion av N10
89 W 4 Albion av SW8
138 L 8 Albion clo W2
39 O 18 Albion clo Rom
135 O 2 Albion dri E8
74 H 10 Albion gdns W6
49 R 11 Albion gro N16
45 V 20 Albion mews NW6
138 L 7 Albion ms W2
133 W 19 Albion pl EC1
142 F 2 Albion pl EC2
33 U 9 Albion rd E17
49 P 10 Albion rd N10
31 W 7 Albion rd N17
8 D 11 Albion rd Bxly Hth
82 H 12 Albion rd Hounsl
117 V 1 Albion rd Kingst
154 E 15 Albion rd Sutton
101 T 2 Albion rd Twick
135 O 1 Albion sq E8
75 P 7 Albion st SE16
138 L 8 Albion st W2
122 H 20 Albion st Croy
135 N 1 Albion ter E8
110 C 6 Albion Vlls rd SE26
93 U 9 Albion way SE13
43 R 10 Albion way Wemb
91 S 8 Albrighton rd SE22
7 U 5 Albuhera clo Enf
97 Y 4 Albury av Bxly Hth
71 W 20 Albury av Islwth
100 J 15 Albury av Hampt
22 A 1 Albury dri Pinn
76 B 17 Albury st SE8
127 V 7 Albyfield Brom
93 P 4 Albyn rd SE4
50 A 6 Alcester rd E5
155 S 9 Alcester rd Wallgtn
155 Y 16 Alcock clo Wallgtn
49 X 8 Aconbury rd E5
153 X 2 Alcorn clo Sutton
49 T 7 Aldam pl N16
56 K 18 Aldborough rd Dgnhm
54 H 1 Aldborough rd Ilf
54 F 5 Aldborough Rd south Ilf
36 K 15 Aldborough Rd south Ilf
74 F 3 Aldbourne rd W12
150 J 9 Aldbridge st SE17
43 S 19 Aldbury av Wemb
148 M 20 Aldebert ter SW8
149 N 20 Aldebert ter SW8
21 T 13 Aldeburgh pl Wdfd Grn
77 S 12 Aldeburgh st SE10
65 N 11 Alden av E15
132 D 10 Aldenham st NW1
74 K 9 Aldensley rd W6
44 H 8 Alder gro NW2
85 X 7 Alder rd SW14
114 J 8 Alder rd Sidcp
151 O 16 Alder st SE15
154 L 1 Alder way Carsh
89 R 18 Alderbrook rd SW12
74 G 17 Alderbury rd SW13
68 B 8 Alderman av Bark
142 C 4 Aldermanbury EC2
142 C 3 Aldermanbury sq EC2
17 O 13 Aldermans hill N13
142 J 3 Aldermans wlk EC2
112 F 20 Aldermary rd Brom
136 F 6 Aldermaston st W10
151 S 9 Alderminster rd SE1
110 M 6 Aldermoor rd SE6
70 K 20 Alderney av Hounsl
40 D 20 Alderney gdns Grnfp
83 T 11 Alderney rd E1
147 X 8 Alderney rd SW1
148 A 10 Alderney rd SW1
20 M 19 Alders av Wdfd Grn
12 H 16 Alders clo Edg
12 H 16 Alders rd Edg
17 U 1 Alders the N21
100 C 11 Alders the Felt
70 E 15 Alders the Hounsl
159 R 1 Alders the W Wkhm
8 E 8 Aldersbrook av Enf
53 V 10 Aldersbrook la E12
52 H 6 Aldersbrook rd E11
53 R 11 Aldersbrook rd E12
142 A 1 Aldersey gdns Bark
142 A 1 Aldersgate st EC1
112 M 7 Aldersgrove av SE9
113 N 6 Aldersgrove av SE9
129 R 3 Aldershot rd NW6
124 G 14 Aldersmead av Croy

128 L 16 Alderson st W10
26 J 17 Alderton cres NW4
90 L 9 Alderton rd SE24
123 V 16 Alderton rd Croy
87 W 5 Alderville rd SW6
83 P 7 Alderwick dri Hounsl
96 F 15 Alderwood rd SE9
139 T 11 Aldford st W1
142 M 6 Aldgate EC3
143 N 4 Aldgate av E1
143 O 5 Aldgate High st E1
136 E 16 Aldine st W12
57 X 15 Aldingham gdns Hornch
106 H 13 Aldis st SW17
45 X 15 Aldred rd NW6
106 D 7 Aldren rd SW17
159 V 19 Aldrich cres Croy
106 E 3 Aldrich ter SW18
20 F 19 Aldriche way E4
12 F 9 Aldridge av Edg
9 Z 2 Aldridge av Enf
24 K 6 Aldridge av Stanm
137 R 3 Aldridge Rd vlls W11
118 A 16 Aldridge ri New Mald
107 V 11 Aldrington rd SW16
114 D 6 Aldwick clo SE9
156 C 7 Aldwick rd Croy
93 T 16 Aldworth gro SE13
51 Z 20 Aldworth rd E15
64 M 1 Aldworth rd E15
64 L 1 Aldworth rd E15
141 O 7 Aldwych WC2
36 C 14 Aldwych av Ilf
97 X 13 Alers rd Bxly Hth
128 A 2 Alexander av NW10
62 K 1 Alexander clo Brom
126 G 20 Alexander clo Brom
96 H 15 Alexander clo Sidcp
101 U 4 Alexander clo Twick
6 G 16 Alexander ct N14
6 G 16 Alexander ct N14
137 W 4 Alexander ms W2
146 J 4 Alexander pl SW7
48 A 8 Alexander rd N4
97 W 4 Alexander rd Bxly Hth
114 A 14 Alexander rd Chisl
113 Z 13 Alexander rd Chisl
146 J 4 Alexander sq SW7
137 N 5 Alexander st W7
29 Y 6 Alexandra av N22
89 O 2 Alexandra av SW11
73 Z 20 Alexandra av W4
40 F 4 Alexandra av Harrow
70 D 1 Alexandra av S'hall
153 X 6 Alexandra av Sutton
40 J 10 Alexandra clo Harrow
92 M 3 Alexandra cotts SE14
112 C 14 Alexandra cres Brom
109 R 13 Alexandra dri SE19
117 R 10 Alexandra dri Surb
29 T 12 Alexandra gdns N10
155 N 18 Alexandra gdns Carsh
82 K 5 Alexandra gdns Hounsl
15 O 18 Alexandra gro N12
48 K 5 Alexandra gro N4
29 W 9 Alexandra palace N22
29 Z 9 Alexandra park N22
40 J 11 Alexandra park Harrow
29 T 6 Alexandra Pk rd N22
123 P 11 Alexandra pl SE25
51 U 10 Alexandra rd E10
32 L 20 Alexandra rd E17
34 G 11 Alexandra rd E18
66 J 9 Alexandra rd E6
27 P 13 Alexandra rd NW4
129 Z 4 Alexandra rd NW8
130 C 3 Alexandra rd NW8
29 S 3 Alexandra rd N10
31 O 15 Alexandra rd N15
30 F 9 Alexandra rd N8
110 E 15 Alexandra rd SE26
85 Z 8 Alexandra rd SW14
105 V 15 Alexandra rd SW19
73 Z 6 Alexandra rd W4
72 G 17 Alexandra rd Brentf
123 R 19 Alexandra rd Croy
9 T 15 Alexandra rd Enf
82 K 7 Alexandra rd Hounsl
103 P 18 Alexandra rd Kingst
106 K 19 Alexandra rd Mitch
18 M 2 Alexandra rd N .
85 N 5 Alexandra rd Rich
37 X 18 Alexandra rd Rom
39 S 18 Alexandra rd Rom
84 F 17 Alexandra rd Twick

119 Y 13 Alexandra sq Mrdn
65 R 14 Alexandra st E16
60 A 20 Alexandria rd W13
151 T 5 Alexis st SE16
50 B 11 Alfearn rd E5
159 W 15 Alford gdns Croy
159 W 15 Alford gdns Croy
89 Y 3 Alford rd SW8
81 Z 13 Alford rd Erith
30 H 13 Alfoxton av N15
58 C 20 Alfred gdns Shall
70 C 1 Alfred gro S'hall
132 E 20 Alfred ms W1
140 E 1 Alfred pl W1
52 C 15 Alfred rd E15
123 Y 10 Alfred rd SE25
71 Y 1 Alfred rd W13
137 U 1 Alfred rd W2
73 W 3 Alfred rd W3
81 P 14 Alfred rd Belvdr
116 L 7 Alfred rd Kingst
154 E 12 Alfred rd Sutton
82 Z 8 Alfred st E3
67 W 5 Alfreds gdns Bark
67 T 6 Alfreds way Bark
122 A 16 Alfriston av Croy
22 H 20 Alfriston av Harrow
89 N 13 Alfriston rd SW11
116 L 13 Alfriston rd Surb
83 Y 9 Algar clo Islwth
83 Y 8 Algar rd Islwth
106 B 2 Algarve rd SW18
26 G 19 Algernon rd NW4
129 S 5 Algernon rd NW6
93 R 7 Algernon rd SE13
93 P 11 Algiers rd SE13
150 H 2 Alice st SE1
24 C 14 Alicia av Harrow
24 D 14 Alicia clo Harrow
24 D 14 Alicia gdns Harrow
113 P 6 Alie st E1
43 V 3 Alington cres NW9
155 W 20 Alington gro Wallgtn
88 J 11 Aliwal rd SW11
74 B 13 Alkerden rd W4
49 V 7 Alkham rd N16
31 S 4 All Hallows rd N17
94 A 4 All Saints dri SE3
106 D 16 All Saints rd SW19
137 O 3 All Saints rd W11
73 V 7 All Saints rd W3
154 B 5 All Saints rd Sutton
132 M 7 All Saints st N1
133 N 7 All Saints st N1
62 J 6 All Souls av NW10
128 A 4 All Souls av NW10
139 Z 2 All Souls pl W1
117 Y 12 Allan clo New Mald
4 D 19 Allan dri Barnt
61 W 13 Allan way W3
27 T 10 Allandale av N3
57 U 1 Allandale rd Hornch
51 N 20 Allanmouth rd E9
10 A 7 Allard cres Bushey
90 C 19 Allardyce st SW4
63 R 9 Allas rd E2
101 T 11 Allbrook clo Tedd
47 O 15 Allcroft rd NW5
89 Z 1 Allen Edwards dri SW8
49 R 12 Allen rd N16
124 E 4 Allen rd Becknhm
122 E 19 Allen rd Croy
145 U 1 Allen st W8
156 M 20 Allenby av S Croy
58 J 10 Allenby rd Grnfd
110 K 8 Allenby rd SE23
58 H 10 Allenby rd S'hall
68 F 17 Allendale av S'hall
91 N 4 Allendale rd SE5
42 A 17 Allendale rd Grnfd
9 R 18 Allens rd Enf
95 S 6 Allenswood rd SE9
22 L 14 Allerford ct Harrow
111 S 10 Allerford rd SE6
48 M 6 Allerton rd N16
49 N 6 Allerton rd N16
144 K 19 Allestree rd SW6
55 T 7 Allgood rd Dgnhm
109 P 6 Alleyn cres SE21
109 P 3 Alleyn pk SE21
70 F 13 Alleyn pk S'hall
109 P 7 Alleyn rd SE21
88 B 17 Allfarthing la SW18
119 O 15 Allgood clo Mrdn
142 E 10 Allhallows la EC4
65 X 13 Alliance rd E13
79 Z 17 Alliance rd SE18
80 A 19 Alliance rd SE18
61 S 12 Alliance rd W3
133 Z 7 Allingham st N1
105 P 13 Allington clo SW19

26 K 18 Allington rd NW4
128 K 10 Allington rd W10
22 M 15 Allington rd Harrow
147 Z 2 Allington st SW1
109 S 1 Allinson gro SE21
30 H 15 Allison rd N8
61 W 19 Allison rd W3
130 K 8 Allitsen rd NW8
89 W 12 Allnutt way SW4
75 U 13 Alloa rd SE8
55 O 6 Alloa rd Ilf
42 E 5 Allonby gdns Wemb
63 W 9 Alloway rd E3
131 R 18 Allsop pl NW1
15 P 6 Allum way N20
33 U 1 Alma av E4
41 P 7 Alma cres Harrow
153 T 10 Alma cres Sutton
151 P 6 Alma gro SE1
109 T 17 Alma pl SE19
122 G 12 Alma pl Thntn Hth
29 R 3 Alma rd N10
88 C 11 Alma rd SW18
154 K 10 Alma rd Carsh
9 U 12 Alma rd Enf
41 O 7 Alma rd Harrow
58 A 20 Alma rd S'hall
115 O 6 Alma rd Sidcp
23 R 3 Alma row Har
130 D 11 Alma sq NW8
51 X 16 Alma st E15
47 T 17 Alma st NW5
88 G 18 Alma ter SW18
50 C 12 Almack rd E5
133 W 3 Almeida st N1
104 G 17 Almer rd SW20
88 K 12 Almeric rd SW11
48 B 4 Almington st N4
72 J 8 Almond av W5
154 L 3 Almond av Carsh
154 L 3 Almond av Carsh
91 Y 5 Almond clo SE15
127 W 17 Almond clo Brom
72 A 19 Almond gro Brentf
31 X 2 Almond rd N17
151 X 6 Almond rd SE16
127 W 17 Almond way Brom
121 Y 10 Almond way Mitch
21 T 9 Almonds av Buck Hl
82 A 2 Almorah rd Hounsl
134 E 2 Almorah st N1
66 A 18 Alnwick av E16
120 A 9 Alnwick gro Mrdn
65 Y 18 Alnwick rd E16
94 H 17 Alnwick rd SE12
60 G 7 Alperton la Wemb
129 N 16 Alperton st W10
130 L 15 Alpha clo NW1
129 U 8 Alpha pl NW6
146 M 13 Alpha pl SW3
20 C 11 Alpha rd E4
18 J 18 Alpha rd N18
92 M 1 Alpha rd SE14
123 R 20 Alpha rd Croy
9 W 15 Alpha rd Enf
116 M 16 Alpha rd Surb
101 P 12 Alpha rd Tedd
91 X 5 Alpha st SE15
127 W 3 Alpine copse Brom
75 S 12 Alpine rd SE16
10 G 8 Alpine wlk Stanm
61 Z 1 Alric av NW10
118 B 6 Alric av New Mald
43 Z 20 Alrick av NW10
30 G 20 Alroy rd N4
150 K 11 Alsace st SE17
151 O 5 Alscot rd SE1
48 D 7 Alsen pl N7
48 D 7 Alsen rd N7
80 J 9 Alsike rd Belvdr
152 F 8 Alsom av Worc Pk
18 M 18 Alston rd N18
106 F 11 Alston rd SW17
4 E 10 Alston rd Barnt
105 U 17 Alt gro SW19
113 U 5 Altash way SE9
72 B 7 Altenburg av W13
88 L 10 Altenburg gdns SW11
22 B 3 Altham rd Pinn
88 B 6 Althea st SW6
117 N 7 Altheston rd Kingst
34 B 13 Althorne gdns E18
106 K 1 Althorp rd SW17
88 G 2 Althorpe gro SW11
23 O 16 Althorpe rd Harrow
53 T 20 Altmore av E6
66 G 4 Altmore av E6
23 W 2 Alton av Stanm
83 X 3 Alton clo Islwth
111 N 19 Alton gdns Becknhm
83 R 17 Alton gdns Twick
31 O 11 Alton rd N17

86 H 19 Alton rd SW15
104 G 1 Alton rd SW15
156 F 6 Alton rd Croy
84 L 11 Alton rd Rich
64 C 16 Alton st E14
124 K 13 Altyre clo Becknhm
157 P 4 Altyre rd Croy
124 L 12 Altyre way Becknhm
46 B 15 Alvanley gdns NW6
123 S 11 Alverston gdns SE25
105 X 5 Alverstone av SW19
15 V 2 Alverstone av Barnt
96 A 20 Alverstone gdns SE9
53 W 14 Alverstone rd E12
44 M 20 Alverstone rd NW2
118 E 8 Alverstone rd New Mald
43 N 3 Alverstone rd Wemb
75 X 16 Alverton st SE8
24 B 11 Alveston av Harrow
150 J 9 Alvey st SE17
49 U 15 Alvington cres E8
94 J 17 Alwald cres SE12
73 X 14 Alwyn av W4
159 S 17 Alwyn clo Croy
61 T 17 Alwyn gdns W3
48 K 19 Alwyne la N1
48 K 19 Alwyne pl N1
48 K 20 Alwyne rd N1
105 V 14 Alwyne rd SW19
71 S 1 Alwyne rd W7
48 L 18 Alwyne sq N1
48 K 20 Alwyne vlls N1
27 X 18 Alyth gdns NW11
82 C 5 Ambassador clo Hounsl
140 C 15 Ambassadors ct SW1
32 H 4 Amber av E17
51 X 19 Amber st E15
27 Z 10 Amberden av N3
149 X 10 Ambergate st SE17
115 U 13 Amberley ct Sidcp
18 F 4 Amberley gdns Enf
152 C 9 Amberley gdns Epsom
109 Z 11 Amberley gro SE26
123 U 18 Amberley gro Croy
33 P 20 Amberley rd E10
17 P 9 Amberley rd N13
80 K 16 Amberley rd SE2
129 W 19 Amberley rd W9
21 Y 9 Amberley rd Buck Hl
18 F 1 Amberley rd Enf
119 W 17 Amberley way Mrdn
118 B 15 Amberwood ri New Mald
112 J 7 Amblecote clo SE12
112 J 7 Amblecote rd SE12
48 H 9 Ambler rd N4
107 X 10 Ambleside av SW16
124 J 12 Ambleside av Becknhm
57 Y 15 Ambleside av Hornch
9 T 11 Ambleside cres Enf
35 S 14 Ambleside gdns Ilf
42 F 3 Ambleside gdns Wemb
62 D 1 Ambleside rd NW10
98 D 4 Ambleside rd Bxly Hth
155 Y 20 Ambrey way Wallgtn
81 S 9 Ambrooke rd Belvdr
148 B 3 Ambrosden av SW1
27 U 20 Ambrose av NW11
151 V 6 Ambrose st SE16
142 F 5 Amelia st EC1
18 H 15 Amelia st N18
154 A 5 Amen corner EC4
107 N 14 Amen corner SW17
141 Y 5 Amen ct EC4
143 N 8 America sq EC3
142 A 15 America st SE1
87 W 15 Amerland rd SW18
75 X 18 Amersham gro SE14
18 B 19 Amersham rd N18
92 L 1 Amersham rd SE14
123 N 13 Amersham rd Croy
23 S 18 Amersham rd Harrow
75 Y 19 Amersham vale SE14
128 A 5 Amersham gdns NW10
62 L 3 Amery gdns NW10
41 Y 7 Amery rd Harrow
108 B 4 Amesbury av SW2
20 D 1 Amesbury dri E4
127 O 5 Amesbury rd Brom
68 J 1 Amesbury rd Dagnhm
51 X 13 Amethyst rd E15
60 C 17 Amherst av W13
60 D 17 Amherst rd W13
83 Y 4 Amhurst gdns Islwth
49 W 13 Amhurst pas E8

31 R 20 Amhurst pk N16
49 Z 15 Amhurst rd E8
50 A 16 Amhurst rd E8
49 U 11 Amhurst rd N16
49 W 12 Amhurst ter E5
55 P 12 Amidas gdns Dgnhm
63 P 11 Amiel st E1
88 L 8 Amies st SW11
118 L 2 Amity gro SW20
65 O 2 Amity rd E15
64 E 7 Ammiel ter E3
89 O 15 Amner rd SW11
74 L 8 Amor rd W6
144 B 2 Amor rd W6
143 W 5 Amos ct E1
91 W 8 Amott rd SE15
64 A 19 Amoy pl E14
80 F 5 Ampleforth rd SE2
133 N 13 Ampton pl WC1
133 N 14 Ampton st WC1
8 B 17 Amwell clo Enf
83 U 5 Amwell rd Islwth
133 S 12 Amwell st EC1
84 A 18 Amyand la Twick
84 A 18 Amyand Pk gdns Twick
83 Z 19 Amyand Pk rd Twick
84 B 17 Amyand Pk rd Twick
93 N 13 Amyruth rd SE4
47 U 6 Anatola rd N19
118 F 15 Ancaster cres New Mald
124 F 7 Ancaster rd Becknhm
79 V 19 Ancaster st SE18
77 X 11 Anchor And Hope la SE7
151 W 6 Anchor st SE16
134 E 18 Anchor yd EC1
105 Z 13 Anchorage clo SW19
144 J 15 Ancill st W6
62 G 6 Ancona rd NW10
79 T 12 Ancona rd SE18
90 A 8 Andalus rd SW9
82 K 11 Anderson pl Hounsl
50 F 17 Anderson rd E9
147 O 9 Anderson st SW3
91 P 8 Anderton clo SE5
58 L 10 Andover clo Grnfd
48 C 8 Andover gdns N7
48 C 8 Andover gro N7
129 X 9 Andover pl NW6
48 C 8 Andover rd N7
101 R 2 Andover rd Twick
48 C 8 Andover row N7
48 C 8 Andover st N7
49 Y 14 Andre st E8
98 M 14 Andrew clo Bxly
89 X 1 Andrew pl SW8
64 G 17 Andrew st E14
78 C 3 Andrew st E14
135 X 6 Andrews rd E8
80 D 6 Andwell clo SE5
109 V 18 Anerley gro SE19
109 W 17 Anerley hill SE19
109 Y 17 Anerley Park rd SE20
110 A 17 Anerley pk SE20
109 Y 18 Anerley pk SE20
109 Y 20 Anerley pk SE20
124 A 1 Anerley rd SE20
109 Z 20 Anerley Station rd SE20
109 W 17 Anerley vale SE19
140 C 14 Angel ct EC1
142 F 5 Angel ct EC1
18 H 15 Angel ct N18
154 A 5 Angel hill Sutton
154 B 4 Angel Hill dri Sutton
51 X 18 Angel la E15
133 T 9 Angel ms N1
142 F 10 Angel pas EC4
18 J 15 Angel pk N18
90 G 7 Angel Pk gdns SW19
19 O 17 Angel rd N18
90 F 5 Angel rd SW9
9 O 14 Angel rd Enf
23 U 18 Angel rd Harrow
142 A 4 Angel st EC1
141 Z 4 Angel st EC1
74 L 12 Angel wlk W6
144 B 8 Angel wlk W6
135 N 12 Angela st E2
82 K 12 Angfield Hounsl
55 U 4 Angle green Dgnhm
51 Y 10 Angle st E11
47 T 17 Anglers la NW5
108 B 9 Angles rd SW16
78 M 12 Anglesea av SE18
78 L 12 Anglesea rd SE18
116 G 9 Anglesea rd Kingst
155 O 15 Anglesey Ct rd Carsh

155 O 15 Anglesey gdns Car
9 O 13 Anglesey rd Enf
22 G 10 Anglesmede cres Pinn
22 F 10 Anglesmede way Pinn
63 Y 6 Anglo rd E3
25 Z 5 Angus gdns NW9
65 Y 10 Angus rd E13
75 X 19 Angus st SE14
146 L 19 Anhalt rd SW11
95 Y 1 Ankerdine cres SE...
78 L 20 Ankerdine cres SE...
101 S 12 Anlaby rd Tedd
136 E 20 Anley rd W14
24 H 6 Anmersh gro Stanr
146 F 16 Ann la SW10
79 R 11 Ann st SE18
64 C 18 Annabel clo E14
39 O 4 Annan way Rom
77 P 14 Annandale rd W4
74 A 13 Annandale rd W4
157 Y 3 Annandale rd Croy
96 J 19 Annandale rd W4
102 K 12 Anne Boleyns wlk Kingst
153 R 16 Anne Boleyns wlk Sutton
65 S 11 Anne st E13
25 Z 10 Annesley av NW9
44 A 10 Annesley clo NW1(
158 M 6 Annesley dri Croy
47 U 7 Annesley rd N19
94 G 2 Annesley rd SE3
48 D 12 Annette rd N7
134 L 15 Anning st EC2
29 N 11 Annington rd N2
50 H 19 Annis rd E9
139 S 19 Anns clo SW1
143 O 2 Anns pl E1
123 N 7 Annsworthy av Thn Hth
123 P 4 Annsworthy cres Thntn Hth
92 C 5 Ansdell rd SE15
137 Y 20 Ansdell st W8
137 Y 20 Ansdell st W8
155 N 1 Ansell gro Carsh
106 K 7 Ansell rd SW17
145 S 15 Anselm rd SW6
22 E 3 Anselm rd Pinn
111 V 11 Ansford rd Brom
136 H 10 Ansleigh pl W11
38 F 7 Anson clo Rom
44 L 14 Anson rd NW2
45 P 14 Anson rd NW2
47 X 12 Anson rd N7
91 X 7 Anstey rd SE15
96 E 16 Anstridge rd SE9
63 W 8 Anthill rd E3
123 X 15 Anthony rd SE25
59 S 7 Anthony rd Grnfd
97 O 2 Anthony rd Welling
31 W 13 Antill rd N15
63 S 17 Antill ter E1
49 Y 14 Anton st E8
46 L 17 Antrim gro NW3
46 L 18 Antrim rd NW3
153 W 13 Antrobus clo Sutton
73 V 10 Antrobus rd W4
85 W 6 Anyscombe pth SW 14
111 S 20 Apex clo Becknhm
112 G 20 Apollo av Brom
146 F 17 Apollo pl SW10
141 W 7 Apotlecary st EC4
90 E 14 Appach rd SW2
72 H 12 Apple garth Brentf
8 E 12 Apple gro Enf
116 H 4 Apple mkt Kingst
140 D 12 Apple Tree yd SW1
20 E 19 Appleby clo E4
65 R 18 Appleby rd E16
49 Y 20 Appleby rd E8
135 N 8 Appleby st E2
98 L 4 Appledore av Bxly Hth
106 L 3 Appledore clo SW1?
126 D 11 Appledore clo Brom
25 O 4 Appledore clo Edg
114 J 8 Appledore cres Sidcp
128 M 8 Appleford rd W10
159 S 15 Applegarth Croy
36 L 13 Applegarth dri Ilf
144 G 3 Applegarth rd W14
118 F 14 Appleton gdns New Mald
95 P 7 Appleton rd SE9
134 J 20 Appold st EC2
63 P 7 Approach rd E2
118 M 3 Approach rd SW20
5 S 15 Approach rd Barnt

| Ref | Entry | Ref | Entry |
|---|---|---|---|
| Z 17 | Approach the W3 | 53 W 6 | Argyle rd Ilf |
| N 8 | Approach the Enf | 101 U 12 | Argyle rd Tedd |
| N 13 | Aprey gdns NW4 | 132 L 12 | Argyle sq WC1 |
| V 13 | April st E8 | 51 Y 9 | Argyle st E11 |
| M 15 | Apsley clo Harrow | 132 L 13 | Argyle st WC1 |
| K 15 | Apsley rd E17 | 132 L 13 | Argyle wlk WC1 |
| Z 9 | Apsley rd SE25 | 70 J 2 | Argyll av Shall |
| W 7 | Apsley rd New Mald | 25 T 7 | Argyll gdns Edg |
| T 14 | Aquinas st SE1 | 137 U 20 | Argyll rd W8 |
| C 10 | Arabella dri SW15 | 140 A 6 | Argyll st W1 |
| C 10 | Arabella dri SW15 | 92 H 9 | Arica rd SE4 |
| H 2 | Arabia clo E4 | 45 X 18 | Ariel rd NW6 |
| K 10 | Arabin rd SE4 | 89 Y 9 | Aristotle rd SW4 |
| H 20 | Aragon av Epsom | 108 X 19 | Arkell clo SE19 |
| H 12 | Aragon rd Kingst | 111 U 8 | Arkindale rd SE6 |
| P 16 | Aragon rd Mrdn | 32 K 17 | Arkley cres E17 |
| O 19 | Arandora cres Rom | 32 K 17 | Arkley rd E17 |
| V 7 | Arbery rd E3 | 75 X 17 | Arklow rd SE14 |
| K 11 | Arbor rd E4 | 46 D 15 | Arkwright rd NW3 |
| R 11 | Arbor sq E1 | 157 V 20 | Arkwright rd S Croy |
| N 2 | Arboreal av N14 | 65 P 18 | Arkwright st E16 |
| R 3 | Arbour clo Becknhm | 90 A 7 | Arlesford rd SW9 |
| T 12 | Arbour rd Enf | 87 S 14 | Arlesley clo SW15 |
| Y 14 | Arbour way Hornch | 90 F 15 | Arlingford rd SW2 |
| S 7 | Arbroath rd SE9 | 14 K 12 | Arlington N12 |
| Y 8 | Arbury ter SE26 | 134 D 6 | Arlington av N1 |
| 7 16 | Arbuthnot la Bxly | 96 C 10 | Arlington clo Didup |
| A 15 | Arbuthnot la Bxly | 153 Y 3 | Arlington clo Sutton |
| F 4 | Arbuthnot rd SE14 | 84 C 14 | Arlington clo Twick |
| R 17 | Arcade pl Rom | 154 L 3 | Arlington dri Carsh |
| J 2 | Arcade the EC2 | 73 V 13 | Arlington gdns W4 |
| X 6 | Arcadia av N3 | 53 V 3 | Arlington gdns Ilf |
| B 16 | Arcadia st E14 | 131 Y 5 | Arlington rd NW1 |
| Y 10 | Arcadian av Bxly | 132 A 8 | Arlington rd NW1 |
| Y 16 | Arcadian clo Bxly | 16 G 6 | Arlington rd N14 |
| E 1 | Arcadian gdns N22 | 60 B 18 | Arlington rd W13 |
| Y 17 | Arcadian rd Bxly | 102 F 5 | Arlington rd Rich |
| D 17 | Archbishops pl SW2 | 116 H 15 | Arlington rd Surb |
| V 11 | Archdale rd SE22 | 101 V 10 | Arlington rd Tedd |
| P 13 | Archel rd W14 | 84 C 15 | Arlington rd Twick |
| Z 8 | Archer rd SE25 | 34 G 3 | Arlington rd Wdfd Grn |
| E 9 | Archer st W1 | 134 C 6 | Arlington sq N1 |
| M 7 | Archery clo W2 | 140 A 13 | Arlington st N1 |
| U 12 | Archery rd SE9 | 133 U 12 | Arlington way EC1 |
| W 11 | Archibald ms W1 | 17 U 6 | Arlow rd N21 |
| X 12 | Archibald rd N7 | 76 B 16 | Armada st SE8 |
| V 6 | Archibald st E3 | 145 T 16 | Armadale rd SW6 |
| V 6 | Archway clo N19 | 63 Y 4 | Armagh rd E3 |
| T 16 | Archway mall N19 | 121 N 3 | Armfield cres Mitch |
| O 18 | Archway rd N6 | 8 B 6 | Armfield rd Enf |
| U 3 | Archway rd N6 | 74 K 3 | Arminger rd W12 |
| B 7 | Archway st SW13 | 45 U 4 | Armitage rd NW1 |
| U 14 | Arcola st E8 | 87 Y 13 | Armoury way SW18 |
| R 15 | Arctic st NW5 | 69 R 1 | Armstead wlk Dgnhm |
| A 14 | Arcus rd Brom | 56 D 20 | Armstead wlk Dgnhm |
| A 3 | Arcwell rd SW2 | 20 M 19 | Armstrong av Wdfd Grn |
| O 14 | Ardbeg rd SE24 | 6 T 12 | Armstrong cres Barnt |
| G 2 | Arden clo Bushey Watf | 77 Y 12 | Armstrong gdns SE7 |
| P 10 | Arden clo Harrow | 79 N 11 | Armstrong pl SE18 |
| W 20 | Arden cres Dgnhm | 74 D 2 | Armstrong rd W3 |
| H 1 | Arden cres Dgnhm | 100 C 13 | Armstrong rd Felt |
| V 0 | Arden rd N3 | 78 M 12 | Armstrong rd SE18 |
| E 5 | Ardfern av SW16 | 87 S 18 | Arnal cres SW18 |
| Y 3 | Ardfillan rd SE6 | 140 L 6 | Arne st WC2 |
| Y 3 | Ardgowan rd SE6 | 94 B 10 | Arne wlk SE3 |
| Y 19 | Ardgowan rd SE6 | 148 F 3 | Arneway st SW1 |
| L 12 | Ardilaun rd N5 | 37 W 11 | Arnewoys av Rom |
| X 19 | Ardleigh gdns Sutton | 121 N 13 | Arneys la Mitch |
| L 5 | Ardleigh rd E17 | 93 W 19 | Arngask rd SE6 |
| P 19 | Ardleigh rd N1 | 91 S 13 | Arnhem way SE22 |
| M 5 | Ardleigh ter E17 | 9 Z 2 | Arnold cir E2 |
| A 9 | Ardley clo NW10 | 135 N 14 | Arnold clr E2 |
| J 7 | Ardley clo SE6 | 25 N 20 | Arnold clo Harrow |
| L 4 | Ardlui rd SE27 | 83 R 13 | Arnold cres Islwth |
| J 12 | Ardmay gdns Surb | 17 U 15 | Arnold gdns N13 |
| X 15 | Ardmere rd SE13 | 64 A 9 | Arnold rd E3 |
| W 4 | Ardmore la Buck Hl | 31 O 11 | Arnold rd N15 |
| W 4 | Ardock rd SE6 | 106 M 17 | Arnold rd SW17 |
| F 5 | Ardrossan gdns Worc Pk | 69 P 2 | Arnold rd Dgnhm |
| C 17 | Ardwell av Ilf | 69 R 1 | Arnold rd Dgnhm |
| X 12 | Ardwick rd NW2 | 40 C 19 | Arnold rd Grnfd |
| G 2 | Argall av E10 | 16 K 12 | Arnos gro N14 |
| Z 16 | Argent st SE1 | 16 J 15 | Arnos rd N11 |
| G 6 | Argon ms SW6 | 150 D 3 | Arnott st SE1 |
| A 9 | Argus clo Rom | 91 P 9 | Arnould av SE5 |
| A 9 | Argus way Grnfd | 42 G 3 | Arnside gdns Wemb |
| J 15 | Argyle av Hounsl | 98 E 2 | Arnside rd Bxly Hth |
| Y 11 | Argyle clo W13 | 111 R 10 | Arnulf st SE6 |
| K 11 | Argyle pl W6 | 108 H 15 | Arnulls rd SW16 |
| S 11 | Argyle rd E1 | 90 D 15 | Arodene rd SW2 |
| Z 13 | Argyle rd E15 | 110 D 19 | Arpley rd SE20 |
| U 18 | Argyle rd E16 | 108 A 18 | Arragon gdns SW16 |
| L 16 | Argyle rd N12 | 159 S 5 | Arragon gdns W Wkhm |
| N 17 | Argyle rd N12 | 66 B 4 | Arragon rd E6 |
| W 4 | Argyle rd N17 | 83 Z 20 | Arragon rd Twick |
| L 13 | Argyle rd N18 | 155 T 8 | Arran clo Wallgtn |
| Z 12 | Argyle rd W13 | 111 S 3 | Arran rd SE6 |
| A 13 | Argyle rd W13 | 120 D 10 | Arras av Mrdn |
| A 13 | Argyle rd Barnt | | |
| J 17 | Argyle rd Harrow | | |
| K 13 | Argyle rd Hounsl | | |

| Ref | Entry | Ref | Entry |
|---|---|---|---|
| 124 E 5 | Arrol rd Becknhm | 56 H 10 | Ashbrook rd Dgnhm |
| 64 D 9 | Arrow rd E3 | 146 A 5 | Ashburn gdns SW7 |
| 95 T 6 | Arsenal rd SE9 | 146 B 5 | Ashburn ms SW7 |
| 105 N 19 | Arterberry rd SW20 | 146 A 5 | Ashburn pl SW7 |
| 137 T 6 | Artesian rd W2 | 23 W 20 | Ashburnham av Harrow |
| 64 M 3 | Arthingworth st E15 | 23 X 20 | Ashburnham gdns Harrow |
| 79 O 11 | Arthur gro SE18 | 76 E 20 | Ashburnham gro SE10 |
| 66 G 6 | Arthur rd E6 | 76 E 20 | Ashburnham pl SE10 |
| 48 D 11 | Arthur rd N7 | 62 M 8 | Ashburnham rd NW10 |
| 18 F 7 | Arthur rd N9 | 128 C 11 | Ashburnham rd NW10 |
| 105 W 7 | Arthur rd SW19 | 146 D 19 | Ashburnham rd SW10 |
| 103 P 19 | Arthur rd Kingst | 81 X 10 | Ashburnham rd Erith |
| 118 K 12 | Arthur rd New Mald | 102 C 7 | Ashburnham rd Rich |
| 37 U 19 | Arthur rd Rom | 123 Z 20 | Ashburton av Croy |
| 142 F 9 | Arthur st EC4 | 54 G 14 | Ashburton av Ilf |
| 143 V 10 | Artichoke hill E1 | 157 W 1 | Ashburton clo Croy |
| 36 D 17 | Artillery clo Ilf | 157 W 1 | Ashburton gdns Croy |
| 142 L 1 | Artillery la E1 | 48 F 13 | Ashburton gro N7 |
| 78 H 12 | Artillery pl SE18 | 65 T 17 | Ashburton rd E16 |
| 148 D 2 | Artillery row SW1 | 123 W 20 | Ashburton rd Croy |
| 142 M 4 | Artizan st E1 | 157 W 1 | Ashburton rd Croy |
| 119 W 9 | Arundel av Mrdn | 37 V 16 | Ashbury gdns Rom |
| 52 A 13 | Arundel clo E15 | 89 N 6 | Ashbury rd SW11 |
| 98 C 15 | Arundel clo Bxly | 48 M 20 | Ashby gro N1 |
| 156 H 7 | Arundel clo Croy | 31 W 15 | Ashby rd N15 |
| 100 L 13 | Arundel clo Hampt | 92 L 5 | Ashby rd SE4 |
| 40 F 14 | Arundel dri Harrow | 93 N 5 | Ashby rd SE4 |
| 34 G 2 | Arundel dri Wdfd Grn | 133 X 13 | Ashby st EC1 |
| 17 U 7 | Arundel gdns N21 | 74 F 8 | Ashchurch ct W12 |
| 137 M 8 | Arundel gdns W11 | 74 A 10 | Ashchurch ct W4 |
| 25 Y 2 | Arundel gdns Edg | 74 F 7 | Ashchurch gro W12 |
| 25 Y 2 | Arundel gdns Edgw | 74 F 8 | Ashchurch Pk vlls W12 |
| 55 N 6 | Arundel gdns Ilf | 74 F 7 | Ashchurch ter W12 |
| 49 R 15 | Arundel gro N16 | 116 G 18 | Ashcombe av Surb |
| 48 F 19 | Arundel pl N1 | 12 B 14 | Ashcombe gdns Edg |
| 5 X 12 | Arundel rd Barnt | 44 C 10 | Ashcombe pk NW2 |
| 123 O 15 | Arundel rd Croy | 105 Y 12 | Ashcombe rd SW19 |
| 117 U 2 | Arundel rd Kingst | 155 O 12 | Ashcombe rd Carsh |
| 153 U 17 | Arundel rd Sutton | 117 V 5 | Ashcombe sq New Mald |
| 48 F 19 | Arundel sq N1 | 87 Z 6 | Ashcombe st SW6 |
| 141 P 8 | Arundel st WC2 | 96 M 15 | Ashcroft av Sidcp |
| 74 K 17 | Arundel ter SW12 | 97 N 16 | Ashcroft cres Sidop |
| 144 A 14 | Arundel ter SW12 | 63 V 9 | Ashcroft rd E3 |
| 74 K 17 | Arundel ter SW13 | 82 I 18 | Ashdale clo Twick |
| 48 G 15 | Arvon rd N5 | 10 K 19 | Ashdale gro Stanm |
| 148 B 20 | Ascalon st SW8 | 112 J 1 | Ashdale rd SE12 |
| 33 P 1 | Ascham dri E4 | 82 L 18 | Ashdale way Twick |
| 32 J 3 | Ascham end E17 | 21 V 19 | Ashdon clo Wdfd Grn |
| 47 V 14 | Ascham st NW5 | 62 C 3 | Ashdon rd NW10 |
| 40 G 10 | Ascot clo Grnfd | 125 S 4 | Ashdown clo Becknhm |
| 9 P 1 | Ascot gdns Enf | 116 J 4 | Ashdown rd Kingst |
| 58 F 15 | Ascot gdns S'hall | 47 O 15 | Ashdown st NW5 |
| 43 Y 15 | Ascot pk NW10 | 38 H 6 | Ashdown wk Rom |
| 66 F 8 | Ascot rd E6 | 99 W 16 | Ashen dri Drtfrd |
| 31 O 16 | Ascot rd N15 | 108 X 5 | Ashen gro SW19 |
| 18 K 13 | Ascot rd N18 | 158 G 20 | Ashen vale S Croy |
| 107 N 15 | Ascot rd SW17 | 50 G 14 | Ashenden rd E5 |
| 72 J 5 | Ascott av W5 | 102 J 1 | Ashfield clo Rich |
| 154 L 2 | Ascott av Carsh | 114 C 17 | Ashfield la Chisl |
| 117 Y 3 | Ash clo New Mald | 63 O 16 | Ashfield rd E1 |
| 38 G 3 | Ash clo Rom | 16 G 11 | Ashfield rd N14 |
| 115 P 9 | Ash clo Sidcp | 30 M 19 | Ashfield rd N4 |
| 10 K 19 | Ash clo Stanm | 74 C 1 | Ashfield rd W3 |
| 135 X 5 | Ash gro E8 | 143 W 3 | Ashfield st E1 |
| 45 R 13 | Ash gro NW2 | 29 Z 14 | Ashford av N8 |
| 124 C 3 | Ash gro SE20 | 9 R 8 | Ashford cres Enf |
| 72 K 7 | Ash gro W5 | 34 J 8 | Ashford rd E18 |
| 18 D 2 | Ash gro Enf | 53 V 20 | Ashford rd E6 |
| 58 J 13 | Ash gro S'hall | 45 O 12 | Ashford rd NW2 |
| 150 V 1 | Ash gro W Wickm | 31 U 2 | Ashford rd N17 |
| 41 Y 13 | Ash gro Wemb | 134 J 12 | Ashford st N1 |
| 52 B 15 | Ash rd E15 | 17 X 12 | Ashgrove N13 |
| 159 O 2 | Ash rd Croy | 111 Y 14 | Ashgrove rd Brom |
| 119 T 19 | Ash rd Sutton | 54 L 5 | Ashgrove rd Ilf |
| 127 W 15 | Ash row Brom | 55 N 4 | Ashgrove rd Ilf |
| 150 B 5 | Ash st SE17 | 87 W 5 | Ashington rd SW6 |
| 124 H 13 | Ash Tree clo Croy | 108 A 10 | Ashlake rd SW16 |
| 25 X 15 | Ash Tree clo NW9 | 139 T 1 | Ashland pl W1 |
| 124 H 14 | Ash Tree way Croy | 102 J 1 | Ashleigh cl Rich |
| 34 H 13 | Ashbourne av E18 | 102 J 2 | Ashleigh clo Rich |
| 27 V 14 | Ashbourne av NW11 | 154 A 3 | Ashleigh gdns Sutton |
| 15 Z 7 | Ashbourne av N20 | 154 C 3 | Ashleigh gdns Sutton |
| 81 N 19 | Ashbourne av Bxly Hth | 124 B 5 | Ashleigh rd SE20 |
| 41 R 7 | Ashbourne av Harrow | 86 A 7 | Ashleigh rd SW14 |
| 107 R 17 | Ashbourne av Mitch | 35 Z 8 | Ashley av Ilf |
| 15 O 14 | Ashbourne clo N12 | 119 Y 12 | Ashley av Mrdn |
| 61 O 13 | Ashbourne clo W5 | 27 N 7 | Ashley clo NW4 |
| 12 L 17 | Ashbourne gro NW7 | 30 G 8 | Ashley cres N22 |
| 91 U 12 | Ashbourne gro SE22 | 82 K 20 | Ashley dri Twick |
| 60 M 14 | Ashbourne gro W4 | 17 Y 14 | Ashley gdns N13 |
| 60 M 11 | Ashbourne rd W5 | 102 G 5 | Ashley gdns Rich |
| 61 O 13 | Ashbourne rd W5 | 42 K 7 | Ashley gdns Wemb |
| 105 W 19 | Ashbourne ter SW19 | 27 N 7 | Ashley la NW4 |
| 27 V 14 | Ashbourne way NW11 | | |
| 24 E 19 | Ashbridge clo Harrow | | |
| 34 A 20 | Ashbridge rd E11 | | |
| 130 K 18 | Ashbridge st NW8 | | |
| 47 X 5 | Ashbrook rd N19 | | |

| | | |
|---|---|---|
| 156 J8 | Ashley la Croy |
| 148 B3 | Ashley pl SW1 |
| 20 A18 | Ashley rd E4 |
| 65 Y1 | Ashley rd E7 |
| 31 Y11 | Ashley rd N17 |
| 48 A2 | Ashley rd N4 |
| 106 A15 | Ashley rd SW19 |
| 9 P10 | Ashley rd Enf |
| 100 H20 | Ashley rd Hampt |
| 84 K8 | Ashley rd Rich |
| 122 D10 | Ashley rd Thntn Hth |
| 27 N2 | Ashley wlk NW7 |
| 51 Y13 | Ashlin rd E15 |
| 123 X20 | Ashling rd Croy |
| 87 N6 | Ashlone rd SW6 |
| 6 H18 | Ashmead clo N14 |
| 93 O4 | Ashmead rd SE4 |
| 125 W3 | Ashmere av Becknhm |
| 90 A11 | Ashmere gro SW2 |
| 130 L19 | Ashmill st NW1 |
| 149 R16 | Ashmole pl SW8 |
| 149 R16 | Ashmole st SW8 |
| 96 F7 | Ashmore gro Welling |
| 129 O11 | Ashmore rd W9 |
| 31 U14 | Ashmount rd N15 |
| 47 W2 | Ashmount rd N19 |
| 38 M8 | Ashmour gdns Rom |
| 39 N8 | Ashmour gdns Rom |
| 42 A19 | Ashness gdns Grnfd |
| 88 M13 | Ashness rd SW11 |
| 24 E19 | Ashridge clo Harrow |
| 79 O20 | Ashridge cres SE18 |
| 16 M15 | Ashridge gdns N13 |
| 17 N16 | Ashridge gdns N13 |
| 22 B13 | Ashridge gdns Pinn |
| 119 U8 | Ashridge way Mrdn |
| 49 X1 | Ashtead rd E5 |
| 153 W9 | Ashton clo Sutton |
| 82 D10 | Ashton gdns Hounsl |
| 37 Z19 | Ashton gdns Rom |
| 51 X16 | Ashton rd E15 |
| 64 G19 | Ashton st E14 |
| 120 H3 | Ashtree av Mitch |
| 35 Z18 | Ashurst dri Ilf |
| 36 C13 | Ashurst dri Ilf |
| 15 X17 | Ashurst rd N12 |
| 5 Z17 | Ashurst rd Barnt |
| 6 A15 | Ashurst rd Barnt |
| 157 Z2 | Ashurst wlk Croy |
| 106 L11 | Ashvale rd SW17 |
| 51 W8 | Ashville rd E11 |
| 112 F2 | Ashwater rd SE12 |
| 18 D16 | Ashwell gro N18 |
| 63 U7 | Ashwell rd E3 |
| 49 T17 | Ashwin st E8 |
| 20 K11 | Ashwood rd E4 |
| 129 Y13 | Ashworth rd W9 |
| 74 F6 | Askew bldgs W12 |
| 97 X11 | Askew clo Bxly Hth |
| 74 E4 | Askew cres W12 |
| 74 G7 | Askew rd W12 |
| 74 F3 | Askham rd W12 |
| 87 T14 | Askill dri SW15 |
| 88 B18 | Aslett st SW18 |
| 45 U14 | Asmara rd NW2 |
| 27 X15 | Asmuns hill NW11 |
| 27 W15 | Asmuns pl NW11 |
| 127 U3 | Aspen copse Brom |
| 74 K13 | Aspen gdns W6 |
| 121 N12 | Aspen gdns Mitch |
| 144 G14 | Aspenlea rd W6 |
| 92 F8 | Aspinal rd SE4 |
| 75 O10 | Aspinden rd SE16 |
| 151 Y5 | Aspinden rd SE16 |
| 50 A16 | Aspland gro E8 |
| 88 B14 | Aspley rd SW18 |
| 31 Y4 | Asplins rd N17 |
| 63 P13 | Assembly pas E1 |
| 120 H18 | Assembly wlk Carsh |
| 81 P13 | Assurance cotts Blvdr |
| 92 B1 | Astbury rd SE15 |
| 76 F6 | Aste st E14 |
| 146 K9 | Astell st SW3 |
| 89 O3 | Astle st SW11 |
| 45 N2 | Astley av NW2 |
| 133 Z1 | Astley row N1 |
| 24 E20 | Aston av Harrow |
| 115 O9 | Aston clo Sidcp |
| 119 N3 | Aston rd SW20 |
| 60 H17 | Aston rd W5 |
| 63 V16 | Aston st E14 |
| 105 X2 | Astonville st SW18 |
| 38 J18 | Astor av Rom |
| 90 E7 | Astoria wlk SW9 |
| 57 Y17 | Astra clo Hornch |
| 136 B20 | Astrop ms W6 |
| 74 L7 | Astrop ms W6 |
| 74 L7 | Astrop ter W6 |
| 136 B20 | Astrop ter W6 |
| 136 B20 | Astropter W6 |
| 146 A6 | Astwood ms SW5 |
| 75 N20 | Asylum rd SE15 |
| 92 A1 | Asylum rd SE15 |
| 151 X16 | Asylum rd SE15 |
| 144 J20 | Atalanta st SW6 |
| 102 C15 | Atbara rd Tedd |
| 83 O10 | Atcham rd Hounsl |
| 88 B19 | Atheldene rd SW18 |
| 111 P6 | Athelney st SE6 |
| 117 N8 | Athelstan rd Kingst |
| 63 X7 | Athelstane gro E3 |
| 48 F6 | Athelstane rd N4 |
| 23 R8 | Athelstone rd Harrow |
| 41 R5 | Athena clo Harrow |
| 29 R11 | Athenaenm pl N10 |
| 15 S6 | Athenaeum rd N20 |
| 92 F13 | Athenlay rd SE15 |
| 50 B12 | Atherden rd E5 |
| 89 Z7 | Atherfold rd SW9 |
| 90 A7 | Atherfold rd SW9 |
| 146 C4 | Atherstone ms SW7 |
| 105 P9 | Atherton dri SW19 |
| 52 D17 | Atherton ms E7 |
| 52 C17 | Atherton rd E7 |
| 74 E20 | Atherton rd SW13 |
| 35 S7 | Atherton rd Ilf |
| 88 K5 | Atherton st SW11 |
| 60 G6 | Athlon rd Wemb |
| 90 E19 | Athlone rd SW2 |
| 47 R17 | Athlone st NW5 |
| 81 X14 | Athol rd Erith |
| 54 M2 | Athol rd Ilf |
| 55 N1 | Athol rd Ilf |
| 64 H18 | Athol st E14 |
| 8 D19 | Athole gdns Enf |
| 93 O13 | Athurdon rd SE4 |
| 33 S19 | Atkins rd E10 |
| 89 Z19 | Atkins rd SW12 |
| 75 Y18 | Atkinson st SE14 |
| 90 F10 | Atlantic rd SW19 |
| 77 X10 | Atlas gdns SE7 |
| 65 S7 | Atlas rd E13 |
| 62 B10 | Atlas rd NW10 |
| 64 A4 | Atley rd E3 |
| 87 S10 | Atney rd SW15 |
| 30 D19 | Atterbury rd N4 |
| 148 H8 | Atterbury st SW1 |
| 44 A9 | Attewood av NW10 |
| 133 R15 | Attneave st WC1 |
| 90 E20 | Atwater clo SW2 |
| 91 Y5 | Atwell rd SE15 |
| 85 R5 | Atwood av Rich |
| 74 J10 | Atwood rd W6 |
| 78 G3 | Auberon st E16 |
| 48 H12 | Aubert pk N5 |
| 48 J12 | Aubert rd N5 |
| 33 P11 | Aubrey rd E17 |
| 30 B18 | Aubrey rd N8 |
| 137 P14 | Aubrey rd W8 |
| 137 R15 | Aubrey wlk W8 |
| 109 N11 | Aubyn hill SE27 |
| 86 G12 | Aubyn sq SW15 |
| 123 U1 | Auckland clo SE19 |
| 123 T1 | Auckland gdns SE19 |
| 108 M9 | Auckland hill SE27 |
| 51 R9 | Auckland rd E10 |
| 109 U19 | Auckland rd SE19 |
| 123 T3 | Auckland rd SE19 |
| 88 J12 | Auckland rd SW11 |
| 53 Z3 | Auckland rd Ilf |
| 54 A2 | Auckland rd Ilf |
| 117 N8 | Auckland rd Kingst |
| 109 T20 | Auckland ri SE19 |
| 149 N11 | Auckland st SE11 |
| 34 C14 | Audley ct E18 |
| 54 K8 | Audley gdns Ilf |
| 26 B19 | Audley rd NW4 |
| 60 M15 | Audley rd W5 |
| 61 N14 | Audley rd W5 |
| 7 V8 | Audley rd Enf |
| 84 M14 | Audley rd Rich |
| 139 V13 | Audley sq W1 |
| 125 R14 | Audrey clo Becknhm |
| 42 B6 | Audrey gdns Wemb |
| 53 Y10 | Audrey rd Ilf |
| 135 T8 | Audrey st E2 |
| 65 X9 | Augurs la E13 |
| 101 N5 | Augusta rd Twick |
| 64 C17 | Augusta st E14 |
| 144 F3 | Augustine rd W14 |
| 105 S1 | Augustus rd SW19 |
| 131 Z11 | Augustus st NW1 |
| 151 R13 | Aulay st SE1 |
| 149 U12 | Aulton pl SE11 |
| 154 L4 | Aultone way Carsh |
| 154 B2 | Aultone way Sutton |
| 122 C13 | Aurelia gdns Croy |
| 122 B14 | Aurelia rd Croy |
| 57 O18 | Auriel av Dgnhm |
| 144 K6 | Auriol W14 |
| 13 O11 | Austell gdns NW7 |
| 40 J6 | Austen rd Harrow |
| 40 J6 | Austen rd Harrow |
| 127 S13 | Austin av Brom |
| 142 G5 | Austin friars EC2 |
| 89 O2 | Austin rd SW11 |
| 134 M14 | Austin st E2 |
| 114 L6 | Austral clo Sidcp |
| 114 L6 | Austral clo Sidcp |
| 149 W4 | Austral st SE11 |
| 62 J19 | Australia rd W12 |
| 74 J1 | Australia rd W12 |
| 117 S19 | Austyn gdns Surb |
| 8 L7 | Autumn clo Enf |
| 64 B4 | Autumn st E3 |
| 59 Y13 | Avalon clo W13 |
| 7 U7 | Avalon clo Enf |
| 88 A1 | Avalon rd SW6 |
| 59 Y12 | Avalon rd W13 |
| 106 M14 | Avarn rd SW17 |
| 141 Y6 | Ave Maria la EC4 |
| 116 G16 | Avebury pk Surb |
| 51 X3 | Avebury rd E11 |
| 105 V19 | Avebury rd SW19 |
| 134 F6 | Avebury st N1 |
| 50 A6 | Aveley rd E5 |
| 39 O13 | Aveley rd Rom |
| 149 R10 | Aveline st SE11 |
| 33 O6 | Avenell rd N5 |
| 48 H10 | Avenell rd N5 |
| 87 Y18 | Avening terr SW18 |
| 65 T12 | Avenons rd E13 |
| 44 L19 | Avenue clo NW2 |
| 130 L6 | Avenue clo NW8 |
| 6 H18 | Avenue clo N14 |
| 73 S5 | Avenue cres W3 |
| 116 J11 | Avenue elmers Surb |
| 123 W3 | Avenue gdns SE25 |
| 86 A8 | Avenue gdns SW14 |
| 73 T5 | Avenue gdns W3 |
| 101 X16 | Avenue gdns Tedd |
| 29 S11 | Avenue ms N10 |
| 108 J3 | Avenue Pk rd SE27 |
| 51 Y12 | Avenue rd E11 |
| 52 H13 | Avenue rd E7 |
| 62 D6 | Avenue rd NW10 |
| 130 J4 | Avenue rd NW8 |
| 15 R14 | Avenue rd N12 |
| 6 G20 | Avenue rd N14 |
| 16 G1 | Avenue rd N14 |
| 31 O16 | Avenue rd N15 |
| 29 W20 | Avenue rd N6 |
| 110 D20 | Avenue rd SE20 |
| 124 E2 | Avenue rd SE20 |
| 123 V4 | Avenue rd SE25 |
| 121 X4 | Avenue rd SW16 |
| 118 K2 | Avenue rd SW20 |
| 71 Y1 | Avenue rd W13 |
| 73 S5 | Avenue rd W3 |
| 81 W11 | Avenue rd Blvdr |
| 72 E13 | Avenue rd Brentf |
| 97 Y9 | Avenue rd Bxly Hth |
| 81 Y19 | Avenue rd Erith |
| 83 U3 | Avenue rd Islwth |
| 116 K6 | Avenue rd Kingst |
| 118 B7 | Avenue rd New Mald |
| 22 A9 | Avenue rd Pinn |
| 55 S2 | Avenue rd Rom |
| 70 F2 | Avenue rd S'hall |
| 101 X16 | Avenue rd Tedd |
| 155 U18 | Avenue rd Wallgtn |
| 21 Z18 | Avenue rd Wdfd Grn |
| 117 V7 | Avenue ter New Mald |
| 142 K8 | Avenue the EC3 |
| 34 J17 | Avenue the E11 |
| 20 J19 | Avenue the E4 |
| 128 J4 | Avenue the NW6 |
| 29 U7 | Avenue the N10 |
| 31 P9 | Avenue the N17 |
| 27 Y7 | Avenue the N3 |
| 30 E11 | Avenue the N8 |
| 76 J19 | Avenue the SE10 |
| 77 X18 | Avenue the SE7 |
| 89 P13 | Avenue the SW4 |
| 60 A19 | Avenue the W13 |
| 74 A9 | Avenue the W4 |
| 4 E13 | Avenue the Barnt |
| 111 U20 | Avenue the Becknhm |
| 127 O7 | Avenue the Brom |
| 97 W18 | Avenue the Bxly |
| 155 O16 | Avenue the Carsh |
| 157 R5 | Avenue the Croy |
| 100 F14 | Avenue the Hampt |
| 23 U12 | Avenue the Harrow |
| 23 V4 | Avenue the Harrow |
| 82 J13 | Avenue the Hounsl |
| 115 R18 | Avenue the Orp |
| 22 E19 | Avenue the Pinn |
| 22 G1 | Avenue the Pinn |
| 85 N4 | Avenue the Rich |
| 39 O13 | Avenue the Rom |
| 117 O15 | Avenue the Surb |
| 153 U20 | Avenue the Sutton |
| 84 D14 | Avenue the Twick |
| 126 A14 | Avenue the W Wkhm |
| 125 W18 | Avenue the W Wkhm |
| 42 K3 | Avenue the Wemb |
| 43 O7 | Avenue the Wemb |
| 152 D3 | Avenue the Worc |
| 108 H16 | Averill gro SW16 |
| 144 G15 | Averill st W6 |
| 147 V8 | Avery Farm row S |
| 35 V16 | Avery gdns Ilf |
| 114 B2 | Avery hill Sidcp |
| 96 B16 | Avery Hill park SE |
| 96 D20 | Avery Hill rd SE9 |
| 139 X8 | Avery row W1 |
| 124 K12 | Aviemore clo Becknhm |
| 124 J12 | Aviemore way Becknhm |
| 92 G8 | Avignon rd SE4 |
| 110 B17 | Avington gro SE20 |
| 63 T17 | Avis sq E1 |
| 107 P8 | Avoca rd SW17 |
| 154 D8 | Avon clo Sutton |
| 152 F2 | Avon clo Worc Pk |
| 157 N14 | Avon path S Croy |
| 142 C19 | Avon pl SE1 |
| 33 X11 | Avon rd E17 |
| 93 O7 | Avon rd SE4 |
| 58 J11 | Avon rd Grnfd |
| 44 B9 | Avondale av NW2 |
| 15 N17 | Avondale av N12 |
| 15 Y4 | Avondale av Barnt |
| 118 C19 | Avondale av Worc |
| 9 V11 | Avondale cres Enf |
| 35 O17 | Avondale cres Ilf |
| 34 G4 | Avondale ct E11 |
| 82 E14 | Avondale gdns Hounsl |
| 136 K11 | Avondale park W11 |
| 136 J10 | Avondale Pk gdns W11 |
| 136 J9 | Avondale Pk rd W |
| 64 M13 | Avondale rd E16 |
| 65 N14 | Avondale rd E16 |
| 51 N1 | Avondale rd E17 |
| 17 U9 | Avondale rd N13 |
| 30 K15 | Avondale rd N15 |
| 28 C5 | Avondale rd N3 |
| 113 R5 | Avondale rd SE9 |
| 85 Z7 | Avondale rd SW14 |
| 105 Z12 | Avondale rd SW19 |
| 106 A12 | Avondale rd SW19 |
| 112 C15 | Avondale rd Brom |
| 23 X9 | Avondale rd Harro |
| 156 M15 | Avondale rd S Croy |
| 97 U5 | Avondale rd Welling |
| 91 U7 | Avondale ri SE15 |
| 151 S11 | Avondale sq SE1 |
| 75 R19 | Avonley ms SE14 |
| 75 R19 | Avonley st SE14 |
| 145 N4 | Avonmore pl W14 |
| 145 N5 | Avonmore rd W14 |
| 150 A1 | Avonmouth st SE1 |
| 82 K4 | Avonwick rd Houns |
| 20 H16 | Avril way E4 |
| 156 A15 | Avro way Wallgtn |
| 31 P5 | Awlfield av N17 |
| 96 L4 | Awliscombe rd Welling |
| 67 O3 | Axe st Bark |
| 25 R4 | Axholme av Edg |
| 80 H20 | Axminster cres Welling |
| 97 S1 | Axminster cres Welling |
| 48 B9 | Axminster rd N7 |
| 139 T2 | Aybrook st W1 |
| 127 V8 | Aycliffe clo Brom |
| 74 F2 | Aycliffe rd W12 |
| 150 H9 | Aylesbury rd SE17 |
| 126 E7 | Aylesbury rd Brom |
| 133 W17 | Aylesbury st EC1 |
| 43 Y10 | Aylesbury st NW10 |
| 124 H13 | Aylesford av Becknhm |
| 148 F11 | Aylesford st SW1 |
| 45 O20 | Aylestone av NW6 |
| 128 F2 | Aylestone av NW6 |
| 123 Z10 | Aylett rd SE25 |
| 124 A10 | Aylett rd SE25 |
| 83 U5 | Aylett rd Islwth |
| 8 K18 | Ayley croft Enf |
| 10 L12 | Aylmer clo Stanm |
| 10 K13 | Aylmer dri Stanm |
| 52 B2 | Aylmer rd E11 |
| 28 K16 | Aylmer rd N2 |
| 74 C6 | Aylmer rd Dgnhm |
| 55 X11 | Aylmer rd Dgnhm |
| 56 A17 | Ayloffe rd Dgnhm |
| 110 G5 | Aylward rd SE23 |
| 119 V5 | Aylward rd SW20 |
| 63 R16 | Aylward st E1 |
| 10 L13 | Aylwards ri Stanm |
| 144 H3 | Aynhoe rd W14 |
| 85 V6 | Aynscombe la SW14 |
| 39 O4 | Ayr grn Rom |

| Ref | Street |
|---|---|
| 39 O 4 | Ayr way Rom |
| 65 T 10 | Ayres clo E13 |
| 42 B 16 | Ayres st SE1 |
| 49 R 8 | Ayrsome rd N16 |
| 91 P 17 | Aysgarth rd SW19 |
| 90 D 5 | Aytoun rd SW19 |
| 91 U 4 | Azenby rd SE15 |
| 77 N 12 | Azof st SE10 |

## B

| Ref | Street |
|---|---|
| 48 J 15 | Baalbec rd N5 |
| 35 P 12 | Babbacombe gdns Ilf |
| 12 G 19 | Babbacombe rd Brom |
| 26 K 13 | Babbington rd NW4 |
| 07 Y 11 | Babington rd SW16 |
| 55 T 14 | Babington rd Dgnhm |
| 57 X 4 | Babington rd Hornch |
| 43 R 18 | Babington ri Wemb |
| 40 E 12 | Babmaes st SW1 |
| 34 G 13 | Baches st N1 |
| 43 T 5 | Back Ch la E1 |
| 33 T 18 | Back hill EC1 |
| 46 E 12 | Back la NW3 |
| 29 Z 17 | Back la N8 |
| 67 N 2 | Back la Bark |
| 72 G 18 | Back la Brentf |
| 98 E 17 | Back la Bxly |
| 25 C 18 | Back la Bxly |
| 25 V 5 | Back la Edg |
| 02 D 8 | Back la Rich |
| 37 X 20 | Back la Rom |
| 15 N 10 | Back rd Sidcp |
| 73 T 2 | Back st W3 |
| 50 M 3 | Bacon gro SE1 |
| 25 T 13 | Bacon la NW9 |
| 25 P 3 | Bacon la Edg |
| 35 R 16 | Bacon st E2 |
| 47 P 4 | Bacons la N6 |
| 63 R 8 | Bacton st E2 |
| 69 S 4 | Baddow clo Dgnhm |
| 42 F 17 | Baden pl SE1 |
| 29 Z 12 | Baden rd N8 |
| 53 Y 14 | Baden rd Ilf |
| 57 X 18 | Bader way Rainhm |
| 52 E 2 | Badgers copse Worc Pk |
| 13 W 7 | Badgers croft SE9 |
| 58 E 8 | Badgers hole Croy |
| 18 E 2 | Badgers wlk New Mald |
| 33 N 9 | Badlis rd E17 |
| 40 H 19 | Badminton clo Grnfd |
| 23 S 14 | Badminton clo Har |
| 89 P 17 | Badminton rd SW12 |
| 90 L 1 | Badsworth rd SE5 |
| 134 E 3 | Bagford st N1 |
| 63 Y 13 | Baggallay st E3 |
| 88 C 3 | Bagleys la SW6 |
| 37 Z 12 | Bagleys spring Rom |
| 18 F 1 | Bagshot rd Enf |
| 75 K 10 | Bagshot st SE17 |
| 57 Z 20 | Baildon st SE8 |
| 110 E 15 | Bailey pl SE26 |
| 36 A 15 | Bailey rd Ilf |
| 56 C 11 | Bainbridge rd Dgnhm |
| 140 G 3 | Bainbridge st WC1 |
| 58 M 19 | Baird av S'hall |
| 25 V 18 | Baird clo NW9 |
| 109 S 10 | Baird gdns SE21 |
| 8 K 14 | Baird rd Enf |
| 94 A 6 | Baizdon rd SE3 |
| 93 Z 6 | Baizdon rd SE3 |
| 121 N 4 | Baker la Mitch |
| 61 Z 4 | Baker rd NW10 |
| 62 A 4 | Baker rd NW10 |
| 131 R 19 | Baker st NW1 |
| 139 S 2 | Baker st W1 |
| 8 D 8 | Baker st Enf |
| 142 K 14 | Bakers all SE1 |
| 33 R 19 | Bakers av E17 |
| 119 T 3 | Bakers end SW20 |
| 50 B 4 | Bakers hill E5 |
| 29 N 17 | Bakers la N6 |
| 72 G 1 | Bakers la W5 |
| 139 T 4 | Bakers ms W1 |
| 133 T 17 | Bakers row EC1 |
| 64 L 5 | Bakers row E15 |
| 65 U 11 | Balaam st E13 |
| 16 K 8 | Balaams la N14 |
| 151 P 6 | Balaclava rd SE1 |
| 116 D 16 | Balaclava rd Surb |
| 95 V 12 | Balcaskie rd SE9 |
| 94 M 4 | Balchen rd SE3 |
| 91 Z 15 | Balchier rd SE22 |
| 131 N 18 | Balcombe st NW1 |
| 63 R 1 | Balcorne st E9 |
| 112 J 6 | Balder ri SE12 |
| 139 U 7 | Balderton st W1 |
| 64 C 7 | Baldock st E3 |
| 108 B 16 | Baldry gdns SW16 |
| 90 K 2 | Baldwin cres SE5 |
| 61 X 19 | Baldwin gdns W3 |
| 134 E 14 | Baldwin st EC1 |
| 134 A 8 | Baldwin ter N1 |
| 141 S 1 | Baldwin's gdns EC1 |
| 133 S 20 | Baldwins pl EC1 |
| 132 L 9 | Balfe st NW1 |
| 74 B 14 | Balfern gro W4 |
| 88 J 4 | Balfern st SW11 |
| 53 Z 7 | Balfour appr Ilf |
| 71 V 2 | Balfour av W7 |
| 15 Z 11 | Balfour gro N20 |
| 139 V 11 | Balfour ms W1 |
| 139 U 11 | Balfour pl W1 |
| 48 M 13 | Balfour rd N5 |
| 123 X 10 | Balfour rd SE25 |
| 106 A 18 | Balfour rd SW19 |
| 72 A 6 | Balfour rd W13 |
| 61 W 15 | Balfour rd W3 |
| 127 P 11 | Balfour rd Brom |
| 154 M 17 | Balfour rd Carsh |
| 23 R 16 | Balfour rd Harrow |
| 82 K 7 | Balfour rd Hounsl |
| 53 Z 7 | Balfour rd Ilf |
| 84 C 3 | Balfour rd Ilf |
| 150 D 5 | Balfour st SE17 |
| 20 J 6 | Balgonie rd E4 |
| 39 Y 11 | Balgores cres Rom |
| 39 X 11 | Balgores la Rom |
| 39 Y 12 | Balgores sq Rom |
| 118 B 10 | Balgowan clo New Mald |
| 124 K 4 | Balgowan rd Becknhm |
| 79 X 11 | Balgowan st SE18 |
| 89 R 19 | Balham gro SW12 |
| 89 R 19 | Balham High rd SW12 |
| 107 P 3 | Balham High rd SW17 |
| 89 S 16 | Balham hill SW12 |
| 89 S 19 | Balham New rd SW12 |
| 106 M 1 | Balham Pk rd SW12 |
| 107 O 2 | Balham Pk rd SW12 |
| 18 L 8 | Balham rd N9 |
| 107 R 1 | Balham Stn rd SW12 |
| 142 G 7 | Ball ct EC3 |
| 112 E 7 | Ballamore rd Brom |
| 50 G 17 | Ballance rd E9 |
| 88 C 11 | Ballantyne st SW18 |
| 103 X 19 | Ballard clo Kingst |
| 69 V 3 | Ballards clo Dgnhm |
| 157 Y 14 | Ballards Farm rd Croy |
| 158 A 14 | Ballards Farm rd Croy |
| 27 Z 3 | Ballards la N3 |
| 44 G 7 | Ballards la NW2 |
| 69 V 2 | Ballards rd Dgnhm |
| 157 X 14 | Ballards ri S Croy |
| 158 C 13 | Ballards way Croy |
| 157 Y 15 | Ballards way S Croy |
| 76 I 13 | Ballast quay SE10 |
| 90 B 11 | Ballater rd SW2 |
| 157 U 11 | Ballater rd S Croy |
| 92 G 17 | Ballina st SE23 |
| 89 N 15 | Ballingdon rd SW11 |
| 20 K 4 | Balliol av E4 |
| 31 P 5 | Balliol rd N17 |
| 136 E 5 | Balliol rd W10 |
| 97 R 4 | Balliol rd Welling |
| 111 X 3 | Balloch rd SE6 |
| 44 B 11 | Ballogie av NW10 |
| 49 O 17 | Balls Pond pl N1 |
| 49 R 17 | Balls Pond rd N1 |
| 63 Y 7 | Balmer rd E3 |
| 134 G 3 | Balmes rd N1 |
| 124 J 9 | Balmoral av Becknhm |
| 71 Y 7 | Balmoral gdns W13 |
| 54 J 5 | Balmoral gdns Ilf |
| 48 B 18 | Balmoral gro N7 |
| 51 S 8 | Balmoral rd E10 |
| 52 L 14 | Balmoral rd E7 |
| 44 K 17 | Balmoral rd NW2 |
| 40 G 12 | Balmoral rd Harrow |
| 116 L 8 | Balmoral rd Kingst |
| 39 Y 15 | Balmoral rd Rom |
| 152 J 4 | Balmoral rd Worc Pk |
| 6 B 16 | Balmore cres Barnt |
| 47 T 7 | Balmore st N19 |
| 87 N 11 | Balmuir gdns SW15 |
| 44 B 12 | Balmacraig av NW10 |
| 106 F 17 | Baltic clo SW19 |
| 134 A 18 | Baltic st EC1 |
| 87 W 20 | Balvernie gro SW18 |
| 136 D 18 | Bamborough gdns W12 |
| 63 T 1 | Bambury rd E9 |
| 60 M 5 | Bamford av Wemb |
| 54 B 19 | Bamford rd Bark |
| 111 W 11 | Bamford rd Brom |
| 155 U 6 | Bamfylde clo Wallgtn |
| 110 E 6 | Bampton rd SE23 |
| 101 U 2 | Banbury cotts Twick |
| 140 K 8 | Banbury rd WC2 |
| 153 Z 17 | Banbury ct Sutton |
| 88 K 4 | Banbury st SW11 |
| 77 V 19 | Banchory rd SE3 |
| 28 K 15 | Bancroft av N2 |
| 21 T 9 | Bancroft av Buck Hl |
| 22 M 20 | Bancroft gdns Harrow |
| 63 T 11 | Bancroft rd E1 |
| 23 N 6 | Bancroft rd Har |
| 22 M 11 | Bancroft rd Harrow |
| 155 X 12 | Bandon ri Wallgtn |
| 87 O 8 | Bangalore st SW15 |
| 40 K 15 | Bangor clo Grnfd |
| 73 N 15 | Bangor rd Brentf |
| 74 K 10 | Banim st W6 |
| 128 G 12 | Banister rd NW10 |
| 144 G 4 | Bank av Mitch |
| 142 D 12 | Bank end SE1 |
| 86 B 13 | Bank la SW15 |
| 102 J 17 | Bank la Kingst |
| 112 A 10 | Bankfoot rd Brom |
| 92 L 18 | Bankhurst rd SE6 |
| 98 B 10 | Banks la Bxly Hth |
| 141 Y 11 | Bankside SE1 |
| 142 A 11 | Bankside SE1 |
| 7 X 7 | Bankside Enf |
| 157 T 15 | Bankside S Croy |
| 154 K 13 | Bankside clo Carsh |
| 90 F 12 | Bankton rd SW2 |
| 94 A 11 | Bankwell rd SE13 |
| 134 B 18 | Banner st EC1 |
| 23 Z 17 | Bannersfield la Harrow |
| 76 M 12 | Banning st SE10 |
| 90 F 20 | Bannister clo SW2 |
| 79 W 11 | Bannockburn rd SE18 |
| 18 F 10 | Banstead gdns N9 |
| 154 K 13 | Banstead rd Carsh |
| 92 B 8 | Banstead rd SE15 |
| 156 A 10 | Banstead way Wallgtn |
| 12 G 20 | Banstock rd Edg |
| 8 M 8 | Banton cl Enf |
| 8 M 9 | Banton clo Enf |
| 75 V 18 | Bantree rd SE14 |
| 75 N 9 | Banyard rd SE16 |
| 151 X 3 | Banyard rd SE16 |
| 47 O 11 | Baptist gdns NW5 |
| 52 B 2 | Bar field E11 |
| 144 D 3 | Barb ms W6 |
| 48 D 10 | Barbara N7 |
| 49 R 10 | Barbauld rd N16 |
| 149 V 1 | Barbel st SE1 |
| 17 U 3 | Barber clo N21 |
| 65 U 8 | Barbers all E13 |
| 64 E 5 | Barbers st E15 |
| 68 L 16 | Barbican rd Grnfd |
| 88 A 13 | Barchard st SW18 |
| 23 R 6 | Barchester rd Harrow |
| 64 D 15 | Barchester st E14 |
| 21 T 14 | Barclay oval Wdfd Grn |
| 52 B 4 | Barclay rd E11 |
| 65 Y 11 | Barclay rd E13 |
| 33 T 16 | Barclay rd E17 |
| 18 B 19 | Barclay rd N18 |
| 145 V 19 | Barclay rd SW6 |
| 157 O 5 | Barclay rd Croy |
| 108 B 4 | Barcombe av SW2 |
| 79 U 19 | Barden st SE18 |
| 37 V 11 | Bardfield av Rom |
| 120 B 8 | Bardney rd Mrdn |
| 158 K 20 | Bardolph av Croy |
| 47 Z 12 | Bardolph rd N7 |
| 85 N 9 | Bardolph rd Rich |
| 18 J 11 | Bardot clo N9 |
| 63 O 13 | Bardsey pl E1 |
| 76 F 17 | Bardsley la SE10 |
| 129 N 15 | Barfett st W10 |
| 15 Y 8 | Barfield av N20 |
| 127 X 5 | Barfield rd Brom |
| 26 H 6 | Barford clo NW4 |
| 133 U 6 | Barford st N1 |
| 92 A 8 | Barforth rd SE15 |
| 92 B 9 | Barforth rd SE15 |
| 79 Y 13 | Bargate clo SE18 |
| 118 G 16 | Bargate clo New Mald |
| 78 M 4 | Barge Ho rd E16 |
| 141 U 11 | Barge Ho st SE1 |
| 111 S 2 | Bargery rd SE6 |
| 110 M 2 | Bargrove cres SE6 |
| 127 G 20 | Barham clo Brom |
| 113 Z 12 | Barham clo Chisl |
| 38 F 9 | Barham clo Rom |
| 42 C 17 | Barham clo Wemb |
| 104 F 18 | Barham rd SW20 |
| 113 Y 12 | Barham rd Chisl |
| 156 M 10 | Barham rd S Croy |
| 112 F 4 | Baring clo SE12 |
| 112 F 2 | Baring rd SE12 |
| 94 D 19 | Baring rd SE12 |
| 94 E 18 | Baring rd SE12 |
| 5 U 12 | Baring rd Barnt |
| 9 V 19 | Baring rd Croy |
| 134 E 5 | Baring st N1 |
| 104 C 20 | Barings clo New Mald |
| 137 X 9 | Bark st W2 |
| 146 B 14 | Barker st SW10 |
| 31 P 1 | Barkham rd N17 |
| 65 Y 14 | Barking By pass E16 |
| 67 T 6 | Barking By pass Bark |
| 54 E 17 | Barking park Bark |
| 65 S 12 | Barking rd E16 |
| 66 F 4 | Barking rd E6 |
| 145 X 7 | Barkston gdns SW5 |
| 75 O 14 | Barkworth rd SE16 |
| 151 Y 11 | Barkworth rd SE16 |
| 75 R 19 | Barlborough st SE14 |
| 128 F 19 | Barlby gdns W10 |
| 139 F 9 | Barlby rd W10 |
| 136 D 1 | Barlby rd W10 |
| 55 O 2 | Barley la Ilf |
| 37 R 14 | Barley la Rom |
| 73 Y 13 | Barley Mow pas W4 |
| 141 Y 1 | Barley Mow pass EC1 |
| 63 Y 20 | Barleycorn way E14 |
| 139 Z 10 | Barlow pl W1 |
| 73 T 2 | Barlow rd W3 |
| 100 J 17 | Barlow rd Hampt |
| 150 G 7 | Barlow st SE17 |
| 111 R 3 | Barmeston rd SE6 |
| 59 X 6 | Barmouth av Grnfd |
| 88 D 17 | Barmouth rd SW18 |
| 158 F 3 | Barmouth rd Croy |
| 11 R 20 | Barn cres Stanm |
| 43 S 7 | Barn hill Wemb |
| 43 R 5 | Barn ri Wemb |
| 49 P 8 | Barn st N16 |
| 43 P 5 | Barn way Wemb |
| 50 F 15 | Barnabas ter E9 |
| 50 G 17 | Barnabus rd E9 |
| 63 S 19 | Barnado st E1 |
| 114 F 20 | Barnard clo Chisl |
| 155 Y 16 | Barnard clo Wallgtn |
| 118 G 9 | Barnard gdns New Mald |
| 29 R 6 | Barnard hill N10 |
| 88 K 10 | Barnard rd SW11 |
| 9 N 8 | Barnard rd Enf |
| 121 O 4 | Barnard rd Mitch |
| 141 T 3 | Barnards inn EC4 |
| 64 I 2 | Barnby sq E15 |
| 64 L 2 | Barnby st E15 |
| 132 C 11 | Barnby st NW1 |
| 98 L 4 | Barnehurst av Bxly Hth |
| 98 K 2 | Barnehurst clo Erith |
| 98 J 5 | Barnehurst rd Bxly Hth |
| 74 F 19 | Barnes av SW13 |
| 99 V 11 | Barnes Cray rd Drtfrd |
| 65 Z 14 | Barnes st E16 |
| 118 H 12 | Barnes end New Mald |
| 86 C 4 | Barnes High st SW13 |
| 72 F 1 | Barnes pickle W5 |
| 54 C 14 | Barnes rd Ilf |
| 63 U 17 | Barnes st E14 |
| 86 B 5 | Barnes ter SW13 |
| 13 T 1 | Barnet Ga la Barnt |
| 135 S 13 | Barnet gro E2 |
| 4 J 14 | Barnet hill Barnt |
| 14 G 5 | Barnet la N20 |
| 4 K 16 | Barnet la Barnt |
| 11 X 1 | Barnet la Brhm Wd |
| 12 L 7 | Barnet way NW7 |
| 118 A 14 | Barnfield New Mald |
| 158 D 2 | Barnfield av Croy |
| 102 J 11 | Barnfield av Kingst |
| 121 T 7 | Barnfield av Mitch |
| 102 K 11 | Barnfield gdns Rich |
| 78 M 17 | Barnfield rd SE18 |
| 79 N 16 | Barnfield rd SE18 |
| 60 C 11 | Barnfield rd W5 |
| 81 P 15 | Barnfield rd Blvdr |
| 25 U 5 | Barnfield rd Edg |
| 157 T 20 | Barnfield rd S Croy |
| 125 X 14 | Barnfield Wood clo W Wkhm |
| 125 X 13 | Barnfield Wood rd Becknhm |
| 58 M 7 | Barnham rd Grnfd |
| 59 N 8 | Barnham rd Grnfd |
| 142 L 16 | Barnham st SE1 |

126 C 13 Barnhill av Brom
43 W 9 Barnhill rd Wemb
100 C 5 Barnlea clo Felt
56 C 15 Barnmead gdns Dgnhm
110 G 20 Barnmead rd Becknhm
56 B 15 Barnmead rd Dgnhm
117 X 10 Barnsbury clo New Mald
117 U 20 Barnsbury cres Surb
48 E 19 Barnsbury gro N7
117 V 20 Barnsbury la Surb
48 F 20 Barnsbury pk N1
133 S 5 Barnsbury rd N1
133 S 1 Barnsbury sq N1
133 V 1 Barnsbury st N1
133 R 1 Barnsbury ter N1
129 P 16 Barnsdale rd W9
129 S 17 Barnsdale yd W9
63 N 12 Barnsley st E1
135 X 17 Barnsley st E1
90 G 13 Barnwell rd SW2
77 T 2 Barnwood ct E16
133 S 9 Baron cl N1
36 C 9 Baron gdns Ilf
120 K 8 Baron gro Mitch
65 O 14 Baron rd E16
55 V 3 Baron rd Dgnhm
133 T 9 Baron st N1
135 N 11 Baroness rd E2
31 X 4 Baronet gro N17
31 X 4 Baronet rd N17
31 X 4 Baronet rd N17
144 L 10 Barons Ct rd W14
145 N 10 Barons Ct rd W14
5 W 18 Barons ga Barnt
144 K 8 Barons keep W14
141 V 18 Barons pl SE1
84 C 15 Barons the Twick
120 H 9 Barons wlk Mitch
84 C 17 Baronsfield rd Twick
86 G 2 Baronsmead rd SW13
72 M 7 Baronsmede W5
28 K 13 Baronsmere rd N2
76 G 13 Barque st E14
82 A 11 Barrack rd Hounsl
30 B 6 Barratt av N22
28 M 6 Barrenger rd N10
33 U 13 Barrett rd E17
139 V 6 Barrett st W1
61 X 7 Barretts Green rd NW10
49 T 13 Barretts gro N16
92 J 4 Barriedale SE14
107 P 9 Barringer sq SW17
53 W 17 Barrington rd E12
29 W 14 Barrington rd N8
90 H 7 Barrington rd SW9
97 W 6 Barrington rd Bxly Hth
153 X 1 Barrington rd Sutton
154 L 18 Barrow av Carsh
17 W 10 Barrow clo N21
154 J 15 Barrow Hedges clo Carsh
154 J 15 Barrow Hedges way Carsh
152 A 2 Barrow hill Worc Pk
152 A 2 Barrow Hill clo Worc
130 J 10 Barrow Hill rd NW8
22 A 8 Barrow Point av Pinn
22 A 6 Barrow Point la Pinn
107 Z 14 Barrow rd SW16
156 G 12 Barrow rd Croy
22 B 7 Barrowdene clo Pinn
17 W 9 Barrowell grn N21
19 O 11 Barrowfield clo N9
73 X 15 Barrowgate rd W4
43 X 20 Barrs rd NW10
31 V 19 Barry av N15
80 L 19 Barry av Bxly Hth
43 X 20 Barry rd NW10
61 X 1 Barry rd NW10
91 X 14 Barry rd SE22
92 B 7 Barset rd SE15
108 M 6 Barston rd SE27
140 L 3 Barter st WC1
79 W 11 Barth rd SE18
141 Z 2 Bartholomew clo EC1
142 F 5 Bartholomew la EC2
47 W 17 Bartholomew rd NW5
150 F 3 Bartholomew st SE1
47 U 18 Bartholomew vlls NW5
66 E 5 Bartle av E6
141 V 4 Bartlett ct EC4
64 E 13 Bartlett st E14
157 N 11 Bartlett st Croy
38 M 3 Bartlow gdns Rom

56 J 5 Barton av Rom
97 Z 12 Barton clo Bxly Hth
117 Z 4 Barton grn New Mald
144 L 10 Barton rd W14
57 V 5 Barton rd Hornch
115 Z 15 Barton rd Sidcp
148 H 2 Barton st SW1
92 J 14 Bartram rd SE4
5 P 3 Bartrams la Barnt
50 K 17 Bartrip st E9
52 H 11 Barwick rd E7
125 S 20 Barwood av W Wkhm
100 G 5 Basden gro Felt
55 P 20 Basedale rd Dgnhm
61 Z 11 Bashley rd NW10
66 E 8 Basil av E6
139 O 19 Basil st SW3
145 O 1 Basil st SW3
35 W 5 Basildon av Ilf
154 B 19 Basildon clo Sutton
80 B 11 Basildon rd SE2
97 Y 6 Basildon rd Bxly Hth
98 A 16 Basing dri Bxly
45 U 4 Basing hill NW11
43 O 5 Basing hill Wemb
137 O 4 Basing st W11
27 Z 10 Basing way N3
28 A 9 Basing way N3
91 O 10 Basingdon way SE5
142 D 3 Basinghall av EC2
154 B 18 Basinghall gdns Sutton
142 D 4 Basinghall st EC2
134 B 3 Basire st N1
88 J 18 Baskerville rd SW18
95 P 13 Basket gdns SE9
89 P 7 Basnett rd SW11
91 U 12 Bassano st SE22
79 W 17 Bassant rd SE18
74 E 7 Bassein Pk rd W12
58 K 16 Basset way Grnfd
154 B 20 Bassett clo Sutton
71 O 19 Bassett gdns Islwth
136 J 3 Bassett rd W10
47 P 17 Bassett st NW5
88 D 18 Bassingham rd SW18
42 G 19 Bassingham rd Wemb
142 C 3 Bassishaw highwalk EC2
67 W 8 Bastable av Bark
68 B 7 Bastable av Bark
79 Z 15 Bastion rd SE2
80 A 14 Bastion rd SE2
133 Z 16 Bastwick st EC1
134 A 16 Bastwick st EC1
87 Y 2 Basuto rd SW6
75 W 20 Batavia rd SE14
133 T 6 Batchelor st N1
63 Y 19 Bate st E14
20 L 18 Bateman rd E4
140 F 6 Bateman st W1
140 F 6 Batemans bldgs W1
134 L 15 Batemans row EC2
156 F 12 Bates cres Croy
133 S 17 Bath ct EC1
53 N 19 Bath rd E12
19 O 8 Bath rd N9
74 B 10 Bath rd W4
99 Z 18 Bath rd Drtfrd
82 D 7 Bath rd Hounsl
37 Y 18 Bath rd Rom
134 D 14 Bath st EC1
150 A 2 Bath ter SE1
105 P 7 Bathgate rd SW19
62 K 7 Bathurst gdns NW10
128 A 10 Bathurst gdns NW10
138 G 8 Bathurst ms W2
53 Z 5 Bathurst rd Ilf
138 G 8 Bathurst st W2
78 K 11 Bathway SE18
49 U 10 Batley pl N16
49 U 10 Batley rd N16
8 A 6 Batley rd Enf
74 K 2 Batman clo W12
74 M 8 Batoum gdns W6
144 D 1 Batoum gdns W6
79 U 11 Batson st SE18
74 H 6 Batson st W12
120 F 5 Batsworth rd Mitch
88 K 9 Batten st SW11
111 Y 6 Battersby rd SE6
146 J 18 Battersea br SW11
88 K 2 Battersea Br rd SW11
146 J 19 Battersea Br rd SW11
88 G 1 Battersea Church rd SW11

88 G 2 Battersea High st SW11
88 M 1 Battersea park SW11
147 M 1 Battersea park SW11
147 Z 20 Battersea Pk rd SW11
89 O 2 Battersea Pk rd SW11
88 J 11 Battersea Pk rd SW11
148 A 18 Battersea Pk rd SW8
88 J 11 Battersea ri SW11
133 W 2 Battishill st N1
142 J 13 Battle Br la SE1
132 J 9 Battle Bridge rd NW1
81 Y 11 Battle rd Erith
48 H 15 Battledean rd N5
143 T 5 Batty st E1
111 Z 5 Baudwin rd SE6
87 X 19 Baulk the SW18
122 B 3 Bavant rd SW16
48 A 7 Bavaria rd N4
90 M 5 Bavent rd SE5
91 V 13 Bawdale rd SE22
36 L 14 Bawdsey av Ilf
15 Y 11 Bawtry rd N20
135 S 11 Baxendale E2
15 R 8 Baxendale N20
65 Z 17 Baxter rd E16
49 O 18 Baxter rd N1
31 X 10 Baxter rd N18
18 M 13 Baxter rd N18
53 Y 15 Baxter rd Ilf
94 M 11 Bayfield rd SE9
128 E 13 Bayford rd NW10
63 N 1 Bayford st E8
135 X 1 Bayford st E8
132 B 7 Bayham pl NW1
72 A 1 Bayham rd W13
73 Y 7 Bayham rd W4
120 B 8 Bayham rd Mrdn
131 Z 3 Bayham st NW1
132 A 4 Bayham st NW1
140 F 2 Bayley st WC1
141 S 19 Baylis rd SE1
8 K 7 Baynes clo Enf
46 G 17 Baynes ms NW3
132 C 2 Baynes st NW1
144 K 16 Bayonne rd W6
49 V 10 Bayston rd N16
137 W 11 Bayswater rd W2
138 K 9 Bayswater rd W2
63 Z 14 Baythorne st E3
90 D 12 Baytree rd SW2
117 X 13 Bazalgette clo New Mald
117 X 13 Bazalgette gdns New Mald
64 F 19 Bazely st E14
7 U 18 Bazile rd N21
100 H 5 Beach gro Felt
100 J 5 Beach way Twick
111 V 10 Beachborough rd Brom
52 A 8 Beachcroft rd E11
106 L 6 Beachcroft rd SW17
64 A 1 Beachy rd E3
48 A 15 Beacon hill N7
93 W 15 Beacon rd SE13
77 S 17 Beaconsfield clo SE3
73 U 14 Beaconsfield clo W4
51 U 8 Beaconsfield rd E10
65 O 12 Beaconsfield rd E16
32 M 20 Beaconsfield rd E17
34 B 7 Beaconsfield rd E18
44 E 18 Beaconsfield rd NW10
16 C 15 Beaconsfield rd N11
31 T 14 Beaconsfield rd N15
18 J 12 Beaconsfield rd N9
77 R 17 Beaconsfield rd SE3
113 R 8 Beaconsfield rd SE9
73 X 9 Beaconsfield rd W4
72 F 5 Beaconsfield rd W5
127 O 6 Beaconsfield rd Brom
123 O 14 Beaconsfield rd Croy
9 U 1 Beaconsfield rd Enf
117 Z 5 Beaconsfield rd New Mald
70 D 4 Beaconsfield rd S'hall
117 N 18 Beaconsfield rd Surb
84 B 17 Beaconsfield rd Twick
66 K 18 Beaconsfield st E6
37 X 19 Beaconsfield ter Rom
144 K 3 Beaconsfield Ter rd W14

33 Y 7 Beacontree av E17
55 T 8 Beacontree av Dgnhm
52 C 2 Beacontree rd E11
108 K 9 Beadman st SE27
92 F 20 Beadnell rd SE23
74 M 11 Beadon rd W6
144 C 6 Beadon rd W6
126 E 10 Beadon rd Brom
119 V 6 Beaford gro SW20
140 B 8 Beak st W1
97 O 2 Beal clo Well
53 W 7 Beal rd Ilf
17 W 17 Beale clo N13
63 X 4 Beale rd E3
65 S 5 Beale st E13
69 V 4 Beam av Dgnhm
56 M 20 Beam way Dgnhm
35 Y 9 Beaminster gdns Ilf
10 A 6 Beamish dri Bushey
18 L 6 Beamish rd N9
97 W 11 Bean rd Bxly Hth
113 X 10 Beanshaw SE9
37 Z 9 Beansland gro Rom
141 W 4 Bear all EC4
142 B 12 Bear gdns SE1
141 Y 14 Bear la SE1
100 A 11 Bear rd Felt
140 G 10 Bear st WC2
109 T 15 Beardell st SE19
102 K 18 Bearfield rd Kingst
92 K 14 Bearstead ri SE4
111 O 20 Bearsted ter Becknhm
122 C 4 Beatrice av SW16
42 L 16 Beatrice av Wemb
33 O 16 Beatrice rd E17
48 G 1 Beatrice rd N4
19 P 2 Beatrice rd N9
151 U 6 Beatrice rd SE1
84 L 13 Beatrice rd Rich
70 D 3 Beatrice rd S'hall
65 S 12 Beatrice st E13
75 U 1 Beatson st SE1
49 T 11 Beatty rd N16
11 S 18 Beatty rd Stanm
132 A 7 Beatty st NW1
35 X 12 Beattyville gdns Ilf
146 M 2 Beauchamp pl SW3
147 N 3 Beauchamp pl SW3
52 H 20 Beauchamp rd E7
123 P 2 Beauchamp rd SE19
88 K 10 Beauchamp rd SW11
153 Y 9 Beauchamp rd Sutton
83 Z 19 Beauchamp rd Twick
141 T 1 Beauchamp st EC1
86 K 8 Beauchamp ter SW15
74 L 8 Beauclerc rd W6
144 A 1 Beauclerc rd W6
24 A 11 Beaufort av Harrow
24 A 11 Beaufort av Harrow
61 N 13 Beaufort clo W5
38 J 12 Beaufort clo Rom
102 C 10 Beaufort ct Rich
27 Y 12 Beaufort dri NW11
26 L 19 Beaufort gdns NW4
147 N 2 Beaufort gdns SW3
146 M 1 Beaufort gdns SW3
82 B 1 Beaufort gdns Hounsl
53 W 4 Beaufort gdns Ilf
60 M 15 Beaufort rd W5
61 N 13 Beaufort rd W5
116 J 10 Beaufort rd Kingst
102 D 10 Beaufort rd Rich
84 E 18 Beaufort rd Twick
146 H 15 Beaufort st SW3
152 G 18 Beaufort way Epsom
31 T 2 Beaufoy rd N17
89 R 6 Beaufoy rd SW11
109 Z 10 Beaulah av SE26
109 P 19 Beaulah hill SE19
110 A 10 Beaulieu av SE26
26 B 12 Beaulieu clo NW9
121 O 1 Beaulieu clo Mitch
84 G 17 Beaulieu clo Twick
17 Y 4 Beaulieu gdns N21
39 R 5 Beauly way Rom
113 W 10 Beaumanor gdns SE9
35 N 2 Beaumaris dri Wdfd Grn
132 C 17 Beaumont WC1
145 O 9 Beaumont av W8
22 L 19 Beaumont av Harrow
84 M 9 Beaumont av Rich
42 E 14 Beaumont av Wemb
145 U 10 Beaumont cres W14

| | |
|---|---|
| 83 S 13 | Beaumont gro E1 |
| 39 V 1 | Beaumont ms W1 |
| 51 R 2 | Beaumont rd E10 |
| 85 W 9 | Beaumont rd E13 |
| 08 L 15 | Beaumont rd SE19 |
| 37 R 18 | Beaumont rd SW19 |
| 73 W 8 | Beaumont rd W4 |
| 47 Z 2 | Beaumont ri N19 |
| 83 T 13 | Beaumont sq E1 |
| 31 V 20 | Beaumont st W1 |
| 39 V 1 | Beaumont st W1 |
| 31 U 15 | Beauval rd SE22 |
| 14 D 2 | Beaverbank rd Sidcp |
| 32 A 9 | Beavers la Hounsl |
| 42 J 14 | Beaverwood rd Chisl |
| 73 C 12 | Deavor la W6 |
| 79 U 12 | Bebbington rd SE18 |
| 54 J 17 | Beccles dri Bark |
| 23 J 19 | Beccles st E14 |
| 24 E 6 | Beck la Becknhm |
| 55 X 4 | Beck rd E8 |
| 20 M 13 | Beck rd Mitch |
| 50 C 11 | Beck st SE17 |
| 18 C 11 | Beckenham gdns N9 |
| 25 X 4 | Beckenham gro Brom |
| 11 S 13 | Beckenham Hill rd Becknhm |
| 26 A 3 | Beckenham la Brom |
| 11 P 18 | Beckenham Pl pk Becknhm |
| 11 T 16 | Beckenham place Becknhm |
| 11 T 15 | Beckenham Place park Becknhm |
| 24 K 2 | Beckenham rd Becknhm |
| 25 U 18 | Beckenham rd W Wkhm |
| 66 J 9 | Becket av E6 |
| 23 X 14 | Becket clo SE25 |
| 23 X 16 | Becket fold Har |
| 10 H 10 | Beckett wlk SE26 |
| 10 H 15 | Beckett wlk Bcknhm |
| 23 V 15 | Beckford rd Croy |
| 74 E 5 | Becklow rd W12 |
| 65 E 15 | Beckton gdns E6 |
| 65 T 15 | Beckton rd E16 |
| 65 H 15 | Beckton rd E16 |
| 24 H 8 | Beckway Becknhm |
| 25 N 7 | Beckway Becknhm |
| 21 X 4 | Beckway rd SW16 |
| 50 H 7 | Beckway st SE17 |
| 91 O 14 | Beckwith rd SE24 |
| 07 R 14 | Beclands rd SW17 |
| 07 Y 8 | Becmead av SW16 |
| 24 B 15 | Becmead av Harrow |
| 09 S 13 | Becondale rd SE19 |
| 56 A 7 | Becontree av Dgnhm |
| 87 U 11 | Bective pl SW15 |
| 52 G 11 | Bective rd E7 |
| 87 U 11 | Bective rd SW15 |
| 66 F 15 | Becton pl E6 |
| 98 H 1 | Becton pl Erith |
| 7 Y 4 | Bedale rd Enf |
| 42 E 14 | Bedale st SE1 |
| 56 C 2 | Beddington Farm rd Croy |
| 22 B 19 | Beddington Farm rd Croy |
| 55 P 14 | Beddington gdns Carsh |
| 55 Y 11 | Beddington gro Wallgtn |
| 21 W 16 | Beddington la Croy |
| 55 Z 3 | Beddington la Wallgtn |
| 55 U 4 | Beddington park Wallgtn |
| 36 K 20 | Beddington rd Ilf |
| 98 C 2 | Beddonwell rd Bxly Hth |
| 63 Y 14 | Bede rd E3 |
| 37 T 18 | Bede rd Rom |
| 15 Y 14 | Bedens rd Sidcp |
| 30 G 2 | Bedford av WC1 |
| 4 J 15 | Bedford av Barnt |
| 29 P 3 | Bedford clo N10 |
| 40 K 10 | Bedford ct WC2 |
| 37 V 15 | Bedford gdns W8 |
| 07 V 6 | Bedford hill SW12 |
| 44 M 17 | Bedford pass SW6 |
| 22 M 20 | Bedford pk Croy |
| 40 K 1 | Bedford pl WC1 |
| 32 K 20 | Bedford pl WC1 |
| 23 O 20 | Bedford pl Croy |
| 33 O 8 | Bedford rd E17 |
| 34 E 9 | Bedford rd E18 |
| 66 H 3 | Bedford rd E6 |
| 13 N 9 | Bedford rd NW7 |
| 31 R 13 | Bedford rd N15 |
| 28 J 10 | Bedford rd N2 |
| 30 A 6 | Bedford rd N22 |

| | |
|---|---|
| 29 Y 17 | Bedford rd N8 |
| 18 M 1 | Bedford rd N9 |
| 19 N 2 | Bedford rd N9 |
| 89 Z 8 | Bedford rd SW9 |
| 72 A 1 | Bedford rd W13 |
| 73 Z 9 | Bedford rd W4 |
| 72 K 15 | Bedford rd Brentf |
| 9 S 10 | Bedford rd Enf |
| 23 N 17 | Bedford rd Harrow |
| 53 Z 10 | Bedford rd Ilf |
| 54 A 10 | Bedford rd Ilf |
| 14 H 7 | Bedford rd Sidcp |
| 101 P 5 | Bedford rd Twick |
| 53 N 4 | Bedford rd Worc Pk |
| 141 O 1 | Bedford row WC1 |
| 140 G 2 | Bedford sq WC1 |
| 140 K 9 | Bedford st WC2 |
| 48 D 7 | Bedford ter N7 |
| 132 H 18 | Bedford way WC1 |
| 140 J 10 | Bedfordbury WC2 |
| 105 T 3 | Bedgebury gdns SW19 |
| 94 M 11 | Bedgebury rd SE9 |
| 112 F 6 | Bedivere rd Brom |
| 80 M 16 | Bedonwell rd SE2 |
| 81 O 16 | Bedonwell rd Blvdr |
| 81 R 17 | Bedonwell rd Bxly Hth |
| 109 R 17 | Bedwardine rd SE19 |
| 31 R 4 | Bedwell rd N17 |
| 81 R 14 | Bedwell rd Blvdr |
| 65 U 15 | Beeby rd E16 |
| 15 X 6 | Beech av N20 |
| 74 B 3 | Beech av W3 |
| 72 B 19 | Beech av Brentf |
| 21 V 8 | Beech av Buck Hl |
| 96 M 17 | Beech av Sidcp |
| 88 G 17 | Beech clo SW15 |
| 104 L 15 | Beech clo SW15 |
| 154 L 2 | Beech clo Carsh |
| 8 L 20 | Beech clo Enf |
| 57 X 11 | Beech clo Hornch |
| 127 T 2 | Beech copse Brom |
| 28 L 9 | Beech dri N2 |
| 72 J 8 | Beech gdns W5 |
| 56 J 20 | Beech gdns Dgnhm |
| 121 X 10 | Beech gro Mitch |
| 117 Y 6 | Beech gro New Mald |
| 33 W 1 | Beech Hall cres E4 |
| 33 V 2 | Beech Hall rd E4 |
| 20 J 20 | Beech Hall rd E4 |
| 5 U 4 | Beech hill Barnt |
| 5 O 6 | Beech Hill av Barnt |
| 5 V 7 | Beech Hill park Barnt |
| 5 V 7 | Beech Hill park Barnt |
| 157 O 6 | Beech Ho rd Croy |
| 21 U 9 | Beech la Buck Hl |
| 15 U 15 | Beech lawns N12 |
| 17 N 19 | Beech rd N11 |
| 122 B 4 | Beech rd SW16 |
| 134 A 20 | Beech st EC1 |
| 38 L 14 | Beech st Rom |
| 11 S 17 | Beech Tree clo Stanm |
| 21 O 4 | Beech Tree glade E4 |
| 154 A 11 | Beech Tree pl Sutton |
| 43 X 20 | Beech way NW10 |
| 12 M 18 | Beech wlk NW7 |
| 99 X 10 | Beech wlk Dtford |
| 113 W 17 | Beechcroft Chisl |
| 45 V 1 | Beechcroft av NW1 |
| 40 G 2 | Beechcroft av Harrow |
| 117 W 2 | Beechcroft av New Mald |
| 70 D 2 | Beechcroft av S'hall |
| 43 N 10 | Beechcroft gdns Wemb |
| 42 M 10 | Beechcroft gdns Wemb |
| 34 H 8 | Beechcroft rd E18 |
| 85 W 9 | Beechcroft rd SW14 |
| 17 R 8 | Beechdale N21 |
| 90 D 16 | Beechdale rd SW2 |
| 22 D 11 | Beechen gro Pinn |
| 106 K 6 | Beeches rd SW17 |
| 119 T 20 | Beeches rd Sutton |
| 154 H 19 | Beeches wlk Carsh |
| 51 W 15 | Beechey pl E15 |
| 156 L 9 | Beechfield ct S Croy |
| 156 L 9 | Beechfield ct S Croy |
| 38 L 20 | Beechfield gdns Rom |
| 31 N 18 | Beechfield rd N4 |
| 110 M 1 | Beechfield rd SE6 |
| 126 M 3 | Beechfield rd Brom |
| 95 V 12 | Beechhill rd SE9 |
| 89 N 2 | Beechmere rd E17 |
| 111 Z 13 | Beechmont clo Brom |
| 153 R 3 | Beechmore gdns Sutton |
| 89 N 2 | Beechmore rd SW8 |
| 59 S 14 | Beechmount av W7 |
| 107 R 19 | Beecholme av Mitch |

| | |
|---|---|
| 50 A 9 | Beecholme rd E5 |
| 98 M 4 | Beechroft av Bxly Hth |
| 102 J 11 | Beechrow Rich |
| 97 W 17 | Beechway Bxly |
| 27 W 17 | Beechwood av N3 |
| 58 J 8 | Beechwood av Grnfd |
| 40 L 9 | Beechwood av Harrow |
| 85 P 2 | Beechwood av Rich |
| 122 H 8 | Beechwood av Thntn Hth |
| 12 M 16 | Beechwood clo NW7 |
| 97 Y 7 | Beechwood cres Bxly Hth |
| 21 P 17 | Beechwood dri Wdfd Grn |
| 40 L 9 | Beechwood gdns Harrow |
| 35 U 14 | Beechwood gdns Ilf |
| 34 E 11 | Beechwood pk E18 |
| 49 U 18 | Beechwood rd E8 |
| 29 Y 11 | Beechwood rd N8 |
| 157 R 19 | Beechwood rd S Croy |
| 45 Z 8 | Beechworth clo NW3 |
| 92 J 12 | Beecroft rd SE4 |
| 35 T 15 | Beehive la Ilf |
| 90 F 9 | Beehive pl SW9 |
| 120 B 8 | Beeleigh rd Mrdn |
| 127 X 2 | Been ct E4 |
| 86 H 20 | Beesborough rd SW15 |
| 147 Y 2 | Beeston pl SW1 |
| 5 U 19 | Beeston rd Barnt |
| 11 T 1 | Beethoven rd Borhm Wd |
| 128 L 11 | Beethoven st W10 |
| 94 K 2 | Begbie rd SE3 |
| 152 E 15 | Beggars hill Epsom |
| 62 E 18 | Begonia wlk W12 |
| 89 T 17 | Beira st SW12 |
| 55 U 1 | Belfairs dri Rom |
| 49 U 6 | Belfast rd N16 |
| 123 Z 10 | Belfast rd SE25 |
| 78 H 12 | Belford gro SE18 |
| 92 C 4 | Belfort rd SE15 |
| 49 T 13 | Belfrade rd N16 |
| 129 Z 7 | Belgrave gdns NW8 |
| 130 A 6 | Belgrave gdns NW8 |
| 6 J 15 | Belgrave gdns N14 |
| 11 S 15 | Belgrave gdns Stanm |
| 147 V 1 | Belgrave Ms w SW1 |
| 147 T 1 | Belgrave Ms w SW1 |
| 147 U 3 | Belgrave pl SW1 |
| 51 U 3 | Belgrave rd E10 |
| 52 F 4 | Belgrave rd E11 |
| 65 X 11 | Belgrave rd E13 |
| 33 O 18 | Belgrave rd E17 |
| 123 V 8 | Belgrave rd SE25 |
| 148 C 8 | Belgrave rd SW1 |
| 74 E 20 | Belgrave rd SW1 |
| 20 D 8 | Belgrave rd Hounsl |
| 53 T 4 | Belgrave rd Ilf |
| 120 F 5 | Belgrave rd Mitch |
| 147 U 1 | Belgrave sq SW1 |
| 63 U 17 | Belgrave st E1 |
| 21 S 11 | Belgrave ter Wdfd Grn |
| 147 X 3 | Belgrave yd SW1 |
| 139 S 20 | Belgrove Ms north SW1 |
| 139 T 20 | Belgrove sq SW1 |
| 132 K 12 | Belgrove st WC1 |
| 91 P 1 | Belham st SE5 |
| 90 J 8 | Belinda rd SW9 |
| 48 E 20 | Belitha vlls N1 |
| 39 Y 4 | Bell av Rom |
| 87 S 18 | Bell drive SW18 |
| 56 K 6 | Bell Farm av Dgnhm |
| 110 J 12 | Bell green SE26 |
| 110 K 10 | Bell Green la SE26 |
| 142 H 7 | Bell Inn yd EC3 |
| 142 M 2 | Bell la E1 |
| 143 N 3 | Bell la E1 |
| 77 R 2 | Bell la E16 |
| 27 N 14 | Bell la NW4 |
| 9 U 4 | Bell la Enf |
| 101 Z 1 | Bell la Twick |
| 8 C 7 | Bell rd Enf |
| 82 J 9 | Bell rd Hounsl |
| 130 K 20 | Bell st NW1 |
| 138 J 1 | Bell st NW1 |
| 78 K 8 | Bell Water ga SE18 |
| 142 D 10 | Bell Wharf la EC4 |
| 141 S 6 | Bell yd WC2 |
| 141 S 7 | Bell yd WC2 |
| 24 B 5 | Bellamy dri Stanm |
| 20 F 20 | Bellamy rd E4 |
| 89 R 18 | Bellamy st SW12 |
| 107 Z 3 | Bellasis av SE2 |
| 110 K 8 | Belle grn SE26 |
| 33 W 7 | Belle Vue rd SW18 |

| | |
|---|---|
| 88 K 20 | Belle Vue rd SW17 |
| 90 E 8 | Bellefields rd SW9 |
| 96 J 5 | Bellegrove clo Welling |
| 91 V 4 | Bellenden rd SE15 |
| 20 B 7 | Bellestaines E4 |
| 88 L 14 | Belleville rd SW11 |
| 59 P 2 | Bellevue Grnfd |
| 10 C 5 | Bellevue la Bushey |
| 122 L 7 | Bellevue pk Thntn Hth |
| 16 B 16 | Bellevue rd N11 |
| 86 G 5 | Bellevue rd SW13 |
| 106 K 1 | Bellevue rd SW13 |
| 60 A 12 | Bellevue rd W13 |
| 98 A 13 | Bellevue rd Bxly Hth |
| 116 K 8 | Bellevue rd Kingst |
| 106 E 7 | Bellevue rd SW17 |
| 10 B 20 | Bellfield av Harrow |
| 96 G 5 | Bellgrove rd Welling |
| 97 O 7 | Bellgrove rd Welling |
| 63 V 8 | Bellhaven st E3 |
| 111 P 8 | Bellingham grn SE6 |
| 111 S 6 | Bellingham rd SE6 |
| 77 N 12 | Bellot st SE10 |
| 81 T 16 | Bellring clo Blvdr |
| 87 X 6 | Bells all SW6 |
| 151 S 20 | Bells Gdns rd SE15 |
| 4 D 14 | Bells hill Barnt |
| 108 E 12 | Belltrees gro SE16 |
| 92 F 11 | Bellwood rd SE15 |
| 17 O 15 | Belmont av N13 |
| 30 L 11 | Belmont av N17 |
| 18 L 5 | Belmont av N9 |
| 5 Z 17 | Belmont av Barnt |
| 6 A 14 | Belmont av Barnt |
| 118 H 10 | Belmont av New Mald |
| 70 B 9 | Belmont av S'hall |
| 96 G 6 | Belmont av Welling |
| 60 M 2 | Belmont av Wemb |
| 24 A 6 | Belmont cir Harrow |
| 6 A 14 | Belmont clo Barnt |
| 21 U 13 | Belmont clo Wdfd Grn |
| 93 X 8 | Belmont gro SE13 |
| 73 X 11 | Belmont gro W4 |
| 93 Y 8 | Belmont hill SE13 |
| 114 B 10 | Belmont la Chisl |
| 24 D 3 | Belmont la Stanm |
| 93 X 10 | Belmont rd SE13 |
| 33 S 19 | Belmont Pk rd E10 |
| 73 Y 12 | Belmont pl W4 |
| 64 M 9 | Belmont rd E15 |
| 30 L 12 | Belmont rd N17 |
| 124 A 13 | Belmont rd SE25 |
| 89 W 8 | Belmont rd SW8 |
| 73 X 12 | Belmont rd W4 |
| 124 L 4 | Belmont rd Becknhm |
| 113 Z 12 | Belmont rd Chisl |
| 81 Z 20 | Belmont rd Erith |
| 98 F 1 | Belmont rd Erith |
| 23 X 10 | Belmont rd Harrow |
| 54 C 9 | Belmont rd Ilf |
| 101 P 0 | Belmont rd Twick |
| 155 T 11 | Belmont rd Wallgtn |
| 153 V 18 | Belmont ri Sutton |
| 47 P 19 | Belmont st NW1 |
| 89 Y 2 | Belmont st SW8 |
| 133 T 1 | Belper st N1 |
| 50 C 17 | Belsham st E9 |
| 46 J 16 | Belsize av NW3 |
| 17 R 19 | Belsize av N13 |
| 72 C 8 | Belsize av W13 |
| 46 G 16 | Belsize cres NW3 |
| 46 H 15 | Belsize ct NW3 |
| 154 B 7 | Belsize gdns Sutton |
| 46 K 17 | Belsize gro NW3 |
| 46 F 18 | Belsize la NW3 |
| 46 G 18 | Belsize ms NW3 |
| 46 F 19 | Belsize ms NW3 |
| 46 J 17 | Belsize Pk gdns NW3 |
| 46 G 17 | Belsize Pk ms NW3 |
| 46 G 16 | Belsize pl NW3 |
| 46 E 20 | Belsize rd NW6 |
| 129 Z 3 | Belsize rd NW6 |
| 130 D 1 | Belsize rd NW6 |
| 23 P 1 | Belsize rd Harrow |
| 46 H 18 | Belsize sq NW3 |
| 46 G 17 | Belsize ter NW3 |
| 78 F 10 | Belson rd SE18 |
| 105 P 6 | Beltane dri SW19 |
| 51 Z 12 | Belton rd E11 |
| 52 J 20 | Belton rd E7 |
| 31 S 10 | Belton rd N17 |
| 115 O 9 | Belton rd Sidcp |
| 64 A 14 | Belton way E3 |
| 87 Z 5 | Beltran rd SW6 |
| 81 W 10 | Beltwood rd Blvdr |
| 105 T 12 | Belvedere av SW19 |
| 35 Z 8 | Belvedere av Ilf |
| 141 Z 19 | Belvedere bldgs SE1 |

| | | |
|---|---|---|
| 101 T 13 | Belvedere clo Tedd |
| 105 T 13 | Belvedere dri SW19 |
| 105 S 13 | Belvedere gro SW19 |
| 141 Z 19 | Belvedere pl SE1 |
| 50 J 3 | Belvedere rd E10 |
| 141 O 18 | Belvedere rd SE1 |
| 109 U 17 | Belvedere rd SE19 |
| 80 H 3 | Belvedere rd SE2 |
| 98 B 7 | Belvedere rd Bxly Hth |
| 105 S 13 | Belvedere sq SW19 |
| 24 K 19 | Belvedere way Harrow |
| 91 Y 19 | Belvoir rd SE22 |
| 40 H 20 | Belvue clo Grnfd |
| 58 H 2 | Belvue park Grnfd |
| 40 J 20 | Belvue rd Grnfd |
| 132 M 2 | Bemerton st N1 |
| 87 P 8 | Bemish rd SW15 |
| 32 L 9 | Bemsted rd E17 |
| 150 H 10 | Ben Cope st SE17 |
| 91 P 2 | Ben Hill rd SE5 |
| 63 U 15 | Ben Johnson rd E1 |
| 68 B 1 | Ben Tillet clo Bark |
| 79 X 11 | Benares rd SE18 |
| 74 K 8 | Benbow rd W6 |
| 144 A 1 | Benbow rd W6 |
| 76 B 15 | Benbow st SE8 |
| 111 U 12 | Benbury clo Brom |
| 157 V 13 | Benchfield S Croy |
| 107 W 17 | Bencroft rd SW16 |
| 130 M 20 | Bendall ms NW1 |
| 87 O 7 | Bendemeer rd SW15 |
| 66 D 2 | Bendish rd E6 |
| 80 A 12 | Bendmore av SE2 |
| 88 A 20 | Bendon valley SW18 |
| 90 E 7 | Benedict rd SW9 |
| 120 G 7 | Benedict rd Mitch |
| 126 D 12 | Benenden grn Brom |
| 121 Z 3 | Benett gdns SW16 |
| 154 D 6 | Benfleet clo Sutton |
| 142 G 7 | Bengal ct EC3 |
| 53 Y 11 | Bengal rd Ilf |
| 23 R 7 | Bengarth dri Harrow |
| 58 A 3 | Bengarth rd Grnfd |
| 90 L 7 | Bengeworth rd SE5 |
| 41 Z 8 | Bengeworth rd Harrow |
| 11 N 15 | Benhale clo Stanm |
| 59 U 15 | Benham rd W7 |
| 88 F 9 | Benham st SW11 |
| 154 B 9 | Benhill av Sutton |
| 150 G 20 | Benhill rd SE5 |
| 154 E 6 | Benhill rd Sutton |
| 154 C 5 | Benhill Wood rd Sutton |
| 154 B 6 | Benhilton gdns Sutton |
| 57 Y 11 | Benhurst av Hornch |
| 108 E 12 | Benhurst la SW16 |
| 93 Y 18 | Benin st SE13 |
| 133 W 20 | Benjamin st EC1 |
| 64 J 17 | Benledi st E14 |
| 50 J 17 | Benn st E9 |
| 88 K 13 | Bennerley rd SW11 |
| 140 A 13 | Bennet st SW1 |
| 96 M 5 | Bennett clo Welling |
| 93 S 3 | Bennett gro SE13 |
| 94 C 6 | Bennett pk SE3 |
| 65 X 13 | Bennett rd E13 |
| 37 Z 20 | Bennett rd Rom |
| 74 A 15 | Bennett st W4 |
| 158 K 4 | Bennetts av Croy |
| 59 S 3 | Bennetts av Grnfd |
| 55 U 7 | Bennetts Castle la Dgnhm |
| 158 K 3 | Bennetts way Croy |
| 148 H 3 | Bennetts yd SW1 |
| 13 N 19 | Benningholme rd Edg |
| 13 N 19 | Benningholme rd Edg |
| 31 P 5 | Bennington rd N17 |
| 33 Y 2 | Bennington rd Wdfd Grn |
| 86 K 19 | Bensby clo SW15 |
| 122 L 10 | Bensham clo Thntn Hth |
| 122 L 3 | Bensham gro Thntn Hth |
| 122 J 10 | Bensham la Thntn Hth |
| 122 M 9 | Bensham Mnr rd Thntn Hth |
| 123 N 10 | Bensham Mnr rd Thntn Hth |
| 65 Z 7 | Benson av E6 |
| 92 D 20 | Benson rd SE23 |
| 156 G 6 | Benson rd Croy |
| 49 X 10 | Benthall rd N16 |
| 134 B 1 | Bentham ct N1 |
| 50 F 18 | Bentham rd E9 |
| 139 V 3 | Bentinck ms W1 |
| 139 V 4 | Bentinck st W1 |
| 36 B 17 | Bentley dri Ilf |
| 10 G 12 | Bentley priory Stanm |
| 49 S 18 | Bentley rd N1 |
| 10 K 17 | Bentley way Stanm |
| 21 S 9 | Bentley way Wdfd Grn |
| 54 D 3 | Benton rd Ilf |
| 108 M 11 | Bentons la SE27 |
| 109 N 11 | Bentons ri SE27 |
| 55 Z 7 | Bentry clo Dgnhm |
| 55 Z 7 | Bentry rd Dgnhm |
| 56 A 7 | Bentry rd Dgnhm |
| 136 A 6 | Bentworth rd W12 |
| 62 J 18 | Bentworth rd W12 |
| 48 F 14 | Benwell rd N7 |
| 63 Z 8 | Benworth st E3 |
| 88 M 13 | Berber rd SW11 |
| 114 A 4 | Bercta rd SE9 |
| 63 T 19 | Bere st E1 |
| 128 F 13 | Berens rd NW10 |
| 15 Y 8 | Beresford av N20 |
| 59 S 15 | Beresford av W7 |
| 117 T 19 | Beresford av Surb |
| 84 F 15 | Beresford av Twick |
| 61 P 2 | Beresford av Wemb |
| 21 Y 13 | Beresford dri Buck Hl |
| 8 D 14 | Beresford gdns Enf |
| 82 E 14 | Beresford gdns Hounsl |
| 37 Z 17 | Beresford gdns Rom |
| 33 R 4 | Beresford rd E17 |
| 20 M 4 | Beresford rd E4 |
| 28 J 11 | Beresford rd N2 |
| 49 N 15 | Beresford rd N5 |
| 30 H 15 | Beresford rd N8 |
| 23 O 16 | Beresford rd Harrow |
| 102 M 20 | Beresford rd Kingst |
| 103 N 20 | Beresford rd Kingst |
| 117 V 8 | Beresford rd New Mald |
| 153 V 18 | Beresford rd Sutton |
| 78 M 10 | Beresford sq SE18 |
| 78 L 9 | Beresford st SE18 |
| 48 M 15 | Beresford ter N5 |
| 74 E 13 | Berestede rd W6 |
| 50 F 17 | Berger rd E9 |
| 50 E 17 | Berger rd E9 |
| 35 P 14 | Bergholt av Ilf |
| 49 R 1 | Bergholt cres N16 |
| 97 X 2 | Berkeley av Bxly Hth |
| 41 S 18 | Berkeley av Grnfd |
| 35 Y 7 | Berkeley av Ilf |
| 38 L 2 | Berkeley av Rom |
| 16 G 1 | Berkeley ct N14 |
| 18 A 2 | Berkeley gdns N21 |
| 137 V 14 | Berkeley gdns W8 |
| 139 R 5 | Berkeley ms W1 |
| 105 P 17 | Berkeley pl SW19 |
| 53 R 16 | Berkeley rd E12 |
| 25 P 14 | Berkeley rd NW9 |
| 31 P 19 | Berkeley rd N15 |
| 29 Y 17 | Berkeley rd N8 |
| 86 F 1 | Berkeley rd SW13 |
| 139 Y 11 | Berkeley sq W1 |
| 139 Z 12 | Berkeley st W1 |
| 70 A 18 | Berkeley waye Hounsl |
| 81 R 12 | Berkhampstead rd Blvdr |
| 81 S 12 | Berkhamstead rd Belv |
| 43 O 18 | Berkhamsted av Wemb |
| 5 U 16 | Berkley cres Barnt |
| 131 R 1 | Berkley rd NW1 |
| 17 S 20 | Berkshire gdns N13 |
| 18 M 17 | Berkshire gdns N18 |
| 50 M 16 | Berkshire rd E9 |
| 51 N 17 | Berkshire rd E9 |
| 121 Z 10 | Berkshire way Mitch |
| 122 A 10 | Berkshire way Mitch |
| 44 C 13 | Bermans way NW10 |
| 150 K 1 | Bermondsey sq SE1 |
| 142 J 17 | Bermondsey st SE1 |
| 143 U 18 | Bermondsey Wall east SE16 |
| 143 S 18 | Bermondsey Wall west SE16 |
| 72 B 7 | Bernard av W13 |
| 105 W 12 | Bernard gdns SW19 |
| 31 V 15 | Bernard rd N15 |
| 56 K 1 | Bernard rd Rom |
| 155 R 9 | Bernard rd Wallgtn |
| 132 K 18 | Bernard st WC1 |
| 11 R 19 | Bernays clo Stanm |
| 90 D 9 | Bernays gro SW9 |
| 122 K 10 | Berne rd Thntn Hth |
| 158 M 4 | Bernel dri Croy |
| 140 C 2 | Berners ms W1 |
| 140 D 4 | Berners pl W1 |
| 133 V 6 | Berners rd N1 |
| 30 E 6 | Berners rd N22 |
| 140 C 3 | Berners st W1 |
| 21 N 11 | Bernhardt rd E4 |
| 109 P 12 | Berridge rd SE19 |
| 48 E 9 | Berriman rd N7 |
| 40 E 5 | Berriton rd Harrow |
| 17 W 4 | Berry clo N21 |
| 11 V 13 | Berry hill Stanm |
| 133 X 14 | Berry pl EC1 |
| 133 X 16 | Berry st EC1 |
| 44 A 19 | Berry st NW10 |
| 72 J 8 | Berry way W5 |
| 149 Y 10 | Berryfield rd SE17 |
| 95 Y 9 | Berryhill SE9 |
| 95 Y 10 | Berryhill gdns SE9 |
| 119 N 7 | Berrylands SW20 |
| 117 R 12 | Berrylands Surb |
| 116 N 13 | Berrylands rd Surb |
| 117 N 13 | Berrylands rd Surb |
| 110 F 10 | Berrymans la SE26 |
| 73 V 4 | Berrymead gdns W3 |
| 73 X 8 | Berrymede rd W4 |
| 122 K 12 | Bert rd Thntn Hth |
| 8 J 14 | Bert way Enf |
| 106 F 11 | Bertal rd SW17 |
| 33 W 15 | Berthan gdns E17 |
| 76 C 18 | Berthon st SE8 |
| 44 G 18 | Bertie rd NW10 |
| 110 G 14 | Bertie rd SE26 |
| 105 X 18 | Bertram cotts SW19 |
| 66 E 14 | Bertram gdns E6 |
| 26 H 19 | Bertram rd NW4 |
| 8 J 14 | Bertram rd Enf |
| 103 O 17 | Bertram rd Kingst |
| 47 S 8 | Bertram st N19 |
| 93 R 7 | Bertrand st SE13 |
| 25 R 3 | Bertridge grn Edg |
| 96 H 17 | Berwick cres Sidcp |
| 65 X 18 | Berwick rd E16 |
| 32 M 14 | Berwick rd E17 |
| 30 H 4 | Berwick rd N22 |
| 97 R 3 | Berwick rd Welling |
| 140 C 5 | Berwick st W1 |
| 82 J 2 | Berwyn av Hounsl |
| 108 J 1 | Berwyn rd SE21 |
| 85 S 10 | Berwyn rd Rich |
| 144 F 11 | Beryl rd W6 |
| 45 S 11 | Besant rd NW2 |
| 107 V 16 | Besley st SW16 |
| 148 G 10 | Bessborough gdns SW1 |
| 148 F 10 | Bessborough ms SW1 |
| 148 F 10 | Bessborough pl SW1 |
| 104 G 1 | Bessborough rd SW15 |
| 41 R 2 | Bessborough rd Harrow |
| 148 F 10 | Bessborough st SW1 |
| 148 G 10 | Bessborough way SW1 |
| 90 M 6 | Bessemer rd SE5 |
| 91 N 5 | Bessemer rd SE5 |
| 92 E 1 | Besson st SE14 |
| 75 T 12 | Bestwood st SE8 |
| 154 F 10 | Betchworth clo Sutton |
| 54 H 8 | Betchworth rd Ilf |
| 159 T 18 | Betchworth way Croy |
| 59 R 10 | Betham rd Grnfd |
| 23 T 14 | Bethecar rd Harrow |
| 97 U 8 | Bethel rd Welling |
| 65 P 11 | Bethell av E16 |
| 53 W 1 | Bethell av Ilf |
| 110 M 19 | Bethersden clo Becknhm |
| 135 U 14 | Bethnal Green rd E2 |
| 135 Z 11 | Bethnel Green museum E2 |
| 15 Z 14 | Bethume av N11 |
| 49 S 3 | Bethune clo N16 |
| 61 Z 12 | Bethune rd NW10 |
| 49 S 4 | Bethune rd N16 |
| 150 C 17 | Bethwin rd SE15 |
| 20 M 13 | Betoyne av E4 |
| 16 F 14 | Betstyle rd N11 |
| 115 Z 4 | Betterton dri Sidcp |
| 140 K 5 | Betterton st WC2 |
| 87 W 5 | Bettridge rd SW6 |
| 65 V 19 | Betts rd E16 |
| 143 V 9 | Betts st E1 |
| 12 E 10 | Beulah clo Edg |
| 122 M 4 | Beulah cres Thntn Hth |
| 122 M 15 | Beulah gro Croy |
| 108 K 16 | Beulah hill SE19 |
| 51 N 2 | Beulah rd E11 |
| 33 T 14 | Beulah rd E17 |
| 105 V 17 | Beulah rd SW19 |
| 153 Y 9 | Beulah rd Sutton |
| 122 L 5 | Beulah rd Thntn Hth |
| 99 W 9 | Beult rd Drtford |
| 68 A 1 | Bevan av Bark |
| 156 F 11 | Bevan ct Croy |
| 80 C 14 | Bevan rd SE2 |
| 5 Z 13 | Bevan rd Barnt |
| 134 B 6 | Bevan st N1 |
| 134 G 12 | Bevenden st N1 |
| 104 E 19 | Beverley av SW20 |
| 82 F 11 | Beverley av Hounsl |
| 96 J 19 | Beverley av Sidcp |
| 17 Y 6 | Beverley clo N21 |
| 86 F 5 | Beverley clo SW13 |
| 8 D 15 | Beverley clo Enf |
| 34 H 3 | Beverley cres Wdfd Grn |
| 92 M 7 | Beverley ct SE4 |
| 25 R 9 | Beverley dri Edg |
| 27 T 20 | Beverley gdns NW11 |
| 86 E 7 | Beverley gdns SW13 |
| 23 Y 5 | Beverley gdns Stanm |
| 43 O 3 | Beverley gdns Wem |
| 104 B 18 | Beverley la Kingst |
| 118 F 7 | Beverley park New Mald |
| 20 K 19 | Beverley rd E4 |
| 66 B 9 | Beverley rd E6 |
| 123 Z 3 | Beverley rd SE20 |
| 86 E 6 | Beverley rd SW13 |
| 74 C 14 | Beverley rd W4 |
| 98 L 6 | Beverley rd Bxly Hth |
| 55 Z 12 | Beverley rd Dgnhm |
| 56 A 12 | Beverley rd Dgnhm |
| 102 E 20 | Beverley rd Kingst |
| 121 W 8 | Beverley rd Mitch |
| 118 F 9 | Beverley rd New Mald |
| 70 C 10 | Beverley rd S'hall |
| 152 L 3 | Beverley rd Worc Pk |
| 118 G 3 | Beverley way SW20 |
| 47 V 10 | Beversbrook rd N19 |
| 90 C 12 | Beverstone rd SW2 |
| 122 H 9 | Beverstone rd Thntr Hth |
| 107 N 13 | Bevill allen SW17 |
| 107 N 13 | Bevill Allen clo SW17 |
| 133 R 11 | Bevin way WC1 |
| 136 M 1 | Bevington rd W10 |
| 137 N 2 | Bevington rd W10 |
| 125 P 3 | Bevington rd Becknhm |
| 143 U 18 | Bevington st SE16 |
| 142 L 5 | Bevis marks EC3 |
| 7 N 14 | Bewcastle gdns Enf |
| 48 F 20 | Bewdley st N1 |
| 89 S 4 | Bewick st SW8 |
| 143 Z 8 | Bewley st E1 |
| 63 O 19 | Bewley st E1 |
| 108 J 11 | Bewlys rd SE27 |
| 100 A 3 | Bexhill clo Felt |
| 16 J 17 | Bexhill rd N11 |
| 92 L 17 | Bexhill rd SE4 |
| 85 W 8 | Bexhill rd SW14 |
| 65 N 5 | Bexhill wlk E15 |
| 99 P 12 | Bexley clo Drtford |
| 18 B 11 | Bexley gdns N9 |
| 98 F 20 | Bexley High st Bxly |
| 99 P 12 | Bexley la Drtford |
| 115 U 8 | Bexley la Sidcp |
| 96 Z 14 | Bexley rd SE9 |
| 154 L 11 | Beynon rd Carsh |
| 151 R 14 | Bianca rd SE15 |
| 27 V 8 | Bibsworth rd N3 |
| 85 S 8 | Bicester rd Rich |
| 131 P 20 | Bickenhall st W1 |
| 106 M 14 | Bickersteth rd SW17 |
| 47 U 8 | Bickerton rd N19 |
| 127 U 5 | Bickler Pk rd Brom |
| 127 R 8 | Bickley cres Brom |
| 33 R 20 | Bickley rd E10 |
| 127 P 4 | Bickley rd Brom |
| 106 L 13 | Bickley st SW17 |
| 90 M 8 | Bicknell rd SE5 |
| 8 F 5 | Bicknoller rd Enf |
| 126 C 12 | Bidborough clo Brom |
| 132 H 13 | Bidborough st WC1 |
| 88 E 11 | Bidcot st SW11 |
| 113 V 9 | Biddenden way SE9 |
| 64 L 14 | Bidder st E16 |
| 48 C 13 | Biddestone rd N7 |
| 129 Y 14 | Biddulph rd W9 |
| 156 L 20 | Biddulph rd S Croy |
| 9 X 3 | Bideford av Enf |
| 60 A 7 | Bideford av Grnfd |
| 25 O 5 | Bideford clo Edg |
| 18 E 2 | Bideford gdns Enf |
| 112 B 7 | Bideford rd Brom |
| 9 X 3 | Bideford rd Enf |
| 100 E 6 | Bideford rd Felt |
| 80 D 20 | Bideford rd Welling |
| 29 V 3 | Bidwell gdns N11 |
| 92 A 3 | Bidwell st SE15 |
| 67 P 5 | Bifrons st Bark |
| 63 A 3 | Big hill E5 |
| 78 M 14 | Big Nell rd SE18 |
| 64 G 2 | Biggerstaff rd E15 |

20 D 10 Boxley rd Mrdn
77 V 3 Boxley st E16
24 A 13 Boxmoor rd Harrow
23 O 3 Boxtree la Harrow
133 R 4 Boxworth gr N1
78 L 13 Boyard rd SE18
65 T 12 Boyce way E13
25 W 18 Boycroft av NW9
70 G 3 Boyd av S'hall
106 F 15 Boyd rd SW19
143 T 7 Boyd st E1
141 Y 19 Boyfield st SE1
112 C 13 Boyland rd Brom
10 M 18 Boyle av Stanm
140 A 9 Boyle st W1
27 R 12 Boyne av NW4
93 W 8 Boyne rd SE13
56 E 10 Boyne rd Dgnhm
137 O 13 Boyne Ter ms W11
150 D 14 Boyson rd SE17
30 A 11 Boyton clo N8
30 A 11 Boyton rd N8
30 D 7 Brabant rd N22
156 A 17 Brabazon av Wallgtn
64 C 16 Brabazon st E14
92 B 6 Brabourne gdns SE15
81 P 18 Brabourne cres Bxly Hth
125 V 11 Brabourne ri Becknhm
41 X 17 Bracewell av Grnfd
62 L 14 Bracewell rd W10
136 B 2 Bracewell rd W10
157 V 5 Bracewood gdns Croy
48 B 6 Bracey st N4
89 P 17 Bracken av SW12
159 P G Bracken av Croy
86 G 4 Bracken gdns SW13
74 K 7 Brackenbury gdns W6
28 D 10 Brackenbury rd N2
74 K 8 Brackenbury rd W6
17 R 7 Brackendale N21
40 B 12 Brackenhill Ruis
40 B 12 Brackenhill Ruis
126 C 1 Brackenhill clo Brom
126 C 1 Brackenhill la Brom
74 B 12 Brackley rd W4
111 O 17 Brackley rd Becknhm
35 N 1 Brackley sq N1
74 B 13 Brackley ter W4
45 Y 13 Bracknell cl NW3
48 A 13 Bracknell gdns NW3
45 Z 13 Bracknell way NW3
46 A 13 Bracknell way NW3
79 Z 10 Bracondale rd SE2
80 C 10 Bracondale rd SE2
141 U 15 Brad st SE1
98 F 18 Bradbourne rd Bxly
87 Y 4 Bradbourne st SW6
49 T 16 Bradbury st N16
85 N 0 Braddon rd Rich
75 N 6 Braddon st SE16
113 Y 19 Braddon st SS16
76 L 13 Braddyll st SE10
129 X 18 Braden st W9
96 M 10 Bradenham av Welling
97 N 10 Bradenham av Welling
24 A 12 Bradenham rd Harrow
54 M 16 Bradfield dri Bark
77 T 4 Bradfield rd E16
40 C 15 Bradfield rd Ruis
9 N 10 Bradfield sq Enf
152 C 14 Bradford dri Epsom
109 Z 9 Bradford rd SE26
74 A 4 Bradford rd W3
54 F 4 Bradford rd Ilf
93 R 17 Bradgate rd SE6
52 H 5 Brading cres E11
90 D 18 Brading rd SW2
122 B 15 Brading rd Croy
129 R 12 Bradiston rd W9
134 J 9 Bradlaugh st N1
60 B 17 Bradley gdns W13
30 C 7 Bradley rd N22
108 L 14 Bradley rd SE19
9 X 1 Bradley rd Enf
133 T 9 Bradleys bldgs N1
144 B 7 Bradmore la W6
74 K 10 Bradmore Pk rd W6
151 X 13 Bradshaw st SE15
50 G 19 Bradstock rd E9
152 H 11 Bradstock rd Epsom
56 E 6 Bradwell av Dgnhm
34 B 12 Bradwell clo E18
57 Z 19 Bradwell clo Hornch
63 T 9 Bradwell st E1
26 N 14 Brady st E1
135 X 20 Brady st E1

43 Y 8 Braemar av NW10
30 B 5 Braemar av N22
105 X 5 Braemar av SW19
98 K 11 Braemar av Bxly Hth
157 N 20 Braemar av S Croy
122 G 5 Braemar av Thntn Heath
60 J 1 Braemar av Wemb
25 Z 6 Braemar gdns NW9
114 F 6 Braemar gdns Sidcp
125 T 20 Braemar gdns W Wkhm
65 R 13 Braemar rd E13
31 R 15 Braemar rd N15
73 T 8 Braemar rd W3
72 H 16 Braemar rd Brentf
152 J 5 Braemar rd Worc Pk
54 K 8 Braemore av Ilf
105 T 20 Braeside SW19
111 P 14 Braeside Beckhm
98 K 11 Braeside cres Bxly Hth
107 V 18 Braeside rd SW16
81 P 11 Braesyde clo Blvdr
156 L 8 Brafferton rd Croy
149 W 10 Braganza st SE17
61 Z 19 Braid av W3
100 C X Braid clo Felt
111 X 2 Braidwood rd SE6
142 K 14 Braidwood st SE1
90 G 15 Brailsford rd SW2
35 P 14 Braintree av Ilf
56 E 9 Braintree rd Dgnhm
63 P 10 Braintree st E2
24 E 5 Braithwaite gdns Stanm
90 G 2 Bramah rd SW9
15 V 18 Bramber rd N12
145 P 14 Bramber rd SW6
159 P 8 Bramble clo Croy
122 C 6 Bramble la SW16
79 P 14 Bramblebury rd SE18
81 Y 11 Bramblecroft Erith
126 A 13 Brambledown clo Brom
157 R 18 Brambledown rd S Croy
72 A 20 Brambles clo Brentf
120 K 20 Bramblewood clo Carsh
120 L 9 Bramcote av Mitch
151 Z 10 Bramcote gro SE16
75 O 13 Bramcote gro SE16
86 K 11 Bramcote rd SW15
112 E 2 Bramdean cres SE12
112 E 2 Bramdean gdns SE12
124 L 6 Bramerton rd Beck
146 J 13 Bramerton st SW3
88 L 14 Bramfield rd SW11
88 C 11 Bramford rd SW18
145 Y 9 Bramham gdns SW5
77 W 16 Bramhope la SE7
6 D 17 Bramley clo Twick
82 M 16 Bramley clo Twick
156 N 10 Bramley clo S Croy
35 X 18 Bramley cres Ilf
156 K 9 Bramley hill S Croy
99 W 12 Bramley pl Drtfrd
6 D 17 Bramley rd N14
136 G 9 Bramley rd W11
72 D 9 Bramley rd W5
6 L 13 Bramley rd Enf
153 N 19 Bramley rd Sutton
154 F 11 Bramley rd Sutton
136 G 6 Bramley st W10
150 O O Bramley way W Wkhm
30 K 16 Brampton gdns N15
26 K 14 Brampton gro NW4
23 Z 12 Brampton gro Harrow
24 A 13 Brampton gro Harrow
43 O 4 Brampton gro Wemb
30 F 10 Brampton Park rd N8
66 C 10 Brampton rd E6
25 R 15 Brampton rd NW9
30 L 16 Brampton rd N15
80 G 16 Brampton rd SE18
80 G 18 Brampton rd Bxly Hth
97 X 1 Brampton rd Bxly Hth
123 T 16 Brampton rd Croy
50 F 19 Bramshaw ri New Mald
118 B 14 Bramshaw ri New Mald
47 T 8 Bramshill gdns NW5
62 C 6 Bramshill rd NW10

77 U 16 Bramshot av SE7
62 G 5 Bramston rd SW17
89 O 5 Bramwell pl SW8
53 U 13 Brancaster rd E12
107 Z 6 Brancaster rd SW16
36 G 19 Brancaster rd Ilf
21 S 9 Brancepeth Buck Hl
46 C 10 Branch hill NW3
134 G 4 Branch pl N1
63 V 19 Branch rd E14
24 F 10 Brancker rd Harrow
76 G 20 Brand st SE10
87 V 11 Brandlehow rd SW15
33 V 12 Brandon rd E17
47 Z 20 Brandon rd N7
70 E 14 Brandon rd S'hall
153 Z 8 Brandon rd Sutton
150 C 7 Brandon st SE17
93 Y 10 Brandram rd SE13
107 R 4 Brandreth rd SW17
155 Z 6 Brandries the Wallgtn
36 A 12 Brandville gdns Ilf
111 U 12 Brangbourne rd Brom
144 J 20 Branksea st SW6
18 F 18 Branksome av N18
105 Y 20 Branksome rd SW19
90 A 12 Branksome rd SW2
24 L 18 Branksome way Harrow
117 X 2 Branksome way New Mald
17 S 3 Branscombe gdns N21
93 R 8 Branscombe st SE13
24 M 3 Bransgrove rd Edg
85 N 5 Branstone rd Rich
59 U 12 Brants wlk W7
81 W 18 Brantwood av Islwth
83 Y 9 Brantwood av Islwth
33 S 11 Brantwood clo E17
6 M 15 Brantwood gdns Enf
35 S 14 Brantwood gdns Ilf
18 L 20 Brantwood rd N17
90 L 12 Brantwood rd SE24
98 H 6 Brantwood rd Bxlyhth
157 N 20 Brantwood rd S Croy
89 O 6 Brassey sq SW11
62 B 18 Brassie av W3
110 B 9 Brasted clo SE26
97 W 13 Brasted clo Bxly Hth
87 Z 18 Brathway rd SW18
58 J 11 Braund av Grnfd
114 J 1 Braundton av Sidcp
96 K 20 Braundton av Sidcup
129 O 15 Bravington pl W9
129 O 16 Bravington rd W9
92 K 11 Braxfield rd SE4
108 C 15 Braxted pk SW16
65 R 10 Bray dri E16
65 R 19 Bray pl E16
147 N 9 Bray pl SW3
91 Z 5 Brayards rd SE15
92 A 5 Brayards rd SE15
62 D 15 Braybrook st W12
89 W 6 Brayburne av SW4
49 W 2 Braydon rd E5
133 S 2 Brayfield ter N1
6 L 14 Brayton gdns Enf
96 E 10 Braywood rd SE9
69 R 9 Breach la Dgnhm
142 B 7 Bread st EC4
93 N 6 Breakspears rd SE4
92 M 9 Breakspears rd SE4
66 J 10 Bream gdns E6
64 A 2 Bream st E3
104 C 2 Breamore clo SW15
55 N 7 Breamore rd Ilf
54 K 8 Breamore rd Ilf
141 S 4 Breams bldgs EC4
102 A 6 Breamwater gdns Rich
86 L 9 Breasley clo SW15
146 C 8 Brechin pl SW7
47 Y 15 Brecknock rd N7
144 L 15 Brecon rd W6
9 O 13 Brecon rd Enf
66 J 8 Brede clo E6
47 V 7 Bredgar rd N19
90 M 6 Bredhurst SE5
123 U 17 Bredon rd Croy
88 A 7 Breer st SW6
143 U 10 Breezers hill E1
138 D 20 Bremner rd SW7
126 D 13 Brenchley clo Brom
127 X 1 Brenchley clo Chisl
92 D 15 Brenchley gdns SE23
106 L 5 Brenda rd SW17
44 A 14 Brendon av NW10

99 P 2 Brendon clo Erith
40 K 11 Brendon gdns Harrow
36 H 15 Brendon gdns Ilf
114 D 4 Brendon rd SE9
56 D 4 Brendon rd Dgnhm
138 M 4 Brendon st W1
18 D 2 Brendon way Enf
121 P 6 Brenley clo Mitch
95 O 9 Brenley gdns SE9
60 M 7 Brent cres Wemb
27 O 16 Brent grn NW4
44 H 2 Brent Park rd NW4
4 J 18 Brent pl Barnt
65 T 16 Brent rd E16
78 L 19 Brent rd SE18
72 E 18 Brent rd Brentf
157 Z 19 Brent rd S Croy
72 E 17 Brent side Brentf
27 O 15 Brent st NW4
26 F 20 Brent View rd NW9
14 K 20 Brent way N3
72 G 19 Brent way Brentf
43 O 17 Brent way Wemb
61 V 1 Brentfield NW10
43 X 17 Brentfield clo NW10
27 P 20 Brentfield ct NW11
43 X 17 Brentfield rd NW10
61 Y 1 Brentfield rd NW10
72 G 18 Brentford high Brentf
30 K 9 Brentham Halt rd W5
60 F 11 Brentham way W5
50 B 19 Brenthouse rd E9
44 E 17 Brenthurst rd NW10
72 D 20 Brentley Brentf
61 N 7 Brentmead gdns NW10
27 P 18 Brentmoor pl NW11
63 W 17 Brenton st E3
59 Y 11 Brentside clo W13
71 P 2 Brentvale av S'hall
60 M 4 Brentvale av Wemb
61 N 5 Brentvale av Wemb
72 J 12 Brentwick gdns Brentf
39 X 18 Brentwood rd Rom
31 V 2 Brereton rd N17
148 A 2 Bressenden pl SW1
34 C 8 Bressey gro E18
55 Y 20 Brett gdns Dgnhm
87 P 17 Brett Ho clo SW15
50 A 16 Brett rd E8
81 X 1 Brett rd NW10
150 F 10 Brettell st SE17
33 O 5 Brettenham av E17
33 O 5 Brettenham rd E17
18 K 13 Brettenham rd N18
18 K 13 Brettenham Rd east N18
140 D 9 Brewer st W1
148 D 1 Brewers grn SW1
84 G 12 Brewers la Rich
47 Z 10 Brewery rd N1
48 A 19 Brewery rd N7
79 R 13 Brewery rd SE18
127 S 19 Brewery rd Bron
64 D 8 Brewery rd E3
143 Y 12 Brewhouse la E1
87 S 9 Brewhouse st SW15
133 W 17 Brewhouse yd EC1
55 R 17 Brewood rd Dgnhm
136 B 2 Brewster gdns W10
62 M 14 Brewster gdns W10
51 S 4 Brewster rd E10
57 Y 11 Brian clo Hornch
37 U 14 Brian rd Rom
92 E 1 Briant st SE14
22 C 6 Briants clo Pinn
108 D 17 Briar av SW16
155 P 20 Briar banks Carsh
17 Z 11 Briar clo N13
83 W 12 Briar clo Islwth
40 J 19 Briar cres Grnfd
153 N 8 Briar ct Sutton
126 B 20 Briar gdns Brom
155 P 20 Briar la Carsh
159 R 7 Briar la Croy
44 M 11 Briar rd NW2
122 B 7 Briar rd SW16
24 D 17 Briar rd Harrow
101 S 2 Briar rd Twick
86 K 10 Briar wlk SW15
25 W 2 Briar wlk Edg
25 W 18 Briar Wood clo NW9
59 V 20 Briarbank rd W13
45 X 10 Briardale gdns NW3
28 B 8 Briarfield av N3
31 Z 3 Briars clo N17
89 X 12 Briarwood rd SW4
152 X 13 Briarwood rd Epsom
115 R 12 Briary ct Sidcp
112 H 12 Briary gdns Brom
18 F 12 Briary la N9

| | | |
|---|---|---|
| 141 S 8 | Brick ct WC2 |
| 85 S 3 | Brick Farm clo Rich |
| 135 P 19 | Brick la E1 |
| 143 P 2 | Brick la E1 |
| 8 L 9 | Brick la Enf |
| 9 O 9 | Brick la Enf |
| 139W 15 | Brick st W1 |
| 79 Y 18 | Brickfield cotts SE18 |
| 64 D 10 | Brickfield rd E3 |
| 122 K 2 | Brickfield rd Thntn Hth |
| 41 R 6 | Brickfields Harrow |
| 157 S 2 | Brickwood rd Croy |
| 141W 6 | Bride la EC4 |
| 48 D 19 | Bride st N7 |
| 141W 7 | Bridewell pl EC4 |
| 131 Y 19 | Bridford ms W1 |
| 47 N 20 | Bridge appr NW3 |
| 74 K 12 | Bridge av W6 |
| 144 A 8 | Bridge av W6 |
| 59 R 14 | Bridge av W7 |
| 9 N 8 | Bridge clo Enf |
| 39 P 19 | Bridge clo Rom |
| 88 F 6 | Bridge ct SW11 |
| 33 U 4 | Bridge end E17 |
| 17 Y 3 | Bridge ga N21 |
| 27 S 14 | Bridge la NW11 |
| 88 K 3 | Bridge la SW11 |
| 147 Y 5 | Bridge pl SW 1 |
| 123 P 18 | Bridge pl Croy |
| 64 K 2 | Bridge rd E15 |
| 50 K 2 | Bridge rd E17 |
| 53 T 20 | Bridge rd E6 |
| 44 A 18 | Bridge rd NW10 |
| 30 A 6 | Bridge rd N22 |
| 18 K 10 | Bridge rd N9 |
| 110 L 18 | Bridge rd Becknhm |
| 97 Z 6 | Bridge rd Bxly Hth |
| 99 V 1 | Bridge rd Erith |
| 83 P 6 | Bridge rd Hounsl |
| 70 E 5 | Bridge rd S'hall |
| 154 B 14 | Bridge rd Sutton |
| 84 A 15 | Bridge rd Twick |
| 99 T 3 | Bridge rd W Erith |
| 155 T 11 | Bridge rd Wallgtn |
| 43 R 9 | Bridge rd Wemb |
| 129W 8 | Bridge st NW6 |
| 140 K 18 | Bridge st SW1 |
| 73 Y 11 | Bridge st W4 |
| 22 A 10 | Bridge st Pinn |
| 84 G 14 | Bridge st Rich |
| 64 K 1 | Bridge ter E15 |
| 23 U 11 | Bridge the Harrow |
| 144 A 9 | Bridge view W6 |
| 27 V 16 | Bridge way NW11 |
| 16 G 12 | Bridge way N11 |
| 83 O 20 | Bridge way Twick |
| 153 X 14 | Bridgefield rd Sutton |
| 148 L 12 | Bridgefoot SE1 |
| 65 T 18 | Bridgeland rd E16 |
| 101 X 14 | Bridgeman rd Tedd |
| 130 J 9 | Bridgeman st NW8 |
| 97 Y 17 | Bridgen rd Bxly |
| 8 H 5 | Bridgenhall rd Enf |
| 156 A 7 | Bridges la Croy |
| 87W 2 | Bridges pl SW6 |
| 105 Z 16 | Bridges rd SW19 |
| 106 A 16 | Bridges rd Stanm |
| 10 H 17 | Bridges rd Stanm |
| 74 L 13 | Bridgeview W6 |
| 24 M 7 | Bridgewater gdns Edg |
| 64 F 3 | Bridgewater rd E15 |
| 42 C 17 | Bridgewater rd Grnfd |
| 42 C 17 | Bridgewater rd Wemb |
| 134 A 20 | Bridgewater st EC1 |
| 67 X 1 | Bridgeway Bark |
| 42 L 19 | Bridgeway Wemb |
| 132 D 9 | Bridgeway st NW1 |
| 107 X 18 | Bridgewood rd SW16 |
| 152 H 7 | Bridgewood rd Worc Pk |
| 106 D 6 | Bridgford st SW18 |
| 73 V 8 | Bridgman rd W4 |
| 140 C 8 | Bridle la W1 |
| 156 B 6 | Bridle path Croy |
| 159 O 1 | Bridle rd Croy |
| 159 P 9 | Bridleway Croy |
| 155W 10 | Bridleway the Wallgtn |
| 19 N 3 | Bridlington rd N9 |
| 18 M 2 | Bridlington rd N9 |
| 38 G 20 | Bridport av Rom |
| 134 F 6 | Bridport pl N1 |
| 134 F 8 | Bridport pl N1 |
| 18 E 18 | Bridport rd N18 |
| 58 K 3 | Bridport rd Grnfd |
| 122 G 6 | Bridport rd Thntn Hth |
| 89 X 2 | Bridport rd SW8 |
| 75 O 18 | Bridson st SE15 |
| 137 U 5 | Bridstow pl W2 |
| 90 H 3 | Brief st SE5 |
| 159 R 15 | Brierley Croy |
| 19 R 6 | Brierley av N9 |
| 51 X 12 | Brierley rd E11 |
| 107 T 4 | Brierley rd SW12 |
| 63 P 8 | Brierly st E2 |
| 76 H 12 | Brig st E14 |
| 8 A 5 | Brigadier av Enf |
| 7 Y 3 | Brigadier hill Enf |
| 64 E 16 | Bright st E14 |
| 94 B 12 | Brightfield rd SE12 |
| 92 M 17 | Brightling rd SE4 |
| 63 X 20 | Brightlingsea pl E14 |
| 106 E 1 | Brightman rd SW18 |
| 32 L 17 | Brighton av E17 |
| 40 G 18 | Brighton dri Grnfd |
| 92 H 1 | Brighton gro SE14 |
| 65 N 5 | Brighton rd E15 |
| 66 K 8 | Brighton rd E6 |
| 49 T 12 | Brighton rd N16 |
| 28 D 8 | Brighton rd N2 |
| 157 N 13 | Brighton rd S Croy |
| 116 E 14 | Brighton rd Surb |
| 154 B 17 | Brighton rd Sutton |
| 90 D 10 | Brighton ter SW9 |
| 93 X 15 | Brightside N4 |
| 9 U 5 | Brightside the Enf |
| 106 L 13 | Brightwell cres SW17 |
| 81 T 10 | Brigstock rd Blvdr |
| 122 L 9 | Brigstock rd Thntn Hth |
| 28 D 13 | Brim hill N2 |
| 92 A 1 | Brimmington rd SE15 |
| 80 C 9 | Brimpsfield clo SE2 |
| 9W 7 | Brimsdown av Enf |
| 92 L 3 | Brindley st SE13 |
| 58 K 19 | Brindley way S'hall |
| 19 Z 10 | Brindwood rd E4 |
| 20 A 10 | Brindwood rd E4 |
| 80 B 10 | Brinkburn clo SE2 |
| 25 S 9 | Brinkburn clo Edg |
| 25 R 9 | Brinkburn gdns Edg |
| 152 J 2 | Brinklow rd Worc Pk |
| 78 M 20 | Brinklow cres SE18 |
| 79 N 19 | Brinklow cres SE18 |
| 35 R 9 | Brinkworth rd Ilf |
| 27 O 11 | Brinsdale rd NW4 |
| 9W 7 | Brinsdown av Enf |
| 23 P 7 | Brinsley rd Harrow |
| 101 P 2 | Brinsworth clo Twick |
| 105 Z 19 | Brisbane av SW19 |
| 51 S 8 | Brisbane rd E10 |
| 71 Z 4 | Brisbane rd W13 |
| 54 A 2 | Brisbane rd Ilf |
| 150 E 20 | Brisbane st SE5 |
| 106 G 15 | Briscoe rd SW19 |
| 95 N 8 | Briset rd SE9 |
| 133W 19 | Briset st EC1 |
| 86 L 19 | Bristol gdns SW15 |
| 129 Z 19 | Bristol gdns W9 |
| 130 A 19 | Bristol gdns W9 |
| 129 Z 19 | Bristol ms W9 |
| 130 A 19 | Bristol ms W9 |
| 52 M 19 | Bristol rd E12 |
| 53 N 18 | Bristol rd E12 |
| 58 K 3 | Bristol rd Grnfd |
| 120 C 10 | Bristol rd Mrdn |
| 30 B 20 | Briston gro N8 |
| 109 R 12 | Bristow rd SE19 |
| 97 Z 3 | Bristow rd Bxly Hth |
| 98 A 3 | Bristow rd Bxly Hth |
| 156 A 9 | Bristow rd Croy |
| 82 M 9 | Bristow rd Hounsl |
| 15 S 12 | Britannia rd N12 |
| 145 X 19 | Britannia rd SW6 |
| 53 Y 11 | Britannia rd Ilf |
| 116 M 16 | Britannia rd Surb |
| 117 N 16 | Britannia rd Surb |
| 133 Y 4 | Britannia row N1 |
| 133 N 12 | Britannia rd WC1 |
| 134 E 12 | Britannia wlk N1 |
| 74 E 12 | British gro W4 |
| 74 E 14 | British Grove pass W6 |
| 21 O 7 | British Legion rd E4 |
| 140 H 2 | British museum WC1 |
| 63 Z 10 | British st E3 |
| 56 A 9 | Brittain rd Dgnhm |
| 134 A 4 | Brittania row N1 |
| 132 M 12 | Brittania st WC1 |
| 146 J 10 | Britten st SW3 |
| 133W 19 | Britton st EC1 |
| 54 H 14 | Brixham gdns Ilf |
| 97 V 2 | Brixham rd Welling |
| 90 C 16 | Brixton hill SW2 |
| 90 A 19 | Brixton Hill pl SW2 |
| 149 T 18 | Brixton rd SW9 |
| 90 F 5 | Brixton rd SW9 |
| 90 F 9 | Brixton Stn rd SW9 |
| 140 L 6 | Broad ct WC2 |
| 122 H 16 | Broad Grn av Croy |
| 31W 14 | Broad la N15 |
| 100 F 16 | Broad la Hampt |
| 113W 2 | Broad lawn SE9 |
| 126 B 11 | Broad Oaks way Brom |
| 51 X 20 | Broad st E15 |
| 56 D 20 | Broad st Dgnhm |
| 69 S 2 | Broad st Dgnhm |
| 101 V 14 | Broad st Tedd |
| 142 H 2 | Broad St av EC2 |
| 142 T 2 | Broad St bldgs EC2 |
| 45 V 1 | Broad Walk la NW1 |
| 23 U 7 | Broad Way the Harrow |
| 95 T 3 | Broad wlk SE18 |
| 94 L 6 | Broad wlk SE18 |
| 82 A 3 | Broad wlk Hounsl |
| 133 V 19 | Broad yd EC1 |
| 139 X 9 | Broadbent st W1 |
| 77 S 19 | Broadbridge clo SE3 |
| 158 F 17 | Broadcoombe S Croy |
| 24 H 7 | Broadcroft av Stanm |
| 10 E 8 | Broadfield ct Bushey Watf |
| 93 Z 20 | Broadfield rd SE6 |
| 111 Z 3 | Broadfield rd SE6 |
| 21 Y 12 | Broadfield way Buck HI |
| 22 K 6 | Broadfields Harrow |
| 17 T 1 | Broadfields av N21 |
| 12 E 14 | Broadfields av Edg |
| 5 O 7 | Broadgates av Barnt |
| 106 G 3 | Broadgates rd SW18 |
| 89 T 7 | Broadhinton rd SW4 |
| 12 E 12 | Broadhurst av Edg |
| 54 K 13 | Broadhurst av Ilf |
| 46 B 18 | Broadhurst clo NW6 |
| 45 Z 19 | Broadhurst gdns NW6 |
| 46 B 18 | Broadhurst gdns NW6 |
| 57W 19 | Broadhurst walk Rainhm |
| 107 Z 4 | Broadlands av SW16 |
| 108 A 5 | Broadlands av SW16 |
| 9 O 12 | Broadlands av Enf |
| 100 A 8 | Broadlands av Felt |
| 100 G 8 | Broadlands av Felt |
| 47 N 1 | Broadlands Av clo N6 |
| 107 Z 5 | Broadlands clo SW16 |
| 9 O 12 | Broadlands clo Enf |
| 29 N 20 | Broadlands rd N6 |
| 112 H 10 | Broadlands rd Brom |
| 118 D 15 | Broadlands way New Mald |
| 30 H 20 | Broadley st NW8 |
| 30 L 18 | Broadley ter NW8 |
| 111 P 7 | Broadmead SE6 |
| 118 F 18 | Broadmead av Worc Pk |
| 22 C 2 | Broadmead clo Pinn |
| 34 K 2 | Broadmead rd Wdfd Gn |
| 35 N 3 | Broadmead rd Wdfd Gn |
| 21 S 18 | Broadmead rd Wdfd Gn |
| 139 S 2 | Broadstone pl W1 |
| 57W 7 | Broadstone rd Hornch |
| 25 P 19 | Broadview NW9 |
| 107W 17 | Broadview rd SW16 |
| 34 B 10 | Broadwalk E18 |
| 17 R 6 | Broadwalk N21 |
| 31 S 6 | Broadwater rd N17 |
| 106 H 9 | Broadwater rd SW17 |
| 65 U 7 | Broadway E13 |
| 51 Y 20 | Broadway E15 |
| 140 F 20 | Broadway SW1 |
| 148 E 1 | Broadway SW1 |
| 72 A 2 | Broadway W13 |
| 71W 2 | Broadway W7 |
| 67 O 3 | Broadway Bark |
| 98 E 11 | Broadway Bxly Hth |
| 152 G 12 | Broadway Epsom |
| 59 N 11 | Broadway Grnfd |
| 39W 9 | Broadway Rom |
| 123 O 12 | Broadway av Croy |
| 84 A 16 | Broadway av Twick |
| 21W 18 | Broadway clo Wdfd Grn |
| 51 X 20 | Broadway ct E15 |
| 120 J 7 | Broadway gdns Mitch |
| 21W 18 | Broadway gdns Wdfd Grn |
| 135 U 5 | Broadway mkt E8 |
| 17W 5 | Broadway ms N21 |
| 20 H 19 | Broadway the E4 |
| 13 P 17 | Broadway the NW7 |
| 29 Z 18 | Broadway the N8 |
| 18 K 9 | Broadway the N9 |
| 105 X 16 | Broadway the SW19 |
| 56 C 6 | Broadway the Dgnhm |
| 57 Y 13 | Broadway the Hornch |
| 22 D 3 | Broadway the Pinn |
| 70 C 1 | Broadway the S'hall |
| 11 S 15 | Broadway the Stanm |
| 153 S 14 | Broadway the Sutton |
| 21W 18 | Broadway the Wdfd Grn |
| 140 C 7 | Broadwick st W1 |
| 64 C 13 | Brock pl E3 |
| 65 U 13 | Brock rd E13 |
| 54 J 16 | Brockdish av Bark |
| 123 Z 18 | Brockenhurst Croy |
| 118 B 18 | Brockenhurst Worc Pk |
| 13 P 17 | Brockenhurst gdns NW7 |
| 54 B 14 | Brockenhurst gdns Ilf |
| 121 Y 3 | Brockenhurst way SW16 |
| 105 V 13 | Brockham clo SW19 |
| 90 C 18 | Brockham dri SW2 |
| 36 A 17 | Brockham dri Ilf |
| 10 H 18 | Brockhurst clo Stanm |
| 92 H 10 | Brockill cres SE14 |
| 88 C 19 | Brocklebank rd SW18 |
| 75 T 19 | Brocklehurst st SE14 |
| 123 Z 10 | Brocklesby rd SE25 |
| 11 X 11 | Brockley av Stanm |
| 11 X 11 | Brockley Av north Stanm |
| 11 X 14 | Brockley clo Stanm |
| 38 K 3 | Brockley cres Rom |
| 92 C 9 | Brockley footpath SE15 |
| 92 L 4 | Brockley gdns SE4 |
| 93 N 12 | Brockley gros SE4 |
| 92 K 14 | Brockley gros SE4 |
| 92 K 14 | Brockley Hall rd SE4 |
| 11 U 9 | Brockley hill Edg |
| 92 J 20 | Brockley pk SE23 |
| 92 J 8 | Brockley rd SE4 |
| 110 H 1 | Brockley rd SE4 |
| 92 J 16 | Brockley ri SE23 |
| 110 H 1 | Brockley ri SE23 |
| 11W 13 | Brockley side Stanm |
| 150 J 9 | Brockley ter SE17 |
| 92 K 18 | Brockley view SE23 |
| 92 G 13 | Brockley way SE4 |
| 11W 9 | Brockman ri Brom |
| 153 S 4 | Brocks dri Sutton |
| 90 H 18 | Brockwell park SE24 |
| 90 H 20 | Brockwell Pk gdns SE24 |
| 80 D 11 | Broderick gro SE2 |
| 49 T 8 | Brodia rd N16 |
| 20 H 7 | Brodie rd E4 |
| 8 A 4 | Brodie rd Enf |
| 151 P 10 | Brodie st SE1 |
| 63 S 19 | Brodlove la E1 |
| 106 K 3 | Brodrick rd SW17 |
| 106 K 3 | Brograve gdns Becknhm |
| 31 Y 11 | Brograve rd N17 |
| 135 R 4 | Broke rd E8 |
| 142 A 9 | Broken wharf EC4 |
| 63 Y 10 | Brokesley st E3 |
| 95 U 3 | Brome rd SE9 |
| 24 E 5 | Bromefield Stanm |
| 89 V 10 | Bromells rd SW4 |
| 89 V 10 | Bromells rd SW4 |
| 91 T 7 | Bromer rd SE5 |
| 89 Y 6 | Bromfelde rd SW4 |
| 133 U 7 | Bromfield st N1 |
| 55 P 18 | Bromhall rd Dgnhm |
| 113 U 7 | Bromhedge SE9 |
| 80 B 9 | Bromholm rd SE2 |
| 112 A 19 | Bromley av Brom |
| 126 L 11 | Bromley comm Brom |
| 127 P 16 | Bromley comm Brom |
| 126 C 5 | Bromley cres Brom |
| 126 C 5 | Bromley gdns Brom |
| 125 X 5 | Bromley gro Brom |
| 64 G 14 | Bromley Hall rd E14 |
| 64 D 8 | Bromley High st E13 |
| 111 Z 15 | Bromley hill Brom |
| 112 A 16 | Bromley hill Brom |
| 114 E 18 | Bromley la Chisl |
| 132 A 19 | Bromley pl W1 |
| 33 S 20 | Bromley rd E10 |
| 33 O 9 | Bromley rd E17 |
| 31W 3 | Bromley rd N17 |
| 18 B 12 | Bromley rd N18 |
| 111 T 8 | Bromley rd SE6 |
| 125 V 2 | Bromley rd Becknhm |

5 R 18 Buxton st E1
8 C 5 Byam st SW6
1 X 1 Byards croft SW16
8 H 13 Bycroft rd S'hall
0 E 17 Bycroft st SE20
7 X 9 Bycullah av Enf
7 V 9 Bycullah rd Enf
2 B 16 Bye the W3
3 U 5 Bye Way the Harrow
0 K 5 Bye ways Twick
6 G 16 Byegrove rd SW19
5 V 8 Byegrove the SW14
7 R 12 Byeways the Surb
6 G 3 Byfeld gdns SW13
3 Y 8 Byfield rd Islwth
9 R 15 Bygrove Croy
4 C 18 Bygrove st E14
7 O 1 Byland clo N21
4 H 3 Byne rd SE26
4 H 3 Byne rd Carsh
7 O 17 Bynes rd S Croy
2 F 18 Byng pl WC1
4 C 11 Byng rd Barnt
5 B 5 Byng st E14
8 A 8 Bynon av Bxly Hth
7 T 2 Byrne rd SW12
3 F 19 Byron av E12
4 B 9 Byron av E18
5 T 11 Byron av NW9
8 G 10 Byron av New Mald
4 G 9 Byron av Sutton
4 G 9 Byron Av east Sutton
0 J 11 Byron rd SE26
7 X 9 Byron ct Enf
8 B 18 Byron dri N2
4 G 7 Byron gdns Sutton
1 R 5 Byron Hill rd Harrow
3 R 3 Byron rd E10
3 P 11 Byron rd E17
4 J 8 Byron rd NW2
3 T 16 Byron rd NW7
2 O 1 Byron rd W5
3 T 18 Byron rd Harrow
3 W 10 Byron rd Harrow
2 E 9 Byron rd Wemb
4 F 16 Byron st E14
9 O 1 Byron terr N9
8 B 9 Byron way Grnfd
5 Z 5 Bysouth clo Ilf
6 M 14 Byton rd SW17
2 L 10 Byward st EC3
7 N 9 Bywater st SW3
2 E 9 Byway the Epsom
4 F 18 Byway the Sutton
4 F 18 Byway the Sutton
0 A 3 Bywell pl W1
4 D 14 Bywood av Croy

# C

38 K 2 Cabbell st NW1
83 N 19 Cable st E1
43 X 8 Cable st E1
88 J 5 Cabul rd SW11
62 D 18 Cactus wlk W12
45 S 10 Caddington rd NW2
93 W 2 Cade rd SE10
76 L 12 Cadeb pl SE10
88 C 17 Cader rd SW18
56 L 19 Cadiz rd Dgnhm
56 C 11 Cadiz st SE17
10 C 3 Cadley ter SE23
89 Y 9 Cadmus clo SW4
54 A 14 Cadogan ct Sutton
47 P 5 Cadogan ga SW3
34 J 10 Cadogan gdns E18
7 S 18 Cadogan gdns N21
28 A 5 Cadogan gdns N3
47 P 5 Cadogan gdns SW3
47 S 3 Cadogan la SW1
47 S 3 Cadogan la SW1
47 R 2 Cadogan la SW1
47 R 1 Cadogan pl SW1
16 G 12 Cadogan rd Surb
47 O 4 Cadogan sq SW1
47 N 7 Cadogan st SW3
50 K 18 Cadogan ter E9
31 V 18 Cadoxton av N15
14 A 4 Cadwallon rd SE9
48 E 12 Caedmon rd N7
80 C 10 Caerleon ter SE2
35 W 4 Caernarvon dri Ilf
134 M 11 Caesar st E2
104 F 13 Caesars camp SW19
120 M 10 Caesars wlk Mitch
121 N 10 Caesars wlk Mitch
76 C 11 Cahir st E14
72 G 4 Cairn av W5
129 N 15 Cairn st W10

10 J 19 Cairn way Stanm
44 C 11 Cairnfield av NW2
88 K 12 Cairns rd SW11
33 O 12 Cairo rd E17
156 K 3 Cairo rd Croy
65 P 3 Caistor Park rd E15
65 P 4 Caistor pk E15
89 R 19 Caistor rd SW12
96 J 17 Caithness gdns Sidcp
144 G 3 Caithness rd W14
107 S 18 Caithness rd Mitch
48 K 17 Calabria rd N5
90 J 1 Calais st SE5
57 Z 14 Calbourne av Hornch
89 N 19 Calbourne rd SW12
113 O 10 Calcott wlk SE9
118 J 19 Caldbeck av Worc Pk
91 N 4 Caldecot rd SE5
10 E 1 Caldecote gdns Bushey Watf
10 G 1 Caldecote la Bushey Watf
59 V 6 Calder av Grnfd
8 C 12 Calder clo Enf
25 O 9 Calder gdns Edg
120 C 11 Calder rd Mrdn
62 M 15 Calderon pl W10
136 C 3 Calderon pl W10
51 V 11 Calderon rd E11
89 X 13 Caldervale rd SW4
78 K 10 Calderwood st SE18
150 E 16 Caldew st SE5
149 P 20 Caldwell st SW9
142 A 9 Caldy rd Blvdr
81 U 7 Caldy rd Blvdr
146 L 8 Cale st SW3
66 F 2 Caledon rd E6
155 P 7 Caledon rd Wallgtn
132 L 10 Caledonia st N1
132 M 9 Caledonian rd N1
123 N 4 Caledonian rd N1
48 C 15 Caledonian rd N7
77 O 13 Caletock st SE10
155 Z 18 Caley clo Wallgtn
10 C 7 California la Bushey Watf
117 U 7 California rd New Mald
111 S 5 Callander rd SE6
17 W 15 Callard av N13
129 O 1 Callcott rd NW6
137 T 13 Callcott st W8
32 I 18 Callis rd F17
146 E 13 Callow st SW3
150 K 13 Calmington rd SE5
111 Y 16 Calmont rd Brom
35 Y 4 Calne av Ilf
105 P 9 Colonne rd SW19
133 O 10 Calshot st N1
115 Y 16 Calt clo Sidcp
11 Y 16 Calthorpe gdns Edg
154 C 4 Calthorpe gdns Sutton
133 P 18 Calthorpe st WC1
91 S 14 Calton av SE21
5 S 19 Calton rd Barnt
56 D 7 Calverley cres Dgnhm
42 G 1 Calverley gdns Harrow
47 Y 4 Calverley gro N19
152 F 14 Calverley rd Epsom
134 M 14 Calvert av E2
81 T 12 Calvert clo Blvdr
77 O 14 Calvert rd SE 10
4 D 10 Calvert rd Barnt
131 T 3 Calvert st NW1
66 J 3 Calverton rd E6
142 D 15 Calverts bldgs SE1
135 N 18 Calvin st E1
77 W 14 Calydon rd SE7
101 R 2 Camac rd Twick
87 P 13 Cambalt rd SW15
32 M 12 Cambell rd E17
118 J 3 Camberley av SW20
8 D 14 Camberley av Enf
91 O 2 Camberwell Church st SE5
91 P 2 Camberwell glebe SE5
91 N 1 Camberwell grn SE5
92 O 2 Camberwell gro SE5
149 W 18 Camberwell New rd SE5
91 N 2 Camberwell pas SE5
150 C 17 Camberwell rd SE5
90 L 2 Camberwell Stn rd SE5
56 K 16 Cambeys rd Dgnhm
87 Y 19 Camborne av SW18
123 W 18 Camborne rd Croy
119 P 12 Camborne rd Mrdn

115 T 8 Camborne rd Sidcp
153 Z 17 Camborne rd Sutton
154 A 16 Camborne rd Sutton
96 J 4 Camborne rd Welling
82 G 1 Camborne way Hounsl
19 S 4 Cambourne av N9
72 C 5 Cambourne av W13
89 W 20 Cambray rd SW12
82 H 11 Cambria clo Hounsl
96 F 20 Cambria clo Sidcp
114 F 1 Cambria clo Sidcp
90 L 7 Cambria rd SE5
145 Z 20 Cambria st SW6
36 H 15 Cambrian av Ilf
108 H 6 Cambrian clo SE27
51 N 2 Cambrian rd E10
84 M 17 Cambrian rd Rich
129 V 7 Cambridge av NW6
41 V 9 Cambridge av Grnfd
118 B 4 Cambridge av New Mald
96 K 10 Cambridge av Welling
140 G 7 Cambridge cir WC2
104 J 20 Cambridge cl SW20
104 J 20 Cambridge clo SW20
82 C 10 Cambridge clo Hounsl
73 O 17 Cambridge cotts Rich
63 N 7 Cambridge cres E2
135 W 9 Cambridge cres E2
101 X 11 Cambridge cres Tedd
94 E 13 Cambridge dri SE12
54 J 4 Cambridge dri Ilf
131 X 15 Cambridge ga NW1
131 Y 15 Cambridge Ga ms NW1
129 V 9 Cambridge gdns NW6
31 N 1 Cambridge gdns N17
18 A 2 Cambridge gdns N21
136 K 4 Cambridge gdns W10
8 K 9 Cambridge gdns Enf
117 P 3 Cambridge gdns Kingst
95 Y 20 Cambridge grn SE9
109 Z 19 Cambridge gro SE20
144 A 7 Cambridge gro W6
74 K 10 Cambridge gro W6
117 P 5 Cambridge Gro rd Kingst
63 O 9 Cambridge Heath rd E2
135 Y 5 Cambridge Heath rd E8
63 N 3 Cambridge Ldge vlls E9
50 D 19 Cambridge pass E11
34 F 19 Cambridge pk E11
84 E 17 Cambridge pk Twick
130 U 11 Cambridge pl NW8
137 Z 19 Cambridge pl W8
34 D 20 Cambridge rd E11
20 K 5 Cambridge rd E4
129 U 12 Cambridge rd NW6
123 Z 5 Cambridge rd SE20
88 L 3 Cambridge rd SW11
86 D 6 Cambridge rd SW13
118 H 1 Cambridge rd SW20
104 L 20 Cambridge rd SW20
71 V 5 Cambridge rd W7
54 B 20 Cambridge rd Bark
112 F 18 Cambridge rd Brom
154 K 11 Cambridge rd Carsh
100 F 17 Cambridge rd Hampt
22 J 18 Cambridge rd Harrow
82 C 9 Cambridge rd Hounsl
54 J 2 Cambridge rd Ilf
117 R 5 Cambridge rd Kingst
121 U 6 Cambridge rd Mitch
117 Z 8 Cambridge rd New Mald
118 B 8 Cambridge rd New Mald
73 O 19 Cambridge rd Rich
70 E 3 Cambridge rd S'hall
114 H 10 Cambridge rd Sidcp
101 X 11 Cambridge rd Tedd
84 G 15 Cambridge rd Twick
73 S 13 Cambridge Rd north W4
73 S 14 Cambridge Rd south W4
79 N 14 Cambridge row SE18
138 K 5 Cambridge sq W2
147 Y 5 Cambridge st SW1
148 A 10 Cambridge st SW1
131 X 14 Cambridge ter NW1

65 T 13 Cambus rd E16
79 X 19 Camdale rd SE18
91 V 1 Camden av SE15
114 B 20 Camden clo Chisl
131 Z 1 Camden gdns NW1
153 Z 12 Camden gdns Sutton
122 J 4 Camden gdns Thntn Hth
91 W 1 Camden gro SE15
151 N 20 Camden gro SE15
113 Z 15 Camden gro Chisl
131 Y 2 Camden High st NW1
132 A 6 Camden High st NW1
109 T 15 Camden Hill rd SE19
63 V 17 Camden Hurst st E14
47 Z 16 Camden la N7
47 X 18 Camden ms NW1
113 X 17 Camden park Chisl
133 V 8 Camden pas N1
47 Y 18 Camden Pk rd NW1
113 Y 20 Camden Pk rd Chisl
113 Y 19 Camden place Chisl
34 H 18 Camden rd E11
32 K 18 Camden rd E17
132 A 2 Camden rd NW1
47 X 18 Camden rd N7
48 A 14 Camden rd N7
98 A 20 Camden rd Bxly
154 L 7 Camden rd Carsh
153 Z 11 Camden rd Sutton
94 A 5 Camden row SE3
47 X 19 Camden sq NW1
131 Z 1 Camden st NW1
132 A 2 Camden st NW1
113 V 18 Camden way Chisl
122 J 5 Camden way Thntn Hth
133 W 6 Camden wlk N1
113 V 17 Camden wood Chisl
79 B 2 Camel rd E16
136 K 6 Camelford rd W11
82 J 18 Camellia pl Twick
151 V 16 Camelot SE15
146 E 14 Camera pl SW10
15 U 8 Cameron clo N12
15 V 8 Cameron clo N20
143 Y 4 Cameron pl E1
110 M 5 Cameron rd SE6
126 E 11 Cameron rd Brom
122 J 15 Cameron rd Croy
54 H 4 Cameron Rd south Ilf
66 I 19 Cameron st F6
151 V 6 Camilla rd SE16
112 D 9 Camlan rd Brom
135 N 16 Camlet st E2
4 L 8 Camlet way Barnt
5 R 5 Camlet way Barnt
132 E 5 Camley st NW1
142 K 4 Camomile st EC3
104 L 13 Camp rd SW19
104 L 12 Camp view SW19
87 Y 2 Campana rd SW6
36 B 14 Campbell av Ilf
101 O 3 Campbell clo Twick
12 C 15 Campbell croft Edg
12 C 15 Campbell croft Edg
83 A 12 Campbell rd E15
64 B 9 Campbell rd E3
60 D 4 Campbell rd E6
31 W 4 Campbell rd N17
71 T 1 Campbell rd W7
122 H 15 Campbell rd Croy
101 P 3 Campbell rd Twick
130 E 19 Campbell st W2
47 W 10 Campdale rd N7
55 I 10 Campden cres Dgnhm
42 B 8 Campden cres Wemb
137 V 16 Campden gro W8
137 S 10 Campden hill W8
137 S 14 Campden Hill gdns W8
137 R 13 Campden Hill pl W8
137 T 15 Campden Hill rd W8
137 R 14 Campden Hill sq W8
137 V 16 Campden Ho clo W8
137 T 11 Campden rd S Croy
137 U 14 Campden st W8
143 O 6 Camperdown st E1
94 M 18 Campfield rd SE9
95 N 18 Campfield rd SE9
142 E 10 Campion la EC4
86 L 12 Campion rd SW15
83 W 1 Campion rd Islwth
45 P 10 Campion ter NW2
24 J 14 Camplin rd Harrow
75 T 19 Camplin st SE14
30 B 12 Campsbourne rd N8
30 A 11 Campsbourne rd N8
30 A 12 Campsbourne the N8

| Ref | Street |
|---|---|
| 4 J 8 | Carthew rd W6 |
| 4 K 8 | Carthew vlls W6 |
| 3 Z 20 | Carthusian st EC1 |
| 0 M 10 | Carting la WC2 |
| 8 D 1 | Cartmel rd Bxly Hth |
| 9 R 4 | Carton st W1 |
| 2 H 14 | Cartwright gdns WC1 |
| 6 A 19 | Cartwright rd Dgnhm |
| 9 N 1 | Cartwright rd Dgnhm |
| 9 P 10 | Cartwright st E1 |
| 0 L 15 | Carver rd SE24 |
| 2 J 12 | Carville cres Brentf |
| 2 B 10 | Cary rd E11 |
| 9 O 11 | Carysfort rd N16 |
| 9 Y 15 | Carysfort rd N8 |
| 9 U 12 | Cascade av N10 |
| 5 T 20 | Casella rd SE19 |
| 8 H 10 | Casewick rd SE27 |
| 0 B 7 | Casimir rd E5 |
| 1 O 12 | Casino av SE24 |
| 5 N 13 | Casket st E2 |
| 5 Y 17 | Caslon pl E1 |
| 1 Z 1 | Casselden rd NW10 |
| 0 A 12 | Cassilda rd SE2 |
| 4 C 14 | Cassilis rd Twick |
| 2 G 17 | Cassiobury rd E17 |
| 0 H 19 | Cassland rd E9 |
| 3 N 9 | Cassland rd Thntn Hth |
| 2 L 19 | Cassles rd SE6 |
| 3 S 1 | Casson st E1 |
| 6 G 7 | Castalia st E14 |
| 9 Z 10 | Castella av Rom |
| 9 X 15 | Castellain rd W9 |
| 0 A 18 | Castellain rd W9 |
| 9 Z 10 | Castellan av Rom |
| 6 M 13 | Castelnau SW15 |
| 4 H 18 | Castelnau SW13 |
| 4 H 7 | Castelnau SW13 |
| 4 F 8 | Casterbridge rd SE3 |
| 7 J 10 | Castile rd SE18 |
| 1 Z 5 | Castillon rd SE6 |
| 2 A 4 | Castillon rd SE6 |
| 0 L 5 | Castlands rd SE6 |
| 0 K 17 | Castle av E4 |
| 2 H 20 | Castle av Epsom |
| 5 S 17 | Castle clo N12 |
| 5 S 17 | Castle clo N12 |
| 05 O 5 | Castle clo SW19 |
| 2 G 7 | Castle ct EC3 |
| 5 R 18 | Castle dri Ilf |
| 8 B 3 | Castle gdns Dgnhm |
| 9 U 18 | Castle Hill av Croy |
| 8 B 1 | Castle la SW1 |
| 7 T 19 | Castle rd NW1 |
| 5 S 17 | Castle rd N12 |
| 8 C 4 | Castle rd Dgnhm |
| 9 V 4 | Castle rd Islwth |
| 0 J 19 | Castle rd Grnfd |
| 3 V 4 | Castle rd Islwth |
| 6 A 6 | Castle st E6 |
| 5 Z 6 | Castle st E6 |
| 6 J 2 | Castle st Kingst |
| 05 O 5 | Castle way SW19 |
| 7 P 1 | Castle yd N6 |
| 1 Y 12 | Castle yd SE1 |
| 0 C 15 | Castlebar hill W5 |
| 0 C 13 | Castlebar ms W5 |
| 0 E 15 | Castlebar pk W5 |
| 0 E 16 | Castlebar rd W5 |
| 7 R 19 | Castlecombe dri SW19 |
| 13 P 11 | Castlecombe rd SE9 |
| 9 Z 19 | Castledine rd SE20 |
| 95 Z 20 | Castleford av SE9 |
| 13 Z 1 | Castleford av SE9 |
| 04 M 9 | Castlegate Rich |
| 47 S 19 | Castlehaven rd NW1 |
| 31 X 1 | Castlehaven rd NW1 |
| 8 C 17 | Castleleigh ct Enf |
| 50 L 16 | Castlemaine av SE15 |
| 57 U 11 | Castlemaine S Croy |
| 52 K 19 | Castlemaine av Epsom |
| 52 K 19 | Castlemaine av Epsom |
| 139 N 3 | Castlereagh st W1 |
| 98 M 3 | Castleton av Bxly Hth |
| 99 N 4 | Castleton av Bxly Hth |
| 42 J 12 | Castleton av Wemb |
| 33 X 7 | Castleton rd E17 |
| 113 O 10 | Castleton rd SE9 |
| 55 O 4 | Castleton rd Ilf |
| 121 W 9 | Castleton rd Mitch |
| 144 M 11 | Castletown rd W14 |
| 145 N 10 | Castletown rd W14 |
| 35 S 18 | Castleview gdns Ilf |
| 95 V 4 | Castlewood dri SE9 |
| 49 W 1 | Castlewood rd E5 |
| 31 X 20 | Castlewood rd N16 |
| 5 V 12 | Castlewood rd Barnt |
| 64 A 19 | Castor st E14 |
| 135 V 5 | Cat & Mutton bndge E8 |
| 5 X 18 | Cat hill Barnt |
| 6 A 17 | Cat hill Barnt |
| 35 V 7 | Caterham av Ilf |
| 93 V 8 | Caterham rd SE13 |
| 150 G 7 | Catesby st SE17 |
| 93 P 19 | Catford bdwy SE6 |
| 111 N 1 | Catford hill SE 6 |
| 93 P 19 | Catford rd SE6 |
| 51 X 8 | Cathall rd E11 |
| 143 X 18 | Cathay st SE16 |
| 75 N 16 | Cathay st SE16 |
| 47 U 10 | Cathcart hill N19 |
| 146 A 13 | Cathcart rd SW10 |
| 47 S 16 | Cathcart st NW5 |
| 141 Z 5 | Cathedral pl EC4 |
| 142 E 13 | Cathedral st SE1 |
| 48 M 10 | Catherine ct N14 |
| 6 H 17 | Catherine ct N14 |
| 83 P 11 | Catherine gdns Hounsl |
| 93 R 1 | Catherine gro SE10 |
| 140 B 20 | Catherine pl SW1 |
| 39 Y 16 | Catherine rd Rom |
| 116 G 11 | Catherine rd Surb |
| 141 N 8 | Catherine rd WC2 |
| 140 B 15 | Catherine wheel SW1 |
| 142 K 2 | Catherine Wheel all E1 |
| 72 G 19 | Catherine Wheel yd Brentf |
| 89 T 17 | Cathles rd SW12 |
| 74 J 7 | Cathnor rd W12 |
| 9 V 1 | Catisfield rd Enf |
| 151 U 10 | Catlin st SE16 |
| 110 D 7 | Catling clo SE23 |
| 89 Y 9 | Cato rd SW4 |
| 138 M 3 | Cato st W1 |
| 108 A 6 | Caton pas SW16 |
| 124 M 2 | Cator la Becknhm |
| 110 J 19 | Cator park Becknhm |
| 110 F 15 | Cator rd SE26 |
| 155 N 11 | Cator rd Carsh |
| 151 O 17 | Cator st SE15 |
| 91 V 1 | Cator st SE15 |
| 151 O 17 | Cator st SE15 |
| 10 A 5 | Catsey woods Bushey Watf |
| 140 M 2 | Catton st WC1 |
| 113 S 11 | Cattistock rd SE9 |
| 66 E 2 | Caulfield rd E6 |
| 92 A 4 | Caulfield rd SE15 |
| 28 H 13 | Causeway the N2 |
| 87 Z 12 | Causeway the SW19 |
| 104 M 12 | Causeway the SW19 |
| 105 N 12 | Causeway the SW19 |
| 30 A 19 | Causeway the N8 |
| 155 O 4 | Causeway the Carsh |
| 154 B 19 | Causeway the Sutton |
| 101 W 14 | Causeway the Tedd |
| 19 O 3 | Causeyware rd N9 |
| 47 T 1 | Causton rd N6 |
| 148 G 8 | Causton st SW1 |
| 89 T 14 | Cautley av SW4 |
| 146 O 12 | Cavaye pl SW10 |
| 65 W 8 | Cave rd E13 |
| 31 O 2 | Cavell rd N17 |
| 63 N 16 | Cavell st E1 |
| 143 Y 4 | Cavell st E1 |
| 130 G 11 | Cavendish av NW8 |
| 27 X 3 | Cavendish av N3 |
| 59 Y 16 | Cavendish av W13 |
| 81 W 17 | Cavendish av Erith |
| 41 T 13 | Cavendish av Harrow |
| 57 Y 18 | Cavendish av Hornch |
| 118 H 10 | Cavendish av New Mald |
| 97 N 12 | Cavendish av Sidcp |
| 34 G 3 | Cavendish av Wdfd Grn |
| 96 M 8 | Cavendish av Welling |
| 130 G 12 | Cavendish clo NW8 |
| 57 Y 18 | Cavendish cres Hornchurch |
| 142 K 3 | Cavendish ct EC2 |
| 51 V 3 | Cavendish dri E11 |
| 12 A 19 | Cavendish dri Edg |
| 54 L 15 | Cavendish gdns Bark |
| 53 W 3 | Cavendish gdns Ilf |
| 37 Z 17 | Cavendish gdns Rom |
| 139 Y 1 | Cavendish ms N1 |
| 139 Y 3 | Cavendish pl W1 |
| 20 H 20 | Cavendish rd E4 |
| 45 U 19 | Cavendish rd NW6 |
| 19 N 16 | Cavendish rd N18 |
| 30 H 18 | Cavendish rd N4 |
| 89 T 16 | Cavendish rd SW12 |
| 106 J 17 | Cavendish rd SW19 |
| 107 T 1 | Cavendish rd SW19 |
| 85 W 1 | Cavendish rd W4 |
| 4 A 12 | Cavendish rd Croy |
| 122 J 19 | Cavendish rd Croy |
| 118 C 10 | Cavendish rd New Mald |
| 154 C 15 | Cavendish rd Sutton |
| 139 Y 4 | Cavendish sq W1 |
| 134 E 9 | Cavendish st N1 |
| 125 P 20 | Cavendish way W Wkhm |
| 54 E 10 | Cavenham gdns Ilf |
| 118 H 18 | Caverleigh way Worc Pk |
| 17 T 10 | Caversham av N13 |
| 153 R 2 | Caversham av Sutton |
| 47 U 17 | Caversham rd NW5 |
| 30 L 13 | Caversham rd N15 |
| 147 N 13 | Caversham st SW3 |
| 136 B 4 | Caverswall st W10 |
| 62 L 16 | Caverswall st W12 |
| 127 W 1 | Caveside clo Chisl |
| 71 Z 10 | Cawdor cres W7 |
| 63 U 2 | Cawley rd E9 |
| 109 T 14 | Cawnpore st SE19 |
| 64 A 7 | Caxton gro E3 |
| 30 D 7 | Caxton rd N22 |
| 106 C 13 | Caxton rd SW19 |
| 136 E 16 | Caxton rd W12 |
| 65 P 19 | Caxton st E16 |
| 148 D 1 | Caxton st SW1 |
| 77 R 1 | Caxton St south E16 |
| 59 U 7 | Cayton rd Grnfd |
| 134 D 14 | Cayton st EC1 |
| 33 O 6 | Cazenove rd E17 |
| 49 Y 5 | Cazenove rd N16 |
| 54 D 20 | Cecil av Bark |
| 8 G 14 | Cecil av Enf |
| 42 M 16 | Cecil av Wemb |
| 140 H 10 | Cecil ct WC2 |
| 22 D 13 | Cecil pk Pinn |
| 121 N 11 | Cecil pl Mitch |
| 52 A 7 | Cecil rd F11 |
| 65 T 4 | Cecil rd E13 |
| 33 O 3 | Cecil rd E17 |
| 62 A 4 | Cecil rd NW10 |
| 25 Z 11 | Cecil rd NW9 |
| 29 T 7 | Cecil rd N10 |
| 16 F 5 | Cecil rd N14 |
| 106 A 18 | Cecil rd SW19 |
| 61 W 5 | Cecil rd W3 |
| 122 C 16 | Cecil rd Croy |
| 7 Z 13 | Cecil rd Enf |
| 8 B 14 | Cecil rd Enf |
| 23 S 10 | Cecil rd Harrow |
| 83 N 6 | Cecil rd Hounsl |
| 53 Y 12 | Cecil rd Ilf |
| 55 X 1 | Cecil rd Rom |
| 153 V 14 | Cecil rd Sutton |
| 126 E 19 | Cecil way Brom |
| 30 A 19 | Cecile pk N8 |
| 49 W 15 | Cecilia rd E8 |
| 15 W 1 | Cedar av Bark |
| 9 P 8 | Cedar av Enf |
| 37 Y 15 | Cedar av Rom |
| 96 M 17 | Cedar av Sidcp |
| 82 M 15 | Cedar av Twick |
| 38 L 12 | Cedar clo Rom |
| 127 T 3 | Cedar copse Brom |
| 105 P 8 | Cedar ct SW19 |
| 28 H 13 | Cedar dri N2 |
| 154 D 14 | Cedar gdns Sutton |
| 72 J 7 | Cedar gro W5 |
| 97 Y 16 | Cedar gro Bxly |
| 58 H 14 | Cedar gro S'hall |
| 102 J 1 | Cedar heights Rich |
| 4 F 7 | Cedar Lawn av Barnt |
| 55 V 1 | Cedar Park gdns Rom |
| 8 A 3 | Cedar Park rd Enf |
| 45 N 12 | Cedar rd NW2 |
| 31 V 4 | Cedar rd N17 |
| 126 L 3 | Cedar rd Brom |
| 157 R 2 | Cedar rd Croy |
| 7 X 4 | Cedar rd Enf |
| 99 W 2 | Cedar rd Erith |
| 38 K 14 | Cedar rd Rom |
| 154 C 14 | Cedar rd Sutton |
| 13 Y 13 | Cedar rd Tedd |
| 16 C 2 | Cedar ri N14 |
| 84 L 10 | Cedar ter Rich |
| 108 J 12 | Cedar Tree gro SE27 |
| 74 C 1 | Cedar way W3 |
| 94 K 14 | Cedarhurst dri SE9 |
| 145 W 19 | Cedarne rd SW6 |
| 33 O 15 | Cedars av E17 |
| 27 O 10 | Cedars clo NW4 |
| 18 E 7 | Cedars ms N9 |
| 89 R 10 | Cedars ms SW4 |
| 52 A 18 | Cedars rd E15 |
| 17 W 7 | Cedars rd N21 |
| 18 J 9 | Cedars rd N9 |
| 86 F 5 | Cedars rd SW13 |
| 89 S 10 | Cedars rd SW4 |
| 73 V 15 | Cedars rd W4 |
| 124 L 3 | Cedars rd Becknhm |
| 156 B 7 | Cedars rd Croy |
| 102 D 20 | Cedars rd Kingst |
| 119 Y 8 | Cedars rd Mrdn |
| 21 T 6 | Cedars the Buck Hl |
| 101 X 15 | Cedars the Tedd |
| 108 D 16 | Cedarville gdns SW16 |
| 39 R 10 | Cedric av Rom |
| 114 B 6 | Cedric rd SE9 |
| 137 Y 3 | Celbridge ms W2 |
| 47 V 12 | Celia rd N19 |
| 125 Z 7 | Celtic av Brom |
| 126 A 7 | Celtic av Brom |
| 64 F 13 | Celtic st E14 |
| 78 D 17 | Cemetery la SE7 |
| 52 D 13 | Cemetery rd E7 |
| 31 T 3 | Cemetery rd N17 |
| 80 C 19 | Cemetery rd SE2 |
| 149 R 1 | Centaur st SE1 |
| 51 X 7 | Central av E11 |
| 28 F 8 | Central av N2 |
| 18 F 10 | Central av N9 |
| 8 M 8 | Central av Enf |
| 9 N 8 | Central av Enf |
| 83 O 12 | Central av Hounsl |
| 22 D 19 | Central av Pinn |
| 156 B 11 | Central av Wallgtn |
| 96 M 4 | Central av Welling |
| 109 P 14 | Central hill SE19 |
| 141 W 2 | Central mkt EC1 |
| 56 L 7 | Central park av Dgnhm |
| 58 H 10 | Central Park av Dgnhm |
| 59 Y 8 | Central pde Grnfd |
| 66 F 6 | Central Pk rd E6 |
| 65 Z 7 | Central Pk rd E6 |
| 120 B 10 | Central rd Mrdn |
| 42 B 15 | Central rd Wemb |
| 152 H 2 | Central rd Worc Pk |
| 85 V 7 | Central School path SW14 |
| 27 Z 17 | Central sq NW11 |
| 133 Z 12 | Central st EC1 |
| 134 A 16 | Central st EC1 |
| 154 J 16 | Central way Carsh |
| 73 Y 3 | Centre av W3 |
| 114 B 17 | Centre Common rd Chisl |
| 52 F 6 | Centre rd E11 |
| 78 H 13 | Centre rd E18 |
| 69 V 5 | Centre rd Dgnhm |
| 63 N 7 | Centre st E2 |
| 35 W 9 | Centre st E2 |
| 19 S 8 | Centre way N9 |
| 32 H 11 | Century av E17 |
| 63 R 12 | Cephas av E1 |
| 63 O 12 | Cephas st E1 |
| 135 Z 17 | Cephas st E1 |
| 79 X 12 | Cerise rd SE15 |
| 91 X 3 | Cerise rd SE15 |
| 120 C 14 | Centre rd Mrdn |
| 144 J 2 | Ceylon rd W14 |
| 148 B 18 | Ceylon st SW8 |
| 63 X 5 | Chad st E3 |
| 35 U 9 | Chadacre av Ilf |
| 152 J 12 | Chadacre rd Epsom |
| 64 E 15 | Chadbourn st E14 |
| 127 S 7 | Chadd dri Brom |
| 37 V 16 | Chadville gdns Rom |
| 55 U 5 | Chadway Dgnhm |
| 55 R 1 | Chadwell av Rom |
| 37 S 17 | Chadwell Heath la Rom |
| 133 U 11 | Chadwell st EC1 |
| 20 L 12 | Chadwick av E4 |
| 34 A 20 | Chadwick av E11 |
| 81 U 5 | Chadwick av SE18 |
| 148 F 3 | Chadwick st SW1 |
| 65 V 14 | Chadwin rd E13 |
| 124 F 13 | Chaffinch av Croy |
| 124 F 13 | Chaffinch clo Croy |
| 124 K 1 | Chaffinch rd Becknhm |
| 37 S 14 | Chaford way Rom |
| 131 P 18 | Chagford st NW1 |
| 8 F 8 | Chailey av Enf |
| 55 C 10 | Chailey st E5 |
| 80 D 8 | Chalcombe rd SE2 |
| 131 R 3 | Chalcot cres NW1 |
| 131 S 2 | Chalcot rd NW1 |
| 131 T 1 | Chalcot sq NW1 |
| 46 L 18 | Chalcote gdns NW3 |
| 93 Z 13 | Chalcroft rd SE13 |
| 144 L 17 | Chaldon rd SW6 |
| 90 A 17 | Chale rd SW2 |
| 43 T 18 | Chalfont av Wemb |
| 26 C 11 | Chalfont ct NW 9 |
| 18 F 10 | Chalfont grn N9 |
| 48 E 17 | Chalfont rd N7 |
| 18 F 11 | Chalfont rd N9 |

| | |
|---|---|
| 123 V 6 | Chalfont rd SE25 |
| 72 A 9 | Chalfont way W13 |
| 109 P 8 | Chalford rd SE21 |
| 35 N 3 | Chalford wlk Wdfd Grn |
| 119 Y 12 | Chalgrove av Mrdn |
| 35 P 7 | Chalgrove cres Ilf |
| 27 T 10 | Chalgrove gdns N3 |
| 50 B 17 | Chalgrove rd E9 |
| 31 Z 4 | Chalgrove rd N17 |
| 154 F 17 | Chalgrove rd Sutton |
| 47 O 20 | Chalk Farm rd NW1 |
| 5 Z 12 | Chalk la Barnt |
| 6 A 13 | Chalk la Barnt |
| 65 W 14 | Chalk rd E13 |
| 43 R 9 | Chalkhill rd Wemb |
| 43 V 9 | Chalklands Wemb |
| 8 C 15 | Chalkwell Pk av Enf |
| 90 D 20 | Challice way SW2 |
| 110 B 19 | Challin st SE20 |
| 72 G 13 | Challis rd Brentf |
| 28 F 8 | Challoner clo N2 |
| 145 O 11 | Challoner cres W14 |
| 145 O 11 | Challoner st W14 |
| 89 U 4 | Chalmers st SW8 |
| 49 T 10 | Chalmers ter N16 |
| 92 M 10 | Chalsey rd SE4 |
| 28 F 18 | Chalton dri N2 |
| 132 D 8 | Chalton st NW1 |
| 143 P 8 | Chamber st E1 |
| 125 P 19 | Chamberlain cres W Wkhm |
| 28 D 8 | Chamberlain rd N2 |
| 131 P 1 | Chamberlain st NW1 |
| 116 K 19 | Chamberlain way Surb |
| 62 M 2 | Chamberlayne rd NW10 |
| 128 D 7 | Chamberlayne rd NW10 |
| 28 F 5 | Chambers gdns N2 |
| 44 L 20 | Chambers la NW10 |
| 128 B 1 | Chambers la NW10 |
| 62 L 1 | Chambers la NW10 |
| 48 A 11 | Chambers rd N7 |
| 143 T 18 | Chambers st SE16 |
| 135 O 13 | Chambord st E2 |
| 110 H 9 | Champion cres SE26 |
| 91 P 6 | Champion gro SE5 |
| 91 O 7 | Champion hill SE5 |
| 91 R 8 | Champion hill SE5 |
| 110 J 9 | Champion rd SE26 |
| 153 T 7 | Champneys clo Sutton |
| 141 X 14 | Chancel st SE1 |
| 109 N 6 | Chancellor gro SE21 |
| 108 M 5 | Chancellor gro SE24 |
| 74 M 15 | Chancellors rd W6 |
| 144 D 11 | Chancellors rd W6 |
| 74 M 14 | Chancellors rd W6 |
| 144 C 10 | Chancellors rd W6 |
| 80 E 11 | Chancelot rd SE2 |
| 141 R 3 | Chancery la WC2 |
| 125 S 3 | Chancery la Becknhm |
| 14 J 14 | Chanctonbury way N12 |
| 65 S 14 | Chandler av E16 |
| 75 N 2 | Chandler st E1 |
| 143 X 12 | Chandler st E1 |
| 33 P 8 | Chandos av E17 |
| 16 H 11 | Chandos av N14 |
| 15 S 5 | Chandos av N20 |
| 72 F 10 | Chandos av W5 |
| 21 V 8 | Chandos clo Buck Hl |
| 25 N 2 | Chandos cres Edg |
| 140 K 10 | Chandos pl WC2 |
| 51 W 14 | Chandos rd E15 |
| 62 A 11 | Chandos rd NW10 |
| 44 M 15 | Chandos rd NW2 |
| 31 S 8 | Chandos rd N17 |
| 28 H 8 | Chandos rd N2 |
| 23 O 16 | Chandos rd Harrow |
| 139 Y 3 | Chandos st W1 |
| 142 G 7 | Change all EC3 |
| 64 J 3 | Channelsea rd E15 |
| 64 K 1 | Chant st E15 |
| 90 D 8 | Chantrey rd SW9 |
| 7 Y 3 | Chantry clo Enf |
| 24 M 16 | Chantry clo Harrow |
| 115 Z 14 | Chantry clo Sidcp |
| 126 M 11 | Chantry la Brom |
| 127 N 11 | Chantry la Brom |
| 22 K 4 | Chantry pl Harrow |
| 22 K 4 | Chantry rd Harrow |
| 133 Y 6 | Chantry st N1 |
| 69 Z 5 | Chantry way Rainhm |
| 99 P 12 | Chapel clo Drtfrd |
| 28 H 10 | Chapel ct N2 |
| 142 E 17 | Chapel ct SE1 |
| 113 T 6 | Chapel Farm rd SE9 |
| 78 F 9 | Chapel hill SE18 |
| 99 P 12 | Chapel hill Drtfrd |

| | |
|---|---|
| 76 E 12 | Chapel Ho pl E14 |
| 76 E 12 | Chapel Ho st E14 |
| 22 A 11 | Chapel la Pinn |
| 55 W 1 | Chapel la Rom |
| 133 S 8 | Chapel mkt N1 |
| 133 T 8 | Chapel pl EC1 |
| 31 V 1 | Chapel pl N17 |
| 139 X 5 | Chapel pl W1 |
| 108 K 10 | Chapel rd SE27 |
| 72 B 2 | Chapel rd W13 |
| 98 E 10 | Chapel rd Bxly Hth |
| 82 M 9 | Chapel rd Hounsl |
| 120 F 5 | Chapel rd Mitch |
| 84 C 19 | Chapel rd Twick |
| 137 W 10 | Chapel side W2 |
| 64 K 1 | Chapel st E15 |
| 138 K 2 | Chapel st NW1 |
| 139 V 19 | Chapel st SW1 |
| 8 A 11 | Chapel st Enf |
| 158 B 15 | Chapel view S Croy |
| 126 F 4 | Chapel way Brom |
| 156 M 2 | Chapel wlk Croy |
| 44 N 18 | Chaplin rd NW2 |
| 31 U 10 | Chaplin rd N17 |
| 55 Z 20 | Chaplin rd Dgnhm |
| 68 M 1 | Chaplin rd Dgnhm |
| 42 H 18 | Chaplin rd Wemb |
| 24 L 17 | Chapman cres Harrow |
| 50 L 18 | Chapman rd E9 |
| 81 T 14 | Chapman rd Blvdr |
| 122 E 19 | Chapman rd Croy |
| 63 N 19 | Chapman st E1 |
| 143 X 8 | Chapman st E1 |
| 80 G 12 | Chapmans la SE2 |
| 44 E 17 | Chapmans pk NW10 |
| 44 F 16 | Chapter rd NW2 |
| 149 Y 12 | Chapter rd SE17 |
| 52 F 14 | Chapter st E7 |
| 148 E 7 | Chapter st SW1 |
| 149 X 13 | Chapter ter SE17 |
| 9 T 13 | Charcroft gdns Enf |
| 74 A 11 | Chardin rd W4 |
| 49 X 4 | Chardmore rd N16 |
| 65 T 15 | Charford rd E16 |
| 65 R 11 | Chargeable la E13 |
| 6 P 12 | Chargeable st E16 |
| 140 G 7 | Charing Cross rd WC2 |
| 130 K 9 | Charlbert st NW8 |
| 11 T 17 | Charlbury av Stanm |
| 54 L 7 | Charlbury gdns Ilf |
| 60 E 16 | Charlbury gro W5 |
| 113 Z 6 | Charldane rd SE9 |
| 110 A 6 | Charlecote gro SE26 |
| 55 Y 11 | Charlecoute rd Dgnhm |
| 66 H 10 | Charlemont rd E6 |
| 115 S 9 | Charles clo Sidcp |
| 41 P 2 | Charles cres Harrow |
| 78 J 10 | Charles Grinling wlk SE18 |
| 140 E 12 | Charles li st SW1 |
| 130 J 9 | Charles la NW8 |
| 65 Y 1 | Charles rd E7 |
| 56 M 19 | Charles rd Dgnhm |
| 37 V 19 | Charles rd Rom |
| 134 H 14 | Charles sq N1 |
| 77 Z 3 | Charles st E16 |
| 86 B 6 | Charles st SW13 |
| 139 W 12 | Charles st W1 |
| 156 L 5 | Charles st Croy |
| 8 G 17 | Charles st Enf |
| 112 M 7 | Charlesfield SE9 |
| 150 C 7 | Charleston st SE17 |
| 81 X 19 | Charlesville rd Erith |
| 48 B 20 | Charlesworth st N7 |
| 109 Y 12 | Charleville cir SE26 |
| 144 M 11 | Charleville rd W14 |
| 145 N 10 | Charleville rd W14 |
| 106 L 14 | Charlmont rd SW17 |
| 89 P 2 | Charlotte Despard av SW8 |
| 132 C 20 | Charlotte ms W1 |
| 134 K 14 | Charlotte rd EC2 |
| 86 D 2 | Charlotte rd SW13 |
| 56 G 18 | Charlotte rd Dgnhm |
| 155 V 14 | Charlotte rd Wallgtn |
| 89 U 7 | Charlotte row SW4 |
| 132 C 20 | Charlotte st W1 |
| 140 D 2 | Charlotte st W1 |
| 133 R 6 | Charlotte ter N1 |
| 81 R 16 | Charlton clo Blvdr |
| 67 X 6 | Charlton cres Bark |
| 78 A 20 | Charlton dene SE18 |
| 77 Z 19 | Charlton dene SE7 |
| 78 A 17 | Charlton house SE18 |
| 47 X 15 | Charlton Kings rd NW5 |
| 78 B 18 | Charlton park SE18 |
| 78 C 18 | Charlton Pk la SE7 |
| 78 B 16 | Charlton Pk rd SE7 |
| 133 W 7 | Charlton pl N1 |

| | |
|---|---|
| 62 C 3 | Charlton rd NW10 |
| 19 T 1 | Charlton rd N9 |
| 77 U 18 | Charlton rd SE 3 |
| 77 W 17 | Charlton rd SE7 |
| 24 J 11 | Charlton rd Harrow |
| 43 N 5 | Charlton rd Wemb |
| 93 Y 2 | Charlton way SE10 |
| 77 P 20 | Charlton way SE3 |
| 94 A 1 | Charlton way SE3 |
| 10 G 20 | Charlwood clo Harrow |
| 148 C 8 | Charlwood pl SW1 |
| 87 O 10 | Charlwood rd SW15 |
| 148 B 9 | Charlwood st SW1 |
| 97 S 2 | Charmaith rd Welling |
| 24 G 9 | Charmian av Stanm |
| 119 Z 4 | Charminster av SW19 |
| 113 O 10 | Charminster rd SE9 |
| 143 O 20 | Charminster rd Worc Pk |
| 49 Z 11 | Charnock rd E5 |
| 119 Z 3 | Charnwood av SW19 |
| 118 B 9 | Charnwood clo New Mald |
| 34 G 12 | Charnwood dri E18 |
| 123 P 10 | Charnwood rd SE25 |
| 49 Y 7 | Charnwood st E5 |
| 132 E 8 | Charrington st NW1 |
| 111 R 4 | Charsley rd SE6 |
| 126 A 2 | Chart clo Brom |
| 134 G 13 | Chart st N1 |
| 54 E 3 | Charter av Ilf |
| 82 A 10 | Charter cres Hounsl |
| 97 Y 18 | Charter dri Bxly |
| 117 T 5 | Charter rd Kingst |
| 20 M 18 | Charter Rd the Wdfd Grn |
| 21 P 18 | Charter Rd the Wdfd Grn |
| 117 T 4 | Charter sq Kingst |
| 16 J 1 | Charter way N14 |
| 27 V 11 | Charter way N3 |
| 42 C 14 | Charterhouse av Wemb |
| 133 Y 19 | Charterhouse sq EC1 |
| 133 Y 20 | Charterhouse sq EC1 |
| 141 W 1 | Charterhouse st EC1 |
| 129 R 5 | Charteris rd NW6 |
| 48 E 5 | Charteris rd N4 |
| 34 G 3 | Charteris rd Wdfd Grn |
| 21 W 19 | Charteris rd Wdfd Grn |
| 109 S 12 | Charters clo SE19 |
| 86 L 14 | Chartfield av SW15 |
| 87 P 14 | Chartfield av SW15 |
| 87 P 13 | Chartfield sq SW15 |
| 108 H 7 | Chartham gro SE27 |
| 123 Z 7 | Chartham rd SE25 |
| 44 B 10 | Chartley av NW2 |
| 10 J 19 | Chartley av Stanm |
| 77 Y 14 | Charton Ch la SE7 |
| 114 D 5 | Chartwell clo SE9 |
| 7 X 9 | Chase Creen av Enf |
| 38 J 2 | Chase Cross rd Rom |
| 7 X 11 | Chase Ct gdns Enf |
| 19 Z 16 | Chase gdns E4 |
| 83 S 17 | Chase gdns Twick |
| 7 Z 11 | Chase grn Enf |
| 7 Y 10 | Chase hill Enf |
| 36 D 15 | Chase la Ilf |
| 34 B 7 | Chase rd E18 |
| 61 Y 10 | Chase rd NW10 |
| 6 H 15 | Chase rd N14 |
| 16 K 2 | Chase rd N14 |
| 7 T 10 | Chase ridings Enf |
| 7 Z 11 | Chase side Enf |
| 119 S 2 | Chase Side av SW20 |
| 53 N 12 | Chase the E12 |
| 108 E 17 | Chase the SW16 |
| 119 T 1 | Chase the SW20 |
| 89 T 9 | Chase the SW4 |
| 126 H 5 | Chase the Brom |
| 98 G 7 | Chase the Bxly Hth |
| 25 S 5 | Chase the Edg |
| 57 T 9 | Chase the Hornch |
| 22 D 12 | Chase the Pinn |
| 39 O 11 | Chase the Rom |
| 37 Y 18 | Chase the Rom |
| 10 L 18 | Chase the Stanm |
| 156 B 11 | Chase the Wallgtn |
| 16 G 5 | Chase way N14 |
| 106 M 10 | Chasefield rd SW17 |
| 107 N 11 | Chasefield rd SW17 |
| 63 V 17 | Chaseley st E14 |
| 8 A 9 | Chaseside av Enf |
| 8 A 7 | Chaseside cres Enf |
| 7 O 18 | Chaseville Pk rd N21 |
| 7 V 7 | Chasewood av Enf |
| 99 X 17 | Chastillan rd Dart |
| 47 N 16 | Chaston st NW5 |
| 60 K 16 | Chatfield pl W5 |

| | |
|---|---|
| 88 E 8 | Chatfield rd SW11 |
| 122 J 19 | Chatfield rd Croy |
| 126 D 18 | Chatham av N1 |
| 134 E 11 | Chatham av N1 |
| 27 Z 16 | Chatham clo NW1 |
| 119 V 18 | Chatham clo Sutton |
| 50 C 17 | Chatham pl E9 |
| 32 H 11 | Chatham rd E17 |
| 34 C 7 | Chatham rd E18 |
| 88 L 15 | Chatham rd SW11 |
| 117 O 2 | Chatham rd Kingst |
| 150 F 5 | Chatham st SE17 |
| 26 L 8 | Chatsworth av NW |
| 119 T 2 | Chatsworth av SW |
| 112 G 11 | Chatsworth av Bro |
| 115 O 1 | Chatsworth av Sidc |
| 43 N 16 | Chatsworth av Wem |
| 26 L 8 | Chatsworth clo NW |
| 83 P 9 | Chatsworth cres Hounsl |
| 18 J 1 | Chatsworth dri Enf |
| 8 K 20 | Chatsworth dri Enf |
| 127 N 11 | Chatsworth gdns N |
| 23 P 19 | Chatsworth gdns Harrow |
| 118 D 11 | Chatsworth gdns New Mald |
| 101 X 9 | Chatsworth pl Tedd |
| 52 B 15 | Chatsworth rd E15 |
| 50 D 9 | Chatsworth rd E5 |
| 45 M 18 | Chatsworth rd NW2 |
| 73 W 17 | Chatsworth rd W4 |
| 60 M 12 | Chatsworth rd W5 |
| 157 O 7 | Chatsworth rd Croy |
| 153 R 9 | Chatsworth rd Sutto |
| 60 M 12 | Chatsworth ri W5 |
| 108 K 6 | Chatsworth way SE27 |
| 150 B 4 | Chatteris rd SE17 |
| 48 J 9 | Chatterton rd N4 |
| 127 N 11 | Chatterton rd Brom |
| 88 M 14 | Chatto rd SW11 |
| 89 N 13 | Chatto rd SW11 |
| 85 R 6 | Chaucer av Rich |
| 16 J 16 | Chaucer clo N11 |
| 35 U 17 | Chaucer gdns Ilf |
| 153 Y 6 | Chaucer gdns Sutto |
| 124 C 17 | Chaucer grn Croy |
| 34 F 18 | Chaucer rd E11 |
| 35 U 6 | Chaucer rd E7 |
| 52 G 18 | Chaucer rd E7 |
| 90 G 14 | Chaucer rd SE24 |
| 73 W 2 | Chaucer rd W3 |
| 39 Z 1 | Chaucer rd Rom |
| 115 U 3 | Chaucer rd Sidcp |
| 153 X 7 | Chaucer rd Sutton |
| 96 J 2 | Chaucer rd Welling |
| 18 J 10 | Chaundry clo SE9 |
| 95 T 16 | Chaundrve clo SE9 |
| 65 W 19 | Chauntler rd E16 |
| 152 L 4 | Cheam Comm rd Worc Pk |
| 153 P 14 | Cheam park Sutton |
| 153 R 13 | Cheam Pk way Sutton |
| 153 P 20 | Cheam rd Sutton |
| 142 B 6 | Cheapside EC2 |
| 18 C 12 | Cheddington rd N18 |
| 111 W 11 | Chelford rd Brom |
| 68 C 7 | Chelmer cres Bark |
| 50 E 9 | Chelmer rd E9 |
| 39 O 1 | Chelmsford av Rom |
| 53 S 1 | Chelmsford gdns Ilf |
| 51 Y 3 | Chelmsford rd E11 |
| 33 N 18 | Chelmsford rd E17 |
| 34 B 4 | Chelmsford rd E18 |
| 16 H 4 | Chelmsford rd N14 |
| 62 L 4 | Chelmsford sq NW10 |
| 128 B 5 | Chelmsford sq NW10 |
| 144 J 12 | Chelmsford st W6 |
| 147 W 13 | Chelsea br SW1 |
| 147 U 11 | Chelsea Br rd SW1 |
| 25 O 7 | Chelsea clo Edg |
| 101 N 13 | Chelsea clo Hampt |
| 147 R 13 | Chelsea emb SW3 |
| 146 L 12 | Chelsea Manor st SW3 |
| 146 K 12 | Chelsea Mnr gdns SW3 |
| 146 F 14 | Chelsea Pk gdns SW3 |
| 146 H 10 | Chelsea sq SW3 |
| 19 S 2 | Chelsfield av N9 |
| 110 D 8 | Chelsfield gdns SE26 |
| 89 Y 7 | Chelsham rd SW4 |
| 157 O 15 | Chelsham rd S Croy |
| 79 S 18 | Chelsworth dri SE18 |
| 83 Y 19 | Cheltenham av Twick |
| 40 J 17 | Cheltenham clo Grnfd |
| 66 D 7 | Cheltenham gdns E6 |

| Ref | Name |
|---|---|
| T 4 | Cheltenham pl W3 |
| J 13 | Cheltenham pl Harrow |
| U 19 | Cheltenham rd E10 |
| D 12 | Cheltenham rd SE15 |
| P 9 | Cheltenham ter SW3 |
| P 10 | Chelverton rd SW15 |
| R 4 | Chelwood gdns Rich |
| G 11 | Chelwood wlk SE4 |
| M 10 | Chemleigh vi Surb |
| J 10 | Cheney rd NW1 |
| K 4 | Cheney row E17 |
| A 10 | Cheneys rd E11 |
| E 18 | Chenies ms WC1 |
| F 8 | Chenies pl NW1 |
| E 20 | Chenies st WC1 |
| W 1 | Cheniston gdns W8 |
| X 1 | Cheniston gdns W8 |
| T 8 | Chepstow cres W2 |
| J 19 | Chepstow cres Ilf |
| F 18 | Chepstow gdns S'hall |
| V 7 | Chepstow ms W2 |
| U 7 | Chepstow pl W2 |
| U 4 | Chepstow pl W2 |
| X 7 | Chepstow rd W2 |
| S 4 | Chepstow rd Croy |
| T 5 | Chepstow ri Croy |
| R 9 | Chepstow vlls W11 |
| D 18 | Chequer st EC1 |
| R 5 | Chequers la Dgnhm |
| R 7 | Chequers La cotts Dgnhm |
| X 15 | Chequers way N13 |
| G 9 | Cherbury st N1 |
| V 2 | Cherington rd W7 |
| D 12 | Cheriton av Brom |
| V 6 | Cheriton av Ilf |
| S 18 | Cheriton dri SE18 |
| P 4 | Cheriton sq SW17 |
| L 2 | Cherry clo Carsh |
| S 9 | Cherry clo Mrdn |
| A 19 | Cherry cres Brentf |
| H 13 | Cherry garth Brentf |
| W 19 | Cherry Gdn st SE6 |
| A 14 | Cherry gdns Dgnhm |
| O 20 | Cherry hill Barnt |
| D 8 | Cherry Hill gdns Croy |
| X 17 | Cherry orchard SE7 |
| P 1 | Cherry orchard Croy |
| R 20 | Cherry Orchard rd Croy |
| R 3 | Cherry rd Enf |
| M 15 | Cherry st Rom |
| L 13 | Cherry Tree rd N2 |
| Z 13 | Cherry Tree ri Buck Hl |
| M 8 | Cherry Tree wlk Becknhm |
| M 8 | Cherry Tree wlk Becknhm |
| L 14 | Cherry Tree woods N2 |
| F 19 | Cherry wlk Brom |
| A 12 | Cherrydown av E4 |
| A 12 | Cherrydown av E4 |
| Z 11 | Cherrydown clo E4 |
| A 11 | Cherrydown clo E4 |
| H 7 | Cherrydown clo Rom |
| W 5 | Cherrydown rd Sidcp |
| O 18 | Cherrytree way Stanm |
| O 13 | Cherrywood dri SW15 |
| S 8 | Cherrywood la Mrdn |
| T 4 | Chertsey dri Sutton |
| X 5 | Chertsey rd E11 |
| P 14 | Chertsey rd W4 |
| D 10 | Chertsey rd W4 |
| L 3 | Chertsey rd Twick |
| W 17 | Chertsey rd Twick |
| N 1 | Chertsey rd Twick |
| N 1 | Chertsey rd Twick |
| N 1 | Chertsey rd Twick |
| N 12 | Chertsey rd Twick |
| A 6 | Cheseman st SE26 |
| L 18 | Chesfield rd Kingst |
| T 14 | Chesham av Brom |
| M 12 | Chesham clo Rom |
| D 1 | Chesham cres SE20 |
| E 1 | Chesham ms SW1 |
| S 2 | Chesham ms SW1 |
| S 2 | Chesham pl SW1 |
| D 2 | Chesham rd SW19 |
| F 13 | Chesham rd SW19 |
| P 2 | Chesham rd Kingst |
| Y 11 | Chesham st NW10 |
| S 3 | Chesham st SW1 |
| A 4 | Chesham ter W13 |
| U 6 | Cheshire ct EC4 |
| P 20 | Cheshire rd N22 |
| C 1 | Cheshire rd N22 |
| S 16 | Cheshire st E2 |
| S 9 | Chesholm rd N16 |
| 52 J 19 | Cheshunt rd E7 |
| 81 R 14 | Cheshunt rd Blvdr |
| 89 R 19 | Chesil pl SW12 |
| 87 U 1 | Chesilton rd SW6 |
| 66 C 8 | Chesley gdns E6 |
| 159 U 15 | Chesney cres Croy |
| 89 N 2 | Chesney st SW11 |
| 31 W 10 | Chesnut rd N17 |
| 27 V 11 | Chessington av N3 |
| 80 M 19 | Chessington av Bxly Hth |
| 81 N 19 | Chessington av Bxly Hth |
| 22 E 14 | Chessington ct Pinn |
| 81 O 19 | Chessington rd Bxly Hth |
| 152 B 20 | Chessington rd Epsom |
| 159 S 3 | Chessington way W Wkhm |
| 145 P 13 | Chesson rd W14 |
| 82 E 20 | Chester av Hounsl |
| 84 M 15 | Chester av Rich |
| 100 D 1 | Chester av Twick |
| 139 W 20 | Chester clo SW1 |
| 06 K 8 | Chester clo SW15 |
| 153 Y 3 | Chester clo Sutton |
| 131 X 13 | Chester Clo north NW1 |
| 131 X 13 | Chester Clo south NW1 |
| 22 H 17 | Chester dri Harrow |
| 131 X 14 | Chester ga NW1 |
| 9 N 19 | Chester gdns Enf |
| 120 C 13 | Chester gdns Mrdn |
| 79 O 13 | Chester gro SE18 |
| 139 W 20 | Chester ms SW1 |
| 131 X 11 | Chester pl NW1 |
| 34 J 19 | Chester rd E11 |
| 53 N 20 | Chester rd E12 |
| 85 N 12 | Chester rd E16 |
| 32 F 17 | Chester rd E17 |
| 131 X 13 | Chester rd NW1 |
| 31 P 9 | Chester rd N17 |
| 47 S 7 | Chester rd N19 |
| 19 N 7 | Chester rd N9 |
| 104 M 15 | Chester rd SW19 |
| 54 L 2 | Chester rd Ilf |
| 96 H 13 | Chester rd Sidcp |
| 147 T 7 | Chester row SW1 |
| 147 U 6 | Chester row SW1 |
| 147 V 4 | Chester sq SW1 |
| 147 W 3 | Chester Sq ms SW1 |
| 51 Y 8 | Chester st E11 |
| 139 W 20 | Chester st SW1 |
| 149 T 7 | Chester way SE11 |
| 30 K 1 | Chesterfield gdns N4 |
| 139 W 13 | Chesterfield gdns Wey |
| 91 U 12 | Chesterfield gro SE22 |
| 139 W 12 | Chesterfield hill W1 |
| 33 U 20 | Chesterfield rd E10 |
| 14 L 18 | Chesterfield rd N3 |
| 73 W 17 | Chesterfield rd W4 |
| 4 B 18 | Chesterfield rd Barnt |
| 9 V 1 | Chesterfield rd Enf |
| 139 W 13 | Chesterfield st W1 |
| 93 X 1 | Chesterfield wlk SE10 |
| 46 B 13 | Chesterford gdns NW3 |
| 53 U 17 | Chesterford rd E12 |
| 104 A 20 | Chesters the New Mald |
| 58 K 6 | Chesterton clo Grnfd |
| 65 T 8 | Chesterton rd E13 |
| 136 H 3 | Chesterton rd W10 |
| 65 S 8 | Chesterton ter E13 |
| 117 P 4 | Chesterton ter Kingst |
| 30 M 5 | Chesthunte rd N17 |
| 145 R 15 | Chestnut all SW6 |
| 52 G 13 | Chestnut av E7 |
| 29 Z 15 | Chestnut av N8 |
| 33 V 14 | Chestnut av SE17 |
| 85 Y 9 | Chestnut av SW14 |
| 72 H 12 | Chestnut av Brentf |
| 11 Y 19 | Chestnut av Edg |
| 152 A 9 | Chestnut av Epsom |
| 100 G 18 | Chestnut av Hampt |
| 57 U 7 | Chestnut av Hornch |
| 101 W 18 | Chestnut av Tedd |
| 42 A 14 | Chestnut av Wemb |
| 33 V 13 | Chestnut Av north E17 |
| 6 J 18 | Chestnut clo N14 |
| 154 L 1 | Chestnut clo Carsh |
| 145 R 15 | Chestnut ct SW6 |
| 34 E 19 | Chestnut dri E11 |
| 97 X 8 | Chestnut dri Bxly Hth |
| 23 V 3 | Chestnut dri Harrow |
| 22 A 19 | Chestnut dri Pinn |
| 57 U 8 | Chestnut glen Hornch |
| 31 V 10 | Chestnut gro N17 |
| 89 O 19 | Chestnut gro W12 |
| 107 P 1 | Chestnut gro W12 |
| 72 G 7 | Chestnut gro W5 |
| 5 Z 18 | Chestnut gro Barnt |
| 83 Y 10 | Chestnut gro Islwth |
| 121 Y 9 | Chestnut gro Mitch |
| 117 Z 6 | Chestnut gro New Mald |
| 118 A 5 | Chestnut gro New Mald |
| 158 B 16 | Chestnut gro S Croy |
| 42 A 14 | Chestnut gro Wemb |
| 108 K 6 | Chestnut rd SE27 |
| 119 R 3 | Chestnut rd SW20 |
| 102 J 18 | Chestnut rd Kingst |
| 103 S 3 | Chestnut rd Twick |
| 79 U 14 | Chestnut ri SE18 |
| 21 S 16 | Chestnut wlk Wdfd Grn |
| 158 J 1 | Cheston av Croy |
| 99 S 3 | Chesworth clo Erith |
| 30 E 18 | Chettle ct N8 |
| 107 N 5 | Chetwode rd SW17 |
| 1b Z 5 | Chetwynd av Barnt |
| 47 S 11 | Chetwynd rd NW5 |
| 146 L 1 | Cheval pl SW7 |
| 128 G 9 | Chevening rd NW6 |
| 77 R 14 | Chevening rd SE10 |
| 109 O 16 | Chevening rd SE19 |
| 115 S 6 | Chevenings the Sidcp |
| 47 X 3 | Cheverton rd N19 |
| 50 H 15 | Chevet st E9 |
| 99 P 4 | Cheviot clo Bxly Hth |
| 8 B 9 | Cheviot clo Enf |
| 154 F 20 | Cheviot clo Sutton |
| 45 S 6 | Cheviot ga NW2 |
| 45 R 7 | Cheviot gdns NW2 |
| 108 J 18 | Cheviot rd SE27 |
| 57 W 2 | Cheviot rd Hornch |
| 36 H 14 | Cheviot way Ilf |
| 32 H 14 | Chewton rd E17 |
| 34 B 10 | Cheyne av E18 |
| 100 F 2 | Cheyne av Twick |
| 146 M 14 | Cheyne gdns SW3 |
| 116 M 9 | Cheyne hill Surb |
| 117 N 10 | Cheyne hill Surb |
| 147 O 13 | Cheyne pl SW3 |
| 146 K 15 | Cheyne row SW3 |
| 146 K 16 | Cheyne walk SW3 |
| 26 M 18 | Cheyne wlk NW4 |
| 7 V 16 | Cheyne wlk N21 |
| 146 F 17 | Cheyne wlk SW10 |
| 146 L 15 | Cheyne wlk SW3 |
| 157 X 3 | Cheyne wlk Croy |
| 11 V 19 | Cheyneys av Edg |
| 24 J 1 | Cheyneys av Edg |
| 157 T 8 | Chichele gdns Croy |
| 45 P 13 | Chichele rd NW2 |
| 22 M 2 | Chicheley gdns Harrow |
| 23 N 3 | Chicheley rd Harrow |
| 141 O 16 | Chicheley st SE1 |
| 24 L 10 | Chichester ct Stanm |
| 53 S 2 | Chichester gdns Ilf |
| 52 A 10 | Chichester rd E11 |
| 129 U 9 | Chichester rd NW6 |
| 18 J 5 | Chichester rd N9 |
| 157 U 6 | Chichester rd Croy |
| 141 R 5 | Chichester rents WC2 |
| 148 D 11 | Chichester st SW1 |
| 143 R 1 | Chicksand st E1 |
| 14 L 11 | Chiddingfold N12 |
| 87 Y 4 | Chiddingstone SW6 |
| 81 P 18 | Chiddingstone Bxly Hth |
| 98 G 10 | Chieveley rd Bxly Hth |
| 71 Y 2 | Chignell pl W13 |
| 143 X 10 | Chigwell hill E1 |
| 34 H 10 | Chigwell rd E18 |
| 64 D 18 | Chilcot clo E14 |
| 107 S 4 | Childeric rd SW17 |
| 75 V 19 | Childeric rd SE14 |
| 87 S 6 | Childerley rd SW6 |
| 75 X 16 | Childers st SE8 |
| 145 V 6 | Childs pl SW5 |
| 145 V 6 | Childs st SW5 |
| 27 W 15 | Childs way NW11 |
| 59 Z 6 | Chilham clo Grnfd |
| 113 R 10 | Chilham rd SE9 |
| 126 D 17 | Chilham way Brom |
| 150 D 17 | Chilham way Brom |
| 107 P 13 | Chillerton rd SW17 |
| 48 E 16 | Chillingworth rd N7 |
| 118 F 15 | Chilmark gdns New Mald |
| 121 X 2 | Chilmark rd SW16 |
| 100 G 2 | Chiltern av Twick |
| 99 P 3 | Chiltern clo Bxly Hth |
| 7 R 14 | Chiltern dene Enf |
| 117 S 13 | Chiltern dri Surb |
| 45 P 8 | Chiltern gdns NW2 |
| 64 B 12 | Chiltern rd E3 |
| 36 J 14 | Chiltern rd Ilf |
| 139 S 2 | Chiltern st W1 |
| 139 S 1 | Chiltern st W1 |
| 21 T 12 | Chiltern way Wdfd Grn |
| 72 G 10 | Chilton av W5 |
| 10 B 1 | Chilton av Bushey Watf |
| 75 U 11 | Chilton gro SE8 |
| 12 C 19 | Chilton rd Edg |
| 85 P 7 | Chilton rd Rich |
| 135 R 15 | Chilton st E2 |
| 154 D 5 | Chilworth gdns Sutton |
| 138 E 6 | Chilworth ms W2 |
| 138 D 6 | Chilworth st W2 |
| 17 U 15 | Chimes av N13 |
| 149 S 3 | China wlk SE11 |
| 112 H 7 | Chinbrook cres SE12 |
| 112 H 7 | Chinbrook rd SE12 |
| 29 U 13 | Chine the N10 |
| 7 X 18 | Chine the N21 |
| 42 C 14 | Chine the Wemb |
| 20 M 11 | Chingdale rd E4 |
| 21 N 11 | Chingdale rd E4 |
| 20 C 9 | Chingford av E4 |
| 21 O 14 | Chingford la Wdfd Grn |
| 20 B 16 | Chingford Mount rd E4 |
| 20 B 19 | Chingford rd E4 |
| 33 P 2 | Chingford rd E4 |
| 112 A 15 | Chingley clo Brom |
| 58 M 6 | Chinnor cres Grnfd |
| 59 N 6 | Chinnor cres Grnfd |
| 89 W 9 | Chip st SW4 |
| 76 F 6 | Chipka st E14 |
| 60 F 10 | Chippendale st E5 |
| 43 U 16 | Chippenham av Wemb |
| 129 T 14 | Chippenham gdns NW6 |
| 129 U 19 | Chippenham ms W9 |
| 129 T 18 | Chippenham rd W9 |
| 122 J 9 | Chipstead av Thntn Hth |
| 44 L 7 | Chipstead gdns NW2 |
| 87 Y 3 | Chipstead st SW6 |
| 63 V 5 | Chisenhale rd E3 |
| 157 S 2 | Chisholm clo Croy |
| 84 M 17 | Chisholm rd Rich |
| 28 C 2 | Chislehurst av N3 |
| 113 Z 14 | Chislehurst High st Chisl |
| 127 S 1 | Chislehurst rd Chisl |
| 84 K 14 | Chislehurst rd Rich |
| 114 M 13 | Chislehurst rd Sidcp |
| 94 H 4 | Chiswell sq SE3 |
| 134 E 20 | Chiswell st EC1 |
| 74 C 13 | Chiswick la NW4 |
| 74 D 15 | Chiswick la SW4 |
| 85 V 4 | Chiswick br W4 |
| 73 Z 11 | Chiswick Comm rd W4 |
| 73 U 12 | Chiswick High rd W4 |
| 74 B 12 | Chiswick High rd W4 |
| 74 D 15 | Chiswick mall W4 |
| 18 L 8 | Chiswick rd N9 |
| 73 V 12 | Chiswick rd W4 |
| 22 E 10 | Chiswick st Pinn |
| 73 S 15 | Chiswick village W4 |
| 132 C 20 | Chitty st W1 |
| 55 V 5 | Chitty's la Dgnhm |
| 88 H 13 | Chivalry rd SW11 |
| 20 E 10 | Olivers rd E4 |
| 68 E 12 | Choats Manor way Bark |
| 69 N 6 | Choats Manor way Dgnhm |
| 68 M 10 | Choats rd Dgnhm |
| 69 N 10 | Choats rd Dgnhm |
| 105 O 4 | Chobham gdns SW19 |
| 51 W 15 | Chobham rd E15 |
| 47 S 1 | Cholmeley cres N6 |
| 47 S 1 | Cholmeley pk N6 |
| 116 A 16 | Cholmley rd Surb |
| 62 F 5 | Cholmondeley av NW10 |
| 84 F 13 | Cholmondeley wlk Rich |
| 143 Y 13 | Choppins ct E1 |
| 91 X 5 | Choumert gro SE15 |
| 91 V 6 | Choumert rd SE15 |
| 91 X 5 | Choumert sq SE15 |
| 64 E 18 | Chrisp st E14 |
| 64 D 15 | Chrisp st E14 |
| 64 D 15 | Chrisp st E14 |

31 S 12 Clyde cir N15
51 P 2 Clyde pl E10
77 T 2 Clyde rd E16
31 T 12 Clyde rd N15
29 X 4 Clyde rd N22
123 U 20 Clyde rd Croy
157 L 12 Clyde rd Croy
153 Y 10 Clyde rd Sutton
155 V 13 Clyde rd Wallgtn
75 Z 17 Clyde st SE8
110 D 4 Clyde ter SE23
110 D 5 Clyde vale SE23
39 P 4 Clyde way Rom
9 S 16 Clydesdale Enf
9 S 16 Clydesdale Enf
24 G 9 Clydesdale av Stanm
85 S 10 Clydesdale gdns Rich
137 P 5 Clydesdale rd W11
57 T 2 Clydesdale rd Hornch
89 W 3 Clyston st SW8
86 M 12 Coalecroft rd SW15
135 U 8 Coate st E2
127 X 4 Coates Hill rd Brom
11 T 2 Coates rd Borehm Wd
142 M 3 Cobb st E1
95 R 8 Cobbett rd SE9
100 J 1 Cobbett rd Twick
149 O 20 Cobbett st SW8
35 O 15 Cobbetts av Ilf
35 O 15 Cobbetts av Ilf
52 C 9 Cobbold rd E11
44 D 18 Cobbold rd NW10
74 C 6 Cobbold rd W12
141 X 7 Cobbs ct EC4
82 E 12 Cobbs rd Hounsl
150 L 16 Cobden pl SE15
52 A 8 Cobden rd E11
123 Y 12 Cobden rd SE25
64 E 15 Cobden st E15
118 G 10 Cobham av New Mald
127 P 16 Cobham clo Brom
33 V 5 Cobham rd E17
30 J 9 Cobham rd N22
67 R 4 Cobham rd Bark
54 H 8 Cobham rd Ilf
117 P 2 Cobham rd Kingst
112 M 10 Cobland rd SE12
63 Y 9 Coborn rd E3
63 Y 9 Coborn st E3
151 N 11 Cobourg rd SE5
132 C 14 Cobourg st NW1
30 D 9 Coburg rd N22
105 U 18 Cochrane rd SW19
130 H 10 Cochrane st NW8
142 L 3 Cock hill E1
141 X 3 Cock la EC1
6 A 13 Cockfosters rd Barnt
5 X 4 Cockfosters rd Barnt
140 F 19 Cockpit steps SW1
133 O 19 Cockpit yd WC1
140 G 13 Cockspur ct SW1
135 P 18 Code st E1
92 J 18 Codrington hill SE23
137 N 7 Codrington ms W11
24 H 11 Cody clo Harrow
64 L 12 Cody rd E16
32 G 3 Cogan av E17
63 Y 17 Cogenhagen pl E14
141 T 13 Coin st SE1
47 P 17 Coity st NW5
143 U 4 Coke st E1
109 N 2 Cokers la SE21
129 V 4 Colas mews NW6
146 A 7 Colbeck ms SW7
41 N 1 Colbeck rd Harrow
49 T 2 Colberg pl N16
153 N 2 Colborne way Worc Pk
152 M 3 Colborne way Worc Pk
154 F 6 Colburn way Sutton
109 T 13 Colby rd SE19
53 U 10 Colchester rd E10
33 V 20 Colchester rd E17
33 N 20 Colchester rd E17
25 W 2 Colchester rd Edg
75 T 17 Cold Blow la SE14
120 M 7 Cold blows Mitch
76 H 4 Cold harbour E14
133 S 17 Coldbath sq EC1
93 S 4 Coldbath st SE13
71 Y 3 Coldershaw rd W13
29 N 7 Coldfall av N10
90 H 9 Coldharbour la SW9
156 F 11 Coldharbour Croy
156 G 11 Coldharbour way Croy
87 V 16 Coldstream gdns SW18
83 Y 14 Cole Pk gdns Twick
83 Y 18 Cole Pk rd Twick

83 Y 15 Cole Pk rd Twick
83 Y 17 Cole rd Twick
142 D 19 Cole st SE1
145 Z 7 Colebeck ms SW5
63 R 11 Colebert av E1
87 P 17 Colebrook clo SW15
33 N 14 Colebrook rd E17
122 A 1 Colebrook rd SW16
60 A 17 Colebrooke av W13
34 K 20 Colebrooke dri E11
133 X 7 Colebrooke row N1
24 D 4 Coledale dri Stanm
88 C 12 Coleford rd SW18
51 W 13 Colegrave rd E15
151 R 16 Colegrove rd SE15
145 Y 12 Coleherne ms SW10
145 X 11 Coleherne rd SW10
87 S 3 Colehill gdns SW6
87 S 3 Colehill la SW6
75 P 2 Coleman clo E1
134 B 4 Coleman fields N1
150 K 18 Coleman rd SE5
81 X 10 Coleman rd Blvdr
55 Z 19 Coleman rd Dgnhm
56 A 19 Coleman rd Dgnhm
142 E 5 Coleman st EC2
142 E 3 Coleman St bldgs EC2
113 X 7 Colemans heath SE9
50 D 11 Colenso rd E5
54 G 4 Colenso rd Ilf
96 D 12 Colepits Wood rd SE9
30 F 10 Coleraine rd N8
77 R 16 Coleraine rd SE3
53 R 17 Coleridge av E12
154 K 8 Coleridge av Sutton
130 B 2 Coleridge gdns NW6
32 L 12 Coleridge rd E17
15 P 17 Coleridge rd N12
48 F 8 Coleridge rd N4
29 X 19 Coleridge rd N8
124 C 16 Coleridge rd Croy
39 Y 3 Coleridge rd Rom
27 X 14 Coleridge wlk NW11
40 K 7 Coles cres Harrow
44 H 5 Coles Green rd NW2
10 B 5 Coles grn Bushey Watf
124 K 5 Colesburg rd Becknhm
101 U 15 Coleshill rd Tedd
88 K 4 Colestown st SW11
144 H 7 Colet gdns W14
133 P 17 Coley st WC1
110 G 1 Colfe rd SE23
26 B 14 Colin clo NW9
158 K 4 Colin clo Croy
26 E 15 Colin cres NW9
26 H 14 Colin Deep gdns NW4
26 F 13 Colin Deep la NW9
26 F 18 Colin dri NW9
26 E 15 Colin gdns NW9
26 A 13 Colin Park rd NW9
44 F 17 Colin rd NW10
30 J 14 Colina ms N15
30 J 15 Colina rd N15
25 Z 11 Colindale av NW9
26 B 10 Colindale av NW9
86 L 10 Colinette rd SW15
55 R 6 Colinton rd Ilf
87 Y 18 Coliston rd SW18
106 H 3 Collamore av SW18
76 G 16 College appr SE10
23 T 4 College av Harrow
23 U 2 College av Harrow
46 F 19 College clo Harrow
133 V 1 College cres NW3
20 D 4 College cross N1
18 H 16 College gdns E4
91 R 20 College gdns SE21
8 B 8 College gdns Enf
35 R 15 College gdns Ilf
118 E 12 College gdns New Mald
109 R 18 College grn SE19
132 D 5 College gro NW1
142 D 9 College hill EC4
23 U 3 College Hill rd Harrow
23 V 4 College Hill rd Harrow
47 S 12 College la NW5
18 F 20 College Pk rd N17
33 Z 12 College pl E17
132 C 4 College pl NW1
33 T 17 College rd E17
62 M 6 College rd NW10
128 B 8 College rd NW10
18 F 20 College rd N17
17 U 8 College rd N21
91 R 19 College rd SE21

109 S 1 College rd SE21
106 G 16 College rd SW19
60 A 18 College rd W13
112 F 18 College rd Brom
126 E 1 College rd Brom
157 O 4 College rd Croy
23 T 3 College rd Harrow
23 U 19 College rd Harrow
83 V 3 College rd Islwth
42 H 5 College rd Wemb
126 E 2 College slip Brom
142 D 9 College st EC4
63 X 8 College ter E3
27 W 6 College ter N3
113 O 3 College view SE9
50 D 18 Collent st E9
31 U 16 Colless rd N15
151 U 2 Collett rd SE16
25 P 7 Collier dri Edg
38 H 3 Collier Row la Rom
38 C 4 Collier Row rd Rom
133 N 9 Collier st N1
122 G 10 Colliers Water la Thntn Hth
106 G 16 Colliers Wood High st SW19
81 V 17 Collindale av Erith
97 O 20 Collindale av Sidcp
74 J 2 Collingbourne rd W12
145 Z 7 Collingham gdns SW5
145 Y 6 Collingham pl SW5
145 Z 26 Collingham rd SW5
110 C 9 Collingtree rd SE26
29 O 11 Collingwood av N10
117 V 18 Collingwood av Surb
82 H 18 Collingwood clo Twick
33 N 18 Collingwood rd E17
31 S 12 Collingwood rd N15
120 G 5 Collingwood rd Mitch
153 W 5 Collingwood rd Sutton
63 N 12 Collingwood st E1
135 X 17 Collingwood st E1
24 K 7 Collins av Stanm
48 C 12 Collins rd N5
94 B 6 Collins st SE3
133 X 5 Collins yd N1
142 A 19 Collinson st SE1
9 P 12 Collinwood av Enf
35 V 5 Collinwood gdns Ilf
92 C 1 Colls rd SE15
156 A 8 Collyer av Croy
91 V 2 Collyer pl SE15
156 A 8 Collyer rd Croy
65 Y 15 Colman rd E16
63 T 11 Colmar st E1
23 P 3 Colmer pl Harrow
108 B 19 Colmer rd SW16
9 R 14 Colmore rd Enf
149 W 2 Colnbrook st SE1
50 H 13 Colne rd E5
18 A 3 Colne rd N21
101 U 2 Colne rd Twick
29 P 2 Colney Hatch la N10
15 Y 18 Colney Hatch la N11
16 A 20 Colney Hatch rd N11
88 G 20 Cologne rd SW11
77 N 14 Colomb st SE10
54 B 2 Colombo rd Ilf
141 W 15 Colombo st SE1
82 M 15 Colonial av Twick
83 N 15 Colonial av Twick
132 K 18 Colonnade WC1
131 Y 15 Colosseum ter NW1
157 R 2 Colson rd Croy
107 V 10 Colson way SW16
31 V 12 Colsterworth rd N15
154 K 8 Colston av Carsh
53 N 18 Colston rd E7
85 W 10 Colston rd SW14
80 C 13 Coltness cres SE2
23 U 14 Colton rd Har
25 S 4 Columbia av Edg
118 E 18 Columbia av Worc Pk
65 R 13 Columbia rd E13
135 S 10 Columbia rd E2
93 W 13 Columbine way SE13
101 T 2 Colus all Twick
49 U 16 Colvestone cres E8
18 L 4 Colvill rd N9
137 P 6 Colville houses W11
137 P 5 Colville ms W11
137 R 6 Colville ms W11
140 D 2 Colville pl W1
51 V 9 Colville rd E11
32 J 8 Colville rd E17
137 R 7 Colville rd W11
73 U 8 Colville rd W3
137 O 6 Colville sq W11

137 O 5 Colville Sq ms W1
137 P 6 Colville ter W11
34 J 13 Colvin gdns E11
20 H 11 Colvin gdns E4
36 B 3 Colvin gdns Ilf
66 D 2 Colvin rd E6
122 F 12 Colvin rd Thntn Hth
74 K 11 Colvin st W6
91 U 14 Colwell rd SE22
144 E 14 Colworth rd E11
106 G 18 Colwood gdns SW
33 Z 19 Colworth rd E11
34 A 20 Colworth rd E11
123 X 20 Colworth rd Croy
59 X 6 Colwyn av Grnfd
82 M 3 Colwyn cres Houns
44 K 9 Colwyn rd NW2
113 Z 4 Colyer clo SE9
98 M 1 Colyers clo Erith
98 L 1 Colyers la Erith
99 S 1 Colyers la Erith
99 P 1 Colyers wlk Erith
97 V 1 Colyton clo Welling
42 C 17 Colyton clo Wemb
92 A 14 Colyton rd SE22
18 H 17 Colyton way N18
77 P 19 Combe av SE3
77 Y 16 Combe lodge SE7
77 P 19 Combe ms SE3
103 Y 14 Combe Wood Golf course Kingst
77 S 14 Combedale rd SE10
87 T 20 Combemartin rd SW18
44 A 8 Comber clo NW2
150 B 20 Comber gro SE5
90 C 7 Combermere rd SW
50 A 6 Comberton rd E5
120 B 13 Comberton rd Mrdn
79 X 20 Combesides SE18
80 A 9 Combwell cres SE2
33 T 15 Comely Bank rd E1
144 M 10 Comerage ms W14
144 L 11 Comeragh rd W14
145 N 10 Comeragh rd W14
92 K 11 Comerford rd SE4
76 A 19 Comet pl SE8
76 A 20 Comet st SE8
30 B 4 Commerce rd N22
72 C 18 Commerce rd Brentf
156 D 4 Commerce way Croy
75 X 8 Commercial Dock pas SE16
131 W 1 Commercial pl NW1
63 O 17 Commercial rd E1
143 U 5 Commercial rd E1
18 F 19 Commercial rd N18
143 O 2 Commercial st E1
151 T 18 Commercial way SE15
150 M 20 Commercial way SE15
77 N 13 Commerell st SE10
63 V 13 Commodore st E1
86 H 7 Common rd SW13
10 D 11 Common rd Stanm
72 K 2 Common the W5
10 H 9 Common the Stanm
86 M 6 Commondale SW15
106 H 13 Commonfield la SW17
106 H 13 Commonfield pas SW17
121 P 7 Commonside east Mitch
121 N 8 Commonside west Mitch
62 K 20 Commonwealth av W12
137 S 20 Commonwealth institute W8
31 X 1 Commonwealth rd N17
80 E 13 Commonwealth way SE2
51 X 16 Community rd E15
110 H 5 Como rd SE23
39 N 14 Como st Rom
45 Z 19 Compayne gdns NW6
46 B 19 Compayne gdns NW6
46 A 6 Compton av E6
48 J 19 Compton av N1
46 J 1 Compton av N6
31 N 2 Compton cres W4
73 V 17 Compton cres W4
58 A 1 Compton cres Grnfd
133 X 16 Compton pas EC1
132 J 15 Compton pl WC1
128 G 13 Compton rd NW10
48 K 19 Compton rd N1
17 V 5 Compton rd N21

V 14 Compton rd SW19
3 Z 20 Compton rd Croy
7 Z 1 Compton rd Croy
2 D 16 Compton ri Pinn
3 X 16 Compton st EC1
5 R 5 Compton st E13
3 H 19 Compton ter N1
7 V 4 Comreddy clo Enf
0 H 6 Comus st SE17
3 J 11 Comyn rd SW11
5 O 14 Comyns clo E16
9 P 1 Comyns rd Dgnhm
0 A 6 Comyns the Bushey Watf
0 B 10 Concanon rd SW2
1 P 14 Concert Hall appr SE1
1 S 12 Concord rd W3
9 O 18 Concord rd Enf
9 W 2 Condell rd SW8
3 V 17 Conder st E14
0 L 7 Conderton rd SE5
8 M 20 Condover cres SE18
0 K 8 Conduit ct WC2
9 U 2 Conduit la N9
9 V 20 Conduit la Enf
9 V 20 Conduit la Enf
7 X 12 Conduit la S Croy
8 F 7 Conduit ms W2
8 G 6 Conduit pl W2
8 M 13 Conduit rd SE18
9 N 13 Conduit rd SE18
9 Z 8 Conduit st W1
0 A 8 Conduit st W1
3 V 20 Conduit way NW10
8 J 11 Conewood st N5
0 G 10 Conference rd SE2
9 T 13 Congo rd SE18
0 F 11 Congress rd SE2
5 S 8 Congreve rd SE9
0 J 7 Congreve st SE17
7 Y 9 Conical corner Enf
8 B 8 Conifer gdns SW16
2 C 18 Conifers clo Tedd
7 X 4 Coniger rd SW6
6 K 19 Coningby rd S Croy
4 H 4 Coningham ms W12
4 J 6 Coningham rd W12
0 D 18 Coningsby gdns E4
2 F 6 Coningsby rd W5
3 T 5 Conington rd SE13
1 U 7 Conisborough cres SE6
7 Z 12 Coniscliffe rd N13
7 U 2 Coniston av Bark
0 B 8 Coniston av Grnfd
6 G 8 Coniston av Welling
5 S 11 Coniston clo N20
7 U 2 Coniston clo Bark
8 K 3 Coniston clo Bxly Hth
5 Y 16 Coniston gdn W9
9 P 6 Coniston gdns N9
5 R 13 Coniston gdns Ilf
54 F 14 Coniston gdns Sutton
42 E 3 Coniston gdns Wemb
29 S 7 Coniston rd N10
18 J 20 Coniston rd N17
11 Y 15 Coniston rd Brom
12 A 17 Coniston rd Brom
98 K 3 Coniston rd Bxly Hth
23 X 17 Coniston rd Croy
82 L 17 Coniston rd Twick
57 V 15 Coniston way Hornch
20 L 17 Conlan st W10
44 C 19 Conley rd NW10
20 J 2 Connaught av E4
65 V 9 Connaught av SW14
16 A 5 Connaught av Barnt
8 F 9 Connaught av Enf
82 C 12 Connaught av Hounsl
50 G 6 Connaught clo E10
38 L 7 Connaught clo W2
8 F 10 Connaught clo Enf
54 F 3 Connaught clo Sutton
27 Z 13 Connaught dri NW11
29 T 15 Connaught gdns N10
17 W 15 Connaught gdns N13
54 D 8 Connaught la Ilf
39 N 7 Connaught ms W2
39 N 7 Connaught pl W2
51 Y 4 Connaught rd E11
78 B 3 Connaught rd E16
66 A 20 Connaught rd E16
33 N 16 Connaught rd E17
20 L 4 Connaught rd E4
62 B 5 Connaught rd NW10
48 F 1 Connaught rd N4
72 A 1 Connaught rd W13
4 D 20 Connaught rd Barnt
54 D 8 Connaught rd Ilf
118 B 8 Connaught rd New Mald
84 L 13 Connaught rd Rich
154 G 4 Connaught rd Sutton
101 S 12 Connaught rd Tedd
139 N 6 Connaught sq W2
138 M 7 Connaught sq W2
78 L 14 Connaught st SE18
138 M 6 Connaught st W2
17 X 14 Connaught way N13
60 M 10 Connell cres W5
61 N 11 Connell cres W5
72 F 6 Conningsby cotts W5
30 H 20 Conningsby rd N4
20 K 10 Connington cres E4
6 H 17 Connisbee ct N14
9 S 2 Connop rd Enf
56 C 11 Connor rd Dgnhm
63 S 3 Connor st E9
71 S 2 Conolly rd W7
149 X 1 Conquest st SE1
119 N 19 Conrad dr Worc Pk
141 U 16 Cons st SE1
91 Z 5 Consort rd SE15
92 A 7 Consert rd SE15
118 G 18 Consfield av New Mald
83 S 14 Consort ms Islwth
91 Z 2 Consort rd SE15
28 B 19 Constable clo NW11
31 X 15 Constable cres N15
25 O 6 Constable gdns Edg
83 O 13 Constable gdns Hounsl
126 C 19 Constance cres Brom
122 J 16 Constance rd Croy
18 D 1 Constance rd Enf
154 E 9 Constance rd Sutton
82 L 19 Constance rd Twick
78 C 3 Constance st E16
46 L 13 Constantine rd NW3
139 Y 17 Constitution hill SW1
95 W 2 Constitution ri SE18
150 C 7 Content st SE17
137 N 6 Convent gdns W11
72 D 11 Convent gdns W5
10 L 19 Conway clo Stanm
59 V 4 Conway cres Grnfd
37 S 19 Conway cres Rom
8 D 3 Conway gdns Enf
121 Z 9 Conway gdns Mitch
42 D 2 Conway gdns Wemb
61 Z 14 Conway gro W3
132 B 19 Conway ms W1
44 L 8 Conway rd NW2
17 O 10 Conway rd N14
30 K 15 Conway rd N15
79 U 12 Conway rd SE18
105 N 20 Conway rd SW20
82 F 18 Conway rd Hounsl
65 S 12 Conway st E13
132 A 19 Conway st W1
46 K 20 Conybeare NW3
20 M 19 Conyers clo Wdfd Grn
107 W 12 Conyers rd SW16
80 C 7 Cookhill rd SE2
7 X 2 Cooks Hole rd Enf
64 E 6 Cooks rd E3
149 X 13 Cooks rd SE17
44 B 3 Cool Oak la NW9
65 U 19 Coolfin rd E16
20 J 16 Coolgardie av E4
29 X 18 Coolhurst rd N8
129 O 15 Coomassie rd W9
157 T 9 Coombe av Croy
24 M 9 Coombe clo Edg
82 H 12 Coombe clo Hounsl
17 V 6 Coombe corner N21
100 D 16 Coombe cres Hampt
103 Y 18 Coombe end Kingst
118 B 12 Coombe Field clo New Mald
118 G 2 Coombe gdns SW20
118 C 8 Coombe gdns New Mald
103 Y 14 Coombe hill Kingst
104 C 18 Coombe Hill glade SW20
104 A 18 Coombe Hill rd Kingst
103 Z 20 Coombe Ho chase Kingst
118 H 1 Coombe la SW20
158 B 12 Coombe la Croy
117 U 1 Coombe la Kingst
103 Y 19 Coombe La west Kingst
104 C 19 Coombe La west Kingst
127 S 7 Coombe lea Brom
103 X 18 Coombe neville Kingst
157 X 8 Coombe park Croy
103 X 13 Coombe pk Kingst
104 A 20 Coombe pk Kingst
43 Y 8 Coombe rd NW10
30 G 7 Coombe rd N22
109 Z 9 Coombe rd SE26
72 B 8 Coombe rd W13
74 B 14 Coombe rd W4
10 B 1 Coombe rd Bushey Watford
157 W 10 Coombe rd Croy
100 D 16 Coombe rd Hampt
117 P 1 Coombe rd Kingst
118 A 3 Coombe rd New Mald
103 V 20 Coombe ri Kingst
103 V 13 Coombe ridings Kingst
153 Z 5 Coombe wlk Sutton
38 C 20 Coombe Wood dri Rom
103 W 13 Coombe Wood rd Kingst
5 Z 9 Coombehurst clo Barnt
69 P 3 Coombes rd Dgnhm
133 Y 10 Coombs st N1
133 Y 10 Coombs st N1
32 G 4 Cooper av E17
154 M 5 Cooper cres Carsh
44 F 16 Cooper rd NW10
156 H 9 Cooper rd Croy
51 S 3 Coopers la E10
112 G 4 Coopers la SE12
151 P 10 Coopers rd SE1
142 M 8 Coopers row EC3
34 L 3 Coopersale clo Wdfd Grn
50 G 15 Coopersale rd E9
50 D 0 Coote gdns Dgnhm
98 A 2 Coote rd Bxly Hth
56 B 9 Coote rd Dgnhm
145 U 2 Cope pl W8
75 T 10 Cope st SE16
33 S 17 Copeland rd E17
91 Y 5 Copeland rd SE15
63 Y 17 Copenhagen pl E14
133 S 6 Copenhagen st N1
132 L 5 Copenhagen st WC1
110 M 18 Copers Cope rd Beckhnm
111 O 20 Copers Cope rd Beckhnm
16 D 14 Copies gro N11
42 F 16 Copland av Wemb
42 E 15 Copland clo Wemb
42 J 17 Copland rd Wemb
91 U 9 Coplestone rd SE15
108 C 15 Copley pk SW16
11 T 15 Copley rd Stanm
63 T 15 Copley st E1
94 C 10 Coppelia rd SE3
56 A 1 Coppen rd Dgnhm
106 C 10 Copper Mill la SW17
76 D 17 Copperas st SE8
63 W 13 Copperfield rd E3
141 Z 16 Copperfield st SE1
142 A 16 Copperfield st SE1
32 D 18 Coppermill la E17
28 K 1 Coppetts clo N12
28 M 2 Coppetts rd N10
29 N 4 Coppetts rd N10
118 M 6 Coppice clo SW20
86 H 17 Coppice dri SW15
7 W 13 Coppice the Enf
34 C 11 Coppice way E18
14 L 10 Coppice wlk N20
159 S 15 Coppins the Croy
159 S 6 Copse av W Wkhm
104 E 20 Copse hill SW20
154 B 16 Copse hill Sutton
21 P 6 Copse the E4
158 G 18 Copse view S Croy
142 F 4 Copthall av EC2
142 F 4 Copthall clo EC2
142 G 5 Copthall ct EC2
13 U 20 Copthall dri NW7
26 G 1 Copthall dri NW7
26 G 1 Copthall gdns NW7
101 X 1 Copthall gdns Twick
89 X 20 Copthorne av SW12
140 J 2 Coptic st WC1
141 T 18 Coral st SE1
132 J 17 Coram st WC1
19 S 2 Coran clo N9
82 H 8 Corban rd Hounsl
5 T 5 Corbar clo Barnt
155 O 2 Corbet clo Wallgtn
34 K 18 Corbett rd E11
33 V 10 Corbett rd E17
75 P 12 Corbetts pas SE16
52 A 1 Corbicum rd E11
105 P 16 Corbiere ct SW19
40 L 10 Corbins la Harrow
7 O 14 Corby cres Enf
61 X 7 Corby rd NW10
96 H 20 Corbylands rd Sidcp
114 H 1 Corbylands rd Sidcp
48 A 5 Corbyn st N4
64 D 17 Cordelia st E14
64 D 16 Cording st E14
63 U 8 Cordova rd E3
95 P 3 Corelli rd SE3
40 F 12 Corfe av Harrow
63 N 10 Corfield st E2
135 X 15 Corfield st E2
60 J 16 Corfton rd W5
47 W 12 Corinne rd N19
140 A 10 Cork st W1
140 A 10 Cork St ms W1
116 H 17 Corkran rd Surb
159 X 5 Corkscrew hill W Wkhm
90 H 3 Cormont rd SE5
24 H 1 Cornbury rd Edg
48 D 19 Cornelia st N7
115 Z 14 Cornell clo Sidcp
94 D 7 Corner grn SE3
74 B 18 Corney rd W4
91 Z 15 Cornflower ter SE22
91 Z 15 Cornflower ter SE22
126 E 13 Cornford clo Brom
107 T 3 Cornford gro SW12
142 G 6 Cornhill EC3
110 A 20 Cornish gro SE20
93 T 8 Cornmill la SE13
93 T 8 Cornmill la SE13
55 W 3 Cornshaw rd Dgnhm
50 B 10 Cornthwaite rd E5
63 O 9 Cornwall av E9
30 B 5 Cornwall av N22
27 Z 2 Cornwall av N3
58 G 15 Cornwall av S hall
96 J 9 Cornwall av Welling
54 L 19 Cornwall clo Bark
136 L 7 Cornwall cres W11
115 T 18 Cornwall dri Orp
44 K 19 Cornwall gdns NW10
145 Z 3 Cornwall gdns SW7
146 A 3 Cornwall gdns SW7
145 Y 3 Cornwall Gdns wlk SW7
74 B 15 Cornwall gro W4
146 A 3 Cornwall Ms south SW7
145 X 2 Cornwall Ms west W8
31 O 5 Cornwall rd N15
18 K 15 Cornwall rd N18
48 F 2 Cornwall rd N4
141 T 14 Cornwall rd SE1
156 H 3 Cornwall rd Croy
22 M 17 Cornwall rd Harrow
22 E 3 Cornwall rd Pinn
153 W 19 Cornwall rd Sutton
83 Z 20 Cornwall rd Twick
63 N 19 Cornwall st E1
19 O 8 Cornwallis av N9
19 N 8 Cornwallis av N9
114 D 5 Cornwallis av SE9
19 O 8 Cornwallis gro N9
32 G 14 Cornwallis rd E17
47 Z 6 Cornwallis rd N19
48 A 7 Cornwallis rd N4
55 X 13 Cornwallis rd Dgnhm
95 U 7 Cornwallis wlk SE9
28 F 14 Cornwood clo N2
55 S 16 Cornworthy rd Dgnhm
94 F 19 Corona rd SE12
97 W 15 Coronation clo Bxly
36 C 13 Coronation clo Ilf
57 Y 14 Coronation dri Hornch
65 Z 10 Coronation rd E13
61 O 9 Coronation rd NW10
82 G 20 Coronation wlk Twick
134 J 13 Coronet st N1
82 A 10 Corporation av Hounsl
133 U 16 Corporation row EC1
65 P 6 Corporation st E15
64 M 7 Corporation st E15
47 Z 16 Corporation st N7
48 E 11 Corrall rd N7
90 A 11 Corrance rd SW2
16 L 13 Corri av N14
45 Z 2 Corrina ct NW11
45 X 1 Corringham rd NW11

D 7 Craven gdns Ilf
D 8 Craven hill W2
C 8 Craven Hill gdns W2
C 9 Craven Hill gdns W2
K 12 Craven pas WC2
C 4 Craven Pk rd NW10
V 19 Craven Pk rd N15
Z 3 Craven rd NW10
D 7 Craven rd W2
D 20 Craven rd W5
Z 20 Craven rd Croy
M 20 Craven rd Kingst
N 20 Craven rd Kingst
K 12 Craven st WC2
D 8 Craven ter W2
W 1 Craven wlk E5
Y 20 Craven wlk N16
G 15 Crawford av Wemb
T 4 Crawford clo Islwth
W 10 Crawford gdns N13
F 8 Crawford gdns Grnfd
O 1 Crawford ms W1
O 1 Crawford ms W1
T 17 Crawford pas EC1
L 3 Crawford pl W1
M 3 Crawford pl W1
N 2 Crawford st W 1
C 9 Crawley ms NW1
S 4 Crawley rd E10
L 7 Crawley rd N22
E 3 Crawley rd Enf
H 2 Crawshay rd SW9
V 11 Crawthew gro SE22
X 12 Cray clo Drtfrd
S 17 Cray rd Blvdr
T 16 Cray rd Sidcp
P 10 Craybrooke rd Sidcp
B 5 Craybury rd SE9
U 1 Crayden rd Erith
K 12 Crayford High st Drtfrd
Z 12 Crayford rd N7
S 12 Crayford way Drtfrd
P 17 Crealock gro Wdfd Grn
B 17 Crealock st SW18
K 3 Creasy clo SE1
Y 16 Crebor st SE22
U 16 Credenhill st SW16
A 15 Crediton hill NW6
T 17 Crediton rd E16
E 6 Crediton rd NW10
X 7 Credon rd E13
N 14 Credon rd SE16
Y 10 Credon rd SE16
R 3 Cree way Rom
L 6 Creechurch la EC3
L 6 Creechurch pl EC3
Y 6 Creed la EC4
D 17 Creek rd SE8
X 9 Creek rd Bark
C 17 Creekside SE8
M 3 Creeland gros SE6
J 14 Creffield rd W6
R 20 Creffield rd W3
A 7 Creighton av E6
N 8 Creighton av N10
N 2 Creighton av N2
H 8 Creighton rd NW6
S 1 Creighton rd N17
F 9 Creighton rd W5
M 10 Cremer st E2
F 16 Cremorne est SW10
E 19 Cremorne rd SW10
T 7 Crescent av Hornch
T 4 Crescent east Barnt
Y 7 Crescent gdns SW19
V 11 Crescent gro SW4
H 10 Crescent gro Mitch
X 13 Crescent la SW4
L 5 Crescent pl SW3
P 5 Crescent rd E10
T 3 Crescent rd E13
K 6 Crescent rd E18
N 6 Crescent rd E4
Y 3 Crescent rd E6
A 15 Crescent rd N11
H 11 Crescent rd N15
Y 4 Crescent rd N22
V 4 Crescent rd N3
Y 19 Crescent rd N8
K 5 Crescent rd N9
M 13 Crescent rd SE18
N 12 Crescent rd SW20
S 3 Crescent rd Becknhm
F 19 Crescent rd Brom
G 10 Crescent rd Dgnhm
W 13 Crescent rd Enf
R 17 Crescent rd Kingst
M 7 Crescent rd Sidcp
X 3 Crescent ri N22
V 17 Crescent ri Barnt
A 17 Crescent row EC1

32 J 17 Crescent the E17
44 K 9 Crescent the NW2
16 A 15 Crescent the N11
31 T 17 Crescent the N15
86 F 4 Crescent the SW13
105 Y 8 Crescent the SW19
5 N 10 Crescent the Barnt
125 O 1 Crescent the Becknhm
97 U 18 Crescent the Bxly
123 O 13 Crescent the Croy
41 P 5 Crescent the Harrow
35 W 18 Crescent the Ilf
117 X 4 Crescent the New Mald
70 D 5 Crescent the S'hall
114 L 10 Crescent the Sidcp
116 H 13 Crescent the Surb
154 F 9 Crescent the Sutton
125 Z 14 Crescent the W Wickhm
42 A 7 Crescent the Wemb
15 V 19 Crescent way N12
93 N 8 Crescent way SE4
108 E 17 Crescent way SW16
6 P 6 Crescent west Barnt
109 W 7 Crescent Wood rd SE26
88 A 2 Cresford rd SW6
26 J 18 Crespigny rd NW4
58 F 11 Cressage clo S'hall
50 D 18 Cresset rd E9
89 W 9 Cresset st SW4
63 R 13 Cressey ct E1
47 W 3 Cressida rd N19
154 C 7 Cressingham gro Sutton
93 U 7 Cressingham rd SE13
12 L 20 Cressingham rd Edg
25 Y 2 Cressingham rd Edg
49 S 13 Cressington rd N16
94 C 7 Cresswell pk SE3
123 Y 9 Cresswell rd SE25
84 F 16 Cresswell rd Twick
17 T 2 Cresswell way N21
63 R 14 Cressy clo E1
63 R 14 Cressy pl E1
46 L 13 Cressy rd NW3
9 P 4 Crest dri Enf
44 G 7 Crest rd NW2
126 B 18 Crest rd Brom
157 Z 16 Crest rd S Croy
27 U 14 Crest the NW4
17 T 13 Crest the N13
117 R 13 Crest the Surb
17 V 10 Crestbrook av N13
132 K 12 Crestfield st WC1
86 H 15 Crestway SW15
146 A 9 Cresswell gdns SW10
146 B 11 Cresswell pl SW10
61 C 10 Creswick rd W3
27 W 13 Creswick wlk NW11
78 K 9 Creton st SE18
76 A 10 Crew st E14
149 S 19 Crewdson rd SW9
62 D 8 Crewe pl NW10
45 W 8 Crewys rd NW2
92 A 5 Crewys rd SE15
155 X 9 Crichton av Wallgtn
154 L 16 Crichton rd Carsh
120 L 8 Cricket grn Mitch
127 Z 1 Cricket Ground rd Chisl
7 Z 9 Cricketers Arms rd Enf
108 B 4 Cricklade av SW2
45 O 12 Cricklewood bdwy NW2
45 T 10 Cricklewood la NW2
65 O 4 Cridland st E15
88 E 16 Crieff rd SW18
107 Y 2 Criffel av SW2
150 L 3 Crimscott st SE1
148 F 20 Crimsworth rd SW8
132 L 7 Crinan st N1
148 C 17 Cringle st SW8
74 M 15 Crisp rd W6
144 C 11 Crisp rd W6
67 P 6 Crispe rd Bark
155 Z 4 Crispin clo Wallgtn
12 J 20 Crispin rd Edg
142 M 1 Crispin st E1
47 V 5 Cristowe rd SW6
47 X 7 Criterion ms N19
106 L 5 Crockerton rd SW17
113 X 10 Crockham way SE9
62 D 18 Crocus field Barnt
159 V 1 Crocus wlk W12
12 M 11 Croft clo NW7
12 M 11 Croft clo NW7
81 O 14 Croft clo Blvdr

113 U 11 Croft clo Chisl
71 X 5 Croft gdns W7
21 V 18 Croft Lodge clo Wdfd Grn
108 G 19 Croft rd SW16
106 D 19 Croft rd SW19
112 G 16 Croft rd Brom
9 V 7 Croft rd Enf
154 H 10 Croft rd Sutton
75 V 12 Croft st SE8
62 D 5 Croft the NW10
60 J 14 Croft the W5
4 D 14 Croft the Barnt
70 C 18 Croft the Hounsl
22 F 20 Croft tho Pinn
42 C 14 Croft the Wemb
102 B 8 Croft way Rich
114 G 7 Croft way Sidcp
47 S 8 Croftdown rd NW5
158 L 19 Crofters mead Croy
158 M 20 Crofters mead Croy
97 V 19 Crofton av Bxly
92 K 16 Crofton Pk rd SE4
65 V 10 Crofton rd E13
91 T 2 Crofton rd SE5
84 M 10 Crofton ter Rich
5 N 19 Crofton way Barnt
23 Y 17 Crofts rd Harrow
45 Y 12 Croftway NW3
47 P 19 Crogsland rd NW1
157 R 15 Croham clo S Croy
157 V 17 Croham hurst Croy
157 T 13 Croham Manor rd S Croy
157 R 16 Croham mt S Croy
157 T 11 Croham Park av S Croy
157 Y 16 Croham Valley rd S Croy
157 W 14 Croham Valley rd S Croy
158 C 17 Croham Valley rd S Croy
122 B 2 Croindene rd SW16
47 Y 2 Cromartie rd N19
114 F 1 Crombie rd Sidcp
96 F 20 Crombie rd Sidcup
33 W 20 Cromer rd E10
31 W 6 Cromer rd N17
123 Z 6 Cromer rd SE25
107 O 15 Cromer rd SW17
5 O 13 Cromer rd Barnt
37 Z 18 Cromer rd Rom
38 K 10 Cromer rd Rom
21 T 14 Cromer rd Wdfd Grn
132 K 14 Cromer st WC1
87 U 17 Cromer Vlls rd SW18
87 X 13 Cromford rd SW18
117 Z 1 Cromford way New Mald
130 F 19 Crompton st W2
47 T 2 Cromwell av N6
74 J 12 Cromwell av W6
126 G 8 Cromwell av Brom
118 C 10 Cromwell av New Mald
28 F 13 Cromwell clo N2
126 H 9 Cromwell clo Brom
145 S 6 Cromwell cres W8
146 H 4 Cromwell gdns SW7
136 D 20 Cromwell gro W6
146 F 5 Cromwell ms SW7
47 T 3 Cromwell pl N6
85 W 7 Cromwell pl SW14
146 G 5 Cromwell pl SW7
33 T 16 Cromwell rd E17
52 K 20 Cromwell rd E7
29 P 1 Cromwell rd N10
16 E 20 Cromwell rd N11
16 E 20 Cromwell rd N11
28 C 6 Cromwell rd N3
105 Z 12 Cromwell rd SW19
106 A 12 Cromwell rd SW19
145 X 5 Cromwell rd SW5
146 C 5 Cromwell rd SW7
124 K 5 Cromwell rd Becknhm
123 N 17 Cromwell rd Croy
82 H 13 Cromwell rd Hounsl
116 K 2 Cromwell rd Kingst
60 J 6 Cromwell rd Wemb
152 A 6 Cromwell rd Worc Pk
73 T 15 Cromwell Rd ext NW4
82 H 10 Cromwell st Hounsl
87 Y 2 Crondace rd SW6
134 J 10 Crondall st N1
150 M 15 Cronin rd SE15
151 N 18 Cronin rd SE15
97 X 9 Crook log Bxly Hth
75 U 12 Crooke rd SE8
104 M 15 Crooked billet SW19

27 S 10 Crooked usage N3
87 V 3 Crookham SW6
95 Y 7 Crookston rd SE9
76 J 20 Crooms hill SE10
76 H 19 Crooms Hill gro SE10
134 E 10 Cropley st N1
56 E 14 Croppath rd Dgnhm
52 E 17 Crosby rd E7
69 U 5 Crosby rd Dgnhm
142 F 18 Crosby row SE1
142 J 5 Crosby sq EC3
101 X 4 Cross deep Rich
101 W 3 Cross Deep gdns Rich
101 W 3 Cross Deep gdns Twick
12 B 11 Cross ga Edg
142 F 3 Cross Key ct EC2
139 U 2 Cross Keys clo W1
142 A 3 Cross Keys sq EC 1
142 J 10 Cross la EC3
30 B 12 Cross la N8
98 C 18 Cross la Bxly
82 K 11 Cross Lances rd Hounsl
20 L 8 Cross rd E4
16 F 15 Cross rd N11
18 F 20 Cross rd N17
30 F 1 Cross rd N22
91 T 4 Cross rd SE5
105 Y 18 Cross rd SW19
123 P 20 Cross rd Croy
8 F 15 Cross rd Enf
100 B 10 Cross rd Felt
23 P 14 Cross rd Harrow
23 Y 8 Cross rd Harrow
40 J 9 Cross rd Harrow
103 N 18 Cross rd Kingst
38 F 12 Cross rd Rom
55 T 2 Cross rd Rom
115 R 11 Cross rd Sidcp
154 G 10 Cross rd Sutton
51 Z 20 Cross st E3
64 A 1 Cross st E3
133 Y 3 Cross st N1
18 J 16 Cross st N18
86 C 6 Cross st SW13
101 N 13 Cross st Hampt
15 U 19 Cross way N12
55 T 10 Cross way Dgnhm
21 Y 14 Cross way Wdfd Grn
23 U 6 Cross Way the Harrow
95 P 6 Crossbrook rd SE3
46 G 19 Crossfield rd NW 3
30 L 11 Crossfield rd N17
76 B 18 Crossfield st SE8
90 B 4 Crossford st SW9
42 B 18 Crossgate Grnfd
122 H 14 Crossland rd Thntn Hth
72 M 3 Crosslands av W5
73 N 3 Crosslands av W5
70 E 14 Crosslands av S'hall
48 F 18 Crossley st N7
113 U 2 Crossmead SE9
58 J 8 Crossmead av Grnfd
91 O 11 Crossthwaite av SE5
135 U 3 Crosston st E8
142 M 8 Crosswall EC3
143 N 7 Crosswall EC3
26 E 14 Crossway NW9
49 T 15 Crossway N16
68 J 20 Crossway SE2
118 M 9 Crossway SW20
59 Y 11 Crossway W13
18 D 2 Crossway Enf
30 K 3 Crossway the N22
113 U 4 Crossway the SE9
23 U 6 Crossway the Harrow
17 Y 1 Crossways N21
39 Z 11 Crossways Rom
158 K 16 Crossways S Croy
154 F 18 Crossways Sutton
125 N 9 Crossways rd Becknhm
145 S 5 Crossways rd Mitch
70 E 20 Crossways the Hounsl
43 R 7 Crossways the Wemb
68 D 7 Crouch av Bark
113 X 7 Crouch croft SE9
29 Z 19 Crouch End hill N8
48 A 1 Crouch hill N4
56 H 1 Crow la Rom
107 P 13 Crowborough rd SW17
143 W 9 Crowder st E1
90 G 5 Crowhurst rd SW9
16 M 3 Crowland gdns N14
31 V 16 Crowland rd N15

| | | |
|---|---|---|
| 123 N 9 | Crowland rd Thntn Hth | |
| 49 N 20 | Crowland ter N1 | |
| 120 B 13 | Crowland wlk Mrdn | |
| 38 H 18 | Crowlands av Rom | |
| 156 H 11 | Crowley cres Croy | |
| 92 D 20 | Crowmarsh gdns SE23 | |
| 13 T 7 | Crown clo NW7 | |
| 13 S 7 | Crown clo NW7 | |
| 142 C 6 | Crown ct EC4 | |
| 94 G 16 | Crown ct SE12 | |
| 140 M 7 | Crown ct WC2 | |
| 108 L 14 | Crown dale SE19 | |
| 156 L 4 | Crown hill Croy | |
| 16 H 5 | Crown la N14 | |
| 108 G 14 | Crown la SW16 | |
| 127 O 13 | Crown la Brom | |
| 119 Z 7 | Crown la Mrdn | |
| 127 O 13 | Crown la Spur Brom | |
| 108 G 13 | Crown La gdns SW16 | |
| 140 C 14 | Crown pas SW1 | |
| 29 P 2 | Crown rd N10 | |
| 31 W 1 | Crown rd N17 | |
| 8 M 14 | Crown rd Enf | |
| 36 D 13 | Crown rd Ilf | |
| 119 Z 8 | Crown rd Mrdn | |
| 117 X 1 | Crown rd New Mald | |
| 153 Z 9 | Crown rd Sutton | |
| 154 A 8 | Crown rd Sutton | |
| 84 C 17 | Crown rd Twick | |
| 150 B 18 | Crown st SE5 | |
| 73 T 3 | Crown st W3 | |
| 56 J 19 | Crown st Dgnhm | |
| 41 S 4 | Crown st Harrow | |
| 84 M 9 | Crown ter Rich | |
| 95 Z 4 | Crown Woods la SE18 | |
| 141 T 8 | Crown-Office row EC4 | |
| 132 B 8 | Crowndale rd NW1 | |
| 36 F 17 | Crownfield av Ilf | |
| 51 W 13 | Crownfield rd E15 | |
| 62 D 4 | Crownhill rd NW10 | |
| 35 R 3 | Crownhill rd Wdfd Grn | |
| 38 H 13 | Crownmead way Rom | |
| 96 A 7 | Crownwoods la SE9 | |
| 96 F 12 | Crownwoods way SE9 | |
| 64 L 8 | Crows rd E15 | |
| 24 F 6 | Crowshott av Stanm | |
| 90 E 13 | Crowstone rd SW2 | |
| 72 K 12 | Crowther av Brentf | |
| 123 X 10 | Crowther rd SE25 | |
| 120 C 14 | Croxden wlk Rom | |
| 30 K 3 | Croxford gdns N22 | |
| 56 L 4 | Croxford way Rom | |
| 129 R 13 | Croxley rd W9 | |
| 90 L 19 | Croxted clo SE21 | |
| 109 N 2 | Croxted rd SE21 | |
| 90 L 18 | Croxted rd SE24 | |
| 59 O 9 | Croyde av Grnfd | |
| 96 E 18 | Croydon clo Sidcp | |
| 122 H 19 | Croydon gro Croy | |
| 65 R 12 | Croydon rd E13 | |
| 110 D 20 | Croydon rd SE20 | |
| 123 Z 4 | Croydon rd SE20 | |
| 124 L 6 | Croydon rd Becknhm | |
| 156 B 8 | Croydon rd Croy | |
| 121 T 11 | Croydon rd Mitch | |
| 155 V 7 | Croydon rd Wallgtn | |
| 18 J 5 | Croyland rd N9 | |
| 50 G 16 | Crozier ter E9 | |
| 142 K 17 | Crucifix la SE1 | |
| 133 Y 6 | Cruden st N1 | |
| 133 R 11 | Cruikshank st WC1 | |
| 52 A 20 | Cruikshank rd E15 | |
| 26 B 16 | Crummock gdns NW9 | |
| 80 F 11 | Crumpsall st SE2 | |
| 25 R 17 | Crundale av NW9 | |
| 157 O 15 | Crunden rd S Croy | |
| 106 M 18 | Crusoe rd Mitch | |
| 142 L 8 | Crutched friars EC3 | |
| 112 A 4 | Crutchley rd SE6 | |
| 109 Y 12 | Crystal Palace park SE26 | |
| 109 V 13 | Crystal Palace pde SE19 | |
| 91 W 10 | Crystal Palace rd SE22 | |
| 109 W 16 | Crystal Palace Stn rd SE19 | |
| 109 O 15 | Crystal ter SE19 | |
| 9 O 9 | Cuba dri Enf | |
| 76 A 4 | Cuba st E14 | |
| 133 O 14 | Cubitt st WC1 | |
| 156 E 11 | Cubitt st Croy | |
| 59 U 13 | Cuckoo av W7 | |
| 59 S 13 | Cuckoo dene W7 | |
| 19 P 2 | Cuckoo Hall la N9 | |
| 59 U 19 | Cuckoo la W7 | |
| 152 D 7 | Cudas clo Epsom | |
| 152 D 6 | Cuddington av Worc Pk | |
| 93 T 18 | Cudham st SE6 | |
| 135 X 16 | Cudworth st E1 | |
| 63 N 11 | Cudworth st E1 | |
| 95 P 17 | Cuff cres SE9 | |
| 147 O 7 | Culford gdns SW3 | |
| 49 R 19 | Culford gro N1 | |
| 49 R 18 | Culford ms N1 | |
| 134 J 2 | Culford rd N1 | |
| 49 R 18 | Culford rd N1 | |
| 7 N 13 | Culgarth gdns Enf | |
| 61 W 12 | Cullen way NW10 | |
| 75 O 7 | Culling rd SE16 | |
| 143 Z 20 | Culling rd SE16 | |
| 23 X 13 | Cullington clo Harrow | |
| 44 H 15 | Cullingworth rd NW10 | |
| 7 V 9 | Culloden rd Enf | |
| 64 G 17 | Culloden st E14 | |
| 142 J 7 | Cullum st EC3 | |
| 51 X 20 | Cullum st E15 | |
| 72 D 3 | Culmington rd W13 | |
| 156 K 18 | Culmington rd S Croy | |
| 107 N 1 | Culmore cross SW4 | |
| 75 O 20 | Culmore rd SE14 | |
| 151 Z 19 | Culmore rd SE15 | |
| 89 O 13 | Culmstock rd SW11 | |
| 133 S 7 | Culpepper st N1 | |
| 30 K 14 | Culross rd N15 | |
| 139 S 9 | Culross st W1 | |
| 24 F 8 | Culver gro Stanm | |
| 108 C 8 | Culverhouse gdns SW16 | |
| 11 N 14 | Culverlands clo Stanm | |
| 93 R 20 | Culverley rd SE6 | |
| 111 U 1 | Culverley rd SE6 | |
| 154 L 2 | Culvers av Carsh | |
| 155 N 1 | Culvers av Carsh | |
| 121 O 19 | Culvers av Mitch | |
| 155 N 2 | Culvers retreat Carsh | |
| 154 L 3 | Culvers way Carsh | |
| 126 C 13 | Culverstone clo Brom | |
| 89 O 6 | Culvert pl SW8 | |
| 31 R 16 | Culvert rd N15 | |
| 89 N 4 | Culvert rd SW8 | |
| 150 B 8 | Culworth gro SE17 | |
| 130 K 10 | Culworth st NW8 | |
| 123 W 7 | Cumbedow av SE25 | |
| 61 T 9 | Cumberland av NW10 | |
| 96 K 10 | Cumberland av Welling | |
| 84 B 15 | Cumberland clo Twick | |
| 144 M 5 | Cumberland cres W14 | |
| 80 M 20 | Cumberland dri Bxly Hth | |
| 98 A 1 | Cumberland dri Bxly Hth | |
| 27 R 6 | Cumberland gdns NW4 | |
| 133 R 12 | Cumberland gdns WC1 | |
| 131 Z 12 | Cumberland mkt NW1 | |
| 61 X 20 | Cumberland pk W3 | |
| 73 W 1 | Cumberland pk W3 | |
| 131 X 12 | Cumberland pl NW1 | |
| 53 N 14 | Cumberland rd E12 | |
| 65 V 11 | Cumberland rd E13 | |
| 32 H 7 | Cumberland rd E17 | |
| 30 D 6 | Cumberland rd N22 | |
| 19 P 7 | Cumberland rd N9 | |
| 86 E 1 | Cumberland rd SW13 | |
| 61 W 20 | Cumberland rd W3 | |
| 71 W 6 | Cumberland rd W7 | |
| 125 Z 8 | Cumberland rd Brom | |
| 126 C 8 | Cumberland rd Brom | |
| 22 K 15 | Cumberland rd Harrow | |
| 73 O 20 | Cumberland rd Rich | |
| 25 N 11 | Cumberland rd Stanm | |
| 147 N 9 | Cumberland st SW1 | |
| 148 A 11 | Cumberland st SW1 | |
| 131 X 10 | Cumberland Terr ms NW1 | |
| 124 A 13 | Cumberland va SE25 | |
| 31 P 5 | Cumberton rd N17 | |
| 99 R 4 | Cumbrian av Bxly Hth | |
| 45 R 7 | Cumbrian gdns NW2 | |
| 133 O 9 | Cumming st N1 | |
| 152 H 15 | Cumnor gdns Epsom | |
| 154 E 13 | Cumnor rd Sutton | |
| 142 K 6 | Cunard pl EC3 | |
| 151 Z 9 | Cunard rd NW10 | |
| 150 H 14 | Cunard st SE5 | |
| 65 X 18 | Cundy rd E16 | |
| 147 V 7 | Cundy st SW1 | |
| 152 F 8 | Cunliffe rd Worc Pk | |
| 107 V 14 | Cunliffe st SW16 | |
| 159 S 3 | Cunningham clo W Wknm | |
| 23 P 15 | Cunningham pk Harrow | |
| 130 F 16 | Cunningham pl NW8 | |
| 130 F 16 | Cunningham pl NW8 | |
| 31 W 13 | Cunningham rd N15 | |
| 73 W 10 | Cunnington st W4 | |
| 89 R 1 | Cupar rd SW11 | |
| 148 G 8 | Cureton st SW1 | |
| 143 O 16 | Curlew st SE1 | |
| 107 U 5 | Curlverden rd SW12 | |
| 108 L 11 | Curnicks la SE27 | |
| 155 P 6 | Curran av Wallgtn | |
| 96 L 14 | Currant av Sidcp | |
| 41 P 18 | Currey rd Grnfd | |
| 74 A 4 | Curricle st W3 | |
| 105 V 10 | Currie Hill clo SW19 | |
| 141 S 4 | Cursitor st EC4 | |
| 134 K 15 | Curtain pl EC2 | |
| 134 K 14 | Curtain rd EC2 | |
| 6 L 15 | Curthwaite gdns Enf | |
| 82 D 20 | Curtis rd Hounsl | |
| 150 M 4 | Curtis st SE1 | |
| 62 F 20 | Curve the W12 | |
| 52 G 12 | Curwen av E7 | |
| 74 F 6 | Curwen rd W12 | |
| 9 U 17 | Curzon av Enf | |
| 23 Y 5 | Curzon av Stanm | |
| 44 B 20 | Curzon cres NW10 | |
| 62 C 1 | Curzon cres NW10 | |
| 67 X 8 | Curzon cres Bark | |
| 139 V 14 | Curzon pl W1 | |
| 29 S 7 | Curzon rd N10 | |
| 60 B 12 | Curzon rd W5 | |
| 122 E 14 | Curzon rd Thntn Hth | |
| 139 W 13 | Curzon st W1 | |
| 101 V 8 | Cusack clo Twick | |
| 81 Z 13 | Cusoe rd Erith | |
| 141 U 17 | Cut the SE1 | |
| 90 M 5 | Cutcombe rd SE5 | |
| 33 V 11 | Cuthbert rd E17 | |
| 18 K 15 | Cuthbert rd N18 | |
| 156 J 3 | Cuthbert rd Croy | |
| 130 F 20 | Cuthbert st W 2 | |
| 91 O 3 | Cuthill rd SE5 | |
| 142 L 4 | Cutler st E1 | |
| 97 X 12 | Cuxton clo Bxly Hth | |
| 135 O 16 | Cygnet st E2 | |
| 133 P 9 | Cynthia st N1 | |
| 83 N 18 | Cypress av Twick | |
| 132 C 19 | Cypress pl W1 | |
| 123 T 3 | Cypress rd SE25 | |
| 23 P 7 | Cypress rd Harrow | |
| 27 U 7 | Cyprus av N3 | |
| 27 T 6 | Cyprus gdns N3 | |
| 63 P 7 | Cyprus pl E2 | |
| 63 R 7 | Cyprus pl E2 | |
| 66 K 19 | Cyprus place E6 | |
| 27 V 8 | Cyprus rd N3 | |
| 18 G 7 | Cyprus rd N9 | |
| 63 R 7 | Cyprus st E2 | |
| 91 V 14 | Cyrena rd SE22 | |
| 98 A 5 | Cyril rd Bxly Hth | |
| 133 X 15 | Cyrus st EC1 | |

## D

| | | |
|---|---|---|
| 40 J 14 | Dabbs Hill la Grnrd | |
| 93 T 2 | Dabia cres SE10 | |
| 75 Z 15 | Dacca st SE8 | |
| 64 A 2 | Dace rd E3 | |
| 35 X 7 | Dacre av Ilf | |
| 93 X 7 | Dacre pk SE13 | |
| 94 A 10 | Dacre pk SE13 | |
| 93 Z 8 | Dacre pl SE13 | |
| 52 B 3 | Dacre rd E11 | |
| 65 U 4 | Dacre rd E13 | |
| 122 A 17 | Dacre rd Croy | |
| 140 F 20 | Dacre st SW1 | |
| 110 D 6 | Dacres clo SE23 | |
| 110 E 7 | Dacres rd SE23 | |
| 74 E 1 | Daffodil rd W12 | |
| 62 E 20 | Daffodil st W12 | |
| 107 N 7 | Dafforne rd SW17 | |
| 68 M 3 | Dagenham av Dgnhm | |
| 56 C 20 | Dagenham av Dgnhm | |
| 69 N 1 | Dagenham av Dgnhm | |
| 69 U 1 | Dagenham Old park Dgnhm | |
| 50 M 3 | Dagenham rd E10 | |
| 56 J 11 | Dagenham rd Dgnhm | |
| 57 N 4 | Dagenham rd Rom | |
| 42 L 13 | Dagmar av Wemb | |
| 43 N 13 | Dagmar av Wemb | |
| 128 E 10 | Dagmar gdns NW | |
| 133 X 3 | Dagmar pas N1 | |
| 31 O 14 | Dagmar rd N15 | |
| 29 Y 4 | Dagmar rd N22 | |
| 123 R 10 | Dagmar rd SE25 | |
| 91 R 3 | Dagmar rd SE5 | |
| 56 L 19 | Dagmar rd Dgnhm | |
| 103 O 19 | Dagmar rd Kingst | |
| 70 C 9 | Dagmar rd S'hall | |
| 133 X 3 | Dagmar ter N1 | |
| 123 P 13 | Dagnall pk SE25 | |
| 123 R 11 | Dagnall rd SE25 | |
| 89 N 3 | Dagnall st SW11 | |
| 89 T 17 | Dagnan rd SW12 | |
| 112 E 8 | Dagonet gdns Bro | |
| 112 E 7 | Dagonet rd Brom | |
| 121 X 9 | Dahlia gdns Mitch | |
| 80 D 12 | Dahlia rd SE2 | |
| 107 U 15 | Dahomey rd SW1 | |
| 156 A 15 | Daimler way Wall | |
| 53 V 10 | Daines clo E12 | |
| 111 W 12 | Dainford clo Brom | |
| 95 Y 7 | Dairsie rd SE9 | |
| 105 R 9 | Dairy wlk SW19 | |
| 87 Y 7 | Daisy la SW6 | |
| 34 H 8 | Daisy rd E18 | |
| 90 F 13 | Dalberg rd SW2 | |
| 88 C 11 | Dalby rd SW18 | |
| 47 R 18 | Dalby st NW5 | |
| 82 A 5 | Dalcross rd Houns | |
| 25 N 7 | Dale av Edg | |
| 24 M 6 | Dale av Edg | |
| 82 C 7 | Dale av Hounsl | |
| 94 D 8 | Dale clo SE3 | |
| 5 N 20 | Dale clo Barnt | |
| 99 U 14 | Dale clo Drtfrd | |
| 99 U 17 | Dale end Drtfrd | |
| 21 V 13 | Dale gdns Wdfd G | |
| 16 F 12 | Dale Green rd N1 | |
| 151 P 18 | Dale gro N12 | |
| 155 N 3 | Dale Park av Carsh | |
| 154 M 3 | Dale Park av Carsh | |
| 109 N 20 | Dale Park rd SE19 | |
| 47 O 15 | Dale rd NW5 | |
| 99 U 16 | Dale rd Drtfrd | |
| 58 K 15 | Dale rd Grnfd | |
| 153 V 9 | Dale rd Sutton | |
| 74 A 14 | Dale st W4 | |
| 99 V 4 | Dale view Erith | |
| 20 H 9 | Dale View av E4 | |
| 20 G 9 | Dale View cres E4 | |
| 20 H 9 | Dale View gdns E4 | |
| 106 K 4 | Dalebury rd SW17 | |
| 46 F 17 | Daleham gdns NW | |
| 46 F 17 | Daleham ms NW3 | |
| 107 S 12 | Daleside rd SW16 | |
| 31 S 19 | Daleview rd N15 | |
| 152 L 2 | Dalewood gdns Worc Pk | |
| 50 F 17 | Daley st E9 | |
| 128 C 20 | Dalgarno gdns W1 | |
| 136 A 1 | Dalgarno gdns W1 | |
| 62 L 14 | Dalgarno gdns W1 | |
| 62 M 12 | Dalgarno way W10 | |
| 128 D 19 | Dalgarno way W10 | |
| 63 X 17 | Dalgleish st E14 | |
| 11 W 17 | Dalkeith gro Stanm | |
| 90 M 20 | Dalkeith rd SE21 | |
| 54 C 10 | Dalkeith rd Ilf | |
| 44 H 1 | Dallas rd NW4 | |
| 109 Z 8 | Dallas rd SE26 | |
| 60 M 14 | Dallas rd W5 | |
| 153 T 14 | Dallas rd Sutton | |
| 78 M 18 | Dallin rd SE18 | |
| 79 N 18 | Dallin rd SE18 | |
| 97 X 10 | Dallin rd Bxly Hth | |
| 74 J 8 | Dalling rd W 6 | |
| 94 B 17 | Dallinger rd SE12 | |
| 133 X 16 | Dallington st EC1 | |
| 92 F 20 | Dalmain rd SE23 | |
| 123 W 17 | Dalmally rd Croy | |
| 47 Z 14 | Dalmeny av N7 | |
| 122 F 4 | Dalmeny av SW16 | |
| 42 E 17 | Dalmeny clo Wemb | |
| 47 X 10 | Dalmeny rd N1 | |
| 5 S 20 | Dalmeny rd Barnt | |
| 98 G 2 | Dalmeny rd Bxly Hth | |
| 155 P 17 | Dalmeny rd Carsh | |
| 152 K 5 | Dalmeny rd Worc Pk | |
| 108 M 3 | Dalmore rd SE21 | |
| 92 J 12 | Dalrymple rd SE4 | |
| 24 J 6 | Dalston gdns Stanm | |
| 50 A 15 | Dalston la E5 | |
| 49 V 18 | Dalston la E8 | |
| 120 H 3 | Dalton av Mitch | |
| 108 K 5 | Dalton st SE27 | |
| 91 S 1 | Dalton st SE5 | |
| 90 C 8 | Dalyell rd SW9 | |

4 A 7 Dame st N1
6 C 19 Damer ter SW10
2 F 12 Dames rd E7
3 N 17 Damien st E1
3 Y 4 Damien st E1
8 B 19 Danbrook rd SW16
7 V 10 Danbury clo Rom
5 S 8 Danbury ms Wallgtn
3 Y 8 Danbury st N1
1 Y 20 Danbury way Wdfd Grn
1 U 7 Danby st SE15
7 V 3 Dancer rd SW6
P 7 Dancer rd Rich
4 G 8 Dando cres SE3
8 E 19 Dane clo Bxly
7 V 5 Dane Court gdns Croy
3 X 6 Dane pl E3
6 D 20 Dane rd SW19
2 D 2 Dane rd W13
4 A 16 Dane rd Ilf
8 C 20 Dane rd S'hall
6 B 16 Danebury av SW15
1 S 5 Daneby rd SE6
1 N 13 Danecroft rd SE24
5 S 17 Danehurst gdns Ilf
7 S 1 Danehurst st SW6
5 Z 20 Daneland Barnt
0 K 15 Danemead gro Grnfd
0 K 15 Danemead gro Grnfd
7 N 7 Danemere st SW15
3 S 11 Danes ga Harrow
8 K 20 Danes rd Rom
9 U 14 Danesbury Croy
4 D 3 Danescourt cres Sutton
7 R 16 Danescroft av NW4
7 R 16 Danescroft gdns NW4
0 H 18 Danesdale rd E9
1 T 7 Daneswood av SE6
2 F 18 Danethorpe rd Wemb
6 D 8 Danette gdns Dgnhm
1 N 3 Daneville rd SE5
4 E 19 Dangan rd E11
4 E 14 Daniel Bolt clo E14
1 O 17 Daniel gdns SE15
6 J 20 Daniel pl NW4
1 O 20 Daniel rd W5
2 C 8 Daniels rd SE15
0 F 9 Dansey pl W1
7 O 9 Dansington rd Welling
7 O 9 Danson cres Welling
7 P 10 Danson la Welling
7 V 9 Danson mead Welling
9 Y 12 Danson rd SE17
7 V 12 Danson rd Bxly Hth
9 X 6 Dante rd SE11
6 L 9 Danube st SW3
29 W 12 Danvers rd N8
46 H 15 Danvers st SW3
20 G 10 Daphne gdns E4
88 B 17 Daphne st SW18
40 D 6 Darblay st W1
43 R 10 Darby st E1
55 V 8 Darcy av Wallgtn
24 H 14 Darcy dri Harrow
69 P 2 Darcy gdns Dgnhm
24 J 13 Darcy gdns Harrow
21 Z 3 Darcy rd SW16
53 O 8 Darcy rd Sutton
55 Z 10 Dare gdns Dgnhm
85 P 7 Darell rd Rich
49 V 2 Darenth rd N16
97 O 2 Darenth rd Welling
92 K 13 Darfield rd SE4
67 O 8 Darfur st SW15
88 G 8 Darien rd SW11
45 R 20 Darlan rd SW6
05 R 18 Darlaston rd SW19
17 Y 3 Darley dri New Mald
18 G 4 Darley rd N9
93 O 7 Darling rd SE4
63 N 13 Darling row E1
35 Y 19 Darling row E1
08 K 12 Darlington rd SE27
50 B 19 Darnley rd E9
34 G 4 Darnley rd Wdfd Grn
36 J 13 Darnley ter W11
91 X 13 Darrell rd SE22
89 Z 1 Darsley dri SW8
29 N 12 Dart st W10
19 R 1 Dartford av N9
99 Y 15 Dartford rd Drtfrd
50 B 13 Dartford st SE17
93 V 3 Dartmouth gro SE10
93 V 3 Dartmouth hill SE10
47 T 5 Dartmouth Pk hill NW5
47 S 10 Dartmouth Pk rd NW5
110 D 4 Dartmouth pl SE23
65 S 17 Dartmouth rd E16
45 O 17 Dartmouth rd NW2
26 G 19 Dartmouth rd NW4
110 C 5 Dartmouth rd SE26
126 F 17 Dartmouth rd Brom
93 V 3 Dartmouth row SE10
140 F 19 Dartmouth st SW1
150 M 12 Dartnell rd SE5
123 U 17 Dartnell rd Croy
146 E 18 Dartrey rd SW10
88 E 11 Darvall sq SW18
88 E 11 Darvall st SW18
49 V 10 Darville rd N16
58 L 17 Darwin dri S'hall
150 F 6 Darwin pl SE17
30 J 7 Darwin rd N22
72 F 12 Darwin rd W5
96 L 8 Darwin rd Welling
150 G 5 Darwin st SE17
59 T 6 Daryngton dri Grnfd
98 E 14 Dashwood clo Bxly Hth
30 C 19 Dashwood rd N8
108 K 12 Dassett rd SE27
91 P 2 Datchelor pl SE5
110 L 6 Datchet rd SE6
150 D 10 Date st SE17
50 H 12 Daubeney rd E5
30 L 2 Daubeney rd N17
88 C 15 Daulte rd SW18
47 Z 7 Davenant rd N19
143 T 2 Davenant st E1
93 T 16 Davenport rd SE6
115 Y 4 Davenport rd Sidcp
33 O 17 Daventry av E17
130 K 20 Daventry st NW1
77 U 13 Daverill st SE18
151 O 15 Davey st SE15
59 T 8 David av Grnfd
131 S 20 David ms W1
55 X 6 David rd Dgnhm
51 Y 16 David st E15
141 X 19 Davidge st SE1
110 C 2 Davids rd SE23
36 G 1 Davids way Ilf
148 J 18 Davidson gdns SW1
123 U 15 Davidson rd Croy
52 A 5 Davies la E11
139 W 8 Davies ms W1
139 W 8 Davies st W1
55 R 16 Davington gdns Dgnhm
55 R 15 Davington rd Dgnhm
135 R 18 Davis av E1
74 D 4 Davis rd W3
65 W 7 Davis st E13
76 G 8 Davis st E14
74 G 6 Davisville rd W12
83 X 11 Dawes av Islwth
144 K 17 Dawes rd SW6
145 P 18 Dawes rd SW6
150 G 9 Dawes st SE17
16 M 14 Dawlish av N13
17 N 15 Dawlish av N13
106 A 4 Dawlish av SW18
59 Z 7 Dawlish av Grnfd
60 A 7 Dawlish av Grnfd
54 H 12 Dawlish dri Ilf
22 B 17 Dawlish dri Pinn
51 T 5 Dawlish rd E10
45 P 17 Dawlish rd NW2
31 W 9 Dawlish rd N17
106 E 4 Dawnay gdns SW18
106 F 3 Dawnay rd SW18
44 E 7 Dawpool rd NW2
13 T 16 Daws la NW7
67 W 2 Dawson av Bark
67 Y 2 Dawson av Bark
67 Y 2 Dawson gdns Bark
137 U 9 Dawson pl W2
45 N 13 Dawson rd NW2
117 N 6 Dawson rd Surb
135 O 9 Dawson st E2
120 A 4 Daybrook rd SW19
86 G 9 Daylesford av SW15
96 G 20 Days la Sidcp
108 C 2 Daysbrook rd SW2
92 C 1 Dayton gro SE15
49 R 20 De Beauvoir rd N1
134 J 2 De Beauvoir rd N1
49 S 20 De Beauvoir sq N1
134 K 1 De Beauvoir sq N1
6 D 20 De Behun av N14
91 O 4 De Crespigny pk SE5
110 H 8 De Frene rd SE26
156 B 16 De Havilland rd Croy
25 S 8 De Havilland rd Edg
156 B 16 De Havillard rd Croy
149 W 11 De Laune st SE17
80 E 10 De Lucy st SE2
107 Z 5 De Montford rd SW16
88 B 7 De Morgan rd SW6
31 O 4 De Quiney rd N17
138 A 19 De Vere gdns W8
53 T 5 De Vere gdns Ilf
138 A 20 De Vere ms W8
139 V 2 De Walden st W1
44 G 16 Deacon rd NW2
116 M 1 Deacon rd Kingst
150 A 6 Deacon st SE17
107 O 15 Deal rd SW17
135 S 19 Deal st E1
86 L 10 Dealtry rd SW15
148 J 4 Dean Bradley st SW1
42 C 9 Dean ct Wemb
24 K 8 Dean dri Stanm
140 F 20 Dean Farrar st SW1
33 W 12 Dean gdns E17
44 M 17 Dean pl NW2
157 O 9 Dean rd Croy
100 F 13 Dean rd Hampt
82 L 14 Dean rd Hounsl
148 J 4 Dean Ryle st SW1
52 E 14 Dean st E7
140 F 7 Dean st W1
148 J 3 Dean Stanley st SW1
148 J 3 Dean Trench st SW1
12 K 20 Dean wlk Edg
143 Z 6 Deancross st E1
63 O 17 Deancross st E1
139 U 13 Deanery ms W1
51 Z 18 Deanery rd E15
52 A 19 Deanery rd E15
139 U 13 Deanery st W1
85 U 10 Deanhill rd SW14
150 F 8 Deans bldgs SE17
73 T 16 Deans clo W4
12 H 20 Deans clo Edg
141 Y 7 Deans ct EC4
12 K 16 Deans dri Edg
73 T 16 Deans la W4
12 H 18 Deans la Edg
139 X 4 Deans ms W1
148 E 8 Deans pl SW1
71 W 4 Deans rd W7
153 Z 7 Deans rd Sutton
154 A 6 Deans rd Sutton
12 G 17 Deans way Edg
148 H 1 Deans yd SW1
140 H 20 Dean's yd SW 1
25 U 1 Deansbrook clo Edg
25 U 1 Deansbrook clo Edgw
13 N 20 Deansbrook rd NW7
12 H 20 Deansbrook rd Edg
13 N 20 Deansbrook rd Edg
43 V 5 Deanscroft av NW9
28 G 13 Deansway N2
18 E 10 Deansway N9
120 J 5 Dearn gdns Mitch
10 L 17 Dearne clo Stanm
64 H 3 Deason st E15
57 Z 18 Debden wlk Hornch
75 P 12 Debnams rd SE16
106 D 17 Deburgh rd SW19
150 J 1 Decima st SE1
27 U 14 Decoy av NW11
85 W 9 Dee rd Rich
64 J 16 Dee st E14
39 P 3 Dee way Rom
89 X 2 Deeley rd SW8
61 O 17 Deena clo W3
105 R 10 Deepdale SW19
157 V 7 Deepdene av Croy
7 W 20 Deepdene ct N21
90 C 18 Deepdene gdns SW2
91 N 9 Deepdene rd SE5
97 O 6 Deepdene rd Welling
120 C 3 Deer Pk rd SW19
108 H 1 Deerbrook rd SE24
90 L 9 Deerdale rd SE24
57 W 19 Deere av Rainhm
26 F 17 Deerfield cotts NW9
45 P 19 Deerhurst rd NW2
108 C 13 Deerhurst rd SW16
106 F 7 Deeside rd SW17
155 Z 16 Defiant way Wallgtn
73 R 20 Defoe av Rich
49 S 8 Defoe rd N16
113 Y 13 Degema rd Chisl
44 F 2 Dehar cres NW9
91 S 16 Dekker rd SE21
77 V 20 Delacourt rd SE3
77 X 13 Delafield rd SE7
75 N 14 Delaford rd SE16
145 N 16 Delaford st SW6
124 C 15 Delamere cres Croy
12 K 18 Delamere gdns NW7
119 P 1 Delamere rd SW20
72 L 4 Delamere rd W5
138 A 1 Delamere st W2
138 A 1 Delamere ter W2
131 Z 6 Delancey pas NW1
131 X 6 Delancey st NW1
88 E 12 Delaporte sq SW18
129 W 16 Delaware rd W9
91 N 16 Delawyk cres SE24
118 L 20 Delcombe av Worc Pk
91 S 12 Delft way SE22
18 G 1 Delhi rd Enf
132 L 4 Delhi st N1
88 B 18 Delia st SW18
64 L 3 Dell clo E15
155 W 7 Dell clo Wallgtn
21 U 11 Dell clo Wdfd Grn
152 F 12 Dell la Epsom
9 P 2 Dell rd Enf
152 G 12 Dell rd Epsom
109 U 19 Dell the SE19
79 Z 14 Dell the SE2
21 U 11 Dell the Wdfd Grn
42 C 14 Dell the Wemb
118 B 4 Dell wlk New Mald
4 C 16 Dellors clo Barnt
63 N 20 Dellow st E1
143 Y 8 Dellow st E1
35 X 11 Dellwood gdns Ilf
83 P 9 Delmany cres Hounsl
94 J 4 Delme cres SE3
90 D 10 Delmere clo SW19
157 V 5 Delmey clo Croy
93 N 2 Deloraine st SE4
144 H 15 Delorme st W6
152 C 5 Delta rd Worc Pk
135 R 12 Delta st E2
81 Y 13 Deluci rd Erith
78 K 17 Delvan st SE18
149 Y 10 Delverton rd SE17
87 X 3 Delvino rd SW6
155 W 7 Demesne rd Wallgtn
88 C 12 Dempster rd SW18
125 X 7 Den clo Becknhm
125 X 7 Den rd Brom
115 S 8 Denberry dri Sidcp
137 R 8 Denbigh clo W11
113 T 15 Denbigh clo Chisl
58 F 17 Denbigh clo S'hall
153 V 10 Denbigh clo Sutton
85 N 14 Denbigh gdns Rich
148 B 9 Denbigh pl SW1
66 B 10 Denbigh rd E6
44 A 20 Denbigh rd NW10
62 A 1 Denbigh rd NW10
137 R 8 Denbigh rd W11
60 C 19 Denbigh rd W13
82 L 4 Denbigh rd Hounsl
58 F 17 Denbigh rd S'hall
148 C 10 Denbigh st SW1
137 R 8 Denbigh ter W11
127 V 2 Denbridge rd Brom
107 O 1 Dendy st SW12
82 E 7 Dene av Hounsl
97 O 10 Dene av Sidcp
92 H 9 Dene clo SE4
126 C 20 Dene clo Brom
152 D 2 Dene clo Worc Pk
11 S 16 Dene gdns Stanm
16 A 7 Dene rd N11
60 A 14 Dene the W13
42 J 12 Dene the Wemb
5 S 17 Dene wood Barnt
26 M 19 Denehurst gdns NW4
73 S 3 Denehurst gdns W3
85 R 10 Denehurst gdns Rich
83 R 19 Denehurst gdns Twick
21 U 13 Denehurst gdns Wdfd Grn
28 M 20 Denewood rd N6
120 M 10 Denham cres Mitch
36 A 18 Denham dri Ilf
15 Y 10 Denham rd N20
67 W 3 Denham way Bark
57 U 18 Denholm wlk Rainhm
129 R 12 Denholme rd W9
28 C 11 Denison clo N2
106 F 16 Denison rd SW19
60 E 11 Denison rd W5
115 Y 3 Deniston av Bxly
17 S 4 Denleigh gdns N21
27 Z 15 Denman dri NW11
27 Z 14 Denman Dri north NW11
27 Z 15 Denman Dri south NW11
91 U 3 Denman rd SE15
140 E 9 Denman st W1
105 S 17 Denmark av SW19
119 Y 13 Denmark ct Mrdn
155 N 5 Denmark gdns Carsh

| | |
|---|---|
| 133 S 7 | Denmark gro N1 |
| 91 O 10 | Denmark hill SE5 |
| 140 G 5 | Denmark pl WC2 |
| 129 R 9 | Denmark rd NW6 |
| 123 Y 11 | Denmark rd SE25 |
| 90 L 4 | Denmark rd SE5 |
| 105 R 16 | Denmark rd SW19 |
| 155 N 6 | Denmark rd Carsh |
| 60 C 20 | Denmark rd Grnfd |
| 116 J 6 | Denmark rd Kingst |
| 101 R 6 | Denmark rd Twick |
| 51 Y 10 | Denmark st E11 |
| 65 U 13 | Denmark st E13 |
| 31 Y 3 | Denmark st N17 |
| 140 H 5 | Denmark st WC2 |
| 108 L 10 | Denmark wlk SE27 |
| 116 L 20 | Dennan rd Surb |
| 135 P 5 | Denne ter E8 |
| 20 B 8 | Denner rd E4 |
| 122 G 18 | Dennett rd Croy |
| 92 E 4 | Dennetts gro SE14 |
| 92 D 3 | Dennetts rd SE14 |
| 156 G 10 | Denning av Croy |
| 46 G 12 | Denning rd NW3 |
| 45 Y 16 | Dennington Pk rd NW6 |
| 42 L 14 | Dennis av Wemb |
| 11 R 15 | Dennis gdns Stanm |
| 11 O 12 | Dennis la Stanm |
| 119 S 1 | Dennis Pk cres SW2 |
| 149 V 8 | Denny cres SE11 |
| 55 S 20 | Denny gdns Dgnhm |
| 18 M 5 | Denny rd N9 |
| 149 T 8 | Denny st SE11 |
| 64 M 2 | Densham rd E15 |
| 65 N 3 | Densham rd E15 |
| 19 P 10 | Densworth gro N9 |
| 61 W 1 | Denton rd NW10 |
| 18 F 14 | Denton rd N18 |
| 30 E 17 | Denton rd N8 |
| 99 S 19 | Denton rd Drtfrd |
| 84 G 17 | Denton rd Twick |
| 80 F 19 | Denton rd Welling |
| 88 B 15 | Denton st SW18 |
| 88 L 17 | Dents rd SW11 |
| 49 R 1 | Denver rd N16 |
| 99 X 19 | Denver rd Drtfrd |
| 146 M 6 | Denyer st SW3 |
| 44 E 16 | Denzil rd NW10 |
| 87 U 9 | Deodar rd SW15 |
| 28 B 6 | Depot appr N3 |
| 54 C 1 | Depot cotts Ilf |
| 83 P 7 | Depot rd Hounsl |
| 150 E 16 | Depot st SE5 |
| 93 O 1 | Deptford bdwy SE4 |
| 93 O 1 | Deptford br SE4 |
| 76 B 17 | Deptford Ch st SE8 |
| 76 B 12 | Deptford Ferry rd E14 |
| 76 B 16 | Deptford grn SE8 |
| 75 Y 12 | Deptford strand SE8 |
| 15 P 17 | Derby av N12 |
| 23 P 5 | Derby av Harrow |
| 38 J 19 | Derby av Rom |
| 140 K 17 | Derby ga SW1 |
| 110 C 4 | Derby hill SE23 |
| 110 B 4 | Derby Hill cres SE23 |
| 53 N 19 | Derby rd E12 |
| 52 M 20 | Derby rd E12 |
| 34 B 4 | Derby rd E18 |
| 63 S 3 | Derby rd E9 |
| 30 K 13 | Derby rd N15 |
| 19 O 16 | Derby rd N18 |
| 85 T 10 | Derby rd SW14 |
| 105 Y 18 | Derby rd SW19 |
| 156 J 1 | Derby rd Croy |
| 9 P 17 | Derby rd Enf |
| 58 K 2 | Derby rd Grnfd |
| 82 K 10 | Derby rd Hounsl |
| 117 O 18 | Derby rd Surb |
| 153 W 14 | Derby rd Sutton |
| 139 V 14 | Derby st W1 |
| 135 U 14 | Derbyshire st E2 |
| 134 K 15 | Dereham pl EC2 |
| 54 L 16 | Dereham rd Bark |
| 155 S 7 | Derek av Wallgtn |
| 43 S 20 | Derek av Wemb |
| 135 V 4 | Dericote st E8 |
| 156 L 9 | Dering pl Croy |
| 156 M 9 | Dering rd Croy |
| 139 X 6 | Dering st W1 |
| 106 M 8 | Derinton rd SW17 |
| 107 N 10 | Derinton rd SW17 |
| 93 W 12 | Dermody gdns SE13 |
| 93 W 12 | Dermody rd SE13 |
| 108 H 1 | Deronda rd SE24 |
| 77 X 10 | Derrick gdns SE7 |
| 124 L 8 | Derrick rd Becknhm |
| 155 Z 4 | Derry rd Wallgtn |
| 137 X 19 | Derry st W8 |
| 53 V 14 | Dersingham av E12 |
| 53 V 12 | Dersingham av E12 |
| 53 V 16 | Dersingham av E12 |
| 45 T 9 | Dersingham rd NW2 |
| 12 L 18 | Derwent av NW7 |
| 26 A 16 | Derwent av NW9 |
| 18 A 17 | Derwent av N18 |
| 103 Z 9 | Derwent av SW15 |
| 104 A 10 | Derwent av SW15 |
| 15 Y 5 | Derwent av Barnt |
| 15 S 11 | Derwent cres N20 |
| 98 D 5 | Derwent cres Bxly Hth |
| 24 E 7 | Derwent cres Stanm |
| 35 R 13 | Derwent gdns Ilf |
| 42 E 2 | Derwent gdns Wemb |
| 91 T 10 | Derwent gro SE22 |
| 17 P 11 | Derwent rd N13 |
| 123 Y 3 | Derwent rd SE20 |
| 72 C 8 | Derwent rd W5 |
| 58 F 16 | Derwent rd S'hall |
| 82 L 16 | Derwent rd Twick |
| 26 A 17 | Derwent rise NW9 |
| 76 M 12 | Derwent st SE10 |
| 57 Y 15 | Derwent way Hornch |
| 73 V 2 | Derwentwater rd W3 |
| 91 S 16 | Desenfans rd SE21 |
| 65 N 12 | Desford rd E16 |
| 47 U 4 | Despard rd N19 |
| 112 E 12 | Detling rd Brom |
| 50 B 7 | Detmold rd E5 |
| 155 N 5 | Devana end Carsh |
| 104 M 20 | Devas rd SW20 |
| 105 N 20 | Devas rd SW20 |
| 64 F 11 | Devas st E3 |
| 80 B 6 | Devenish rd SE2 |
| 91 S 12 | Deventer cres SE22 |
| 150 E 3 | Deverell st SE1 |
| 141 R 7 | Devereux ct WC2 |
| 88 M 16 | Devereux rd SW11 |
| 39 P 4 | Deveron way Rom |
| 101 O 1 | Devon av Twick |
| 31 W 9 | Devon clo N17 |
| 21 V 7 | Devon clo Buck Hl |
| 60 E 3 | Devon clo Grnfd |
| 60 E 3 | Devon cres Grnfd |
| 30 K 18 | Devon gdns N4 |
| 67 U 3 | Devon rd Bark |
| 153 S 19 | Devon rd Sutton |
| 28 G 14 | Devon ri N2 |
| 151 X 15 | Devon st SE15 |
| 75 N 17 | Devon st SE15 |
| 38 J 8 | Devon way Rom |
| 70 E 19 | Devon waye Hounsl |
| 83 Z 19 | Devoncroft gdns Twick |
| 17 Y 19 | Devonia gdns N18 |
| 133 X 7 | Devonia rd N1 |
| 35 T 19 | Devonport gdns Ilf |
| 74 K 4 | Devonport rd W12 |
| 63 R 18 | Devonport st E1 |
| 64 C 11 | Devons rd E3 |
| 154 C 17 | Devonshire av Sutton |
| 52 A 13 | Devonshire clo E15 |
| 17 S 12 | Devonshire clo N13 |
| 131 X 20 | Devonshire clo W1 |
| 27 P 1 | Devonshire cres NW7 |
| 17 Y 19 | Devonshire ct N18 |
| 76 D 20 | Devonshire dri SE10 |
| 93 S 1 | Devonshire dri SE10 |
| 17 Z 20 | Devonshire gdns N18 |
| 17 Z 20 | Devonshire gdns N18 |
| 17 Z 2 | Devonshire gdns N21 |
| 73 U 20 | Devonshire gdns W4 |
| 75 N 17 | Devonshire gro SE15 |
| 151 Y 16 | Devonshire gro SE15 |
| 31 O 1 | Devonshire Hill la N17 |
| 18 A 20 | Devonshire Hill la N17 |
| 17 X 20 | Devonshire Hill la N18 |
| 45 X 9 | Devonshire ms NW2 |
| 74 A 13 | Devonshire ms W4 |
| 131 X 20 | Devonshire Ms north W1 |
| 131 W 20 | Devonshire Ms south W1 |
| 131 V 19 | Devonshire Ms west W1 |
| 131 V 19 | Devonshire pl W1 |
| 131 V 19 | Devonshire Pl ms W1 |
| 52 A 13 | Devonshire rd E16 |
| 65 W 17 | Devonshire rd E16 |
| 33 O 18 | Devonshire rd E17 |
| 27 N 1 | Devonshire rd NW7 |
| 17 Z 20 | Devonshire rd N18 |
| 17 Z 20 | Devonshire rd N18 |
| 19 P 6 | Devonshire rd N9 |
| 92 E 19 | Devonshire rd SE23 |
| 110 B 20 | Devonshire rd SE23 |
| 113 P 4 | Devonshire rd SE9 |
| 106 L 16 | Devonshire rd SW19 |
| 74 A 13 | Devonshire rd W4 |
| 72 D 8 | Devonshire rd W5 |
| 97 Z 10 | Devonshire rd Bxly Hth |
| 123 N 16 | Devonshire rd Croy |
| 100 B 8 | Devonshire rd Felt |
| 23 O 18 | Devonshire rd Harrow |
| 36 G 20 | Devonshire rd Ilf |
| 22 D 3 | Devonshire rd Pinn |
| 58 G 13 | Devonshire rd S'hall |
| 154 D 16 | Devonshire rd Sutton |
| 155 O 7 | Devonshire rd Wallgtn |
| 142 K 3 | Devonshire row E1 |
| 131 Y 19 | Devonshire Row ms W1 |
| 142 L 3 | Devonshire sq E1 |
| 126 J 8 | Devonshire sq Brom |
| 151 X 15 | Devonshire st SE15 |
| 131 X 19 | Devonshire st W1 |
| 74 A 15 | Devonshire st W4 |
| 138 C 7 | Devonshire ter W2 |
| 158 K 2 | Devonshire way Croy |
| 159 N 1 | Devonshire way Croy |
| 91 X 8 | Dewar st SE15 |
| 64 F 15 | Dewberry st E14 |
| 22 C 19 | Dewesbury clo Pinn |
| 133 S 7 | Dewey rd N1 |
| 56 J 18 | Dewey rd Dgnhm |
| 106 M 12 | Dewey st SW17 |
| 144 F 2 | Dewhurst rd W14 |
| 152 F 4 | Dewsbury gdns Worc Pk |
| 44 G 15 | Dewsbury rd NW10 |
| 90 G 12 | Dexter rd SE24 |
| 4 B 19 | Dexter rd Barnt |
| 31 N 4 | Deyncourt rd N17 |
| 34 L 14 | Deynecourt gdns E11 |
| 91 O 1 | Deynsford rd SE5 |
| 140 E 5 | Diadem ct W1 |
| 40 A 13 | Diamond rd Pinn |
| 150 L 19 | Diamond st SE15 |
| 93 V 1 | Diamond ter SE10 |
| 32 M 9 | Diana rd E17 |
| 80 C 13 | Dianthus clo SE2 |
| 57 Y 12 | Diban av Hornch |
| 153 Y 4 | Dibdin clo Sutton |
| 153 Y 4 | Dibdin rd Sutton |
| 44 L 13 | Dicey av NW2 |
| 28 D 5 | Dickens av N3 |
| 102 J 3 | Dickens clo Rich |
| 66 B 6 | Dickens rd E6 |
| 150 C 1 | Dickens sq SE1 |
| 89 T 4 | Dickens st SW8 |
| 30 B 20 | Dickenson rd N8 |
| 47 R 18 | Dickenson st NW5 |
| 123 X 14 | Dickensons la SE25 |
| 123 X 15 | Dickensons pl SE25 |
| 117 X 1 | Dickerage la New Mald |
| 117 V 2 | Dickerage rd Kingst |
| 95 R 8 | Dickson rd SE9 |
| 88 E 11 | Didcot st SW11 |
| 48 K 7 | Digby cres N4 |
| 69 R 2 | Digby gdns Dgnhm |
| 50 F 16 | Digby rd E9 |
| 67 W 1 | Digby rd Bark |
| 63 R 9 | Digby st E2 |
| 63 S 15 | Diggon st E2 |
| 88 C 12 | Dighton rd SW18 |
| 133 S 6 | Dignum st N1 |
| 48 G 18 | Digswell st N7 |
| 112 H 6 | Dilhorne clo SE9 |
| 147 P 13 | Dilke st SW3 |
| 110 J 8 | Dillwyn rd SE26 |
| 75 P 11 | Dilston gro SE16 |
| 151 Z 4 | Dilston gro SE16 |
| 104 H 1 | Dilton gdns SW15 |
| 74 K 11 | Dimes pl W6 |
| 43 W 4 | Dimsdale dri NW9 |
| 18 J 1 | Dimsdale dri Enf |
| 64 B 20 | Dingle gdns E14 |
| 134 B 13 | Dingley pl EC1 |
| 134 B 13 | Dingley rd EC1 |
| 156 M 3 | Dingwall av Croy |
| 157 N 3 | Dingwall av Croy |
| 27 X 19 | Dingwall gdns NW11 |
| 88 C 19 | Dingwall rd SW18 |
| 154 M 19 | Dingwall rd Carsh |
| 157 O 2 | Dingwall rd Croy |
| 135 V 9 | Dinmont st E2 |
| 5 O 18 | Dinsdale gdns Barnt |
| 77 O 15 | Dinsdale rd SE3 |
| 89 S 18 | Dinsmore rd SW12 |
| 106 G 14 | Dinton rd SW19 |
| 103 N 17 | Dinton rd Kingst |
| 65 O 3 | Dirleton rd E15 |
| 144 L 15 | Disbrowe rd W6 |
| 142 C 17 | Disney pl SE1 |
| 142 C 17 | Disney st SE1 |
| 9 S 6 | Dison clo Enf |
| 52 F 17 | Disraeli rd E7 |
| 61 X 6 | Disraeli rd NW10 |
| 87 R 11 | Disraeli rd SW15 |
| 72 F 3 | Disraeli rd W5 |
| 135 O 11 | Diss st E2 |
| 142 A 7 | Distaff la EC4 |
| 144 E 11 | Distillery la W6 |
| 149 S 6 | Distin st SE11 |
| 42 B 16 | District rd Wemb |
| 93 R 2 | Ditch all SE10 |
| 64 G 20 | Ditchburn st E14 |
| 113 R 10 | Dittisham rd SE9 |
| 116 F 20 | Ditton Grange clo Surb |
| 116 F 20 | Ditton Grange dri Surb |
| 116 C 20 | Ditton Hill rd Surb |
| 110 A 20 | Ditton pl SE20 |
| 97 Y 13 | Ditton rd Bxly Hth |
| 70 E 13 | Ditton rd S'hall |
| 116 K 20 | Ditton rd Surb |
| 159 R 1 | Dixon pl W Wkhm |
| 92 K 1 | Dixon rd SE14 |
| 123 T 6 | Dixon rd SE25 |
| 95 U 13 | Dobell rd SE9 |
| 62 K 1 | Dobree av NW10 |
| 128 A 1 | Dobree av NW10 |
| 46 F 20 | Dobson clo NW6 |
| 142 C 9 | Doby ct EC4 |
| 65 P 20 | Dock rd E16 |
| 77 P 1 | Dock rd E16 |
| 72 H 18 | Dock rd Brentf |
| 143 P 18 | Dockhead SE1 |
| 78 J 3 | Dockland st E16 |
| 151 S 2 | Dockley rd SE16 |
| 49 R 17 | Docwras bldgs N1 |
| 63 Z 17 | Dod st E14 |
| 64 A 17 | Dod st E14 |
| 108 H 8 | Dodbrooke rd SE27 |
| 149 X 16 | Doddington gro SE17 |
| 149 W 13 | Doddington pl SE17 |
| 141 V 20 | Dodson st SE1 |
| 141 O 1 | Dog And Duck yd WC1 |
| 91 S 8 | Dog Kennel hill SE |
| 44 B 13 | Dog la NW10 |
| 93 O 19 | Doggett rd SE6 |
| 5 W 18 | Doggetts ct Barnt |
| 65 T 11 | Doherty rd E13 |
| 141 X 14 | Dolben st SE1 |
| 87 V 6 | Dolby rd SW6 |
| 149 N 11 | Dolland st SE11 |
| 27 V 4 | Dollis av N3 |
| 4 D 20 | Dollis Brook wlk Barnt |
| 44 L 8 | Dollis Hill av NW2 |
| 44 H 10 | Dollis Hill la NW2 |
| 27 V 3 | Dollis pk N3 |
| 27 T 3 | Dollis rd NW7 |
| 4 H 18 | Dollis Valley way Barnt |
| 90 B 9 | Dolman st SW4 |
| 116 G 13 | Dolphin clo Surb |
| 64 C 20 | Dolphin la E14 |
| 148 D 12 | Dolphin sq SW1 |
| 148 D 12 | Dolphin sq SW1 |
| 133 N 20 | Dombey st WC1 |
| 109 V 9 | Dome Hill pk SE26 |
| 91 P 9 | Domett clo SE5 |
| 134 F 3 | Domingo st EC1 |
| 123 U 16 | Dominion rd Croy |
| 142 G 1 | Dominion st EC2 |
| 113 Z 8 | Domonic dri SE9 |
| 114 A 7 | Domonic dri SE9 |
| 150 M 11 | Domville gro SE5 |
| 39 P 3 | Don way Rom |
| 37 T 16 | Donald dri Rom |
| 65 V 4 | Donald rd E13 |
| 122 E 16 | Donald rd Croy |
| 129 P 6 | Donaldson rd NW6 |
| 78 L 20 | Donaldson rd SE18 |
| 95 X 2 | Donaldson rd SE18 |
| 40 E 17 | Doncaster dri Grnfd |
| 30 L 19 | Doncaster gdns N4 |
| 40 D 15 | Doncaster gdns Grnfd |
| 18 M 3 | Doncaster rd N9 |
| 133 R 9 | Donegal row N1 |
| 133 R 9 | Donegal st N1 |
| 87 P 3 | Doneraile st SW6 |
| 65 V 9 | Dongola rd E13 |
| 65 U 9 | Dongola rd E13 |
| 31 R 11 | Dongola rd N17 |
| 8 K 8 | Donkey la Enf |
| 51 X 13 | Donmow rd E15 |
| 90 M 16 | Donne clo SE24 |
| 146 L 5 | Donne pl SW3 |
| 121 T 8 | Donne pl Mitch |
| 55 T 6 | Donne rd Dgnhm |
| 24 K 1 | Donnefield av Edg |

| Ref | Entry |
|---|---|
| 6 C 15 | Donnington av Ilf |
| 2 K 2 | Donnington rd NW10 |
| 8 A 3 | Donnington rd NW10 |
| 4 G 18 | Donnington rd Harrow |
| 2 H 3 | Donnington rd Worc Pk |
| 7 W 18 | Donnybrook rd SW16 |
| 9 T 8 | Donovan av N10 |
| 1 X 14 | Doone clo Tedd |
| 5 X 10 | Dora rd SW19 |
| 3 Y 16 | Dora st E14 |
| 4 M 11 | Doral way Carsh |
| 9 U 19 | Doran grn SE18 |
| 7 Y 13 | Dorchester av N13 |
| 7 X 19 | Dorchester av Bxly |
| 2 L 20 | Dorchester av Harrow |
| 0 L 14 | Dorchester clo Grnfd |
| 6 F 2 | Dorchester ct N14 |
| 0 B 14 | Dorchester gdns E4 |
| 7 Y 12 | Dorchester gdns NW11 |
| 4 B 15 | Dorchester gro W4 |
| 0 L 12 | Dorchester rd SE24 |
| 0 L 14 | Dorchester rd Grnfd |
| 0 B 17 | Dorchester rd Mrdn |
| 2 L 1 | Dorchester rd Worc Pk |
| 43 N 1 | Dorchester wora Pk |
| 24 M 18 | Dorchester way Harrow |
| 25 N 17 | Dorchester way Harrow |
| 97 Y 4 | Dorcis av Bxly Hth |
| 74 B 4 | Dordrecht rd W3 |
| 53 W 15 | Dore av E12 |
| 20 B 16 | Dore gdns Mrdn |
| 43 Y 3 | Doreen av NW9 |
| 15 X 10 | Dorell clo S'hall |
| 37 W 4 | Doria rd SW6 |
| 57 X 5 | Dorian rd Hornch |
| 25 S 1 | Doric ct Becknhm |
| 32 E 13 | Doric way NW1 |
| 32 F 13 | Doric way NW1 |
| 19 P 3 | Dorien rd SW20 |
| 93 J 2 | Doris av Erith |
| 52 F 20 | Doris rd E7 |
| 75 X 16 | Dorking rd SE8 |
| 88 H 1 | Dorlcote rd SW18 |
| 87 Z 12 | Dormay st SW18 |
| 4 B 18 | Dormer clo Barnt |
| 68 G 17 | Dormers av S'hall |
| 68 L 18 | Dormers ri S'hall |
| 68 J 19 | Dormers Wells la S'hall |
| 70 K 1 | Dormers Wells la S'hall |
| 77 U 19 | Dornberg rd SE3 |
| 87 T 4 | Dorncliffe rd SW6 |
| 45 W 16 | Dornfell st NW6 |
| 07 T 4 | Dornton rd SW12 |
| 57 P 12 | Dornton rd S Croy |
| 60 L 1 | Dorothy av Wemb |
| 98 G 10 | Dorothy Evans clo Bxly Hth |
| 55 S 13 | Dorothy gdns Dgnhm |
| 88 L 8 | Dorothy rd SW11 |
| 41 T 1 | Dorrington st EC1 |
| 43 Y 3 | Dors clo NW9 |
| 39 O 10 | Dorset av Rom |
| 70 G 10 | Dorset av S'hall |
| 96 K 10 | Dorset av Welling |
| 41 V 7 | Dorset bldgs EC4 |
| 131 O 19 | Dorset clo NW1 |
| 11 Z 20 | Dorset dri Edg |
| 22 B 8 | Dorset gdns Mitch |
| 147 W 1 | Dorset ms SW1 |
| 51 W 17 | Dorset pl E15 |
| 48 F 9 | Dorset pl SW 1 |
| 65 Z 1 | Dorset rd E7 |
| 31 P 13 | Dorset rd N15 |
| 30 A 6 | Dorset rd N22 |
| 13 P 4 | Dorset rd SE9 |
| 19 Z 2 | Dorset rd SW19 |
| 120 A 3 | Dorset rd SW19 |
| 105 X 20 | Dorset rd SW19 |
| 148 M 18 | Dorset rd SW8 |
| 149 P 19 | Dorset rd SW8 |
| 72 F 7 | Dorset rd W5 |
| 124 E 6 | Dorset rd Becknhm |
| 23 O 18 | Dorset rd Harrow |
| 120 K 3 | Dorset rd Mitch |
| 141 V 7 | Dorset ri EC4 |
| 131 O 18 | Dorset sq NW1 |
| 139 S 1 | Dorset st W1 |
| 101 O 7 | Dorset way Twick |
| 70 E 20 | Dorset waye Hounsl |
| 74 H 9 | Dorville cres W6 |
| 94 D 14 | Dorville rd SE12 |
| 79 P 19 | Dothill rd SE18 |
| 133 N 17 | Doughty ms WC1 |
| 133 O 17 | Doughty st WC1 |
| 33 N 4 | Douglas av E17 |
| 32 M 5 | Douglas av E17 |
| 118 K 9 | Douglas av New Mald |
| 42 K 19 | Douglas av Wemb |
| 10 M 17 | Douglas clo Stanm |
| 159 N 5 | Douglas dri Croy |
| 76 G 12 | Douglas gro E17 |
| 102 G 1 | Douglas house Rich |
| 148 F 8 | Douglas pth SW 1 |
| 65 T 14 | Douglas rd E16 |
| 20 M 4 | Douglas rd E4 |
| 21 N 4 | Douglas rd E4 |
| 129 P 3 | Douglas rd NW6 |
| 48 L 19 | Douglas rd N1 |
| 30 G 4 | Douglas rd N22 |
| 39 U 19 | Douglas rd Hornch |
| 57 U 1 | Douglas rd Hornch |
| 82 L 8 | Douglas rd Hounsl |
| 37 N 19 | Douglas rd Ilf |
| 117 T 5 | Douglas rd Kingst |
| 117 N 19 | Douglas rd Surb |
| 97 R 2 | Douglas rd Welling |
| 119 Y 14 | Douglas sq Mrdn |
| 148 F 7 | Douglas st SW1 |
| 75 Z 19 | Douglas way SE8 |
| 105 Z 2 | Dounceforth gdns SW18 |
| 106 A 2 | Dounesforth gdns SW18 |
| 137 Z 20 | Douro pl W8 |
| 64 A 5 | Douro st E3 |
| 20 A 8 | Dove House gdns E4 |
| 146 B 8 | Dove ms SW5 |
| 22 F 2 | Dove pk Pinn |
| 49 O 18 | Dove rd N1 |
| 135 T 7 | Dove row E2 |
| 30 G 10 | Dovecote av N22 |
| 24 E 18 | Dovedale av Harrow |
| 35 X 6 | Dovedale av Ilf |
| 97 N 3 | Dovedale clo Welling |
| 92 A 15 | Dovedale rd SE22 |
| 106 M 19 | Dovedale ri Mitch |
| 146 J 11 | Dovehouse st SW3 |
| 154 B 6 | Dover Ct la Sutton |
| 86 K 16 | Dover Pk dri SW15 |
| 52 K 6 | Dover rd E12 |
| 19 P 9 | Dover rd N9 |
| 109 O 15 | Dover rd SE19 |
| 37 Z 19 | Dover rd Rom |
| 139 Z 11 | Dover st W1 |
| 140 A 12 | Dover st W 1 |
| 122 G 10 | Dovercourt av Thntn Hth |
| 11 W 16 | Dovercourt gdns Stanm |
| 91 T 15 | Dovercourt rd SE22 |
| 90 B 18 | Doverfield rd SW2 |
| 86 H 10 | Doverhouse rd SW15 |
| 17 W 14 | Doveridge gdns N13 |
| 157 P 12 | Doveton rd S Croy |
| 63 P 12 | Doveton st E1 |
| 111 X 2 | Dowanhill rd SE6 |
| 112 A 2 | Dowanhill rd SE6 |
| 10 L 18 | Dowding pl Stanm |
| 155 T 19 | Dower av Wallgtn |
| 142 D 9 | Dowgate hill EC4 |
| 150 J 18 | Dowlas st SE5 |
| 116 G 1 | Down Hall rd Kingst |
| 74 K 12 | Down pl W6 |
| 144 A 8 | Down pl W6 |
| 102 B 16 | Down rd Tedd |
| 139 W 15 | Down st W1 |
| 26 M 8 | Downage NW4 |
| 99 O 4 | Downbank av Bxly Hth |
| 111 Y 8 | Downderry rd Brom |
| 80 F 18 | Downe clo Welling |
| 89 U 9 | Downers cotts SW4 |
| 17 T 5 | Downes ct N1 |
| 118 E 20 | Downfield Worc Pk |
| 134 E 2 | Downham rd N1 |
| 111 Y 11 | Downham way Brom |
| 112 A 11 | Downham way Brom |
| 31 O 10 | Downhills av N17 |
| 31 O 11 | Downhills Pk rd N17 |
| 30 L 11 | Downhills Pk rd N17 |
| 30 M 9 | Downhills way N17 |
| 12 L 17 | Downhurst av NW7 |
| 59 S 4 | Downing dri Grnfd |
| 56 C 20 | Downing rd Dgnhm |
| 69 O 1 | Downing rd Dgnhm |
| 140 J 20 | Downing st SW1 |
| 113 T 3 | Downleys clo SE9 |
| 95 S 8 | Downman rd SE9 |
| 113 T 13 | Downs av Chisl |
| 22 D 20 | Downs av Pinn |
| 125 X 1 | Downs hill Becknhm |
| 111 W 20 | Downs hill Becknhm |
| 50 A 13 | Downs Pk rd E5 |
| 49 X 14 | Downs Pk rd E8 |
| 49 Y 12 | Downs rd E5 |
| 125 R 2 | Downs rd Becknhm |
| 8 F 15 | Downs rd Enf |
| 108 L 20 | Downs rd Thntn Hth |
| 105 O 18 | Downs the SW20 |
| 83 X 1 | Downs view Islwth |
| 51 V 12 | Downsell rd E15 |
| 32 J 19 | Downsfield rd E17 |
| 36 J 19 | Downshall av Ilf |
| 46 G 13 | Downshire hill NW3 |
| 101 V 6 | Downside Twick |
| 46 K 16 | Downside cres NW3 |
| 59 Y 12 | Downside cres W13 |
| 154 H 14 | Downside rd Sutton |
| 108 K 19 | Downsview gdns SE19 |
| 108 L 17 | Downsview rd SE19 |
| 154 C 18 | Downsway the Sutton |
| 108 B 3 | Downton av SW2 |
| 28 H 1 | Downway N12 |
| 133 T 4 | Dowrey st N1 |
| 31 V 8 | Dowsett rd N17 |
| 91 P 10 | Dowson clo SE5 |
| 142 B 16 | Doyce st SE1 |
| 62 H 3 | Doyle gdns NW10 |
| 128 A 8 | Doyle gdns NW10 |
| 123 X 9 | Doyle rd SE25 |
| 147 S 5 | Doyley st SW1 |
| 47 T 2 | Doynton st N19 |
| 107 S 7 | Dr Johnson av SW17 |
| 150 A 13 | Draco st SE17 |
| 120 G 7 | Dragmire la Mitch |
| 75 X 14 | Dragoon rd SE8 |
| 61 X 11 | Dragor rd NW10 |
| 93 O 8 | Drake rd SE4 |
| 121 N 13 | Drake rd Croy |
| 122 D 17 | Drake rd Croy |
| 40 F 6 | Drake rd Harrow |
| 8 B 6 | Drake st Enf |
| 92 F 6 | Drakefell rd SE14 |
| 107 O 6 | Drakefield rd SW17 |
| 48 H 12 | Drakeley ct N5 |
| 107 X 18 | Drakewood rd SW16 |
| 51 V 13 | Drapers rd E15 |
| 7 V 8 | Drapers rd Enf |
| 151 T 4 | Drappers rd SE16 |
| 76 K 4 | Drawdock rd SE10 |
| 104 F 18 | Drax av SW20 |
| 105 T 14 | Draxmont appr SW19 |
| 90 D 13 | Dray gdns SW2 |
| 34 G 19 | Draycot rd E11 |
| 146 K 6 | Draycott av SW3 |
| 147 N 7 | Draycott av SW3 |
| 274 B 10 | Draycott av Harrow |
| 42 D 1 | Draycott av Harrow |
| 24 C 18 | Draycott clo Harrow |
| 147 N 7 | Draycott pl SW3 |
| 147 O 0 | Draycott ter SW3 |
| 137 V 18 | Drayson ms W8 |
| 59 Z 20 | Drayton av W13 |
| 59 V 19 | Drayton Br rd W7 |
| 17 W 2 | Drayton gdns N21 |
| 146 B 9 | Drayton gdns SW10 |
| 50 Z 19 | Drayton gdns W13 |
| 72 B 1 | Drayton Gr rd W13 |
| 72 B 1 | Drayton Green rd W13 |
| 59 Z 19 | Drayton grn W13 |
| 59 Z 19 | Drayton grn W13 |
| 48 G 15 | Drayton pk N5 |
| 51 X 3 | Drayton rd E11 |
| 62 E 3 | Drayton rd NW10 |
| 31 S 8 | Drayton rd N17 |
| 60 A 19 | Drayton rd W13 |
| 156 K 2 | Drayton rd Croy |
| 24 C 17 | Drayton wlk Harrow |
| 47 X 2 | Dresden rd N19 |
| 41 W 17 | Drew gdns Grnfd |
| 78 D 3 | Drew rd E16 |
| 107 X 4 | Drewstead rd SW16 |
| 108 A 5 | Drewstead rd SW16 |
| 63 R 18 | Drewton st E1 |
| 63 W 5 | Driffield rd E3 |
| 107 P 20 | Driftway the Mitch |
| 40 K 6 | Drinkwater rd Harrow |
| 33 S 11 | Drive the E17 |
| 34 E 9 | Drive the E4 |
| 20 K 3 | Drive the E4 |
| 27 S 20 | Drive the NW11 |
| 45 T 1 | Drive the NW11 |
| 16 H 20 | Drive the N11 |
| 28 L 15 | Drive the N2 |
| 14 L 20 | Drive the N3 |
| 122 C 6 | Drive the SW16 |
| 104 M 18 | Drive the SW20 |
| 61 X 17 | Drive the W3 |
| 54 L 20 | Drive the Bark |
| 5 P 20 | Drive the Barnt |
| 4 E 12 | Drive the Barnt |
| 125 N 2 | Drive the Becknham |
| 21 Y 3 | Drive the Buck Hl |
| 97 W 18 | Drive the Bxly |
| 12 E 15 | Drive the Edg |
| 8 C 7 | Drive the Enf |
| 152 C 14 | Drive the Epsom |
| 81 V 18 | Drive the Erith |
| 22 H 20 | Drive the Harrow |
| 40 H 2 | Drive the Harrow |
| 35 R 18 | Drive the Ilf |
| 53 T 2 | Drive the Ilf |
| 83 P 4 | Drive the Islwth |
| 103 V 19 | Drive the Kingst |
| 120 E 11 | Drive the Mrdn |
| 38 L 3 | Drive the Rom |
| 39 N 2 | Drive the Rom |
| 115 R 9 | Drive the Sidcp |
| 116 J 18 | Drive the Surb |
| 123 N 8 | Drive the Thntn Hth |
| 125 W 18 | Drive the W Wckhm |
| 155 X 20 | Drive the Wallgtn |
| 43 V 8 | Drive the Wemb |
| 109 X 9 | Droitwich clo SE20 |
| 87 S 16 | Dromore rd SW15 |
| 55 T 14 | Dronfield gdns Dgnhm |
| 128 J 14 | Droop st W10 |
| 75 N 18 | Drovers la SE15 |
| 157 N 12 | Drovers rd S Croy |
| 91 T 10 | Druce rd SE21 |
| 142 L 16 | Druid st SE1 |
| 143 O 19 | Druid st SE1 |
| 125 Y 8 | Druids way Brom |
| 38 M 14 | Drummond av Rom |
| 132 E 12 | Drummond cres NW1 |
| 23 W 2 | Drummond dri Stanm |
| 34 K 18 | Drummond rd E11 |
| 143 W 20 | Drummond rd SE16 |
| 151 W 1 | Drummond rd SE16 |
| 156 L 2 | Drummond rd Croy |
| 38 L 13 | Drummond rd Rom |
| 140 L 5 | Drury la WC2 |
| 41 N 2 | Drury rd Harrow |
| 23 N 20 | Drury rd Harrow |
| 87 O 8 | Dryad st SW15 |
| 25 R 10 | Dryburgh gdns NW9 |
| 88 M 3 | Dryburgh rd SW15 |
| 59 V 18 | Dryden av W7 |
| 149 U 7 | Dryden ct Housing est SE11 |
| 141 U 5 | Dryden pass EC4 |
| 106 C 14 | Dryden rd SW19 |
| 8 F 19 | Dryden rd Enf |
| 23 W 6 | Dryden rd Harrow |
| 96 K 1 | Dryden rd Welling |
| 140 L 6 | Dryden rd WC2 |
| 43 V 18 | Dryfield clo NW10 |
| 12 J 19 | Dryfield rd Edg |
| 81 O 16 | Dryhill rd Blvdr |
| 30 B 18 | Drylands rd N8 |
| 20 E 1 | Drysdale av E4 |
| 93 T 3 | Drysdale pl SE13 |
| 134 L 13 | Drysdale st N1 |
| 107 O 2 | Du Cane ct SW11 |
| 62 E 18 | Du Cane rd W12 |
| 136 A 5 | Du Cane rd W12 |
| 11 U 18 | Du Cros dri Stanm |
| 139 X 2 | Duchess ms W1 |
| 137 T 18 | Duchess Of Bedfords wlk W8 |
| 139 Y 2 | Duchess st W1 |
| 5 U 2 | Duchy rd Barnt |
| 141 T 12 | Duchy st SE1 |
| 90 B 10 | Ducie st SW4 |
| 140 D 7 | Duck la W1 |
| 9 V 15 | Duck Lees la Enf |
| 30 H 18 | Duckett rd N4 |
| 63 U 13 | Duckett st E1 |
| 99 T 13 | Ducketts rd Drtfrd |
| 84 D 13 | Ducks wlk Twick |
| 142 E 9 | Ducksfoot la EC4 |
| 74 A 4 | Ducros rd W3 |
| 44 E 14 | Dudden Hill la NW10 |
| 24 D 10 | Dudley av Harrow |
| 119 S 18 | Dudley dri Mrdn |
| 72 C 5 | Dudley gdns Harrow |
| 41 O 5 | Dudley gdns Harrow |
| 33 O 9 | Dudley rd E17 |
| 129 N 8 | Dudley rd NW6 |
| 28 A 8 | Dudley rd N3 |
| 105 Y 15 | Dudley rd SW19 |
| 40 M 6 | Dudley rd Harrow |
| 41 N 5 | Dudley rd Harrow |
| 53 Z 11 | Dudley rd Ilf |
| 54 A 11 | Dudley rd Ilf |
| 116 L 5 | Dudley rd Kingst |
| 85 O 6 | Dudley rd Rich |

| | | |
|---|---|---|
| 70 A 7 | Dudley rd S'hall |
| 138 E 2 | Dudley st W2 |
| 50 C 6 | Dudlington rd E5 |
| 146 H 9 | Dudmaston ms SW3 |
| 99 X 14 | Dudsbury rd Drtfrd |
| 115 S 14 | Dudsbury rd Sidcp |
| 64 C 18 | Duff st E14 |
| 134 D 18 | Dufferin st EC1 |
| 23 W 16 | Duffield clo Harrow |
| 88 K 7 | Duffield st SW11 |
| 140 C 7 | Dufours pl W1 |
| 93 Z 2 | Duke Humphrey rd SE3 |
| 94 A 2 | Duke Humphrey rd SE3 |
| 83 R 16 | Duke Of Cambridge clo Twick |
| 154 F 4 | Duke Of Edinburgh rd Sutton |
| 140 D 12 | Duke Of York st SW1 |
| 73 Z 13 | Duke rd W4 |
| 36 E 13 | Duke rd Ilf |
| 140 C 12 | Duke st SW1 |
| 139 U 7 | Duke st W1 |
| 84 H 12 | Duke st Rich |
| 154 E 8 | Duke st Sutton |
| 142 G 13 | Duke St hill SE1 |
| 102 F 11 | Duke's av Kingst |
| 29 U 9 | Dukes av N10 |
| 27 Z 4 | Dukes av N3 |
| 28 A 4 | Dukes av N3 |
| 73 Z 15 | Dukes av W4 |
| 11 Z 18 | Dukes av Edg |
| 40 D 20 | Dukes av Grnfd |
| 58 C 1 | Dukes av Grnfd |
| 22 F 20 | Dukes av Harrow |
| 23 T 12 | Dukes av Harrow |
| 82 A 10 | Dukes av Hounsl |
| 102 G 11 | Dukes av Kingst |
| 118 C 7 | Dukes av New Mald |
| 100 D 11 | Dukes clo Hampt |
| 137 V 17 | Dukes la W8 |
| 29 T 10 | Dukes ms N10 |
| 139 U 4 | Dukes ms W1 |
| 142 M 6 | Dukes pl EC3 |
| 66 J 3 | Dukes rd E6 |
| 132 G 14 | Dukes rd WC1 |
| 61 P 12 | Dukes rd W3 |
| 110 F 10 | Dukesthorpe rd SE26 |
| 48 E 5 | Dulas st N4 |
| 48 E 5 | Dulas st N4 |
| 136 J 8 | Dulford st W11 |
| 88 M 14 | Dulka rd SW11 |
| 114 D 4 | Dulverton rd SE9 |
| 109 T 1 | Dulwich comm SE21 |
| 91 U 19 | Dulwich park SE21 |
| 90 G 14 | Dulwich rd SE 24 |
| 91 P 15 | Dulwich village SE21 |
| 109 S 11 | Dulwich Wood av SE19 |
| 109 T 11 | Dulwich Wood pk SE19 |
| 90 B 17 | Dumbarton rd SW2 |
| 95 V 9 | Dumbreck rd SE9 |
| 49 T 8 | Dumont rd N16 |
| 131 T 1 | Dumpton pl NW1 |
| 122 F 5 | Dunbar av SW16 |
| 124 J 8 | Dunbar av Becknhm |
| 56 E 10 | Dunbar av Dgnhm |
| 56 F 15 | Dunbar gdns Dgnhm |
| 52 G 18 | Dunbar rd E7 |
| 30 H 5 | Dunbar rd N22 |
| 108 L 7 | Dunbar rd SE27 |
| 117 W 8 | Dunbar rd New Mald |
| 108 K 7 | Dunbar st SE27 |
| 95 S 6 | Dunblane rd SE9 |
| 46 M 14 | Dunboyne st NW5 |
| 135 V 16 | Dunbridge st E2 |
| 62 A 17 | Duncan gro W3 |
| 135 V 4 | Duncan rd E8 |
| 84 L 10 | Duncan rd Rich |
| 133 V 8 | Duncan st N1 |
| 133 W 9 | Duncan ter N1 |
| 140 J 11 | Duncannon st WC2 |
| 92 J 18 | Duncombe hill SE23 |
| 47 X 4 | Duncombe rd N19 |
| 93 Y 16 | Duncrievie rd SE13 |
| 79 U 20 | Duncroft SE18 |
| 92 G 8 | Dundalk rd SE4 |
| 92 C 4 | Dundas rd SE15 |
| 65 V 7 | Dundee rd E13 |
| 124 A 12 | Dundee rd SE25 |
| 143 X 15 | Dundee st E1 |
| 152 K 9 | Dundela gdns Worc Pk |
| 128 F 6 | Dundonald rd NW10 |
| 105 U 19 | Dundonald rd SW19 |
| 51 S 9 | Dunedin rd E10 |
| 54 C 3 | Dunedin rd Ilf |
| 63 S 17 | Dunelm st E1 |
| 111 S 11 | Dunfield gdns SE6 |
| 111 S 11 | Dunfield rd SE6 |

| | | |
|---|---|---|
| 48 D 13 | Dunford rd N7 |
| 86 F 9 | Dungarvan av SW15 |
| 122 F 13 | Dunheved clo Thntn Hth |
| 122 G 14 | Dunheved Rd south Thntn Hth |
| 122 F 14 | Dunheved Rd west Thntn Hth |
| 18 G 10 | Dunholme grn N9 |
| 18 G 12 | Dunholme la N9 |
| 18 G 12 | Dunholme rd N9 |
| 143 S 1 | Dunk st E1 |
| 123 O 8 | Dunkeld rd SE25 |
| 55 S 6 | Dunkeld rd Dgnhm |
| 113 O 8 | Dunkery rd SE9 |
| 108 L 9 | Dunkirk st SE27 |
| 50 D 13 | Dunlace rd E5 |
| 82 F 19 | Dunleary clo Hounsl |
| 159 W 14 | Dunley dri Croy |
| 31 O 10 | Dunloe av N17 |
| 135 P 9 | Dunloe st E2 |
| 134 M 9 | Dunloe st E2 |
| 151 P 3 | Dunlop pl SE16 |
| 128 K 5 | Dunmore rd NW6 |
| 105 O 20 | Dunmore rd SW20 |
| 119 N 1 | Dunmore rd SW20 |
| 37 S 15 | Dunmow clo Rom |
| 49 U 14 | Dunn st E8 |
| 57 U 14 | Dunningford clo Hornch |
| 47 V 14 | Dunollie rd NW5 |
| 92 D 18 | Dunoon rd SE23 |
| 7 U 8 | Dunraven dri Enf |
| 74 H 2 | Dunraven rd W12 |
| 139 S 8 | Dunraven st W1 |
| 144 E 3 | Dunsany rd W14 |
| 123 T 10 | Dunsdale rd SE3 |
| 159 T 17 | Dunsfold way Croy |
| 49 T 3 | Dunsmure rd N16 |
| 35 Y 8 | Dunspring la Ilf |
| 131 V 20 | Dunstable ms W1 |
| 84 K 11 | Dunstable rd Rich |
| 104 L 16 | Dunstall rd SW20 |
| 45 X 5 | Dunstan rd NW11 |
| 91 Z 15 | Dunstans gro SE22 |
| 91 Y 17 | Dunstans rd SE22 |
| 119 P 19 | Dunster av Mrdn |
| 38 J 8 | Dunster clo Rom |
| 43 V 4 | Dunster dri NW9 |
| 45 V 20 | Dunster gdns NW6 |
| 129 P 1 | Dunster gdns NW6 |
| 40 B 9 | Dunster way Harrow |
| 135 N 5 | Dunston rd E8 |
| 150 M 8 | Dunston rd SE1 |
| 134 M 4 | Dunston st E8 |
| 33 R 20 | Dunton rd E10 |
| 151 O 5 | Dunton rd SE1 |
| 39 O 13 | Dunton rd Rom |
| 106 A 1 | Duntshill rd SW18 |
| 95 V 11 | Dunvegan rd SE9 |
| 98 B 2 | Dunwich rd Bxly Hth |
| 139 H 18 | Duplex ride SW1 |
| 119 P 3 | Dupont rd SW20 |
| 63 X 16 | Dupont st E14 |
| 156 K 7 | Duppas Hill la Croy |
| 156 G 7 | Duppas Hill rd Croy |
| 156 J 7 | Duppas Hill ter Croy |
| 156 H 7 | Duppas rd Croy |
| 77 U 13 | Dupree rd SE7 |
| 120 L 20 | Durand clo Carsh |
| 154 M 1 | Durand clo Carsh |
| 90 D 2 | Durand gdns SW9 |
| 61 U 1 | Durand way NW10 |
| 135 T 10 | Durant st E2 |
| 9 R 11 | Durants park Enf |
| 9 U 15 | Durants pk Enf |
| 9 S 13 | Durants Pk av Enf |
| 9 R 14 | Durants rd Enf |
| 69 Y 1 | Durban gdns Dgnhm |
| 69 Y 2 | Durban gdns Dgnhm |
| 64 M 8 | Durban rd E15 |
| 32 K 4 | Durban rd E17 |
| 18 F 20 | Durban rd N17 |
| 108 M 9 | Durban rd SE27 |
| 109 N 9 | Durban rd SE27 |
| 124 L 4 | Durban rd Becknhm |
| 54 G 3 | Durban rd Ilf |
| 58 F 17 | Durdans rd S'hall |
| 55 W 14 | Durell gdns Dgnhm |
| 55 V 14 | Durell rd Dgnhm |
| 104 H 1 | Durford cres SW15 |
| 126 C 9 | Durham av Brom |
| 70 F 15 | Durham av Hounsl |
| 50 D 17 | Durham gro E9 |
| 140 L 11 | Durham Ho st WC2 |
| 147 O 11 | Durham pl SW3 |
| 53 N 13 | Durham rd E12 |
| 65 O 12 | Durham rd E16 |
| 31 R 11 | Durham rd N17 |
| 28 L 11 | Durham rd N2 |
| 48 D 7 | Durham rd N7 |
| 18 J 8 | Durham rd N9 |
| 104 K 20 | Durham rd SW20 |

| | | |
|---|---|---|
| 118 L 2 | Durham rd SW20 |
| 72 G 9 | Durham rd W5 |
| 126 C 6 | Durham rd Brom |
| 56 J 15 | Durham rd Dgnhm |
| 22 L 16 | Durham rd Harrow |
| 115 P 12 | Durham rd Sidcp |
| 79 R 14 | Durham ri SE18 |
| 63 U 15 | Durham row E11 |
| 149 O 12 | Durham rd SE11 |
| 137 W 4 | Durham ter W2 |
| 72 E 18 | Durham wharf Brentf |
| 122 F 13 | Durheved Rd north Thntn Hth |
| 22 B 19 | Durley av Pinn |
| 49 R 1 | Durley rd N16 |
| 49 X 7 | Durlston rd E5 |
| 102 J 15 | Durlston rd Kingst |
| 31 T 17 | Durnford st N15 |
| 109 P 13 | Durning rd SE19 |
| 105 Y 4 | Durnsford av SW19 |
| 29 V 1 | Durnsford rd N11 |
| 87 U 3 | Durrell rd SW6 |
| 104 M 19 | Durrington av SW20 |
| 104 M 20 | Durrington pk SW20 |
| 50 G 13 | Durrington rd E5 |
| 94 K 4 | Dursley clo SE3 |
| 95 N 2 | Dursley gdns SE3 |
| 94 K 4 | Dursley rd SE3 |
| 95 N 2 | Dursley rd SE3 |
| 135 W 20 | Durward st E1 |
| 143 V 1 | Durward st E1 |
| 139 R 1 | Durweston ms W1 |
| 139 P 1 | Durweston st W1 |
| 4 H 7 | Dury rd Barnt |
| 87 V 14 | Dutch yd SW18 |
| 76 H 1 | Duthie st E14 |
| 93 U 1 | Dutton st SE10 |
| 57 Z 19 | Duxford clo Hornch |
| 141 T 3 | Dyers bldgs EC1 |
| 51 Y 5 | Dyers Hall rd E11 |
| 86 K 9 | Dyers la SW15 |
| 39 X 3 | Dyers way Rom |
| 126 B 5 | Dykes way Brom |
| 81 S 8 | Dylan rd Blvdr |
| 91 P 10 | Dylways SE5 |
| 35 W 9 | Dymchurch clo Ilf |
| 88 A 7 | Dymock st SW6 |
| 39 T 20 | Dymoke rd Hornch |
| 145 V 20 | Dyne rd NW6 |
| 129 N 1 | Dyne rd NW6 |
| 112 L 8 | Dyneley rd SE12 |
| 49 S 10 | Dynevor rd N16 |
| 84 K 13 | Dynevor rd Rich |
| 45 Y 20 | Dynham rd NW6 |
| 140 H 3 | Dyott st WC1 |
| 102 E 11 | Dysart av Kingst |
| 134 H 19 | Dysart st EC2 |
| 34 A 19 | Dyson rd E11 |
| 52 C 18 | Dyson rd E15 |
| 19 N 17 | Dysons rd N18 |

# E

| | | |
|---|---|---|
| 30 M 20 | Eade rd N4 |
| 31 O 20 | Eade rd N4 |
| 48 L 1 | Eade rd N4 |
| 9 R 15 | Eagle clo Enf |
| 133 W 20 | Eagle ct EC1 |
| 109 O 16 | Eagle hill SE19 |
| 34 E 14 | Eagle la E11 |
| 140 D 11 | Eagle pl SW1 |
| 140 M 2 | Eagle pl WC1 |
| 42 H 20 | Eagle pl Wemb |
| 141 O 2 | Eagle st WC1 |
| 34 H 2 | Eagle ter Wdfd Grn |
| 134 D 7 | Eagle Wharf rd N1 |
| 95 Z 3 | Eaglesfield rd SE18 |
| 96 A 1 | Eaglesfield rd SE18 |
| 78 M 20 | Eaglesfield rd SE18 |
| 63 P 12 | Eaglet pl E1 |
| 64 C 9 | Eagling rd E3 |
| 94 M 11 | Ealdham sq SE9 |
| 72 G 2 | Ealing grn W5 |
| 72 D 11 | Ealing Pk gdns W5 |
| 72 J 16 | Ealing rd Brentf |
| 58 G 7 | Ealing rd Grnfd |
| 42 J 17 | Ealing rd Wemb |
| 60 J 6 | Ealing rd Wemb |
| 60 L 18 | Ealing village W5 |
| 130 L 9 | Eamont st NW8 |
| 99 T 10 | Eardemont clo Drtfrd |
| 145 U 11 | Eardley cres SW5 |
| 107 X 17 | Eardley rd SW16 |
| 81 S 13 | Eardley rd Blvdr |
| 151 L 4 | Earl cotts SE1 |
| 151 N 9 | Earl rd SE1 |
| 85 W 9 | Earl rd SW14 |
| 79 S 12 | Earl ri SE18 |
| 134 H 20 | Earl st EC2 |
| 87 N 9 | Earldom rd SW15 |

| | | |
|---|---|---|
| 52 F 16 | Earlham gro E7 |
| 30 D 3 | Earlham gro N22 |
| 140 J 6 | Earlham st WC2 |
| 23 T 12 | Earls cres Harrow |
| 145 T 10 | Earls Ct Exhibition building SW5 |
| 145 X 7 | Earls Ct gdns SW6 |
| 145 T 2 | Earls Ct rd W8 |
| 145 W 10 | Earls Ct sq SW5 |
| 145 R 3 | Earls ter W8 |
| 145 T 3 | Earls wlk W8 |
| 106 C 1 | Earlsfield rd SW18 |
| 88 D 19 | Earlsfield rd SW18 |
| 95 V 10 | Earlshall rd SE9 |
| 40 F 13 | Earlsmead Harrow |
| 128 A 11 | Earlsmead rd NW1 |
| 62 L 8 | Earlsmead rd NW1 |
| 31 U 15 | Earlsmead rd N15 |
| 110 E 11 | Earlsthorpe rd SE23 |
| 133 W 13 | Earlstoke st EC1 |
| 63 N 3 | Earlston gro E9 |
| 122 G 12 | Earlswood av Thnt Hth |
| 35 W 12 | Earlswood gdns Ilf |
| 77 N 14 | Earlswood st SE10 |
| 131 X 3 | Early ms NW1 |
| 73 T 17 | Earnest gdns W14 |
| 140 H 4 | Earnshaw st WC2 |
| 144 M 5 | Earsby st W14 |
| 120 A 15 | Easby cres Mrdn |
| 55 S 16 | Easebourne rd Dgnhm |
| 57 X 15 | Easedale dri Hornc |
| 139 V 4 | Easleys ms W1 |
| 63 S 17 | East Abour st E1 |
| 62 B 20 | East Acton la W3 |
| 73 Z 3 | East Acton la W3 |
| 53 R 20 | East av E12 |
| 33 R 14 | East av E17 |
| 58 D 20 | East av S'hall |
| 156 C 11 | East av Wallgtn |
| 5 V 18 | East Barnet la Barr |
| 73 Y 2 | East Churchfield rd W3 |
| 61 O 12 | East clo W5 |
| 6 C 14 | East clo WC2 |
| 59 O 6 | East clo Grnfd |
| 16 A 12 | East cres N11 |
| 8 G 17 | East cres Enf |
| 42 E 8 | East ct Wemb |
| 154 K 19 | East drive Carsh |
| 91 R 14 | East Dulwich gro SE22 |
| 91 V 10 | East Dulwich rd SE22 |
| 28 C 10 | East End rd N2 |
| 27 Y 8 | East End rd N3 |
| 22 C 9 | East End way Pinn |
| 76 E 9 | East Ferry rd E14 |
| 106 J 15 | East gdns SW17 |
| 65 Y 14 | East Ham And Barking By pass E16 |
| 66 F 13 | East Ham And Barking By pass E6 |
| 67 S 7 | East Ham By pass Bark |
| 66 H 14 | East Ham Manor wa E6 |
| 141 V 5 | East Harding st EC |
| 46 G 10 | East Heath rd NW3 |
| 88 B 13 | East hill SW 18 |
| 43 P 5 | East hill Wemb |
| 98 L 1 | East holme Erith |
| 64 J 20 | East India dock E14 |
| 64 K 18 | East India Dock rd E14 |
| 116 G 3 | East la Kingst |
| 42 D 10 | East la Wemb |
| 143 O 9 | East minster E1 |
| 143 X 1 | East Mount st E1 |
| 37 X 16 | East Park clo Rom |
| 141 Z 1 | East pas EC1 |
| 108 L 9 | East pl SE27 |
| 141 X 1 | East Poultry av EC1 |
| 141 X 1 | East Poultry av EC1 |
| 65 R 3 | East rd E15 |
| 134 F 12 | East rd N1 |
| 106 E 15 | East rd SW19 |
| 16 B 4 | East rd Barnt |
| 25 U 4 | East rd Edgw |
| 9 R 3 | East rd Enf |
| 102 K 20 | East rd Kingst |
| 37 X 14 | East rd Rom |
| 57 N 2 | East rd Rom |
| 97 P 4 | East rd Welling |
| 98 F 15 | East Rochester way Bxly Hth |
| 98 K 18 | East Rochester way Bxly Hth |

| | | | |
|---|---|---|---|
| 8 L 17 East row W10 | 119 R 10 Eastway Mrdn | 124 M 12 Eden way Becknhm | 88 J 3 Edna st SW11 |
| 5 Y 10 East Sheen av SW14 | 155 U 9 Eastway Wallgtn | 125 O 14 Eden way Becknhm | 75 S 18 Edric rd SE14 |
| 3 R 11 East smithfield E1 | 34 G 8 Eastwood clo E18 | 63 T 1 Edenbridge rd E9 | 12 G 20 Edrick rd Edg |
| 7 P 1 East st Bark | 34 F 6 Eastwood rd E18 | 18 E 1 Edenbridge rd Enf | 12 G 20 Edrick wlk Edg |
| 7 O 2 East st Bark | 29 O 8 Eastwood rd N10 | 107 T 15 Edencourt rd SW16 | 157 N 7 Edridge rd Croy |
| 2 D 19 East st Brentf | 55 N 2 Eastwood rd Ilf | 99 O 4 Edendale rd Bxly Hth | 20 C 18 Edward av E4 |
| 6 F 2 East st Brom | 37 N 20 Eastwood rd Ilf | 152 E 4 Edenfield gdns Worc | 120 F 11 Edward av Mrdn |
| 6 E 10 East st Bxly Hth | 107 U 16 Eastwood st SW16 | Pk | 18 H 3 Edward clo N9 |
| 1 N 17 East Surrey gro SE15 | 33 W 16 Eatington rd E10 | 87 U 7 Edenhurst av SW6 | 101 N 13 Edward clo Hampt |
| 3 P 6 East Tenter st E1 | 147 T 6 Eaton clo SW1 | 74 B 19 Edensor gdns W4 | 5 T 16 Edward gro Barnt |
| 20 G 15 East view E4 | 11 P 14 Eaton clo Stanm | 74 A 19 Edensor rd W4 | 75 Z 17 Edward pl SE8 |
| 4 H 10 East view Barnt | 103 S 18 Eaton dri Kingst | 107 P 18 Edenvale rd Mitch | 32 G 16 Edward rd E17 |
| 48 J 4 East way Croy | 38 F 3 Eaton dri Rom | 88 C 6 Edenvale st SW6 | 110 F 16 Edward rd SE20 |
| 6 B 4 East wlk Barnt | 147 U 4 Eaton gate SW1 | 122 E 5 Ederline av SW16 | 5 T 16 Edward rd Barnt |
| 7 Z 20 East woodside Bxly | 55 Y 20 Eaton gdns Dgnhm | 64 D 9 Edgar rd E3 | 112 J 17 Edward rd Brom |
| 41 N 13 Eastbank rd Hampt | 25 R 12 Eaton gro NW9 | 82 E 18 Edgar rd Hounsl | 114 A 13 Edward rd Chisl |
| 41 Y 19 Eastbourne av W3 | 147 Y 2 Eaton la SW1 | 37 V 20 Edgar rd S Croy | 123 T 16 Edward rd Croy |
| 45 V 8 Eastbourne gdns | 147 V 3 Eaton la SW1 | 157 O 20 Edgar rd S Croy | 101 N 12 Edward rd Hampt |
| SW14 | 147 U 5 Eaton Ms west SW1 | 87 S 2 Edgarley ter SW6 | 23 N 11 Edward rd Harrow |
| 48 D 5 Eastbourne ms W2 | 17 U 9 Eaton Pk rd N21 | 78 M 16 Edge hill SE18 | 37 X 18 Edward rd Rom |
| 45 N 5 Eastbourne rd E15 | 147 U 2 Eaton pl SW1 | 105 O 17 Edge hill SW19 | 133 N 6 Edward sq N1 |
| 36 K 8 Eastbourne rd E6 | 26 M 15 Eaton rd NW4 | 27 X 11 Edge Hill av N3 | 65 S 13 Edward st E16 |
| 31 S 19 Eastbourne rd N15 | 90 H 12 Eaton rd SW9 | 137 V 14 Edge st W8 | 75 Z 17 Edward st SE8 |
| 73 X 16 Eastbourne rd SW17 | 8 E 13 Eaton rd Enf | 114 A 10 Edgebury Chisl | 76 A 17 Edward st SE8 |
| 72 F 14 Eastbourne rd W4 | 83 R 11 Eaton rd Hounsl | 113 Z 10 Edgebury Chisl | 145 R 3 Edwardes sq W 8 |
| 70 A 3 Eastbourne rd Brentf | 115 W 5 Eaton rd Sidcp | 114 A 10 Edgebury wlk Chisl | 48 H 19 Edwards cotts N 1 |
| 48 D 5 Eastbourne rd Felt | 154 E 14 Eaton rd Sutton | 103 X 18 Edgecombe clo | 49 P 8 Edwards la N16 |
| 19 O 10 Eastbournia av N9 | 34 L 14 Eaton ri E11 | Kingst | 139 T 5 Edwards mans W 1 |
| 19 P 3 Eastbrook av N9 | 60 F 17 Eaton ri W5 | 91 R 5 Edgecombe rd SE5 | 81 R 9 Edwards rd Blvdr |
| 56 K 12 Eastbrook av Dgnhm | 147 W 2 Eaton row SW1 | 158 E 18 Edgecoombe S Croy | 66 K 8 Edwin av E6 |
| 57 P 8 Eastbrook dri Rom | 147 T 6 Eaton ter SW1 | 31 R 15 Edgecot gro N15 | 81 O 17 Edwin clo Bxly Hth |
| 94 J 1 Eastbury av SE3 | 147 S 5 Eaton Ter ms SW1 | 54 L 20 Edgefield av Bark | 12 K 20 Edwin rd Edg |
| 87 V 3 Eastbury av Bark | 20 A 8 Eatons mead E4 | 56 E 12 Edgefield gdns Dgnhm | 101 U 1 Edwin rd Twick |
| 8 F 6 Eastbury av Enf | 106 M 4 Eatonville rd SW17 | 60 C 15 Edgehill rd W13 | 63 R 12 Edwin st E1 |
| 74 B 14 Eastbury gro W4 | 107 N 4 Eatonville rd SW17 | 114 B 9 Edgehill rd Chisl | 65 S 15 Edwin st E16 |
| 102 J 19 Eastbury rd Kingst | 107 N 4 Eatonville vils SW17 | 121 R 1 Edgehill rd Mitch | 35 P 16 Edwina gdns Ilf |
| 38 M 18 Eastbury rd Rom | 152 M 2 Ebbisham rd Worc | 88 A 11 Edgel st SW4 | 4 A 18 Edwyn clo Barnt |
| 87 X 3 Eastbury sq Bark | Pk | 89 X 8 Edgeley la SW4 | 145 U 19 Effie pl SW6 |
| 40 C 4 Eastcastle st W1 | 94 H 9 Ebdon way SE3 | 89 X 8 Edgeley rd SW4 | 145 U 19 Effie rd SW6 |
| 42 M 9 Eastchean EC3 | 45 X 9 Ebenezer ms NW2 | 108 J 13 Edgepoint clo SE27 | 154 B 17 Effingham clo Sutton |
| 55 Y 8 Eastcombe av SE7 | 149 V 7 Ebenezer row SE11 | 26 G 15 Edgeworth av NW4 | 30 H 14 Effingham rd N8 |
| 41 Z 16 Eastcote av Grnfd | 134 E 13 Ebenezer st N1 | 26 F 18 Edgeworth clo NW4 | 94 G 12 Effingham rd SE12 |
| 40 L 8 Eastcote av Harrow | 121 U 1 Ebenezer wlk SW16 | 26 G 15 Edgeworth cres NW4 | 122 D 18 Effingham rd Croy |
| 58 G 1 Eastcote la Grnfd | 88 B 12 Ebner st SW18 | 95 N 11 Edgeworth rd SE9 | 116 C 18 Effingham rd Surb |
| 40 E 17 Eastcote la Grnfd | 134 M 16 Ebor st E2 | 94 L 10 Edgeworth rd SE9 | 106 J 12 Effort st SW17 |
| 40 E 11 Eastcote la Harrow | 24 F 19 Ebrington rd Harrow | 5 X 13 Edgeworth rd Barnt | 90 G 13 Effra pde SW2 |
| 41 N 10 Eastcote rd Harrow | 94 G 9 Ebsfleet rd SE3 | 107 W 16 Eddington rd SW16 | 105 Z 14 Effra rd SW19 |
| 22 B 14 Eastcote rd Pinn | 45 R 13 Ebsfleet rd NW2 | 12 C 20 Edgware High st Edg | 90 E 13 Effra rd SW2 |
| 96 F 6 Eastcote rd Welling | 92 G 19 Ebsworth st SE23 | 44 L 6 Edgware rd NW2 | 75 N 14 Egan st SE16 |
| 90 B 5 Eastcote st SW19 | 48 B 10 Eburne rd N7 | 25 W 9 Edgware rd NW9 | 151 X 10 Egan way SE16 |
| 52 B 17 Eastcroft rd Epsom | 147 W 9 Ebury br SW1 | 26 D 18 Edgware way NW9 | 131 T 3 Egbert pl NW1 |
| 93 X 11 Eastdown pk SE13 | 147 V 11 Ebury Br rd SW1 | 130 F 19 Edgware rd W2 | 146 L 4 Egerton cres SW3 |
| 34 K 17 Eastern av Ilf | 147 W 4 Ebury ms SW1 | 138 K 3 Edgware rd W2 | 76 E 20 Egerton dri SE10 |
| 61 T 12 Eastern av W3 | 147 W 4 Ebury Ms east SW1 | 139 N 6 Edgware rd W2 | 93 S 1 Egerton dri SE10 |
| 35 F 18 Eastern av Ilf | 147 V 7 Ebury pl SW1 | 12 A 18 Edgware rd Edg | 62 M 3 Egerton gdns NW10 |
| 57 S 18 Eastern av Ilf | 147 V 6 Ebury sq SW1 | 12 B 17 Edgware way Edg | 128 C 5 Egerton gdns NW10 |
| 40 A 1 Eastern av Pinn | 88 L 9 Eccles rd SW11 | 11 Y 11 Edgware way Edg | 26 K 13 Egerton gdns SW3 |
| 40 A 1 Eastern av Pinn | 17 S 10 Ecclesbourne clo | 12 C 16 Edgwarebury gdns | 140 K 4 Egerton gdns SW3 |
| 39 V 5 Eastern av Rom | N13 | Edg | 60 B 17 Egerton gdns SW13 |
| 40 A 1 Eastern av Rom | 17 S 16 Ecclesbourne gdns | 11 X 3 Edgwarebury house | 54 K 10 Egerton gdns Ilf |
| 37 T 13 Eastern av Rom | N13 | Borhm Wd | 146 L 3 Egerton Gdns ms |
| 39 S 5 Eastern Av east Rom | 134 R 2 Ecclesbourne rd N1 | 11 Y 3 Edgwarebury la | SW3 |
| 38 M 10 Eastern Av west Rom | 122 L 11 Ecclesbourne rd | Borhm Wd | 31 U 20 Egerton rd N16 |
| 05 V 6 Eastern rd E13 | Thntn Hth | 12 B 8 Edgwarebury la Edg | 123 R 7 Egerton rd SE25 |
| 33 V 15 Eastern rd E17 | 147 Y 5 Eccleston br SW1 | 12 C 14 Edgwarebury la Edg | 118 E 8 Egerton rd New Mald |
| 28 M 12 Eastern rd N2 | 37 O 20 Eccleston clo Rom | 12 A 10 Edgwarebury park | 83 U 17 Egerton rd Twick |
| 30 A 4 Eastern rd N22 | 55 P 1 Eccleston cres Rom | Edg | 60 L 1 Egerton rd Wemb |
| 93 O 11 Eastern rd SE4 | 147 V 2 Eccleston ms SW1 | 65 V 7 Edinburgh rd E13 | 146 K 3 Egerton ter SW3 |
| 39 T 16 Eastern rd Rom | 147 W 6 Eccleston pl SW1 | 32 M 16 Edinburgh rd E17 | 153 R 3 Egham clo Sutton |
| 58 D 13 Easternville gdns Ilf | 71 X 2 Eccleston rd W13 | 18 L 15 Edinburgh rd N18 | 153 R 4 Egham cres Sutton |
| 33 O 12 Eastfield rd E17 | 147 Z 7 Eccleston sq SW1 | 71 V 5 Edinburgh rd W7 | 65 W 14 Egham rd E13 |
| 30 A 11 Eastfield rd N8 | 147 Z 7 Eccleston Sq ms | 154 E 4 Edinburgh rd Sutton | 88 C 14 Eglantine rd SW18 |
| 61 V 14 Eastfield rd W3 | SW1 | 80 D 7 Edington rd SE2 | 120 A 15 Egleston rd Mrdn |
| 56 C 13 Eastfield rd Dgnhm | 147 X 5 Eccleston st SW1 | 9 P 10 Edington rd Enf | 20 K 2 Eglington rd E4 |
| 9 S 3 Eastfield rd Enf | 42 K 15 Ecclestone ct Wemb | 131 U 2 Edis st NW1 | 78 M 19 Eglinton hills SE18 |
| 21 P 3 Eastfields rd Mitch | 42 K 15 Ecclestone mews | 57 T 4 Edison av Hornch | 78 K 17 Eglinton rd SE18 |
| 22 C 10 Eastgade Pinn | Wemb | 57 S 4 Edison clo Hornch | 86 L 8 Egliston rd SW15 |
| 28 B 14 Eastholm NW11 | 42 J 15 Ecclestone ms Wemb | 58 K 17 Edison dri S'hall | 117 O 20 Egmont av Surb |
| 90 K 6 Eastlake rd SE5 | 43 N 15 Ecclestone pl Wemb | 79 X 20 Edison gro SE18 | 118 E 7 Egmont rd New Mald |
| 51 U 17 Eastlands cres SE21 | 20 D 6 Echo heights E4 | 29 Z 19 Edison rd N8 | 117 O 20 Egmont rd Surb |
| 40 K 8 Eastleigh av Harrow | 135 R 18 Eckersley st E1 | 79 Y 20 Edison rd SE18 | 154 C 18 Egmont rd Sutton |
| 44 B 10 Eastleigh clo NW2 | 75 S 19 Eckington gdns SE14 | 79 Y 20 Edison rd S18 | 75 T 20 Egmont st SE14 |
| 98 L 7 Eastleigh rd Bxly Hth | 88 J 10 Eckstein rd SW11 | 126 D 3 Edison rd Brom | 108 G 7 Egremont rd SE27 |
| 86 G 19 Eastleigh wlk SW15 | 65 U 14 Eclipse rd E13 | 96 K 2 Edison rd Welling | 53 U 11 Eighth av E12 |
| 58 K 9 Eastmead av Grnfd | 111 Y 5 Ector rd SE6 | 117 S 16 Edith gdns Surb | 123 P 12 Eileen rd SE25 |
| 108 M 4 Eastmearn rd SE21 | 129 U 18 Edbrooke rd W9 | 146 B 15 Edith gro SW10 | 66 D 14 Eisenhower dri E6 |
| 09 N 4 Eastmearn rd SE21 | 48 E 5 Eddington st N4 | 51 X 14 Edith rd E15 | 47 N 14 Elaine gro NW5 |
| 78 A 10 Eastmoor pl SE7 | 87 W 4 Eddiscombe rd SW6 | 68 A 1 Edith rd E6 | 90 J 5 Elam st SE25 |
| 78 A 10 Eastmoor st SE7 | 38 G 19 Eddy clo Rom | 29 Y 2 Edith rd N11 | 156 H 5 Eland pl Croy |
| 76 K 15 Eastney st SE10 | 92 J 14 Eddystone rd SE4 | 31 Y 12 Edith rd N17 | 89 N 7 Eland rd SW11 |
| 14 C 2 Easton rd Bxly | 60 F 4 Eden clo Wemb | 123 P 12 Edith rd SE25 | 156 H 5 Eland rd Croy |
| 33 S 15 Easton st WC1 | 33 S 15 Eden gro E17 | 106 B 15 Edith rd SW19 | 150 C 5 Elba pl SE17 |
| 126 D 15 Eastry av Brom | 48 D 15 Eden gro N7 | 144 J 6 Edith rd W14 | 88 C 4 Elbe st SW6 |
| 81 S 18 Eastry rd Erith | 125 T 13 Eden park Becknhm | 145 N 8 Edith rd W14 | 121 W 15 Elberon av Croy |
| 27 U 14 Eastside rd NW11 | 124 K 8 Eden Pk av Becknhm | 146 C 17 Edith ter SW10 | 123 W 11 Elborough rd SE25 |
| 79 V 19 Eastview av SE18 | 125 P 10 Eden Pk av Becknhm | 145 O 8 Edith vils wk W14 | 105 X 2 Elborough st SW18 |
| 27 U 17 Eastville av NW11 | 33 S 15 Eden rd E17 | 90 B 7 Edithna st SW9 | 65 T 19 Elbury dri E16 |
| 34 H 15 Eastway E11 | 108 K 11 Eden rd SE27 | 120 J 5 Edmund rd Mitch | 146 L 19 Elcho st SW11 |
| 51 N 14 Eastway E9 | 124 G 8 Eden rd Becknhm | 97 O 6 Edmund rd Welling | 129 P 19 Elcom st W10 |
| 50 L 16 Eastway E9 | 157 O 8 Eden rd Croy | 150 F 18 Edmund st SE5 | 151 V 18 Elcot av SE15 |
| 126 E 17 Eastway Brom | 116 J 9 Eden st Kingst | 28 H 14 Edmunds wlk N2 | 30 A 17 Elder av N8 |
| | | 119 O 3 Edna rd SW20 | 108 M 13 Elder rd SE27 |

| | |
|---|---|
| 134 M 19 | Elder st E1 |
| 72 K 7 | Elderberry rd W5 |
| 50 D 12 | Elderfield rd E5 |
| 34 H 15 | Elderfield wlk E11 |
| 125 P 13 | Elderslie clo Becknhm |
| 95 X 14 | Elderslie rd SE9 |
| 110 H 10 | Elderton rd SE26 |
| 121 U 1 | Eldertree pl Mitch |
| 121 T 2 | Eldertree way Mitch |
| 158 D 2 | Eldon av Croy |
| 70 G 19 | Eldon av Hounsl |
| 46 G 14 | Eldon gro NW3 |
| 123 Z 8 | Eldon pk SE25 |
| 32 L 14 | Eldon rd E17 |
| 30 K 5 | Eldon rd N22 |
| 19 O 7 | Eldon rd N9 |
| 145 Z 2 | Eldon rd W8 |
| 146 A 2 | Eldon rd W8 |
| 142 G 1 | Eldon st EC2 |
| 67 U 3 | Eldred rd Bark |
| 14 B 15 | Eleanor cres NW7 |
| 56 A 8 | Eleanor gdns Dgnhm |
| 86 C 8 | Eleanor gro SW13 |
| 52 D 19 | Eleanor rd E15 |
| 49 Z 18 | Eleanor rd E8 |
| 17 N 20 | Eleanor rd N11 |
| 64 A 9 | Eleanor st E3 |
| 64 B 10 | Eleanor st E3 |
| 90 E 10 | Electric av SW9 |
| 149 Z 4 | Elephant And castle SE1 |
| 143 Z 17 | Elephant la SE16 |
| 75 O 5 | Elephant la SE16 |
| 150 A 4 | Elephant rd SE17 |
| 72 D 6 | Elers rd W13 |
| 35 R 20 | Eley gdns Ilf |
| 19 R 16 | Eley rd N18 |
| 63 R 19 | Elf row E1 |
| 101 V 13 | Elfin gro Tedd |
| 90 M 13 | Elfindale rd SE24 |
| 91 N 14 | Elfindale rd SE24 |
| 48 G 12 | Elfort rd N5 |
| 111 O 9 | Elfrida cres SE6 |
| 59 U 13 | Elfwine rd W7 |
| 122 A 5 | Elgar av SW16 |
| 72 K 5 | Elgar av W5 |
| 117 R 19 | Elgar av Surb |
| 11 S 2 | Elgar clo Borehm Wd |
| 75 W 7 | Elgar st SE16 |
| 130 A 14 | Elgin av W9 |
| 129 T 17 | Elgin av W9 |
| 24 A 7 | Elgin av Harrow |
| 136 M 8 | Elgin cres W11 |
| 137 N 7 | Elgin cres W11 |
| 129 Z 12 | Elgin Ms north W 9 |
| 130 A 13 | Elgin Ms south W9 |
| 29 V 7 | Elgin rd N22 |
| 157 V 2 | Elgin rd Croy |
| 123 U 20 | Elgin rd Croy |
| 54 J 1 | Elgin rd Ilf |
| 154 D 6 | Elgin rd Sutton |
| 155 U 13 | Elgin rd Wallgtn |
| 149 S 16 | Elia pl SE11 |
| 133 W 9 | Elia st N1 |
| 95 V 10 | Elibank rd SE9 |
| 110 A 3 | Eliot bank SE23 |
| 40 J 6 | Eliot dri Harrow |
| 93 V 5 | Eliot hill SE13 |
| 93 V 5 | Eliot pk SE13 |
| 93 Y 5 | Eliot pl SE13 |
| 55 W 13 | Eliot rd Dgnhm |
| 93 X 5 | Eliot vale SE13 |
| 156 J 4 | Elis David pl Croy |
| 156 J 4 | Elis David pl Croy |
| 156 J 4 | Elis David rd Croy |
| 156 J 4 | Elis David rd Croy |
| 134 D 2 | Elizabeth av N1 |
| 7 X 10 | Elizabeth av Enf |
| 54 E 6 | Elizabeth av Ilf |
| 147 X 7 | Elizabeth br SW1 |
| 64 D 17 | Elizabeth clo E14 |
| 130 D 17 | Elizabeth clo W9 |
| 4 B 12 | Elizabeth clo Barnt |
| 38 G 5 | Elizabeth clo Rom |
| 85 O 2 | Elizabeth cotts Rich |
| 74 D 4 | Elizabeth gdns W3 |
| 46 L 18 | Elizabeth ms NW3 |
| 66 A 2 | Elizabeth rd E6 |
| 31 S 16 | Elizabeth rd N15 |
| 19 O 3 | Elizabeth ride N9 |
| 147 W 6 | Elizabeth st SW1 |
| 95 U 15 | Elizabeth ter SE9 |
| 31 P 12 | Elizabethan pl N15 |
| 65 U 12 | Elkington rd E13 |
| 30 B 20 | Ella rd N8 |
| 144 F 15 | Ellaline rd W6 |
| 19 N 16 | Ellanby cres N 18 |
| 92 C 11 | Elland rd SE15 |
| 22 A 16 | Ellement clo Pinn |
| 127 O 6 | Ellen clo Brom |
| 19 P 10 | Ellen ct N9 |
| 143 T 7 | Ellen st E1 |
| 30 K 5 | Ellenborough rd N20 |
| 115 Y 13 | Ellenborough rd Sidcp |
| 157 T 20 | Ellenbridge way S Croy |
| 101 V 14 | Elleray rd Tedd |
| 87 P 2 | Ellerby st SW6 |
| 46 D 14 | Ellerdale clo NW3 |
| 46 D 14 | Ellerdale rd NW3 |
| 93 R 9 | Ellerdale st SE13 |
| 83 O 11 | Ellerdine rd Hounsl |
| 84 J 15 | Ellerker gdns Rich |
| 64 B 17 | Ellerman st E14 |
| 74 J 2 | Ellerslie rd W12 |
| 89 Z 12 | Ellerslie sq SW4 |
| 68 E 1 | Ellerton gdns Dgnhm |
| 86 F 2 | Ellerton rd SW13 |
| 88 F 20 | Ellerton rd SW18 |
| 106 G 1 | Ellerton rd SW18 |
| 104 G 17 | Ellerton rd SW20 |
| 68 F 2 | Ellerton rd Dgnhm |
| 116 M 20 | Ellerton rd Surb |
| 92 A 6 | Ellery st SE15 |
| 12 K 10 | Ellesmere av NW7 |
| 125 S 4 | Ellesmere av Becknhm |
| 34 D 16 | Ellesmere clo E11 |
| 35 R 17 | Ellesmere gdns Ilf |
| 4 G 16 | Ellesmere gro Barnt |
| 77 T 2 | Ellesmere rd E16 |
| 63 V 5 | Ellesmere rd E3 |
| 44 H 15 | Ellesmere rd NW10 |
| 73 X 15 | Ellesmere rd W4 |
| 58 M 12 | Ellesmere rd Grnfd |
| 84 D 15 | Ellesmere rd Twick |
| 64 C 17 | Ellesmere st E14 |
| 50 A 19 | Ellingfort rd E8 |
| 51 X 13 | Ellingham rd E15 |
| 74 G 5 | Ellingham rd W12 |
| 29 S 13 | Ellington rd N10 |
| 82 L 5 | Ellington rd Hounsl |
| 48 F 18 | Ellington st N7 |
| 26 K 19 | Elliot rd NW4 |
| 126 M 9 | Elliot rd Brom |
| 127 N 9 | Elliot rd Brom |
| 122 K 9 | Elliot rd Thntn Hth |
| 39 Y 4 | Elliott gdns Rom |
| 149 V 20 | Elliott rd SW9 |
| 90 H 1 | Elliott rd SW9 |
| 74 A 11 | Elliott rd W4 |
| 10 M 18 | Elliott rd Stanm |
| 149 X 4 | Elliotts row SE11 |
| 77 X 16 | Ellis ms SE7 |
| 147 R 4 | Ellis st SW1 |
| 77 Y 15 | Elliscombe rd SE7 |
| 86 F 17 | Ellisfield dri SW15 |
| 70 D 10 | Ellison gdns S'hall |
| 86 E 5 | Ellison rd SW13 |
| 108 A 19 | Ellison rd SW16 |
| 107 Y 18 | Ellison rd SW16 |
| 114 F 2 | Ellison rd Sidcp |
| 39 Y 4 | Ellora clo Rom |
| 107 Y 13 | Ellora rd SW16 |
| 63 N 9 | Ellsworth st E2 |
| 135 X 17 | Ellsworth st E2 |
| 72 L 4 | Elm av W5 |
| 17 O 2 | Elm bank N14 |
| 86 C 5 | Elm Bank gdns SW13 |
| 34 J 18 | Elm clo E11 |
| 27 O 17 | Elm clo NW4 |
| 113 M 8 | Elm clo SW20 |
| 120 L 20 | Elm clo Carsh |
| 22 J 19 | Elm clo Harrow |
| 38 G 6 | Elm clo Rom |
| 157 P 14 | Elm clo S Croy |
| 117 W 17 | Elm clo Twick |
| 100 K 5 | Elm cres W5 |
| 116 K 1 | Elm cres Kingst |
| 22 J 18 | Elm dri Harrow |
| 28 E 10 | Elm gdns N2 |
| 8 A 2 | Elm gdns Enf |
| 121 X 6 | Elm gdns Mitch |
| 62 A 17 | Elm grn W3 |
| 45 R 12 | Elm gro NW2 |
| 30 B 19 | Elm gro N8 |
| 91 W 4 | Elm gro SE15 |
| 105 S 18 | Elm gro SW19 |
| 81 Z 18 | Elm gro Erith |
| 40 G 2 | Elm gro N9 |
| 116 L 1 | Elm gro Kingst |
| 154 B 9 | Elm gro Sutton |
| 21 R 17 | Elm gro Wdfd Grn |
| 155 P 6 | Elm Gro pde Wallgtn |
| 86 G 4 | Elm Grove rd SW 13 |
| 124 A 18 | Elm Grove rd Croy |
| 34 J 18 | Elm Hall gdns E11 |
| 110 M 3 | Elm la SE6 |
| 31 W 18 | Elm Park av N15 |
| 90 C 17 | Elm pk SW2 |
| 11 P 17 | Elm pk Stanm |
| 57 U 12 | Elm Pk av Hornch |
| 27 O 17 | Elm Pk gdns NW4 |
| 146 F 11 | Elm Pk gdns SW10 |
| 146 E 12 | Elm Pk la SW3 |
| 50 J 4 | Elm Pk rd E10 |
| 17 X 4 | Elm Pk rd N21 |
| 27 W 2 | Elm Pk rd N3 |
| 123 T 6 | Elm Pk rd SE25 |
| 146 E 13 | Elm Pk rd SW3 |
| 146 F 10 | Elm pl SW7 |
| 33 V 16 | Elm rd E10 |
| 51 V 7 | Elm rd E11 |
| 33 V 16 | Elm rd E17 |
| 52 D 18 | Elm rd E7 |
| 46 E 10 | Elm rd NW3 |
| 85 W 9 | Elm rd SW14 |
| 124 L 2 | Elm rd Becknhm |
| 152 E 15 | Elm rd Epsom |
| 99 W 1 | Elm rd Erith |
| 82 B 5 | Elm rd Hounsl |
| 102 M 19 | Elm rd Kingst |
| 103 O 18 | Elm rd Kingst |
| 116 L 1 | Elm rd Kingst |
| 117 X 4 | Elm rd New Mald |
| 38 G 7 | Elm rd Rom |
| 114 M 12 | Elm rd Sidcp |
| 123 N 10 | Elm rd Thntn Hth |
| 121 P 20 | Elm rd Wallgtn |
| 42 K 15 | Elm rd Wemb |
| 119 V 16 | Elm Rd west Sutton |
| 133 P 17 | Elm st WC1 |
| 45 X 9 | Elm ter NW2 |
| 95 W 15 | Elm ter SE9 |
| 23 R 3 | Elm ter Harrow |
| 11 P 17 | Elm ter Stanm |
| 130 F 12 | Elm Tree clo NW8 |
| 130 F 12 | Elm Tree clo NW8 |
| 58 F 7 | Elm Tree clo Grnfd |
| 130 F 13 | Elm Tree rd NW8 |
| 43 Z 11 | Elm way NW10 |
| 44 A 11 | Elm way NW10 |
| 152 M 4 | Elm way Worc Pk |
| 45 Z 8 | Elm wlk NW3 |
| 118 M 8 | Elm wlk SW20 |
| 119 O 9 | Elm wlk SW20 |
| 39 W 9 | Elm wlk Rom |
| 31 P 14 | Elmar rd N15 |
| 4 A 15 | Elmbank av Barnt |
| 59 S 13 | Elmbank way W7 |
| 107 R 7 | Elmbourne rd SW17 |
| 117 W 16 | Elmbridge av Surb |
| 95 S 10 | Elmbrook gdns SE9 |
| 153 V 8 | Elmbrook rd Sutton |
| 108 K 3 | Elmcourt rd SE27 |
| 34 H 14 | Elmcroft av E11 |
| 45 W 1 | Elmcroft av NW11 |
| 9 N 20 | Elmcroft av Enf |
| 116 L 17 | Elmcroft av Sidcp |
| 34 J 13 | Elmcroft clo E11 |
| 60 G 16 | Elmcroft clo W5 |
| 45 R 1 | Elmcroft cres NW11 |
| 22 J 11 | Elmcroft cres Harrow |
| 25 P 14 | Elmcroft gdns NW9 |
| 50 C 11 | Elmcroft st E5 |
| 17 R 17 | Elmdale rd N13 |
| 144 D 12 | Elmdale st W6 |
| 117 X 20 | Elmdene Surb |
| 124 K 13 | Elmdene clo Becknhm |
| 78 M 15 | Elmdene rd SE18 |
| 82 A 4 | Elmdon rd Hounsl |
| 7 P 11 | Elmer clo Enf |
| 25 S 2 | Elmer gdns Edg |
| 83 R 8 | Elmer gdns Islwth |
| 93 U 19 | Elmer rd SE6 |
| 124 H 8 | Elmer Side rd Becknhm |
| 102 B 16 | Elmers dri Tedd |
| 124 D 6 | Elmers End rd Becknhm |
| 123 Y 16 | Elmers rd SE25 |
| 30 A 16 | Elmfield av N8 |
| 120 O 1 | Elmfield av Mitch |
| 101 X 12 | Elmfield av Tedd |
| 126 F 5 | Elmfield pk Brom |
| 32 E 17 | Elmfield rd E17 |
| 20 J 7 | Elmfield rd E4 |
| 28 F 9 | Elmfield rd N2 |
| 27 F 9 | Elmfield rd N2 |
| 107 P 3 | Elmfield rd SW17 |
| 126 G 5 | Elmfield rd Brom |
| 70 C 8 | Elmfield rd S'hall |
| 157 U 19 | Elmfield way S Croy |
| 12 K 15 | Elmgate gdns Edg |
| 23 X 15 | Elmgrove cres Harrow |
| 23 Y 15 | Elmgrove gdns Harrow |
| 72 K 4 | Elmgrove rd W5 |
| 80 M 17 | Elmhurst Blvdr |
| 81 N 16 | Elmhurst Blvdr |
| 28 F 11 | Elmhurst av N2 |
| 107 R 19 | Elmhurst av Mitch |
| 34 F 6 | Elmhurst dri E18 |
| 52 H 20 | Elmhurst rd E7 |
| 31 T 7 | Elmhurst rd N17 |
| 113 P 6 | Elmhurst rd SW4 |
| 89 X 7 | Elmhurst st SW4 |
| 98 F 17 | Elmington clo Bxly |
| 150 G 20 | Elmington rd SE5 |
| 93 S 8 | Elmira st SE13 |
| 113 U 15 | Elmlee clo Chisl |
| 79 S 12 | Elmley st SE18 |
| 51 V 10 | Elmore rd E11 |
| 9 S 4 | Elmore rd Enf |
| 49 N 20 | Elmore st N1 |
| 27 O 17 | Elms av NW4 |
| 29 T 9 | Elms av N10 |
| 89 X 14 | Elms cres SW4 |
| 41 X 13 | Elms ct Wemb |
| 56 A 11 | Elms gdns Dgnhm |
| 41 X 13 | Elms gdns Wemb |
| 41 Z 9 | Elms la Harrow |
| 41 Z 12 | Elms la Wemb |
| 138 E 9 | Elms ms W2 |
| 41 Y 12 | Elms Pk av Wemb |
| 89 U 13 | Elms rd SW4 |
| 23 S 2 | Elms rd Harrow |
| 10 G 20 | Elms rd Harrow |
| 86 D 8 | Elms the SW13 |
| 7 Z 20 | Elmscott gdns N21 |
| 18 A 1 | Elmscott gdns N21 |
| 112 A 12 | Elmscroft ct Brom |
| 32 L 12 | Elmsdale rd E17 |
| 86 H 13 | Elmshaw rd SW15 |
| 28 F 12 | Elmshurst cres N2 |
| 28 F 12 | Elmshurst cres N2 |
| 228 F 12 | Elmshurst cres N2 |
| 9 R 1 | Elmshurst rd Enf |
| 159 S 14 | Elmside Croy |
| 43 O 9 | Elmside rd Wemb |
| 24 C 13 | Elmsleigh av Harrow |
| 101 R 4 | Elmsleigh rd Twick |
| 113 V 12 | Elmstead av Chisl |
| 43 N 7 | Elmstead av Wemb |
| 42 K 5 | Elmstead av Wemb |
| 14 K 8 | Elmstead clo N20 |
| 152 B 12 | Elmstead clo Epsom |
| 80 F 17 | Elmstead cres Bxly Hth |
| 152 F 5 | Elmstead gdns Worc Pk |
| 113 T 14 | Elmstead glade Chis |
| 113 U 10 | Elmstead la Chisl |
| 99 P 1 | Elmstead rd Erith |
| 54 J 7 | Elmstead rd Ilf |
| 87 W 1 | Elmstone rd SW6 |
| 82 K 4 | Elmsworth av Houns |
| 101 U 11 | Elmtree rd Tedd |
| 17 O 15 | Elmwood av N13 |
| 24 A 18 | Elmwood av Harrow |
| 23 Z 16 | Elmwood av Harrow |
| 155 R 4 | Elmwood clo Wallgt |
| 25 W 13 | Elmwood cres NW9 |
| 41 Z 11 | Elmwood ct Wemb |
| 97 Y 18 | Elmwood dri Bxly |
| 152 G 16 | Elmwood dri Epsom |
| 59 T 18 | Elmwood gdns W7 |
| 91 O 14 | Elmwood rd SE24 |
| 73 V 16 | Elmwood rd W4 |
| 122 J 17 | Elmwood rd Croy |
| 120 M 6 | Elmwood rd Mitch |
| 109 N 4 | Elmworth gro SE21 |
| 109 N 4 | Elmworth gro SE21 |
| 129 Y 18 | Elnathan ms W 9 |
| 32 L 7 | Elphinstone rd E17 |
| 48 J 11 | Elphinstone st N5 |
| 49 X 18 | Elrington rd E8 |
| 97 R 4 | Elsa rd Welling |
| 63 U 15 | Elsa st E1 |
| 50 D 18 | Elsdale st E9 |
| 31 U 6 | Elsden rd N17 |
| 53 V 16 | Elsenham rd E12 |
| 105 V 3 | Elsenham st SW18 |
| 52 A 11 | Elsham rd E11 |
| 51 Z 11 | Elsham rd E11 |
| 136 K 19 | Elsham rd W14 |
| 91 U 10 | Elsie rd SE22 |
| 17 Z 3 | Elsiedene rd N21 |
| 92 M 13 | Elsiemaud rd SE4 |
| 110 J 2 | Elsinore rd SE23 |
| 89 N 7 | Elsley rd SW11 |
| 88 M 7 | Elsley rd SW11 |
| 82 D 8 | Elsma ter Hounsl |
| 88 M 9 | Elspeth rd SW11 |
| 42 J 15 | Elspeth rd Wemb |
| 119 Y 12 | Elsrick av Mrdn |
| 124 H 17 | Elstan way Croy |
| 150 G 8 | Elsted st SE17 |
| 95 V 13 | Elstow clo SE9 |
| 68 L 2 | Elstow gdns Dgnhm |
| 68 L 3 | Elstow rd Dgnhm |
| 19 N 7 | Elstree gdns N9 |
| 80 M 10 | Elstree gdns Blvdr |
| 81 N 10 | Elstree gdns Blvdr |
| 112 A 17 | Elstree gdns Blvdr |
| 54 B 15 | Elstree gdns Ilf |

Y 19 Farnaby rd Brom
A 20 Farnaby rd Brom
B 1 Farnaby rd Brom
R 10 Farnan av E17
A 12 Farnan rd SW16
G 11 Farnborough av E17
H 17 Farnborough av S Croy
H 18 Farnborough cres S Croy
U 18 Farncombe st SE16
X 9 Farndale av N13
N 8 Farndale cres Grnfd
R 8 Farnell rd Islwth
R 2 Farnham clo N20
Y 14 Farnham pl SE1
M 20 Farnham rd Ilf
U 4 Farnham rd Welling
P 12 Farnham royal N1
Y 2 Farningham rd N17
L 2 Farnley rd E4
P 9 Farnley rd SE25
H 2 Faroe rd W14
S 5 Farorna wlk Enf
U 14 Farquhar rd SE19
Y 7 Farquhar rd SW19
L 19 Farquharson rd Croy
Z 6 Farr av Bark
B 7 Farr rd Enf
Z 20 Farrance rd Rom
Z 1 Farrance rd Rom
A 17 Farrance st E14
J 6 Farrant av N22
L 14 Farrant st W10
G 4 Farren rd SE23
Z 18 Farrence st E14
X 13 Farrer rd N8
J 14 Farrer rd Harrow
U 20 Farrier st NW1
U 18 Farringdon rd EC1
H 17 Farringdon rd EC1
W 5 Farringdon rd EC4
Y 12 Farthing fields E1
S 9 Farwell rd Sidcp
E 20 Farwig la Brom
O 2 Fashion st E1
N 8 Fashoda rd Brom
X 17 Fassett rd E8
J 8 Fassett rd Kingst
X 17 Fassett sq E8
V 17 Fauconberg rd W4
S 20 Fauna clo Rom
X 11 Faunce st SE17
Y 2 Favart rd SW6
O 6 Faversham av E4
B 19 Faversham av Enf
M 21 Faversham rd SE6
M 3 Faversham rd Becknhm
B 14 Faversham rd Mrdn
K 6 Fawcett rd Croy
A 14 Fawcett st SW10
V 11 Fawe Pk rd SW15
D 16 Fawe st E14
Z 16 Fawley rd NW6
A 16 Fawley rd NW6
Y 12 Fawley rd N17
X 6 Fawn rd E13
K 12 Fawnbrake av SE24
Y 1 Fawood av NW10
E 13 Faygate cres Bxly Hth
C 4 Faygate rd SW2
V 12 Fayland av SW16
R 4 Fearnley rd SE5
S 12 Fearon st SE10
L 17 Featherbed la Croy
N 20 Featherbed la Croy
K 10 Feathers pl SE10
B 4 Featherstone av SE23
X 20 Featherstone rd NW7
A 8 Featherstone rd S'hall
E 16 Featherstone st EC1
C 7 Featherstone ter S'hall
H 6 Featley rd SW9
E 5 Federal rd Grnfd
F 12 Federation rd SE2
Z 5 Felbridge av Stanm
A 5 Felbridge av Stanm
F 9 Felbridge clo SW16
C 19 Felbridge clo Sutton
L 5 Felbrigge rd Ilf
R 16 Felday rd SE13
U 2 Felden st SW6
C 3 Felden clo Pinn
J 11 Felgate ms W6
Y 5 Felhampton rd SE9
J 12 Felhurst cres Dgnhm
A 17 Felix av N8
Z 20 Felix rd W13

71 X 1 Felix rd W13
63 N 6 Felix st E2
62 K 8 Felixstowe rd NW10
31 U 10 Felixstowe rd N17
18 L 12 Felixstowe rd N9
80 E 9 Felixstowe rd SE2
156 M 5 Fell rd Croy
91 V 13 Fellbrigg rd SE22
135 Y 18 Fellbrigg st E1
102 B 8 Fellbrook Rich
154 J 4 Fellowes rd Carsh
46 N 19 Fellows rd NW3
77 T 12 Felltram way SE7
89 Z 11 Felmersham rd SW4
124 C 4 Felmingham rd SE20
56 G 10 Fels clo Dgnhm
56 L 10 Fels Farm av Dgnhm
90 B 17 Felsberg rd SW2
86 M 78 Felsham rd SW15
87 R 9 Felsham rd SW15
79 Y 14 Felspar clo SE18
35 V 6 Felstead av Ilf
34 G 20 Felstead rd E11
65 Z 18 Felstead rd E16
38 K 1 Felstead rd Rom
50 M 10 Felstead st E9
121 N 3 Feltham rd Mitch
127 Z 15 Felton clo Brom
67 W 5 Felton gdns Bark
114 K 11 Felton lea Sidcp
114 K 12 Felton lea Sidcp
72 C 5 Felton rd W13
67 V 5 Felton rd Bark
134 G 5 Felton st N1
142 K 7 Fen ct EC3
96 J 14 Fen gro Sidcp
65 P 19 Fen st E16
36 D 3 Fencepiece rd Ilf
142 J 7 Fenchurch av EC3
142 L 7 Fenchurch bldgs EC3
142 J 8 Fenchurch st EC3
142 M 8 Fenchurch St station EC3
150 L 2 Fendall st SE1
65 R 18 Fendt clo E16
80 H 9 Fendyke rd Blvdr
145 R 6 Fenelon pl W14
151 U 19 Fenham rd SE15
32 A 4 Fenman ct N17
112 E 15 Fenn clo Brom
50 D 15 Fenn st E9
78 K 1 Fennell st SE18
152 C 20 Fennells mead Epsom
151 W 1 Fenner rd SE16
15 T 18 Fenstanton av N12
148 L 15 Fentiman rd SW8
149 R 18 Fentiman rd SW8
30 M 1 Fenton rd N17
65 U 8 Fentons av E13
91 X 8 Fenwick gro SE15
89 Z 8 Fenwick rd SE15
91 X 8 Fenwick rd SE15
47 R 20 Ferdinand pl NW1
47 P 20 Ferdinand st NW1
48 J 16 Fergus rd N5
117 N 11 Ferguson av Surb
48 D 1 Ferme Pk rd N4
30 B 16 Ferme Pk rd N8
110 K 2 Fermor rd SE23
129 P 18 Fermoy rd W9
58 K 13 Fermoy rd Grnfd
121 Y 8 Fern av Mitch
60 B 14 Fern dene W13
70 D 15 Fern la Hounsl
64 B 12 Fern la Hounsl
41 V 14 Fernbank av Wemb
96 H 14 Fernbrook av Sidcp
40 J 2 Fernbrook dri Harrow
93 Y 15 Fernbrook rd SE13
94 A 15 Fernbrook rd SE13
49 W 14 Ferncliffe rd E8
45 Z 11 Ferncroft av NW3
15 Y 18 Ferncroft av N12
126 L 4 Ferndale Brom
33 W 15 Ferndale av E17
82 C 8 Ferndale av Hounsl
52 B 6 Ferndale rd E11
52 J 20 Ferndale rd E7
31 V 17 Ferndale rd N15
124 A 12 Ferndale rd SE25
89 Z 9 Ferndale rd SW4
90 D 9 Ferndale rd SW9
38 L 7 Ferndale rd Rom
66 L 19 Ferndale st E6
23 V 13 Ferndale ter Harrow
38 F 19 Ferndene way Rom
90 M 10 Ferndene rd SE24
91 N 8 Ferndene rd SE24
95 N 19 Ferndown rd SE9
16 B 4 Ferney rd Barnt
35 P 16 Fernhall dri Ilf

129 P 11 Fernhead rd W9
129 P 15 Fernhead yd W9
33 X 8 Fernhill ct E17
102 H 13 Fernhill gdns Kingst
78 G 3 Fernhill st E16
92 F 13 Fernholme rd SE15
12 B 18 Fernhurst gdns Edg
87 T 1 Fernhurst rd SW6
123 Z 19 Fernhurst rd Croy
107 T 2 Fernlea rd SW12
121 C 2 Fernlea rd Mitch
22 L 6 Fernleigh ct Harrow
42 J 6 Fernleigh ct Wemb
17 U 7 Fernleigh rd N21
52 B 18 Ferns rd E15
133 S 13 Fernsbury st WC1
146 B 16 Fernshaw SW10
45 Y 6 Fernside NW3
21 U 4 Fernside Buck HI
12 L 10 Fernside av NW7
89 N 19 Fernside av SW12
107 V 15 Fernthorpe rd SW16
49 O 14 Ferntower rd N5
107 Y 10 Fernwood av SW16
42 C 17 Fernwood av Wemb
15 Z 10 Fernwood cres N20
6 U 5 Ferny Hill Barnt
A6 A 10 Findhorn st E14
155 X 8 Ferrers av Wallgtn
107 Y 13 Ferrers rd SW16
30 C 14 Ferrestone rd N8
131 T 9 Ferrett pas NW1
88 B 11 Ferrier st SW18
41 N 4 Ferring clo Harrow
109 S 6 Ferrings rd SE21
158 L 6 Ferris av Croy
91 X 11 Ferris rd SE22
49 Z 10 Ferron rd E5
78 J 8 Ferry appr SE18
31 Y 12 Ferry la N17
74 E 17 Ferry la SW13
72 J 18 Ferry la Brentf
73 N 17 Ferry la Rich
74 F 20 Ferry rd SW13
86 G 1 Ferry rd SW13
118 A 16 Ferry rd Surb
102 A 12 Ferry rd Tedd
76 F 13 Ferry st E14
58 L 7 Ferrymead av Grnfd
58 H 8 Ferrymead dri Grnfd
59 O 6 Ferrymead gdns Grnfd
102 R 7 Ferrymore Rich
87 O 7 Festing rd SW15
115 V 3 Festival clo Bxly
154 M 9 Festival wlk Carsh
141 T 4 Fetter la EC4
37 V 12 Fews la Rom
76 A 18 Ffinch st SE8
20 C 19 Field clo E4
126 L 4 Field clo Brom
21 Y 11 Field clo Buck HI
141 R 1 Field ct WC1
101 W 10 Field end Tedd
40 C 14 Field End rd Ruis
72 D 19 Field la Brentf
101 Y 13 Field la Tedd
133 U 10 Field pl SE11
118 C 14 Field pl New Mald
33 N 14 Field rd E17
52 E 14 Field rd E7
31 P 10 Field rd N17
144 L 13 Field rd W6
133 N 11 Field st WC1
61 W 1 Field way NW10
159 S 15 Field way Croy
159 T 13 Field way Croy
107 W 20 Fieldend rd SW16
120 K 4 Fieldgate la Mitch
143 T 3 Fieldgate st E1
107 W 2 Fieldhouse rd SW12
101 N 8 Fielding av Twick
136 H 20 Fielding rd W14
74 A 7 Fielding rd W3
73 Z 8 Fielding rd W4
110 C 1 Fieldings the SE23
37 V 15 Fields Park cres Rom
153 S 11 Fieldsend rd Sutton
111 X 13 Fieldside rd Brom
106 F 2 Fieldview SW18
55 S 11 Fieldway Dgnhm
48 G 16 Fieldway cres N5
65 S 15 Fife rd E16
30 K 3 Fife rd N22
85 V 14 Fife rd SW14
116 H 3 Fife rd Kingst
133 O 7 Fife ter N1
53 T 12 Fifth av E12
128 K 15 Fifth av W10
8 H 17 Fifth av Enf
101 P 6 Fifth Cross rd Twick
107 O 18 Figges rd Mitch
49 W 5 Filey av N16
8 F 8 Fillebrook av Enf

52 A 1 Fillebrook rd E11
51 Y 3 Fillebrook rd E11
87 T 1 Filmer rd SW6
145 N 19 Filmer rd SW6
81 W 14 Filton rd Erith
145 X 12 Finborough rd SW10
106 M 16 Finborough rd SW17
9 N 11 Finch av SE27
43 X 17 Finch clo NW10
142 G 6 Finch la EC2
65 V 18 Finch rd E16
80 A 8 Finchale rd SE2
34 M 1 Finchingfield av Wdfd Grn
15 N 20 Finchley ct N12
27 O 12 Finchley la NW4
15 S 12 Finchley pk N12
130 E 8 Finchley pl NW8
27 W 15 Finchley rd NW11
45 X 4 Finchley rd NW11
46 D 18 Finchley rd NW3
130 F 3 Finchley rd NW8
27 Y 1 Finchley way N3
14 K 20 Finchley way N3
141 P 19 Finck st SE1
52 K 16 Finden rd E7
44 O 10 Findhorn av E14
40 K 10 Findon clo Harrow
18 L 5 Findon rd N9
74 G 4 Findon rd W12
92 G 8 Finland rd SE4
87 P 2 Finlay st SW6
37 N 1 Finnemore rd Ilf
37 N 1 Finnemore rd Ilf
135 X 15 Finnis st E2
63 N 11 Finnis st E2
55 Z 20 Finnymore rd Dgnhm
56 A 20 Finnymore rd Dgnhm
142 H 1 Finsbury av EC2
142 G 2 Finsbury cir EC2
134 J 19 Finsbury mkt EC2
134 F 20 Finsbury pav EC2
48 J 3 Finsbury pk N4
30 K 20 Finsbury Pk av N4
48 H 7 Finsbury Pk rd N4
30 B 4 Finsbury rd N22
134 G 20 Finsbury sq EC2
134 E 20 Finsbury sq EC2
90 M 9 Finsen rd SE5
136 F 4 Finstock rd W10
57 W 17 Finucane gdns Rainhm
10 B 7 Finucane rd Bushey Watford
118 E 13 Fir gro New Mald
119 U 20 Fir rd Sutton
159 O 7 Fir Tree gdns Croy
155 N 18 Fir Tree gro Carsh
82 C 11 Fir Tree rd Hounsl
56 K 10 Fir Tree wlk Dgnhm
8 C 11 Fir Tree wlk Enf
92 B 4 Firbank rd SE15
41 S 9 Fircroft gdns Harrow
106 M 6 Fircroft rd SW17
110 K 15 Firebell all Surb
155 Z 16 Firefly clo Wallgtn
121 T 3 Firework rd Mitch
111 N 9 Firhill rd SE6
29 P 12 Firs av N10
85 W 11 Firs av SW14
29 P 12 Firs clo N10
17 Y 3 Firs la N21
18 B 6 Firs Park av N21
18 A 6 Firs Park gdns N21
60 F 15 Firs the W5
21 S 15 Firs wlk Wdfd Grn
158 F 1 Firsby av Croy
49 V 3 Firsby rd N16
17 Y 10 Firscroft N13
53 R 13 First av E12
65 T 10 First av E13
33 P 14 First av E17
27 N 13 First av NW4
19 P 15 First av N18
86 A 7 First av SW14
146 M 4 First av SW3
129 N 16 First av W10
74 D 3 First av W3
69 V 5 First av Dgnhm
8 G 18 First av Enf
152 A 19 First av Epsom
37 V 14 First av Rom
80 G 19 First av Welling
42 H 6 First av Wemb
101 S 3 First Cross rd Twick
43 T 12 First way Wemb
118 L 4 Firstway SW20
152 E 12 Firswood av Epsom
152 E 12 Firswood av Epsom
87 S 3 Firth gdns SW6
121 N 2 Firtree av Mitch
152 E 10 Firtree clo Epsom
142 G 10 Fish St hill EC3

58 G 8 Fisher clo Grnfd
23 X 6 Fisher rd Harrow
65 R 14 Fisher st E16
140 M 2 Fisher st WC1
81 Y 3 Fisher's way Blvdr
73 Z 12 Fishers la W4
130 F 17 Fisherton st NW8
142 F 10 Fishmongers Hall st EC4
106 L 7 Fishponds rd SW17
106 K 8 Fishponds rd SW17
100 M 13 Fitz Dygram clo Hampt
144 M 6 Fitz James av W14
144 L 7 Fitz-George av W14
27 V 10 Fitzalan rd N 3
149 S 5 Fitzalan st SE11
103 Z 19 Fitzgeorge av Kingst
86 B 9 Fitzgerald av SW14
34 F 17 Fitzgerald rd E11
85 Y 7 Fitzgerald rd SW14
139 T 4 Fitzhardinge st W1
88 H 16 Fitzhugh gro SW18
157 Z 4 Fitzjames av Croy
4 H 14 Fitzjohn av Barnt
46 F 17 Fitzjohn's av NW3
139 X 12 Fitzmaurice pl W1
62 D 17 Fitzneal st W12
46 M 5 Fitzroy clo N6
132 B 18 Fitzroy ct W1
109 S 18 Fitzroy gdns SE19
132 A 19 Fitzroy ms W1
46 M 5 Fitzroy pk N6
47 N 3 Fitzroy pk N6
131 T 2 Fitzroy rd NW1
132 A 18 Fitzroy sq W1
132 B 19 Fitzroy st W1
55 T 15 Fitzstephen rd Dgnhm
47 V 3 Fitzwarren gdns N19
84 M 6 Fitzwilliam av Rich
85 N 6 Fitzwilliam av Rich
89 V 7 Fitzwilliam rd SW4
56 A 11 Five Elms rd Dgnhm
31 O 19 Fladbury rd N15
34 A 18 Fladgate rd E11
23 Z 18 Flambard rd Harrow
63 V 17 Flamborough st E14
78 C 14 Flamstead rd SE7
68 F 2 Flamstead rd Dgnhm
55 T 20 Flamstead rd Dgnhm
43 P 19 Flamsted av Wemb
74 E 8 Flanchford rd W12
66 G 7 Flanders rd E6
74 C 10 Flanders rd W4
50 E 17 Flanders way E9
143 R 9 Flank st E1
46 E 12 Flask walk NW3
119 Z 16 Flaxley rd Mrdn
140 E 6 Flaxman ct W1
90 L 5 Flaxman rd SE5
132 H 14 Flaxman ter WC1
79 R 19 Flaxton rd SE18
10 J 16 Flecker clo Stanm
116 D 19 Fleece rd Surb
32 L 6 Fleeming clo E17
32 M 7 Fleeming rd E17
141 X 5 Fleet la EC4
46 K 14 Fleet rd NW3
141 T 6 Fleet st EC4
44 H 15 Fleetwood rd NW10
117 W 5 Fleetwood rd New Mald
117 W 6 Fleetwood sq New Mald
49 S 7 Fleetwood st N16
156 F 11 Fleming ct Croy
106 L 18 Fleming mead Mitch
149 X 13 Fleming rd SE17
58 M 17 Fleming rd S'hall
50 K 3 Flempton rd E10
51 U 1 Fletcher la E10
73 W 7 Fletcher rd W4
143 T 8 Fletcher st E1
50 C 10 Fletching rd E5
29 Z 1 Fletton rd N 11
141 T 5 Fleur De Lis ct WC2
134 M 19 Fleur De Lis st E1
87 P 20 Fleur gates SW19
31 P 3 Flexmere gdns N17
31 R 4 Flexmere rd N17
111 Z 13 Flimwell clo Brom
150 G 8 Flint st SE17
150 K 9 Flinton st SE17
140 H 5 Flitcroft st WC2
143 S 19 Flockton st SE16
90 K 1 Flodden rd SE5
146 L 11 Flood st SW3
146 K 12 Flood wlk SW3
64 C 17 Flora clo E14
74 H 10 Flora gdns W6
37 S 19 Flora gdns Rom
81 P 14 Flora st Blvdr
140 L 7 Floral st WC2
7 Y 11 Florence av Enf
120 D 12 Florence av Mrdn
92 M 1 Florence cotts SE4
7 Y 10 Florence dri Enf
73 V 17 Florence gdns W4
65 R 7 Florence rd E13
26 L 12 Florence rd NW4
48 E 2 Florence rd N4
92 M 2 Florence rd SE14
80 G 10 Florence rd SE2
106 A 15 Florence rd SW19
73 X 7 Florence rd W4
60 V 20 Florence rd W5
72 J 1 Florence rd W5
124 G 4 Florence rd Becknhm
126 F 1 Florence rd Brom
103 N 19 Florence rd Kingst
157 N 20 Florence rd S Croy
70 A 9 Florence rd S'hall
65 P 12 Florence st E16
133 X 2 Florence st N1
92 M 1 Florence terr SE14
154 F 7 Florian av Sutton
87 U 10 Florian rd SW15
10 C 7 Florida clo Bushey (watf)
108 J 20 Florida rd Thntn Hth
122 J 1 Florida rd Thntn Hth
135 T 13 Florida st E2
24 C 4 Floriston clo Stanm
24 C 4 Floriston gdns Stanm
105 S 1 Florys ct SW19
86 M 6 Floss st SW15
143 O 2 Flower And Dean st E1
13 R 18 Flower la NW7
111 V 12 Flowerhouse clo SE6
111 V 11 Flowerhouse est SE6
107 O 4 Flowersmead SW17
77 Y 13 Floyd rd SE7
93 Z 10 Fludyer st SE13
140 B 1 Foley st W1
134 M 20 Folgate sq E1
134 L 20 Folgate st EC2
62 C 18 Foliot st W12
65 N 5 Folkestone rd E15
33 R 13 Folkestone rd E17
66 K 7 Folkestone rd E6
18 K 14 Folkestone rd N18
14 H 17 Folkington corner N12
64 F 18 Follett st E14
5 T 11 Folly house Barnt
32 J 3 Folly la E17
76 H 6 Folly wall E14
108 C 17 Fontaine rd SW16
89 P 9 Fontarabia rd SW8
39 P 9 Fontayne av Rom
149 W 8 Fontenoy pas SE11
107 U 4 Fontenoy rd SW4
34 M 6 Fonteyne gdns Ilf
48 E 6 Fonthill rd N4
86 F 20 Fontley way SW15
40 H 17 Fontwell clo Grnfd
23 T 1 Fontwell clo Harrow
127 V 12 Fontwell dri Brom
41 V 3 Football la Harrow
115 V 15 Footscray High st Sidcp
115 U 3 Footscray la Sidcp
115 U 9 Footscray place Sidcp
114 B 4 Footscray rd SE9
95 X 15 Footscray rd SE9
143 T 8 Forbes st E1
49 X 4 Forburg rd N16
41 P 1 Ford clo Harrow
63 W 5 Ford rd E3
69 R 1 Ford rd Dgnhm
56 C 20 Ford rd Dgnhm
69 P 1 Ford rd Dgnhm
68 N 16 Ford sq E1
143 Y 3 Ford sq E1
65 P 17 Ford st E16
63 W 5 Ford st E3
126 K 5 Forde av Brom
93 W 20 Fordel rd E6
5 V 12 Fordham clo Barnt
5 W 13 Fordham rd Barnt
143 V 3 Fordham st E1
73 O 1 Fordhook av W5
129 R 14 Fordingley rd W9
28 M 14 Fordington rd N6
111 O 3 Fordmill rd SE6
17 X 5 Fords gro N21
65 T 17 Fords Park rd E16
45 S 13 Fordwych rd NW2
93 U 14 Fordyce rd SE13
56 A 5 Fordyke rd Dgnhm
142 D 2 Fore st EC2
142 E 2 Fore st EC2
18 H 19 Fore st N18
90 K 5 Foreign st SE5
27 R 5 Foreland ct NW4
79 S 10 Foreland st SE18
144 D 7 Foreman ct W6
75 Y 12 Foreshore SE8
20 M 2 Forest appr E4
34 D 1 Forest appr Wdfd Grn
21 N 2 Forest av E4
34 D 16 Forest clo E11
21 U 12 Forest clo Wdfd Grn
34 A 13 Forest ct E11
21 P 6 Forest ct E4
53 O 10 Forest dri E12
33 Z 2 Forest dri Wdfd Grn
33 X 20 Forest Dri east E11
51 V 1 Forest Dri west E10
21 Z 12 Forest edge Buck Hl
26 A 14 Forest gate NW9
31 U 7 Forest gdns N17
33 Z 18 Forest glade E11
34 A 18 Forest glade E11
20 M 17 Forest glade E4
49 U 19 Forest gro E8
92 B 16 Forest Hill rd SE22
35 W 1 Forest house Wdfd Grn
52 D 15 Forest la E15
51 Z 16 Forest la E 15
33 X 2 Forest Mt rd Wdfd Grn
51 V 1 Forest rd E11
33 X 20 Forest rd E11
51 Z 16 Forest rd E15
32 C 13 Forest rd E17
33 O 10 Forest rd E17
52 F 11 Forest rd E7
49 T 19 Forest rd E8
19 N 5 Forest rd N9
99 W 2 Forest rd Erith
36 H 4 Forest rd Ilf
73 P 19 Forest rd Rich
38 H 11 Forest rd Rom
119 X 18 Forest rd Sutton
21 S 11 Forest rd Wdfd Grn
33 Y 12 Forest ri E17
33 X 14 Forest ri E17
125 O 5 Forest ridge Becknhm
21 O 3 Forest side E4
52 G 11 Forest side E7
21 X 5 Forest side Buck Hl
118 D 19 Forest side Worc Pk
52 F 15 Forest st E7
34 A 13 Forest the E11
52 C 1 Forest view E11
20 K 1 Forest view E4
33 X 16 Forest View av E10
53 P 12 Forest View rd E12
33 U 4 Forest View rd E17
26 E 20 Forest way Sidcp
21 W 13 Forest way Wdfd Grn
21 U 12 Forest way Wdfd Grn
16 K 13 Forestdale N14
92 A 9 Forester rd SE15
63 W 11 Forester st E3
155 X 16 Foresters clo Wallgtn
98 F 10 Foresters cres Bxly Hth
33 X 14 Foresters dri E17
155 Y 17 Foresters dri Wallgtn
156 A 20 Foresters dri Wallgtn
110 B 4 Forestholme clo SE23
30 H 4 Forfar rd N22
89 P 1 Forfar rd SW11
100 B 13 Forge la Felt
153 S 16 Forge la Sutton
24 D 10 Formby av Stanm
129 Z 18 Formosa st W9
27 X 19 Forres gdns NW11
122 C 7 Forrest gdns SW16
139 N 5 Forset st W1
111 W 7 Forster Memorial park SE6
31 U 9 Forster rd N17
89 Z 18 Forster rd SW2
124 H 6 Forster rd Bcknhm
122 L 15 Forster rd Croy
134 C 8 Forston st N1
149 X 14 Forsyte gdns SE17
8 D 18 Forsyth pl Enf
109 S 20 Forsythe cres SE19
123 S 1 Forsythe cres SE19
151 T 7 Fort rd SE1
58 H 2 Fort rd Grnfd
142 L 1 Fort st E1
134 L 20 Fort st E 1
77 V 3 Fort st E16
54 L 11 Forterie gdns Ilf
135 X 1 Fortescue av E8
63 N 1 Fortescue av E8
101 N 6 Fortescue av Twick
106 G 19 Fortescue rd SW
25 X 2 Fortescue rd Edg
47 U 12 Fortess rd NW5
47 T 14 Fortess wlk NW5
89 O 9 Forthbridge rd SV
28 K 12 Fortis green N 2
29 N 12 Fortis Green av N
29 P 11 Fortis Green rd N
29 P 11 Fortismere av N1
47 Z 7 Fortnam rd N19
62 B 2 Fortune Ga rd NW
45 Y 14 Fortune Green rd NW6
11 V 1 Fortune la Borehn
134 B 19 Fortune st EC1
65 R 15 Forty Acre la E16
43 O 8 Forty av Wemb
42 M 9 Forty av Wemb
43 N 8 Forty clo Wemb
85 V 8 Forty footpath SW
8 H 2 Forty hill Enf
43 T 8 Forty la Wemb
12 C 20 Forum way Edg
12 D 19 Forumside Edg
137 Z 10 Fosbury ms W2
26 J 19 Foscote rd NW4
87 V 5 Foskett rd SW6
156 F 12 Foss av Croy
77 W 14 Fossdene rd SE7
59 Z 14 Fosse way W13
93 P 9 Fossil rd SE13
80 J 10 Fossington rd Blv
55 U 5 Fossway Dgnhm
142 A 4 Foster la EC2
26 M 14 Foster pl NW4
65 S 11 Foster rd E13
32 H 18 Foster rd E17
62 A 19 Foster rd W3
73 Y 14 Foster rd W4
113 T 12 Fosters clo Chisl
8 F 13 Fotheringham rd E
140 B 7 Foubert's pl W1
49 U 11 Foulden rd N16
146 F 9 Foulis ter SW7
107 N 8 Foulser rd SW17
123 N 7 Foulsham rd Thntn Hth
148 H 19 Fount st SW8
141 S 8 Fountain ct WC2
109 V 11 Fountain dri SE19
106 H 10 Fountain rd SW17
120 L 4 Fountain rd Mitch
122 K 4 Fountain rd Thntn Hth
100 F 6 Fountains av Felt
100 F 5 Fountains clo Felt
17 N 1 Fountains cres N1
16 M 2 Fountains cres N1
31 X 14 Fountayne rd N15
49 W 7 Fountayne rd N16
82 G 16 Four Square ct Hounsl
10 C 2 Four tubs Bushey (watfd)
20 L 6 Four wents E4
9 V 7 Fouracres Enf
12 J 19 Fourland wlk Edg
143 O 1 Fournier st E1
53 S 12 Fourth av E12
128 L 15 Fourth av W10
8 H 17 Fourth av Enf
56 M 5 Fourth av Rom
101 P 4 Fourth Cross rd Twick
43 U 13 Fourth way Wemb
136 J 8 Fowell st W11
35 O 15 Fowey av Ilf
88 G 8 Fowler clo SW11
52 E 12 Fowler rd E7
133 Y 2 Fowler rd N1
121 P 2 Fowler rd Mitch
91 R 4 Fowler st SE5
60 G 11 Fowlers wlk W5
88 K 7 Fownes st SW11
133 Y 20 Fox And Knot st EC
63 R 11 Fox clo E1
65 S 16 Fox clo E16
141 S 1 Fox ct EC1
109 V 19 Fox hill SE19
109 U 19 Fox Hill gdns SE19
81 V 12 Fox Ho rd Blvdr
17 O 8 Fox la N13
60 J 12 Fox lane W5
65 O 16 Fox st E16
120 H 4 Fox's path Mitch
92 K 8 Foxberry rd SE4
93 N 14 Foxborough gdns SE4
107 R 4 Foxbourne rd SW1
114 F 16 Foxbury av Chisl
114 F 16 Foxbury av Sidcp
112 G 16 Foxbury clo Brom
112 G 16 Foxbury rd Brom

9 T 14 Foxcombe Croy
6 G 20 Foxcombe rd SW15
5 Z 2 Foxcroft rd SE18
6 A 2 Foxcroft rd SE18
8 C 20 Foxearth rd S Croy
8 C 19 Foxearth spur S Croy
4 D 8 Foxes dale SE3
5 X 6 Foxes dale Brom
1 S 18 Foxgrove av Becknhm
1 U 19 Foxgrove rd Becknhm
7 X 9 Foxham rd N19
5 P 12 Foxhole rd SE9
1 V 1 Foxholt gdns NW10
6 K 14 Foxlands cres Dgnhm
6 K 16 Foxlands rd Dgnhm
8 V 18 Foxley rd SW9
2 H 8 Foxley rd Thntn Hth
8 L 3 Foxmore st SW11
2 H 7 Foxwell st SE4
4 B 10 Foxwood rd SE3
1 Y 4 Foyle rd N17
7 O 17 Foyle rd SE3
K 12 Framfield clo N12
8 J 14 Framfield rd N5
9 V 17 Framfield rd W7
7 O 19 Framfield rd Mitch
3 S 9 Framlington cres SE9
6 C 20 Frampton Pk rd E9
2 B 12 Frampton rd Hounsl
H 17 Frampton st NW8
3 O 13 Francemary rd SE4
0 C 18 Frances rd E4
2 J 16 Frances rd Croy
8 G 12 Frances st SE18
6 D 7 Franche Ct rd SW17
8 F 4 Francis av Bxly Hth
Y 15 Francis av Harrow
4 E 6 Francis av Ilf
0 D 0 Francis Chichester way SW11
5 U 16 Francis gro SW19
1 T 4 Francis rd E10
8 M 12 Francis rd N2
0 C 4 Francis rd Grnfd
3 Z 15 Francis rd Harrow
2 A 6 Francis rd Hounsl
4 E 6 Francis rd Ilf
5 V 14 Francis rd Wallgtn
6 Y 16 Francis st E15
8 B 4 Francis st SW1
4 D 6 Francis st Ilf
1 T 7 Francis Taylor bldng EC4
7 V 9 Francis ter N19
6 M 12 Franciscan rd SW17
7 O 10 Franciscan rd SW17
2 C 10 Francklin gdns Edg
2 C 10 Francklyn gdns Edg
9 W 14 Franconia rd SW4
1 S 20 Frank Dixon clo SE21
1 T 20 Frank Dixon way SE21
9 T 1 Frank Dixon way SE21
5 T 12 Frank st E13
0 M 13 Frankfurt rd SE24
1 N 13 Frankfurt rd SE24
6 B 19 Frankham st SE8
1 Y 17 Frankland rd Wdfd Grn
0 A 15 Frankland rd E4
5 R 2 Franklin clo N20
5 R 2 Franklin clo N20
1 V 8 Franklin cres Mitch
5 R 8 Franklin pass SE9
0 D 20 Franklin rd SE20
7 Z 2 Franklin rd Bxly Hth
P 5 Franklin rd Kingst
4 E 9 Franklin rd E3
R 19 Franklin rd N15
7 R 10 Franklins row SW3
4 D 19 Franklyn rd NW10
7 W 9 Franks av New Mald
7 Z 13 Frankswood av Brom
1 X 1 Frankton rd SE15
7 Z 14 Franlaw cres N13
7 V 4 Franmil rd Hornch
0 A 7 Fransfield gro SE26
2 H 11 Frant rd Thntn Hth
3 T 17 Fraser rd E17
8 L 11 Fraser rd N9
0 D 4 Fraser rd Grnfd
74 A 14 Fraser st W4
2 Fraser rd Erith
41 T 19 Frazier st SE1
51 S 1 Frean st SE16
39 S 18 Frederic ms SW1
32 H 17 Frederic st E17
20 K 2 Frederica rd E4

48 B 20 Frederica st N7
139 N 7 Frederick clo W2
153 V 10 Frederick clo Sutton
149 W 20 Frederick cres SW9
Frederick cres Enf
163 U 10 Frederick gdns Sutton
78 M 13 Frederick pl SE18
79 N 13 Frederick pl SE18
149 Y 12 Frederick rd SE17
153 V 10 Frederick rd Sutton
51 W 20 Frederick st E15
133 O 13 Frederick st WC1
134 M 2 Frederick rd E8
142 D 6 Frederick's pl EC2
15 R 14 Fredericks pl N12
57 V 18 Freeborne gdns Rainham
88 M 5 Freedom st SW11
48 B 15 Freegrove rd N7
27 R 7 Freeland pk NW4
60 M 20 Freeland rd W5
158 F 18 Freelands av S Croy
112 J 20 Freelands gro Brom
112 J 20 Freelands rd Brom
26 J 1 Freelands rd Brom
133 N 2 Freeling st N1
9 T 16 Freemantle av Enf
81 T 11 Freemantle av Blvdr
36 B 8 Freemantle rd Ilf
150 K 8 Freemantle st SE17
150 K 8 Freemantle st SE17
65 U 15 Freemasons rd E16
123 R 18 Freemasons rd Croy
135 Z 4 Freemont st E9
89 P 9 Freke rd SW11
63 O 3 Fremont st E9
92 G 10 Frendsbury rd SE4
104 F 5 Frensham dri SW15
159 U 17 Frensham dri Croy
114 E 5 Frensham rd SE9
151 T 15 Fremantle rd Sutton
88 K 5 Frere st SW11
67 N 5 Fresh Wharf rd Bark
106 D 6 Freshford st SW18
107 P 14 Freshwater clo SW17
138 M 2 Freshwater pl W1
55 W 3 Freshwater rd Dgnhm
37 S 14 Freshwell av Rom
6 A 18 Freston gdns Barnt
27 V 7 Freston pk N3
98 A 12 Freston rd Bxly Hth
106 G 1 Frewin rd SW18
141 X 7 Friar st EC4
15 X 12 Friars av N20
61 Y 18 Friars gdns W3
84 F 13 Friars la Rich
61 Z 19 Friars Place la W3
62 A 20 Friars Place la W3
66 B 4 Friars rd E6
84 K 16 Friars Stile rd Rich
16 D 4 Friars walk N14
61 Y 19 Friars way W3
16 D 2 Friars wlk N14
6 H 19 Friars wlk N14
80 K 14 Friars wlk SE2
23 U 3 Friars wlk Harrow
158 H 19 Friarswood Croy
15 X 15 Friary clo N12
140 C 15 Friary clo N12
21 S 14 Friary la Wdfd Grn
15 W 14 Friary park N12
15 W 13 Friary rd N12
151 U 18 Friary rd SE15
61 X 17 Friary rd W3
15 V 14 Friary way N12
20 L 8 Friday Hill E4
20 M 11 Friday Hill east E4
20 L 10 Friday Hill east E4
20 L 9 Friday Hill west E4
81 Z 13 Friday rd Erith
106 L 19 Friday rd Mitch
142 A 7 Friday st EC4
47 U 16 Frideswide pl NW5
133 W 12 Friend st EC1
93 N 4 Friendly st SE4
93 N 4 Friendly St ms SE4
157 O 6 Friends rd Croy
15 S 9 Friern Barnet la N20
16 C 17 Friern Barnet rd N11
15 R 3 Friern Mount dri N20
15 S 16 Friern pk N12
91 W 18 Friern rd SE22
15 S 14 Friern Watch av N12
156 B 11 Frimley av Wallgtn
159 V 16 Frimley clo Croy
159 V 17 Frimley cres Croy
115 T 13 Frimley ct Sidcp
120 J 6 Frimley gdns Mitch
54 H 10 Frimley rd Ilf
63 T 12 Frimley way E1

33 X 2 Frinton dri Wdfd Grn
35 W 18 Frinton mews Ilf
66 B 9 Frinton rd E6
31 T 19 Frinton rd N15
107 P 16 Frinton rd SW17
38 D 1 Frinton rd Rom
115 Z 4 Frinton rd Sidcp
87 Z 6 Friston st SW6
88 A 6 Friston st SW6
27 T 2 Frith ct NW7
14 F 19 Frith la NW7
27 T 1 Frith la NW7
51 W 11 Frith rd E11
156 L 3 Frith rd Croy
140 F 7 Frith st W1
118 A 14 Fritham clo New Mald
136 B 13 Frithville gdns W12
74 L 3 Frithville gdns W12
56 G 9 Frizlands la Dgnhm
30 G 13 Frobisher rd N8
91 V 11 Frogley rd SE22
87 V 12 Frogmore SW18
153 R 7 Frogmore clo Sutton
70 F 12 Frogmore ct S'hall
153 R 7 Frogmore gdns Sutton
46 C 12 Frognal NW3
23 V 14 Frognal av Harrow
115 O 20 Frognal av Orp
46 C 14 Frognal clo NW3
46 D 17 Frognal ct NW3
46 C 12 Frognal gdns NW3
46 B 14 Frognal la NW3
115 O 15 Frognal pl Sidcp
46 C 11 Frognal ri NW3
46 C 13 Frognal way NW3
95 P 13 Froissart rd SE9
30 H 10 Frome rd N15
133 Z 7 Frome st N1
134 A 7 Frome st N1
150 C 11 Fromondes rd Sutton
89 T 5 Froude st SW8
66 A 2 Fry rd E6
31 O 3 Fryatt rd N17
64 M 18 Fryatt st E14
133 U 8 Frye's bldgs N1
25 P 18 Fryent clo NW9
26 A 19 Fryent cres NW9
26 A 19 Fryent gro NW9
25 P 17 Fryent way NW9
43 S 2 Fryent way NW9
142 M 2 Frying Pan all E1
157 T 3 Fryston rd Bxly Hth
80 C 13 Fuchsia st SE2
22 M 8 Fulbeck way Harrow
33 T 4 Fulbourne rd E17
47 V 11 Fulbrook ms N19
47 V 11 Fulbrook rd N19
75 N 6 Fulford st SE16
87 V 18 Fulford st SE16
145 T 18 Fulham bdy SW6
87 T 5 Fulham High st SW6
87 P 5 Fulham palace SW6
144 H 18 Fulham Palace rd SW 6
87 R 3 Fulham Palace rd SW 6
144 E 11 Fulham Palace rd W6
110 U 5 Fulham Pk gdns SW13
87 U 4 Fulham Pk rd SW6
146 G 9 Fulham rd SW3
145 T 19 Fulham rd SW6
87 U 3 Fulham rd SW6
118 D 19 Fullbrooks av Worc Pk
135 R 15 Fuller st E2
26 L 12 Fuller st NW4
34 C 3 Fullers av Wdfd Grn
38 J 3 Fullers clo Rom
38 J 2 Fullers la Rom
34 B 3 Fullers rd E18
123 U 17 Fullerton rd SE25
88 C 13 Fullerton rd SW18
154 H 18 Fullerton rd Carsh
100 K 8 Fullwell park Twick
88 B 2 Fulmead st SW6
72 A 9 Fulmer way W13
33 W 16 Fulready rd E10
82 B 10 Fulstone clo Hounsl
94 E 5 Fulthorpe rd SE3
138 A 9 Fulton ms W2
43 R 11 Fulton rd Wemb
36 B 6 Fulwell av Ilf
35 W 4 Fulwell av Ilf
100 L 4 Fulwell Pk av Twick
101 N 4 Fulwell Pk av Twick
101 P 10 Fulwell rd Tedd
60 L 5 Fulwood av Wemb
83 X 16 Fulwood gdns Twick
141 R 2 Fulwood pl WC1
22 G 1 Furham feild Pinn

151 T 18 Furley pl SE15
151 T 20 Furley rd SE15
48 F 18 Furlong rd N7
88 A 18 Furmage st SW18
108 K 12 Furneaux av SE27
62 G 7 Furness rd NW10
88 B 4 Furness rd SW6
40 L 3 Furness rd Harrow
120 B 15 Furness rd Mrdn
57 V 15 Furness way Hornch
141 T 3 Furnival st EC4
50 D 15 Furrow la E9
14 L 19 Fursby av N3
94 A 20 Further Green rd SE6
112 A 1 Further Green rd SE6
122 M 5 Furze rd Thntn Hth
64 B 14 Furze st E3
107 S 12 Furzedown dri SW17
107 T 11 Furzedown rd SW17
113 Z 14 Furzefield clo Chisl
77 V 18 Furzefield rd SE3
33 W 9 Fyfield rd E17
90 G 7 Fyfield rd SW9
8 D 12 Fyfield rd Enf
34 L 1 Fyfield rd Wdfd Grn
148 F 5 Fynes st SW1

# G

99 W 13 Gable clo Dartford
92 G 18 Gabriel st SE23
43 O 18 Gaddesden av Wemb
65 N 13 Gage rd E16
132 M 20 Gage st WC1
133 R 4 Gainford st N1
41 T 17 Gainsboro gdns Grnfd
55 P 11 Gainsborough Dgnm
53 W 14 Gainsborough av E12
45 U 1 Gainsborough gdns NW11
46 G 11 Gainsborough gdns NW3
25 O 7 Gainsborough gdns Edgw
83 P 13 Gainsborough gdns Islwth
52 A 1 Gainsborough rd E11
65 N 10 Gainsborough rd E15
64 M 10 Gainsborough rd E15
15 O 16 Gainsborough rd N12
74 C 10 Gainsborough rd W4
117 Y 15 Gainsborough rd New Mald
85 N 6 Gainsborough rd Rich
50 L 18 Gainsborough sq E9
32 K 13 Gainsford rd E17
143 O 17 Gainsford st SE1
122 K 13 Galahgreen Thntn Hth
91 S 4 Gairloch rd SE5
47 U 17 Gairstand st NW5
114 B 2 Gaitskell rd SE9
112 G 8 Galahad rd Brom
74 F 20 Galata rd SW13
91 Z 7 Galatea rd SE15
76 F 7 Galbraith st E14
64 B 14 Gale st E3
55 V 20 Gale st Dgnhm
68 H 4 Gale st Dgnhm
33 X 2 Galeborough av Wdfd Grn
140 K 2 Galen pl WC1
74 K 11 Galena rd W6
63 N 10 Gales gdns E2
35 S 1 Gales way Wdfd Grn
88 D 17 Galesbury rd SW18
15 Y 0 Gallants Farm rd Barnt
58 A 7 Gallery gdns Grnfd
91 R 20 Gallery rd SE21
109 P 2 Gallery rd SE21
151 W 7 Galley Wall rd SE16
75 N 12 Galley Wall rd SE16
48 J 16 Gallia rd N5
9 N 20 Galliard av Enf
9 P 20 Galliard clo Enf
9 P 20 Galliard clo Enf
18 K 4 Galliard rd N9
19 O 1 Galliard rd N9
158 B 16 Gallop S Croy
154 F 19 Gallop Sutton
79 U 12 Gallosson rd SE18
74 G 2 Galloway rd W12
7 R 20 Gallus clo N21
94 G 8 Gallus sq SE3
122 B 10 Galpin's rd Thntn Hth
132 K 17 Galsen rd WC1

| | | | |
|---|---|---|---|
| 37 P 20 Galsworthy av Rom | 58 L 12 Garrick rd Grnfd | 48 D 15 Geary st N7 | 43 Z 19 Gibbons rd NW10 |
| 45 T 12 Galsworthy rd NW2 | 85 R 6 Garrick rd Rich | 30 M 4 Gedeney rd N17 | 19 P 14 Gibbs av N18 |
| 103 S 19 Galsworthy rd Kingst | 140 J 9 Garrick st WC2 | 31 N 3 Gedeney rd N17 | 109 O 13 Gibbs clo SE19 |
| 63 X 17 Galt st E14 | 27 O 12 Garrick way NW4 | 133 Z 16 Gee st EC1 | 109 P 13 Gibbs clo SE19 |
| 128 K 15 Galton st W10 | 140 J 9 Garrick yd WC1 | 134 A 16 Gee st EC1 | 12 K 14 Gibbs grn Edg |
| 87 W 13 Galveston rd SW15 | 4 H 19 Garrows field Barnt | 65 P 3 Geere rd E15 | 109 O 13 Gibbs sq SE19 |
| 134 C 14 Galway st EC1 | 39 R 3 Garry clo Rom | 139 V 6 Gees st W1 | 145 P 14 Gibraltar wlk E2 |
| 89 T 5 Gambetta st SW8 | 39 O 2 Garry way Rom | 113 S 6 Gefferys homes SE9 | 63 R 11 Gibson clo E8 |
| 141 X 15 Gambia st SE1 | 100 K 16 Garside clo Hampt | 134 M 9 Geffrye museum E2 | 49 U 7 Gibson gdns N16 |
| 106 H 11 Gambole rd SW17 | 25 N 18 Garth SE9 | 134 M 9 Geffrye st E2 | 133 V 4 Gibson sq N1 |
| 5 Z 12 Games rd Barnet | 100 L 14 Garth Hampt | 151 W 19 Geldart st SE15 | 76 L 14 Gibson st SE10 |
| 87 O 9 Gamlen rd SW15 | 102 L 12 Garth clo Kingst | 49 Y 7 Geldestone rd E5 | 108 H 15 Gibson's hill SW1 |
| 153 W 13 Gander Grn la Sutton | 119 O 17 Garth clo Mrdn | 92 P 5 Gellatly rd SE14 | 39 V 9 Gidea clo Rom |
| 156 B 16 Gant clo Croy | 45 U 8 Garth rd NW2 | 38 G 2 Gelsthorpe rd Rom | 39 V 8 Gidea park Rom |
| 140 B 7 Ganton st W1 | 73 X 15 Garth rd W4 | 18 L 10 General Gordon pl | 81 U 10 Gideon clo Blvdr |
| 35 V 15 Gantshill cres Ilford | 102 L 13 Garth rd Kingstn | SE18 | 89 O 7 Gideon rd SW11 |
| 105 Z 11 Gap rd SW19 | 119 O 18 Garth rd Mrdn | 93 X 1 General Wolfe rd | 39 V 10 Gidea av Rom |
| 106 A 11 Gap rd SW19 | 25 N 18 Garth the Harrow | SE10 | 47 W 6 Giesbach rd N19 |
| 139 U 1 Garbutt pl W1 | 15 V 20 Garth way N12 | 78 M 17 Genesta rd SE18 | 18 D 18 Giffard rd N18 |
| 133 Y 12 Gard st EC1 | 92 F 18 Garthorne rd SE23 | 79 N 17 Genesta rd SE18 | 76 B 19 Giffin st SE8 |
| 98 D 6 Garden av Bxlyhth | 105 V 2 Gartmoor gdns | 37 Y 16 Genesta gdns Rom | 59 S 14 Gifford gdns W7 |
| 107 R 19 Garden av Mitch | SW19 | 90 G 10 Geneva rd SW9 | 132 L 2 Gifford st N1 |
| 12 C 19 Garden city Edg | 54 L 5 Gartmore rd Ilf | 116 K 8 Geneva rd Kingst | 133 N 1 Gifford st N1 |
| 12 C 19 Garden city Edg | 88 B 16 Garton pl SW18 | 122 L 10 Geneva rd Thntn Hth | 65 N 3 Gift la E15 |
| 19 Z 16 Garden cl E4 | 144 K 14 Garvan rd W6 | 90 H 11 Geneva ter SW9 | 25 W 4 Gilbert gro Edg |
| 90 D 7 Garden clo SW9 | 65 W 17 Garvary rd E16 | 20 C 15 Genever clo E4 | 140 J 2 Gilbert pl WC1 |
| 58 B 3 Garden clo Grnfd | 137 W 7 Garway rd W2 | 19 N 18 Genista rd N18 | 149 V 6 Gilbert rd SE11 |
| 100 F 13 Garden clo Hampt | 34 A 2 Gascoigne gdns | 86 M 13 Genoa av SW15 | 106 C 17 Gilbert rd SW19 |
| 156 A 11 Garden clo Wallgtn | Wdfd Grn | 87 N 14 Genoa st SW15 | 81 R 9 Gilbert rd Belvdr |
| 115 U 14 Garden cotts Sidcp | 135 N 12 Gascoigne pl E2 | 124 B 1 Genoa rd SE20 | 112 E 18 Gilbert rd Brom |
| 108 B 1 Garden la SW2 | 67 R 6 Gascoigne rd Bark | 8 C 13 Genotin rd Enf | 39 T 13 Gilbert rd Rom |
| 112 J 15 Garden la Brom | 159 W 20 Gascoigne rd Croy | 7 Z 12 Gentlemans row Enf | 51 Y 13 Gilbert st E15 |
| 137 U 10 Garden ms W2 | 119 T 1 Gascony av NW6 | 65 T 10 Gentry gdns E13 | 139 V 7 Gilbert st W1 |
| 130 E 11 Garden rd NW8 | 50 G 19 Gascoyne rd E9 | 92 K 7 Geoffrey rd SE4 | 106 J 11 Gilbey rd SW17 |
| 124 C 1 Garden rd SE20 | 76 H 1 Gaselee st E14 | 150 H 19 Geogian clo Brom | 79 X 17 Gilbourne rd SE18 |
| 112 J 17 Garden rd Brom | 149 R 12 Gasholder pl SE11 | 146 G 3 Geological museum | 9 V 16 Gilda av Enf |
| 85 P 9 Garden rd Rich | 89 T 17 Gaskarth rd SW12 | SW7 | 49 Y 5 Gilda cres N16 |
| 149 W 1 Garden row SE1 | 25 V 6 Gaskarth rd Edg | 29 O 3 George cres N10 | 139 Z 2 Gildea st W1 |
| 139 W 2 Garden row SE1 | 28 M 18 Gaskell rd N6 | 140 L 11 George ct WC2 | 47 O 15 Gilden rd NW5 |
| 63 T 15 Garden st E1 | 89 Z 5 Gaskell st SW4 | 142 F 15 George Inn yd SE1 | 78 K 16 Gildersome st SE1 |
| 148 E 8 Garden ter SW1 | 133 X 4 Gaskin st N1 | 34 G 8 George la E18 | 109 T 10 Giles coppice SE19 |
| 43 X 17 Garden way NW10 | 106 M 10 Gassiot rd SW17 | 93 S 16 George la SE13 | 91 R 15 Gilkes cres SE21 |
| 134 J 15 Garden wlk EC2 | 107 N 11 Gassiot rd SW17 | 126 H 19 George la Brom | 91 R 16 Gilkes pl SE21 |
| 142 A 9 Gardeners la EC4 | 154 G 5 Gassiot way Sutton | 20 B 19 George rd E4 | 65 S 19 Gill av E16 |
| 63 U 7 Gardeners rd E3 | 144 H 13 Gastein rd W6 | 72 J 15 George rd Brentf | 63 Z 19 Gill st E14 |
| 18 E 1 Gardenia rd Enf | 121 O 5 Gaston rd Mitch | 103 V 18 George rd Kingst | 15 Y 5 Gillam clo Barnt |
| 91 X 10 Gardens SE22 | 151 X 2 Gataker st SE16 | 118 E 10 George rd New Mald | 57 X 18 Gillam way Rainhm |
| 125 V 2 Gardens Becknhm | 47 Y 10 Gatcombe rd N19 | 143 S 19 George row SE16 | 10 A 7 Gillan grn Bushey |
| 22 M 18 Gardens Harrow | 138 L 19 Gate ms SW7 | 65 O 18 George st E16 | Watf |
| 22 E 18 Gardens Pinn | 18 K 14 Gate rd N18 | 139 T 3 George st W1 | 48 G 10 Gillespie rd N5 |
| 44 M 14 Gardiner av NW2 | 141 N 3 Gate st WC2 | 71 U 3 George st W7 | 66 D 6 Gillett av E6 |
| 34 H 18 Gardner clo E11 | 130 J 17 Gateforth st NW8 | 80 B 20 George st Bark | 123 N 9 Gillett rd Thntn Hth |
| 100 F 4 Gardner gro Felt | 103 W 19 Gatehouse clo Kingst | 156 M 4 George st Croy | 49 S 16 Gillette rd N16 |
| 65 U 12 Gardner rd E13 | 90 D 8 Gateley rd SW9 | 157 O 3 George st Croy | 143 V 19 Gillian Pk rd Sutton |
| 142 B 9 Gardners la EC4 | 134 J 16 Gatesborough st EC2 | 82 E 4 George st Hounsl | 93 P 12 Gillian st SE13 |
| 46 F 12 Gardnor rd NW3 | 106 L 7 Gateside rd SW17 | 84 H 12 George st Rich | 47 R 15 Gillies st NW5 |
| 119 Z 16 Garendon gdns Mrdn | 109 S 16 Gatestone rd SE19 | 37 T 17 George st Rom | 147 Z 5 Gillingham ms SW1 |
| 119 Z 16 Garendon rd Mrdn | 150 C 13 Gateway SE17 | 70 B 11 George st S'hall | 45 S 10 Gillingham rd NW2 |
| 120 A 18 Garendon rd Mrdn | 100 G 5 Gatfield gro Felt | 154 A 10 George st Sutton | 148 A 5 Gillingham row SW1 |
| 112 F 9 Gareth gro Brom | 30 F 6 Gathorne rd N22 | 22 F 10 George V av Pinn | 147 Z 6 Gillingham st SW1 |
| 65 P 13 Garfield rd E13 | 147 W 11 Gatliff rd SW1 | 22 G 11 George V clo Pinn | 147 Z 5 Gillingham st SW1 |
| 20 L 4 Garfield rd E4 | 79 Z 13 Gatling rd SE2 | 60 B 3 George V way Gnfd | 148 A 5 Gillingham st SW7 |
| 16 F 17 Garfield rd N11 | 80 A 14 Gatling rd SE2 | 139 V 8 George yd W1 | 65 O 3 Gillman dri E15 |
| 89 P 8 Garfield rd SW11 | 91 U 1 Gatonby st SE15 | 48 E 15 George's rd N7 | 146 G 17 Gillray av SW10 |
| 106 D 14 Garfield rd SW19 | 154 C 19 Gatton clo Sutton | 134 K 12 George's sq N1 | 93 W 10 Gilmore rd SE13 |
| 9 R 16 Garfield rd Enf | 106 K 9 Gatton rd SW17 | 76 H 20 Georgette pl SE10 | 85 Z 10 Gilpin av SW14 |
| 83 Z 20 Garfield rd Twick | 17 V 1 Gatward clo N21 | 35 Z 12 Georgeville gdns Ilf | 18 H 17 Gilpin cres N18 |
| 64 A 20 Garford st E14 | 87 V 19 Gatwick rd SW18 | 122 J 2 Georgia rd Thntn Hth | 82 K 17 Gilpin cres Twick |
| 79 U 11 Garibaldi st SE18 | 89 X 6 Gauden clo SW4 | 10 K 20 Georgian clo Stanm | 50 H 12 Gilpin rd E5 |
| 79 T 19 Garland rd SE18 | 89 X 7 Gauden rd SW4 | 43 R 17 Georgian ct Wemb | 57 T 19 Gilroy clo Rainham |
| 24 J 4 Garland rd Stanm | 41 Z 14 Gauntlet ct Wemb | 132 B 3 Georgiana st NW1 | 123 O 9 Gilsland rd Thntn Ht |
| 142 C 9 Garlick hill EC4 | 42 A 14 Gauntlett ct Wemb | 135 O 12 Georgina gdns E2 | 88 B 4 Gilstead rd SW6 |
| 110 J 6 Garlie's rd SE23 | 154 G 12 Gauntlett st Sutton | 112 G 9 Geraint rd Brom | 146 C 12 Gilston rd SW10 |
| 45 U 18 Garlinge rd NW2 | 92 C 4 Gautrey rd SE15 | 147 V 6 Gerald ms SW1 | 111 Z 6 Gilton rd SE6 |
| 32 B 2 German rd N17 | 76 A 9 Gaverick st E14 | 65 O 12 Gerald rd E16 | 141 X 3 Giltspur st EC1 |
| 133 T 13 Garnault ms EC1 | 94 H 19 Gavestone cres SE12 | 147 U 6 Gerald rd SW1 | 109 S 15 Gipsy hill SE19 |
| 133 U 14 Garnault pl EC1 | 94 G 18 Gavestone rd SE12 | 88 C 14 Gerald rd Dgnhm | 86 H 9 Gipsy la SW15 |
| 8 H 4 Garnault rd Enf | 79 U 11 Gavin st SE18 | 73 P 16 Geraldine rd W4 | 108 M 10 Gipsy rd SE27 |
| 33 T 4 Garner rd E17 | 63 P 8 Gawber st E2 | 149 V 3 Geraldine st SE1 | 109 O 11 Gipsy rd SE27 |
| 135 U 9 Garner st E2 | 64 A 6 Gawthorne st E3 | 82 G 19 Gerard av Hounsl | 80 H 20 Gipsy rd Welling |
| 44 B 18 Garnet rd NW10 | 44 K 14 Gay clo NW2 | 86 D 2 Gerard rd SW13 | 97 W 3 Gipsy rd Welling |
| 123 N 9 Garnet rd Thntn Hth | 56 J 13 Gay gdns Dgnhm | 23 Z 18 Gerard rd Harrow | 108 M 11 Gipsy Rd gdns SE27 |
| 63 O 20 Garnet st E1 | 64 H 6 Gay rd E15 | 114 A 4 Gerda rd SE9 | 120 H 4 Girdlers rd W14 |
| 75 O 1 Garnet st E1 | 35 T 9 Gayfere rd Ilf | | 47 U 7 Girdlestone rd N19 |
| 143 Z 10 Garnet st E1 | 148 J 2 Gayfere st SW1 | 6 H 15 Gerrads clo N14 | 87 T 18 Girdwood rd SW18 |
| 46 L 14 Garnett rd NW3 | 74 E 6 Gayford rd W12 | 140 G 8 Gerrard pl W1 | 145 R 19 Gironde rd SW6 |
| 49 U 8 Garnham st N16 | 49 X 20 Gayhurst rd E8 | 133 X 8 Gerrard rd N1 | 64 C 17 Girsud st E1 |
| 151 O 17 Garnies st SE15 | 40 E 15 Gaylor rd Grnfd | 140 G 8 Gerrard st W1 | 25 R 11 Girton av NW9 |
| 107 X 8 Garrad's rd SW16 | 35 R 1 Gaynes Hill rd Edfd | 141 U 20 Gerridge st SE1 | 40 M 19 Girton clo Grnfd |
| 98 F 8 Garrard clo Bxly Hth | Grn | 81 U 9 Gertrude rd Belv | 159 N 4 Girton gdns Croy |
| 113 Z 10 Garrard clo Chisl | 110 F 4 Gaynesford rd SE23 | 146 D 15 Gertrude st SW10 | 110 F 12 Girton rd SE26 |
| 106 G 9 Garratt la SW17 | 154 M 17 Gaynesford rd Carsh | 25 X 5 Gervase clo Edg | 40 M 18 Girton rd Grnfd |
| 88 A 14 Garratt la SW18 | 35 W 17 Gaysham av Ilf | 25 X 5 Gervase rd Edgw | 41 N 17 Girton rd Grnfd |
| 25 R 1 Garratt rd Edgw | 35 Y 11 Gaysham hall Ilf | 75 N 18 Gervase st SE14 | 30 C 19 Gisburn rd N8 |
| 106 J 11 Garratt ter SW17 | 46 F 12 Gayton cres NW3 | 151 Y 17 Gervase st SE15 | 53 O 11 Gladding rd E12 |
| 12 D 20 Garratt rd Edg | 46 E 12 Gayton rd NW3 | 111 O 4 Ghent st SE6 | 124 H 16 Glade gdns Croy |
| 144 B 17 Garrett st EC1 | 23 W 19 Gayton rd Harrow | 10 B 7 Giant Tree hill | 70 J 6 Glade la S'hall |
| 10 B 2 Garretts rd Bushey | 88 M 16 Gayville rd SW11 | Bushey | 17 O 1 Glade the N21 |
| Watf | 33 O 10 Gaywood rd E17 | 92 D 5 Gibbon rd SE15 | 77 X 19 Glade the SE7 |
| 27 U 19 Garrick av NW11 | 139 X 2 Gaywood st SE1 | 61 Z 19 Gibbon rd W3 | 127 O 4 Glade the Brom |
| 84 F 12 Garrick cl Rich | 149 W 11 Gaza st SE17 | 62 A 19 Gibbon rd W3 | 124 H 15 Glade the Croy |
| 27 N 9 Garrick dri NW4 | 36 A 12 Geariesville gdns Ilf | 102 K 19 Gibbon rd Kingst | 7 T 10 Glade the Enf |
| 26 E 18 Garrick rd NW9 | 44 H 14 Geary rd NW10 | 86 H 12 Gibbon wlk SW15 | 152 H 12 Glade the Epsom |

| Ref | Street |
|---|---|
| 5 T 5 | Glade the Ilf |
| 3 T 19 | Glade the Sutton |
| 8 T 19 | Glade the W Wkhm |
| 4 U 12 | Glade the Wdfd Grn |
| 7 P 1 | Gladeside N21 |
| 8 F 17 | Gladeside Croy |
| 4 V 17 | Gladesmore rd N15 |
| 4 U 10 | Gladeswood rd Belvdr |
| 2 J 18 | Gladiator st SE23 |
| 9 U 11 | Glading ter N16 |
| 7 V 4 | Gladsmuir rd N19 |
| 4 G 10 | Gladsmuir rd Barnt |
| 3 R 19 | Gladstone av E12 |
| 3 J 6 | Gladstone av N22 |
| 3 R 19 | Gladstone av Twick |
| 4 G 12 | Gladstone park NW2 |
| 4 L 10 | Gladstone Pk Gdn est NW2 |
| 4 L 9 | Gladstone Pk gdns NW2 |
| 5 P 1 | Gladstone rd E15 |
| 5 X 18 | Gladstone rd SW19 |
| 3 X 9 | Gladstone rd W4 |
| 1 X 5 | Gladstone rd Buck Hl |
| 3 P 17 | Gladstone rd Croy |
| 7 R 6 | Gladstone rd Kingst |
| 0 L 3 | Gladstone rd Mitch |
| 0 B 7 | Gladstone rd S'hall |
| 9 W 1 | Gladstone st SE1 |
| 9 T 1 | Gladstone ter SW8 |
| 0 C 19 | Gladwell N8 |
| 2 G 15 | Gladwell rd Brom |
| 7 O 7 | Gladwyn rd SW15 |
| 6 Y 19 | Gladys rd NW6 |
| 6 F 18 | Glaisher st SE10 |
| 3 R 20 | Glamis pl E1 |
| 8 R 1 | Glamis rd E1 |
| 5 R 1 | Glamis rd E1 |
| 0 M 19 | Glamis way Grnfd |
| 2 E 19 | Glamorgan rd Kingst |
| 4 M 8 | Glanfield rd Beckenhm |
| 1 U 13 | Glanleam rd Stanm |
| 6 J 7 | Glanville rd Brom |
| 0 F 2 | Glasbrook av Twick |
| 9 T 2 | Glaserton rd NW2 |
| 6 M 15 | Glasford st SW17 |
| 5 U 6 | Glasgow rd E13 |
| 8 L 15 | Glasgow rd N18 |
| 3 S 19 | Glass House fields E1 |
| 1 Y 18 | Glasshill st SE1 |
| 0 C 10 | Glasshouse st W1 |
| 8 M 9 | Glasshouse wlk SE11 |
| 9 N 9 | Glasshouse wlk SE11 |
| 9 W 17 | Glasslyn rd N8 |
| 8 D 5 | Glastonbury la Brom |
| 9 Z 16 | Glastonbury rd Mrdn |
| 8 W 10 | Glastonby st NW6 |
| 4 C 13 | Glaucus st E3 |
| 1 U 17 | Glazbrook rd Tedd |
| 4 L 9 | Glazbury rd W14 |
| 9 O 3 | Glazebrook clo SE21 |
| 7 W 11 | Glebe av Enf |
| 4 J 10 | Glebe av Harrow |
| 4 H 4 | Glebe av Mitch |
| 1 S 20 | Glebe av Wdfd Grn |
| 7 N 12 | Glebe cres NW4 |
| 4 K 11 | Glebe cres Harrow |
| 0 G 7 | Glebe ct Felt |
| 4 L 5 | Glebe ct Mitch |
| 1 P 16 | Glebe ct Stanm |
| 8 B 16 | Glebe gdns New Mald |
| 4 J 12 | Glebe la Harrow |
| 0 K 0 | Glebe path Mitch |
| 6 K 13 | Glebe pl SW3 |
| 9 U 20 | Glebe rd E8 |
| 4 E 18 | Glebe rd NW10 |
| 8 E 5 | Glebe rd N3 |
| 0 C 14 | Glebe rd N8 |
| 2 F 4 | Glebe rd SW13 |
| 2 F 20 | Glebe rd Brom |
| 4 M 13 | Glebe rd Carsh |
| 5 N 14 | Glebe rd Carsh |
| 6 H 19 | Glebe rd Dgnhm |
| 8 R 1 | Glebe rd Stanm |
| 1 R 17 | Glebe rd Stanm |
| 3 S 18 | Glebe rd Sutton |
| 3 W 16 | Glebe side Twick |
| 0 K 6 | Glebe sq Mitch |
| 3 Z 13 | Glebe st W4 |
| 4 C 8 | Glebe ter E3 |
| 2 Z 7 | Glebe the SE3 |
| 3 Z 7 | Glebe the SE3 |
| 0 D 19 | Glebe the Worc Pk |
| 0 G 7 | Glebe way Felt |
| 9 Y 3 | Glebe way W Wkhm |
| 1 Y 17 | Glebe way Wdfd Grn |
| 99 T 10 | Glebelands Drtfrd |
| 34 E 8 | Glebelands av E18 |
| 36 F 19 | Glebelands av Ilf |
| 54 E 1 | Glebelands av Ilf |
| 146 A 8 | Gledhow gdns SW5 |
| 120 L 11 | Gledstanes rd W14 |
| 10 B 7 | Gleed Bushey |
| 10 B 7 | Gleed av Bushey Watf |
| 105 P 4 | Glen Albyn rd SW19 |
| 21 V 20 | Glen cres Wdfd Grn |
| 156 G 2 | Glen gdns Croy |
| 65 X 11 | Glen rd E13 |
| 21 V 19 | Glen ri Wdfd Grn |
| 155 S 18 | Glen Road end Wallgtn |
| 125 Z 3 | Glen the Brom |
| 158 G 4 | Glen the Croy |
| 7 W 1 | Glen the Enf |
| 22 C 20 | Glen the Pinn |
| 70 F 13 | Glen the S'hall |
| 42 H 12 | Glen the Wemb |
| 24 K 12 | Glenalmond rd Harrow |
| 50 C 13 | Glenam rd E5 |
| 52 A 20 | Glenavon rd E15 |
| 95 Y 8 | Glenbarr clo SE9 |
| 111 Z 14 | Glenbow rd Brom |
| 112 A 13 | Glenbow rd Brom |
| 7 P 13 | Glenbrook North Enf |
| 7 R 13 | Glenbrook South Enf |
| 45 X 16 | Glenbrook rd NW6 |
| 116 J 15 | Glenbuck rd Surb |
| 106 M 6 | Glenburnie rd SW17 |
| 60 C 13 | Glencairn dri W5 |
| 108 B 18 | Glencairn rd SW16 |
| 54 F 2 | Glencoe av Ilf |
| 56 E 11 | Glencoe dri Dgnhm |
| 30 E 2 | Glendale av N22 |
| 12 B 15 | Glendale av Edg |
| 55 S 1 | Glendale av Rom |
| 95 X 8 | Glendale clo SE9 |
| 105 V 12 | Glendale dri SW19 |
| 42 J 5 | Glendale gdns Wemb |
| 81 Y 10 | Glendale rd Erith |
| 90 C 9 | Glendall st SW9 |
| 87 P 7 | Glendarvon st SW15 |
| 31 Z 5 | Glendish rd N17 |
| 12 M 14 | Glendor gdns NW7 |
| 85 Y 8 | Glendower gdns SW14 |
| 146 F 6 | Glendower pl SW7 |
| 20 K 5 | Glendown rd SE2 |
| 79 Z 14 | Glendown rd SE2 |
| 62 B 20 | Glendun rd W3 |
| 107 V 11 | Gleneagle rd SW16 |
| 11 O 20 | Gleneagles Stanm |
| 107 Z 10 | Gleneldon ms SW16 |
| 108 D 10 | Gleneldon rd SW16 |
| 90 A 12 | Glenelg rd SW2 |
| 95 Y 13 | Glenesk rd SE9 |
| 93 W 20 | Glenfarg rd SE6 |
| 107 V 1 | Glenfield rd SW4 |
| 72 A 4 | Glenfield rd W13 |
| 72 B 5 | Glenfield rd W13 |
| 76 A 8 | Glengall causeway E14 |
| 76 F 8 | Glengall gro E14 |
| 161 P 12 | Glengall ms SE15 |
| 129 T 4 | Glengall rd NW6 |
| 151 P 12 | Glengall rd SE15 |
| 97 Z 7 | Glengall rd Bxly Hth |
| 12 F 10 | Glengall rd Edg |
| 21 U 19 | Glengall rd Wdf Grn |
| 151 P 13 | Glengall ter SE15 |
| 76 G 12 | Glengarnock av E14 |
| 91 U 12 | Glengarry rd SE22 |
| 35 Z 16 | Glenham dri Ilf |
| 90 Y 8 | Glenhead clo SE9 |
| 27 Y 7 | Glenhill clo N7 |
| 95 W 12 | Glenhouse rd SE9 |
| 47 P 12 | Glenhurst av NW5 |
| 15 U 15 | Glenhurst rd N12 |
| 72 E 15 | Glenhurst rd Brentf |
| 108 M 18 | Glenhurst ri SE19 |
| 46 J 17 | Glenilla rd NW3 |
| 107 Y 19 | Glenister Pk rd SW16 |
| 77 P 13 | Glenister rd SE10 |
| 78 K 4 | Glenister st E16 |
| 95 X 11 | Glenlea rd SE9 |
| 46 J 16 | Glenloch rd NW3 |
| 9 R 9 | Glenloch rd Enf |
| 77 T 18 | Glenluce rd SE3 |
| 95 X 12 | Glenlyon rd SE9 |
| 13 T 20 | Glenmere av NW7 |
| 46 J 17 | Glenmore rd NW3 |
| 96 K 2 | Glenmore rd Welling |
| 68 A 8 | Glenmore way Bark |
| 108 F 7 | Glennie rd SE27 |
| 54 B 18 | Glenny rd Bark |
| 52 H 17 | Glenparke rd E7 |
| 88 C 5 | Glenrosa st SW6 |
| 136 B 4 | Glenroy st W10 |
| 62 M 16 | Glenroy st W12 |
| 62 M 16 | Glenroy st W12 |
| 92 L 8 | Glensdale rd SE4 |
| 95 X 12 | Glenshiel rd SE9 |
| 79 W 10 | Glenside rd SE18 |
| 108 F 7 | Glentanner way SW17 |
| 74 J 16 | Glentham gdns SW13 |
| 74 J 16 | Glentham rd SW13 |
| 124 B 19 | Glenthorne av Croy |
| 119 X 19 | Glenthorne clo Sutton |
| 35 Y 11 | Glenthorne gdns Ilf |
| 119 X 19 | Glenthorne gdns Sutton |
| 32 H 15 | Glenthorne rd E17 |
| 16 B 16 | Glenthorne rd N11 |
| 144 A 6 | Glenthorne rd W6 |
| 74 K 11 | Glenthorne rd W6 |
| 116 L 8 | Glenthorne rd Kingst |
| 119 P 12 | Glenthorpe rd Mrdn |
| 39 P 1 | Glenton clo Rom |
| 93 Y 10 | Glenton rd SE13 |
| 39 P 2 | Glenton way Rom |
| 131 P 18 | Glentworth st NW1 |
| 95 X 13 | Glenure rd SE9 |
| 80 K 16 | Glenview SE2 |
| 127 O 4 | Glenview Brom |
| 8 A 4 | Glenville av Enf |
| 75 Z 20 | Glenville gro SE8 |
| 103 O 20 | Glenville rd Kingst |
| 43 Z 3 | Glenwood av NW9 |
| 44 A 3 | Glenwood av NW9 |
| 23 W 16 | Glenwood clo Harrow |
| 39 V 14 | Glenwood dri Rom |
| 35 V 15 | Glenwood gdns Ilf |
| 43 V 4 | Glenwood gro NW9 |
| 13 O 10 | Glenwood rd N15 |
| 30 K 15 | Glenwood rd N15 |
| 110 M 1 | Glenwood rd SE6 |
| 111 N 1 | Glenwood rd SE6 |
| 152 G 13 | Glenwood rd Epsom |
| 83 P 8 | Glenwood rd Hounsl |
| 95 X 13 | Glenwood rd Croy |
| 64 E 8 | Glergion way E3 |
| 144 N 8 | Gliddon rd W14 |
| 52 B 15 | Globe cres E15 |
| 52 B 15 | Globe rd E15 |
| 63 P 7 | Globe rd E15 |
| 39 V 19 | Globe rd Hornch |
| 57 W 1 | Globe rd Hornch |
| 21 Z 18 | Globe rd Wdfd Grn |
| 142 D 20 | Globe st SE1 |
| 139 X 7 | Globe yd W1 |
| 157 P 19 | Glossop rd S Croy |
| 118 B 9 | Gloster rd New Mald |
| 131 T 2 | Gloucester av NW1 |
| 114 J 5 | Gloucester av Sidcup |
| 96 K 11 | Gloucester av Welling |
| 76 G 19 | Gloucester cir SE10 |
| 43 X 20 | Gloucester clo NW10 |
| 131 X 4 | Gloucester cres NW1 |
| 73 O 20 | Gloucester ct Rich |
| 27 Y 13 | Gloucester dri NW11 |
| 48 K 6 | Gloucester dri N4 |
| 131 W 7 | Gloucester ga NW1 |
| 131 W 7 | Gloucester Ga ms NW1 |
| 27 U 20 | Gloucester gdns NW11 |
| 6 C 15 | Gloucester gdns Barnt |
| 53 S 1 | Gloucester gdns Ilf |
| 154 B 1 | Gloucester gdns Sutton |
| 150 K 17 | Gloucester gro SE15 |
| 25 X 5 | Gloucester gro Edg |
| 138 D 6 | Gloucester ms W2 |
| 138 C 6 | Gloucester ms W2 |
| 131 O 18 | Gloucester pl NW1 |
| 139 R 2 | Gloucester pl W1 |
| 139 P 2 | Gloucester Pl ms W1 |
| 51 N 2 | Gloucester rd E10 |
| 34 J 16 | Gloucester rd E11 |
| 53 T 11 | Gloucester rd E12 |
| 32 F 7 | Gloucester rd E17 |
| 31 P 11 | Gloucester rd N17 |
| 18 G 17 | Gloucester rd N18 |
| 146 C 8 | Gloucester rd SW7 |
| 73 X 4 | Gloucester rd W3 |
| 72 E 7 | Gloucester rd W5 |
| 5 O 17 | Gloucester rd Barnt |
| 81 O 13 | Gloucester rd Blvdr |
| 123 P 18 | Gloucester rd Croy |
| 99 Z 18 | Gloucester rd Dartford |
| 7 Z 3 | Gloucester rd Enf |
| 100 L 17 | Gloucester rd Hampt |
| 22 K 16 | Gloucester rd Harrow |
| 82 A 11 | Gloucester rd Hounsl |
| 73 P 19 | Gloucester rd Richm |
| 39 S 18 | Gloucester rd Rom |
| 101 S 13 | Gloucester rd Tedd |
| 101 N 1 | Gloucester rd Twick |
| 138 H 7 | Gloucester sq W2 |
| 148 B 8 | Gloucester st SW 1 |
| 148 B 8 | Gloucester st SW7 |
| 138 C 6 | Gloucester ter W2 |
| 133 U 14 | Gloucester way EC1 |
| 137 U 16 | Gloucester wlk W8 |
| 22 A 18 | Glover rd Pinn |
| 5 T 14 | Glyn av Barnt |
| 152 F 20 | Glyn clo Epsom |
| 115 S 11 | Glyn dri Sidcp |
| 50 F 11 | Glyn rd E5 |
| 9 P 14 | Glyn rd Enf |
| 153 O 4 | Glyn rd Worc Pk |
| 149 N 11 | Glyn st SE11 |
| 89 N 7 | Glyncena rd SW11 |
| 146 M 3 | Glynde ms SW3 |
| 97 X 8 | Glynde rd Bxly Hth |
| 92 M 15 | Glynde st SE4 |
| 70 N 12 | Glyndon rd SE18 |
| 62 B 1 | Glynfield rd NW10 |
| 110 C 5 | Glynwood dri SE23 |
| 8 H 3 | Goat la Enf |
| 121 N 15 | Goat rd Mitch |
| 143 N 16 | Goat st SE1 |
| 145 P 19 | Goater's all SW6 |
| 38 M 1 | Gobions av Rom |
| 39 N 2 | Gobions av Rom |
| 156 B 10 | Godalming av Wallgtn |
| 64 C 16 | Godalming rd E14 |
| 64 M 10 | Godbold rd E15 |
| 148 G 9 | Goddard rd Becknhm |
| 83 R 18 | Godfrey av Twick |
| 78 F 12 | Godfrey hill SE18 |
| 78 F 12 | Godfrey rd SE18 |
| 64 G 4 | Godfrey st E15 |
| 146 L 9 | Godfrey st SW3 |
| 148 M 11 | Goding st SE11 |
| 108 F 2 | Godley rd SW18 |
| 141 Z 7 | Godliman st EC4 |
| 91 Z 6 | Godman rd SE15 |
| 74 J 4 | Godolphin rd W12 |
| 58 B 3 | Godric av Grnfd |
| 159 X 20 | Godric cres Croy |
| 155 F 6 | Godson rd Croy |
| 133 S 9 | Godson st N1 |
| 154 E 7 | Godstone rd Sutton |
| 84 A 17 | Godstone rd Twick |
| 80 E 6 | Godstow rd SE2 |
| 52 J 12 | Godwin rd E7 |
| 126 L 7 | Godwin rd Brom |
| 94 A 4 | Goffers rd SE3 |
| 93 Y 3 | Goffers rd SE3 |
| 155 Y 8 | Goidel clo Wallgtn |
| 128 M 18 | Golborne gdns W10 |
| 119 N 19 | Golborne rd W10 |
| 136 L 1 | Golborne rd W10 |
| 12 L 19 | Gold hill Edg |
| 12 L 20 | Gold la Edg |
| 4 C 18 | Golda clo Barnt |
| 26 A 2 | Goldbesters gro Edg |
| 12 M 19 | Goldbesters gro Edg |
| 13 N 20 | Goldbesters gro Edg |
| 128 M 20 | Goldborne rd W10 |
| 159 X 18 | Goldcrest way Croy |
| 84 G 13 | Golden ct Rich |
| 134 B 17 | Golden la EC1 |
| 59 T 20 | Golden manor W7 |
| 71 T 1 | Golden manor W7 |
| 140 C 9 | Golden sq W1 |
| 12 F 15 | Golders clo Edg |
| 40 U 1 | Golders gdns NW11 |
| 45 W 2 | Golders Green cres NW11 |
| 46 V 1 | Golders Green rd NW11 |
| 27 T 18 | Golders Green rd NW11 |
| 45 Z 6 | Golders Hill park NW3 |
| 46 A 5 | Golders Hill park NW3 |
| 27 R 19 | Golders Manor dri NW11 |
| 45 Z 5 | Golders Pk clo NW11 |
| 27 O 15 | Golders ri NW4 |
| 45 W 2 | Golders way NW11 |
| 74 K 6 | Goldhawk mews W12 |
| 74 K 6 | Goldhawk ms W12 |
| 74 G 8 | Goldhawk rd N12 |
| 136 B 19 | Goldhawk rd N12 |
| 130 B 1 | Goldhurst st NW6 |
| 46 D 20 | Goldhurst ter NW6 |

7 X 18 Granville rd SW18
5 Y 18 Granville rd SW19
8 B 13 Granville rd Barnt
3 Y 5 Granville rd Ilf
5 O 9 Granville rd Sidcp
7 U 8 Granville rd Welling
3 R 13 Granville sq WC1
3 P 13 Granville st WC1
0 J 4 Grape st WC1
8 G 1 Gras Mere rd SW16
0 A 18 Grasdene rd SE19
3 Z 10 Grasmere av SW15
4 A 9 Grasmere av SW19
9 Y 6 Grasmere av W3
1 X 19 Grasmere av W3
2 J 16 Grasmere av Hounsl
2 J 4 Grasmere av Wemb
3 Z 8 Grasmere gdns Harrow
5 S 14 Grasmere gdns Ilf
9 S 6 Grasmere rd N10
8 J 20 Grasmere rd N17
7 Z 13 Grasmere rd SE25
8 A 13 Grasmere rd SE25
2 B 19 Grasmere rd Brom
K 4 Grasmere rd Bxly Hth
7 V 5 Grass pk N3
5 U 8 Grass way Wallgtn
5 N 11 Grassington rd Sidcp
0 B 3 Grassmount SE23
4 M 19 Grasvenor av Barnt
K 2 Gratton rd W14
5 O 10 Gratton ter NW12
7 W 7 Gravel hill N3
8 G 13 Gravel hill Bxly Hth
8 H 14 Gravel hill Croy
2 M 4 Gravel la E1
0 G 6 Gravel pits Brom
1 S 2 Gravel rd Twick
5 P 1 Gravel st E1
4 B 8 Gravelwood clo Chisl
6 J 10 Graveney rd SW17
4 G 1 Gravesend rd W12
6 C 4 Gray av Dgnhm
7 V 16 Gray gdns Rainhm
8 B 3 Gray st E16
1 V 18 Gray st SE1
1 P 1 Gray's Inn pl WC1
3 O 16 Gray's Inn rd WC1
1 R 1 Gray's Inn sq WC1
7 Y 9 Grayham cres New Mald
7 X 9 Grayham rd New Mald
7 O 2 Grayland clo Brom
0 L 17 Graylands rd SE15
9 P 6 Grayling rd N16
7 X 18 Grayscroft rd SW16
9 N 7 Grayshott rd SW11
8 D 1 Graywood ct N12
8 D 1 Graywood ct N12
9 O 7 Grazebrook rd N16
8 K 12 Grazeley av Bxly Hth
9 R 11 Grazeley ct SE19
8 G 8 Great North rd N2
4 H 8 Great North rd Barnt
4 J 14 Great West rd W6
9 V 13 Greatdown rd W7
6 G 11 Greatfield av E6
3 O 11 Greatfield clo SE4
7 T 4 Greatfields rd Bark
3 S 2 Greatorex st E1
6 H 10 Greaves pl SW17
8 K 15 Grecian cres SE19
5 Greek st W1
1 X 4 Green Arbour ct EC1
2 M 12 Green av NW7
3 N 12 Green av NW7
2 C 8 Green av W13
5 N 3 Green bank E1
3 Y 14 Green bank E1
5 O 13 Green bank N12
7 S 13 Green Bank cres NW4
8 C 20 Green clo NW11
5 W 17 Green clo NW9
5 Z 5 Green clo Brom
4 M 3 Green clo Carsh
0 C 12 Green clo Hampt
8 A 1 Green Ct av Croy
8 A 1 Green Ct gdns Croy
9 R 11 Green dale SE5
7 T 19 Green Dragon la N21
7 X 1 Green Dragon la N21
0 J 2 Green dri S'hall
7 X 8 Green end N21
6 F 14 Green hill NW3
1 X 1 Green Hills rents EC1
1 V 15 Green Hundred rd SE15
7 P 16 Green la NW4
0 E 18 Green la SE20
3 X 4 Green la SE9

95 Y 19 Green la SE9
108 F 19 Green la SW16
71 T 4 Green la W7
114 A 14 Green la Chisl
56 B 6 Green la Dgnhm
11 Z 12 Green la Edg
12 A 14 Green la Edg
100 A 12 Green la Felt
54 D 8 Green la Ilf
55 O 5 Green la Ilf
119 X 14 Green la Mrdn
120 B 17 Green la Mrdn
117 W 11 Green la New Mald
11 O 18 Green la Stanm
122 J 2 Green la Thntn Hth
118 H 19 Green la Worc Pk
122 K 2 Green La gdns Thntn Hth
49 N 12 Green lanes N16
17 X 4 Green lanes N21
48 L 4 Green lanes N4
30 H 16 Green lanes N8
152 B 18 Green lanes Epsom
71 Z 1 Green Man la W13
72 A 1 Green Man la W13
17 W 2 Green Moor link N21
139 X 16 Green park SW1
99 S 12 Green pl Drtfrd
32 J 9 Green Pond rd E17
6 D 19 Green rd N14
15 S 10 Green rd N20
65 X 2 Green st E13
52 K 20 Green st E7
139 S 8 Green st W1
9 P 9 Green st Enf
133 U 13 Green ter EC1
34 H 19 Green the E11
52 A 18 Green the E15
16 K 10 Green the N14
17 V 4 Green the N21
18 X 4 Green the N9
62 B 17 Green the W3
126 E 18 Green the Brom
98 D 3 Green the Bxly Hth
155 O 9 Green the Carsh
158 M 19 Green the Croy
70 F 17 Green the Hounsl
119 S 9 Green the Mrdn
117 X 5 Green the N Mald
115 R 18 Green the Orp
84 G 12 Green the Rich
70 C 8 Green the S'hall
154 A 6 Green the Sutton
101 T 2 Green the Twick
21 T 16 Green the Wdfd Grn
96 J 11 Green the Welling
41 Z 6 Green the Wemb
60 M 16 Green vale E4
97 W 13 Green vale Bxly Hth
24 F 1 Green verges Stanm
95 N 13 Green way SE9
151 S 14 Green way Brom
21 Y 15 Green way Wdfd Grn
20 H 4 Green wlk E4
27 P 14 Green wlk NW4
150 H 2 Green wlk SE 1
99 T 11 Green wlk Drtfrd
158 K 15 Green wlk S Croy
70 G 14 Green wlk S'hall
154 K 1 Green Wrythe cres Carsh
144 G 15 Green Wrythe gdns Carsh
144 H 17 Green Wrythe la Carsh
140 D 8 Green's ct W1
78 L 10 Green's end SE18
95 W 16 Greenacres SE9
11 N 20 Greenacres dri Stanm
46 B 13 Greenaway gdns NW3
41 Y 15 Greenbank av Wemb
78 B 19 Greenbay rd SE7
130 K 10 Greenberry st NW8
5 S 6 Greenbrook av Barnt
148 C 4 Greencoat pl SW1
148 D 3 Greencoat row SW1
25 R 5 Greencourt av Edg
46 D 19 Greencroft gdns NW6
129 Y 1 Greencroft gdns NW6
8 E 11 Greencroft gdns Enf
82 D 2 Greencroft rd Hounsl
74 A 6 Greenend rd W4
76 M 7 Greenfell st SE10
117 T 15 Greenfield av Surb
45 T 9 Greenfield gdns NW2
68 H 3 Greenfield gdns Dgnhm
143 U 4 Greenfield rd E1

31 S 15 Greenfield rd N15
68 G 3 Greenfield rd Dgnhm
22 J 10 Greenfield way Harrow
58 H 18 Greenfields S'hall
59 T 14 Greenford av W7
70 E 1 Greenford av S'hall
58 E 20 Greenford av S'hall
58 M 8 Greenford gdns Grnfd
59 N 8 Greenford gdns Grnfd
59 O 10 Greenford rd Grnfd
41 T 17 Greenford rd Grnfd
71 N 1 Greenford rd S'hall
154 A 9 Greenford rd Sutton
42 A 17 Greengate Grnfd
65 V 8 Greengate st E13
28 D 14 Greenhalgh wlk N2
29 P 6 Greenham rd N10
34 C 9 Greenheys dri E18
21 X 4 Greenhill Buck Hl
154 D 3 Greenhill Sutton
43 U 6 Greenhill Wemb
23 V 17 Greenhill cres Harrow
58 E 6 Greenhill gdns Grnfd
53 P 14 Greenhill gro E12
62 A 4 Greenhill pk NW10
5 O 18 Greenhill pk Barnt
62 A 4 Greenhill rd NW10
23 U 18 Greenhill rd Harrow
58 E 7 Greenhill ter Grnfd
43 T 6 Greenhill way Wemb
96 F 18 Greenhithe clo Sidcp
95 V 14 Greenholm rd SE9
95 Y 13 Greenholm rd SE9
108 G 12 Greenhurst rd SE27
80 F 11 Greening st SE2
132 A 3 Greenland rd NW1
131 Z 4 Greenland rd NW1
4 A 19 Greenland rd Barnt
131 Z 4 Greenland rd NW1
78 H 9 Greenlaw st SE18
32 M 11 Greenleaf rd E17
33 N 11 Greenleaf rd E17
65 Y 4 Greenleaf rd E6
35 Z 10 Greenleafe dri Ilf
134 A 2 Greenman st N1
9 P 8 Greenmoor rd Enf
107 X 20 Greenock rd SW16
73 U 9 Greenock rd W4
55 T 5 Greenside Dgnhm
84 G 12 Greenside Rich
74 G 7 Greenside rd W12
74 A 6 Greenside rd W4
122 G 16 Greenside rd Croy
34 L 1 Greenstead av Wdfd Grn
21 Z 20 Greenstead av Wdfd Grn
34 K 1 Greenstead av Wdfd Grn
21 Y 19 Greenstead clo Wdfd Grn
86 H 14 Greenstead gdns SW15
21 Y 19 Greenstead gdns Wdfd Grn
95 U J 1 Greenvale rd SE9
124 J 14 Greenview av Becknhm
124 H 15 Greenview av Croy
17 N 7 Greenway N14
16 M 9 Greenway N14
14 L 7 Greenway N20
15 N 8 Greenway N20
118 M 8 Greenway SW20
113 X 11 Greenway Chisl
55 U 5 Greenway Dgnhm
24 K 16 Greenway Harrow
82 D 9 Greenway Hounsl
155 U 9 Greenway Wallgtn
33 W 12 Greenway av E17
25 X 9 Greenway clo NW9
14 L 9 Greenway clo N20
48 M 7 Greenway clo N4
23 U 6 Greenway ct Harrow
25 X 8 Greenway gdns NW9
158 K 6 Greenway gdns Croy
58 J 8 Greenway gdns Grnfd
25 Y 9 Greenway the SE9
23 U 6 Greenway the Harrow
22 E 19 Greenway the Pinn
63 T 8 Greenways E2
25 O 4 Greenways Becknhm
131 Z 4 Greenwell st W1
76 G 16 Greenwich Ch st SE10

76 L 18 Greenwich park SE10
76 L 16 Greenwich Pk st SE10
93 S 2 Greenwich South st SE10
56 H 11 Greenwood av Dgnhm
9 U 7 Greenwood av Enf
10 E 4 Greenwood clo Bushey Watf
119 S 9 Greenwood clo Mrdn
17 V 10 Greenwood gdns N13
36 C 3 Greenwood gdns Ilf
104 B 17 Greenwood pk Kingst
47 T 14 Greenwood pl NW5
65 S 5 Greenwood rd E13
49 X 16 Greenwood rd E8
122 K 16 Greenwood rd Croy
83 U 7 Greenwood rd Islwth
121 X 7 Greenwood rd Mitch
61 Y 4 Greenwood ter NW10
23 O 4 Greer rd Harrow
72 J 15 Greet rd Brentf
141 V 16 Greet st SE1
77 T 20 Gregor ms SE3
95 O 19 Gregory cres SE9
137 W 18 Gregory pl W8
65 X 19 Gregory rd E16
70 H 8 Gregory rd S'hall
30 A 15 Greig clo N8
85 N 11 Grena gdns Rich
85 N 11 Grena rd Rich
123 O 18 Grenaby av Croy
123 O 18 Grenaby rd Croy
77 Z 20 Grenada rd SE7
63 Z 20 Grenade st E14
78 H 4 Grenadier st E16
150 M 18 Grenard rd SE15
43 P 7 Grendon gdns Wemb
57 T 4 Grenfell av Hornch
24 J 20 Grenfell gdns Harrow
136 H 9 Grenfell rd W11
107 N 17 Grenfell rd Mitch
154 E 3 Grennell clo Sutton
154 E 4 Grennell rd Sutton
117 V 20 Grenville clo Surb
84 A 18 Grenville clo Twick
34 K 3 Grenville gdns Wdfd Grn
12 K 16 Grenville pl NW7
146 A 4 Grenville pl SW7
48 A 4 Grenville rd N4
159 V 20 Grenville rd Croy
132 L 18 Grenville st WC1
15 Y 13 Gresham av N20
98 A 16 Gresham clo Bxly
37 R 18 Gresham dri Rom
45 T 3 Gresham gdns NW11
65 W 18 Gresham rd E16
80 D 7 Gresham rd E6
43 Z 16 Gresham rd NW10
123 W 10 Gresham rd SE25
90 G 8 Gresham rd SW9
124 G 3 Gresham rd Becknhm
12 A 20 Gresham rd Edg
83 N 2 Gresham rd Hounsl
142 C 5 Gresham st EC2
47 W 2 Gresley rd N19
140 E 3 Gresse st W1
87 V 17 Gressenhall rd SW18
115 O 7 Gresswell clo Sidcp
87 O 2 Greswell st SW6
31 T 3 Gretton rd N17
129 W 6 Greville ms NW6
129 Y 8 Greville pl NW6
33 U 13 Greville rd E17
129 Z 0 Greville rd NW6
85 N 15 Greville rd Rich
141 T 1 Greville st EC1
28 C 18 Grey clo NW11
148 E 3 Greycoat pl SW 1
148 E 3 Greycoat st SW 1
111 O 12 Greycot rd Becknhm
78 L 16 Greydon st SE18
135 O 19 Greyeagle st E1
141 Z 4 Greyfriars pas EC4
26 H 11 Greyhound hill NW4
107 Z 15 Greyhound la SW16
62 L 8 Greyhound rd NW10
31 T 10 Greyhound rd N17
128 A 12 Greyhound rd W10
144 J 13 Greyhound rd W6
154 D 10 Greyhound rd Sutton
107 V 20 Greyhound ter SW16
92 C 18 Greystead rd SE23
22 H 10 Greystoke av Pinn
60 L 12 Greystoke av W5

## H

5 N 2 Hackbridge Pk gdns Carsh  
5 P 1 Hackbridge rd Wallgtn  
9 R 20 Hackford rd SW9  
0 E 2 Hackford rd SW9  
1 O 15 Hackington cres Becknhm  
0 A 19 Hackney gro E8  
5 T 9 Hackney rd E2  
8 C 11 Hadden clo New Mald  
9 U 9 Hadden way SE18  
1 X 9 Haddington rd Brom  
6 F 17 Haddo st SE10  
7 P 1 Haddo gdns Ilf  
6 M 18 Haddon gro Sidcp  
4 A 9 Haddon rd Sutton  
3 P 11 Hadleigh clo E1  
9 N 2 Hadleigh rd N9  
8 M 2 Hadleigh rd N9  
3 P 10 Hadleigh st E2  
7 U 19 Hadley clo N21  
5 N 9 Hadley common Barnt  
4 Y 12 Hadley gdns W4  
70 D 14 Hadley gdns S'hall  
4 G 8 Hadley green West Barnt  
4 H 9 Hadley Green rd Barnt  
4 G 10 Hadley gro Barnt  
4 H 6 Hadley highstone Barnt  
4 J 8 Hadley house Barnt  
6 G 3 Hadley rd Barnt  
5 O 10 Hadley rd Barnt  
31 O 9 Hadley rd Belvdr  
7 R 4 Hadley rd Enf  
45 X 9 Hadley rd Mitch  
4 O 11 Hadley ridge Barnt  
47 S 18 Hadley st NW1  
7 T 20 Hadley way N21  
4 K 9 Hadley Wood Barnt  
5 O 9 Hadley Wood rd Barnt  
09 W 17 Hadlow pl SE19  
15 O 10 Hadlow rd Sidcp  
80 Q 19 Hadlow rd Welling  
56 B 15 Hadrian clo Croy  
76 M 14 Hadyn Pk rd W12  
14 F 5 Hadyn Pk rd W12  
88 K 11 Hafer rd SW11  
12 A 2 Hafton rd SE6  
64 A 19 Haggard rd Twick  
35 N 2 Haggerston rd E8  
34 M 1 Haggerston rd E8  
35 U 14 Hague st E2  
1 R 17 Haig rd Stanm  
65 Y 8 Haig Rd east E13  
65 X 8 Haig Rd west E13  
81 R 6 Hailey rd Belvdr  
8 H 20 Halleybury av Enf  
08 C 5 Hailsham av SW16  
07 P 16 Hailsham rd SW17  
A 15 Hailsham terr N18  
95 O 12 Halmo rd SE9  
37 S 11 Hainault gore Rom  
38 A 17 Hainault house Rom  
33 Z 20 Hainault rd E11  
28 B 18 Hainault rd Rom  
38 L 10 Hainault rd Rom  
14 A 2 Hainault st SE 9  
54 A 7 Hainault st Ilf  
54 C 17 Haines st SW6  
08 M 8 Hainthorpe rd SE27  
56 B 11 Halbutt gdns Dgnhm  
56 B 11 Halbutt st Dgnhm  
34 J 6 Halcomb st N1  
98 H 12 Halcot av Bxly Hth  
63 O 16 Halcrow st E1  
43 Y 1 Halcrow st E1  
20 G 20 Haldan rd E4  
33 V 1 Haldan rd E4  
88 A 20 Haldane pl SW18  
66 D 8 Haldane rd E6  
66 D 8 Haldane rd E6  
145 R 17 Haldane rd SW16  
58 M 18 Haldane rd Shall  
87 W 15 Haldon rd SW18  
20 G 10 Hale clo E4  
12 J 16 Hale clo Edg  
12 K 19 Hale dri NW7  
33 W 8 Hale End rd E17  
20 J 19 Hale End rd E4  
31 X 11 Hale gdns N17  
73 P 2 Hale gdns W3  
12 M 16 Hale Gro gdns NW7  
13 N 17 Hale Gro gdns NW7  
12 L 16 Hale la NW7  
13 O 17 Hale la NW7  

12 E 16 Hale la Edg  
66 D 12 Hale rd E6  
31 X 11 Hale rd N17  
64 D 19 Hale st E14  
33 W 2 Hale the E4  
31 X 11 Hale the N17  
59 U 15 Hale wlk W7  
31 Z 6 Halefield rd N17  
119 Z 18 Halesowen rd Mrdn  
120 A 19 Halesowen rd Mrdn  
93 P 7 Halesworth rd SE13  
72 F 17 Half acre Brentf  
71 S 2 Half Acre rd W7  
135 R 7 Half Moon la N1  
90 L 15 Half Moon la SE24  
91 N 15 Half Moon la SE24  
139 Y 14 Half Moon st W1  
143 O 5 Halfmoon pass E1  
33 W 16 Halford rd E10  
145 T 15 Halford rd SW6  
84 J 13 Halford rd E10  
96 F 20 Halfway st Sidcp  
114 J 2 Halfway st Sidcp  
83 Z 12 Haliburton rd Twick  
49 O 17 Haliday wlk N1  
50 D 15 Halidon st E9  
8 A 0 Halifax rd Enf  
58 L 3 Halifax rd Grnfd  
110 A 8 Halifax st SE26  
156 L 19 Haling Down pas S Croy  
156 C 16 Haling gro S Croy  
156 K 15 Haling Pk rd S Croy  
157 N 14 Haling Pk rd S Croy  
156 M 14 Haling Pk rd S Croy  
157 O 13 Haling rd S Croy  
139 S 20 Halkin ms SW1  
147 S 1 Halkin pl SW1  
139 U 19 Halkin st SW1  
110 B 11 Hall dri SE26  
50 U 16 Hall dri W7  
11 O 13 Hall Farm clo Stanm  
83 R 18 Hall Farm dri Twick  
19 Z 14 Hall gdns E4  
19 Y 14 Hall la E4  
20 B 14 Hall la E4  
26 G 7 Hall la NW4  
130 F 19 Hall pl W 2  
98 L 14 Hall Pl cres Bxly  
51 X 12 Hall rd E6  
66 G 3 Hall rd E6  
130 C 14 Hall rd W4  
83 R 12 Hall rd Islwth  
37 U 18 Hall rd Ro.  
155 T 18 Hall rd Wallgtn  
133 X 11 Hall st EC1  
15 P 16 Hall st N12  
94 E 8 Hall the SE3  
113 T 13 Hallam clo Chisl  
22 C 2 Hallam gdns Pinn  
131 Y 20 Hallam ms W1  
139 Z 1 Hallam st W 1  
131 Y 10 Hallam st W1  
52 K 12 Halley rd E7  
53 P 15 Halley rd E7  
63 V 15 Halley st E14  
134 D 1 Halliford st N1  
90 B 15 Halliwell rd SW2  
28 O 4 Halliwick rd N10  
153 Z 5 Hallmead rd Sutton  
154 A 5 Hallmead rd Sutton  
155 Z 7 Hallowell av Wallgtn  
121 O 5 Hallowell clo Mitch  
8 G 4 Hallside rd Enf  
65 O 18 Hallsville rd E16  
65 O 17 Hallsville rd E16  
27 V 15 Hallswelle rd NW11  
49 Y 11 Hallway wlk N1  
95 X 17 Halons rd SE9  
150 G 7 Halpin pl SE17  
94 M 6 Halsbrook rd SE3  
95 P 11 Halsbrook rd SE3  
11 O 15 Halsbury clo Stanm  
74 H 3 Halsbury rd W12  
41 O 13 Halsbury Rd east Grnfd  
40 L 14 Halsbury Rd west Grnfd  
147 N 6 Halsey st SW3  
54 K 16 Halsham cres Bark  
90 K 2 Halsmere rd SE5  
18 A 5 Halstead gdns N21  
34 G 15 Halstead rd E11  
18 A 5 Halstead rd N21  
8 E 14 Halstead rd Enf  
99 P 1 Halstead rd Erith  
128 F 13 Halstow rd NW10  
77 R 15 Halstow rd SE10  
81 V 10 Halt Robin la Belvdr  
81 T 10 Halt Robin rd Belvdr  
133 Y 3 Halton Cross st N1  
133 Y 2 Halton rd N1  

48 J 20 Halton rd N1  
102 D 6 Ham clo Rich  
102 H 9 Ham Farm rd Rich  
102 H 8 Ham Ga av Rich  
102 C 2 Ham house Rich  
52 E 20 Ham Pk rd E7  
110 A 20 Ham pl SE20  
102 M 11 Ham ridings Rich  
102 C 3 Ham st Rich  
72 E 20 Ham the Brentf  
124 J 15 Ham view Croy  
124 J 15 Ham view Croy  
140 D 9 Ham yd W1  
89 V 14 Hambalt rd SW4  
88 B 7 Hamble st SW6  
123 U 6 Hambledon gdns SE25  
87 U 19 Hambledon rd SW18  
96 F 19 Hambledown rd Sidcp  
126 F 19 Hambro av Brom  
107 Y 13 Hambro rd SW16  
123 Z 6 Hambrook rd SE25  
70 B 2 Hambrough rd S'hall  
56 G 9 Hamden cres Dgnhm  
64 G 18 Hamelin st E14  
66 J 10 Hameway E6  
52 H 1 Hamfrith rd E15  
18 K 2 Hamilton av N9  
36 B 14 Hamilton av Ilf  
39 N 8 Hamilton av Rom  
38 M 9 Hamilton av Rom  
153 S 1 Hamilton av Sutton  
130 E 15 Hamilton clo NW8  
5 X 14 Hamilton clo Barnt  
17 U 14 Hamilton cres N13  
40 F 9 Hamilton cres Harrow  
82 K 14 Hamilton cres Hounsl  
130 D 11 Hamilton gdns NW8  
139 V 15 Hamilton mans W1  
48 I 13 Hamilton nk N5  
48 H 13 Hamilton Pk west N5  
139 V 15 Hamilton pl W1  
65 N 10 Hamilton rd E15  
32 J 9 Hamilton rd E17  
44 G 14 Hamilton rd NW10  
45 R 1 Hamilton rd NW11  
28 D 10 Hamilton rd N2  
18 J 3 Hamilton rd N9  
109 O 9 Hamilton rd SE27  
106 B 19 Hamilton rd SW19  
74 A 7 Hamilton rd W4  
60 L 19 Hamilton rd W5  
5 X 14 Hamilton rd Barnt  
72 G 16 Hamilton rd Brentf  
97 Z 4 Hamilton rd Bxly Hth  
23 U 15 Hamilton rd Harrow  
53 Z 12 Hamilton rd Ilf  
39 Y 16 Hamilton rd Rom  
70 E 2 Hamilton rd S'hall  
114 M 9 Hamilton rd Sidcp  
123 N 5 Hamilton rd Thntn Hth  
101 U 1 Hamilton rd Twick  
78 A 18 Hamilton st SE8  
130 B 12 Hamilton ter NW8  
129 Z 9 Hamilton ter NW8  
14 K 20 Hamilton way N3  
155 X 19 Hamilton way Wallgtn  
149 O 6 Hamlet st SE11  
94 D 12 Hamlea clo SE12  
39 D 2 Hamlet clo Rom  
74 F 11 Hamlet gdns W6  
109 W 10 Hamlet rd SE19  
38 C 2 Hamlet rd Rom  
91 P 7 Hamlet the SE5  
63 Y 11 Hamlets way E3  
109 R 19 Hamlyn gdns SE19  
112 E 20 Hammel rd Brom  
13 U 14 Hammers la NW1  
65 R 17 Hammersley av E16  
144 D 7 Hammersmith bdwy W6  
74 K 15 Hammersmith br W6  
144 A 11 Hammersmith br W6  
74 L 13 Hammersmith Br rd W6  
144 B 10 Hammersmith Br rd W6  
144 D 9 Hammersmith flyover W6  
136 A 19 Hammersmith gro W6  
144 C 5 Hammersmith gro W6  
74 L 7 Hammersmith gro W6  
144 H 6 Hammersmith rd W6  
74 G 14 Hammersmith rd W6  
121 R 4 Hammond av Mitch  
9 N 10 Hammond rd Enf  

70 D 9 Hammond rd S'hall  
47 U 17 Hammond st NW5  
12 E 9 Hamonde clo Edg  
148 K 4 Hampden av Becknhm  
139 O 6 Hampden Gurney st W1  
31 W 5 Hampden la N17  
29 P 1 Hampden rd N10  
31 X 4 Hampden rd N17  
30 G 13 Hampden rd N8  
148 J 4 Hampden rd Becknhm  
23 O 5 Hampden rd Harrow  
117 R 5 Hampden rd Kingst  
117 R 5 Hampden rd Kingst  
88 H 2 Hampden rd Rom  
16 E 6 Hampden way N14  
18 M 17 Hampshire clo N18  
74 H 12 Hampshire Hog la W6  
30 D 1 Hampshire rd N22  
47 X 16 Hampshire st NW5  
90 C 1 Hampson way SW8  
27 X 19 Hampstead gdns NW11  
46 I 14 Hampstead grn NW3  
46 D 11 Hampstead gro NW3  
46 G 6 Hampstead heath NW3  
28 E 11 Hampstead heights N2  
28 E 11 Hampstead heights N2  
46 F 13 Hampstead High st NW3  
46 H 13 Hampstead Hill gdns NW3  
47 N 2 Hampstead la N6  
46 K 2 Hampstead la N6  
132 B 11 Hampstead rd NW1  
46 E 10 Hampstead sq NW3  
46 C 4 Hampstead way NW11  
27 X 16 Hampstead way NW11  
104 L 18 Hampton clo SW20  
116 C 8 Hampton Court park Kingst  
48 H 18 Hampton ct N1  
100 C 10 Hampton la Felt  
51 X 5 Hampton rd E11  
20 A 16 Hampton rd E4  
19 X 16 Hampton rd E4  
52 G 15 Hampton rd E7  
129 U 14 Hampton rd NW6  
146 M 14 Hampton rd Croy  
147 N 15 Hampton rd Croy  
54 B 13 Hampton rd Ilf  
101 R 13 Hampton rd Tedd  
101 R 9 Hampton rd Twick  
152 H 3 Hampton rd Worc Pk  
100 G 9 Hampton Rd east Felt  
100 C 6 Hampton Rd west Felt  
24 K 19 Hampton ri Harrow  
129 Z 6 Hampton st SE17  
77 U 3 Hanameel st E10  
31 Y 7 Hanbury rd N17  
89 P 6 Hanbury rd SW11  
73 T 7 Hanbury rd W3  
135 S 20 Hanbury st E1  
64 F 9 Hancock rd E3  
109 O 16 Hancock rd SE19  
141 P 2 Hand ct WC2  
122 H 19 Handcroft rd Croy  
156 J 1 Handcroft rd Croy  
11 Z 19 Handel clo Edg  
132 K 16 Handel st WC1  
12 C 20 Handel way Edg  
50 O 1 Handel way Edg  
94 C 14 Handen rd SE12  
145 S 18 Handforth rd SW9  
139 S 18 Handforth rd SW9  
63 R 2 Handley rd E9  
20 J 19 Handsworth av E4  
31 P 11 Handsworth rd N17  
67 N 5 Handtrough way Barking  
104 M 14 Hanford row SW19  
61 O 11 Hanger grn W5  
60 K 12 Hanger Hill park W5  
60 L 14 Hanger la W5  
60 M 17 Hanger vale W5  
61 O 15 Hanger Vale la W5  
141 V 6 Hanging Sword all EC4  
142 F 19 Hankey pl SE1  
13 N 10 Hankins la NW7  
48 A 5 Hanley rd N4  
108 K 8 Hannen rd SE27  
63 R 14 Hannibal rd E1  
50 L 17 Hannington point E9

89 S 8 Hannington rd SW4
153 T 8 Hanover clo Sutton
130 M 13 Hanover gate NW1
139 S 16 Hanover gdns SE11
36 B 2 Hanover gdns Ilf
91 X 3 Hanover pk SE15
140 L 7 Hanover pl WC2
62 M 2 Hanover rd NW10
128 C 3 Hanover rd NW10
31 V 13 Hanover rd N15
139 Z 7 Hanover st W 1
139 Y 7 Hanover sq W1
131 N 14 Hanover ter NW1
131 N 15 Hanover Ter ms NW1
139 O 20 Hans cres SW3
147 O 2 Hans pl SW1
147 N 1 Hans rd SW3
147 P 2 Hans st SW1
7 U 7 Hansart way Enf
136 J 18 Hansard ms W14
105 Y 1 Hansford clo SW18
25 X 4 Hanshaw dri Edgw
91 V 13 Hansler rd SE22
97 Y 12 Hansol rd Bxly Hth
70 C 5 Hanson gdns S'hall
132 A 20 Hanson st W1
140 A 1 Hanson st W1
140 F 3 Hanway pl W1
140 F 4 Hanway st W 1
100 A 9 Hanworth clo Felt
100 J 14 Hanworth rd Hampt
82 H 14 Hanworth rd Hounsl
82 K 10 Hanworth ter Hounsl
143 T 9 Harads pl E1
46 E 20 Harben rd NW6
65 P 3 Harberson rd E15
89 R 20 Harberson rd SW12
47 V 4 Harberton rd N19
19 U 17 Harbet rd E4
98 F 18 Harbex clo Bxly
76 D 12 Harbinger rd E14
87 X 1 Harbledown rd SW6
87 P 1 Harbord st SW6
96 J 18 Harborough av Sidcp
108 D 9 Harborough rd SW16
90 L 7 Harbour rd SE5
86 F 18 Harbridge av SW15
154 H 17 Harbury rd Carsh
88 F 11 Harbut rd SW11
49 R 10 Harcombe rd N16
53 T 14 Harcourt av E12
12 G 11 Harcourt av Edg
97 T 18 Harcourt av Sidcp
155 T 9 Harcourt av Wallgtn
155 T 8 Harcourt field Wallgtn
65 O 6 Harcourt rd E15
29 W 4 Harcourt rd N22
92 K 8 Harcourt rd SE4
105 Y 19 Harcourt rd SW19
97 Z 9 Harcourt rd Bxly Hth
122 D 14 Harcourt rd Thntn Hth
155 S 8 Harcourt rd Wallgtn
138 M 2 Harcourt st W1
145 Z 11 Harcourt ter SW10
146 A 12 Harcourt ter SW10
159 T 7 Hardcourts clo W Wkhm
108 G 2 Hardel ri SW2
78 D 10 Harden st SE18
78 A 9 Hardens manorway SE18
91 Z 2 Harders rd SE15
92 A 2 Harders Rd ms SE15
90 K 8 Hardess st SE24
56 K 10 Hardie rd Dgnhm
98 A 4 Harding rd Bxly Hth
62 L 4 Hardinge rd NW10
128 C 6 Hardinge rd NW10
18 D 18 Hardinge rd N18
63 R 19 Hardinge st E1
110 E 16 Hardings la SE20
77 U 13 Hardman rd SE7
116 K 2 Hardman rd Kingst
82 H 2 Hardwick av Hounsl
11 R 16 Hardwick clo Stanm
133 T 13 Hardwick st EC1
67 O 4 Hardwick st Bark
17 N 18 Hardwicke rd N13
73 X 11 Hardwicke rd W4
102 C 9 Hardwicke rd Rich
87 Z 14 Hardwicks way SW18
142 J 17 Hardwidge st SE1
77 R 17 Hardy rd SE3
106 B 18 Hardy rd SW19
7 U 6 Hardy way Enf
93 X 4 Hare And Billet rd SE13

141 S 7 Hare ct EC4
39 Y 12 Hare Hall la Rom
78 J 9 Hare st SE18
134 L 9 Hare wlk N1
48 L 17 Harecourt rd N1
90 M 11 Haredale av SE24
29 X 15 Harefield av N8
153 R 20 Harefield av Sutton
92 K 7 Harefield ms SE4
31 O 19 Harefield rd N15
92 L 8 Harefield rd SE4
93 N 8 Harefield rd SE4
108 D 18 Harefield rd SW16
115 W 6 Harefield rd Sidcp
56 F 19 Haresfield rd Dgnhm
131 N 20 Harewood av NW1
130 M 17 Harewood av NW1
58 D 1 Harewood clo Grnfd
58 D 1 Harewood clo Grnfd
35 T 7 Harewood dri Ilf
139 Y 6 Harewood pl W1
106 K 16 Harewood rd SW19
83 W 1 Harewood rd Islwth
71 V 20 Harewood rd Islwth
157 S 14 Harewood rd S Croy
130 M 20 Harewood row NW1
70 F 11 Harewood ter S'hall
91 R 7 Harfield gdns SE5
20 E 2 Harford clo E4
20 E 2 Harford rd E4
63 U 12 Harford st E1
28 G 14 Harford wlk N2
94 L 4 Hargood rd SE3
47 U 8 Hargrave pk N19
47 X 16 Hargrave pl NW5
47 W 7 Hargrave rd N19
36 A 13 Hargville gdns Ilf
90 B 8 Hargwyne st SW9
30 D 13 Haringey gro N8
30 A 19 Haringey pk N8
30 A 14 Haringey rd N8
18 A 12 Harington ter N13
157 W 5 Harland av Croy
114 E 16 Harland av Sidcp
94 E 20 Harland rd SE12
112 F 1 Harland rd SE12
17 O 11 Harlech rd N14
71 Z 17 Harlequin av Brentf
102 A 17 Harlequin rd Tedd
102 A 17 Harlequin rd Tedd
92 F 10 Harlescott rd SE15
62 D 3 Harlesden gdns NW10
62 F 4 Harlesden la NW10
62 H 2 Harlesden rd NW10
44 J 20 Harlesden rd NW10
42 G 17 Harley clo Wemb
146 C 11 Harley gdns SW10
63 Z 9 Harley gro E3
139 W 2 Harley pl W1
62 B 6 Harley rd NW10
130 H 2 Harley rd NW3
23 R 12 Harley rd Harrow
139 X 2 Harley st W1
131 W 19 Harley st W1
112 K 20 Harleyford Brom
149 O 13 Harleyford rd SE11
149 S 15 Harleyford rd SE11
150 G 14 Harling st SE 5
98 A 7 Harlington rd Bxly Hth
18 A 10 Harlow rd N13
21 O 20 Harman av Wdfd Grn
45 T 11 Harman clo NW2
45 T 11 Harman dri NW2
96 L 15 Harman dri Sidcp
8 G 16 Harman rd Enf
30 A 15 Harmiston av N8
47 R 20 Harmood pl NW1
47 R 20 Harmood st NW1
149 W 12 Harmsworth st SE17
14 J 6 Harmsworth way N20
79 Z 6 Harness rd SE18
25 X 4 Harnshaw dri Edg
81 O 14 Harold av Belvdr
149 R 12 Harold pl SE11
51 Z 4 Harold rd E11
65 X 3 Harold rd E13
20 F 2 Harold rd E4
61 X 8 Harold rd NW10
31 V 14 Harold rd N15
30 C 14 Harold rd N8
109 R 16 Harold rd SE19
154 F 9 Harold rd Sutton
34 G 4 Harold rd Wdfd Grn
32 G 16 Haroldstone rd E17
141 V 4 Harp all EC4
142 J 10 Harp la EC3
59 V 12 Harp rd W7
52 K 6 Harpenden rd E12
108 H 5 Harpenden rd SE27

150 C 1 Harper rd SE1
142 B 20 Harper rd SE1
63 S 10 Harpley sq E1
54 B 19 Harpour rd Bark
89 O 3 Harpsden st SW11
133 N 20 Harpur ms WC1
133 N 20 Harpur st WC1
94 L 2 Harraden rd SE3
139 R 20 Harrett st SW1
139 R 19 Harriet wlk SW1
30 J 14 Harringay gdns N15
30 G 15 Harringay pass N8
30 J 14 Harringay rd N15
30 J 13 Harringay rd N15
146 A 7 Harrington gdns SW7
50 B 4 Harrington hill E5
52 A 4 Harrington rd E11
124 B 8 Harrington rd SE25
123 Y 9 Harrington rd SE25
146 E 6 Harrington rd SW7
132 B 9 Harrington sq NW1
98 A 2 Harris rd Bxly Hth
56 B 15 Harris rd Dgnhm
50 L 1 Harris st E17
150 G 19 Harris st SE5
56 F 19 Harrison rd Dgnhm
132 M 14 Harrison st WC1
156 J 5 Harrison's ri Croy
55 R 15 Harrold rd Dgnhm
18 H 1 Harrow av Enf
39 Z 3 Harrow cres Rom
18 G 4 Harrow dri N9
57 Z 3 Harrow dri Hornch
51 Z 9 Harrow grn E11
64 F 20 Harrow la E14
57 V 7 Harrow Lodge park Hornch
80 F 2 Harrow Lodge park Hornch
68 F 20 Harrow Manor way SE2
41 U 6 Harrow pk Harrow
142 M 3 Harrow pl E1
52 D 9 Harrow rd E11
66 D 2 Harrow rd E6
128 D 14 Harrow rd NW10
62 J 8 Harrow rd NW10
138 B 2 Harrow rd W2
129 O 17 Harrow rd W9
67 V 3 Harrow rd Bark
154 J 12 Harrow rd Carsh
54 C 14 Harrow rd Ilf
41 X 12 Harrow rd Wemb
43 P 17 Harrow rd Wemb
23 R 14 Harrow view Harrow
60 C 12 Harrow View rd W5
10 D 18 Harrow Weald pk Harrow
88 F 5 Harroway rd SW11
139 N 4 Harrowby st W1
138 M 4 Harrowby st W1
139 N 4 Harrowby st W1
42 F 14 Harrowdene clo Wemb
42 G 10 Harrowdene rd Wemb
12 D 10 Harrowes meade Edg
50 G 19 Harrowgate rd E9
73 O 2 Hart gro W5
58 G 14 Hart gro S'hall
142 L 8 Hart st EC3
67 O 4 Hart st Bark
141 S 1 Hart yd EC1
82 F 5 Harte rd Hounsl
105 V 17 Hartfield cres SW19
110 B 20 Hartfield gro SE20
105 W 18 Hartfield rd SW19
64 B 7 Hartfield ter E3
24 A 10 Hartford av Harrow
23 Z 10 Hartford av Harrow
98 F 17 Hartford rd Bxly
27 H 14 Hartford wlk N2
48 A 15 Hartham clo N7
83 X 1 Hartham clo Islwth
31 U 6 Hartham rd N17
48 A 15 Hartham rd N7
83 X 2 Hartham rd Islwth
113 P 8 Harting rd SE9
7 Z 4 Hartingdon rd Enf
65 V 17 Hartington rd E16
32 H 19 Hartington rd E17
31 X 6 Hartington rd N17
18 J 10 Hartington rd N8
148 J 20 Hartington rd SW8
89 Z 1 Hartington rd SW8
72 B 1 Hartington rd W13
85 W 3 Hartington rd W4
73 U 20 Hartington rd W4
70 B 7 Hartington rd S'hall
84 B 17 Hartington rd Twick
145 R 17 Hartismore rd SW6

50 G 18 Hartlake rd E9
12 C 9 Hartland clo Edg
12 B 9 Hartland dri Edg
52 B 20 Hartland rd E15
65 O 1 Hartland rd E15
147 R 20 Hartland rd NW1
129 O 7 Hartland rd NW6
15 Z 17 Hartland rd N11
100 K 10 Hartland rd Hampt
57 W 8 Hartland rd Hornch
83 Z 7 Hartland rd Islwth
119 Z 18 Hartland rd Mrdn
158 H 4 Hartland way Croy
158 H 2 Hartland way Croy
119 W 16 Hartland way Mrdn
66 D 4 Hartley av NW7
13 R 17 Hartley av NW7
13 R 17 Hartley clo NW7
127 V 4 Hartley clo Brom
52 C 3 Hartley rd E11
122 K 16 Hartley rd Croy
80 F 18 Hartley rd Welling
63 R 8 Hartley st E2
48 D 15 Hartnoll st N7
19 N 9 Harton rd N9
93 N 1 Harton st SE4
120 L 17 Hartopp av SW4
92 G 1 Harts la SE14
53 Z 18 Harts la Bark
9 O 15 Harts way Enf
10 B 8 Hartsbourne av Bushey Watf
10 D 8 Hartsbourne rd Bushey Watf
142 L 7 Hartshorn all EC3
66 J 11 Hartshorn gdns E6
80 H 4 Hartslock dr SE 2
113 T 3 Hartsmead rd SE9
74 C 7 Hartswood rd W12
79 V 11 Hartville rd SE18
20 F 19 Hartwell dri E4
49 U 17 Hartwell st E8
73 U 15 Harvard hill W4
73 V 15 Harvard la W4
93 V 14 Harvard rd SE13
73 T 14 Harvard rd W4
83 T 3 Harvard rd Islwth
80 J 14 Harvel cres SE2
134 G 5 Harvey ct N1
77 Z 13 Harvey gdns SE7
52 B 3 Harvey rd E11
30 C 15 Harvey rd N8
91 O 1 Harvey rd SE5
82 F 19 Harvey rd Hounsl
53 Z 16 Harvey rd Ilf
54 A 16 Harvey rd Ilf
57 P 6 Harvey's la Rom
115 X 13 Harvill rd Sidcp
128 H 11 Harvist rd NW6
129 O 9 Harviste st NW6
129 N 9 Harviste rd NW6
28 L 12 Harwell pas N2
126 G 3 Harwood av Mitch
120 J 6 Harwood av Mitch
145 V 19 Harwood rd SW6
88 A 1 Harwood ter SW6
18 F 12 Haselbury grn N9
18 E 12 Haselbury la N9
18 F 8 Haselbury rd N9
92 C 20 Haseley end SE23
89 Y 11 Haselrigge rd SW4
110 K 10 Haseltine rd SE26
55 W 13 Haskard rd Dgnhm
55 W 14 Haskard rd Dgnhm
146 M 4 Hasker st SW3
119 T 19 Haslam av Sutton
27 O 18 Haslemere av NW4
106 A 3 Haslemere av SW18
72 A 8 Haslemere av E4
15 Z 6 Haslemere av Barnt
144 F 3 Haslemere av Mitch
71 Z 9 Haslemere Av 1-84 W13
100 F 12 Haslemere clo Hampt
156 A 12 Haslemere clo Wallgtn
156 A 12 Haslemere clo Wallgtn
27 U 11 Haslemere gdns N3
17 V 7 Haslemere rd N21
29 Z 20 Haslemere rd N8
98 C 5 Haslemere rd Bxly Hth
54 K 6 Haslemere rd Ilf
122 H 11 Haslemere rd Thntn Hth
159 U 17 Hasley dri Croy
5 O 19 Hasluck gdns Barnt
135 P 12 Hassard st E2
77 W 18 Hassendean rd SE10
50 G 17 Hassett rd E9
110 A 6 Hassocks clo SE26
145 X 1 Hassocks rd SW16

45 O 11 Hassop rd NW2
13 P 9 Hassop wlk SE9
78 B 13 Hasted rd SE18
36 B 14 Hastings av Ilf
8 N 5 Hastings rd E15
16 J 17 Hastings rd N11
31 O 9 Hastings rd N8
60 B 20 Hastings rd W13
23 Y 17 Hastings rd Croy
39 Y 17 Hastings rd Rom
32 J 14 Hastings rd WC1
26 H 11 Hatch croft NW4
37 Z 13 Hatch gro Rom
20 K 12 Hatch la E4
46 A 3 Hatch rd SW16
9 S 7 Hatch the Enf
75 U 20 Hatcham Pk rd SE14
92 F 1 Hatcham Pk rd SE14
75 P 16 Hatcham rd SE15
47 Z 6 Hatchard rd N19
46 C 8 Hatcliffe rd SE3
35 Z 9 Hatfield clo Ilf
20 E 9 Hatfield clo Mitch
19 X 12 Hatfield mead Mrdn
52 A 14 Hatfield rd E15
71 Y 3 Hatfield rd W13
73 Z 5 Hatfield rd W4
55 Z 20 Hatfield rd Dgnhm
68 M 1 Hatfield rd Dgnhm
134 A 18 Hatfield rd EC1
141 U 12 Hatfields SE1
10 K 17 Hathaway clo Stanm
53 U 17 Hathaway cres E12
59 Y 14 Hathaway gdns W13
37 V 15 Hathaway gdns Rom
122 K 18 Hathaway rd Croy
119 Y 9 Hatherleigh rd Mrdn
115 O 6 Hatherley cres Sidcp
66 B 8 Hatherley gdns E6
137 X 5 Hatherley gro W2
32 M 13 Hatherley rd E17
33 N 12 Hatherley rd E7
85 N 3 Hatherley rd Rich
115 O 8 Hatherley rd Sidcp
148 D 6 Hatherley st SW1
113 W 10 Hathern gdns SE9
100 D 18 Hatherop rd Hampt
92 D 6 Hathway st SE15
36 B 13 Hatley av Ilf
15 Y 15 Hatley clo N11
48 E 7 Hatley rd N4
75 P 5 Hatteraick st SE16
133 T 20 Hatton gdn EC1
141 I 1 Hatton gdn EC1
120 M 11 Hatton gdns Mitch
122 G 19 Hatton rd Croy
130 G 19 Hatton row W2
130 G 18 Hatton st NW 8
133 T 19 Hatton wall EC1
133 U 20 Hatton yd EC1
139 X 7 Haunch Of Venison rd W1
39 R 17 Havana cl Rom
105 Z 4 Havana rd SW19
76 A 6 Havannah st E14
33 U 11 Havant rd E17
23 U 19 Havelock pl Harrow
31 Y 7 Havelock rd N17
106 C 12 Havelock rd SW19
81 O 12 Havelock rd Blvdr
150 L 8 Havelock rd Brom
126 L 8 Havelock rd Brom
157 V 2 Havelock rd Croy
99 Y 18 Havelock rd Drtfrd
23 T 10 Havelock rd Harrow
70 D 8 Havelock rd S'hall
132 M 4 Havelock st Ilf
54 A 8 Havelock st Ilf
89 T 1 Havelock ter SW8
147 Z 20 Havelock ter SW8
110 C 2 Havelock wlk SE23
105 O 6 Haven clo SW19
60 G 19 Haven grn W5
60 J 17 Haven la W5
60 G 19 Haven pl W5
7 T 10 Havenhurst ri Enf
43 U 8 Havenwood Wemb
73 P 19 Haverfield gdns Rich
63 U 8 Haverfield rd E3
25 N 5 Haverford way Edg
20 H 6 Haverhill rd E4
107 V 2 Haverhill rd SW12
107 V 1 Haverhill rd SW4
39 P 11 Havering dri Rom
37 W 14 Havering gdns Rom
38 M 9 Havering rd Rom
39 N 3 Havering rd Rom
63 S 18 Havering st E1
58 D 4 Havering way Bark
84 H 17 Haversham clo Twick
46 K 17 Haverstock hill NW3
47 N 15 Haverstock rd NW5
133 Y 10 Haverstock st N1

126 J 20 Havil st SE5
91 S 1 Havil st SE5
90 L 18 Hawarden gro SE24
32 F 13 Hawarden rd E17
51 W 3 Hawbridge rd E11
125 V 19 Hawes la W Wkham
159 X 1 Hawes la W Wkhm
18 L 19 Hawes rd N18
112 H 20 Hawes rd Brom
133 X 2 Hawes st N1
64 B 14 Hawgood st E3
30 K 9 Hawke Park rd N22
109 P 14 Hawke rd SE19
156 B 16 Hawker clo Croy
116 L 4 Hawkes pass Kingst
106 L 20 Hawkes rd Mitch
86 J 13 Hawkesbury rd SW15
110 K 5 Hawkesfield rd SE23
107 Y 19 Hawkhurst rd SW16
117 X 11 Hawkhurst way New Mald
159 S 2 Hawkhurst way W Wkhm
41 P 1 Hawkins cres Harrow
108 K 5 Hawkley gdns SE27
37 T 19 Hawkridge clo Rom
117 N 4 Hawks rd Kingst
116 M 4 Hawks rd Kingst
44 D 20 Hawkshead rd NW10
74 A 7 Hawkshead rd W4
92 E 13 Hawkslade rd SE15
49 P 8 Hawksley ct N16
49 P 9 Hawksley rd N16
120 H 15 Hawksmoor st W6
20 F 3 Hawksmouth E4
75 R 10 Hawkstone rd SE16
50 A 3 Hawkwood mt E5
40 A 1 Hawlands dri Pinn
40 A 1 Hawlands dri Pinn
131 Y 1 Hawley cres NW1
47 S 20 Hawley rd NW1
47 S 20 Hawley st NW1
93 R 17 Hawstead rd SE6
17 O 16 Hawthorn av N13
122 H 1 Hawthorn av Thntn Hth
100 F 13 Hawthorn clo Hampt
22 G 19 Hawthorn dri Harrow
72 H 8 Hawthorn gdns W5
110 A 19 Hawthorn gro SE20
8 C 4 Hawthorn gro Enf
72 C 20 Hawthorn hatch Brentf
27 S 5 Hawthorn ms NW7
44 H 19 Hawthorn rd NW10
18 F 18 Hawthorn rd N18
29 Y 11 Hawthorn rd N8
72 B 20 Hawthorn rd Brentf
21 Z 14 Hawthorn rd Buck Hl
98 B 12 Hawthorn rd Bxly Hth
154 H 12 Hawthorn rd Sutton
155 T 15 Hawthorn rd Wallgtn
18 F 9 Hawthorn way N9
156 P 16 Hawthorne av Carsh
144 G 3 Hawthorne av Mitch
127 T 7 Hawthorne clo Brom
154 C 3 Hawthorne clo Sutton
58 C 4 Hawthorne Farm av Grnfd
25 W 20 Hawthorne gro NW9
33 O 10 Hawthorne rd E17
127 U 6 Hawthorne rd Brom
21 S 10 Hawthorns Buck Hl
130 K 1 Hawtrey rd NW3
112 H 20 Haxted rd Brom
139 Z 11 Hay Hl W1
25 X 13 Hay la NW9
149 H 13 Hay's la SE1
139 W 11 Hay's mans W1
57 U 4 Hayburn way Hornch
62 H 4 Haycroft gdns NW10
90 B 3 Haycroft rd SW2
64 E 16 Haycurrie st E14
65 S 14 Hayday rd E16
38 K 7 Hayden way Rom
137 N 5 Hayden's pl W11
40 G 17 Haydock av Grnfd
40 G 17 Haydock grn Grnfd
25 W 14 Haydon clo NW9
105 Z 12 Haydon Pk rd SW19
106 A 12 Haydon Pk rd SW19
55 V 7 Haydon rd Dgnhm
143 O 7 Haydon st EC3
106 B 13 Haydon's rd SW19
125 V 19 Hayes chase W Wkhm
94 A 8 Hayes clo SE13
27 V 15 Hayes cres NW11
153 P 7 Hayes cres Sutton
126 A 20 Hayes hill Brom
126 B 20 Hayes Hill rd Brom

125 U 7 Hayes la Becknhm
126 G 14 Hayes la Brom
126 A 20 Hayes mead Brom
125 Z 20 Hayes mead W Wkhm
130 M 19 Hayes pl NW1
126 F 10 Hayes rd Brom
126 G 20 Hayes st Brom
153 P 20 Hayes walk Sutton
125 U 8 Hayes way Becknhm
126 H 20 Hayes Wood av Brom
126 D 12 Hayesford Pk dri Brom
63 S 14 Hayfield pass E1
25 X 14 Hayland clo NW9
149 X 3 Hayles st SE11
49 T 15 Hayling rd N16
133 X 2 Hayman st N1
140 F 11 Haymarket SW1
127 S 15 Haymerle rd SE15
124 L 2 Hayne rd Becknhm
133 Y 20 Hayne st EC1
141 Z 1 Hayne st EC1
109 S 16 Haynes la SE19
42 K 20 Haynes rd Wemb
119 T 5 Haynt wlk SW20
133 P 8 Hays bldgs N1
123 Y 4 Haysleigh gdns SE20
90 C 12 Hayter rd SW2
141 P 13 Hayward Art gallery SE 1
86 M 16 Hayward gdns SW15
87 N 16 Hayward gdns SW15
15 P 8 Hayward rd N20
133 W 17 Hayward's pl EC1
98 M 13 Haywood cl Bxly
141 P 13 Haywood gallery SE1
127 N 8 Haywood rd Brom
18 A 11 Hazel clo N13
91 Y 5 Hazel clo Brentf
72 B 18 Hazel clo Brentf
121 Z 9 Hazel clo Mitch
83 O 18 Hazel clo Twick
99 X 2 Hazel dri Erith
12 E 13 Hazel gdns Edg
110 G 11 Hazel gro SE26
37 X 20 Hazel gro Rom
60 K 5 Hazel gro Wemb
102 J 4 Hazel la Rich
62 L 8 Hazel rd NW10
128 B 12 Hazel rd NW10
99 X 2 Hazel rd Erith
19 X 19 Hazel way E4
127 X 15 Hazel wlk Brom
8 J 19 Hazel Wood rd Enf
112 A 4 Hazelbank rd SE6
111 Z 4 Hazelbank rd SE6
89 T 16 Hazelbank rd SW12
36 F 1 Hazelbrook gdns Ilf
88 A 4 Hazelbury rd SW6
61 Z 1 Hazeldean rd NW10
73 V 16 Hazeldene rd W4
55 P 6 Hazeldene rd Ilf
97 T 5 Hazeldene rd Welling
92 J 13 Hazeldon rd SE4
125 V 1 Hazelhurst Becknhm
106 E 9 Hazelhurst rd SW17
38 G 3 Hazels cres Rom
47 X 2 Hazellville rd N19
129 S 6 Hazelmere way Brom
87 N 12 Hazelwell rd SW15
120 B 9 Hazelwood av Mrdn
72 K 5 Hazelwood clo W5
17 T 13 Hazelwood cres N13
116 J 14 Hazelwood crt Surb
7 W 13 Hazelwood la N13
17 T 13 Hazelwood la N13
32 H 16 Hazelwood rd E17
151 R 4 Hazledean rd Croy
118 H 19 Hazlemere gdns Worc Park
72 H 8 Hazlenut rd W5
86 L 12 Hazlewell rd SW15
128 M 17 Hazlewood cres W10
129 N 18 Hazlewood cres W10
144 K 2 Hazlitt ms W14
144 K 3 Hazlitt rd W14
63 S 16 Head st E1
31 U 2 Headcorn rd N17
112 D 12 Headcorn rd Brom
122 D 8 Headcorn rd Thntn Hth
139 V 19 Headford pl SW1
26 K 12 Heading st NW4
106 E 2 Headington rd SW18
89 X 17 Headlam rd SW4
18 S 16 Headlam st E1
63 N 12 Headlam st E1
35 Y 17 Headley appr Ilf

156 D 10 Headley av Wallgtn
159 T 16 Headley dri Croy
35 Y 17 Headley dri Ilf
36 A 18 Headley dri Ilf
92 A 6 Headley st SE15
23 P 11 Headstone dri Harrow
23 O 12 Headstone gdns Harrow
22 L 8 Headstone la Harrow
22 M 11 Headstone manor Harrow
23 S 18 Headstone rd Harrow
152 D 20 Headway the Epsom
106 C 8 Headworth rd SW17
93 N 2 Heald st SE4
47 S 18 Healey st NW1
150 G 8 Hearn bldgs SE17
134 K 18 Hearn st EC2
73 P 15 Hearne rd W4
89 O 20 Hearnville rd SW12
80 J 17 Heath av Bxly Hth
46 C 8 Heath brow NW3
46 A 2 Heath clo NW11
61 O 12 Heath clo W5
8 C 9 Heath clo Enf
39 W 10 Heath clo Rom
46 A 12 Heath dri NW3
45 Z 13 Heath dri NW3
119 N 8 Heath dri SW20
118 M 8 Heath dri SW20
39 W 8 Heath dri Rom
154 C 19 Heath dri Sutton
101 V 2 Heath gdns Twick
110 B 18 Heath gro SE20
46 J 13 Heath Hurst rd NW3
157 R 19 Heath Hurst rd S Croy
93 H 7 Heath la SE3
105 O 6 Heath mead SW19
39 X 15 Heath Pk rd Rom
89 R 7 Heath rd SW8
53 T 17 Heath rd Drtford
23 N 20 Heath rd Harrow
83 P 10 Heath rd Hounsl
82 L 11 Heath rd Hounsl
55 Y 1 Heath rd Romford
122 M 5 Heath rd Thntn Hth
101 W 2 Heath rd Twick
87 R 16 Heath ri SW15
128 D 14 Heath ri Brom
46 H 11 Heath side NW3
67 N 3 Heath st Barking
28 E 12 Heath view N2
28 D 12 Heath View clo N2
79 W 15 Heath vlle SE18
77 S 20 Heath way SE3
98 L 2 Heath way Erith
21 Z 15 Heath way Wdfd Grn
83 V 19 Heatham pk Twick
10 G 8 Heathbourne rd Stanm
99 V 20 Heathclose av Drtfrd
35 U 7 Heathcote av Ilf
20 F 9 Heathcote gro E4
84 C 14 Heathcote rd Twick
141 N 15 Heathcote st WC1
61 Z 1 Heathcroft NW11
60 M 11 Heathcroft W5
61 N 4 Heathcroft W5
82 B 8 Heathdale av Hounsl
108 C 18 Heathdene rd SW16
155 T 16 Heathdene rd Wallgtn
39 O 7 Heather av Rom
39 N 5 Heather clo Rom
99 V 19 Heather dri Drtfd
39 O 7 Heather dri Rom
27 S 19 Heather gdns NW11
39 O 6 Heather gdns Rom
39 N 7 Heather glen Rom
161 R 2 Heather Pk dri Wemb
44 D 7 Heather rd NW2
112 F 2 Heather rd SE12
39 N 6 Heather way Rom
158 T 18 Heather way S Croy
10 J 20 Heather way Stanm
12 E 16 Heather wlk Edg
95 V 5 Heatherbank SE9
144 H 10 Heatherdean clo Mitch
93 U 13 Heathergrove est SE13
35 S 9 Heatherley dri Ilf
49 W 10 Heatherley pl N16
49 W 11 Heatherley st E5
108 D 19 Heatherset gdns SW16
115 V 6 Heatherside rd Sidcp
20 G 10 Heathfield E4
114 C 16 Heathfield Chisl
158 D 14 Heathfield S Croy

88 G 17 Heathfield ave SW18
73 X 13 Heathfield ct W4
27 P 20 Heathfield gdns NW11
88 F 15 Heathfield gdns SW18
73 V 14 Heathfield gdns W4
114 B 17 Heathfield la Chisl
83 V 17 Heathfield north Twick
44 M 19 Heathfield pk NW2
88 F 16 Heathfield rd SW18
73 S 6 Heathfield rd W3
112 D 18 Heathfield rd Brom
98 A 11 Heathfield rd Bxly Hth
157 N 9 Heathfield rd Croy
83 V 18 Heathfield south Twick
88 F 18 Heathfield sq SW18
136 K 10 Heathfield st W11
136 K 10 Heathfield st W11
79 W 16 Heathfield ter SE18
73 W 13 Heathfield ter W4
158 G 18 Heathfield vale S Croy
28 A 19 Heathgate NW11
27 A 19 Heathgate NW11
49 P 3 Heathland rd N16
99 Y 17 Heathlands ri Drtfrd
94 B 10 Heathlee rd SE3
114 C 15 Heathley end Chisl
87 W 3 Heathmans rd SW6
82 E 19 Heathside Hounsl
98 A 4 Heathside av Bxly Hth
97 Z 3 Heathside av Bxly Hth
62 H 18 Heathstan rd W12
99 S 17 Heathview av Drtfrd
99 X 20 Heathview cres Drtfrd
86 L 19 Heathview gdns SW15
122 F 8 Heathview rd Thntn Hth
48 A 2 Heathville rd N4
88 M 8 Heathwall st SW11
158 M 5 Heathway Croy
56 C 12 Heathway Dgnhm
69 R 2 Heathway Dgnhm
78 D 13 Heathwood gdns SE18
99 O 20 Heathwood lodge Bxly
39 Y 2 Heaton av Rom
39 U 6 Heaton Grange rd Rom
51 V 16 Heaton pl E15
91 Y 6 Heaton rd SE15
107 O 17 Heaton rd Mitch
88 H 6 Heaver rd SW11
79 S 14 Heavitree rd SE18
107 K 7 Hebdon rd SW17
45 O 14 Heber rd NW2
91 V 15 Heber rd SE22
144 A 2 Hebron rd W6
74 L 9 Hebron rd W6
145 T 19 Heckfield pl SW6
63 T 19 Heckford st E1
79 U 12 Hector st SE18
83 Y 9 Heddon clo Islwth
6 A 15 Heddon Court av Bark
5 Z 16 Heddon rd Barnt
140 B 10 Heddon st W1
7 W 6 Hedge hill Enf
17 V 11 Hedge la N13
94 B 12 Hedgeley st SE12
56 C 19 Hedgemans rd Dgnhm
55 W 20 Hedgemans rd Dgnhm
55 Y 19 Hedgemans way Dgnhm
58 M 7 Hedgerly gdns Grnfd
50 H 18 Hedgers gro E9
35 V 14 Hedgewood gdns Ilf
35 T 13 Hedgley Ilf
55 P 16 Hedingham rd Dgnhm
115 R 7 Hedley clo Sidcp
8 A 8 Heene rd Enf
66 C 2 Heigham rd E6
156 J 10 Heighton gdns Croy
77 Z 15 Heights the SE7
40 F 15 Heights the Grnfd
139 Z 15 Heiron st SE17
89 Y 16 Helby rd SW4
94 C 19 Helder gro SE12
157 O 13 Helder st S Croy
83 R 9 Heldman clo Islwth
78 M 11 Helen st SE18

156 C 16 Helena clo Croy
60 G 14 Helena ct W5
65 R 7 Helena rd E13
33 N 17 Helena rd E17
44 J 14 Helena rd NW10
60 H 14 Helena rd W5
5 U 2 Helens clo Barnt
45 X 4 Helenslea av NW11
90 D 15 Helix gdns SW2
90 E 16 Helix rd SW2
143 U 14 Hellings st E1
134 B 14 Helmet row EC1
39 R 2 Helmsdale clo Rom
107 W 19 Helmsdale rd SW16
39 R 1 Helmsdale rd Rom
135 X 1 Helmsley st E8
22 E 3 Helston clo Pinn
110 L 5 Helvetia st E8
90 A 7 Hemberton rd SW9
25 S 1 Heming rd Edg
133 P 2 Hemingford rd N1
153 N 8 Hemingford rd Sutton
15 Y 16 Hemington av N11
62 E 20 Hemlock rd W12
135 U 17 Hemming st E1
126 F 6 Hemp row SE17
21 S 8 Hempstead clo Buck Hl
33 X 9 Hempstead rd E17
63 N 2 Hemsley st E8
45 Y 20 Hemstal rd NW6
134 J 7 Hemsworth st N1
146 K 11 Hemus pl SW3
142 L 5 Henage la EC3
143 P 1 Hencage st E1
62 D 17 Henchman st W12
26 H 10 Hendale av NW4
52 K 17 Henderson rd E7
18 M 4 Henderson rd N9
88 H 18 Henderson rd SW18
123 N 13 Henderson rd Croy
106 K 4 Hendham rd SW17
27 V 6 Hendon av N3
27 U 9 Hendon la N3
13 S 7 Hendon park NW7
27 V 17 Hendon Pk row NW11
18 K 7 Hendon rd N9
11 P 3 Hendon Urban motorway Edg
45 T 6 Hendon way NW2
26 L 18 Hendon way NW4
13 T 4 Hendon Wood la NW7
150 K 7 Hendre rd SE1
88 M 18 Hendrick av SW12
98 E 15 Henfield clo Bxly
119 V 1 Henfield rd SW19
105 V 20 Henfield rd SW19
120 F 9 Hengelo gdns Mitch
94 J 18 Hengist rd SE12
81 X 18 Hengist rd Erith
125 Y 9 Hengist way Brom
92 E 17 Hengrave rd SE23
46 E 12 Heniker ms SW3
153 R 5 Henley av Sutton
59 O 6 Henley clo Grnfd
83 V 3 Henley clo Islwth
104 C 18 Henley dri Kingst
37 Y 15 Henley gdns Rom
78 H 5 Henley rd E16
128 D 3 Henley rd NW10
18 D 13 Henley rd N18
54 B 13 Henley rd Ilf
89 O 4 Henley st SW11
110 E 7 Hennel clo SE23
66 D 7 Henniker gdns E6
66 C 8 Henniker gdns E6
51 Y 15 Henniker rd E15
88 H 3 Henning st SW11
31 P 3 Henningham rd N17
139 W 5 Henrietta pl W 1
31 R 18 Henrietta rd N15
124 K 9 Henrietta st WC2
143 T 6 Henriques st E1
87 O 8 Henry Jackson rd SW15
66 E 6 Henry rd E6
48 K 5 Henry rd N4
5 T 17 Henry rd Barnt
112 J 20 Henry st Brom
21 P 16 Henrys av Wdfd Grn
36 D 2 Henrys wlk Ilf
92 M 13 Henryson rd SE4
93 N 13 Henryson rd SE4
110 A 9 Hensford gdns SE26
49 P 18 Henshall st N1
150 E 5 Henshaw st SE17
55 X 9 Henshawe rd Dgnhm
91 Y 13 Henslowe rd SE22
44 L 14 Henson av NW2
24 G 11 Henson path Harrow

130 J 7 Henstridge pl NW8
86 J 14 Henty wlk SW15
126 J 1 Henville rd Brom
95 P 8 Henwick rd SE9
75 P 9 Henwood rd SE16
51 N 19 Hepscott rd E9
55 N 15 Hepworth gdns Bark
108 B 19 Hepworth rd SW16
155 Z 17 Heracles clo Wallgtn
135 Y 15 Herald st E2
133 T 18 Herbal hill EC1
133 T 18 Herbal pl EC1
147 O 1 Herbert cres SW1
62 J 5 Herbert gdns NW10
128 A 8 Herbert gdns NW10
73 T 17 Herbert gdns W4
55 W 1 Herbert gdns Rom
78 M 16 Herbert pl SE18
53 R 14 Herbert rd E12
32 L 20 Herbert rd E17
26 E 19 Herbert rd NW9
16 M 20 Herbert rd N 11
31 W 15 Herbert rd N15
18 M 8 Herbert rd N9
78 J 19 Herbert rd SE18
105 W 18 Herbert rd SW19
127 P 11 Herbert rd Brom
98 A 5 Herbert rd Bxly Hth
97 Z 4 Herbert rd Bxly Hth
54 G 6 Herbert rd Ilf
116 L 7 Herbert rd Kingst
70 E 2 Herbert rd S'hall
65 T 8 Herbert st E13
47 O 17 Herbert st NW5
78 L 18 Herbert ter SE18
132 J 17 Herbrand st WC1
48 B 10 Hercules pl N7
149 R 1 Hercules rd SE1
48 A 10 Hercules st N7
15 Y 6 Hereford av Barnt
35 S 20 Hereford gdns Ilf
22 B 15 Hereford gdns Pinn
101 N 2 Hereford gdns Twick
137 V 6 Hereford ms W2
75 Y 19 Hereford pl SE14
34 J 15 Hereford rd E11
137 V 5 Hereford rd W2
61 U 19 Hereford rd W3
72 E 9 Hereford rd W5
146 C 7 Hereford sq SW7
135 T 15 Hereford st E2
17 U 17 Hereward gdns N13
106 K 8 Hereward rd SW17
41 T 8 Herga ct Harrow
23 V 12 Herga rd Harrow
20 A 9 Heriot av E4
47 N 14 Heriot pl NW5
26 M 15 Heriot rd NW4
27 N 15 Heriot rd NW4
19 W 16 Heriot way E4
10 L 13 Heriots clo Stanm
106 K 8 Herlwyn gdns SW17
148 H 18 Hermans st SW8
133 R 9 Hermes st N1
155 Y 15 Hermes way Wallgtn
30 A 15 Hermiston av N8
129 W 4 Hermit pl NW6
65 P 13 Hermit rd E16
133 W 12 Hermit st EC1
34 C 13 Hermitage clo E18
7 W 9 Hermitage clo Enf
34 E 13 Hermitage ct E18
45 Y 9 Hermitage gdns NW2
108 M 16 Hermitage gdns SE19
45 X 9 Hermitage la NW2
18 B 17 Hermitage la N18
108 C 19 Hermitage la SW16
123 X 16 Hermitage la Croy
30 K 20 Hermitage rd N4
31 N 18 Hermitage rd N4
108 M 16 Hermitage rd SE19
109 D 14 Hermitage rd SE19
138 F 2 Hermitage st W2
86 E 3 Hermitage the SW13
84 J 14 Hermitage the Rich
143 T 14 Hermitage wall E1
23 Z 5 Hermitage way Stanm
34 C 12 Hermitage wlk E18
34 F 14 Hermon hill E11
88 C 14 Herndon rd SWU8
43 Y 16 Herne la NW10
90 L 14 Herne hill SE24
90 L 9 Herne Hill rd SE24
90 J 14 Herne pl SE24
32 K 7 Heron clo E17
114 H 8 Heron cres Sidcp
126 L 10 Heron ct Brom
84 G 14 Heron ct Rich
81 P 12 Heron hill Belvdr

53 Y 2 Heron mews Ilf
44 B 19 Heron rd NW10
90 K 10 Heron rd SE24
83 Z 11 Heron rd Twick
84 A 11 Heron rd Twick
21 Y 15 Heron way Wdfd Gr
106 H 1 Herondale av SW18
8 F 9 Herongate clo Enf
52 L 7 Herongate rd E12
21 T 4 Herons clo Buck Hl
12 C 17 Herons ga Edg
60 D 16 Heronsforde W13
11 W 16 Heronslea dri Stanm
48 L 9 Herrick rd N5
148 H 7 Herrick st SW1
129 N 13 Herries st W10
128 M 11 Herries st W10
150 L 14 Herring st SE5
77 Y 9 Herringham rd SE7
78 A 8 Herringham rd SE7
62 H 3 Hersant clo NW10
92 G 13 Herschell rd SE13
86 G 19 Hersham clo SW15
9 P 9 Hertfield rd Enf
85 Z 12 Hertford av SW14
86 A 11 Hertford av SW13
5 T 11 Hertford clo Barnt
132 B 19 Hertford pl W1
66 L 1 Hertford rd E6
144 L 2 Hertford rd N1
49 T 20 Hertford rd N1
28 J 10 Hertford rd N2
18 L 8 Hertford rd N9
53 X 20 Hertford rd Bark
5 S 11 Hertford rd Barnt
36 G 18 Hertford rd Ilf
139 V 14 Hertford st W1
121 Z 10 Hertford way Mitch
48 C 11 Hertslet rd N7
27 Y 4 Hervey clo N3
32 J 12 Hervey pk E17
94 G 2 Hervey rd SE3
94 G 2 Hervey rd SE3
27 Y 5 Hervey wlk N3
136 J 10 Hesketh pl W11
52 E 11 Hesketh rd E7
107 N 2 Heslop rd SW12
145 Y 8 Hesper ms SW5
76 D 11 Hesperus cres E14
71 Z 6 Hessel rd W13
74 A 5 Hessel rd W13
143 V 5 Hessel st E1
18 J 17 Hester rd N18
146 K 18 Hester rd SW11
87 T 3 Hestercombe av SW6
70 C 18 Heston av Hounsl
70 G 15 Heston av Hounsl
70 H 19 Heston rd Hounsl
92 M 2 Heston st SE4
93 N 2 Heston st SE4
89 Z 11 Hetherington rd SW4
74 J 4 Hetley rd W12
74 L 11 Hetton st W6
113 X 10 Hever croft SE9
127 W 4 Hever gdns Brom
79 U 11 Hever rd SE16
98 E 3 Heversham rd Bxly Hth
128 H 20 Hewer st W10
11 O 13 Hewett clo Stanm
55 V 13 Hewett rd Dgnhm
134 K 18 Hewett st EC2
18 D 14 Hewish rd N18
30 H 8 Hewitt av N22
30 H 16 Hewitt rd N8
63 W 6 Hewlett rd E3
111 Z 6 Hexal rd SE6
71 Z 19 Hexham gdns Islwth
108 L 4 Hexham rd SE27
5 O 14 Hexham rd Barnt
119 Z 18 Hexham rd Mrdn
32 A 2 Heybourne rd N17
108 B 17 Heybridge av SW16
36 E 9 Heybridge gdns Ilf
148 M 17 Heyford av SW20
119 W 7 Heyford av SW8
120 K 2 Heyford rd Mitch
148 L 17 Heyford ter SW8
150 A 6 Heygate st SE17
55 T 12 Heynes rd Dgnhm
31 P 19 Heysham rd N15
105 W 3 Heythorp st SW18
52 B 14 Heyworth rd E15
49 Z 11 Heyworth rd E5
50 L 2 Hibbert rd E17
23 W 7 Hibbert rd Harrow
88 E 9 Hibbert st SW11
82 H 12 Hibernia gdns Hounsl
82 H 12 Hibernia rd Hounsl
92 E 12 Hichisson rd SE15
76 F 7 Hickin st E14

53 Z14 Hickling rd Ilf
55 T1 Hickman rd Rom
59 S8 Hicks av Grnfd
75 V13 Hicks st SE8
148 E6 Hide pl SW1
23 P13 Hide st Harrow
157 S17 High beech S Croy
15 Z12 High beeches Sidcp
125 R17 High Broom cres W Wkhm
31 V11 High Cross rd N17
86 H20 High Cross way SW15
117 W1 High dri New Mald
21 R17 High elms Wdfd Grn
21 R17 High elms Wdfd Grn
95 F1 High gro SE18
5 S20 High gro S18
79 S20 High grove S18
50 B3 High Hill ferry E5
140 K4 High holborn WC1
141 P2 High holborn WC1
59 R17 High la W7
109 X10 High Level dri SE26
62 M14 High Lever rd W10
23 U15 High mead Harrow
159 Y3 High mead W Wkhm
25 X16 High Meadow cres NW9
7 R4 High oaks Enf
85 P3 High Park av Rich
85 P3 High Park rd Rich
106 B20 High path SW19
116 H20 High Pk cres SE17
34 E7 High rd E18
44 J18 High rd NW10
16 E16 High rd N11
28 E1 High rd N12
31 V4 High rd N17
15 R11 High rd N20/N12
30 D6 High rd N22
10 C5 High rd Bushey Watf
23 S3 High rd Harrow
53 Y9 High rd Ilf
54 B8 High rd Ilf
116 F4 High rd Kingst
37 X20 High rd Rom
55 O2 High rd Rom
21 S18 High rd Wdfd Grn
42 L16 High rd Wemb
28 G7 High Rd e.finchley N12
33 R19 High Rd leyton E10
51 S5 High Rd leyton E10
51 U13 High Rd leyton E15
51 Y11 High Rd leytonstone E11
52 B2 High Rd leytonstone E11
28 E2 High Rd n.finchley N12
34 F16 High st E11
65 T7 High st E13
51 X20 High st E15
54 G4 High st E15
33 N13 High st E17
62 F6 High st NW10
13 X15 High st NW7
16 K7 High st N14
110 D17 High st SE20
147 V8 High st SE25
105 R13 High st SW19
87 U7 High st SW6
73 U3 High st W3
36 C9 High st Barkingside Ilf
4 G12 High st Barnt
125 N2 High st Becknhm
126 F5 High st Brom
155 O9 High st Carsh
114 A16 High st Chisl
166 M5 High st Croy
169 S1 High st Croy
9 P17 High st Enf
101 N15 High st Hampt
41 T4 High st Harrow
23 T7 High st Harrow
82 K8 High st Hounsl
82 L8 High st Hounsl
116 G6 High st Kingst
118 C9 High st New Mald
22 B11 High st Pinn
39 O16 High st Rom
70 G2 High st S'hall
115 O10 High st Sidcp
153 T14 High st Sutton
154 B9 High st Sutton
101 X13 High st Tedd
123 O8 High st Thntn Hth
122 M8 High st Thntn Hth
82 M18 High st Twick
183 W18 High st Twick
43 N13 High st Wemb

42 M13 High st Wemb
116 E3 High St hamptonwick Kingst
30 C13 High St hornsey N8
53 P14 High St north E12
66 F4 High St north E6
66 F5 High St south E6
142 A9 High Timber st EC4
108 P1 High trees SW2
124 J19 High trees Croy
123 T3 High View clo SE19
34 A9 High View rd E18
115 R9 High View rd Sidcp
40 E3 High worple Harrow
32 J10 Higham Hill rd E17
32 H9 Higham pl E17
31 O9 Higham rd N17
21 S20 Higham rd Wdfd Grn
20 C19 Higham Stn av E4
20 F18 Highams park E4
21 N16 Highams park E4
80 B20 Highbanks clo Welling
147 W19 Highbarrow rd Croy
76 K14 Highbridge SE10
66 M4 Highbridge rd Bark
94 M7 Highbrook rd SE3
95 N7 Highbrook rd SE3
122 H3 Highbury av Thntn Hth
117 W10 Highbury clo New Mald
159 S3 Highbury clo W Wkhm
48 H17 Highbury cres N5
54 G6 Highbury gdns Ilf
48 K13 Highbury grange N5
48 K16 Highbury gro N5
48 G11 Highbury hill N5
48 M16 Highbury New pk N5
48 K11 Highbury pk N5
48 H17 Highbury pl N5
48 K10 Highbury quadrant N5
105 T12 Highbury rd SW19
48 G19 Highbury Stn rd N1
48 J15 Highbury ter N5
48 H15 Highbury Ter ms N5
110 H10 Highclare st SE25
117 Y7 Highclere rd New Mald
86 E16 Highcliffe dri SW15
35 R16 Highcliffe gdns Ilf
77 W16 Highcombe SE7
113 P2 Highcombe clo SE9
25 Z15 Highcroft NW9
61 O1 Highcroft av Wemb
27 V10 Highcroft gdns NW11
48 A2 Highcroft rd N4
122 R8 Highdaun dri Mitch
152 C2 Highdown Worc Pk
86 J15 Highdown rd SW15
27 S19 Highfield av NW11
25 W10 Highfield av NW9
81 W17 Highfield av Erith
41 U16 Highfield av Grnfd
22 D16 Highfield av Pinn
42 L8 Highfield av Wemb
25 W15 Highfield clo NW9
116 E20 Highfield clo Surb
6 H19 Highfield ct N14
126 A8 Highfield dri Brom
152 D14 Highfield dri Epsom
159 T4 Highfield dri W Wkhm
27 S19 Highfield gdns NW11
109 P19 Highfield hill SE19
27 T18 Highfield rd NW11
17 W7 Highfield rd N21
61 U13 Highfield rd W3
127 T10 Highfield rd Brom
98 C14 Highfield rd Bxly Hth
83 U1 Highfield rd Islwth
117 U17 Highfield rd Surb
154 J10 Highfield rd Sutton
35 R3 Highfield rd Wdfd Grn
29 S20 Highgate av N6
47 O4 Highgate clo N6
47 R3 Highgate High st N6
47 U5 Highgate hill N19
47 S13 Highgate rd NW5
47 O6 Highgate West hill N6
47 O7 Highgate West hill N6
55 S14 Highgrove rd Dgnhm
59 T16 Highland av W7
56 K9 Highland av Dgnhm

111 R13 Highland croft Becknhm
109 R15 Highland rd SE19
126 B1 Highland rd Brom
112 B19 Highland rd Brom
98 E12 Highland rd Bxly Hth
61 V20 Highlands av W3
82 U3 Highlands clo Hounsl
53 T2 Highlands gdns Ilf
84 L20 Highlands heath SW15
4 M16 Highlands rd Barnt
25 T6 Highlands the Edg
79 X20 Highmead SE18
42 M20 Highmead cres Wemb
77 N18 Highmore rd SE3
91 W3 Highshore rd SE15
34 E20 Highstone av E11
12 M11 Highview NW7
12 G14 Highview av Edg
156 C11 Highview av Waltgn
16 H17 Highview gdns N11
27 S11 Highview gdns N3
12 G14 Highview gdns Edg
109 P16 Highview rd SE19
55 Z10 Highview rd W10
143 W10 Highway the E1
63 S20 Highway the E1
23 X1 Highway the Stanm
154 D20 Highway the Sutton
31 T16 Highweek rd N15
15 R13 Highwood av N12
35 U14 Highwood gdns Ilf
12 M15 Highwood gro NW7
13 S10 Highwood hill NW7
13 R9 Highwood house NW7
47 Z10 Highwood rd N19
16 L17 Highworth rd N11
121 N5 Hilary av Mitch
145 X19 Hilary clo SW6
98 H2 Hilary clo Bxly Hth
62 D20 Hilary rd W12
153 P6 Hilbert rd Sutton
135 O2 Hilborough rd E8
65 N12 Hilda rd E16
66 A1 Hilda rd E6
112 B14 Hildenborough gdns Brom
90 F4 Hilder rd SW9
107 R1 Hildreth st SW12
145 U14 Hildyard rd SW6
62 L8 Hiley rd NW10
128 B11 Hiley rd NW10
130 D2 Hilgrove rd NW6
24 E8 Hiliary gdns Stanm
127 P2 Hill brow Brom
113 O20 Hill brow Chisl
99 U17 Hill brow Drtfrd
27 Z18 Hill clo NW11
44 J10 Hill clo NW2
113 Y12 Hill clo Chisl
41 T11 Hill clo Harrow
11 N3 Hill clo Stanm
40 H15 Hill court Grnfd
15 N7 Hill cres N20
23 Y16 Hill cres Harrow
117 O10 Hill cres Surb
153 N3 Hill cres Worc Pk
57 V1 Hill crest Hornch
97 O19 Hill crest Sidcp
44 F10 Hill Crest gdns NW2
43 U4 Hill dri NW9
146 C5 Hill dri SW16
95 X2 Hill end SE18
136 E1 Hill Farm rd W10
128 E20 Hill Farm rd W 10
39 P9 Hill gro Rom
23 W1 Hill Ho av Stanm
108 D13 Hill Ho rd SW16
17 T2 Hill House clo N21
108 D13 Hill path SW16
130 D10 Hill rd NW8
29 N6 Hill rd N10
154 K14 Hill rd Carsh
23 Y16 Hill rd Harrow
107 T19 Hill rd Mitch
22 A17 Hill rd Pinn
154 A11 Hill rd Sutton
42 A8 Hill rd Wemb
28 B14 Hill ri NW11
59 O2 Hill ri Grnfd
84 H14 Hill ri Rich
139 V12 Hill st W1
84 H14 Hill st Rich
28 B13 Hill top NW11
119 T18 Hill top Sutton
35 T18 Hill View cres Ilf
96 G4 Hill View dri Welling
25 Y15 Hill View gdns NW9
14 B14 Hill View rd NW7

70 H8 Hillary rd S'hall
70 H7 Hillary rd S'hall
127 Z16 Hillbeck clo SE15
59 P3 Hillbeck way Grnfd
109 O9 Hillbrook rd SW17
128 E7 Hillbrow New Mald
111 Z16 Hillbrow rd Brom
24 C16 Hilbury av Harrow
107 T6 Hilbury rd SW17
68 E18 Hillcote av SW16
15 N18 Hillcourt av N12
91 Z17 Hillcourt rd SE22
17 U2 Hillcrest N21
29 P20 Hillcrest N6
27 U14 Hillcrest av NW11
12 E14 Hillcrest av Edg
124 K13 Hillcrest clo Becknhm
27 S11 Hillcrest gdns N3
33 Y7 Hillcrest rd E17
34 D7 Hillcrest rd E18
109 X11 Hillcrest rd SE26
73 R3 Hillcrest rd W3
60 L13 Hillcrest rd W5
112 E11 Hillcrest rd Brom
99 S18 Hillcrest rd Drtfd
30 Y20 Hillcrest rd Hornch
124 K14 Hillcrest view Becknhm
22 E20 Hillcroft av Pinn
60 H16 Hillcroft cres W5
42 M12 Hillcroft cres Wemb
43 N12 Hillcroft cres Wemb
154 G13 Hillcroome rd Sutton
119 S11 Hillcross av Mrdn
153 V9 Hilldale rd Sutton
108 B17 Hilldown rd SW16
126 B19 Hilldown rd Brom
47 Y15 Hilldrop cres N1
47 Y15 Hilldrop la N1
47 Z14 Hilldrop rd N1
112 G15 Hilldrop rd Brom
95 Y3 Hillend SE18
86 F4 Hillersdon av SW13
12 A16 Hillersdon av Edg
150 F7 Hillery rd SE17
20 D15 Hillfield av NW0
30 B13 Hillfield av N8
120 H13 Hillfield av Mrdn
42 M20 Hillfield av Wemb
23 N13 Hillfield clo Harrow
46 J16 Hillfield ct NW3
29 S12 Hillfield pk N10
17 S9 Hillfield pk N21
45 X14 Hillfield rd NW6
100 D19 Hillfield rd Hampt
38 K5 Hillfoot av Rom
38 J5 Hillfoot rd Rom
137 T13 Hillgate pl W8
137 T13 Hillgate st W8
76 O2 Hilliards ct E1
143 Z13 Hilliards ct E1
5 N20 Hillier clo Barnt
156 G11 Hillier gdns Croy
88 M15 Hillier rd SW11
89 N16 Hillier rd SW11
155 Z6 Hilliers la Wallgtn
98 L8 Hillingdon rd Bxly Hth
149 W17 Hillingdon st SE5
35 O7 Hillington gdns Wdfd Grn
50 A18 Hillman st E8
48 A14 Hillmarton rd N7
110 G12 Hillmore gro SE26
78 E13 Hillreach SE18
47 Z1 Hillrise rd N19
140 B6 Hills pl W1
21 V6 Hills rd Buck Hl
91 S13 Hillsboro rd SE22
61 W2 Hillside NW10
25 X14 Hillside NW9
105 P16 Hillside SW19
5 S17 Hillside Barnt
15 Z18 Hillside av N11
21 X18 Hillside av Wdfd Grn
42 L12 Hillside av Wemb
143 S8 Hillside clo Mrdn
21 Y17 Hillside clo Wdfd Grn
8 B2 Hillside cres Enf
40 M5 Hillside cres Harrow
12 B18 Hillside dri Edg
31 U20 Hillside est N15
33 X9 Hillside gdns E17
29 R19 Hillside gdns N6
108 F4 Hillside gdns SW2
4 E16 Hillside gdns Barnt
12 A14 Hillside gdns Edg
42 K1 Hillside gdns Harrow
155 V17 Hillside gdns Wallgtn
26 F1 Hillside gro NW7
16 K3 Hillside gro N14
31 T19 Hillside rd N15

| | |
|---|---|
| 108 F 3 | Hillside rd SW2 |
| 60 J 15 | Hillside rd W5 |
| 150 B 5 | Hillside rd Brom |
| 156 J 8 | Hillside rd Croy |
| 99 V 15 | Hillside rd Drtfrd |
| 58 G 11 | Hillside rd S'hall |
| 117 O 10 | Hillside rd Surb |
| 153 V 16 | Hillside rd Sutton |
| 137 R 13 | Hillsleigh rd W8 |
| 50 E 8 | Hillstowe st E5 |
| 45 Y 19 | Hilltop rd NW6 |
| 10 L 11 | Hilltop way Stanm |
| 104 J 19 | Hillview SW20 |
| 24 J 16 | Hillview av Harrow |
| 27 R 13 | Hillview gdns NW4 |
| 22 H 11 | Hillview gdns Harrow |
| 113 X 11 | Hillview rd Chisl |
| 22 D 1 | Hillview rd Pinn |
| 22 E 2 | Hillview rd Pinn |
| 154 E 4 | Hillview rd Sutton |
| 83 Y 16 | Hillview rd Twick |
| 44 A 2 | Hillway NW9 |
| 47 P 7 | Hillway N6 |
| 90 F 9 | Hillworth rd SW2 |
| 93 N 9 | Hilly Fields cres SE4 |
| 7 X 1 | Hilly Fields park Enf |
| 59 U 14 | Hillyard rd W13 |
| 90 E 3 | Hillyard st SW9 |
| 50 C 11 | Hilsea st E5 |
| 15 U 18 | Hilton av N12 |
| 91 S 11 | Hilversum cres SE22 |
| 106 K 14 | Himley rd SW17 |
| 156 C 14 | Hinchliffe clo Croy |
| 91 W 9 | Hinckley rd SE15 |
| 81 Z 18 | Hind cres Erith |
| 141 U 5 | Hind ct EC4 |
| 64 B 17 | Hind gro E14 |
| 129 U 4 | Hinde st W1 |
| 23 R 17 | Hindes rd Harrow |
| 58 B 3 | Hindhead gdns Grnfd |
| 156 A 10 | Hindhead way Croy |
| 91 X 13 | Hindmans rd SE22 |
| 69 O 10 | Hindmans way Dgnhm |
| 50 A 15 | Hindrey pl E5 |
| 110 D 3 | Hindsleys pl SE23 |
| 156 B 17 | Hinkler clo Croy |
| 24 G 11 | Hinkler rd Harrow |
| 79 P 18 | Hinstock rd SE18 |
| 82 A 10 | Hinton av Hounsl |
| 18 D 14 | Hinton rd N18 |
| 90 K 9 | Hinton rd SE24 |
| 155 V 14 | Hinton rd Wallgtn |
| 136 L 11 | Hippodrome pl W11 |
| 50 K 3 | Hitcham rd E17 |
| 93 V 14 | Hither Green la SE13 |
| 108 E 5 | Hitherfield rd SW16 |
| 55 Y 7 | Hitherfield rd Dgnhm |
| 23 O 4 | Hitherwell dri Harrow |
| 109 U 10 | Hitherwood dri SE19 |
| 10 E 9 | Hive rd Bushey Watf |
| 107 X 5 | Hoadly rd SW16 |
| 15 W 8 | Hobart clo N20 |
| 123 N 6 | Hobart gdns Thntn Hth |
| 147 W 2 | Hobart pl SW1 |
| 55 X 12 | Hobart rd Dgnhm |
| 36 C 8 | Hobart rd Ilf |
| 152 J 5 | Hobart rd Worc Pk |
| 86 J 14 | Hobbes wlk SW15 |
| 28 E 10 | Hobbs grn N2 |
| 109 N 11 | Hobbs rd SE27 |
| 64 C 16 | Hobday st E14 |
| 114 H 15 | Hoblands end Chisl |
| 135 R 20 | Hobson pl E1 |
| 135 N 14 | Hocker st E2 |
| 66 D 6 | Hockley av E6 |
| 45 U 10 | Hocroft av NW2 |
| 45 V 10 | Hocroft wlk NW2 |
| 59 W 6 | Hodder dri Grnfd |
| 81 S 14 | Hoddesdon rd Blvdr |
| 45 W 3 | Hodford rd NW11 |
| 75 R 10 | Hodnet gro SE16 |
| 149 Y 7 | Hodson pl SE17 |
| 8 L 4 | Hoe la Enf |
| 9 P 3 | Hoe la Enf |
| 33 O 12 | Hoe st E17 |
| 144 J 1 | Hofland rd W14 |
| 38 B 2 | Hog Hill rd Rom |
| 122 M 17 | Hogarth cres Croy |
| 142 K 7 | Hogarth ct EC 3 |
| 70 H 20 | Hogarth gdns Hounsl |
| 27 W 13 | Hogarth hill NW11 |
| 74 A 16 | Hogarth la W 4 |
| 145 W 6 | Hogarth rd SW5 |
| 25 O 6 | Hogarth rd Edg |
| 18 E 8 | Hoggin rd E8 |
| 96 J 16 | Holbeach gdns Sidcp |
| 93 R 18 | Holbeach rd SE6 |
| 151 U 19 | Holbeck row SE15 |
| 147 S 8 | Holbein ms SW1 |
| 147 S 9 | Holbein ms SW1 |
| 147 S 9 | Holbein pl SW1 |

| | |
|---|---|
| 62 J 8 | Holberton gdns NW10 |
| 141 T 2 | Holborn EC1 |
| 141 S 2 | Holborn bldgs EC4 |
| 65 V 13 | Holborn rd E13 |
| 141 W 3 | Holborn viaduct EC1 |
| 8 J 4 | Holbrook clo Enf |
| 114 G 19 | Holbrook la Chisl |
| 65 O 5 | Holbrook rd E15 |
| 127 U 13 | Holbrook way Brom |
| 94 K 3 | Holburne clo SE3 |
| 94 M 3 | Holburne gdns SE3 |
| 94 K 4 | Holburne rd SE3 |
| 94 L 3 | Holburne rd SE3 |
| 95 P 3 | Holburne rd SE3 |
| 13 T 11 | Holcombe hill NW7 |
| 31 W 9 | Holcombe rd N17 |
| 53 W 2 | Holcombe rd Ilf |
| 74 K 12 | Holcombe st W6 |
| 63 R 1 | Holcroft rd E9 |
| 43 W 4 | Holden av NW9 |
| 15 N 15 | Holden av N12 |
| 64 C 9 | Holden rd E3 |
| 15 N 13 | Holden rd N12 |
| 89 O 6 | Holden st SW11 |
| 92 J 13 | Holdenby rd SE4 |
| 28 C 2 | Holdenhurst av N12 |
| 108 K 13 | Holderness way SE27 |
| 107 N 5 | Holdernesse rd SW17 |
| 27 P 9 | Holders Hill av NW4 |
| 27 S 3 | Holders Hill circus NW7 |
| 27 P 8 | Holders Hill cres NW4 |
| 27 R 9 | Holders Hill dri NW4 |
| 27 R 8 | Holders Hill gdns NW4 |
| 27 S 4 | Holders Hill rd NW7 |
| 46 E 9 | Holford rd NW3 |
| 133 R 11 | Holford st WC1 |
| 88 F 8 | Holgate av SW11 |
| 56 D 17 | Holgate gdns Dgnhm |
| 56 D 16 | Holgate rd Dgnhm |
| 104 E 20 | Holland av SW20 |
| 153 X 19 | Holland av Sutton |
| 15 T 1 | Holland clo Barnt |
| 144 L 1 | Holland gdns W14 |
| 149 V 19 | Holland gro SW9 |
| 145 O 2 | Holland ms W14 |
| 137 P 17 | Holland park W8 |
| 137 N 15 | Holland pk W11 |
| 136 M 15 | Holland pk W14 |
| 137 O 14 | Holland Pk av W11 |
| 136 J 16 | Holland Pk av W11 |
| 36 J 18 | Holland Pk av Ilf |
| 136 L 16 | Holland Pk gdns W14 |
| 137 N 15 | Holland Pk ms W11 |
| 145 P 2 | Holland Pk rd W14 |
| 137 W 17 | Holland pl W8 |
| 65 N 8 | Holland rd E15 |
| 66 J 2 | Holland rd E6 |
| 62 H 5 | Holland rd NW10 |
| 30 A 14 | Holland rd N8 |
| 123 Y 10 | Holland rd SE 25 |
| 136 K 19 | Holland rd W14 |
| 145 N 2 | Holland rd W14 |
| 42 F 19 | Holland rd Wemb |
| 137 U 18 | Holland st W8 |
| 73 T 5 | Holland ter W11 |
| 136 L 19 | Holland Vlls rd W14 |
| 137 P 14 | Holland wlk W8 |
| 137 P 14 | Holland wlk W8 |
| 137 R 16 | Holland wlk W8 |
| 10 M 16 | Holland wlk Stanm |
| 118 E 20 | Hollands the Worc Pk |
| 152 D 1 | Hollands the Worc Pk |
| 49 U 9 | Hollar rd N16 |
| 140 D 5 | Hollen st W1 |
| 139 Y 5 | Holles st W1 |
| 15 Y 5 | Holles st W1 |
| 15 Y 19 | Hollick Wood av N12 |
| 56 G 20 | Hollidge way Dgnhm |
| 114 J 2 | Hollies av Sidcp |
| 114 J 2 | Hollies av Sidcp |
| 100 M 14 | Hollies clo Hampt |
| 72 D 11 | Hollies rd W5 |
| 114 L 1 | Hollies the Sidcp |
| 89 P 17 | Hollies the Sidcp |
| 112 F 20 | Holligrave rd Brom |
| 98 B 1 | Hollingbourne av Bxly Hth |
| 60 A 15 | Hollingbourne gdns W13 |
| 90 L 14 | Hollingbourne rd SE24 |
| 158 A 14 | Hollingsworth rd Croy |
| 48 E 17 | Hollingsworth st N7 |

| | |
|---|---|
| 118 E 15 | Hollington cres New Mald |
| 66 F 9 | Hollington rd E6 |
| 31 X 6 | Hollington rd N17 |
| 127 Z 16 | Hollingworth rd Brom |
| 51 Y 9 | Holloway rd E11 |
| 66 H 9 | Holloway rd E6 |
| 47 X 7 | Holloway rd N19 |
| 48 B 13 | Holloway rd N7 |
| 143 R 5 | Holloway st E1 |
| 82 L 7 | Holloway st Hounsl |
| 73 N 15 | Hollows the Brentf |
| 24 K 8 | Holly av Stanm |
| 24 K 9 | Holly av Stanm |
| 114 D 19 | Holly Brake clo Chisl |
| 46 D 11 | Holly Bush hill NW3 |
| 100 G 18 | Holly Bush la Hampt |
| 100 C 12 | Holly clo Felt |
| 148 L 13 | Holly cres Becknhm |
| 33 X 1 | Holly cres Wdfd Grn |
| 20 E 2 | Holly dri E4 |
| 43 W 1 | Holly gro NW9 |
| 91 W 4 | Holly gro SE15 |
| 46 D 12 | Holly hill NW3 |
| 7 P 19 | Holly hill N21 |
| 81 X 13 | Holly Hill rd Blvdr |
| 44 A 19 | Holly la NW10 |
| 47 P 6 | Holly Lodge gdns N6 |
| 46 D 11 | Holly mt NW3 |
| 16 B 15 | Holly Park rd N11 |
| 27 W 10 | Holly pk N3 |
| 48 B 2 | Holly pk N4 |
| 27 X 10 | Holly Pk gdns N3 |
| 71 V 1 | Holly Pk rd W7 |
| 34 D 20 | Holly rd E11 |
| 73 Y 12 | Holly rd W4 |
| 100 M 14 | Holly rd Hampt |
| 82 L 9 | Holly rd Hounsl |
| 101 X 1 | Holly rd Twick |
| 49 V 19 | Holly st E8 |
| 135 O 1 | Holly st E8 |
| 15 R 9 | Holly ter N20 |
| 121 X 7 | Holly way Mitch |
| 46 D 12 | Holly wlk NW3 |
| 100 G 13 | Hollybank clo Hampt |
| 34 D 16 | Hollybush clo E11 |
| 135 Y 12 | Hollybush gdns E2 |
| 63 N 8 | Hollybush gdns E2 |
| 34 D 16 | Hollybush hill E11 |
| 63 N 8 | Hollybush pl E2 |
| 102 L 13 | Hollybush rd Kingst |
| 65 W 8 | Hollybush st E13 |
| 46 D 12 | Hollybush vlls NW3 |
| 45 Y 10 | Hollycroft av NW3 |
| 42 M 8 | Hollycroft av Wemb |
| 92 B 4 | Hollydale rd SE15 |
| 51 X 9 | Hollydown way E11 |
| 70 A 13 | Hollyfarm rd S'hall |
| 15 Z 18 | Hollyfield av N11 |
| 117 N 17 | Hollyfield av N11 |
| 116 M 19 | Hollyfield rd Surb |
| 117 N 17 | Hollyfield rd Surb |
| 10 D 3 | Hollygrove Bushey Watf |
| 93 V 12 | Hollyhouse ter SE13 |
| 154 L 7 | Hollymead Carsh |
| 93 U 2 | Hollymount cres SE10 |
| 96 L 18 | Hollyoak Wood park Sidcp |
| 105 P 1 | Hollytree clo SW19 |
| 19 W 16 | Hollywood rd E4 |
| 146 B 13 | Hollywood rd SW10 |
| 33 X 1 | Hollywood way Wdfd Grn |
| 88 F 5 | Holman rd SW11 |
| 9 T 14 | Holmbridge gdns Enf |
| 27 R 14 | Holmbrook dri NW4 |
| 50 F 15 | Holmbrook st E8 |
| 106 L 7 | Holmbury ct SW17 |
| 50 A 3 | Holmbury view E5 |
| 87 S 16 | Holmbush rd SW15 |
| 150 E 15 | Holmby st SE17 |
| 127 U 13 | Holmcote gdns N5 |
| 27 R 15 | Holmcroft way Brom |
| 45 Y 15 | Holmdale gdns NW4 |
| 113 B 13 | Holmdale rd NW6 |
| 31 T 19 | Holmdale rd Chisl |
| 13 U 19 | Holmdale ter N15 |
| 90 M 13 | Holmdene av NW7 |
| 91 N 14 | Holmdene av SE24 |
| 22 J 11 | Holmdene av SE24 |
| 149 T 4 | Holmdene av Harrow |
| 94 C 16 | Holmdene clo Becknhm |
| 66 E 3 | Holme Lacey rd SE12 |
| 10 J 19 | Holme rd E6 |
| 145 Z 19 | Holme way Stanm |
| 10 E 8 | Holmead rd SW6 |
| 32 K 10 | Holmebury clo Bushey Watf |
| | Holmes av E17 |

| | |
|---|---|
| 47 T 16 | Holmes rd NW5 |
| 101 W 4 | Holmes rd Twick |
| 141 T 17 | Holmes ter SE1 |
| 10 E 8 | Holmesbury clo Bushey Watf |
| 85 U 9 | Holmesdale av SW14 |
| 123 U 7 | Holmesdale clo SE25 |
| 16 C 14 | Holmesdale rd N11 |
| 29 T 20 | Holmesdale rd N6 |
| 123 U 7 | Holmesdale rd SE25 |
| 127 N 6 | Holmesdale rd Brom |
| 97 W 5 | Holmesdale rd Bxly Hth |
| 85 N 2 | Holmesdale rd Rich |
| 102 D 16 | Holmesdale rd Tedd |
| 92 H 15 | Holmesley rd SE23 |
| 114 G 17 | Holmewood cres Chisl |
| 123 S 7 | Holmewood rd SE25 |
| 90 B 20 | Holmewood rd SW2 |
| 27 Y 14 | Holmfield NW11 |
| 27 P 15 | Holmfield av NW4 |
| 36 H 16 | Holmfield av Ilf |
| 81 V 13 | Holmhurst rd Belv |
| 49 T 3 | Holmleigh rd N16 |
| 99 R 7 | Holmsdale gro Bxly Hth |
| 16 D 14 | Holmsdale rd N11 |
| 126 M 6 | Holmsdale rd Brom |
| 110 J 9 | Holmshaw rd SE26 |
| 89 P 16 | Holmside rd SW12 |
| 118 C 16 | Holmsley clo New Mald |
| 25 V 8 | Holmstall av Edg |
| 90 C 19 | Holmswood rd SW2 |
| 40 K 18 | Holmwood clo Grnfd |
| 22 M 9 | Holmwood clo Harrow |
| 153 P 18 | Holmwood clo Sutton |
| 27 Y 8 | Holmwood gdns N3 |
| 155 R 14 | Holmwood gdns Wallgtn |
| 12 L 17 | Holmwood gro NW7 |
| 54 H 8 | Holmwood rd Ilf |
| 153 N 19 | Holmwood rd Sutton |
| 28 E 18 | Holne chase N2 |
| 143 W 15 | Holne chase Mrdn |
| 52 B 19 | Holness rd E15 |
| 86 M 12 | Holroyd rd SW15 |
| 22 M 15 | Holsworth clo Harrow |
| 133 R 19 | Holsworthy sq WC1 |
| 78 D 3 | Holt rd E16 |
| 42 C 9 | Holt rd Wemb |
| 155 U 7 | Holt the Wallgtn |
| 63 S 11 | Holton st E1 |
| 7 Z 7 | Holtwhites av Enf |
| 7 V 6 | Holtwhites hill Enf |
| 22 A 14 | Holwell pl Pinn |
| 89 X 11 | Holwood pl SW4 |
| 150 G 4 | Holwood rd Brom |
| 86 G 19 | Holybourne av SW15 |
| 149 W 6 | Holyoak rd SE11 |
| 28 C 12 | Holyoak wlk N2 |
| 60 E 11 | Holyoake wlk W5 |
| 144 E 18 | Holyport rd SW6 |
| 40 C 13 | Holyrood av Harrow |
| 25 T 8 | Holyrood gdns Edg |
| 5 T 20 | Holyrood rd Barnt |
| 142 J 16 | Holyrood st SE1 |
| 134 L 17 | Holywell la EC2 |
| 134 J 18 | Holywell row EC2 |
| 154 L 3 | Home clo Carsh |
| 58 E 8 | Home clo Grnfd |
| 56 K 10 | Home gdns Dgnhm |
| 24 F 3 | Home mead Stanm |
| 105 V 9 | Home Pk rd SW19 |
| 116 G 10 | Home Pk wlk Kingst |
| 88 J 4 | Home rd SW11 |
| 151 Y 19 | Home st SE15 |
| 30 K 4 | Homecroft rd N22 |
| 110 D 12 | Homecroft rd SE26 |
| 59 V 17 | Homefarm rd W7 |
| 43 X 19 | Homefield clo NW10 |
| 120 E 2 | Homefield gdns Mitch |
| 105 R 14 | Homefield rd SW19 |
| 74 C 12 | Homefield rd W4 |
| 126 K 1 | Homefield rd Brom |
| 12 L 20 | Homefield rd Edg |
| 42 A 12 | Homefield rd Wemb |
| 134 K 10 | Homefield st N1 |
| 109 R 19 | Homelands dri SE19 |
| 92 F 12 | Homeleigh rd SE15 |
| 127 U 11 | Homemead rd Brom |
| 121 W 14 | Homemead rd Croy |
| 98 J 3 | Homer ct Bxly Hth |
| 50 J 18 | Homer rd E9 |
| 124 F 15 | Homer rd Croy |
| 138 M 2 | Homer row W1 |

38 M 2 Homer st W1
17 R 3 Homersham rd Kingst
50 E 15 Homerton gro E9
50 F 16 Homerton High st E9
50 M 14 Homerton rd E9
51 N 13 Homerton rd E9
50 D 15 Homerton row E9
50 D 11 Homerton ter E9
92 C 14 Homestall SE22
6 D 17 Homestead paddock N14
44 E 10 Homestead pk NW2
45 P 19 Homestead rd SW6
56 A 8 Homestead rd Dgnhm
14 H 16 Homewood cres Chisl
20 F 5 Homewood rd Mitch
34 A 17 Honduras st EC1
49 P 5 Hone pde SE11
42 C 6 Honey lane EC2
45 Z 15 Honeybourne rd NW6
89 U 18 Honeybrook rd SW12
83 Z 10 Honeywood rd Islwth
54 M 9 Honeywood wlk Carsh
24 C 3 Honister clo Stanm
24 C 3 Honister gdns Stanm
24 C 4 Honister pl Stanm
29 P 7 Honiton rd NW6
00 N 12 Honiton rd Dam
96 K 4 Honiton rd Welling
93 T 18 Honley rd SE6
92 D 17 Honor Oak pk SE23
10 B 1 Honor Oak rd SE23
92 C 19 Honor Oak rd SE23
92 D 17 Honor Oak ri SE23
6 F 20 Hood av N14
16 F 1 Hood av N14
85 W 13 Hood av SW14
104 E 18 Hood rd SW20
38 G 4 Hood wlk Rom
7 V 20 Hoodcote gdns N21
17 V 2 Hoodcote gdns N21
126 M 12 Hook Farm rd Brom
97 O 8 Hook la Welling
96 J 12 Hook la Welling
12 J 20 Hook wlk Edg
32 F 11 Hookers rd E17
22 J 14 Hooking grn Harrow
56 L 9 Hooks Hall dri Dgnhm
92 A 3 Hooks rd SE15
46 W 1 Hoop la NW11
27 X 20 Hoop la NW11
65 T 18 Hooper rd E16
13 S 7 Hooper st E1
140 J 10 Hop gdns WC2
112 D 19 Hope pk Brom
71 Y 1 Hope rd W13
88 E 9 Hope st SW11
77 V 17 Hopedale rd SE7
128 M 7 Hopefield av NW6
143 R 2 Hopetown st E1
150 F 19 Hopewell st SE5
74 M 4 Hopgood W12
136 C 15 Hopgood st W12
140 D 7 Hopkins st W1
17 U 5 Hoppers rd N21
20 M 8 Hoppett rd E4
118 B 5 Hoppingwood av New Mald
118 G 14 Hopton gdns New Mald
108 A 12 Hopton rd SW16
107 Z 12 Hopton rd SW16
141 X 12 Hopton st SE1
150 H 9 Hopwood st SE17
56 L 4 Horace av Romford
52 H 12 Horace rd E7
36 B 9 Horace rd Ilf
116 L 7 Horace rd Kingst
135 P 10 Horatio st E2
137 S 11 Horbury cres W11
137 R 11 Horbury ms W11
146 D 15 Horbury st SW10
87 T 2 Horder sq NW6
32 L 17 Hore av E17
98 D 13 Horley clo Bxly Hth
113 P 9 Horley rd SE9
219 P 19 Hormead rd W9
77 S 11 Horn la SE10

61 V 18 Horn la W3
73 U 2 Horn la W3
21 T 20 Horn la Wdfd Grn
94 F 13 Horn Park la SE12
72 C 18 Hornbeam cres Brentf
21 N 10 Hornbeam gro E4
127 X 16 Hornbeam way Brom
150 L 18 Hornby rd SE15
94 F 18 Horncastle rd SE12
57 Y 3 Hornchurch rd Hrnch
86 H 20 Horndean clo SW15
38 L 4 Horndon clo Rom
38 K 4 Horndon grn Rom
38 I 5 Horndon rd Rom
94 F 18 Horne clo SE12
86 M 5 Horne way SW15
77 Z 17 Hornfair rd SE7
78 A 19 Hornfair rd SE7
57 R 2 Hornford way Romf
110 A 1 Horniman dri SE23
92 B 20 Horniman dri SE23
110 A 1 Horniman museum SE20
110 A 1 Horniman museum SE23
30 D 17 Horns of Ilf
47 V 13 Hornsey la N6
47 U 1 Hornsey La gdns N6
30 E 11 Hornsey Park rd N8
48 B 7 Hornsey ri N4
47 Z 2 Hornsey ri N19
47 X 1 Hornsey Ri gdns N19
48 D 14 Hornsey st N7
75 R 17 Hornshay pl SE15
75 R 17 Hornshay st SE15
137 W 9 Hornton pl W8
137 V 17 Hornton st W8
156 B 16 Horsa clo Croy
94 K 18 Horsa rd SE12
81 W 19 Horsa rd Erith
140 F 9 Horse & Dolphin yd W1
116 H 2 Horse fair Kingst
104 M 3 Horse ride SW19
142 C 12 Horse Shoe all SE1
154 B 3 Horse Shoe grn Sutton
7 Z 11 Horse Shoe la Enf
139 X 7 Horse Shoe yd W1
25 Y 2 Horsecroft rd Edg
76 F 16 Horseferry pl SE10
148 F 4 Horseferry rd SW1
140 K 15 Horseguards av SW1
140 J 15 Horseguards pde SW1
48 F 15 Horsell rd N5
143 N 16 Horselydown la SE1
150 B 16 Horseman st SE5
41 U 14 Horsenden av Grnfd
41 V 15 Horsenden crs Grnfd
41 U 17 Horsenden La north Grntd
59 Y 2 Horsenden La north Grnfd
59 Z 7 Horsenden La south Grnfd
95 P 12 Horsfeld gdns SE9
95 P 12 Horsfeld rd SE9
90 C 13 Horsford rd SW2
15 S 17 Horsham av N12
98 C 14 Horsham rd Bxly Hth
159 V 17 Horsley dr Croy
159 V 17 Horsley dri Croy
20 G 8 Horsley rd E4
112 H 20 Horsley rd Brom
150 D 13 Horsley rd Brom
92 L 15 Horsmonden rd SE4
146 A 17 Hortensia rd SW10
73 X 14 Horticultural pl W4
45 T 12 Horton av NW2
49 Z 18 Horton rd E8
93 S 7 Horton st SE13
20 H 7 Hortus rd E4
70 D 6 Hortus rd S'hall
107 N 3 Hosack rd SW17
141 X 2 Hosier la EC1
100 K 2 Hosiotal Br rd Twick
76 L 14 Hoskins st SE10
82 J 19 Hospital Br rd Twick
83 V 13 Hospital la Islwth
82 G 9 Hospital rd Hounsl
87 O 9 Hotham rd SW15
106 D 18 Hotham rd SW19
64 L 3 Hotham st E15
75 R 8 Hothfield pl SE16
149 S 8 Hotspur st SE11
84 L 12 Houblon rd Rich
78 K 9 Hough st SE18
31 T 14 Houghton rd N15
141 O 6 Houghton st WC2
156 H 12 Houlder cres Croy
17 R 1 Houndsden rd N21

142 L 4 Houndsditch EC3
18 M 3 Houndsfield rd N9
100 B 4 Hounslow av Felt
82 L 13 Hounslow av Hounsl
82 L 13 Hounslow gdns Hounsl
82 B 5 Hounslow heath Hounsl
82 K 9 Hounslow High st Hounsl
82 M 16 Hounslow rd Twick
140 K 20 House Of parliament SW1
110 K 6 Houston rd SE23
32 L 17 Hove av E17
75 O 20 Hove st SE15
45 R 14 Hoveden rd NW2
97 U 20 Howard av Bxly
45 S 11 Howard cl NW2
16 B 9 Howard clo N11
61 S 16 Howard clo W3
100 M 17 Howard clo Hampt
149 U 2 Howard ct Becknhm
52 A 9 Howard rd E11
33 P 10 Howard rd E17
66 G 6 Howard rd E6
45 O 10 Howard rd NW2
31 S 18 Howard rd N15
49 R 13 Howard rd N16
110 C 20 Howard rd SE20
147 Y 12 Howard rd SE25
67 S 4 Howard rd Bark
112 E 19 Howard rd Brom
53 Z 12 Howard rd Ilf
83 V 7 Howard rd Islwth
128 C 7 Howard rd New Mald
58 L 17 Howard rd S'hall
141 P 8 Howard st WC2
116 A 17 Howard st Surb
28 E 13 Howard wlk N2
87 N 11 Howards la SW15
86 I 12 Howards la SW15
65 T 9 Howards rd E13
80 B 13 Howberry clo Edgw
11 U 20 Howberry clo Edgw
22 H 1 Howberry rd Edgw
11 V 19 Howberry rd Edgw
123 N 2 Howberry rd Thntn Hth
99 V 5 Howbury la Erith
92 C 7 Howbury rd SE15
14 L 20 Howcroft cres N3
27 V 1 Howcroft cres N3
123 T 4 Howden rd SE25
91 W 7 Howden st SE15
38 F 6 Howes clo Rom
37 V 16 Howell clo Rom
130 E 20 Howell st W 2
85 X 8 Howgate rd SE14
148 C 2 Howick pl SW1
140 K 19 Howie st SW11
46 K 17 Howitt rd NW3
132 C 20 Howland Ms east W1
132 B 20 Howland st W1
91 N 15 Howlett's SE24
130 D 20 Howley pl W2
156 K 5 Howley rd Croy
135 N 7 Howley rd Croy
74 G 18 Howsman rd SW13
92 J 10 Howson rd SE4
10 B 6 Howton pl Bushey Watf
134 J 13 Hoxton sq N1
134 J 7 Hoxton st N1
65 P 18 Hoy st E16
62 A 18 Hoylake rd W3
151 V 17 Hoyland SE15
106 J 11 Hoyle rd SW17
108 M 8 Hubbard rd SE27
64 L 4 Hubbard st E15
90 B 8 Hubert gro SW9
66 A 8 Hubert rd E6
80 Z 14 Huddart st E3
47 V 10 Huddleston rd N1
52 C 12 Huddlestone rd E7
44 J 18 Huddlestone rd NW2
98 A 5 Hudson rd Bxly Hth
102 L 20 Hudson rd Kingstn
147 Z 5 Hudsons pl SW1
65 R 14 Hudsons rd E16
24 B 8 Huggin hill EC4
147 Y 7 Hugh ms SW1
147 Y 6 Hugh st SW1
51 Y 14 Hughan rd E15
24 B 14 Hughenden av Harrow
118 H 16 Hughenden rd Worc Park
51 U 11 Hughendon ter E15
57 U 19 Hugo gdns Rainhm
47 V 12 Hugo rd N19
88 A 7 Hugon rd SW6
91 Y 6 Huguenot rd SE15

88 D 14 Huguenot terr SW
37 Y 18 Hull rd Rom
134 A 13 Hull st EC1
54 F 18 Hulse av Bark
38 H 4 Hulse av Bark
44 K 7 Humber rd NW2
77 O 16 Humber rd SE3
65 Y 10 Humberstone rd E13
144 L 15 Humbolt rd W6
71 V 6 Humes av W7
35 U 5 Humphrey clo Ilf
151 N 9 Humphrey st SE1
141 N 13 Hungerford Foot br SE1
140 K 12 Hungerford la WC2
47 Z 16 Hungerford rd N1
48 A 15 Hungerford rd N7
75 S 18 Hunsdon rd SE14
63 R 8 Hunslett st E2
144 A 19 Hunston rd Mrdn
70 G 8 Hunt rd S'hall
104 M 20 Hunter clo SW20
105 N 20 Hunter clo SW20
53 Z 16 Hunter rd Bark
53 Z 16 Hunter rd Ilf
54 A 15 Hunter rd Ilf
123 N 6 Hunter rd Thntn Hth
56 E 13 Hunter sq Dgnhm
132 K 16 Hunter st WC1
24 E 13 Hunters gro Harrow
56 F 14 Hunters Hall rd Dgnhm
157 T 9 Hunters way Croy
7 U 5 Hunters way Enf
152 M 6 Huntingdon gdns Worc Pk
8 K 10 Huntingdon rd N2
19 R 7 Huntingdon rd N9
65 P 19 Huntingdon st E16
158 M 18 Huntingfield Croy
86 H 13 Huntingfield rd SW15
56 E 19 Huntings rd Dgnhm
147 T 7 Huntley rd SE25
132 D 18 Huntley st WC1
118 F 3 Huntley way SW20
14 M 19 Huntly dri N3
135 R 19 Hunton ct st E1
135 R 19 Hunton st E1
140 H 10 Hunts ct WC2
64 F 7 Hunts la E15
9 T 10 Hunts mead Enf
9 T 10 Hunts mead Enf
63 P 20 Hunts ms E1
109 S 5 Hunts Slip rd SE21
150 H 8 Huntsman st SE17
88 D 12 Huntsmoor rd SW18
106 E 7 Huntspill st SW17
131 O 18 Huntsworth ms NW1
149 Y 7 Hurlbutt pl SE17
149 W 7 Hurley rd SE11
58 K 15 Hurley rd Grnfd
87 V 7 Hurlingham gdns SW6
87 X 8 Hurlingham house SW6
87 W 7 Hurlingham park SW6
87 U 6 Hurlingham rd SW6
81 P 20 Hurlingham rd Bxly Hth
48 J 10 Hurlock st N5
123 R 10 Hurlstone rd SE25
107 P 6 Huron rd SW17
20 B 11 Hurst av E4
29 W 10 Hurst av N6
20 A 12 Hurst clo E4
28 A 10 Hurst clo NW11
126 C 20 Hurst clo Brom
40 C 16 Hurst ale Grnfd
80 H 14 Hurst la SE2
80 H 15 Hurst Pl est SE2
33 R 10 Hurst rd F17
17 U 6 Hurst rd N21
98 D 20 Hurst rd Bxly
115 Y 2 Hurst rd Bxly
157 O 10 Hurst rd Croy
81 Y 20 Hurst rd Erith
4 L 12 Hurst ri Barnt
115 Z 2 Hurst springs Bxly
90 J 15 Hurst st SE24
157 S 15 Hurst View rd S Croy
157 S 15 Hurst way S Croy
54 F 18 Hurstbourne gdns Bark
110 J 2 Hurstbourne rd SE23
153 Z 2 Hurstcourt rd Sutton
126 C 20 Hurstdene av Brom
31 T 20 Hurstdene gdns N15
126 E 11 Hurstfield Brom
35 V 5 Hurstleigh gdns Ilf
12 F 12 Hurstmead ct Edg
34 J 12 Hurstmead av E18

7 U 20 Jeffreys st NW1
9 Z 3 Jeffreys wlk SW4
3 V 9 Jeffs rd Sutton
4 L 11 Jeken rd SE9
40 F 12 Jelf rd SW2
1 O 3 Jellicoe rd N17
7 O 8 Jenkins la Bark
45 W 12 Jenkins rd E13
49 W 9 Jenner rd N16
66 F 4 Jennett rd Croy
2 D 6 Jennifer rd Brom
41 V 15 Jennings rd SE22
41 Y 3 Jenningtree way Blvdr
17 Y 3 Jenton av Bxly Hth
32 L 19 Jephson rd E7
41 O 3 Jephson st SE5
7 X 16 Jephtha rd SW18
20 L 9 Jeppos la Mitch
45 U 18 Jerdan pl SW6
44 C 18 Jeremiah st E14
19 P 14 Jeremys grn N18
45 Y 7 Jerningham av Ilf
49 T 18 Jernson way SE13
50 A 13 Jerome pl SE17
35 N 19 Jerome st E1
33 S 7 Jerrard st SE13
24 D 8 Jersey av Stanm
51 W 5 Jersey rd E11
65 X 15 Jersey rd E16
07 R 16 Jersey rd SW17
77 Y 7 Jersey rd W7
82 L 1 Jersey rd Hounsl
70 L 20 Jersey rd Hounsl
73 Z 13 Jersey rd Ilf
71 P 18 Jersey rd Islwth
33 W 18 Jerusalem pass EC1
08 F 14 Jerviston gdns SW18
43 O 17 Jesmond av Wemb
23 U 17 Jesmond rd Croy
50 G 9 Jesmond st SE17
11 Y 15 Jesmond way Stanm
49 Z 4 Jessam av E5
71 V 3 Jessamine rd W7
71 T 5 Jesse rd E10
68 E 15 Jessica rd SW18
90 K 11 Jessop rd SE24
88 A 10 Jetstar way Grnfd
12 J 2 Jevington way SE12
33 N 10 Jewel rd E17
42 M 7 Jewry st EC3
88 B 10 Jews row SW18
10 A 9 Jews wlk SE26
44 L 16 Jeymer av NW2
58 M 4 Jeymer dri Grnfd
59 N 3 Jeymer dri Grnfd
58 M 4 Jeymer dri Grnfd
88 D 17 Jeypore rd SW18
00 H 18 Jillian clo Hampt
95 O 19 Joan cres SE9
55 Y 6 Joan gdns Dgnhm
55 Y 6 Joan rd Dgnhm
41 V 15 Joan st SE1
58 C 3 Joave clo Grnfd
84 K 8 Jocelyn rd Rich
41 P 1 Jockeys fields WC1
63 Z 2 Jodrell rd E3
41 S 18 Johanna st SE1
40 L 11 John Adam st WC2
67 V 2 John Burns dri Bark
49 T 15 John Campbell rd N16
41 V 8 John Carpenter st EC4
143 S 20 John Felton rd SE16
R 10 John Fisher st E1
148 H 8 John Islip st SW7
97 S 8 John Newton ct Wellng
56 G 20 John Parker clo Dgnhm
93 S 2 John Penn st SE13
139 Z 5 John Prince's st W 1
149 Y 17 John Ruskin st SE5
150 B 15 John Ruskin st SE5
48 K 18 John Spencer sq N1
65 O 4 John st E15
123 Y 9 John st SE25
133 P 19 John st WC1
8 G 16 John st Enf
82 C 4 John st Hounsl
78 J 10 John Wilson st SE18
26 L 12 Johns av NW4
120 D 12 Johns la Mrdn
133 O 18 Johns ms WC1
143 Y 4 Johns pl E1
127 M 12 Johnson rd Brom
23 N 17 Johnson rd Croy
63 P 18 Johnson st E1

154 M 4 Johnsons clo Carsh
141 U 6 Johnsons ct EC4
148 B 11 Johnsons pl SW1
21 S 18 Johnston Wdfd Grn
66 H 10 Johnstone rd E6
45 O 10 Johnstone ter NW2
142 G 14 Joiner st SE1
41 P 4 Jollys la Harrow
149 O 8 Jonathan st SE11
120 M 14 Jones la Mitch
65 W 13 Jones rd E13
139 X 10 Jones st W1
121 T 8 Jonson clo Mitch
87 P 11 Jordan ct SW15
60 D 2 Jordan rd Grnfd
83 U 3 Jorden clo Islwth
63 Y 13 Joseph st SE1
90 D 14 Joshua rd av SW2
64 F 16 Joshua st E14
88 M 5 Joubert st SW11
151 P 19 Jowett st SE15
18 H 17 Joyce av N18
90 G 16 Joyce wlk SW2
37 P 18 Joydon dri Rom
83 O 20 Jubilee av Twick
25 Y 18 Jubilee clo NW9
18 K 4 Jubilee cres N9
40 A 12 Jubilee dri Ruisl
58 H 15 Jubilee gdns S'hall
18 L 3 Jubilee park N9
146 M 10 Jubilee pl SW3
60 A 2 Jubilee rd Grnfd
115 U 15 Jubilee rd Sidcp
153 P 15 Jubilee rd Sutton
63 P 17 Jubilee st E1
132 J 14 Judd st WC1
65 P 18 Jude st E16
44 C 9 Judges wlk NW3
146 L 19 Juer st SW11
69 J 5 Julia gdns Bark
47 O 14 Julia st NW5
61 U 20 Julian av W3
41 T 8 Julian hill Harrow
72 D 9 Julien rd W5
93 T 7 Junction appr SE13
138 K 4 Junction ms W2
138 H 4 Junction pl W2
65 V 6 Junction rd E13
31 X 9 Junction rd N17
47 V 9 Junction rd N19
18 K 6 Junction rd N9
72 F 11 Junction rd W5
23 S 19 Junction rd Harrow
55 Z 1 Junction rd Rom
55 X 1 Junction rd Rom
39 T 14 Junction rd Rom
157 O 12 Junction rd S Croy
63 P 19 Juniper st E1
75 T 17 Juno way SE14
64 J 1 Jupp rd E15
64 H 2 Jupp Rd west E15
63 V 10 Jupps rd E3
146 L 19 Justice wlk SW3
9 W 10 Jute la Enf
65 T 12 Jutland rd E13
93 T 19 Jutland rd SE6
38 H 19 Jutsums av Rom
38 G 19 Jutsums la Rom
149 P 5 Juxon st SE11

# K

80 K 6 Kale rd Belvdr
88 G 6 Kambala rd SW11
110 L 10 Kangley Br rd SE26
59 R 5 Karoline gdns Grnfd
79 X 12 Kashgar rd SE18
78 A 18 Kashmir rd SE7
88 M 2 Kassala rd SW11
107 O 1 Kate st SW12
156 M 4 Katharine st Croy
157 N 4 Katharine st Croy
95 N 12 Katharine gdns SE9
36 C 1 Katherine gdns Ilf
66 C 3 Katherine rd E6
52 L 16 Katherine rd E7
83 Z 20 Katherine rd Twick
61 W 13 Kathleen av W3
60 K 1 Kathleen av Wemb
42 K 20 Kathleen rd SW11
88 L 8 Kathleen rd SW11
90 B 6 Kay rd SW9
64 K 1 Kay st E2
135 T 9 Kay st E2
97 R 2 Kay st Welling
154 H 15 Kayemoor rd Sutton
45 P 14 Kayes rd NW2
141 N 6 Kean st WC2

108 X 11 Keary house SW15
58 J 15 Keat's way Grnfd
39 Y 2 Keats av Rom
46 H 12 Keats gro NW3
96 J 1 Keats rd Welling
124 D 15 Keats way Croy
41 O 16 Keble clo Grnfd
118 E 20 Keble clo Worc Pk
106 D 9 Keble clo SW17
126 F 17 Kechill gdns Brom
112 B 11 Keedonwood rd Brom
111 Z 11 Keedonwood rd Brom
156 L 3 Keeley rd Croy
141 N 5 Keeley st W1
94 M 13 Keeling rd SE9
95 N 13 Keeling rd SE9
156 M 8 Keen's rd Croy
48 J 18 Keens yd N1
94 E 6 Keep the SE3
150 F 14 Keesey st SE17
151 V 1 Keeton's rd SE16
87 R 19 Keevil dri SW19
114 D 2 Keightley dri SE9
88 L 11 Keildon rd SW11
00 A 1 Keir Hardie way Bark
74 G 4 Keith gro W12
32 L 6 Keith rd E17
67 S 6 Keith rd Bark
95 P 6 Kelbrook rd SE3
114 A 8 Kelby path SE9
44 H 5 Kelceda clo NW2
136 E 4 Kelfield gdns W10
141 Y 20 Kell st SE1
65 T 11 Kelland rd E13
94 M 5 Kellaway rd SE3
95 O 3 Kellaway rd SE3
93 Y 13 Kellerton rd SE13
90 F 11 Kellett rd SW2
106 L 9 Kellino st SW17
79 X 8 Kellner rd SE18
47 T 18 Kelly st NW1
37 Y 17 Kelly way Rom
91 X 10 Kelmore gro SE22
74 G 7 Kelmscot gdns W12
32 K 6 Kelmscott clo E17
88 L 14 Kelmscott rd SW11
48 K 12 Kelross rd N5
94 H 4 Kelsall clo SE3
125 N 7 Kelsey la Becknhm
125 R 5 Kelsey Pk av Becknhm
125 P 3 Kelsey Pk rd Becknhm
125 O 3 Kelsey sq Becknhm
135 V 15 Kelsey st E2
125 O 6 Kelsey way Becknhm
145 Y 2 Kelso pl W8
120 C 17 Kelso rd Carsh
45 W 19 Kelson st NW6
36 A 6 Kelston rd Ilf
35 Z 7 Kelston rd Ilf
103 O 15 Kelvedon clo Kingst
145 P 20 Kelvedon rd SW6
17 R 18 Kelvin av N13
101 T 15 Kelvin av Tedd
10 G 20 Kelvin cres Harrow
84 C 15 Kelvin dri Twick
58 G 17 Kelvin gdns S'hall
110 A 7 Kelvin gro SE26
48 K 13 Kelvin rd N5
96 M 7 Kelvin rd Welling
124 C 16 Kelvington clo Croy
92 E 14 Kelvington rd SE15
145 P 12 Kelway pl W14
31 W 6 Kemble rd N17
110 G 2 Kemble rd SE23
156 H 4 Kemble rd Croy
141 N 6 Kemble st WC2
90 L 8 Kemerton rd SE5
123 U 17 Kemerton rd Becknhm
125 S 4 Kemerton rd Becknhm
50 H 16 Kemeys st E9
114 E 9 Kemnal manor Chisl
114 D 13 Kemnal rd Chisl
55 W 4 Kemp rd Dgnhm
128 G 10 Kempe rd NW6
91 S 13 Kempis way SE22
46 G 12 Kemplay rd NW3
145 V 11 Kempsford gdns SW5
149 V 1 Kempsford rd SE11
150 L 12 Kempshead rd SE5
107 Z 17 Kempshott rd SW16
108 A 17 Kempshott rd SW16
87 Z 1 Kempson rd SW6
40 H 16 Kempton av Grnfd
100 B 20 Kempton park Felt
66 F 3 Kempton rd E6
124 K 14 Kempton wlk Croy

97 Z 17 Kemsing clo Bxly
122 N 9 Kemsing clo Thntn Hth
77 S 14 Kemsing rd SE10
90 L 4 Kenbury st SE5
148 K 19 Kenchester st SW8
18 B 14 Kendal av E3
61 S 14 Kendal av W3
67 U 2 Kendal av Bark
21 R 9 Kendal clo Wdfd Grn
18 B 14 Kendal gdns N18
44 H 13 Kendal rd NW10
138 M 6 Kendal st W2
111 Z 13 Kendale rd Brom
124 H 3 Kendall av Becknhm
157 R 20 Kendall av S Croy
139 T 3 Kendall pl W1
124 H 3 Kendall rd Becknhm
83 X 5 Kendall rd Islwth
75 R 20 Kender st SE14
89 Y 9 Kendoa rd SW4
120 A 4 Kendor gdns SW19
156 J 16 Kendra Hall rd S Croy
83 S 17 Kendrey gdns Twick
140 E 6 Kendrick ms SW7
146 E 6 Kendrick pl SW7
41 Y 9 Kenelm clo Harrow
4 D 17 Kenerne dri Barnt
4 D 18 Kenerne dri Barnt
89 T 18 Kenilford rd SW12
33 P 9 Kenilworth av E17
105 X 11 Kenilworth av SW19
40 D 12 Kenilworth av Harrow
8 E 6 Kenilworth cres Enf
54 K 6 Kenilworth gdns Ilf
58 F 10 Kenilworth gdns S'hall
63 V 6 Kenilworth rd E3
129 R 3 Kenilworth rd NW6
110 E 20 Kenilworth rd SE20
72 J 3 Kenilworth rd W5
12 G 12 Kenilworth rd Edg
152 F 12 Kenilworth rd Epsom
98 F 19 Kenley clo Bxly
122 H 9 Kenley gdns Thntn Hth
120 A 5 Kenley rd SW19
119 X 4 Kenley rd SW19
117 U 3 Kenley rd Kingst
84 A 16 Kenley rd Twick
136 K 12 Kenley st W11
153 N 9 Kenley wlk Sutton
106 G 13 Kenlor rds SW17
106 M 19 Kenmare dri Mitch
17 Y 14 Kenmare gdns N13
122 E 14 Kenmare rd Thntn Hth
61 P 1 Kenmere gdns N Wemb
97 I 4 Kenmere rd Welling
62 J 8 Kenmont gdns NW10
23 Z 13 Kenmore av Har
22 A 7 Kenmore av Harrow
23 Z 8 Kenmore av Harrow
25 T 7 Kenmore gdns Edg
24 G 12 Kenmore rd Harrow
50 A 16 Kenmure rd E8
64 H 1 Kennard rd E15
15 Z 17 Kennard rd N11
78 F 3 Kennard st E16
9 K 19 Kennedy av Enf
65 T 7 Kennedy clo E13
59 V 12 Kennedy path W7
59 U 13 Kennedy rd W7
67 U 4 Kennedy rd Bark
129 P 17 Kennet rd W9
83 V 7 Kennet rd Islwth
142 B 9 Kennet Wharf la EC4
53 X 11 Kenneth av Ilf
44 L 15 Kenneth cres NW2
10 K 19 Kenneth gdns Stanm
55 X 1 Kenneth rd Rom
99 X 8 Kennet st Drtfrd
75 R 5 Kenning st SE16
49 Y 10 Kenninghall rd E5
19 P 16 Kenninghall rd N18
149 V 9 Kennings way SE11
149 O 12 Kennington gro SE11
149 V 8 Kennington la SE11
149 P 15 Kennington oval SE11
149 P 14 Kennington park SE11
149 W 14 Kennington Pk gdns SE11
149 V 13 Kennington Pk pl SE11

149 T11 Kennington rd SE11
37 N1 Kennylands Ilf
139 S1 Kenrick pl W1
129 N18 Kensal rd W10
128 J16 Kensal rd W10
53 R18 Kensington av E12
122 F1 Kensington av Thntn Hth
137 W18 Kensington Ch ct W8
137 V14 Kensington Ch st W8
137 W18 Kensington Ch wlk W8
137 W17 Kensington Church ct W18
137 W17 Kensington Church ct W8
137 Z19 Kensington ct W8
137 Z20 Kensington Ct pl W8
35 O6 Kensington dri Wdfd Grn
138 B20 Kensington ga W8
53 U4 Kensington gdns Ilf
137 X7 Kensington Gdns sq W2
138 F19 Kensington gore SW7
137 W19 Kensington High st W8
145 R2 Kensington High st W8
137 V13 Kensington mall W8
137 W12 Kensington Pal gdns W8
187 Z15 Kensington Palace London museum W8
137 P10 Kensington Pk gdns W11
137 N6 Kensington Pk ms W11
137 O7 Kensington Pk rd W11
137 T14 Kensington pl W8
138 D19 Kensington rd SW7
58 G5 Kensington rd Grnfd
38 L18 Kensington rd Rom
137 X20 Kensington sq W8
157 O17 Kensington ter S Croy
60 A15 Kent av W13
69 T6 Kent av Dgnhm
96 L11 Kent av Welling
6 C15 Kent dri Barnt
101 S13 Kent dri Tedd
60 B14 Kent gdns W13
110 J14 Kent House la Becknhm
110 F19 Kent House rd Becknhm
131 N15 Kent pas NW1
18 A3 Kent rd N21
73 V8 Kent rd W4
56 H15 Kent rd Dgnhm
116 G5 Kent rd Kingst
73 P19 Kent rd Rich
125 S20 Kent rd W Wkhm
65 X10 Kent st E13
135 P7 Kent st E2
130 M14 Kent ter NW1
54 H7 Kent View gdns Ilf
138 L19 Kent yd SW7
58 B4 Kentford way Grnfd
142 E16 Kentish bldgs SE1
81 S11 Kentish rd Blvdr
131 Z2 Kentish Town rd NW1
47 T18 Kentish Town rd NW5
79 V11 Kentmere rd SE18
23 W20 Kenton av Harrow
58 H20 Kenton av S'hall
24 D15 Kenton gdns Harrow
10 H19 Kenton la Harrow
24 C10 Kenton la Harrow
23 X5 Kenton la Harrow
24 F14 Kenton Pk av Harrow
24 F15 Kenton Pk clo Harrow
24 F13 Kenton Pk cres Harrow
24 E14 Kenton Pk rd Harrow
50 E18 Kenton rd E9
23 Z19 Kenton rd Harrow
24 C17 Kenton rd Harrow
132 K17 Kenton st WC1
6 F17 Kentwins N14
74 G19 Kentwode grn SW15
15 S20 Kenver av N12
94 L13 Kenward rd SE9
38 J7 Kenway Rom
145 N7 Kenway rd SW5
92 D1 Kenwood av SE14
6 L17 Kenwood av Enf

46 F3 Kenwood clo NW3
125 U6 Kenwood dri Becknhm
35 W14 Kenwood gdns Ilf
46 J3 Kenwood house NW3
28 M17 Kenwood rd N6
18 K6 Kenwood rd N9
50 H15 Kenworthy rd E9
44 C8 Kenwyn dri NW2
118 M1 Kenwyn rd SW20
89 Y9 Kenwyn rd SW4
77 Z20 Kenya rd SE7
24 D17 Kenyngton pl Harrow
87 O1 Kenyon st SW6
144 G20 Kenyon st SW6
52 A17 Keogh rd E15
90 A10 Kepler rd SW4
66 E1 Keppel rd E6
55 X12 Keppel rd Dgnhm
142 A15 Keppel row SE1
135 R15 Kerbela st E2
64 D18 Kerbey st E14
91 O3 Kerfield cres SE5
91 O3 Kerfield pl SE5
72 H3 Kerrison pl W5
64 J3 Kerrison rd E15
88 J7 Kerrison rd SW11
72 H4 Kerrison rd W5
11 T13 Kerry av Stanm
65 U18 Kerry clo E16
11 T14 Kerry ct Stanm
75 X17 Kerry rd SE14
113 P9 Kersey gdns SE9
87 P15 Kersfield rd SW15
56 F9 Kershaw rd Dgnhm
88 L3 Kersley ms SW11
49 T9 Kersley rd N16
88 L3 Kersley st SW11
128 G9 Keslake rd NW6
18 C12 Keston clo N18
80 E19 Keston clo Welling
31 O12 Keston rd N17
91 W8 Keston rd SE15
159 X18 Kestral way Croy
90 L13 Kestrel av SE24
104 A12 Keswick av SW15
119 X4 Keswick av SW19
154 D8 Keswick clo Sutton
35 S13 Keswick gdns Ilf
42 J14 Keswick gdns Wemb
87 T15 Keswick rd SW15
98 D3 Keswick rd Bxly Hth
82 M17 Keswick rd Twick
159 Z1 Keswick rd W Wkhm
90 D13 Kett gdns SW2
9 S1 Kettering rd Enf
9 S1 Kettering rd Enf
107 U16 Kettering st SW16
50 K4 Kettlebaston rd E10
31 N6 Kevelioc rd N17
73 O15 Kew Br ct W4
73 O16 Kew bridge Brentf
72 L16 Kew Bridge rd Brentf
153 L15 Kew cres Sutton
84 K8 Kew Foot rd Rich
72 L20 Kew gardens Brentf
85 O1 Kew Gardens rd Rich
73 N18 Kew grn Rich
85 S3 Kew Meadow path Rich
84 C7 Kew observatory Rich
72 L18 Kew palace Brentf
73 N17 Kew rd Rich
85 N2 Kew rd Rich
141 Y20 Key North st SE1
108 D5 Keymer rd SW2
29 N12 Keynes clo N2
21 N14 Keynsham av Wdfd Grn
95 P12 Keynsham gdns SE9
95 P13 Keynsham rd SE9
119 Z19 Keynsham rd Mrdn
151 O4 Keyse rd SE1
132 M10 Keystone cres N1
149 Y1 Keyworth st SE1
75 U14 Kezia st SE8
106 J10 Khama rd SW17
65 V10 Khartoum rd E13
106 G10 Khartoum rd SW17
54 A15 Khartoum rd Ilf
53 Z15 Khartoum rd Ilf
88 J6 Khyber rd SW11
149 O19 Kibworth st SW8
94 F3 Kidbrooke gdns SE3
94 F2 Kidbrooke gro SE3
95 S11 Kidbrooke la SE9
94 H3 Kidbrooke Pk clo SE3
94 G2 Kidbrooke Pk rd SE3

45 Y12 Kidderpore av NW3
45 Z12 Kidderpore gdns NW3
134 G17 Kiffen st EC2
129 T3 Kilburn High rd NW6
45 V20 Kilburn High rd NW6
128 K11 Kilburn la W10
129 O10 Kilburn la W9
129 V12 Kilburn Pk rd NW6
129 V5 Kilburn pl NW6
129 X7 Kilburn priory NW6
129 T5 Kilburn sq NW6
129 V5 Kilburn vale NW6
137 V5 Kildare gdns W2
65 T14 Kildare rd E16
137 V4 Kildare ter W2
90 A15 Kildoran rd SW4
55 N5 Kildowan rd Ilf
92 H15 Kilgow rd SE23
88 C5 Kilkie st SW6
88 D16 Killarney rd SW18
111 X1 Killearn rd SE6
152 L9 Killester gdns Worc Pk
133 N10 Killick st N1
108 A2 Killieser av SW2
107 Z3 Killieser av SW2
65 R17 Killip clo E16
41 O13 Killowen av Grnfd
50 E19 Killowen rd E9
89 V5 Killyon rd SW8
144 M20 Kilmaine rd SW6
74 L10 Kilmarsh rd W6
144 A5 Kilmarsh rd W6
122 E6 Kilmartin av SW16
55 O7 Kilmartin rd Ilf
57 Y16 Kilmartin way Hornch
74 F17 Kilmington rd SW13
84 A11 Kilmorey gdns Twick
84 B11 Kilmorey rd Twick
110 H2 Kilmorie rd SE23
47 P13 Kiln pl NW5
64 A15 Kilner st E14
128 L13 Kilravock st W10
8 C3 Kilvington dri Enf
87 S2 Kimbell gdns SW6
88 A19 Kimber rd SW18
66 L6 Kimberley av E6
92 B6 Kimberley av SE15
54 F2 Kimberley av Ilf
38 J19 Kimberley av Rom
115 X5 Kimberley dri Sidcp
30 J17 Kimberley gdns N4
8 G13 Kimberley gdns Enf
51 X6 Kimberley rd E11
65 O12 Kimberley rd E16
32 K4 Kimberley rd E4
20 M5 Kimberley rd E4
21 N6 Kimberley rd E4
128 M3 Kimberley rd NW6
31 X9 Kimberley rd N17
19 N19 Kimberley rd N18
90 B6 Kimberley rd SW9
122 K13 Kimberley rd Croy
21 N5 Kimberley way E4
124 G3 Kimberly rd Becknhm
10 A2 Kimble cres Bushey Watf
106 G14 Kimble rd SW19
113 R10 Kimmeridge rd SE9
153 V2 Kimpton clo Sutton
91 O1 Kimpton rd SE5
151 V20 Kincaid rd SE15
24 L20 Kinch gro Harrow
42 L1 Kinch gro Harrow
55 O4 Kinfauns rd Ilf
108 G4 Kinfauns rd SW2
111 O10 King Alfred av SE6
150 C9 King And Queen st SE17
92 B1 King Arthur st SE15
151 Z20 King Arthur st SE15
140 J17 King Charles st SW1
117 N16 King Charles' cres Surb
116 M13 King Charles' cres Surb
63 O20 King David la E1
51 T4 King Edward rd E10
32 G11 King Edward rd E17
63 R1 King Edward rd E9
18 M2 King Edward rd N9
5 N15 King Edward rd Barnt
4 M14 King Edward rd Barnt
39 T17 King Edward rd Rom
141 Z4 King Edward st EC1
149 T1 King Edward wlk SE1
73 R3 King Edward's gdns W3
102 C15 King Edward's gro Tedd

9 U14 King Edward's rd E9
135 Y3 King Edwards rd E
19 N3 King Edwards rd N
156 H10 King gdns Croy
65 Z17 King George av E1
152 B7 King George Field Auriol park Epso
87 Z20 King George park SW18
76 H20 King George st SE
121 N8 King George vi Mit
80 M18 King Harold's way Bxly Hth
49 S15 King Henry st N16
159 V18 King Henry's dri Cr
131 O1 King Henry's rd NV
130 K1 King Henry's rd NV
117 T5 King Henry's rd Kingst
49 R17 King Henry's wlk E8
141 Y19 King James st SE1
63 T15 King John st E1
134 L16 King John's ct EC2
95 P19 King John's wlk SE
142 C6 King st EC2
65 S12 King st E13
31 U3 King st N17
28 G9 King st N2
140 D14 King st SW1
140 K9 King st WC2
73 U3 King st W3
74 F12 King st W6
144 B7 King st W6
84 G13 King st Rich
70 C8 King st S'hall
101 Y1 King st Twick
76 K15 King William la SE1
142 F7 King William st EC
76 H16 King William wlk SE10
29 P10 King's av N10
89 Z14 King's av SW4
60 H16 King's av W5
58 L16 King's av Grnfd
21 W18 King's av Wdfd Grn
141 Y17 King's Bench st SE1
141 T8 King's Bench wlk EC4
99 O11 King's clo Drtfrd
46 H20 King's College rd NW3
129 V2 King's gdns NW6
75 N20 King's gro SE15
151 Y20 King's gro SE15
142 G10 King's Head ct EC 3
89 X12 King's Head pass SW4
142 F15 King's Head yd SE1
79 X17 King's highway SE1
50 K13 King's Mead way E9
133 P19 King's ms WC1
95 S15 King's orchard SE9
51 Y1 King's rd E11
147 T4 King's rd SW1
85 Z9 King's rd SW13
105 Y14 King's rd SW19
145 Z20 King's rd SW6
60 G15 King's rd W5
116 D20 King's rd Surb
101 P12 King's rd Tedd
148 B4 King's scholars' SW1
132 A6 King's ter NW1
57 V20 Kingaby gdns Rainham
75 S5 Kingburn st SE16
45 Y17 Kingdon rd NW6
156 K20 Kingdown av S Croy
60 H10 Kingfield rd W5
76 G11 Kingfield st E14
102 C9 Kingfisher dri Rich
141 Z2 Kinghorn st EC1
150 L9 Kinglake st SE17
140 B8 Kingly ct W1
140 B7 Kingly st W1
143 S2 Kings Arms ct E1
142 F4 Kings Arms yd EC2
17 V5 Kings av N21
112 B16 Kings av Brom
21 Z7 Kings av Buck Hl
154 K18 Kings av Carsh
82 L2 Kings av Hounsl
118 C8 Kings av New Mald
38 C18 Kings av Rom
89 Y13 Kings Av gdns SW4
51 R2 Kings clo E10
27 R13 Kings clo NW4
133 O12 Kings Cross rd WC1
132 K9 Kings Cross station N1
65 W4 Kings ct E13
7 Z14 Kings dri Edg
11 Z14 Kings dri Edg
12 A14 Kings dri Edg
117 P15 Kings dri Surb

43 S 7 Kings dri Wemb
35 O 11 Kings Farm av Rich
54 D 4 Kings gdns Ilf
39 V 17 Kings gro Rom
10 F 18 Kings Hall rd SE20
20 E 3 Kings Head hill E4
54 G 12 Kings la Sutton
34 D 9 Kings Park ct E18
02 H 19 Kings pas Kingst
13 G 4 Kings pas Kingst
42 B 20 Kings pl SE1
13 V 12 Kings pl W4
21 Z 8 Kings pl Buck Hl
20 J 5 Kings rd E4
65 Y 3 Kings rd E6
44 J 20 Kings rd NW10
31 V 3 Kings rd N17
18 L 15 Kings rd N17
30 E 4 Kings rd N22
2 Y 6 Kings rd SE25
46 J 12 Kings rd SW3
4 A 13 Kings rd Barnt
40 E 9 Kings rd Harrow
03 O 17 Kings rd Kingst
02 J 19 Kings rd Kingst
21 P 5 Kings rd Mitch
84 M 12 Kings rd Rich
39 V 17 Kings rd Rom
84 C 17 Kings rd Twick
85 P 12 Kings Ride ga Rich
56 D 11 Kings way Croy
23 T 12 Kings way Harrow
19 V 17 Kings way Wdfd Grn
48 L 8 Kings's cres N4
12 G 3 Kingsand SE12
73 N 5 Kingsbridge av W3
58 E 15 Kingsbridge cres S'hall
36 E 3 Kingsbridge rd W10
67 T 7 Kingsbridge rd Bark
19 P 17 Kingsbridge rd Mrdn
20 J 13 Kingsbridge rd S'hall
25 U 15 Kingsbury rd NW9
49 S 17 Kingsbury rd N1
49 S 17 Kingsbury ter N1
86 F 17 Kingsclere clo SW15
05 V 3 Kingscliffe gdns SW19
73 X 10 Kingscote rd W4
23 Z 18 Kingscote rd Croy
17 Y 7 Kingscote rd New Mald
141 W 8 Kingscote st EC4
107 Z 7 Kingscourt rd SW16
45 U 17 Kingscroft rd NW2
73 X 15 Kingsdale rd SE18
10 F 19 Kingsdale rd SE20
72 C 5 Kingsdown av W13
62 B 18 Kingsdown av W3
52 A 10 Kingsdown rd E11
47 Z 8 Kingsdown rd N19
48 A 7 Kingsdown rd N4
153 S 11 Kingsdown rd Sutton
126 E 15 Kingsdown way Brom
116 M 19 Kingsdowne rd Surb
104 D 1 Kingsfarm lodge SW15
22 L 14 Kingsfield av Harrow
23 N 16 Kingsfield av Harrow
41 S 2 Kingsfield rd Harrow
156 B 17 Kingsford ac Croy
156 B 17 Kingsford av Croy
46 M 15 Kingsford st NW5
43 U 8 Kingsgate Wemb
27 Y 10 Kingsgate av N3
97 Y 1 Kingsgate clo Bxly Hth
129 T 2 Kingsgate pl NW6
129 U 2 Kingsgate rd NW6
45 X 20 Kingsgate rd NW6
95 O 18 Kingsground SE9
24 D 13 Kingshill av Harrow
118 H 16 Kingshill av Worc Pk
24 B 11 Kingshill dri Harrow
63 P 1 Kingshold rd E9
95 P 9 Kingsholme gdns SE9
94 F 19 Kingshurst rd SE12
49 T 17 Kingsland High st E8
49 T 17 Kingsland pass N1
65 Y 9 Kingsland rd E13
134 L 6 Kingsland rd E2
49 T 19 Kingsland rd E8
59 Y 16 Kingsley av W13
83 N 4 Kingsley av Hounsl
58 G 20 Kingsley av S'hall
154 G 8 Kingsley av Sutton
28 C 15 Kingsley clo N2
28 C 15 Kingsley clo N2
56 G 12 Kingsley clo Dgnhm
20 B 15 Kingsley gdns E4
145 Z 2 Kingsley ms W8

47 R 2 Kingsley pl N6
33 T 8 Kingsley rd E17
52 F 20 Kingsley rd E7
129 P 3 Kingsley rd NW6
17 U 13 Kingsley rd N13
106 C 12 Kingsley rd SW19
122 F 19 Kingsley rd Croy
41 N 10 Kingsley rd Harrow
83 N 6 Kingsley rd Hounsl
82 L 4 Kingsley rd Hounsl
36 C 4 Kingsley rd Ilf
22 E 14 Kingsley rd Pinn
89 N 6 Kingsley st SW11
88 M 7 Kingsley st SW11
28 C 15 Kingsley way N2
113 U 7 Kingsley Wood dri SE9
123 R 1 Kingslyn cres SE18
78 G 9 Kingsman pk SE18
78 G 9 Kingsman SE18
4 L 14 Kingsmead Barnt
43 Y 1 Kingsmead av NW9
18 M 6 Kingsmead av N9
121 V 5 Kingsmead av Mitch
39 S 18 Kingsmead av Rom
152 J 4 Kingsmead av Worc Pk
114 M 5 Kingsmead clo Sidcp
40 E 20 Kingsmead dri Grnfd
108 F 5 Kingsmead rd SW12
43 U 5 Kingsmere pk NW9
105 R 4 Kingsmill rd SW19
56 B 16 Kingsmill gdns Dgnhm
56 B 16 Kingsmill rd Dgnhm
130 G 9 Kingsmill ter NW8
103 T 16 Kingsnympton pk Kingst
110 E 10 Kingsthorpe rd SE26
153 T 5 Kingston av Sutton
104 B 15 Kingston By-pass SW20
118 B 12 Kingston By-pass New Mald
58 E 2 Kingston clo Grnfd
37 Y 9 Kingston clo Rom
124 L 1 Kingston cres Becknhm
116 F 3 Kingston dr Kingst
103 P 17 Kingston gate Kingst
116 H 5 Kingston Hall rd Kingst
103 S 18 Kingston hill Kingst
37 Z 9 Kingston Hill av Rom
103 W 10 Kingston Hill place Rich
102 A 15 Kingston la Tedd
101 Z 13 Kingston la Tedd
51 V 12 Kingston rd E11
18 L 8 Kingston rd N9
86 M 20 Kingston rd SW15
86 M 20 Kingston rd SW15
104 H 3 Kingston rd SW15
105 Y 19 Kingston rd SW19
110 P 2 Kingston rd SW20
5 U 17 Kingston rd Barnt
152 C 12 Kingston rd Epsom
54 B 12 Kingston rd Ilf
117 V 7 Kingston rd New Mald
39 U 13 Kingston rd Rom
70 D 7 Kingston rd S'hall
102 B 15 Kingston rd Tedd
104 A 8 Kingston vale SW15
103 Y 9 Kingston vale SW15
131 S 4 Kingstown st NW1
15 R 18 Kingsway N12
85 U 8 Kingsway SW14
141 N 5 Kingsway WC2
9 N 15 Kingsway Enf
118 L 10 Kingsway New Mald
42 K 12 Kingsway Wemb
168 D 20 Kingsway av S Croy
22 M 14 Kingsway cres Harrow
140 M 4 Kingsway hall WC2
153 S 15 Kingsway rd Sutton
47 S 9 Kingswear rd NW5
79 Z 17 Kingswick rd SE18
128 L 7 Kingswood av NW6
81 O 10 Kingswood av Blvdr
125 Y 8 Kingswood av Brom
100 K 15 Kingswood av Hampt
82 D 4 Kingswood av Hounsl
122 G 13 Kingswood av Thntn Hth
15 R 1 Kingswood clo N20
15 R 1 Kingswood clo N20
116 K 16 Kingswood clo Surb
109 S 10 Kingswood dri SE19
27 V 5 Kingswood pk N3
93 Z 9 Kingswood pl SE13

110 B 16 Kingswood rd SE20
73 V 9 Kingswood rd SW19
90 A 18 Kingswood rd SW2
189 Z 17 Kingswood rd SW2
126 A 5 Kingswood rd Brom
125 Y 6 Kingswood rd Brom
54 M 3 Kingswood rd Ilf
55 N 2 Kingswood rd Ilf
156 A 10 Kingswood way Croy
43 Y 20 Kingthorpe rd NW10
143 T 1 Kingward st E1
5 U 3 Kingwell rd Barnt
144 L 20 Kingwood rd SW6
96 B 1 Kinlet rd SE18
43 Z 1 Kinloch dri NW9
44 A 1 Kinloch dri NW9
48 D 10 Kinloch st N7
120 D 18 Kinlos rd Carsh
27 U 11 Kinloss gdns N3
73 U 20 Kinnaird av W4
112 C 16 Kinnaird av Brom
112 D 16 Kinnaird clo Brom
74 C 5 Kinnear rd W12
139 R 18 Kinnerton Pl north W1
139 R 19 Kinnerton Pl south W1
139 S 20 Kinnerton st SW1
139 S 19 Kinnerton yd SW1
144 L 14 Kinnowl rd W6
152 F 4 Kinross av Worc Pk
24 L 16 Kinross clo Harrow
91 X 8 Kinsale rd SE15
151 N 4 Kintore st SE1
78 C 13 Kinveachy gdns SE7
110 D 9 Kinver rd SE26
10 H 18 Kipling pl Stanm
97 Z 1 Kipling rd Bxly Hth
142 G 18 Kipling st SE1
18 C 9 Kipling terr N21/N9
152 D 12 Kirby clo Epsom
142 J 17 Kirby gro SE1
141 U 1 Kirby st EC1
133 U 20 Kirby st EC1
72 A 1 Kirchen rd W13
79 O 16 Kirk la SE18
133 O 18 Kirk st WC1
90 A 18 Kirkby st SW2
110 B 9 Kirkdale SE26
52 A 2 Kirkdale rd E11
79 V 18 Kirkham st SE18
35 W 7 Kirkland av Ilf
76 M 3 Kirkland pl SE10
122 E 10 Kirklees rd Thntn Hth
55 S 16 Kirkless rd Dgnhm
105 Z 19 Kirkley rd SW19
157 S 20 Kirkly clo S Croy
140 E 1 Kirkman pl W1
64 H 17 Kirkmichael rd E14
63 X 15 Kirks pl E3
77 S 17 Kirkside rd SE3
31 U 12 Kirkstall av N17
107 Z 1 Kirkstall gdns SW2
107 Z 1 Kirkstall rd SW2
108 A 1 Kirkstall rd SW2
119 Z 19 Kirksted rd Mrdn
112 A 17 Kirkstone way Brom
63 R 6 Kirkwall pl E2
47 O 19 Kirkwood rd NW1
72 A 1 Kirn rd W13
110 J 9 Kirtley rd SE26
148 B 17 Kirtling st SW8
65 X 5 Kirton rd E13
25 W 2 Kirton wlk Edg
64 B 8 Kitcat ter E3
33 R 4 Kitchener rd E17
52 H 18 Kitchener rd E7
28 H 11 Kitchener rd N2
56 J 17 Kitchener rd Dgnhm
123 N 5 Kitchener rd Thntn Hth
135 T 12 Kite pl E2
123 U 1 Kitley gdns SE19
150 D 17 Kitson rd SE5
86 F 3 Kitson rd SW13
92 F 6 Kitto rd SE14
4 H 5 Kitts End rd Barnt
47 Z 7 Kiver rd N19
89 U 15 Klea av SW4
139 Y 20 Knackers yd SW1
110 A 4 Knapdale clo SE23
111 P 5 Knapmill rd SE6
111 P 5 Knapmill way SE6
64 B 12 Knapp rd E3
145 X 6 Knaresborough pl SW5
61 Z 3 Knatchbull rd NW10
90 J 3 Knatchbull rd SE5
33 O 4 Knebworth av E17
80 G 13 Knee hill SE2
80 G 11 Knee Hill cres SE2
83 P 15 Kneller gdns Islwth
83 P 15 Kneller gdns Islwth

83 R 16 Kneller hall Twick
92 J 10 Kneller rd SE4
117 Z 17 Kneller rd New Mald
83 O 16 Kneller rd Twick
82 M 16 Kneller rd Twick
72 L 7 Knight's av W5
49 Z 6 Knightland rd E5
38 M 18 Knighton clo Rom
53 J 17 Knighton clo S Croy
21 V 13 Knighton clo Wdfd Grn
21 V 13 Knighton dri Wdfd Grn
21 V 9 Knighton la Buck Hl
110 G 12 Knighton Pk rd SE26
52 F 11 Knighton rd E7
38 L 18 Knighton rd Rom
141 Z 8 Knightrider st EC4
70 A 14 Knights arbour Shall
108 J 12 Knights hill SE27
108 K 9 Knights hill SE27
18 K 10 Knights la N9
116 J 5 Knights pk Kingst
77 T 4 Knights rd E16
11 S 13 Knights rd Stanm
139 O 18 Knightsbridge SW7
138 L 19 Knightsbridge SW7
139 N 15 Knightsbridge grn SW7
12 G 8 Knightswood clo Edg
12 G 7 Knightswood clo Edg
118 B 14 Knightwood cres New Mald
145 T 15 Knivett rd SW6
64 D 2 Knobs Hill rd E15
95 N 12 Knockholt rd SE9
113 W 10 Knole SE9
99 X 19 Knole rd Drtfrd
60 C 15 Knoll W13
125 R 1 Knoll Becknhm
16 C 3 Knoll dri N14
09 D 17 Knoll rd Bxly
115 R 12 Knoll rd Sidcp
88 C 14 Knolle rd SW18
117 X 20 Knollmead Surb
108 G 6 Knolly's clo SW16
108 E 6 Knolly's rd SW16
63 S 8 Knottisford st E2
33 T 18 Knotts Green rd E10
81 N 18 Knowle av Bxly Hth
101 T 2 Knowle rd Twick
93 W 13 Knowles Hill cres SE13
88 M 6 Knowlsey rd SW11
126 D 12 Knowlton grn Brom
70 K 3 Knowsley av S'hall
52 D 18 Knox rd E7
139 O 1 Knox st W1
106 B 12 Kohat rd SW19
76 M 13 Kossuth st SE10
108 D 19 Kuala gdns SW16
45 Y 19 Kylemore rd NW6
23 T 19 Kymberley rd Harrow
39 T 20 Kyme rd Hornch
24 D 5 Kynance gdns Stanm
146 A 2 Kynance ms SW7
146 A 2 Kynance pl SW7
49 T 9 Kynaston av N16
122 L 11 Kynaston av Thntn Hth
23 H 1 Kynaston clo Harrow
122 M 11 Kynaston cres Thntn Hth
49 S 9 Kynaston rd N16
112 G 12 Kynaston rd Brom
18 B 7 Kynaston rd Enf
122 M 10 Kynaston rd Thntn Hth
19 R 16 Kynoch rd N18
89 O 14 Kyrle rd SW11
49 V 4 Kyverdale rd N16

# L

74 D 1 Labrum way W3
3 O 1 Laburnham av N17
154 H 6 Laburnham av Sutton
11 P 15 Laburnham ct Stanm
54 A 7 Laburnham gro Ilf
127 Y 16 Laburnham way Brom
18 F 3 Laburnum av N9
57 U 9 Laburnum av Hornch
19 Y 19 Laburnum clo E4
121 P 4 Laburnum est Bxly
17 Y 17 Laburnum gdns N21
25 W 20 Laburnum gro NW9
25 W 20 Laburnum gro NW9
17 Y 7 Laburnum gro N21

4 F 19 Leeside Barnt
27 U 18 Leeside cres NW11
90 H 12 Leeson rd SE24
105 U 14 Leeward gdns SW19
75 Y 13 Leeway SE8
64 A 5 Lefevre rd E3
63 Z 4 Lefevre wk E3
74 H 6 Leffern rd W12
74 C 5 Lefroy rd W12
48 J 11 Legard rd N5
94 M 13 Legatt rd SE9
95 N 12 Legatt rd SE9
64 G 6 Leggatt rd E15
93 T 12 Legge st SE13
62 F 5 Leghorn rd NW10
79 T 14 Leghorn rd SE18
119 Y 14 Legion ct Mrdn
56 L 5 Legon av Rom
122 A 9 Leicester av Mitch
140 G 9 Leicester ct EC2
152 M 7 Leicester ct Worc Pk
36 J 20 Leicester gdns Ilf
140 G 9 Leicester pl W1
34 J 16 Leicester rd E11
43 Z 20 Leicester rd E11
28 K 11 Leicester rd N2
5 R 14 Leicester rd Barnt
123 S 18 Leicester rd Croy
140 G 10 Leicester sq WC2
140 G 9 Leicester st W1
35 O 13 Leigh av Ilf
159 T 16 Leigh cres Croy
41 S 5 Leigh ct Harrow
62 M 6 Leigh gdns NW10
128 C 9 Leigh gdns NW10
142 A 17 Leigh Hunt st SE1
108 D 7 Leigh Orchard clo SW6
97 O 4 Leigh pl Welling
51 V 2 Leigh rd E10
53 V 19 Leigh rd E6
48 J 13 Leigh rd N5
83 P 10 Leigh rd Hounsl
132 J 15 Leigh st WC1
108 A 7 Leigham av SW16
108 B 5 Leigham Ct rd SW16
71 U 19 Leigham dri Islwth
108 E 6 Leigham vale SW16
53 W 16 Leighton av E12
22 B 10 Leighton av Pinn
25 R 7 Leighton clo NW9
47 W 14 Leighton cres NW8
62 L 5 Leighton gdns NW10
128 C 7 Leighton gdns NW10
47 W 14 Leighton gro NW5
47 V 16 Leighton pl NW5
47 V 15 Leighton rd NW5
72 A 5 Leighton rd W13
71 Z 5 Leighton rd W13
8 H 18 Leighton rd Enf
122 H 20 Leighton St east Croy
122 H 20 Leighton St west Croy
85 V 9 Leinster av SW14
138 B 7 Leinster gdns W2
138 B 10 Leinster ms W2
138 A 7 Leinster pl W2
129 U 11 Leinster rd NW6
29 T 13 Leinster rd N10
137 W 2 Leinster sq W2
138 B 10 Leinster ter W2
43 Y 4 Leith clo NW9
63 X 14 Leith rd E3
30 H 4 Leith rd N22
108 C 9 Leithcote gdns SW16
143 R 7 Leman st E1
11 R 17 Lemark clo Stanm
52 A 2 Lemna rd E11
96 A 15 Lemonwell dri SE9
144 D 2 Lena gdns W6
74 M 9 Lena gdns W6
89 Y 8 Lendal ter SW9
117 P 20 Lenelby rd Surb
94 B 11 Lenham rd SE12
81 O 17 Lenham rd Bxly Hth
154 B 9 Lenham rd Sutton
123 O 4 Lenham rd Thntn Hth
110 K 17 Lennard rd Becknhm
127 U 20 Lennard rd Brom
122 K 19 Lennard rd Croy
32 M 18 Lennox av E17
44 E 13 Lennox gdns NW10
147 N 4 Lennox gdns SW1
156 K 9 Lennox gdns Croy
53 S 3 Lennox gdns Ilf
147 N 4 Lennox Gdns ms SW1
32 M 18 Lennox rd E17
48 E 7 Lennox rd N4
65 X 1 Lens rd E7
80 G 7 Lensbury way SE18

80 G 8 Lensbury way SE18
142 A 18 Lent st SE1
146 B 5 Lenthall pl SW7
49 W 20 Lenthall rd E8
77 O 12 Lenthorp rd SE10
112 C 7 Lentmead rd Brom
79 R 10 Lenton st SE18
75 O 19 Leo st SE14
151 Z 17 Leo st SE15
111 P 12 Leof cres SE6
120 D 13 Leominster rd Mrdn
120 C 13 Leominster wlk Mrdn
120 D 12 Leonard av Mrdn
56 M 4 Leonard av Rom
20 B 19 Leonard rd E4
52 E 13 Leonard rd E7
18 J 12 Leonard rd N9
107 U 20 Leonard rd SW16
134 G 16 Leonard st EC2
78 D 3 Leonard st E16
19 N 18 Leopald rd N18
133 T 20 Leopards ct EC1
105 W 12 Leopold av SW19
33 O 16 Leopold rd E17
62 B 1 Leopold rd NW10
28 G 9 Leopold rd N2
105 X 11 Leopold rd SW19
73 N 2 Leopold rd W5
72 M 2 Leopold rd W5
63 Z 14 Leopold st E3
149 N 10 Leopold wlk SE11
89 X 13 Leppoc rd SW4
150 J 3 Leroy st SE1
50 C 14 Lesbia rd E5
110 J 7 Lescombe clo SE23
110 J 7 Lescombe rd SE23
98 G 18 Lesley clo Bxly
129 R 20 Leslie gro Croy
123 S 20 Leslie Pk rd Croy
51 V 12 Leslie rd E11
65 V 18 Leslie rd E16
28 G 10 Leslie rd N2
63 O 14 Leslie st E1
48 D 18 Leslie st N7
80 L 12 Lesnes Abbey park SE2
80 L 10 Lesnes Abbey remains Blvdr
81 Z 16 Lesney pk Erith
63 U 7 Lessada st E3
89 T 14 Lessar av SW4
92 G 17 Lessing st SE23
106 M 8 Lessingham av SW17
107 N 10 Lessingham av SW17
35 U 9 Lessingham av Ilf
38 K 19 Lessington av Rom
80 J 18 Lessness av Bxly Hth
81 P 12 Lessness pk Blvdr
81 R 15 Lessness rd Blvdr
120 E 13 Lessness rd Mrdn
65 N 1 Lester av E15
49 U 10 Leswin pl N16
49 U 9 Leswin rd N16
62 H 8 Letchford gdns NW10
62 H 8 Letchford mews NW10
22 K 4 Letchford terr Har
126 F 11 Letchworth clo Brom
126 F 12 Letchworth dri Brom
106 M 9 Letchworth st SW17
93 T 4 Lethbridge rd SE10
64 G 2 Lett rd E15
145 N 19 Letterstone rd SW6
87 W 3 Lettice st SW6
91 R 4 Lettsom st SE5
32 H 16 Leucha rd E17
64 J 16 Leven rd E14
110 K 4 Levendale rd SE23
134 A 14 Lever st EC1
133 Y 14 Lever st EC1
113 W 9 Leverholme gdns SE9
90 A 4 Leverhurst way SW4
107 V 16 Leverson st SW16
47 U 15 Leverton pl NW5
47 U 14 Leverton st NW5
54 H 17 Levett rd Bark
54 H 18 Levett rd Bark
54 K 11 Levett rd Ilf
68 K 6 Levine gdns Bark
40 H 14 Lewes clo Grnfd
15 W 18 Lewes rd N12
151 N 3 Lewes rd Brom
127 N 3 Lewes rd Brom
49 U 2 Leweston pl N16
25 W 18 Lewgars av NW9
85 Z 9 Lewin rd SW14
107 Z 13 Lewin rd SW16
97 Z 11 Lewin rd Bxly Hth
33 O 12 Lewis av E17

43 X 16 Lewis cres NW10
28 G 6 Lewis gdns N2
93 U 9 Lewis gro SE13
120 J 3 Lewis rd Mitch
84 H 13 Lewis rd Rich
70 C 5 Lewis rd S'hall
115 T 7 Lewis rd Sidcp
154 B 7 Lewis rd Sutton
97 U 8 Lewis rd Welling
47 T 19 Lewis st NW1
93 T 12 Lewisham High st SE13
93 U 6 Lewisham hill SE13
93 T 14 Lewisham pk SE13
93 T 3 Lewisham rd SE13
140 G 19 Lewisham st SW1
92 L 2 Lewisham way SE14
93 O 5 Lewisham way SE4
37 O 18 Lexden dri Rom
73 T 2 Lexden rd W3
121 W 8 Lexden rd Mitch
145 X 4 Lexham gdns W8
145 Y 4 Lexham Gdns ms SW7
145 V 4 Lexham ms W8
145 X 3 Lexham wlk W8
140 D 8 Lexington st W1
4 C 15 Lexington way Barnt
89 Z 20 Lexton gdns SW12
36 D 20 Ley st Ilf
53 Y 8 Ley st Ilf
54 C 5 Ley st Ilf
72 D 5 Leyborne av W13
85 O 1 Leyborne pk Rich
126 E 13 Leybourne clo Brom
52 C 4 Leybourne rd E11
25 O 15 Leybourne rd NW9
94 E 13 Leybridge ct SE12
33 T 13 Leyburn clo E17
157 S 3 Leyburn gdns Croy
18 K 19 Leyburn gro N18
18 L 19 Leyburn rd N18
142 M 2 Leyden st E1
143 N 3 Leyden st E1
66 A 19 Leyes rd E16
65 Z 19 Leyes rd E16
152 C 1 Leyfield Worc Pk
9 V 8 Leyland av Enf
21 Y 17 Leyland gdns Wdfd Grn
94 D 13 Leyland rd SE12
75 T 19 Leylang rd SE14
69 Y 2 Leys av Dgnhm
69 X 1 Leys clo Dgnhm
23 R 14 Leys clo Harrow
6 B 16 Leys gdns Barnt
9 V 5 Leys Rd east Enf
9 V 5 Leys Rd west Enf
28 D 13 Leys the N2
24 L 18 Leys the Harrow
98 K 11 Leysdown av Bxly Hth
113 S 4 Leysdown rd SE9
74 H 7 Leysfield rd W12
52 C 3 Leyspring rd E11
36 G 14 Leyswood dri Ilf
73 V 6 Leythe rd W3
33 T 20 Leyton Grn rd E10
51 U 8 Leyton Pk rd E10
51 V 14 Leyton rd E15
106 E 18 Leyton rd SW19
151 T 15 Leyton sq SE15
57 Y 13 Leytonstone rd E15
75 X 18 Liardet gro SE14
48 J 17 Liberia rd N5
90 D 1 Liberty st SW9
65 S 5 Libra rd E3
63 Y 4 Libra rd E3
141 X 19 Library st SE1
84 J 11 Lichfield gdns Rich
27 Y 5 Lichfield gro N3
28 A 7 Lichfield gro N3
66 B 10 Lichfield rd E6
45 S 11 Lichfield rd NW2
18 J 8 Lichfield rd N9
55 S 10 Lichfield rd Dgnhm
85 N 2 Lichfield rd Rich
21 N 14 Lichfield rd Wdfd Grn
90 E 5 Lidcote gdns SW9
24 H 11 Liddell clo Harrow
62 M 5 Liddell gdns NW10
128 C 7 Liddell gdns NW10
126 M 6 Lidden rd Brom
24 H 16 Lidding rd Harrow
65 P 3 Liddington rd E15
65 U 10 Liddon rd E13
127 N 6 Liddon rd Brom
49 O 13 Lidfield rd N16
150 M 19 Lidgate rd SE15
106 E 3 Lidiard rd SW18
132 B 10 Lidlington pl NW1
47 V 5 Lidyard rd N19

79 T 13 Liffler rd SE18
87 P 10 Lifford st SW15
17 U 12 Lightcliffe rd N13
30 A 15 Lightfoot rd N8
19 Y 19 Lilac av W5
72 G 8 Lilac gdns W5
159 O 5 Lilac gdns Croy
57 O 4 Lilac gdns Rom
62 F 19 Lilac st W12
95 R 13 Lilburne gdns SE9
95 S 13 Lilburne rd SE9
59 U 15 Lile cres W7
90 J 4 Lilford rd SE5
34 J 4 Lilian gdns Wdfd
107 U 20 Lilian rd SW16
55 T 15 Lillechurch rd Dgn
120 F 14 Lilleshall rd Mrdn
12 M 15 Lilley la NW7
73 O 7 Lillian av W3
74 H 16 Lillian rd SW13
144 H 16 Lille rd SW6
145 P 14 Lillie road SW6
89 T 7 Lillieshall rd SW4
148 C 7 Lillington st SW1
58 D 3 Lilliput av Grnfd
57 N 1 Lilliput rd Rom
60 E 7 Lily gdns Wemb
33 P 19 Lily rd E17
87 V 1 Lilyville rd SW6
56 B 2 Limbourne av Dgn
88 K 1 Limburg rd SW11
154 L 1 Lime clo Carsh
38 J 14 Lime clo Rom
14 F 4 Lime gro N20
74 L 4 Lime gro W12
136 B 16 Lime gro W12
117 Z 6 Lime gro New Mald
96 L 15 Lime gro Sidcp
83 X 16 Lime gro Twick
142 J 7 Lime st EC3
32 H 13 Lime st E17
142 J 7 Lime St pas EC3
142 J 7 Lime St pass EC3
159 N 5 Lime Tree gro Croy
82 K 1 Lime Tree rd Houns
158 L 6 Lime Tree rd Houns
7 X 3 Lime Tree wlk Enf
70 K 20 Lime Trees rd Houn
63 Z 20 Limehouse causeway E14
146 E 15 Limerston st SW10
34 J 14 Limes av E11
27 T 20 Limes av NW7
13 N 18 Limes av NW7
16 G 16 Limes av N11
15 R 12 Limes av N12
86 C 5 Limes av SW13
154 L 1 Limes av Carsh
156 E 6 Limes av Croy
86 A 7 Limes Field rd SW1
87 Y 17 Limes gdns SW18
93 U 10 Limes gro SE13
11 N 9 Limes house Stanm
125 S 3 Limes rd Becknhm
123 N 16 Limes rd Croy
72 H 7 Limes wlk W5
25 V 8 Limesdale gdns Edg
92 E 10 Limesford rd SE15
121 S 1 Limetree pl Mitch
60 C 16 Limewood clo W13
81 Y 19 Limewood rd Erith
105 P 3 Limpsfield av SW19
122 D 12 Limpsfield av Thntn Hth
151 T 18 Limpston Gdn estate SE15
44 K 18 Linacre rd NW2
94 D 19 Linchmere rd SE12
16 G 10 Lincoln av N14
105 O 7 Lincoln av SW19
57 O 4 Lincoln av Rom
101 O 2 Lincoln av Twick
100 M 3 Lincoln av Twick
99 T 5 Lincoln clo Erith
58 M 3 Lincoln clo Grnfd
59 N 3 Lincoln clo Grnfd
22 E 16 Lincoln clo Harrow
8 F 17 Lincoln cres Enf
53 S 1 Lincoln gdns Ilf
129 N 3 Lincoln ms NW6
53 N 19 Lincoln rd E12
65 U 13 Lincoln rd E13
34 D 6 Lincoln rd E18
31 W 11 Lincoln rd N17
28 K 11 Lincoln rd N2
123 Z 7 Lincoln rd SE25
9 P 18 Lincoln rd Enf
8 L 17 Lincoln rd Enf
99 U 4 Lincoln rd Erith
100 D 7 Lincoln rd Felt
22 F 16 Lincoln rd Harrow
117 V 6 Lincoln rd New Mald
115 R 12 Lincoln rd Sidcp

G 18 Lincoln rd Wemb
H 19 Lincoln rd Worc Pk
Y 7 Lincoln st E11
O 8 Lincoln st SW3
M 16 Lincoln way Enf
O 5 Lincolns Inn fields WC2
S 9 Lincolns the NW7
C 7 Lincombe rd Brom
E 11 Lind rd Sutton
P 4 Lind st SE4
O 15 Lindal cres Enf
L 14 Lindal rd SE4
Z 18 Lindbergh rd Wallgtn
E 11 Linden av NW10
K 6 Linden av Enf
K 12 Linden av Hounsl
H 8 Linden av Thntn Hth
N 14 Linden av Wemb
M 14 Linden av Wemb
G 19 Linden clo N14
V 17 Linden cres Grnfd
N 4 Linden cres Kingst
U 18 Linden cres Wdfd Grn
L 2 Linden ct W12
V 11 Linden gdns W2
Z 13 Linden gdns W4
K 5 Linden gdns Enf
A 8 Linden gro SE15
D 16 Linden gro SE20
A 6 Linden gro New Mald
V 11 Linden gro Tedd
L 14 Linden lawns Wemb
E 17 Linden lea N2
X 2 Linden leas W Wkhm
U 11 Linden ms W11
L 15 Linden rd E17
T 13 Linden rd N10
A 8 Linden rd N11
L 13 Linden rd N15
G 20 Linden rd Hampt
H 20 Linden way N14
H 1 Linden way N14
U 13 Lindens Croy
B 14 Lindfield gdns NW3
D 11 Lindfield rd W5
V 15 Lindfield rd Croy
B 17 Lindfield st E14
G 19 Lindisfarne rd SW20
T 9 Lindisfarne rd Dgnhm
T 6 Lindley rd E10
O 14 Lindley st E1
Z 1 Lindley st E1
B 12 Lindore rd SW11
C 18 Lindores rd Carsh
C 4 Lindrop st SW6
M 16 Lindsay dri Harrow
L 10 Lindsay rd Hampt
K 7 Lindsay rd Worc Pk
O 4 Lindsell st Bark
T 1 Lindsell st SE10
A 12 Lindsey est E3
S 11 Lindsey rd Dgnhm
Y 1 Lindsey st EC1
C 18 Lindum rd Tedd
J 13 Lindway SE27
V 11 Linford rd E17
U 2 Linford st SW8
T 14 Ling rd E13
Y 17 Ling rd Erith
D 10 Lingards rd SE13
K 9 Lingfield av Kingst
D 10 Lingfield clo Enf
E 10 Lingfield cres SE9
N 2 Lingfield gdns N9
P 14 Lingfield rd SW19
M 6 Lingfield rd Worc Pk
B 5 Lingham st SW9
C 16 Lingholm way Barnt
O 3 Lings coppice SE21
K 6 Lingwell rd SW17
T 18 Lingwood gdns Islwth
Y 1 Lingwood rd E5
X 20 Lingwood rd N16
N 18 Linhope st NW1
Y 13 Link la Wallgtn
A 13 Link la Wallgtn
B 13 Link rd N11
O 1 Link rd Wallgtn
D 16 Link st E9
S 16 Link the W3
V 5 Link the Enf
D 16 Link the Grnfd
D 4 Link the Wemb
R 16 Link way Brom
E 14 Linkfield Brom
Y 5 Linkfield rd Islwth
Y 8 Links av Mrdn

39 Z 6 Links av Rom
14 M 6 Links dri N20
108 F 18 Links gdns SW16
44 C 8 Links rd NW2
107 R 17 Links rd SW17
61 P 16 Links rd W3
125 V 20 Links rd W Wkhm
21 S 16 Links rd Wdfd Grn
7 S 12 Links side Enf
10 L 20 Links View clo Watf
159 O 4 Links View rd Croy
101 O 1 Links View rd Hampt
107 N 15 Links way SW17
125 O 13 Links way Becknhm
14 J 18 Linkside N12
118 B 4 Linkside New Mald
7 S 12 Linkside gdns Enf
7 R 11 Linkside gdns Enf
27 O 8 Linksway NW4
118 L 6 Linkway SW20
55 U 11 Linkway Dgnhm
102 B 5 Linkway Rich
4 M 20 Linkway the Barnt
154 E 20 Linkway the Sutton
38 J 9 Linley cres Rom
31 S 7 Linley rd N17
27 Z 19 Linnell clo NW11
27 Z 20 Linnell dri NW11
18 K 15 Linnell rd N18
91 S 3 Linnell rd SE5
90 A 11 Linnell rd SW9
50 C 13 Linscott rd E5
151 S 5 Linsey st SE16
87 S 18 Linstead way SW18
45 X 19 Linsteads NW6
42 F 17 Linthorpe av Wemb
49 T 1 Linthorpe rd N16
5 W 12 Linthorpe rd Barnt
97 O 3 Linton clo Well
108 L 11 Linton gro SE27
54 D 20 Linton rd Bark
67 O 1 Linton rd Bark
67 P 1 Linton rd Bark
134 C 5 Linton st N1
87 W 5 Linver rd SW6
29 Z 13 Linzee rd N8
101 V 2 Lion av Twick
84 M 6 Lion Ga gdns Rich
85 N 5 Lion gdns Rich
18 J 9 Lion rd N9
08 A 10 Lion rd Bxly Hth
122 L 13 Lion rd Croy
101 V 1 Lion rd Twick
150 A 4 Lion st SE17
72 F 18 Lion way Brentf
84 A 3 Lion wharf Islwth
95 O 12 Lionel gdns SE9
128 K 20 Lionel ms W10
95 O 12 Lionel rd SE9
72 L 13 Lionel rd Brentf
73 O 14 Lionel rd Brentf
92 R 19 Liphook cres SE23
101 N 4 Lisbon av Twick
100 M 5 Lisbon av Twick
63 N 13 Lisbon st E1
46 M 13 Lisburne rd NW3
91 V 1 Lisford st SE15
145 N 6 Lisgar ter W14
94 F 2 Liskeard gdns SE3
140 G 9 Lisle st W1
47 N 14 Lismore cir NW5
83 Y 5 Lismore clo Islwth
31 O 11 Lismore rd N17
157 R 15 Lismore rd S Croy
47 P 12 Lissenden gdns NW5
130 G 15 Lisson gro NW8
130 K 20 Lisson st NW1
17 Z 16 Lister gdns N18
18 A 16 Lister gdns N18
17 Z 16 Lister gdns N18
52 A 5 Lister rd E11
31 W 5 Liston rd N17
89 V 8 Liston rd SW4
34 L 2 Liston way Wdfd Grn
56 L 8 Listowel rd Dgnhm
149 X 20 Listowel st SW9
49 T 6 Listria pk N16
51 Z 18 Litchfield av E15
119 V 16 Litchfield av Mrdn
44 G 19 Litchfield gdns NW10
63 W 9 Litchfield rd E3
154 B 9 Litchfield rd Sutton
140 H 8 Litchfield st WC2
28 C 16 Litchfield way NW11
46 C 17 Lithos rd NW3
75 O 10 Litlington st SE16
151 Y 5 Litlington st SE16
140 A 6 Little Argyll st W1
114 H 5 Little birches Sidcp
135 Z 10 Little Boltons the E2

109 S 8 Little bornes SE21
142 A 3 Little britain EC1
141 Y 2 Little britain EC1
18 C 4 Little Bury st N9
10 C 1 Little Bushey la Bushey Watf
148 J 2 Little College st SW1
87 R 18 Little Cote clo SW19
159 Z 3 Little court W Wkhm
159 Z 3 Little ct W Wkhm
107 T 3 Little dimocks SW4
142 C 16 Little Dorrit ct SE1
72 F 9 Little Ealing la W5
131 Y 11 Little Edward st NW1
35 Z 13 Little gearies Ilf
140 J 19 Little George st SW1
47 S 12 Little Green st NW5
5 X 20 Little gro Barnt
78 D 14 Little heath SE7
37 P 14 Little heath Rom
81 P 20 Little Heath rd Bxly Hth
98 A 1 Little Heath rd Bxly Hth
157 Z 17 Little Heath rd S Croy
53 U 11 Little Ilford la E12
59 V 16 Little John rd W7
140 B 7 Little Marlborough st W1
22 C 7 Little Moss la Pinn
141 V 5 Little New st EC4
140 G 9 Little Newport st WC2
100 A 4 Little Park dri Felt
8 A 12 Little Park gdns Enf
21 Z 5 Little Plucketts la Buck Hl
140 A 3 Little Portland st W1
10 D 2 Little potters Watf
10 D 2 Little potters Watf
101 V 15 Little Queens rd Tedd
127 P 2 Little redlands Brom
127 P 2 Little redlands Brom
140 J 2 Little Russell st WC1
140 H 19 Little sanctuary SW1
140 H 19 Little sanctuary SW1
148 H 1 Little St SW7
143 N 6 Little Somerset st E1
140 B 15 Little St James st SW1
85 W 8 Little St leonards SW14
140 A 3 Little Titchfield st W1
141 N 3 Little turnstile WC 1
89 X 8 Littlebury st SW18
77 W 16 Littlecombe SE7
22 C 3 Littlecote pl Pinn
95 V 7 Littlecroft SE9
80 A 17 Littledale SE2
25 U 1 Littlefield rd Edg
158 A 20 Littleheath rd S Croy
113 U 7 Littlemede rd SE9
54 E 10 Littlemoor rd Ilf
80 A 7 Littlemore rd SE2
106 F 20 Littlers clo SW19
21 O 6 Littleton av Ev
41 W 7 Littleton cres Harrow
41 X 8 Littleton rd Harrow
106 D 5 Littleton st SW18
93 V 15 Littlewood SE13
135 O 2 Livermere rd E8
150 D 11 Liverpool gro SE17
33 V 17 Liverpool rd E10
65 N 15 Liverpool rd E16
133 U 2 Liverpool rd N1
48 F 17 Liverpool rd N7
72 H 5 Liverpool rd W5
103 R 17 Liverpool rd Kingst
122 M 7 Liverpool rd Thntn Hth
142 J 2 Liverpool st EC2
142 K 2 Liverpool St station EC2
151 T 14 Livesey pl SE15
64 H 4 Livingstone rd E15
33 R 18 Livingstone rd E17
17 N 18 Livingstone rd N13
88 G 8 Livingstone rd SW11
83 N 9 Livingstone rd Hounsl
82 M 9 Livingstone rd Hounsl
58 A 20 Livingstone rd S'hall
123 N 4 Livingstone rd Thntn Hth
66 L 18 Livingstone st E6
140 D 7 Livonia st W1
77 Y 19 Lizban st SE10
45 W 8 Llanelly rd NW2
78 K 18 Llanover rd SE18

42 G 10 Llanover rd Wemb
120 F 13 Llanthony rd Mrdn
45 W 7 Llanvanor rd NW2
143 T 18 Llewellyn st SE16
122 B 1 Lloyd av SW16
133 S 12 Lloyd Baker st WC1
33 N 7 Lloyd park E17
157 V 8 Lloyd park Croy
157 U 9 Lloyd Pk av Croy
32 F 13 Lloyd rd E17
66 F 4 Lloyd rd E6
56 C 19 Lloyd rd Dgnhm
153 N 4 Lloyd rd Worc Pk
133 R 13 Lloyd sq WC1
133 S 12 Lloyd st WC1
142 L 7 Lloyds av EC3
94 A 5 Lloyds pl SE3
133 V 13 Lloyds row EC1
124 K 11 Lloyds way Becknhm
93 P 6 Loampit hills SE13
93 S 7 Loampit vale SE13
143 P 10 Loats bldgs E1
59 P 10 Locarno rd Grnfd
93 Z 11 Lochaber rd SE13
144 E 12 Lochaline st W6
89 R 19 Lochinvar st SW12
64 G 14 Lochnagar st E14
94 B 8 Lock chase SE3
102 E 8 Lock rd Rich
57 V 19 Locke clo Rainhm
23 U 9 Locket rd Harrow
9 X 8 Lockfield av Enf
63 Z 19 Lockhart st E3
50 F 12 Lockhurst st E5
89 T 1 Lockington rd SW8
31 Y 18 Lockmead rd N15
93 V 7 Lockmead rd SE13
81 V 17 Lockmere clo Erith
121 N 2 Locks la Mitch
63 Y 15 Locksley st E14
151 W 2 Lockwood rd SE16
54 C 8 Lockwood rd Ilf
142 F 18 Lockyer st SE1
50 C 20 Loddiges rd E9
75 P 20 Loder st SE15
85 Z 8 Lodge av SW14
156 E 6 Lodge av Croy
55 P 13 Lodge av Dgnhm
68 B 3 Lodge av Dgnhm
24 J 14 Lodge av Harrow
39 U 12 Lodge av Rom
18 A 17 Lodge clo N18
155 O 1 Lodge clo Wallgtn
6 K 13 Lodge cres Enf
17 T 14 Lodge dri N13
124 M 12 Lodge gdns Becknhm
80 E 18 Lodge hill Welling
15 P 15 Lodge la N12
97 V 14 Lodge la Bxly
159 P 15 Lodge la Croy
38 D 3 Lodge la Rom
26 M 12 Lodge rd NW4
130 H 15 Lodge rd NW8
112 K 17 Lodge rd Brom
122 K 15 Lodge rd Croy
122 L 17 Lodge rd Croy
154 B 9 Lodge rd Sutton
101 V 13 Lodge rd Tedd
155 R 10 Lodge rd Wallgtn
21 P 20 Lodge vlls Wdfd Grn
26 A 15 Lodore gdns NW9
64 F 13 Lodore st E14
143 U 18 Loftie st SE16
133 O 2 Lofting rd N1
74 K 3 Loftus rd W12
9 T 7 Logan clo Enf
145 T 5 Logan ms W8
145 T 5 Logan pl W8
19 O 9 Logan rd N9
42 J 6 Logan rd Wemb
113 R 19 Logs hill Chisl
127 S 1 Logs hill Chisl
113 R 20 Logs Hill clo Chisl
143 O 2 Lolesworth st E1
149 S 7 Lollard st SE11
141 Y 16 Loman st SE1
9 R 7 Lombard av Enf
54 G 5 Lombard av Ilf
142 G 8 Lombard ct EC3
16 F 16 Lombard rd N11
88 F 5 Lombard rd SW11
120 B 2 Lombard rd SW19
142 G 7 Lombard st EC3
77 V 12 Lombard wall SE7
137 Y 10 Lombardy pl W2
43 N 20 Lommed clo Wemb
150 D 19 Lomond gro SE5
150 L 13 Loncroft rd SE5
49 R 11 Londesborough rd N16
142 F 12 London br EC4
142 F 14 London Br st SE1

142 H 14 London Bridge station SE1
135 W 3 London fields E8
49 Y 20 London Fields W side E8
50 A 20 London la E8
112 F 17 London la Brom
138 G 5 London ms W2
137 Z 15 London museum W8
65 R 7 London rd E13
149 X 2 London rd SE 1
110 B 2 London rd SE23
122 D 4 London rd SW16
66 M 2 London rd Bark
67 O 1 London rd Bark
112 C 19 London rd Brom
99 P 13 London rd Drtfrd
8 C 14 London rd Enf
152 K 11 London rd Epsom
41 T 7 London rd Harrow
83 X 2 London rd Islwth
84 B 1 London rd Islwth
117 N 2 London rd Kingst
121 P 17 London rd Mitch
120 K 8 London rd Mitch
107 N 19 London rd Mitch
119 X 11 London rd Mrdn
38 F 18 London rd Rom
11 U 14 London rd Stanm
153 O 4 London rd Sutton
83 Y 17 London rd Twick
155 S 3 London rd Wallgtn
42 M 17 London rd Wemb
142 L 8 London st EC3
138 G 6 London st W2
142 G 3 London wall EC2
140 L 6 Long acre WC2
155 P 14 Long Acre pl Carsh
20 M 6 Long Deacon rd E4
62 B 16 Long dri W3
58 L 4 Long dri Grnfd
40 B 11 Long drive Pinn
23 R 4 Long elmes Harrow
22 M 5 Long elmes Harrow
82 H 3 Long hedges Hounsl
141 Y 1 Long la EC1
28 D 8 Long la N2
27 Z 3 Long la N3
142 D 18 Long la SE1
97 Z 1 Long la Bxly Hth
80 K 20 Long la Bxly Hth
124 B 14 Long la Croy
20 E 19 Long leys E4
47 X 16 Long meadow NW5
114 G 2 Long Meadow rd Sidcp
93 Z 3 Long Pond rd SE3
94 A 2 Long Pond rd SE3
89 U 10 Long rd SW4
134 M 11 Long st E8
150 L 1 Long wlk SE1
86 C 6 Long wlk SW13
117 W 5 Long wlk New Mald
133 N 18 Long yd WC1
33 W 4 Longacre rd E17
189 N 9 Longbeach rd SW11
45 V 8 Longberrys NW2
54 G 16 Longbridge rd Bark
55 N 12 Longbridge rd Dgnhm
93 T 12 Longbridge way SE13
113 V 7 Longcroft SE9
24 H 1 Longcrofte rd Edg
111 O 9 Longdown rd SE6
32 L 20 Longfellow rd E17
33 N 18 Longfellow rd E17
63 V 10 Longfellow rd E3
152 H 1 Longfellow rd Worc Pk
112 D 20 Longfield Brom
32 G 14 Longfield av E17
26 G 3 Longfield av NW7
60 E 20 Longfield av W5
9 R 2 Longfield av Enf
57 T 1 Longfield av Hornch
121 P 20 Longfield av Wallgtn
155 P 1 Longfield av Wallgtn
42 J 5 Longfield av Wemb
110 C 6 Longfield cres SE26
85 S 13 Longfield dri SW14
60 F 18 Longfield rd W5
87 X 19 Longfield wlk SW18
60 E 18 Longfield wlk W5
70 J 1 Longford av S'hall
58 J 20 Longford av S'hall
100 G 10 Longford clo Hampt
154 D 4 Longford gdns Sutton
100 J 2 Longford rd Twick
131 Z 16 Longford st NW1
37 W 12 Longhayes av Rom
124 D 12 Longheath gdns Croy

89 P 3 Longhedge st SW11
111 X 6 Longhill rd SE6
93 Z 14 Longhurst rd SE13
94 A 14 Longhurst rd SE13
124 B 14 Longhurst rd Croy
124 A 14 Longhurst rd Croy
115 N 9 Longland dri N20
115 N 6 Longlands la Sidcp
114 H 6 Longlands Pk cres Sidcp
114 J 6 Longlands rd Sidcp
8 F 19 Longleat rd Enf
80 E 16 Longleigh la SE2
61 N 4 Longley av Wemb
106 J 14 Longley rd SW17
122 H 18 Longley rd Croy
23 P 14 Longley rd Harrow
151 S 6 Longley st SE1
115 X 4 Longmead dri Sidcp
106 L 11 Longmead rd SW17
148 B 6 Longmoore st SW1
5 R 19 Longmore av Barnt
63 U 10 Longnor rd E1
67 X 12 Longreach rd Bark
58 L 18 Longridge la S'hall
145 T 7 Longridge rd SW5
140 G 10 Longs ct WC2
20 K 11 Longshaw rd E4
75 Y 11 Longshore SE8
87 Z 17 Longstaff cres SW18
87 Z 17 Longstaff rd SW18
62 E 3 Longstone av NW10
107 S 13 Longstone rd SW17
121 W 3 Longthornton rd SW16
109 Y 10 Longton av SE26
110 A 9 Longton gro SE26
109 Z 10 Longton gro SE26
38 L 5 Longview way Rom
149 X 5 Longville rd SE11
86 H 17 Longwood dri SW15
35 U 14 Longwood gdns Ilf
26 B 12 Loning the NW9
9 O 2 Loning the Enf
66 G 11 Lonsdale av E6
38 J 18 Lonsdale av Rom
42 L 16 Lonsdale av Wemb
22 C 3 Lonsdale clo Pinn
35 Y 18 Lonsdale cres Ilf
7 O 14 Lonsdale dri Enf
6 K 14 Lonsdale dri Enf
122 C 8 Lonsdale gdns Thntn Hth
137 R 6 Lonsdale ms W11
85 O 2 Lonsdale ms Rich
133 U 2 Lonsdale pl N1
34 D 20 Lonsdale rd E11
129 O 6 Lonsdale rd NW6
124 Z 8 Lonsdale rd SE25
74 F 18 Lonsdale rd SW13
86 D 3 Lonsdale rd SW13
137 R 7 Lonsdale rd W11
74 C 10 Lonsdale rd W4
98 B 5 Lonsdale rd Bxly Hth
133 T 2 Lonsdale sq N1
31 T 11 Loobert rd N15
36 A 9 Looe gdns Ilf
114 A 16 Loop rd Chisl
18 D 13 Lopen rd N18
48 C 13 Loraine rd N7
23 S 17 Loraine rd W4
75 P 12 Lorbetts la SE16
35 U 10 Lord av Ilf
103 X 20 Lord Chancellor wlk Kingst
35 S 12 Lord gdns Ilf
129 Y 20 Lord Hills rd W9
148 J 2 Lord North st SW1
78 E 3 Lord st E16
78 F 9 Lord Warwick st SE18
100 C 5 Lords clo Felt
130 G 13 Lords Cricket grd NW8
49 P 7 Lordship gro N16
31 O 6 Lordship la N17
30 G 6 Lordship la N22
91 V 15 Lordship la SE22
48 M 7 Lordship pk N16
49 O 6 Lordship pk N16
146 K 15 Lordship pl SW3
49 O 4 Lordship rd N16
49 P 8 Lordship ter N16
31 S 6 Lordsmead rd N17
133 O 11 Lorenzo st WC1
24 J 13 Loretto gdns Harrow
15 V 8 Loring rd N20
83 V 4 Loring rd Islwth
144 D 2 Loris rd W6
90 E 4 Lorn rd SW9
124 F 16 Lorne av Croy
130 L 15 Lorne clo NW8
34 K 17 Lorne gdns E11

136 J 17 Lorne gdns W11
124 G 16 Lorne gdns Croy
33 N 17 Lorne rd E17
52 K 11 Lorne rd E7
48 E 3 Lorne rd N4
23 V 8 Lorne rd Harrow
84 L 13 Lorne rd Rich
9 P 17 Lorraine clo Enf
149 Y 14 Lorrimore rd SE17
149 Z 13 Lorrimore sq SE17
30 J 20 Lothair rd N4
72 F 7 Lothair rd W5
30 H 20 Lothair Rd south N4
88 H 8 Lothair st SW11
142 F 5 Lothbury EC2
149 Y 20 Lothian rd SW9
90 J 1 Lothian rd SW9
128 L 13 Lothrop st W10
146 C 19 Lots rd SW10
106 M 14 Loubet st SW17
36 A 15 Loudoun av Ilf
35 Z 14 Loudoun av Ilf
130 D 5 Loudoun rd NW8
130 C 3 Loudoun Rd ms NW8
48 D 16 Lough rd N7
90 J 9 Loughborough pk SW9
90 J 7 Loughborough rd SW9
90 F 4 Loughborough rd SW9
149 R 10 Loughborough st SE11
63 S 13 Louisa st E1
52 A 17 Louise rd E15
107 O 6 Louisville rd SW17
88 G 11 Louvaine rd SW11
44 D 11 Lovat clo NW2
142 H 10 Lovat la EC3
12 E 18 Lovatt clo Edg
12 E 18 Lovatt clo Edg
142 C 4 Love la EC2
31 U 2 Love la N17
78 L 11 Love la SE18
124 A 7 Love la SE25
98 D 17 Love la Bxly
120 K 4 Love la Mitch
119 Z 17 Love la Mrdn
120 A 16 Love la Mrdn
22 A 10 Love la Pinn
153 T 13 Love la Sutton
126 G 3 Love lane Brom
91 N 4 Love walk SE5
72 B 3 Loveday rd W13
151 T 12 Lovegrove st SE1
96 M 5 Lovel av Well
97 N 4 Lovel av Welling
127 X 15 Lovelace av Brom
54 M 14 Lovelace gdns Bark
116 F 17 Lovelace gdns Surb
95 T 7 Lovelace grn SE9
108 L 2 Lovelace rd SE21
15 W 2 Lovelace rd Barnt
116 H 17 Lovelace rd Surb
75 R 17 Lovelinch st SE15
102 D 7 Lovell rd Rich
58 J 17 Lovell rd S'hall
57 V 17 Lovell wlk Rainhm
45 V 18 Loveridge rd NW6
14 H 19 Lovers wlk NW7
27 X 1 Lovers wlk N3
109 V 7 Low Cross Wood la SE21
20 L 9 Low Hall clo E4
32 J 19 Low Hall la E17
19 N 5 Lowden rd N9
90 K 11 Lowden rd SE24
58 B 19 Lowden rd S'hall
65 T 15 Lowe av E16
63 W 17 Lowells st E14
69 Z 6 Lowen rd Rainhm
123 W 20 Lower Addiscombe rd Croy
147 W 3 Lower Belgrave st SW1
71 T 4 Lower Boston rd W7
69 R 3 Lower Broad st Dgnhm
113 U 20 Lower camden Chisl
127 V 1 Lower camden Chisl
156 J 3 Lower Church st Croy
50 B 12 Lower Clapton rd E5
86 K 8 Lower Common south SW15
156 M 7 Lower Coombe st Croy
105 P 20 Lower Downs rd SW20
18 K 13 Lower Fore st N9
127 T 20 Lower Gravel rd Brom

147 Y 1 Lower Grosvenor SW1
19 W 15 Lower Hall la E4
102 G 13 Lower Ham rd Kir
116 H 1 Lower Ham rd Kir
96 A 7 Lower Jackwood SE9
140 C 9 Lower John st W
6 M 16 Lower Kenwood a N14
16 H 18 Lower Maidstone N11
74 K 14 Lower mall W6
144 B 11 Lower mall W6
69 Y 7 Lower Mardyke a R'hm
141 R 19 Lower marsh SE1
117 R 9 Lower Marsh la Kingst
116 M 8 Lower Marsh la Kingst
119 P 14 Lower Morden la Mrdn
84 L 9 Lower Mortlake rd Rich
39 T 19 Lower Moss la N11
16 G 18 Lower Pk rd N11
81 T 9 Lower Pk rd Blvdr
65 R 10 Lower rd E13
48 E 16 Lower rd N7
75 R 8 Lower rd SE16
81 U 9 Lower rd Blvdr
81 Z 10 Lower rd Erith
41 P 4 Lower rd Harrow
154 E 9 Lower rd Sutton
85 S 7 Lower Richmond SW14
87 O 7 Lower Richmond re SW15
147 R 8 Lower Sloane st SW1
99 P 16 Lower Station rd Drtfd
102 F 18 Lower Teddington Kingst
116 F 2 Lower Teddington Kingst
46 D 9 Lower ter NW3
142 G 10 Lower Thames st EC3
10 B 1 Lower tub Watford
45 X 19 Lowfield rd NW6
61 V 17 Lowfield rd W3
23 T 15 Lowick rd Harrow
38 H 17 Lowlands gdns Ror
23 T 20 Lowlands rd Harrow
48 D 13 Lowman rd N7
147 U 2 Lowndes clo SW1
140 B 7 Lowndes ct W1
147 T 2 Lowndes pl SW1
139 R 19 Lowndes sq SW1
147 S 1 Lowndes st SW1
126 F 4 Lowndes av Brom
63 O 20 Lowood st E1
143 Y 9 Lowood st E1
38 F 4 Lowshoe la Rom
90 M 4 Lowth rd SE5
6 M 13 Lowther dri Enf
7 N 14 Lowther dri Enf
92 J 19 Lowther hill SE23
86 E 2 Lowther rd SW13
74 E 20 Lowther rd SW13
103 N 19 Lowther rd Kingst
24 M 10 Lowther rd Stanm
66 B 7 Loxford av E6
54 C 14 Loxford la Ilf
54 A 18 Loxford rd Bark
33 P 1 Loxham rd E4
132 L 13 Loxham st WC1
88 H 20 Loxley rd SW18
110 G 2 Loxton rd SE23
31 S 11 Loxwood rd N17
113 V 19 Lubbock rd Chisl
75 R 20 Lubbock st SE14
88 K 7 Lubeck st SW11
146 K 6 Lucan pl SW3
4 F 10 Lucan rd Barnt
65 W 3 Lucas av E13
40 G 6 Lucas av Harrow
110 D 16 Lucas rd SE20
93 N 3 Lucas st SE4
17 N 12 Lucern clo N14
33 X 14 Lucerne gro E17
137 V 13 Lucerne ms W8
48 J 12 Lucerne rd N5
122 K 10 Lucerne rd Thntn Hth
151 T 4 Lucey rd SE16
107 O 10 Lucien rd SW17
105 Z 4 Lucien rd SW18
21 Y 4 Luctons av Buck Hl
61 V 13 Lucy cres W3
56 A 10 Lucy gdns Dgnhm
81 S 18 Luddesdon rd Erith

X 6 Ludgate broadway EC4
W 6 Ludgate cir EC4
X 6 Ludgate hill EC4
X 7 Ludgate sq EC4
F 12 Ludlow clo Harrow
E 11 Ludlow rd W5
C 12 Ludlow way N2
C 10 Ludovick wlk SW15
C 10 Ludovick wlk SW15
V 18 Ludwick rd SE14
D 8 Luffield rd SE2
J 6 Luffman rd SE12
A 4 Lugard rd SE15
H 17 Luke st EC2
J 12 Lukin cres E4
P 18 Lukin st E1
P 17 Lullingstone clo Orp
O 18 Lullingstone cres Orp
O 14 Lullingstone rd Blvdr
G 17 Lullington garth N12
X 18 Lullington rd SE20
L 1 Lullington rd Dgnhm
Y 20 Lullington rd Dgnhm
S 6 Lulot st N19
L 1 Lulworth av Hounsl
L 20 Lulworth av Hounsl
D 1 Lulworth av Wemb
C 9 Lulworth clo Harrow
A 20 Lulworth dri Pinn
C 8 Lulworth gdns Harrow
B 5 Lulworth rd SE15
P 5 Lulworth rd SE9
K 6 Lulworth rd Welling
L 9 Lumley ct WC2
S 12 Lumley gdns Sutton
S 12 Lumley rd Sutton
U 7 Lumley st W1
N 5 Luna rd Thntn Hth
R 15 Lunham rd SE19
H 3 Lupin clo SW2
U 13 Lupton rd NW5
Y 11 Lupus st SW1
A 11 Lupus st SW7
G 13 Lurgan av W6
A 9 Lurgan av W6
R 1 Lurline gdns SW11
U 6 Luscombe way SW8
J 6 Lushington rd NW10
P 1 Lushington rd SE6
V 12 Luther rd Tedd
H 20 Luton pl SE10
R 12 Luton rd E13
K 10 Luton rd E17
T 6 Luton rd NW8
H 18 Luton st NW8
K 13 Luttrell av SW15
K 4 Lutwyche rd SE6
T 19 Luxborough st W1
F 5 Luxemburg gdns W6
R 2 Luxfield rd SE9
L 3 Luxford st SE4
L 3 Luxmore st SE4
K 0 Luxor st SE5
R 1 Lwr Downs rd SW20
C 9 Lwr James st W1
K 1 Lwr Merton rd NW3
W 7 Lyal rd E3
S 3 Lyall Ms w SW1
S 3 Lyall st SW1
T 1 Lyalla av SE21
T 3 Lyalla ms SW1
K 18 Lyconby gdns Croy
J 8 Lyd clo SW2
O 18 Lydd rd Bxly Hth
A 19 Lydden gro SW18
A 20 Lydden rd SW18
T 20 Lydeard rd E6
Z 9 Lydenberg st SE7
O 17 Lydford rd NW2
D 17 Lydford rd N15
R 15 Lydford rd W9
D 5 Lydhurst av SW2
U 8 Lydon rd SW4
X 11 Lydstep rd Chisl
H 20 Lyford rd SW18
J 1 Lyford rd SW18
D 11 Lyford st SE18
A 15 Lyham rd SW2
Z 13 Lyham rd SW4
G 11 Lyme Farm rd SE12
B 19 Lyme gro E9
S 2 Lyme rd Welling
A 2 Lyme st NW1
A 2 Lyme st NW1
U 12 Lymer av SE19
Y 3 Lymescote gdns Sutton
L 9 Lyminge clo Sidcp
J 2 Lyminge gdns SW18
H 8 Lymington av N22
W 3 Lymington clo SW16

152 D 10 Lymington gdns Epsom
45 Z 17 Lymington rd NW6
46 B 16 Lymington rd NW6
55 W 3 Lymington rd Dgnhm
18 H 1 Lymouth av Enf
17 V 14 Lynbridge gdns N13
75 Z 15 Lynch wlk SE8
89 R 9 Lyncott cres SW4
22 A 16 Lyncroft av Pinn
45 Z 14 Lyncroft gdns NW 6
72 D 4 Lyncroft gdns W13
152 E 20 Lyncroft gdns Epsom
83 N 12 Lyncroft gdns Hounsl
45 W 11 Lyndale NW2
45 W 10 Lyndale av NW2
77 P 17 Lyndale clo SE10
13 O 20 Lyndhurst av NW7
17 V 13 Lyndhurst av N12
121 Y 4 Lyndhurst av SW16
70 K 3 Lyndhurst av S'hall
117 U 19 Lyndhurst av Surb
100 G 2 Lyndhurst av Twick
100 H 2 Lyndhurst av Twick
100 H 2 Lyndhurst av Twick
43 Z 8 Lyndhurst clo NW10
98 H 7 Lyndhurst clo Bxly Hth
51 V 1 Lyndhurst dri E10
118 C 16 Lyndhurst dri New Mald
46 G 15 Lyndhurst gdns NW3
27 U 4 Lyndhurst gdns N3
54 G 17 Lyndhurst gdns Bark
8 D 15 Lyndhurst gdns Enf
36 E 19 Lyndhurst gdns Ilf
91 T 4 Lyndhurst gro SE15
33 U 1 Lyndhurst rd E4
46 G 14 Lyndhurst rd NW3
17 S 20 Lyndhurst rd N18
18 K 14 Lyndhurst rd N18
98 H 7 Lyndhurst rd Bxly Hth
58 K 10 Lyndhurst rd Grnfd
122 F 9 Lyndhurst rd Thntn Hth
91 U 3 Lyndhurst sq SE15
46 F 14 Lyndhurst ter NW3
91 U 2 Lyndhurst way SE15
96 K 13 Lyndon av Sidcp
155 P 6 Lyndon av Wallgtn
81 S 9 Lyndon rd Blvdr
108 J 13 Lyndway SE27
32 K 5 Lyne cres E17
89 T 15 Lynette av SW4
12 E 12 Lynford gdns Edg
54 L 7 Lynford gdns Ilf
97 R 5 Lynmere rd Welling
119 O 15 Lynmouth av Mrdn
60 C 2 Lynmouth gdns Grnfd
32 H 18 Lynmouth rd E17
49 U 4 Lynmouth rd N16
28 M 12 Lynmouth rd N2
27 M 12 Lynmouth rd N2
60 C 3 Lynmouth rd Grnfd
23 P 9 Lynn clo Harrow
51 Z 8 Lynn rd E11
89 T 17 Lynn rd SW12
54 D 1 Lynn rd Ilf
8 A 6 Lynn st Enf
55 X 5 Lynnett rd Dgnhm
98 F 12 Lynsted clo Bxly Hth
95 P 10 Lynsted gdns SE9
26 C 12 Lynton av NW9
15 T 13 Lynton av N12
59 Y 17 Lynton av N13
59 Z 17 Lynton av W13
38 F 5 Lynton av Rom
83 W 10 Lynton clo Islwth
35 Z 19 Lynton cres Ilf
18 E 4 Lynton gdns Enf
14 M 9 Lynton mead N20
51 X 12 Lynton rd E11
20 D 16 Lynton rd E4
129 P 7 Lynton rd NW6
29 Z 16 Lynton rd N8
151 X 8 Lynton rd SE1
61 T 18 Lynton rd W3
122 Y 11 Lynton rd Croy
40 C 8 Lynton rd Harrow
117 Y 11 Lynton rd New Mald
34 K 4 Lynwood clo E18
40 B 9 Lynwood clo Harrow
38 H 1 Lynwood dri Rom
152 G 3 Lynwood dri Worc Pk
156 D 8 Lynwood gdns Croy
58 E 16 Lynwood gdns S'hall
106 M 8 Lynwood rd SW17
60 H 10 Lynwood rd W5
24 F 5 Lyon meade Stanm
61 N 1 Lyon Pk av Wemb

42 J 18 Lyon Pk av Wemb
120 D 1 Lyon rd SW19
23 V 19 Lyon rd Harrow
57 T 1 Lyon rd Hornch
130 F 17 Lyons pl NW8
5 R 19 Lyonsdown av Barnt
5 K 18 Lyonsdown rd Barnt
149 W 8 Lyric pl SW11
86 D 3 Lyric rd SW13
47 W 4 Lysander gro N19
144 G 18 Lysia st SW6
89 R 17 Lysias rd SW12
86 H 12 Lysons wlk SW15
112 G 17 Lytchet rd Brom
91 T 13 Lytcott gro SE22
63 O 5 Lyte st E2
60 L 8 Lytham gro W5
150 E 12 Lytham st SE17
30 F 11 Lyttelton rd N2
29 F 11 Lyttelton rd N8
130 K 1 Lyttleton clo NW3
51 S 9 Lyttleton rd E10
17 V 8 Lytton av N13
9 X 3 Lytton av Enf
28 F 19 Lytton clo N2
58 E 1 Lytton gdns Wallgtn
155 X 7 Lytton gdns Wallgtn
87 S 16 Lytton gro SW15
33 Z 20 Lytton rd E11
5 R 14 Lytton rd Barnt
22 B 3 Lytton rd Pinn
39 Z 17 Lytton rd Rom
77 V 18 Lyveden rd SE10
106 L 16 Lyveden rd SW17

# M

109 W 18 Maberley cres SE19
109 W 19 Maberley rd SE19
124 F 6 Maberley rd Becknhm
132 M 14 Mabledon pl WC1
144 K 18 Mablethorpe rd SW6
50 J 15 Mabley st E0
79 W 10 Mabyn rd SE18
78 B 16 Macarthur ter SE7
66 C 6 Macaulay rd E6
89 T 9 Macaulay rd SW4
89 T 9 Macaulay sq SW4
78 K 9 Macbean st SE18
74 K 12 Macbeth st W6
134 A 12 Macclesfield rd EC1
134 B 12 Macclesfield rd SE25
140 F 9 Macclesfield st W1
56 J 10 Macdonald av Dgnhm
33 V 7 Macdonald rd E17
52 E 13 Macdonald rd E7
16 A 17 Macdonald rd N11
47 V 0 Macdonald rd N19
89 P 1 Macduff rd SW11
136 C 14 Macfarlane rd W12
74 M 3 Macfarlane rd W12
136 C 13 Macfarlane pl W12
74 M 2 Macfarlane pl W12
113 U 18 Macfarren pl NW1
66 A 14 Macgregor rd E16
65 Z 14 Macgregor rd E16
92 C 7 Machell rd SE15
89 S 7 Mackay rd SW4
130 L 9 Mackennal st NW8
48 C 17 Mackenzie rd N7
124 D 4 Mackenzie rd Becknhm
46 L 13 Mackeson rd NW3
90 E 19 Mackie rd SW2
50 F 16 Mackintosh la E9
140 L 4 Macklin st WC2
151 T 5 Macks rd SE16
132 A 11 Mackworth st NW1
50 H 12 Maclaren st E5
92 H 16 Maclean rd SE23
150 B 12 Macleod st SE17
144 K 3 Maclise rd W14
79 S 17 Macoma rd SE18
79 S 17 Macoma ter SE18
76 E 11 Macquarie way E14
129 R 12 Macroom rd W9
131 S 19 Madame tussauds NW8
64 C 13 Maddams st E3
101 V 16 Maddison clo Tedd
115 X 14 Maddocks clo Sidcp
139 Z 8 Maddox st W1
140 A 7 Maddox st W1
111 Z 17 Madeira av Brom
112 A 20 Madeira av Brom
21 X 18 Madeira gro Wdfd Grn
51 Y 5 Madeira rd E11

17 W 12 Madeira rd N13
108 B 11 Madeira rd SW16
120 M 8 Madeira rd Mitch
121 N 8 Madeira rd Mitch
60 L 18 Madeley rd W5
109 X 19 Madeline rd SE20
80 G 19 Madison cres Welling
80 G 19 Madison gdns Welling
48 F 17 Madras pl N7
53 Z 12 Madras rd Ilf
74 G 20 Madrid rd SW13
86 G 1 Madrid rd SW13
150 L 8 Madron st SE17
66 C 6 Mafeking av E6
72 H 16 Mafeking av Brentf
54 F 2 Mafeking av Ilf
65 S 11 Mafeking rd E16
31 X 8 Mafeking rd N17
8 G 13 Mafeking rd Enf
47 U 6 Magdala rd N19
157 O 16 Magdala rd Croy
83 Z 8 Magdala rd Islwth
143 P 8 Magdalen pas E1
88 G 19 Magdalen rd SW18
108 C 3 Magdalen rd SW18
142 K 15 Magdalen st SE1
66 J 11 Magdalene gdns E6
149 T 14 Magee st SE11
10 G 3 Magnaville rd Bushey Watf
24 L 20 Magnolia ct Harrow
73 S 17 Magnolia rd W4
141 V 7 Magpie all EC4
141 U 8 Magpie all EC4
127 S 16 Magpie Hall clo Brom
127 T 15 Magpie Hall la Brom
10 G 6 Magpie Hall rd Bushey Watf
102 E 10 Maguire dri Rich
143 P 16 Maguire st SE1
84 F 12 Maid Of Honour row Rich
20 D 3 Maida av E9
130 E 19 Maida av W2
81 S 8 Maida rd Blvdr
130 C 14 Maida vale W9
99 X 14 Maida Vale rd Drtfrd
20 D 3 Maida way E4
97 Z 20 Maiden Frlegh av Bxly
140 L 0 Maiden la WC2
99 W 10 Maiden la Drtfrd
132 L 7 Maiden Lane bridge N1
52 A 20 Maiden rd E15
93 U 2 Maidenstone hill SE10
00 W 11 Maidman st E3
38 K 7 Maidstone av Rom
142 D 15 Maidstone bldgs SE1
16 K 18 Maidstone rd N11
115 Y 11 Maidstone rd Sidcp
135 T 7 Maidstone st E2
8 K 17 Main av Enf
39 X 10 Main rd Rom
114 J 8 Main rd Sidcp
113 X 11 Mainridge rd Chisl
151 T 16 Maismore st SE15
66 D 15 Maitland gdns E6
47 N 18 Maitland Pk rd NW3
47 N 17 Maitland Pk vlls NW5
52 B 19 Maitland rd E15
110 E 15 Maitland rd SE26
50 H 10 Maiwand rd E5
79 S 13 Majendie rd SE18
51 V 14 Major rd E15
151 U 1 Major rd SE16
47 O 7 Makepeace av N6
146 L 7 Makins st SW3
64 C 19 Malam gdns E14
57 X 17 Malan sq Rainhm
86 L 11 Malbrook rd SW15
26 F 17 Malcolm cres NW4
11 R 17 Malcolm ct Stanm
63 O 10 Malcolm pl E2
63 O 11 Malcolm rd E1
110 B 17 Malcolm rd SE20
123 X 15 Malcolm rd SE25
105 T 16 Malcolm rd SW19
123 Z 7 Malden av SE25
124 A 7 Malden av SE25
41 S 17 Malden av Grnfd
47 P 19 Malden cres NW1
118 J 6 Malden ct New Mald
118 F 19 Malden Green av Worc Pk
118 C 7 Malden hill New Mald

Mal–Mar


152 A 1 Malden la Worc Pk
118 D 14 Malden pk New Mald
47 N 15 Malden pl NW5
47 O 16 Malden rd NW5
118 C 13 Malden rd New Mald
153 N 7 Malden rd Sutton
117 Z 15 Malden way New Mald
91 R 7 Maldon clo SE5
18 H 10 Maldon rd N9
61 W 20 Maldon rd W3
56 J 1 Maldon rd Rom
155 T 10 Maldon rd Wallgtn
21 Y 20 Maldon wlk Wdfd Grn
132 E 18 Malet pl WC1
132 F 19 Malet st WC1
108 K 3 Maley av SE27
34 D 9 Malford gro E18
91 T 7 Malfort rd SE5
110 F 1 Malham rd SE23
74 K 13 Mall rd W6
16 L 10 Mall the N14
17 O 9 Mall the N14
140 D 15 Mall the SW1
85 V 13 Mall the SW14
60 H 19 Mall the W5
24 M 20 Mall the Harrow
116 F 13 Mall the Surb
15 U 1 Mallard clo Barnt
43 V 2 Mallard way NW9
34 J 2 Mallards rd Wdfd Grn
40 E 15 Mallet dri Grnfd
93 X 16 Mallet rd SE13
119 C 13 Malling gdns Mrdn
126 C 16 Malling way Brom
155 Z 4 Mallinson rd Wallgtn
88 K 12 Mallison rd SW11
146 G 13 Mallord st SW3
92 G 10 Mallory clo SE4
66 D 14 Mallory gdns E6
16 B 3 Mallory gdns Barnt
27 T 2 Mallow mead NW7
134 E 16 Mallow st EC1
125 V 10 Malmains clo Becknhm
125 V 9 Malmains way Becknhm
65 N 15 Malmesbury rd E16
64 M 13 Malmesbury rd E16
34 C 5 Malmesbury rd E18
63 Z 8 Malmesbury rd E3
120 C 16 Malmesbury rd Mrdn
65 O 14 Malmesbury ter E16
92 L 3 Malpas rd SE4
55 V 19 Malpas rd Dgnhm
151 S 13 Malt st SE1
51 N 2 Malta rd E10
133 X 15 Malta st EC1
151 N 1 Maltby st SE1
143 N 19 Maltby st SE1
79 V 17 Malton st SE18
141 P 8 Maltravers st WC2
88 A 15 Malva rd SW18
33 W 1 Malvern av E4
80 L 20 Malvern av Bxly Hth
40 G 8 Malvern av Harrow
121 V 6 Malvern clo Mitch
116 K 20 Malvern clo Surb
111 T 20 Malvern ct Becknhm
54 K 13 Malvern dri Ilf
21 X 15 Malvern dri Wdfd Grn
45 S 6 Malvern gdns NW2
129 P 11 Malvern gdns W9
24 L 12 Malvern gdns Harrow
129 S 13 Malvern ms W9
129 R 11 Malvern pl W9
52 B 6 Malvern rd E11
66 C 3 Malvern rd E6
135 S 1 Malvern rd E8
49 W 20 Malvern rd E8
129 S 12 Malvern rd NW6
31 W 9 Malvern rd N17
30 E 10 Malvern rd N8
100 H 19 Malvern rd Hampt
39 V 20 Malvern rd Hornch
122 F 10 Malvern rd Thntn Hth
133 S 3 Malvern ter N1
18 H 6 Malvern ter N9
60 B 14 Malvern way W13
89 R 17 Malwood rd SW12
93 P 13 Malyions rd SE13
93 P 13 Malyions ter SE13
76 G 3 Managers st E14
58 G 16 Manaton cres S'hall
91 Z 7 Manaton rd SE15
51 Z 17 Manbey gro E15
51 Z 17 Manbey Pk rd E15
51 Z 18 Manbey rd E15
51 Z 18 Manbey st E15
52 A 18 Manbey st E15
66 H 9 Manbrough rd E6
76 F 12 Manchester gro E14
139 T 3 Manchester ms W1
76 G 6 Manchester rd E14
31 P 19 Manchester rd N15
122 M 6 Manchester rd Thntn Hth
139 U 4 Manchester sq W1
139 T 2 Manchester st W1
89 P 14 Manchuria rd SW11
142 F 20 Manciple st SE1
89 U 14 Mandalay rd SW4
77 R 20 Mandeville clo SE10
139 V 5 Mandeville pl W1
16 F 9 Mandeville rd N14
40 H 19 Mandeville rd Grnfd
58 D 2 Mandeville rd Grnfd
83 Y 4 Mandeville rd Islwth
50 G 10 Mandeville st E5
106 M 6 Mandrake rd SW17
96 A 13 Mandrell rd SW2
140 G 6 Manette st W1
87 V 13 Manfred rd SW15
76 B 5 Manilla st E14
80 A 8 Manister rd SE2
131 T 3 Manley st NW1
150 F 12 Mann st SE17
37 P 20 Mannin rd Rom
42 H 1 Manning gdns Harrow
56 E 20 Manning rd Dgnhm
143 R 5 Manningtree st E1
30 J 10 Mannock rd N22
83 W 12 Manns clo Islwth
12 C 19 Manns rd Edg
100 M 5 Manoel rd Twick
74 B 13 Manor alley W4
92 M 4 Manor av SE4
58 D 1 Manor av Grnfd
94 F 10 Manor brook SE3
25 R 14 Manor clo NW9
57 O 19 Manor clo Dgnhm
99 O 10 Manor clo Drtfrd
39 V 16 Manor clo Rom
118 C 20 Manor clo Worc Pk
28 C 9 Manor Cottages appr N2
90 K 19 Manor cotts SE24
28 D 8 Manor Cotts appr N2
59 T 20 Manor Court rd W7
20 M 10 Manor Court rd W7
117 O 14 Manor cres Surb
108 A 7 Manor ct SW16
71 S 1 Manor Ct rd W7
152 C 1 Manor Dr the Worc Pk
118 B 20 Manor Dr the Worc Pk
12 L 16 Manor dri NW7
16 F 4 Manor dri N14
15 Y 11 Manor dri N20
152 B 14 Manor dri Epsom
117 Y 16 Manor dri North Surb
118 A 19 Manor dri North Worc Pk
117 O 15 Manor dri Surb
43 N 11 Manor dri Wemb
21 N 9 Manor Farm dri E4
122 F 2 Manor Farm rd SW16
60 F 5 Manor Farm rd Wemb
87 O 15 Manor fields SW15
48 A 9 Manor gdns N7
119 V 2 Manor gdns SW20
73 R 10 Manor gdns W3
100 L 18 Manor gdns Hampt
85 O 10 Manor gdns Rich
157 U 14 Manor gdns S Croy
75 O 17 Manor gro SE14
125 R 3 Manor gro Becknhm
85 R 9 Manor gro Rich
27 O 7 Manor Hall av NW4
27 O 8 Manor Hall dri NW4
45 P 20 Manor Ho dri NW6
128 H 1 Manor Ho dri NW6
99 O 9 Manor house Bxly Hth
94 B 18 Manor la SE12
93 Z 12 Manor la SE13
154 B 10 Manor la Sutton
93 Z 12 Manor La ter SE13
110 C 1 Manor mt SE23
53 R 10 Manor park E12
118 E 17 Manor park New Mald
93 Y 11 Manor pk SE13
94 A 14 Manor pk SE13
85 O 10 Manor pk Rich
125 R 20 Manor Pk clo W Wkhm
12 C 19 Manor Pk cres Edg
22 K 10 Manor Pk dri Harrow
12 C 18 Manor Pk gdns Edg
53 O 13 Manor Pk rd E12
62 C 4 Manor Pk rd NW10
28 E 10 Manor Pk rd N2
114 D 20 Manor Pk rd Chisl
154 C 11 Manor Pk rd Sutton
125 R 20 Manor Pk rd W Wkhm
149 Y 10 Manor pl SE17
150 A 9 Manor pl SE17
121 V 7 Manor pl Mitch
154 B 9 Manor pl Sutton
51 O 2 Manor rd E10
64 L 9 Manor rd E15
32 H 6 Manor rd E17
49 P 5 Manor rd N16
31 Y 3 Manor rd N17
17 O 20 Manor rd N22
119 V 3 Manor rd SE25
123 W 8 Manor rd SW20
60 A 20 Manor rd W13
59 Z 20 Manor rd W13
54 L 19 Manor rd Bark
4 F 14 Manor rd Barnt
125 R 2 Manor rd Becknhm
98 H 20 Manor rd Bxly
56 L 19 Manor rd Dgnhm
57 N 19 Manor rd Dgnhm
99 P 9 Manor rd Drtfrd
8 A 9 Manor rd Enf
23 Y 17 Manor rd Harrow
21 X 1 Manor rd Lghtn
121 V 7 Manor rd Mitch
155 R 8 Manor rd North Wallgtn
85 O 9 Manor rd Rich
37 U 19 Manor rd Rom
39 W 17 Manor rd Rom
114 M 6 Manor rd Sidcp
153 U 18 Manor rd Sutton
101 Z 11 Manor rd Tedd
101 O 4 Manor rd Twick
59 R 1 Manor rd W Wkhm
155 S 10 Manor rd Wallgtn
55 V 7 Manor sq Dgnhm
72 D 14 Manor vale Brentf
28 A 8 Manor view N3
27 Z 8 Manor view N3
78 M 2 Manor way E16
20 J 13 Manor way E4
26 A 12 Manor way NW9
94 D 10 Manor way SE3
125 P 5 Manor way Becknhm
127 S 15 Manor way Brom
98 L 8 Manor way Bxly Hth
157 U 14 Manor way Croy
18 D 1 Manor way Enf
22 K 13 Manor way Harrow
121 L 17 Manor way Mitch
21 Z 16 Manor way Wdfd Grn
118 C 20 Manor way Worc Pk
155 T 8 Manor Way the Wallgtn
117 R 1 Manorgate rd Kingst
4 F 15 Manorside Barnt
86 F 19 Manresa house SW15
146 J 11 Manresa rd SW3
49 V 11 Manse rd N16
33 N 4 Mansel gro E17
105 T 15 Mansel rd SW19
73 Y 4 Mansell rd W3
58 L 13 Mansell rd Grnfd
143 O 7 Mansell st E1
31 O 13 Mansfield av N15
6 B 18 Mansfield av Barnt
20 C 5 Mansfield hill E4
139 X 2 Mansfield ms W1
20 B 6 Mansfield park E4
34 H 19 Mansfield rd E11
32 L 13 Mansfield rd E17
46 M 14 Mansfield rd NW3
47 O 13 Mansfield rd NW3
61 T 12 Mansfield rd W3
53 X 6 Mansfield rd Ilf
157 O 15 Mansfield rd S Croy
139 X 2 Mansfield st W1
135 U 10 Mansford st E2
107 O 20 Manship rd Mitch
142 E 7 Mansion House pl EC4
142 E 6 Mansion House st EC2
146 E 7 Manson ms SW 7
146 E 7 Manson pl SW 7
55 U 1 Manstead gdns Rom
70 G 11 Manston av S'hall
57 Z 19 Manston way Hornch
45 S 14 Manstone rd NW2
133 T 7 Mantell st N1
79 P 13 Manthorpe rd SE18
107 P 10 Mantilla rd SW17
92 J 8 Mantle rd SE4
71 X 6 Manton av W7
79 Z 11 Manton rd SE2
80 A 11 Manton rd SE2
63 P 10 Mantus rd E1
88 H 7 Mantus st SW11
15 P 6 Manus way N20
107 R 5 Manville gdns SW
107 R 5 Manville rd SW17
92 M 15 Manwood rd SE4
78 L 4 Manwood st E16
107 T 3 Many gates SW12
135 V 16 Mape st E2
45 S 17 Mapesbury rd NW
19 Y 19 Maple av E4
74 B 3 Maple av W3
40 L 8 Maple av Harrow
57 Y 10 Maple clo Hornch
121 S 1 Maple clo Mitch
97 N 15 Maple cres Sidcp
117 Z 7 Maple ct New Mal
118 A 6 Maple ct New Mal
26 A 2 Maple gdns Edg
43 V 1 Maple gro NW9
72 H 7 Maple gro W5
72 B 18 Maple gro Brentf
58 F 13 Maple gro S'hall
63 N 15 Maple pl E1
132 B 19 Maple pl W1
34 A 19 Maple rd E11
110 C 18 Maple rd SE20
116 F 15 Maple rd Surb
132 C 19 Maple st W1
38 K 14 Maple st Rom
157 Y 4 Mapledale av Croy
157 Y 4 Mapledale av W Wkhm
114 C 14 Mapledene Chisl
49 W 20 Mapledene rd E8
35 Z 11 Mapleleafe gdns Il
90 C 19 Maplestead rd SW
68 D 4 Maplestead rd Dgnhm
122 G 9 Maplethorpe rd Thntn Hth
126 E 13 Mapleton clo Brom
9 O 3 Mapleton cres Enf
87 Z 16 Mapleton rd SW18
9 N 10 Mapleton rd Enf
7 R 18 Maplin clo N21
65 U 17 Maplin rd E16
63 X 10 Maplin st E3
33 Z 1 Mapperley dri Wdf Grn
80 J 7 Maran way Belvdr
129 N 11 Marban pl W9
129 O 12 Marban rd W9
73 S 3 Marble clo W3
84 B 18 Marble Hill clo Twi
84 A 18 Marble Hill gdns Twick
84 E 19 Marble Hill park Twick
112 K 6 Marbrook ct SE12
48 C 9 Marcellus rd N7
83 X 18 March rd Twick
51 Y 8 Marchant rd E11
75 U 17 Marchant st SE14
84 M 14 Marchmont rd Rich
85 N 14 Marchmont rd Rich
155 V 17 Marchmont rd Wallgtn
132 K 17 Marchmont st WC1
150 K 19 Marchwood clo SE
60 F 16 Marchwood cres W
150 M 7 Marcia rd SE1
88 E 13 Marcilly rd SW18
74 L 8 Marco rd W6
144 A 3 Marco rd W6
49 Z 16 Marcon pl E8
58 K 18 Marconi way S'hall
65 N 4 Marcus ct E15
99 W 19 Marcus rd Drtfrd
65 O 4 Marcus st E15
65 O 4 Marcus st E15
88 B 15 Marcus st SE18
25 Z 17 Mardale dri NW9
74 L 6 Mardale st W12
124 E 12 Mardell rd Croy
126 D 15 Marden av Brom
98 L 13 Marden cres Bxly
122 D 14 Marden cres Croy
31 R 9 Marden rd N17
151 X 3 Marden rd SE16
75 O 8 Marden rd SE16
122 D 15 Marden rd Croy
71 Z 6 Marder rd W13
72 A 6 Marder rd W13
39 S 18 Mardon rd Rom
135 Y 2 Mare st E8
50 A 19 Mare st E8
63 N 3 Mare st E8

Mar–Maw


3 E 18 Maresfield gdns NW3
7 M 1 Marg Bonfield av Bark
) E 1 Margaret av E4
9 Y 16 Margaret clo Rom
) A 4 Margaret ct W1
9 U 5 Margaret gdns N16
9 U 5 Margaret rd N16
5 V 14 Margaret rd Barnt
7 W 15 Margaret rd Bxly
9 Y 16 Margaret rd Rom
9 Z 4 Margaret st W1
) A 4 Margaret st W1
5 P 17 Margaret way Ilf
8 L 14 Margaretta ter SW3
2 L 5 Margaretting rd E12
0 A 13 Margate rd SW2
2 E 18 Margery Pk rd E7
5 X 8 Margery rd Dgnhm
3 R 15 Margery st WC1
5 P 11 Margin dri SW19
4 H 10 Margravine gdns W6
4 H 12 Margravine rd W6
6 H 3 Marham gdns SW18
0 C 14 Marham gdns SW18
3 S 13 Maria ter E1
3 Z 11 Marian ct Sutton
5 V 7 Marian pl E2
2 D 1 Marian way NW10
3 P 4 Maricas av Harrow
3 V 19 Marigold st SE16
9 Y 20 Marigold way E4
8 J 13 Marina av New Mald
6 H 4 Marina dri Welling
8 U 17 Marina gdns Rom
2 F 17 Marina way Tedd
3 S 20 Marine st SE16
8 B 4 Marinefield rd SW6
2 C 8 Mariner gdns Rich
6 D 1 Marion clo Ilf
1 O 14 Marion gro Wdfd Grn
3 T 16 Marion rd NW7
7 V 20 Marion rd SW16
3 N 11 Marion rd Thntn Hth
3 W 9 Marischal rd SE13
3 W 9 Marishal rd SE13
6 J 17 Maritime museum SE10
3 Y 12 Maritime st E 3
7 O 3 Marius rd SW17
9 N 10 Marjorie gro SW11
0 E 1 Mark av E4
0 J 2 Mark clo Shall
2 K 8 Mark la EC3
0 K 6 Mark rd N22
4 H 16 Mark st EC2
1 Z 20 Mark st E15
0 A 5 Market ct W1
8 L 8 Market hill SE18
5 U 5 Market la Edg
5 V 5 Market la Edgw
9 P 14 Market link Rom
9 X 14 Market ms W1
8 C 14 Market pl NW11
8 H 11 Market pl N2
0 A 5 Market pl W1
2 F 18 Market pl Brentf
8 E 10 Market pl Bxly Hth
6 G 4 Market pl Kingst
9 R 14 Market pl Rom
7 Z 19 Market rd N7
8 A 18 Market rd N7
5 P 9 Market rd Rich
4 E 18 Market sq E14
4 C 18 Market sq E14
6 E 13 Market sq Brom
6 G 6 Market st E6
8 K 11 Market st SE18
4 E 18 Market way E14
2 J 16 Market way Wemb
0 D 1 Markfield gdns E4
1 X 14 Markfield rd N15
7 N 9 Markham sq SW3
6 M 9 Markham st SW3
00 E 19 Markhole clo Hampt
2 J 18 Markhouse av E17
2 K 18 Markhouse rd E17
0 M 1 Markhouse rd E17
0 K 1 Markmanor av E17
8 A 12 Marks hall Rom
8 L 16 Marks rd Rom
5 R 8 Marksbury av Rich
09 Z 9 Markwell clo SE26
5 R 16 Markyate rd Dgnhm
8 B 11 Marl st SW18
5 S 10 Marlanda rd Ilf
5 T 8 Marlands rd Ilf
5 T 2 Marlborough av E8
16 G 10 Marlborough av N14
12 F 11 Marlborough av Edg
15 Z 12 Marlborough clo N20
73 Z 8 Marlborough cres W4
140 B 7 Marlborough ct W1
35 R 10 Marlborough dri Ilf
15 Z 11 Marlborough gdns N20
151 T 12 Marlborough gro SE1
130 D 6 Marlborough hill NW8
23 T 13 Marlborough hill Harrow
140 D 15 Marlborough house SW1
77 Y 18 Marlborough la SE7
97 N 20 Marlborough Pk av Sidcp
130 B 9 Marlborough pl NW8
52 A 13 Marlborough rd E15
34 G 9 Marlborough rd E18
20 C 19 Marlborough rd E4
52 K 19 Marlborough rd E7
48 A 6 Marlborough rd N19
47 Y 7 Marlborough rd N19
17 O 20 Marlborough rd N22
30 B 1 Marlborough rd N22
18 H 7 Marlborough rd N9
140 D 15 Marlborough rd SW1
106 H 16 Marlborough rd SW19
73 U 13 Marlborough rd W4
72 H 5 Marlborough rd W5
72 A 20 Marlborough rd Brentf
126 M 9 Marlborough rd Brom
97 W 7 Marlborough rd Bxly Hth
55 T 14 Marlborough rd Dgnhm
100 H 15 Marlborough rd Hampt
23 U 13 Marlborough rd Harrow
84 L 16 Marlborough rd Rich
38 H 13 Marlborough rd Rom
156 M 16 Marlborough rd S Croy
156 M 16 Marlborough rd S Croy
153 Z 4 Marlborough rd Sutton
146 K 8 Marlborough st SW3
110 K 2 Marler rd SE23
80 J 17 Marley av Bxly Hth
58 G 7 Marley clo Grnfd
100 G 16 Marlingdene clo Hampt
145 W 4 Marloes rd W8
124 A 5 Marlow clo SE20
83 V 15 Marlow cres Twick
153 P 4 Marlow dri Sutton
66 F 9 Marlow rd E6
124 B 4 Marlow rd SE20
70 E 8 Marlow rd S'hall
114 D 17 Marlowe clo Chisl
36 L 5 Marlowe clo Ilf
33 U 12 Marlowe rd E17
121 U 8 Marlowe sq Mitch
130 F 4 Marlowes the NW8
79 X 10 Marmadon rd SE18
20 A 13 Marmion av E4
19 Y 13 Marmion av E4
20 A 13 Marmion clo E4
89 P 9 Marmion rd SW11
91 Y 1 Marmont rd SE15
151 U 20 Marmont rd SE15
92 C 15 Marmora rd SE22
16 D 13 Marne av N11
96 M 8 Marne av Welling
90 M 3 Marne rd SE5
128 L 12 Marne st W10
89 O 10 Marney rd SW11
45 S 11 Marnham av NW2
58 K 8 Marnham cres Grnfd
92 K 14 Marnock rd SE4
63 V 15 Maroon st E14
49 N 18 Marquess gro N1
49 N 18 Marquess rd N1
61 O 1 Marquis clo Wemb
47 Z 19 Marquis rd NW1
17 R 20 Marquis rd N22
48 M 19 Marquis rd N4
48 E 3 Marquis rd N4
86 H 9 Marrick clo SW15
9 X 3 Marrilyne av Enf
64 L 2 Marriott rd E15
28 M 5 Marriott rd N10
29 N 5 Marriott rd N10
48 C 5 Marriott rd N4
4 D 12 Marriott rd Barnt
105 S 10 Marryat pl SW19
105 P 12 Marryat rd SW19
93 S 10 Marsala rd SE13
18 M 8 Marsden rd N9
18 M 8 Marsden rd N9
91 V 8 Marsden rd SE15
47 P 18 Marsden st NW5
121 N 2 Marsh av Mitch
13 R 11 Marsh clo NW7
101 U 1 Marsh Farm rd Twick
83 V 20 Marsh Farm rd Twick
69 R 4 Marsh Green rd Dgnhm
50 H 15 Marsh hill E9
51 N 5 Marsh la E10
12 M 12 Marsh la NW7
11 S 18 Marsh la NW7
13 O 11 Marsh la NW7
32 A 3 Marsh la N 17
24 G 1 Marsh la Stanm
60 H 8 Marsh rd W5
22 C 14 Marsh rd Pinn
76 C 11 Marsh st E14
149 X 2 Marshall gdns SE1
31 P 4 Marshall rd N17
140 C 7 Marshall st W1
39 P 9 Marshalls dri Rom
78 E 10 Marshalls gro SE18
38 M 14 Marshalls rd Rom
154 B 8 Marshalls rd Sutton
142 C 17 Marshalsea rd SE1
113 Y 12 Marsham clo Chisl
148 H 3 Marsham st SW1
95 N 7 Marshbrook clo SE18
76 G 8 Marshfield st E14
64 D 3 Marshgate la E15
149 Y 11 Marsland rd SE17
56 D 8 Marston av Dgnhm
46 E 20 Marston clo NW6
56 D 8 Marston gdns Dgnhm
35 R 6 Marston rd Ilf
102 B 13 Marston rd Tedd
22 A 3 Marsworth av Pinn
140 L 8 Mart st E2
140 L 8 Mart st WC2
49 T 6 Martaban rd N16
109 N 7 Martell rd SE21
50 A 20 Martello st E8
33 P 6 Marten rd E17
98 L 11 Martens av Bxly Hth
98 J 10 Martens av Bxly Hth
98 J 11 Martens clo Bxly Hth
98 J 9 Martens Grove park Bxly Hth
52 B 17 Martha rd E15
63 O 19 Martha st E1
23 R 8 Marthorne cres Harrow
95 U 8 Martin Bowes rd SE9
156 E 1 Martin cres Croy
98 B 13 Martin dene Bxly Hth
40 E 15 Martin dri Grnfd
55 U 13 Martin gdns Dgnhm
119 X 7 Martin gro Mrdn
142 F 9 Martin la EC4
55 V 13 Martin rd Dgnhm
98 B 19 Martin ri Bxly Hth
51 W 20 Martin st E15
119 R 4 Martin way SW20
119 T 7 Martin way Mrdn
85 V 12 Martindale SW14
82 B 7 Martindale rd SW12
89 T 19 Martindale rd SW12
48 H 13 Martineau rd N5
102 G 7 Martingale clo Rich
126 A 3 Martins rd Brom
140 L 7 Martlett ct WC2
35 Z 16 Martley dr Ilf
112 J 5 Marvels clo SE12
112 K 5 Marvels la SE12
122 M 11 Marvels la Thntn Hth
135 O 20 Marville rd SW6
97 P 8 Marwood clo Welling
70 B 10 Mary Anns bldgs SE8
78 F 10 Mary bank SE18
136 K 10 Mary pl W11
65 P 15 Mary st E16
134 B 5 Mary st N1
131 Z 6 Mary ter NW1
40 J 7 Maryatt av Harrow
51 Z 15 Maryland pk E15
51 Y 16 Maryland rd E15
17 S 20 Maryland rd N22
122 J 1 Maryland rd Thntn Hth
108 K 20 Maryland rd Thntn Hth
52 A 15 Maryland sq E15
51 Y 16 Maryland st E15
129 V 18 Marylands rd W9
139 U 1 Marylebond High st W1
139 W 5 Marylebond la W1
131 V 18 Marylebond rd NW1
140 B 4 Marylebone pas W1
139 U 2 Marylebone st W1
131 N 19 Marylebone station NW1
78 D 12 Maryon gro SE7
46 J 13 Maryon ms NW3
78 D 12 Maryon rd SE7
83 Y 19 Marys ter Twick
136 J 20 Masbro rd W14
77 X 17 Mascalls rd SE7
87 R 9 Mascotte rd SW15
6 G 19 Masefield av N14
58 H 19 Masefield av S Hall
10 J 17 Masefield av Stanm
99 U 3 Masefield clo Erith
120 F 5 Masefield clo Mitch
6 G 18 Masefield cres NW4
66 J 11 Masefield gdns E6
62 A 17 Mashie rd W3
38 M 5 Mashiters hill Rom
39 R 9 Mashiters wlk Rom
106 C 8 Maskell rd SW17
88 K 1 Maskelyne clo SW11
65 S 19 Mason clo E16
43 O 7 Mason ct Wemb
21 N 14 Mason rd Wdfd Grn
150 H 5 Mason st SE17
133 Y 13 Mason's pl EC1
139 Z 7 Masons Arm ms W1
142 D 4 Masons av EC2
157 N 7 Masons av Croy
23 V 12 Masons av Harrow
61 P 12 Masons Grn la W3
78 M 12 Masons hill SE18
126 G 7 Masons hill Brom
133 Z 12 Masons pl EC1
106 L 20 Masons pl Mitch
140 C 12 Masons yd SW1
35 Z 8 Massford ct Ilf
49 X 18 Massie rd E8
150 J 6 Massinger st SE17
63 S 11 Massingham st E1
76 B 11 Mast Ho ter E14
95 R 1 Master Gunners pl SE18
63 U 14 Masters st E6
82 M 17 Maswell Park cres Hounslw
82 L 17 Maswell Park rd Hounslw
52 A 9 Matcham rd E11
126 E 13 Matfield clo Brom
81 S 16 Matfield rd Blvdr
91 U 11 Matham gro SE22
135 O 6 Matheson rd W14
140 G 19 Mathew Parker st SW1
66 K 7 Mathews av E6
52 C 19 Mathews Pk av E15
140 U 5 Mathews yd EC1
133 O 4 Matilda st N1
153 T 8 Matlock cres Sutton
153 T 9 Matlock gdns Sutton
153 T 0 Matlock pl Sutton
33 U 18 Matlock rd E10
63 U 16 Matlock st E1
117 Y 1 Matlock way New Mald
88 L 6 Matthews st SW11
49 R 14 Matthias rd N16
49 R 14 Matthias sq N16
30 H 17 Mattison rd N4
72 E 2 Mattock la W13
65 R 5 Maud gdns E13
67 X 6 Maud gdns Bark
51 U 10 Maud rd E10
65 R 5 Maud rd E13
32 H 15 Maud rd E17
91 R 3 Maude rd SE5
32 H 15 Maude ter E17
95 U 7 Maudslay rd SE9
71 T 4 Maudsville cotts W7
90 A 13 Mauleverer rd SW2
71 V 4 Maunder rd W7
148 E 4 Maunsel st SW1
30 K 8 Maurice av N22
62 J 18 Maurice st W12
28 C 14 Maurice wlk NW11
77 N 12 Mauritius rd SE10
49 W 8 Maury rd N16
64 F 17 Mauve st E14
113 P 19 Mavalstone clo Chisl
113 P 20 Mavelstone rd Chisl
64 A 4 Maverton rd E3
152 B 10 Mavis av Epsom
152 B 10 Mavis clo Epsom
151 P 10 Mawbey pl SE1
151 P 11 Mawbey rd SE1
148 L 20 Mawbey st SW8
38 G 9 Mawney clo Rom
38 J 10 Mawney park Rom

57 T 1 Melton gdns Rom
32 D 15 Melton st NW1
04 F 19 Melville av SW20
41 W 16 Melville av Grnfd
57 V 12 Melville av S Croy
17 U 17 Melville gdns N13
32 L 12 Melville rd SW4
61 X 2 Melville rd NW10
86 F 2 Melville rd SW13
38 H 3 Melville rd Rom
15 T 5 Melville rd Sidcp
34 A 2 Melville st N1
10 B 20 Melvin rd SE20
65 N 9 Memorial av E15
64 M 8 Memorial av E15
70 E 17 Memorial clo Hounsl
45 R 8 Mendip dri NW2
88 D 8 Mendip rd SW11
99 P 3 Mendip rd Bxly Hth
57 W 2 Mendip rd Hornch
36 Y 16 Mendip rd Ilf
55 N 16 Mendora rd SW6
45 T 13 Menelik rd NW2
09 N 18 Menlo gdns SE19
24 A 17 Mennel st EC1
24 E 17 Mentmore clo Harrow
60 A 20 Mentmore ter LU
35 X 1 Mentmore ter E8
73 W 5 Meon rd W3
21 U 2 Meopham rd Mitch
23 N 2 Mepham cres Harrow
23 N 2 Mepham gdns Harrow
41 R 15 Mepham st SE1
98 F 9 Mera dri Bxly Hth
93 X 9 Mercator st SE13
40 H 6 Mercer st WC21
35 X 18 Merceron st E1
47 Y 10 Mercers rd N19
23 N 4 Mercham rd Thntn Hth
63 Z 10 Merchant st E3
11 W 3 Merchiston rd SE6
14 C 2 Merchland rd SE9
93 V 9 Mercia gro SE13
87 S 13 Mercier rd SW15
72 F 15 Mercury rd Brentf
87 R 18 Mere clo SW19
74 Mere end Croy
56 D 10 Merebank la Croy
45 N 14 Meredith av NW2
33 V 14 Meredith st EC1
15 T 10 Meredith st E13
86 G 4 Meredyth rd SW13
20 D 14 Merevale cres Mrdn
01 S 1 Mereway rd Twick
27 V 3 Merewood clo Brom
98 J 2 Merewood rd Bxly Hth
26 C 12 Mereworth clo Brom
79 O 20 Mereworth dri SE18
36 B 4 Meriden clo Ilf
78 A 18 Meridian rd SE7
84 C 10 Merifield rd SE9
87 T 10 Meridian rd SW15
41 O 2 Merivale rd Harrow
27 U 1 Merlewood clo Chisl
13 T 20 Merlewood dri Chisl
43 W 3 Merley ct NW9
25 N 4 Merlin cres Edgw
12 E 8 Merlin gdns Brom
24 M 10 Merlin gro Becknhm
25 N 10 Merlin gro Becknhm
36 A 1 Merlin gro Ilf
52 M 7 Merlin rd E12
96 M 9 Merlin rd Well
97 O 10 Merlin rd Welling
33 T 14 Merlin st WC1
40 F 9 Merlins av Harrow
42 E 16 Mermaid ct SE1
50 D 1 Merrick sq SE1
7 V 19 Merridene N21
18 M 20 Merrilands rd Worc Pk
96 G 20 Merrilees rd Sidcp
95 N 1 Merriman rd SE3
94 M 1 Merriman rd SE3
35 U 14 Merrington rd SW6
11 T 15 Merrion av Stanm
92 L 13 Merritt rd SE4
6 K 18 Merrivale N14
25 U 4 Merrivale Edg
25 U 4 Merrivale Edgw
35 O 13 Merrivale av Ilf
52 O 19 Merrow rd Sutton
50 F 11 Merrow st SE17
59 V 14 Merrow way Croy
11 T 18 Merryfield gdns Stanm
94 D 5 Merryfield rd SE3
20 D 3 Merryhill clo E4

7 N 15 Merryhills dri Enf
6 K 14 Merryhills dri Enf
32 L 9 Mersey rd E17
25 R 16 Mersham rd NW9
110 A 20 Mersham pl SE20
74 K 17 Merthyr ter SW13
74 C 11 Merton av W4
41 N 15 Merton av Grnfd
92 G 10 Merton clo SE4
127 Z 12 Merton gdns Brom
105 T 20 Merton Hall gdns SW20
105 T 20 Merton Hall rd SW19
119 U 1 Merton Hall rd SW19
106 D 19 Merton High st SW19
47 N 6 Merton la N6
33 T 17 Merton rd E17
123 W 11 Merton rd SE25
106 A 18 Merton rd SW19
67 Y 1 Merton rd Bark
8 A 4 Merton rd Enf
41 N 4 Merton rd Harrow
36 K 20 Merton rd Ilf
55 Z 1 Merton rd Rom
18 J 10 Merton ri NW3
92 F 12 Merttins rd SE15
90 F 12 Mervan rd SW2
114 C 6 Mervyn av SE9
71 Z 8 Mervyn rd W13
61 X 18 Messaline av W3
94 L 12 Messent rd SE9
95 W 15 Messeter pl SE9
129 U 1 Messina av NW6
89 T 10 Meteor st SW11
156 A 16 Meteor wy Wallgtn
149 U 11 Methley st SE11
25 P 2 Methuen clo Edg
25 O 3 Methuen clo Edg
29 T 9 Methuen pk N10
81 V 10 Methuen rd Blvdr
98 B 11 Methuen rd Bxly Hth
25 O 3 Methuen rd Edg
136 F 1 Methwold rd W10
35 O 16 Mews the Ilf
87 W 13 Mexfield rd SW15
8 K 3 Meyer gro Enf
81 Y 16 Meyer rd Erith
141 W 14 Meymott st SE1
50 E 20 Meynell cres E9
50 F 20 Meynell rd E9
39 Z 1 Meynell rd Rom
44 F 17 Meyrick rd NW10
88 H 8 Meyrick rd SW11
116 K 9 Miall rd SE24
134 C 12 Micawber ct N1
134 C 11 Micawber st N1
52 A 4 Michael rd E11
123 R 7 Michael rd SE25
88 B 1 Michael rd SW6
88 B 1 Michael rd SW6
84 J 9 Michaels row Rich
94 C 15 Micheldever rd SE12
101 X 6 Micheham gdns Twick
53 S 12 Michigan av E12
14 J 13 Michleham down N12
153 R 13 Mickleham gdns Sutton
159 X 15 Mickleham way Croy
145 U 15 Micklethwaite rd SW6
12 L 11 Middle dene NW7
130 F 3 Middle field NW8
29 Z 16 Middle la N8
101 V 14 Middle la Tedd
113 S 1 Middle Park av SE9
95 N 17 Middle Park av SE9
94 M 15 Middle Park av SE9
41 P 5 Middle path Harrow
65 S 8 Middle rd E13
121 W 3 Middle rd SW16
5 V 19 middle rd Barnt
41 R 5 Middle rd Harrow
118 K 17 Middle row W10
141 Z 1 Middle st EC1
156 L 4 Middle st Croy
141 S 7 Middle Temple la EC4
121 X 4 Middle way SW16
23 V 7 Middle Way the Harrow
142 H 19 Middle yd SE1
130 F 3 Middlefield NW8
60 A 14 Middlefield W13
36 A 19 Middlefield gdns Ilf
35 A 20 Middlefield gdns Ilf
18 K 19 Middleham gdns N18
18 K 19 Middleham rd N18

8 K 18 Middlesborough rd N18
74 E 12 Middlesex ct W4
141 Z 2 Middlesex pas EC1
143 N 5 Middlesex st E1
142 M 3 Middlesex st E1
50 D 5 Middlesex wharf E5
20 A 11 Middleton av E4
19 Z 12 Middleton av E4
59 S 5 Middleton av Grnfd
115 S 14 Middleton av Sidcp
19 Y 12 Middleton clo E4
35 Z 19 Middleton gdns Ilf
36 A 20 Middleton gdns Ilf
47 Z 15 Middleton gro N7
134 M 1 Middleton rd E8
135 O 1 Middleton rd E8
45 X 1 Middleton rd NW11
120 C 14 Middleton rd Mrdn
120 J 17 Middleton rd Mrdn
119 Z 15 Middleton rd Mrdn
117 V 5 Middleton rd New Mald
135 W 11 Middleton st E2
63 N 8 Middleton st E2
93 X 9 Middleton way SE13
120 G 17 Middleton way Carsh
98 K 7 Midfield av Bxly Hth
115 R 20 Midfield way Orp
132 C 18 Midford pl W1
28 A 14 Midholm NW11
28 A 13 Midholm clo NW11
158 J 4 Midholm rd Croy
132 K 13 Midhope st WC1
29 O 11 Midhurst av N10
122 G 16 Midhurst av Croy
98 D 15 Midhurst hill Bxly Hth
71 Z 6 Midhurst rd W13
72 A 8 Midhurst rd W13
44 M 3 Midland Brent ter NW2
51 U 3 Midland rd E10
132 H 12 Midland rd NW1
62 B 13 Midland ter NW10
45 O 10 Midland ter NW2
63 X 13 Midlothian rd E3
107 V 1 Midmoor rd SW12
105 R 19 Midmoor rd SW12
44 B 12 Midstrath rd NW10
82 D 11 Midsummer av Hounsl
119 V 17 Midway Sutton
66 K 2 Miers clo E6
35 O 14 Mighell av Ilf
146 C 12 Milborne gro SW10
50 D 19 Milborne st E9
94 A 17 Milborough cres SE12
141 X 19 Milcote st SE1
50 B 11 Mildenhall rd E5
49 O 16 Mildmay av N1
49 O 16 Mildmay av N1
49 P 16 Mildmay pk N1
49 P 15 Mildmay pk N1
38 K 15 Mildmay rd Rom
49 P 17 Mildmay st N1
40 L 16 Mildred av Grnfd
63 T 12 Mile End pl E1
63 O 13 Mile End rd E1
91 U 16 Mile rd SE22
121 U 16 Mile rd Wallgtn
32 F 6 Milend the E17
142 F 10 Miles la EC4
116 M 9 Miles pl NW8
120 H 5 Miles rd Mitch
148 K 15 Miles rd SW8
15 Y 9 Miles way N20
13 Y 17 Milespit hill NW7
109 U 16 Milestone rd SE19
62 G 20 Milfoil st W12
80 M 15 Milford clo SE2
25 P 3 Milford gdns Edg
42 G 14 Milford gdns Wemb
154 C 7 Milford gro Sutton
141 R 7 Milford la WC2
93 R 19 Milford rd SE6
72 A 3 Milford rd W13
58 H 20 Milford rd S'hall
70 H 1 Milford rd S'hall
89 S 6 Milford st SW8
142 B 5 Milk st EC2
78 L 4 Milk st E16
112 H 14 Milk st Brom
75 P 1 Milk yd E1
34 J 1 Milkwell gdns Wdfd Grn
90 K 11 Milkwood rd SE24
4 H 19 Mill bridge Barnt
155 O 3 Mill clo Carsh
4 H 7 Mill corner Barnt
100 C 1 Mill Farm cres Twick

110 A 8 Mill gdns SE26
121 O 16 Mill Grn rd Mitch
13 R 16 Mill Hill cir NW7
14 D 20 Mill Hill East sta NW7
14 D 20 Mill Hill Estate sta NW7
73 U 4 Mill Hill gro W3
13 T 17 Mill Hill park NW7
86 G 6 Mill Hill rd SW13
73 S 4 Mill Hill rd W3
73 T 4 Mill Hill ter W3
121 U 11 Mill house Mitch
45 T 16 Mill la NW6
155 N 8 Mill la Carsh
156 E 6 Mill la Carsh
152 E 18 Mill la Epsom
37 Y 19 Mill la Rom
21 R 17 Mill la Wdfd Grn
31 Z 11 Mill Mead rd N17
63 X 18 Mill pl E14
155 N 7 Mill pl Chisl
113 Y 20 Mill pl Chisl
99 X 11 Mill pl Drtfrd
116 K 5 Mill pl Kingst
83 Z 6 Mill plat Islwth
84 A 6 Mill plat Islwth
83 Y 6 Mill Plat av Islwth
77 W 3 Mill rd E16
106 E 17 Mill rd SW19
81 X 20 Mill rd Erith
53 W 9 Mill rd Ilf
101 O 4 Mill rd Twick
12 B 17 Mill ridge Edg
134 L 5 Mill row N1
143 P 18 Mill st SE1
139 Z 8 Mill st W1
116 K 6 Mill st Kingst
126 D 4 Mill vale Brom
158 E 5 Mill View gdns Croy
13 N 15 Mill way NW7
53 W 16 Millais av E12
25 P 7 Millais gdns Edg
51 V 12 Millais rd E11
8 H 18 Millais rd Enf
117 Z 16 Millais rd New Mald
150 D 14 Millais st SE17
49 S 15 Millard rd N18
148 K 7 Millbank SW1
100 C 9 Millbourne rd Felt
96 F 10 Millbrook av Welling
39 S 6 Millbrook gdns Rom
38 A 17 Millbrook gdns Rom
18 L 6 Millbrook rd N9
90 H 8 Millbrook rd SW9
75 N 14 Milledge st SE16
106 G 15 Miller rd SW19
122 E 20 Miller rd Croy
132 A 7 Miller st NW1
49 U 13 Millers av E8
49 U 14 Millers ter E8
58 J 5 Millfield av E17
47 N 8 Millfield la N6
47 O 7 Millfield pl N6
18 C 14 Millfield rd N18
25 W 7 Millfield rd Edg
82 C 20 Millfield rd Hounsl
50 G 10 Millfield rd E5
50 M 3 Millicent rd E10
25 Y 1 Milling rd Edg
133 N 18 Millman ms WC1
133 O 19 Millman pl WC1
128 J 8 Millman rd NW6
133 N 18 Millman st WC1
92 J 6 Millmark gro SE14
9 Y 8 Millmarsh la Enf
55 S 7 Millner rd Dgnhm
64 F 16 Mills gro E14
154 M 2 Millside Carsh
76 B 8 Millwall Dock rd E14
63 N 15 Millward st E1
40 E 19 Millway gdns Grnfd
83 N 13 Millwood rd Hounsl
136 J 2 Millwood st W10
146 G 16 Milmans st SW10
95 P 13 Milne gdns SE9
22 G 1 Milnefeild Pinn
83 P 18 Milner dri Twick
133 V 3 Milner pl N1
155 N 9 Milner pl Carsh
64 M 9 Milner rd E15
106 A 19 Milner rd SW19
116 G 7 Milner rd Kingst
120 F 11 Milner rd Mrdn
123 N 5 Milner rd Thntn Hth
133 V 2 Milner sq N1
147 N 4 Milner st SW3
73 X 16 Milnthorpe rd W4
144 J 1 Milton W14
66 B 1 Milton av E6
61 X 4 Milton av NW10

| | | |
|---|---|---|
| 25 U 11 | Milton av NW9 |
| 47 V 1 | Milton av N6 |
| 4 J 15 | Milton av Barnt |
| 123 P 18 | Milton av Croy |
| 57 U 6 | Milton av Hornch |
| 154 H 8 | Milton av Sutton |
| 28 C 17 | Milton clo N2 |
| 154 G 6 | Milton clo Sutton |
| 36 A 19 | Milton cres Ilf |
| 134 D 20 | Milton ct EC 2 |
| 75 W 18 | Milton Ct rd SE14 |
| 16 J 16 | Milton gro N11 |
| 49 P 13 | Milton gro N16 |
| 47 U 1 | Milton pk N6 |
| 33 O 12 | Milton rd E17 |
| 13 T 15 | Milton rd NW7 |
| 30 J 12 | Milton rd N15 |
| 47 V 1 | Milton rd N6 |
| 90 H 14 | Milton rd SE24 |
| 85 X 9 | Milton rd SW14 |
| 106 C 15 | Milton rd SW19 |
| 73 X 2 | Milton rd W3 |
| 59 W 20 | Milton rd W7 |
| 81 R 11 | Milton rd Blvdr |
| 147 P 18 | Milton rd Croy |
| 100 H 19 | Milton rd Hampt |
| 23 U 13 | Milton rd Harrow |
| 107 P 18 | Milton rd Mitch |
| 39 V 18 | Milton rd Rom |
| 153 Y 7 | Milton rd Sutton |
| 155 W 14 | Milton rd Wallgtn |
| 96 J 1 | Milton rd Welling |
| 134 D 20 | Milton st EC 2 |
| 65 T 5 | Milton st E13 |
| 54 K 6 | Milverton gdns Ilf |
| 45 N 20 | Milverton rd NW6 |
| 128 D 1 | Milverton rd NW6 |
| 149 T 11 | Milverton st SE11 |
| 113 X 9 | Milverton way SE9 |
| 143 X 1 | Milward st E1 |
| 87 V 2 | Mimosa st SW6 |
| 150 M 9 | Mina rd SE17 |
| 105 Z 20 | Mina rd SW19 |
| 111 Z 3 | Minard rd SE6 |
| 93 Y 19 | Minard rd SE6 |
| 16 J 11 | Minchenden cres N14 |
| 142 K 8 | Mincing la EC3 |
| 109 Z 20 | Minden rd SE20 |
| 108 C 13 | Minehead rd SW16 |
| 40 G 9 | Minehead rd Harrow |
| 147 U 6 | Minera ms SW1 |
| 79 T 12 | Mineral st SE18 |
| 114 G 9 | Minerva clo Sidcp |
| 33 R 1 | Minerva rd E4 |
| 61 X 10 | Minerva rd NW10 |
| 116 L 3 | Minerva rd Kingst |
| 135 W 9 | Minerva st E2 |
| 62 A 5 | Minet av NW10 |
| 62 A 5 | Minet gdns NW10 |
| 90 J 5 | Minet rd SW9 |
| 136 E 19 | Minford gdns W14 |
| 64 B 20 | Ming st E14 |
| 116 M 11 | Minniedale Surb |
| 117 N 10 | Minniedale rd Surb |
| 150 K 8 | Minnow st SE17 |
| 143 N 8 | Minories EC3 |
| 89 X 3 | Minshull st SW8 |
| 63 T 2 | Minson rd E9 |
| 86 D 17 | Minstead gdns SW15 |
| 118 A 15 | Minstead way New Mald |
| 153 Y 4 | Minster av Sutton |
| 45 T 15 | Minster rd NW2 |
| 112 H 17 | Minster rd Brom |
| 155 R 9 | Mint rd Wallgtn |
| 142 B 17 | Mint st SE1 |
| 156 M 5 | Mint wk Croy |
| 157 N 5 | Mint wlk Croy |
| 17 W 11 | Mintern clo N13 |
| 25 O 17 | Mintern rd Harrow |
| 134 G 8 | Mintern st N1 |
| 70 H 10 | Minterne av S'hall |
| 25 O 17 | Minterne rd Harrow |
| 135 P 17 | Mirabel rd SW6 |
| 47 W 4 | Miranda rd N19 |
| 78 A 10 | Mirfield st SE7 |
| 79 U 13 | Miriam rd SE18 |
| 112 M 7 | Mirror path SE9 |
| 120 D 14 | Missenden gdns Mrdn |
| 32 J 15 | Mission gro E17 |
| 121 T 15 | Mitcham common Mitch |
| 107 V 13 | Mitcham la SW16 |
| 120 L 9 | Mitcham pk Mitch |
| 66 E 9 | Mitcham rd E6 |
| 121 Z 14 | Mitcham rd SW16 |
| 106 L 12 | Mitcham rd SW17 |
| 122 C 16 | Mitcham rd Croy |
| 36 L 20 | Mitcham rd Ilf |
| 80 F 13 | Mitchell clo SE2 |
| 17 X 15 | Mitchell rd N13 |
| 134 B 15 | Mitchell st EC1 |
| 43 W 18 | Mitchell way NW10 |
| 49 O 19 | Mitchison rd N1 |
| 31 W 9 | Mitchley rd N17 |
| 48 A 7 | Mitford rd N4 |
| 142 B 5 | Mitre ct EC2 |
| 141 U 17 | Mitre rd SE1 |
| 142 M 6 | Mitre sq EC3 |
| 142 L 6 | Mitre st EC3 |
| 27 Z 10 | Moat cres N3 |
| 65 Y 8 | Moat dri E13 |
| 23 O 13 | Moat dri Harrow |
| 40 F 19 | Moat Farm clo Grnfd |
| 90 D 7 | Moat pl SW9 |
| 61 T 16 | Moat pl W3 |
| 9 S 13 | Moat side Enf |
| 89 Y 17 | Moberly rd SW4 |
| 47 N 18 | Modbury gdns NW5 |
| 47 O 17 | Modbury st NW5 |
| 87 P 9 | Modder pl SW15 |
| 72 B 4 | Model cotts W13 |
| 113 R 6 | Model Farm clo SE9 |
| 129 P 20 | Modena st W10 |
| 141 W 5 | Modern ct EC4 |
| 120 G 7 | Moffat gdns Mitch |
| 17 N 18 | Moffat rd N13 |
| 106 K 9 | Moffat rd SW17 |
| 122 M 4 | Moffat rd Thntn Hth |
| 123 N 3 | Moffat rd Thnth Hth |
| 83 X 12 | Mogden la Islwth |
| 76 A 7 | Moiety rd E14 |
| 157 W 20 | Moir clo S Croy |
| 95 U 9 | Moira rd E9 |
| 75 S 12 | Moland mead SE16 |
| 114 B 7 | Molescroft SE9 |
| 153 S 4 | Molesey dri Sutton |
| 87 Y 3 | Molesford rd SW6 |
| 93 T 8 | Molesworth st SE13 |
| 9 W 8 | Mollison av Enf |
| 9 X 4 | Mollison av Enf |
| 156 B 14 | Mollison dri Wallgtn |
| 155 Z 17 | Mollison dri Wallgtn |
| 24 M 9 | Mollison way Edg |
| 25 O 8 | Mollison way Edgw |
| 138 M 3 | Molyneux st W1 |
| 92 D 4 | Mona rd SE15 |
| 65 P 15 | Mona st E16 |
| 81 S 9 | Monarch rd Blvdr |
| 8 B 9 | Monastery gdns Enf |
| 148 G 3 | Monck st SW1 |
| 91 R 9 | Monclar rd SE5 |
| 138 J 20 | Moncorvo clo SW7 |
| 91 X 4 | Moncrieff st SE15 |
| 53 P 17 | Monega rd E12 |
| 52 K 18 | Monega rd E7 |
| 64 K 16 | Moness st E14 |
| 64 A 1 | Monier rd E3 |
| 110 L 19 | Monivea rd Becknhm |
| 65 R 19 | Monk dri E16 |
| 78 J 10 | Monk st SE18 |
| 16 E 1 | Monkfrith av N14 |
| 6 D 20 | Monkfrith clo N14 |
| 16 D 2 | Monkfrith way N14 |
| 21 V 18 | Monkhams av Wdfd Grn |
| 21 V 17 | Monkhams dri Wdfd Grn |
| 21 X 11 | Monkhams la Buck Hl |
| 21 T 18 | Monkhams la Wdfd Grn |
| 119 T 8 | Monkleigh rd Mrdn |
| 5 S 20 | Monks av Barnt |
| 15 S 1 | Monks av Barnt |
| 80 H 10 | Monks clo SE2 |
| 7 X 9 | Monks clo Enf |
| 61 P 16 | Monks dri W3 |
| 125 O 13 | Monks Orchard rd Becknhm |
| 43 U 16 | Monks park Wemb |
| 43 T 19 | Monks Park gdns Wemb |
| 7 X 8 | Monks rd Enf |
| 125 P 16 | Monks way Becknhm |
| 154 B 4 | Monksdene gdns Sutton |
| 35 W 11 | Monkswood gdns Ilf |
| 96 L 4 | Monkton rd Welling |
| 149 V 5 | Monkton st SE11 |
| 27 V 13 | Monkville av NW11 |
| 142 B 2 | Monkwell sq EC2 |
| 34 H 11 | Monmouth av E18 |
| 102 F 19 | Monmouth av Kingst |
| 97 N 9 | Monmouth clo Welling |
| 137 W 6 | Monmouth pl W2 |
| 66 F 10 | Monmouth rd E6 |
| 18 M 8 | Monmouth rd N9 |
| 19 P 10 | Monmouth rd N9 |
| 137 W 7 | Monmouth rd W2 |
| 56 B 15 | Monmouth rd Dgnhm |
| 140 J 7 | Monmouth st WC2 |
| 47 V 10 | Monnery rd N19 |
| 151 T 6 | Monnow rd SE1 |
| 23 S 1 | Monro gdns Harrow |
| 8 M 7 | Monroe cres Enf |
| 127 R 14 | Mons way Brom |
| 48 J 9 | Monsell rd N4 |
| 33 X 2 | Monserratt av Wdfd Grn |
| 62 H 6 | Monson rd NW10 |
| 75 S 20 | Monson rd SE14 |
| 92 L 18 | Montacute rd SE6 |
| 10 G 2 | Montacute rd Bushey Watf |
| 159 T 20 | Montacute rd Croy |
| 120 E 15 | Montacute rd Mrdn |
| 19 N 15 | Montagu cres N18 |
| 19 N 14 | Montagu gdns N18 |
| 139 R 2 | Montagu mans W1 |
| 139 P 2 | Montagu Ms north W1 |
| 139 P 4 | Montagu Ms south W1 |
| 139 P 4 | Montagu Ms west W1 |
| 139 P 2 | Montagu pl W1 |
| 140 H 1 | Montagu pl W1 |
| 26 G 19 | Montagu rd NW4 |
| 19 O 12 | Montagu rd N18 |
| 139 R 2 | Montagu row W1 |
| 139 P 3 | Montagu sq W1 |
| 139 R 4 | Montagu st W1 |
| 92 M 10 | Montague av SE4 |
| 93 N 10 | Montague av SE4 |
| 71 V 3 | Montague av W7 |
| 142 F 13 | Montague clo SE1 |
| 61 P 19 | Montague gdns W3 |
| 155 V 9 | Montague gdns Wallgtn |
| 64 F 20 | Montague pl E14 |
| 64 F 19 | Montague pl E14 |
| 64 F 20 | Montague pl E14 |
| 132 H 20 | Montague pl WC1 |
| 52 B 8 | Montague rd E11 |
| 49 W 15 | Montague rd E8 |
| 31 W 12 | Montague rd N15 |
| 30 C 16 | Montague rd N8 |
| 105 Z 18 | Montague rd SW19 |
| 60 B 17 | Montague rd W13 |
| 71 V 4 | Montague rd W7 |
| 122 J 19 | Montague rd Croy |
| 82 K 7 | Montague rd Hounsl |
| 84 K 15 | Montague rd Rich |
| 70 B 10 | Montague rd S'hall |
| 140 J 1 | Montague st WC 1 |
| 70 B 9 | Montague waye S'hall |
| 21 O 16 | Montalt rd Wdfd Grn |
| 21 P 15 | Montalt rd Wdfd Grn |
| 107 O 8 | Montana rd SW17 |
| 105 O 20 | Montana rd SW20 |
| 113 Z 7 | Montbelle rd SE9 |
| 126 F 15 | Montcalm clo Brom |
| 78 A 18 | Montcalm rd SE7 |
| 135 O 15 | Montclare st E2 |
| 54 C 18 | Monteagle av Bark |
| 89 S 5 | Montefiore st SW8 |
| 63 Y 3 | Monteith rd E3 |
| 92 K 19 | Montem rd SE23 |
| 118 A 9 | Montem rd New Mald |
| 48 C 5 | Montem st N4 |
| 117 Z 8 | Monten rd New Mald |
| 29 W 17 | Montenotte rd N8 |
| 149 S 11 | Montford pl SE11 |
| 87 R 20 | Montford pl SW19 |
| 96 J 15 | Montgomery clo Sidcp |
| 66 E 13 | Montgomery gdns E6 |
| 73 V 10 | Montgomery rd W4 |
| 12 A 20 | Montgomery rd Edg |
| 88 M 16 | Montholme rd SW11 |
| 143 R 2 | Monthorpe st WC1 |
| 86 L 12 | Montolieu gdns SW15 |
| 60 E 15 | Montpelier av W5 |
| 97 W 19 | Montpelier av Bxly |
| 66 B 8 | Montpelier gdns E6 |
| 55 T 1 | Montpelier gdns Rom |
| 47 V 14 | Montpelier gro NW5 |
| 138 M 20 | Montpelier ms SW7 |
| 138 L 20 | Montpelier pl SW7 |
| 28 C 6 | Montpelier rd N3 |
| 151 X 20 | Montpelier rd SE15 |
| 92 A 1 | Montpelier rd SE15 |
| 60 G 15 | Montpelier rd W5 |
| 154 E 8 | Montpelier rd Sutton |
| 45 S 1 | Montpelier ri NW11 |
| 42 F 5 | Montpelier ri Wemb |
| 94 C 4 | Montpelier row SE3 |
| 84 D 19 | Montpelier row Twick |
| 138 L 20 | Montpelier sq SW7 |
| 138 M 20 | Montpelier st SW7 |
| 138 M 20 | Montpelier st SW7 |
| 94 B 5 | Montpelier vale SE3 |
| 45 S 1 | Montpelier way NW11 |
| 138 L 20 | Montpelier wlk SW7 |
| 110 C 16 | Montrave rd SE20 |
| 141 O 8 | Montreal pl WC2 |
| 54 A 2 | Montreal rd Ilf |
| 90 A 20 | Montrell rd SW2 |
| 128 M 7 | Montrose av NW6 |
| 25 W 7 | Montrose av Edg |
| 97 O 18 | Montrose av Sidcp |
| 82 L 20 | Montrose av Twick |
| 96 G 8 | Montrose av Welling |
| 96 J 7 | Montrose clo Welling |
| 42 J 17 | Montrose cres Wem |
| 138 G 20 | Montrose ct SW7 |
| 120 M 5 | Montrose gdns Mitc |
| 154 B 4 | Montrose gdns Sutton |
| 139 U 20 | Montrose pl SW1 |
| 23 W 8 | Montrose rd Harrow |
| 87 S 10 | Montserrat rd SW18 |
| 142 H 10 | Monument st EC3 |
| 75 P 1 | Monza st E1 |
| 75 R 7 | Moodkey st SE16 |
| 63 T 10 | Moody st E1 |
| 4 H 12 | Moon la Barnt |
| 133 V 4 | Moon st N1 |
| 94 F 11 | Moons ct SE12 |
| 134 E 20 | Moor la EC2 |
| 142 D 1 | Moor la EC2 |
| 142 F 2 | Moor pl EC2 |
| 140 G 7 | Moor st W1 |
| 107 Z 6 | Moorcroft rd SW16 |
| 22 A 16 | Moorcroft way Pinn |
| 95 Y 1 | Moordown SE18 |
| 78 L 20 | Moordown SE18 |
| 156 A 18 | Moore clo Wallgtn |
| 135 X 19 | Moore Pk rd SW6 |
| 145 W 20 | Moore Pk rd SW6 |
| 108 K 14 | Moore rd SE19 |
| 147 O 5 | Moore st SW3 |
| 31 U 9 | Moorefield rd SW16 |
| 112 D 19 | Mooreland rd Brom |
| 65 O 3 | Moorey clo E15 |
| 65 O 4 | Moorey clo E15 |
| 60 H 11 | Moorfield av W5 |
| 142 E 2 | Moorfields EC2 |
| 142 F 2 | Moorgate EC2 |
| 137 T 5 | Moorhouse rd W2 |
| 24 H 10 | Moorhouse rd Harrow |
| 38 H 3 | Moorland clo Rom |
| 152 M 11 | Moormead dri Epsom |
| 83 Z 16 | Moormead rd Twick |
| 112 A 7 | Moorside rd Brom |
| 25 O 17 | Moot ct NW9 |
| 45 N 11 | Mora rd NW2 |
| 44 M 11 | Mora rd NW2 |
| 134 C 13 | Mora st EC1 |
| 64 B 19 | Morant st E14 |
| 90 E 1 | Morat st SW9 |
| 46 G 16 | Moravian pl SW3 |
| 63 P 8 | Moravian st E2 |
| 39 O 3 | Moray clo Rom |
| 48 D 6 | Moray ms N4 |
| 48 E 5 | Moray rd N4 |
| 39 O 3 | Moray way Rom |
| 103 T 17 | Morcoombe clo Kingst |
| 61 Z 4 | Mordaunt rd NW10 |
| 90 C 8 | Mordaunt st SW9 |
| 93 U 3 | Morden clo SE13 |
| 119 Z 9 | Morden ct Mrdn |
| 41 X 15 | Morden gdns Grnfd |
| 120 G 9 | Morden gdns Mrdn |
| 120 C 7 | Morden hall Mrdn |
| 120 D 6 | Morden Hall park Mrdn |
| 120 B 7 | Morden Hall rd Mrdn |
| 93 W 4 | Morden hill SE13 |
| 119 U 13 | Morden park Mrdn |
| 94 F 5 | Morden rd SE3 |
| 94 E 4 | Morden rd SE3 |
| 106 A 20 | Morden rd SW19 |
| 36 K 20 | Morden rd Ilf |
| 120 A 3 | Morden rd Mitch |
| 37 Z 20 | Morden rd Rom |
| 38 A 20 | Morden rd Rom |
| 94 E 5 | Morden Rd ms SE3 |
| 93 S 5 | Morden st SE13 |
| 119 X 18 | Morden way Sutton |
| 76 M 9 | Morden Wharf rd SE10 |
| 65 P 17 | More clo E16 |
| 57 Z 16 | Morecambe clo Hornch |
| 11 V 14 | Morecambe gdns Stanm |
| 150 C 8 | Morecambe st SE17 |
| 18 A 13 | Morecombe terr N18 |

18 J 15 Moree way N18
94 H 8 Morehead way SE3
33 Y 12 Moreland st EC1
20 E 10 Moreland av E4
88 L 18 Morella rd SW12
10 H 9 Moremead rd SE6
11 O 10 Moremead rd SE6
93 R 18 Morena st SE6
17 T 17 Moresby av Surb
49 Z 5 Moresby rd E5
A4 A 4 Moresby rd E5
83 S 1 Moreton av Islwth
50 B 5 Moreton clo E5
13 Z 20 Moreton clo NW7
31 O 18 Moreton clo N15
48 C 9 Moreton pl SW1
31 P 18 Moreton rd N15
57 P 11 Moreton rd S Croy
52 H 3 Moreton rd Worc Pk
48 E 8 Moreton st SW1
48 D 10 Moreton st SW 1
48 C 9 Moreton ter SW1
33 Y 13 Morgan av E17
48 F 16 Morgan rd N7
12 E 19 Morgan rd Brom
65 P 14 Morgan st E16
93 V 7 Morgan st E3
42 J 14 Morgans la SE1
46 J 19 Morgans wlk SW11
88 A 12 Morie st SW18
50 L 4 Morieux rd E10
90 R 17 Moring rd SW17
23 S 19 Morland av Croy
24 L 2 Morland av Drtfrd
46 B 4 Morland clo NW11
70 L 3 Morland gdns S'hall
32 G 17 Morland rd E17
10 F 16 Morland rd SE20
23 T 18 Morland rd Croy
69 T 2 Morland rd Dgnhm
24 J 14 Morland rd Harrow
63 Y 6 Morland rd Ilf
54 E 4 Morland rd Sutton
33 W 2 Morley av E4
18 K 14 Morley av N18
30 J 8 Morley av N22
12 G 9 Morley cres Edg
24 E 9 Morley cres Stanm
24 F 9 Morley Cres east Stanm
24 E 10 Morley Cres west Stanm
8 B 4 Morley hill Enf
51 U 5 Morley rd E10
65 P 6 Morley rd E15
93 U 11 Morley rd SE13
67 S 4 Morley rd Bark
37 Y 17 Morley rd Rom
19 V 20 Morley rd Sutton
84 F 10 Morley rd Twick
41 U 19 Morley st SE1
13 Z 20 Morlison clo NW7
91 N 3 Morna rd SE5
50 B 17 Morning la E9
52 L 3 Morningside rd Worc Pk
35 N 8 Mornington av W14
26 M 7 Mornington av Brom
35 V 20 Mornington av Ilf
21 S 13 Mornington clo Wdfd Grn
32 A 8 Mornington cres NW1
64 A 9 Mornington gro E3
32 A 9 Mornington pl NW1
31 Z 8 Mornington pl NW1
52 B 2 Mornington rd E11
20 J 2 Mornington rd E4
75 Z 20 Mornington rd SE8
58 K 12 Mornington rd Grnfd
21 S 13 Mornington rd Wdfd Grn
131 Y 8 Mornington st NW1
32 A 9 Mornington ter NW1
31 Y 7 Mornington ter NW1
102 E 9 Mornington wlk Rich
142 J 19 Morocco st SE1
63 S 4 Morpeth gro E9
63 S 4 Morpeth rd E9
63 S 9 Morpeth st E2
148 B 3 Morpeth ter SW1
54 K 9 Morrab gdns Ilf
53 T 15 Morris av E12
87 X 17 Morris gdns SW18
64 D 15 Morris rd E14
51 Y 12 Morris rd E15
56 C 7 Morris rd Dgnhm
83 V 7 Morris rd Islwth
39 Z 1 Morris rd Rom
63 N 18 Morris st E1
90 A 19 Morrish rd SW2
31 S 10 Morrison av N17
68 K 6 Morrison rd Bark

89 O 6 Morrison st SW11
129 W 14 Morshead rd W9
113 T 10 Morston gro SE9
89 X 16 Morten clo SW4
31 O 4 Morteyne rd N17
64 L 4 Mortham st E15
107 X 3 Mortimer clo SW16
129 Y 6 Mortimer cres NW6
132 D 18 Mortimer mkt WC1
129 X 6 Mortimer pl NW6
66 F 9 Mortimer rd E6
128 D 12 Mortimer rd NW10
128 D 12 Mortimer rd NW10
134 K 2 Mortimer rd N1
49 S 20 Mortimer rd N1
60 C 17 Mortimer rd W13
81 Z 17 Mortimer rd Erith
120 L 2 Mortimer rd Mitch
136 H 11 Mortimer sq W11
139 Z 4 Mortimer st W1
140 B 3 Mortimer st W 1
47 N 12 Mortimer ter NW5
85 Y 6 Mortlake High st SW14
65 W 16 Mortlake rd E16
54 D 13 Mortlake rd Ilf
85 S 4 Mortlake rd Ilf
73 P 19 Mortlake rd Rich
91 Z 2 Mortlock gdns SE15
16 J 13 Morton cres N14
155 V 10 Morton gdns Wallgtn
135 X 6 Morton ms SW5
149 S 2 Morton pl SE1
65 O 2 Morton rd E15
134 D 2 Morton rd N1
120 F 12 Morton rd Mrdn
16 H 12 Morton way N14
90 F 14 Morval rd SW2
100 L 6 Morvon rd SW17
64 A 6 Morville st E3
140 F 2 Morwell st WC1
137 X 8 Moscow pl W2
137 W 9 Moscow rd W 2
91 P 1 Mosedale st SE5
30 H 6 Moselle av N22
30 B 12 Moselle clo N8
31 V 2 Moselle pl N17
22 B 8 Moss clo Pinn
15 O 19 Moss Hall cres N12
15 N 19 Moss Hall gro N12
22 C 8 Moss la Pinn
00 V 10 Moss la Rom
56 F 20 Moss rd Dgnhm
36 A 9 Moss ter Ilf
88 K 9 Mossbury rd SW11
81 T 12 Mossdown clo Blvdr
35 Z 8 Mossford clo Ilf
36 B 10 Mossford grn Ilf
36 B 5 Mossford la Ilf
03 X 12 Mossford st E3
151 Z 6 Mossington rd SE16
75 P 11 Mossington rd SE16
110 C 16 Mosslea rd SE20
127 O 12 Mosslea rd Brom
146 M 6 Mossop st SW3
119 V 7 Mossville gdns Mrdn
43 N 14 Mostyn av Wemb
42 L 14 Mostyn av Wemb
128 F 11 Mostyn gdns NW10
63 Z 7 Mostyn gro E3
119 W 1 Mostyn rd SW19
90 F 3 Mostyn rd SW9
26 A 3 Mostyn rd Edg
25 Z 2 Mostyn rd Edg
127 R 15 Mosul way Brom
139 S 20 Motcomb st SW 1
13 R 7 Mote end NW7
89 U 4 Motley st SW8
12 N 17 Motorway m1 NW7
118 G 13 Motspur pk New Mald
113 O 2 Mottingham gdns SE9
112 K 2 Mottingham hall SE9
112 L 1 Mottingham la SE9
113 N 2 Mottingham la SE9
94 K 19 Mottingham rd SE9
19 S 1 Mottingham rd N9
113 U 8 Mottingham rd SE9
80 A 10 Mottisfont rd SE2
79 Z 9 Mottisfont rd SE2
63 R 2 Moulins rd E9
82 D 4 Moulton av Hounsl
113 V 8 Mound the SE9
31 X 19 Moundfield rd N16
91 X 19 Mount Adon pk SE22
86 E 19 Mount Angelus rd SW15
84 K 13 Mount Ararat rd Rich
109 Z 7 Mount Ash rd SE26
110 A 6 Mount Ash rd SE26
20 C 11 Mount av E4

60 G 14 Mount av W5
58 G 18 Mount av S'hall
60 E 15 Mount clo W5
6 B 15 Mount clo Barnt
113 P 20 Mount clo Chisl
155 H 19 Mount clo Wallgtn
159 Z 2 Mount ct W Wkhm
115 X 15 Mount Culver av Sidcp
97 Y 13 Mount dri Bxly Hth
22 E 15 Mount dri Harrow
43 V 7 Mount dri Wemb
108 C 6 Mount Earl gdns SW16
20 D 6 Mount Echo av E4
20 E 4 Mount Echo dri E4
107 K 5 Mount Ephraim rd SW16
109 Z 6 Mount gdns SE26
12 K 12 Mount gro Edg
48 K 9 Mount Grove rd N5
49 L 7 Mount house Barnt
133 Y 15 Mount mills EC1
108 C 6 Mount Nod rd SW16
155 P 18 Mount pk Wallgtn
41 S 7 Mount Pk av Harrow
156 J 20 Mount Pk av S Croy
60 G 17 Mount Pk cres W5
60 G 15 Mount Pk rd W5
41 R 9 Mount Pk rd Harrow
133 R 17 Mount pleasant WC1
133 R 18 Mount pleasant WC1
5 Y 14 Mount pleasant Barnt
6 A 14 Mount pleasant Barnt
60 K 2 Mount pleasant Wemb
61 N 2 Mount pleasant Wemb
48 C 2 Mount Pleasant cres N4
50 B 6 Mount Pleasant hill E5
50 A 4 Mount Pleasant la E5
32 H 7 Mount Pleasant rd E17
128 C 2 Mount Pleasant rd NW10
31 R 7 Mount Pleasant rd N17
93 T 15 Mount Pleasant rd SE13
60 E 13 Mount Pleasant rd W5
117 X 5 Mount Pleasant rd New Mald
48 C 1 Mount Pleasant vlls N4
98 K 14 Mount Pleasant wlk Bxly
44 L 9 Mount rd NW 2
28 G 20 Mount rd NW4
105 Z 4 Mount rd SW19
5 W 16 Mount rd Barnt
97 X 13 Mount rd Bxly Hth
56 C 3 Mount rd Dgnhm
99 U 15 Mount rd Drtfrd
120 G 2 Mount rd Mitch
117 X 6 Mount rd New Mald
139 W 1 Mount row W1
139 W 10 Mount st W1
24 F 20 Mount Stewart av Harrow
143 V 2 Mount ter E1
46 D 10 Mount the NW10
118 E 7 Mount the New Mald
43 U 7 Mount the Wemb
152 K 9 Mount the Worc Pk
46 C 12 Mount vernon NW3
12 L 11 Mount view NW7
20 J 3 Mount View rd E4
25 X 14 Mount View rd NW9
30 F 19 Mount View rd N4
48 B 1 Mount View rd N4
108 J 7 Mount vills SE27
155 P 20 Mount way Wallgtn
23 Y 6 Mountbell st Stanm
116 J 18 Mountcombe clo Surb
66 H 8 Mountfield rd E6
27 X 9 Mountfield rd N3
60 H 18 Mountfield rd W5
93 W 15 Mountfields ct SE13
49 W 15 Mountford rd E8
133 R 1 Mountfort ter N1
126 C 18 Mounthurst rd Brom
80 D 5 Mountjoy clo SE2
93 W 4 Mounts Pond rd SE3
23 X 4 Mountside Stanm
67 T 4 Movers la Bark
45 T 19 Mowbray rd NW6
109 V 19 Mowbray rd SE19
12 D 13 Mowbray rd Edg
102 D 7 Mowbray rd Rich

38 K 6 Mowbrays clo Rom
38 K 7 Mowbrays rd Rom
63 O 5 Mowlem st E2
135 Y 7 Mowlem st E9
149 S 20 Mowll st SW9
139 V 2 Moxon st W1
4 H 13 Moxon st Barnt
135 T 7 Moye st E2
51 U 2 Moyers rd E10
144 M 15 Moylan rd W6
61 R 7 Moyne pl NW10
107 U 14 Moyser rd SW16
129 N 14 Mozart st W10
107 Y 5 Mt Ephraim la SW16
120 C 14 Muchelney rd Mrdn
56 G 12 Muggeridge rd Dgnhm
78 F 3 Muir st E16
85 X 10 Muirdown av SW14
62 C 18 Muirfield W3
111 V 2 Muirkirk rd SE6
20 C 8 Mulberry clo E4
58 A 6 Mulberry clo Grnfd
72 C 19 Mulberry cres Brentf
54 K 19 Mulberry ct Bark
157 V 1 Mulberry la W Wkhm
74 E 14 Mulberry pl W6
143 S 3 Mulberry st E1
143 S 3 Mulberry st E1
81 Y 5 Mulberry way Blvdr
140 G 13 Mulberry wlk SW3
44 E 13 Mulgrave rd NW10
135 O 14 Mulgrave rd SW6
60 H 10 Mulgrave rd W5
157 O 7 Mulgrave rd Croy
153 V 16 Mulgrave rd Sutton
154 A 14 Mulgrave rd Sutton
41 X 8 Mulgrave rd Wemb
47 Y 4 Mulkern rd N19
89 Y 17 Muller rd SW4
85 Y 7 Mullins path SW14
22 J 3 Mullion ct Har
130 J 19 Mulready st NW8
88 G 20 Multon rd SW18
142 C 5 Mumford ct EC2
90 H 14 Mumford rd SE24
89 N 12 Muncaster rd SW11
135 P 11 Mund st W14
92 B 15 Mundania rd SE22
65 S 19 Munday rd E16
144 K 6 Munden st W14
50 C 8 Mundford rd E5
54 E 4 Mundon gdns Ilf
10 A 8 Mungo Pk clo Bushey Watf
57 W 17 Mungo Pk rd Rainhm
83 P 14 Munnings gdns Islwth
128 M 20 Munro ms W10
85 T 13 Munroe dri SW14
82 C 12 Munster av Hounsl
17 X 13 Munster gdns N13
87 U 2 Munster rd SW6
144 K 18 Munster rd W6
102 C 16 Munster rd Tedd
131 Z 14 Munster sq NW1
150 D 5 Munton rd SE17
97 Y 20 Murchison rd Bxly
51 U 5 Murchison rd E10
128 K 19 Murchison rd W 10
63 W 10 Murdock cottages E3
133 P 7 Muriel st N1
93 Y 11 Murillo rd SE13
141 S 19 Murphy st SE1
126 J 3 Murray av Brom
82 K 14 Murray av Hounsl
134 E 10 Murray gro N1
47 X 19 Murray ms NW1
14 C 20 Murray rd NW7
105 P 15 Murray rd SW19
72 D 12 Murray rd W5
102 C 4 Murray rd Rich
65 U 19 Murray sq E16
47 W 19 Murray st NW1
144 L 14 Muscard rd W6
91 V 8 Muschamp rd SE15
154 J 3 Muschamp rd Carsh
142 L 9 Muscovy st EC3
140 J 2 Museum st WC1
5 R 6 Musgrave clo Barnt
87 Z 1 Musgrave cres SW6
145 V 20 Musgrave cres SW6
83 V 1 Musgrave rd Islwth
92 G 3 Musgrove rd SE14
88 H 6 Musjid rd SW11
49 Z 6 Muston rd E5
29 R 6 Muswell av N10
29 T 11 Muswell hill N10
29 R 12 Muswell Hill bdwy N10
29 T 12 Muswell Hill pl N10
29 R 16 Muswell Hill rd N10
29 S 9 Muswell ms N10

| | | |
|---|---|---|
| 29 T 9 | Muswell rd N10 |
| 129 V 3 | Mutrix rd NW6 |
| 117 V 4 | Muybridge rd New Mald |
| 149 X 20 | Myatt rd SW9 |
| 90 J 1 | Myatt rd SW9 |
| 77 S 18 | Mycenae rd SE3 |
| 17 X 2 | Myddelton gdns N21 |
| 133 T 12 | Myddelton pas EC1 |
| 15 V 8 | Myddelton pk N20 |
| 30 C 1 | Myddelton rd N22 |
| 30 B 11 | Myddelton rd N8 |
| 133 T 11 | Myddelton sq EC1 |
| 133 U 14 | Myddelton st EC1 |
| 8 F 4 | Myddleton av Enf |
| 8 G 5 | Myddleton clo Enf |
| 30 B 12 | Myddleton rd N8 |
| 110 A 9 | Mylis clo SE26 |
| 133 T 11 | Mylne st EC1 |
| 80 A 11 | Myra st SE2 |
| 143 V 4 | Myrdle st E1 |
| 93 V 8 | Myron pl SE13 |
| 16 A 5 | Myrtle clo Barnt |
| 99 S 1 | Myrtle clo Erith |
| 99 R 1 | Myrtle clo Erith |
| 71 T 2 | Myrtle gdns W7 |
| 110 G 10 | Myrtle gro SE26 |
| 8 C 4 | Myrtle gro Enf |
| 117 W 4 | Myrtle gro New Mald |
| 32 J 19 | Myrtle rd E17 |
| 66 E 4 | Myrtle rd E6 |
| 17 Z 11 | Myrtle rd N13 |
| 73 W 2 | Myrtle rd W3 |
| 159 P 5 | Myrtle rd Croy |
| 100 M 16 | Myrtle rd Hampt |
| 82 M 6 | Myrtle rd Hounsl |
| 53 Z 7 | Myrtle rd Ilf |
| 154 D 10 | Myrtle rd Sutton |
| 134 J 11 | Myrtle st N1 |
| 49 V 19 | Myrtleberry st E8 |
| 80 A 19 | Myrtledene rd SE2 |
| 88 M 9 | Mysore rd SW11 |
| 89 N 9 | Mysore rd SW8 |
| 109 N 7 | Myton rd SE21 |
| 72 B 14 | M4 motorway Brentf |
| 70 G 15 | M4 motorway Hounsl |

## N

| | | |
|---|---|---|
| 32 G 18 | N Access rd E17 |
| 32 L 4 | N Countess rd E17 |
| 77 Y 15 | Nadine st SE7 |
| 97 P 7 | Nags Head la Welling |
| 48 B 20 | Nailour st N7 |
| 64 G 15 | Nairn st E14 |
| 91 P 12 | Nairne gro SE24 |
| 122 C 8 | Namton dri Thntn Hth |
| 150 H 9 | Namur ter SE17 |
| 13 S 8 | Nan Clarks la NW7 |
| 64 B 19 | Nankin st E14 |
| 64 H 5 | Nansen rd E15 |
| 89 P 9 | Nansen rd SW11 |
| 45 V 6 | Nant rd NW2 |
| 87 V 7 | Napier av SW6 |
| 134 C 9 | Napier gro N1 |
| 145 O 2 | Napier pl W14 |
| 51 Z 11 | Napier rd E11 |
| 52 A 9 | Napier rd E11 |
| 65 N 6 | Napier rd E15 |
| 66 H 4 | Napier rd E6 |
| 62 K 8 | Napier rd NW10 |
| 31 S 10 | Napier rd N17 |
| 123 Z 10 | Napier rd SE25 |
| 145 N 2 | Napier rd W14 |
| 81 P 12 | Napier rd Blvdr |
| 126 J 8 | Napier rd Brom |
| 157 O 16 | Napier rd Croy |
| 9 U 17 | Napier rd Enf |
| 83 Y 11 | Napier rd Islwth |
| 42 H 17 | Napier rd Wemb |
| 75 Y 18 | Napier st SE8 |
| 133 V 3 | Napier ter N1 |
| 84 B 18 | Napoleon rd Twick |
| 89 U 14 | Narbonne av SW4 |
| 87 Z 6 | Narborough st SW6 |
| 45 X 16 | Narcissus rd NW6 |
| 11 R 18 | Naresby fold Stanm |
| 49 X 8 | Narford rd E5 |
| 63 U 20 | Narrow st E14 |
| 127 R 14 | Narrow way Brom |
| 62 M 17 | Nascot st W12 |
| 136 B 5 | Nascot st W12 |
| 46 E 19 | Naseby clo NW6 |
| 83 U 2 | Naseby clo Islwth |
| 109 O 15 | Naseby rd SE19 |
| 56 E 10 | Naseby rd Dgnhm |
| 35 T 5 | Naseby rd Ilf |
| 112 F 17 | Nash grn Brom |

| | | |
|---|---|---|
| 19 P 8 | Nash rd N9 |
| 92 G 12 | Nash rd SE4 |
| 74 J 8 | Nasmyth st W6 |
| 86 D 3 | Nassau rd SW13 |
| 140 B 2 | Nassau st W1 |
| 46 L 12 | Nassington rd NW3 |
| 16 M 17 | Natal rd N11 |
| 107 Y 13 | Natal rd SW16 |
| 53 Y 13 | Natal rd Ilf |
| 123 N 6 | Natal rd Thntn Hth |
| 79 V 9 | Nathan way SE18 |
| 42 E 6 | Nathans rd Wemb |
| 20 G 4 | Nation way E4 |
| 141 P 13 | National Film theatre SE1 |
| 140 H 11 | National gallery WC2 |
| 140 H 11 | National Portrait gallery WC2 |
| 146 F 3 | Natural History museum SW7 |
| 64 H 20 | Naval row E14 |
| 49 Y 17 | Navarino gro E8 |
| 49 Y 16 | Navarino rd E8 |
| 66 E 5 | Navarre rd E6 |
| 134 M 15 | Navarre st E2 |
| 34 L 4 | Navestock cres Wdfd Grn |
| 89 X 7 | Navy st SW4 |
| 15 P 8 | Naylor rd N20 |
| 151 W 18 | Naylor rd SE15 |
| 58 F 10 | Neal av S'hall |
| 140 J 6 | Neal st WC2 |
| 140 J 6 | Neal yd WC2 |
| 90 B 7 | Nealden st SW9 |
| 28 D 12 | Neale clo N2 |
| 98 J 1 | Neals yd Erith |
| 44 B 14 | Neasden clo NW10 |
| 44 B 11 | Neasden la NW10 |
| 43 Y 9 | Neasden la NW10 |
| 44 C 17 | Neasden la NW10 |
| 55 P 16 | Neasham rd Dgnhm |
| 151 O 14 | Neate st SE5 |
| 150 K 14 | Neate st SE5 |
| 120 C 15 | Neath gdns Mrdn |
| 142 D 19 | Nebraska st SE1 |
| 151 O 1 | Neckinger SE1 |
| 93 S 4 | Nectavine way SE13 |
| 137 T 6 | Needham rd W11 |
| 45 P 10 | Needham ter NW2 |
| 26 J 16 | Neeld cres NW4 |
| 43 P 16 | Neeld cres Wemb |
| 93 P 19 | Nelgarde rd SE6 |
| 144 F 14 | Nella rd W6 |
| 151 Z 6 | Nelldale rd SE16 |
| 75 O 11 | Nelldale rd SE16 |
| 38 G 6 | Nelson clo Rom |
| 82 G 15 | Nelson gdns Hounsl |
| 106 C 20 | Nelson Gro rd SW19 |
| 133 X 10 | Nelson pl N1 |
| 73 T 2 | Nelson pl W3 |
| 115 N 10 | Nelson pl Sidcp |
| 34 G 13 | Nelson pl E11 |
| 20 C 20 | Nelson rd E4 |
| 31 S 12 | Nelson rd N15 |
| 30 C 18 | Nelson rd N8 |
| 19 N 9 | Nelson rd N9 |
| 76 H 17 | Nelson rd SE10 |
| 106 B 18 | Nelson rd SW19 |
| 81 P 12 | Nelson rd Blvdr |
| 126 M 9 | Nelson rd Brom |
| 9 T 19 | Nelson rd Enf |
| 41 S 3 | Nelson rd Harrow |
| 118 A 11 | Nelson rd New Mald |
| 117 Z 12 | Nelson rd New Mald |
| 115 N 10 | Nelson rd Sidcp |
| 11 R 18 | Nelson rd Stanm |
| 82 G 16 | Nelson rd Twick |
| 83 N 17 | Nelson rd Twick |
| 141 X 16 | Nelson sq SE1 |
| 63 N 16 | Nelson st E1 |
| 143 W 4 | Nelson st E1 |
| 65 P 19 | Nelson st E6 |
| 66 K 4 | Nelson st E6 |
| 133 X 10 | Nelson ter N1 |
| 89 X 10 | Nelsons row SW4 |
| 61 V 20 | Nemoure rd W3 |
| 88 J 6 | Nepaul rd SW11 |
| 86 G 17 | Nepean st SW15 |
| 75 P 7 | Neptune st SE16 |
| 95 O 9 | Nesbit rd SE9 |
| 151 S 2 | Nest st SE16 |
| 21 O 18 | Nesta rd Wdfd Grn |
| 75 R 4 | Neston st SE16 |
| 7 W 19 | Nestor av N21 |
| 27 Y 1 | Nether clo N3 |
| 14 L 18 | Nether Court av N3 |
| 14 L 18 | Nether Court Golf course N3 |
| 15 P 17 | Nether st N12 |
| 27 X 3 | Nether st N3 |
| 14 L 20 | Nether st N3 |
| 74 D 15 | Netheravon rd SW4 |
| 74 D 12 | Netheravon rd W4 |

| | | |
|---|---|---|
| 71 V 2 | Netheravon rd W7 |
| 72 F 9 | Netherbury rd W5 |
| 6 M 14 | Netherby gdns Enf |
| 92 C 18 | Netherby rd SE23 |
| 14 L 19 | Nethercourt N3 |
| 14 L 19 | Nethercourt N3 |
| 54 E 19 | Netherfield gdns Bark |
| 15 O 16 | Netherfield rd N12 |
| 107 O 7 | Netherfield rd SW17 |
| 89 N 9 | Netherford rd SW4 |
| 46 E 15 | Netherhall gdns NW3 |
| 46 D 16 | Netherhall way NW3 |
| 15 V 2 | Netherland rd N20 |
| 5 T 19 | Netherlands rd Barnt |
| 39 S 7 | Netherpark dri Rom |
| 46 C 15 | Netherton gdns SW10 |
| 83 Z 13 | Netherton rd Twick |
| 84 A 14 | Netherton rd Twick |
| 136 F 20 | Netherwood rd W14 |
| 45 V 19 | Netherwood st NW6 |
| 128 F 20 | Nethwood rd W10 |
| 159 V 16 | Netley clo Croy |
| 153 P 11 | Netley clo Sutton |
| 120 C 16 | Netley gdns Mrdn |
| 36 E 16 | Netley rd Ilf |
| 120 C 16 | Netley rd Mrdn |
| 132 A 14 | Netley st NW1 |
| 43 P 17 | Nettleden av Wemb |
| 108 J 8 | Nettleford clo SE27 |
| 92 G 1 | Nettleton rd SE14 |
| 107 Y 19 | Nettlewood rd SW16 |
| 110 K 4 | Neuchatel rd SE6 |
| 76 H 18 | Nevada st SE10 |
| 135 V 6 | Nevern pl SW5 |
| 135 T 7 | Nevern rd SW5 |
| 135 T 7 | Nevern sq SW5 |
| 49 S 9 | Nevill rd N16 |
| 103 Z 20 | Neville av Kingst |
| 114 M 9 | Neville clo Sidcp |
| 28 D 19 | Neville dri N2 |
| 55 U 8 | Neville gdns Dgnhm |
| 65 T 2 | Neville rd E7 |
| 129 S 9 | Neville rd NW6 |
| 60 P 10 | Neville rd W5 |
| 123 P 17 | Neville rd Croy |
| 55 V 8 | Neville rd Dgnhm |
| 36 C 4 | Neville rd Ilf |
| 117 R 3 | Neville rd Kingst |
| 102 C 5 | Neville rd Rich |
| 146 F 9 | Neville st SW7 |
| 146 F 10 | Neville ter SW 7 |
| 120 J 18 | Neville wlk Carsh |
| 20 F 6 | Nevin dri E4 |
| 39 R 1 | Nevis clo Rom |
| 107 N 3 | Nevis rd SW17 |
| 65 U 12 | New Barn st E13 |
| 121 X 10 | New Barns av Mitch |
| 139 Y 7 | New Bond st W1 |
| 81 Y 10 | New br Erith |
| 141 W 7 | New Br st EC4 |
| 26 M 15 | New Brent st NW4 |
| 27 N 14 | New Brent st NW4 |
| 142 H 3 | New Broad st EC2 |
| 60 F 20 | New broadway W5 |
| 140 A 9 | New Burlington ms W1 |
| 140 A 8 | New Burlington pl W1 |
| 140 A 9 | New Burlington st W1 |
| 139 X 1 | New Cavendish st W 1 |
| 142 A 6 | New change EC4 |
| 150 D 18 | New Church rd SE5 |
| 65 Y 8 | New City rd E13 |
| 120 D 4 | New clo SW19 |
| 100 B 12 | New clo Felt |
| 140 H 5 | New Compton st WC2 |
| 140 G 10 | New Coventry st W1 |
| 92 H 1 | New Cross rd SE14 |
| 75 P 19 | New Cross rd SE14 |
| 141 P 5 | New ct WC2 |
| 141 R 8 | New ct WC2 |
| 46 E 11 | New end NW3 |
| 46 F 11 | New End sq NW3 |
| 126 E 8 | New Farm av Brom |
| 141 U 3 | New Fetter la EC4 |
| 142 H 10 | New Fresh wharf EC3 |
| 143 N 4 | New Goulston st E1 |
| 70 F 18 | New Heston rd Hounsl |
| 144 C 17 | New House wlk Mrdn |
| 134 L 15 | New Inn sq EC2 |
| 134 K 15 | New Inn st EC2 |
| 134 K 16 | New Inn yd EC2 |
| 150 D 4 | New Kent rd SE1 |
| 76 A 16 | New King st SE8 |
| 87 W 4 | New Kings rd SW6 |
| 142 L 8 | New London st EC 3 |

| | | |
|---|---|---|
| 143 R 10 | New Martan st E1 |
| 64 K 2 | New Mount st E15 |
| 134 J 17 | New North pl EC2 |
| 36 D 1 | New North rd Ilf |
| 132 M 20 | New North st WC1 |
| 28 F 8 | New Oak rd N2 |
| 140 H 4 | New Oxford st WC |
| 140 K 19 | New Palace yd SW |
| 17 Z 12 | New Park av N13 |
| 18 A 12 | New Park av N13 |
| 89 Z 20 | New Pk rd SW2 |
| 107 Y 1 | New Pk rd SW2 |
| 65 O 4 | New Plaistow rd E15 |
| 51 U 15 | New Providence st E15 |
| 139 R 6 | New Quebec st W1 |
| 143 V 4 | New rd E1 |
| 20 F 13 | New rd E4 |
| 13 S 2 | New rd NW7 |
| 27 R 1 | New rd NW7 |
| 31 U 3 | New rd N17 |
| 30 L 5 | New rd N22 |
| 29 Z 16 | New rd N8 |
| 18 L 10 | New rd N9 |
| 80 J 13 | New rd SE2 |
| 72 H 15 | New rd Brentf |
| 69 U 6 | New rd Dgnhm |
| 100 B 11 | New rd Felt |
| 82 K 11 | New rd Hounsl |
| 54 H 6 | New rd Ilf |
| 103 P 17 | New rd Kingst |
| 121 O 19 | New rd Mitch |
| 102 E 8 | New rd Rich |
| 97 P 6 | New rd Welling |
| 41 V 12 | New rd Wemb |
| 17 V 12 | New River cres N13 |
| 48 L 18 | New River wlk N1 |
| 140 J 9 | New row WC2 |
| 141 R 5 | New sq WC2 |
| 142 L 3 | New st E1 |
| 141 U 4 | New St sq EC4 |
| 141 U 5 | New Street hill EC4 |
| 112 J 13 | New Street hill Brom |
| 28 F 9 | New Trinity rd N2 |
| 34 E 17 | New wanstead E11 |
| 26 C 14 | New Way rd NW9 |
| 132 M 8 | New Wharf rd N1 |
| 61 Y 9 | Newark cres SW13 |
| 157 O 14 | Newark rd S Croy |
| 143 W 2 | Newark st E1 |
| 63 N 16 | Newark st E1 |
| 26 H 11 | Newark way NW4 |
| 99 T 1 | Newberry rd Erith |
| 92 B 2 | Newbold rd SE15 |
| 153 O 10 | Newbolt av Sutton |
| 10 H 18 | Newbolt rd Stanm |
| 117 Y 9 | Newborough grn New Mald |
| 73 V 2 | Newburgh rd W3 |
| 140 B 7 | Newburgh st W1 |
| 149 P 9 | Newburn st SE11 |
| 9 X 2 | Newbury clo Grnfd |
| 40 D 17 | Newbury clo Grnfd |
| 152 D 8 | Newbury gdns Epsom |
| 20 H 20 | Newbury rd E4 |
| 126 E 7 | Newbury rd Brom |
| 36 G 19 | Newbury rd Ilf |
| 141 Z 1 | Newbury st E 1 |
| 40 C 17 | Newbury way Grnfd |
| 8 F 9 | Newby clo Enf |
| 64 F 19 | Newby pl E14 |
| 89 T 6 | Newby st SW8 |
| 133 U 16 | Newcastle row EC1 |
| 141 W 4 | Newcastle st EC4 |
| 108 B 8 | Newcombe gdns SW16 |
| 13 O 16 | Newcombe pk NW7 |
| 61 N 2 | Newcombe pk Wemb |
| 137 U 13 | Newcombe st W8 |
| 52 B 9 | Newcomen rd E11 |
| 88 F 7 | Newcomen rd SW11 |
| 142 E 16 | Newcomen st SE1 |
| 130 K 10 | Newcourt st NW8 |
| 63 Y 19 | Newell st E14 |
| 100 G 20 | Newfield clo Hamp |
| 100 H 19 | Newfield clo Hampt |
| 100 G 20 | Newfield clo Hampt |
| 24 M 4 | Newgale gdns Edgw |
| 122 M 19 | Newgate Croy |
| 100 C 6 | Newgate clo Felt |
| 141 X 4 | Newgate st EC1 |
| 20 M 12 | Newgate st E4 |
| 142 L 20 | Newhams row SE1 |
| 95 N 9 | Newhaven gdns SE9 |
| 123 P 11 | Newhaven rd SE25 |
| 149 S 1 | Newhaven ter SE1 |
| 37 W 10 | Newhome av Rom |
| 37 W 10 | Newhouse av Rom |
| 118 B 18 | Newhouse clo New Mald |
| 98 G 15 | Newick clo Bxly |

B 10 Newick rd E5
Y 6 Newington butts SE11
Z 2 Newington causeway SE1
Y 8 Newington cres SE17
O 16 Newington grn N16
O 16 Newington Grn rd N1
P 7 Newland ct Wemb
Y 6 Newland gdns W13
A 10 Newland rd N8
E 3 Newland st E16
X 10 Newlands clo Edg
B 13 Newlands clo S'hall
E 17 Newlands clo Wemb
D 13 Newlands pk SE26
B 16 Newlands pl Barnt
B 3 Newlands rd SW16
R 9 Newlands rd Wdfd Grn
X 17 Newlands the Wallgtn
K 19 Newlands wood Croy
C J Newlyn gdns Harrow
U 6 Newlyn rd N17
G 15 Newlyn rd Barnt
K 5 Newlyn rd Welling
D 3 Newman pas W1
U 10 Newman rd E13
G 2 Newman rd Brom
C 2 Newman st W1
R 20 Newman ter SE1
G 6 Newmans ct EC2
P 3 Newmans row WC2
S 7 Newmans way Barnt
K 16 Newmarket av Grnfd
P 18 Newmarket grn SE9
D 15 Newminster rd Mrdn
M 10 Newnham ala Grnfd
M 16 Newnham gdns Grnfd
E 4 Newnham rd N22
P 7 Newnham st E1
L 14 Newnham way Harrow
V 6 Newnhams clo Brom
E 8 Newnorth rd N1
O 1 Newnton clo N4
G 8 Newport ct WC2
G 8 Newport pl WC2
V 6 Newport rd E10
J 14 Newport rd E17
H 1 Newport rd SW13
O 6 Newport st SE11
C 7 Newquay cres Harrow
S 4 Newquay rd SE6
Z 12 Newry rd Twick
O 15 Newsam av N15
C 17 Newstead rd SE12
R 8 Newstead way SW19
D 17 Newstead wlk Carsh
R 3 Newton av N10
V 6 Newton av W3
H 7 Newton gro N1
A 10 Newton gro W4
H 7 Newton park Harrow
U C
Y 14 Newton rd E15
M 11 Newton rd NW2
W 14 Newton rd N15
U 18 Newton rd SW19
W 5 Newton rd W2
T 6 Newton rd Harrow
V 4 Newton rd Islwth
M 8 Newton rd Welling
M 1 Newton rd Wemb
M 4 Newton st WC2
Z 16 Newton way N18
Z 14 Newtons yd SW18
C 10 Niagra av W5
T 15 Nibthwaite rd Harrow
G 17 Nichol la Brom
F 4 Nicholas gdns W5
N 13 Nicholas glebe SW17
G 8 Nicholas la EC3
R 12 Nicholas rd E1
B 8 Nicholas rd Croy
B 8 Nicholas rd Dgnhm
Y 5 Nicholay rd N19
G 11 Nicholes rd Hounsl
S 7 Nicholl st E2
J 14 Nichols grn W5
V 20 Nicholson rd Croy
X 14 Nicholson st SE1
R 7 Nicola clo Harrow
L 14 Nicola clo S Croy
K 26 Nicoll pl NW4
B 4 Nicolle rd NW10

10 A 7 Nicolson dri Bushey Watford
88 H 18 Nicosia rd SW18
110 G 8 Niederwald rd SE26
74 J 12 Nigel Playfair av W6
52 M 15 Nigel rd E7
91 Y 7 Nigel rd SE15
77 Z 19 Nigeria rd SE7
20 L 15 Nightingale av E4
20 L 13 Nightingale clo E4
73 V 18 Nightingale clo W4
155 N 3 Nightingale clo Carsh
93 X 13 Nightingale gro SE13
34 G 15 Nightingale la E11
29 Z 13 Nightingale la N8
88 L 19 Nightingale la SW12
89 O 17 Nightingale la SW12
126 L 4 Nightingale la Brom
127 N 5 Nightingale la Brom
84 K 18 Nightingale la Rich
78 K 16 Nightingale pl SE18
49 Y 10 Nightingale rd E5
62 E 7 Nightingale rd NW10
30 C 3 Nightingale rd N22
19 S 7 Nightingale rd N9
136 L 14 Nightingale rd W7
155 N 4 Nightingale rd Carsh
100 H 15 Nightingale rd Hampt
89 O 18 Nightingale sq SW12
78 K 16 Nightingale vale SE18
89 R 15 Nightingale wlk SW4
65 X 7 Nile rd E13
134 D 12 Nile st N1
151 O 12 Nile ter SE15
91 S 12 Nimegen way SE22
10 D 4 Nimmo dri Bushey Watford
107 T 12 Nimrod rd SW16
148 H 15 Nine Elms la SW8
79 N 19 Nithdale rd SE18
78 M 18 Nithdale rd SE18
4 B 19 Niton rd Barnt
85 P 8 Niton rd Rich
144 G 17 Niton st SW6
19 S 17 Nobel rd N18
142 B 4 Noble st EC2
30 F 9 Noel Park rd N22
66 C 12 Noel rd E6
133 X 8 Noel rd N1
61 P 17 Noel rd W3
55 T 11 Noel st Dgnhm
140 C 6 Noel st W1
152 L 15 Nonsuch park Epsom Sutton
153 N 13 Nonsuch park Epsom Sutton
153 P 20 Nonsuch wlk Sutton
153 O 19 Nonsuch wlk Sutton
27 P 13 Nora gdns NW4
41 T 3 Nora ter Harrow
135 U 13 Norah st E2
117 R 3 Norbiton av Kingst
117 U 0 Norbiton Comm rd Kingst
63 X 17 Norbiton rd E14
62 D 19 Norbroke st W12
136 J 2 Norbury av SW16
108 C 20 Norbury av SW16
122 E 1 Norbury av SW16
83 P 14 Norbury av Hounsl
108 H 19 Norbury clo SW16
122 C 1 Norbury cres SW16
121 Z 5 Norbury cross SW16
122 C 4 Norbury Ct rd SW16
121 Z 4 Norbury Ct rd SW16
37 V 16 Norbury gdns Rom
13 O 10 Norbury gro NW7
108 J 17 Norbury hill SW16
20 A 15 Norbury rd E4
122 M 4 Norbury rd Thntn Hth
123 N 4 Norbury rd Thntn Hth
121 Z 5 Norbury ri SW16
122 A 5 Norbury ri SW16
24 D 17 Norcombe gdns Harrow
49 W 8 Norcott rd N16
91 W 17 Norcroft gdns SE22
101 T 1 Norcutt rd Twick
17 X 20 Norfolk av N13
31 V 18 Norfolk av N15
17 X 19 Norfolk clo N13
28 H 10 Norfolk clo N2
6 B 14 Norfolk clo Barnt
84 B 15 Norfolk clo Twick
138 L 5 Norfolk cres E4
96 H 18 Norfolk cres Sidcp
98 B 1 Norfolk gdns Bxly Hth
82 E 13 Norfolk gdns Hounsl
107 Z 6 Norfolk ho rd SW16
138 H 5 Norfolk pl W2
96 M 4 Norfolk pl Welling

32 G 7 Norfolk rd E17
66 H 3 Norfolk rd E6
62 B 1 Norfolk rd NW10
44 B 20 Norfolk rd NW10
130 J 5 Norfolk rd NW8
106 J 16 Norfolk rd SW19
67 U 2 Norfolk rd Bark
4 M 12 Norfolk rd Barnt
56 H 15 Norfolk rd Dgnhm
9 O 18 Norfolk rd Enf
22 L 16 Norfolk rd Harrow
54 H 1 Norfolk rd Ilf
38 L 18 Norfolk rd Rom
122 M 6 Norfolk rd Thntn Hth
149 O 4 Norfolk row SE11
138 G 5 Norfolk Sq W2
138 H 6 Norfolk Sq ms W2
52 F 14 Norfolk st E7
141 P 8 Norfolk st WC2
89 P 20 Norgrove rd SW12
123 U 5 Norhyrst av SE25
136 G 14 Norland gdns W11
136 L 14 Norland pl W11
136 H 15 Norland rd W11
136 L 14 Norland sq W11
104 H 1 Norley vale SW15
51 V 4 Norlington rd E10
30 K 4 Norman av N22
100 C 4 Norman av Felt
58 C 19 Norman av S'hall
84 C 18 Norman av Twick
134 B 15 Norman bldgs EC1
38 J 6 Norman clo Rom
63 X 7 Norman gro E3
126 J 14 Norman park Brom
51 X 8 Norman rd E11
66 H 11 Norman rd E6
31 V 15 Norman rd N15
76 E 17 Norman rd SE10
106 D 17 Norman rd SE19
81 U 4 Norman rd Blvdr
57 X 1 Norman rd Horch
54 A 16 Norman rd Ilf
53 Z 16 Norman rd Ilf
153 X 11 Norman rd Sutton
153 W 10 Norman rd Sutton
122 J 11 Norman rd Thntn Hth
134 B 15 Norman st EC1
17 N 9 Norman way N14
16 L 9 Norman way N14
61 T 16 Norman way W3
44 E 13 Normanby rd NW10
144 M 13 Normand ms W14
145 N 13 Normand rd W14
4 H 14 Normandy av Barnt
90 F 2 Normandy rd SW9
99 P 2 Normandy way Erith
97 W 3 Normanhurst av Bxly Hth
83 Z 13 Normanhurst dri Twick
84 D 15 Normanhurst dri Twick
108 D 3 Normanhurst rd SW2
43 X 18 Normans clo NW10
43 X 18 Normans mead NW10
102 E 18 Normansfield av Tedd
20 C 14 Normanshire dri E4
105 X 5 Normanton av SW19
20 M 10 Normanton pk E4
21 N 9 Normanton pk E4
157 R 13 Normanton rd S Croy
110 G 5 Normanton st SE23
108 F 11 Normington clo SW16
28 F 17 Norrice lea N2
140 E 11 Norris st SW1
87 R 11 Norroy rd SW15
5 Z 15 Norrys clo Barnt
5 Y 15 Norrys rd Barnt
104 F 4 Norstead pl SW15
32 G 18 North Access rd E17
61 Y 8 North Acton rd NW10
139 T 8 North Audley st W1
18 L 13 North av N18
60 B 15 North av W13
155 N 16 North av Carsh
22 L 18 North av Harrow
85 O 3 North av Rich
58 F 20 North av S'hall
130 J 4 North bank NW8
51 X 10 North Birbeck rd E11
53 R 16 North Circular rd E12
33 X 5 North Circular rd E17
19 W 17 North Circular rd E4
66 F 10 North Circular rd E6
61 R 2 North Circular rd NW10

44 D 6 North Circular rd NW2
45 N 1 North Circular rd NW2
17 V 16 North Circular rd N13
18 F 15 North Circular rd N18
28 C 8 North Circular rd N2
27 X 11 North Circular rd N3
60 L 8 North Circular rd Wemb
97 W 10 North clo Bxly Hth
69 S 4 North clo Dgnhm
119 S 8 North clo Mrdn
60 L 20 North Common rd W5
32 L 6 North Countess rd E17
115 Y 15 North Cray rd Sidcp
27 V 9 North cres N3
132 E 20 North Cross rd WC1
91 V 12 North Cross rd SE22
36 A 14 North Cross rd Ilf
132 C 20 North ct W1
12 I 10 North dene NW7
82 J 3 North dene Hounsl
159 T 20 North Downs cres Croy
159 S 20 North Downs cres Croy
107 U 9 North dri SW16
83 O 6 North dri Hounsl
46 C 5 North end NW3
21 Y 3 North end Buck Hl
156 L 3 North end Croy
46 D 6 North End av NW3
145 N 7 North End cres W14
45 Z 4 North End rd NW11
46 A 4 North End rd NW11
144 L 5 North End rd SW6
145 R 13 North End rd W14
43 R 10 North End rd Wemb
46 C 7 North End way NW3
74 E 13 North Eydt gdns W6
106 G 17 North gdns SW19
98 B 20 North glade Bexley
31 O 16 North gro N15
47 O 2 North gro N6
29 N 19 North hill N6
29 N 17 North Hill av N6
70 A 13 North Hyde la S'hall
78 G 11 North Kent gro SE18
101 V 14 North la Tedd
87 P 14 North Lodge clo SW15
133 P 18 North ms WC1
87 Y 12 North pas SW18
91 U 17 North pk SE9
135 S 18 North pl E1
106 L 17 North pl Mitch
101 V 15 North pl Tedd
136 B 3 North Pole rd W10
62 M 15 North Pole rd W10
47 Z 17 North rd N1
47 P 1 North rd N6
48 B 16 North rd N7
18 M 4 North rd N9
79 W 9 North rd SE18
106 D 15 North rd SW19
72 G 9 North rd W5
81 U 6 North rd Blvdr
112 H 20 North rd Brom
99 U 17 North rd Drtfrd
25 T 3 North rd Edg
54 G 7 North rd Ilf
95 O 8 North rd Rom
37 X 16 North rd Rom
58 F 20 North rd S'hall
70 G 1 North rd Shall
116 G 14 North rd Surb
125 S 20 North rd W Wkhm
139 T 7 North row W1
93 Y 4 North several SE3
27 Z 17 North sq NW11
65 T 6 North st E13
27 N 15 North st NW4
89 U 6 North st SW4
54 A 20 North st Bark
67 N 1 North st Bark
126 E 2 North st Brom
98 E 9 North st Bxly Hth
154 M 8 North st Carsh
155 N 9 North st Carsh
83 Y 6 North st Islwth
39 O 14 North st Rom
143 P 6 North Tenter st E1
146 J 4 North ter SW3
104 L 12 North.view SW19
60 D 11 North view N5
35 N 7 North View dri Wdfd Grn
29 Y 11 North View rd N8

| Ref | Grid | Street |
|---|---|---|
| 47 | Y 18 | North vlls NW1 |
| 25 | S 10 | North way NW9 |
| 19 | S 8 | North way N9 |
| 138 | F 3 | North Wharf rd W2 |
| 159 | U 13 | North wlk Croy |
| 77 | X 3 | North Woolwich rd E16 |
| 78 | A 4 | North Woolwich rd E16 |
| 85 | Z 7 | North Worple way SW14 |
| 84 | A 7 | North Worple way SW14 |
| 98 | J 6 | Northall rd Bxly Hth |
| 133 | U 16 | Northampton bldgs EC1 |
| 49 | N 16 | Northampton gro N1 |
| 49 | N 16 | Northampton pk N1 |
| 133 | T 16 | Northampton rd EC1 |
| 157 | X 2 | Northampton rd Croy |
| 133 | X 13 | Northampton sq EC1 |
| 48 | L 20 | Northampton st N1 |
| 107 | Z 16 | Northanger rd SW16 |
| 130 | J 14 | Northbank NW8 |
| 33 | T 7 | Northbank rd E17 |
| 121 | Y 5 | Northborough rd SW16 |
| 122 | C 4 | Northborough rd SW16 |
| 126 | F 16 | Northbourne Brom |
| 89 | Y 12 | Northbourne rd SW4 |
| 93 | Y 12 | Northbrook rd SE13 |
| 4 | F 20 | Northbrook rd Barnt |
| 123 | N 11 | Northbrook rd Croy |
| 53 | V 7 | Northbrook rd Ilf |
| 30 | B 1 | Northbrook rd N22 |
| 133 | X 17 | Northburgh st EC1 |
| 49 | O 20 | Northchurch rd N1 |
| 43 | O 18 | Northchurch rd Wemb |
| 134 | J 1 | Northchurch ter N1 |
| 14 | H 5 | Northcliffe dr N20 |
| 60 | J 20 | Northcote av W5 |
| 58 | C 19 | Northcote av S'hall |
| 70 | D 1 | Northcote av S'hall |
| 117 | S 16 | Northcote av Surb |
| 83 | Y 12 | Northcote av Twick |
| 32 | J 14 | Northcote rd E17 |
| 62 | B 1 | Northcote rd NW10 |
| 88 | K 12 | Northcote rd SW11 |
| 123 | O 14 | Northcote rd Croy |
| 117 | X 7 | Northcote rd New Mald |
| 114 | H 10 | Northcote rd Sidcp |
| 84 | A 12 | Northcote rd Twick |
| 83 | Z 12 | Northcote rd Twick |
| 30 | A 4 | Northcott av N22 |
| 72 | B 7 | Northcroft rd W13 |
| 152 | A 17 | Northcroft rd Epsom |
| 31 | U 19 | Northdene gdns N15 |
| 36 | G 15 | Northdown rd Ilf |
| 57 | Y 2 | Northdown rd Hornch |
| 97 | R 5 | Northdown rd Welling |
| 132 | M 10 | Northdown st N1 |
| 99 | S 2 | Northend rd Erith |
| 18 | F 9 | Northern av N9 |
| 142 | J 8 | Northern Langbourn champs EC3 |
| 65 | W 5 | Northern rd E13 |
| 9 | X 15 | Northern rd Enf |
| 119 | T 10 | Northernhay wlk Mrdn |
| 63 | W 20 | Northey st E14 |
| 72 | B 3 | Northfield av W13 |
| 153 | S 9 | Northfield cres Sutton |
| 56 | B 12 | Northfield gdns Dgnhm |
| 53 | V 20 | Northfield rd E6 |
| 49 | T 1 | Northfield rd N16 |
| 72 | A 5 | Northfield rd W13 |
| 5 | W 12 | Northfield rd Barnt |
| 56 | B 12 | Northfield rd Dgnhm |
| 9 | P 19 | Northfield rd Enf |
| 87 | X 11 | Northfields SW18 |
| 61 | U 14 | Northfields W3 |
| 14 | M 12 | Northiam N12 |
| 63 | O 4 | Northiam st E8 |
| 135 | Y 6 | Northiam st E8 |
| 133 | O 19 | Northington st WC1 |
| 90 | L 6 | Northlands st SE5 |
| 12 | K 14 | Northolm Edg |
| 25 | P 4 | Northolme gdns Edg |
| 48 | K 11 | Northolme rd N5 |
| 41 | W 15 | Northolt gdns Grnfd |
| 40 | K 12 | Northolt rd Harrow |
| 41 | O 7 | Northolt rd Harrow |
| 112 | C 7 | Northover Brom |
| 134 | H 7 | Northport st N1 |
| 14 | K 12 | Northram N12 |
| 108 | G 4 | Northstead rd SW2 |
| 142 | M 7 | Northumberland all EC3 |
| 52 | L 4 | Northumberland av E12 |
| 9 | N 5 | Northumberland av Enf |
| 71 | X 20 | Northumberland av Islwth |
| 83 | V 1 | Northumberland av Islwth |
| 96 | G 9 | Northumberland av Welling |
| 140 | K 13 | Northumberland ave WC2 |
| 18 | H 10 | Northumberland gdns N9 |
| 121 | Y 11 | Northumberland gdns Mitch |
| 31 | Z 2 | Northumberland gro N17 |
| 31 | Y 1 | Northumberland pk N17 |
| 81 | X 19 | Northumberland pk Erith |
| 137 | U 5 | Northumberland pl W2 |
| 51 | N 1 | Northumberland rd E17 |
| 15 | P 1 | Northumberland rd Barnt |
| 22 | H 16 | Northumberland rd Harrow |
| 140 | J 12 | Northumberland st WC2 |
| 99 | N 2 | Northumberland way Erith |
| 64 | B 17 | Northumbria st E14 |
| 44 | C 13 | Northview cres NW10 |
| 28 | B 15 | Northway NW11 |
| 27 | A 15 | Northway NW11 |
| 119 | T 8 | Northway Mrdn |
| 119 | S 8 | Northway Mrdn |
| 155 | V 8 | Northway Wllgtn |
| 12 | L 12 | Northway cir NW7 |
| 12 | M 13 | Northway cres NW7 |
| 90 | L 8 | Northway rd SE5 |
| 123 | U 16 | Northway rd Croy |
| 23 | Z 19 | Northwick av Harrow |
| 24 | A 20 | Northwick av Harrow |
| 24 | D 18 | Northwick cir Harrow |
| 130 | F 17 | Northwick clo NW8 |
| 42 | B 2 | Northwick park Harrow |
| 23 | X 18 | Northwick Pk rd Harrow |
| 60 | H 4 | Northwick rd Wemb |
| 130 | E 17 | Northwick ter NW8 |
| 41 | W 1 | Northwick wlk Harrow |
| 49 | Y 2 | Northwold rd E5 |
| 57 | X 12 | Northwood av Hornch |
| 15 | T 16 | Northwood gdns N12 |
| 41 | W 15 | Northwood gdns Grnfd |
| 35 | W 12 | Northwood gdns Ilf |
| 47 | T 1 | Northwood rd N6 |
| 110 | K 2 | Northwood rd SE23 |
| 155 | O 14 | Northwood rd Carsh |
| 122 | L 3 | Northwood rd Thnt Hth |
| 117 | T 16 | Norton av Surb |
| 20 | B 15 | Norton clo E4 |
| 8 | M 9 | Norton clo Enf |
| 122 | A 3 | Norton gdns SW16 |
| 50 | M 3 | Norton rd E10 |
| 57 | N 18 | Norton rd Dgnhm |
| 42 | G 18 | Norton rd Wemb |
| 42 | C 5 | Norval rd Wemb |
| 63 | X 18 | Norway pl E14 |
| 76 | E 16 | Norway st SE10 |
| 52 | E 16 | Norwich rd E7 |
| 135 | U 5 | Norwich rd E8 |
| 69 | S 7 | Norwich rd Dgnhm |
| 58 | L 3 | Norwich rd Thntn Hth |
| 122 | M 7 | Norwich rd Thntn Hth |
| 141 | T 3 | Norwich st EC4 |
| 25 | W 2 | Norwich wlk Edg |
| 57 | P 3 | Norwood av Rom |
| 60 | M 5 | Norwood av Wemb |
| 159 | V 13 | Norwood bank Croy |
| 16 | D 3 | Norwood clo N14 |
| 154 | D 4 | Norwood clo Sutton |
| 62 | C 17 | Norwood comm W3 |
| 71 | S 6 | Norwood dri Harrow |
| 60 | A 14 | Norwood dene W13 |
| 39 | Y 19 | Oak Dene clo Rom |
| 159 | O 1 | Oak gdns Croy |
| 25 | U 7 | Oak gdns Edg |
| 45 | R 12 | Oak gro NW2 |
| 70 | F 12 | Norwood clo S'hall |
| 70 | D 10 | Norwood gdns S'hall |
| 70 | H 12 | Norwood Grn rd S'hall |
| 108 | K 8 | Norwood High st SE27 |
| 108 | M 12 | Norwood Pk rd SE27 |
| 109 | N 12 | Norwood Pk rd SE27 |
| 108 | J 5 | Norwood rd SE27 |
| 70 | E 10 | Norwood rd S'hall |
| 32 | L 15 | Notley rd E17 |
| 150 | E 18 | Notley st SE5 |
| 123 | Z 10 | Notson rd SE25 |
| 137 | T 12 | Notting Hill ga W11 |
| 65 | Y 16 | Nottingham av E16 |
| 140 | K 6 | Nottingham ct WC2 |
| 131 | T 19 | Nottingham pl W1 |
| 33 | U 18 | Nottingham rd E10 |
| 106 | L 2 | Nottingham rd SW17 |
| 83 | V 4 | Nottingham rd Islwth |
| 156 | L 10 | Nottingham rd S Croy |
| 131 | U 20 | Nottingham st W1 |
| 122 | K 18 | Nova rd Croy |
| 114 | B 2 | Novar rd SE9 |
| 87 | X 2 | Novello st SW6 |
| 74 | G 17 | Nowell rd SW13 |
| 22 | E 12 | Nower hill Pinn |
| 106 | M 6 | Noyna rd SW17 |
| 93 | P 8 | Nuding clo SE13 |
| 48 | A 4 | Nugent rd N4 |
| 123 | T 6 | Nugent rd SE25 |
| 130 | C 11 | Nugent ter NW8 |
| 22 | C 4 | Nugents pk Pinn |
| 142 | E 3 | Nun ct EC2 |
| 68 | K 1 | Nuneaton rd Dgnhm |
| 91 | Y 8 | Nunhead cres SE15 |
| 92 | A 7 | Nunhead grn SE15 |
| 92 | B 8 | Nunhead gro SE15 |
| 92 | A 8 | Nunhead la SE15 |
| 7 | Z 8 | Nunns rd Enf |
| 4 | A 19 | Nupton dri Barnt |
| 28 | C 7 | Nursery av N2 |
| 98 | C 7 | Nursery av Bxly Hth |
| 158 | E 3 | Nursery av Croy |
| 158 | E 4 | Nursery clo Croy |
| 9 | T 6 | Nursery clo Enf |
| 37 | W 19 | Nursery clo Rom |
| 21 | U 16 | Nursery clo Wdfd Grn |
| 31 | U 3 | Nursery ct N17 |
| 9 | T 6 | Nursery gdns Enf |
| 52 | G 17 | Nursery la E7 |
| 16 | H 3 | Nursery rd N14 |
| 105 | R 19 | Nursery rd SW19 |
| 90 | D 9 | Nursery rd SW9 |
| 120 | J 7 | Nursery rd Mitch |
| 120 | A 1 | Nursery rd Mrdn |
| 154 | D 9 | Nursery rd Sutton |
| 123 | O 9 | Nursery rd Thntn Hth |
| 150 | D 8 | Nursery row SE17 |
| 31 | U 3 | Nursery st N17 |
| 26 | L 10 | Nursery walk NW4 |
| 39 | N 20 | Nursery wlk Rom |
| 81 | T 20 | Nurstead rd Erith |
| 128 | K 12 | Nutbourne st W10 |
| 91 | W 8 | Nutbrook st SE15 |
| 69 | P 3 | Nutbrowne rd Dgnhm |
| 151 | V 18 | Nutcroft rd SE16 |
| 54 | L 7 | Nutfield gdns Ilf |
| 51 | V 12 | Nutfield rd E15 |
| 44 | F 9 | Nutfield rd NW2 |
| 91 | V 11 | Nutfield rd SE22 |
| 122 | H 9 | Nutfield rd Thntn Hth |
| 139 | N 4 | Nutford pl W1 |
| 108 | D 3 | Nuthurst av SW2 |
| 46 | E 17 | Nutley ter NW3 |
| 11 | U 8 | Nutt gro Edg |
| 151 | P 18 | Nutt st SE15 |
| 134 | L 7 | Nuttall st N1 |
| 34 | K 16 | Nutter la E11 |
| 81 | R 14 | Nuxley rd Blvdr |
| 79 | T 18 | Nyanza st SE18 |
| 85 | P 4 | Nylands av Rich |
| 75 | V 18 | Nynehead st SE14 |
| 110 | K 5 | Nyon gro SE6 |

# O

| Ref | Grid | Street |
|---|---|---|
| 29 | S 2 | Oak av N10 |
| 31 | P 1 | Oak av N17 |
| 29 | Z 14 | Oak av N8 |
| 159 | P 1 | Oak av Croy |
| 7 | P 3 | Oak av Enf |
| 100 | D 14 | Oak av Hampt |
| 70 | A 20 | Oak av Hounsl |
| 159 | V 13 | Oak bank Croy |
| 16 | D 3 | Oak clo N14 |
| 154 | D 4 | Oak clo Sutton |
| 62 | C 17 | Oak comm W3 |
| 71 | S 6 | Oak Cottage clo SE6 |
| 60 | A 14 | Oak cotts W7 |
| 39 | Y 19 | Oak Dene clo Rom |
| 159 | O 1 | Oak gdns Croy |
| 25 | U 7 | Oak gdns Edg |
| 45 | R 12 | Oak gro NW2 |
| 159 | V 1 | Oak gro W Wkhm |
| 34 | H 19 | Oak Hall rd E11 |
| 116 | K 16 | Oak hill Surb |
| 34 | A 2 | Oak hill Wdfd Grn |
| 33 | Z 1 | Oak hill Wdfd Grn |
| 33 | X 1 | Oak hill Wdfd Grn |
| 34 | B 3 | Oak hill Wdfd Grn |
| 33 | X 2 | Oak hill clo Wdfd Grn |
| 33 | Y 1 | Oak Hill cres Wdf Grn |
| 34 | A 3 | Oak Hill gdns Wdf Grn |
| 46 | C 12 | Oak Hill pk NW3 |
| 46 | B 11 | Oak Hill way NW3 |
| 63 | X 19 | Oak la E14 |
| 16 | L 19 | Oak la N11 |
| 28 | F 7 | Oak la N2 |
| 83 | Z 19 | Oak la Twick |
| 83 | U 9 | Oak la Twick |
| 21 | R 13 | Oak la Wdfd Grn |
| 103 | O 3 | Oak lodge Rich |
| 125 | S 18 | Oak Lodge dri W Wkhm |
| 44 | A 20 | Oak rd NW10 |
| 81 | X 20 | Oak rd Erith |
| 99 | X 3 | Oak rd Erith |
| 117 | X 3 | Oak rd New Mald |
| 72 | H 1 | Oak st W5 |
| 38 | J 14 | Oak st Rom |
| 60 | E 18 | Oak Tree clo W13 |
| 24 | C 3 | Oak Tree clo Stan |
| 25 | X 16 | Oak Tree dell NW9 |
| 15 | O 6 | Oak Tree dri N20 |
| 112 | J 11 | Oak Tree gdns Brc |
| 130 | J 14 | Oak Tree rd NW8 |
| 124 | K 19 | Oak View grn Croy |
| 47 | O 13 | Oak village NW5 |
| 16 | D 2 | Oak way N14 |
| 119 | N 9 | Oak way SW20 |
| 74 | A 2 | Oak way W3 |
| 124 | G 13 | Oak way Croy |
| 90 | L 10 | Oakbank gro SE24 |
| 88 | A 5 | Oakbury rd SW6 |
| 93 | W 5 | Oakcroft rd SE13 |
| 16 | G 4 | Oakdale N14 |
| 24 | K 15 | Oakdale av Harrow |
| 51 | W 7 | Oakdale rd E11 |
| 34 | J 8 | Oakdale rd E18 |
| 52 | J 20 | Oakdale rd E7 |
| 30 | M 18 | Oakdale rd N4 |
| 31 | N 18 | Oakdale rd N4 |
| 108 | B 12 | Oakdale rd SW16 |
| 149 | U 6 | Oakden st SE11 |
| 113 | V 11 | Oakdene av Chisl |
| 81 | X 17 | Oakdene av Erith |
| 117 | V 19 | Oakdene dri Surb |
| 27 | W 1 | Oakdene pk N3 |
| 116 | K 17 | Oakenshaw clo Surb |
| 47 | P 6 | Oakeshott av N6 |
| 24 | B 11 | Oakfield av Harrow |
| 118 | D 10 | Oakfield clo New Mald |
| 8 | C 14 | Oakfield gdns N18 |
| 109 | T 12 | Oakfield gdns SE1 |
| 125 | P 13 | Oakfield gdns Bcknhm |
| 120 | K 20 | Oakfield gdns Cars |
| 59 | P 10 | Oakfield gdns Grnf |
| 32 | J 7 | Oakfield rd E17 |
| 66 | C 4 | Oakfield rd E6 |
| 17 | N 9 | Oakfield rd N14 |
| 28 | A 5 | Oakfield rd N3 |
| 48 | F 1 | Oakfield rd N4 |
| 30 | F 20 | Oakfield rd N4 |
| 110 | B 17 | Oakfield rd SE20 |
| 105 | R 6 | Oakfield rd SW19 |
| 122 | L 20 | Oakfield rd Cars |
| 54 | A 9 | Oakfield rd Ilf |
| 146 | A 13 | Oakfields rd NW11 |
| 27 | V 17 | Oakfields rd NW11 |
| 47 | V 12 | Oakford rd NW5 |
| 124 | C 2 | Oakgrove rd SE20 |
| 34 | J 18 | Oakhall ct E11 |
| 126 | D 10 | Oakham dri Brom |
| 27 | P 3 | Oakhampton rd NW |
| 46 | A 12 | Oakhill av NW3 |
| 22 | A 7 | Oakhill av Pinn |
| 116 | K 16 | Oakhill cres Surb |
| 116 | L 17 | Oakhill dri Surb |
| 116 | J 15 | Oakhill gro Surb |
| 16 | B 1 | Oakhill gro Surb |
| 15 | Z 1 | Oakhill park Barnt |
| 116 | J 15 | Oakhill path Surb |
| 87 | X 12 | Oakhill pl SW15 |
| 87 | X 12 | Oakhill rd SW15 |
| 122 | B 2 | Oakhill rd SW16 |
| 125 | T 4 | Oakhill rd Bcknhm |
| 116 | K 16 | Oakhill rd Surb |
| 154 | B 6 | Oakhill rd Sutton |
| 98 | E 12 | Oakhouse rd Bxly Hth |
| 15 | V 1 | Oakhurst av Barnt |

| | |
|---|---|
| G 6 | Paget av Sutton |
| O 10 | Paget clo Hampt |
| E 14 | Paget gdns E6 |
| P 4 | Paget rd N16 |
| Y 13 | Paget rd Ilf |
| K 18 | Paget ri SE18 |
| W 12 | Paget st EC1 |
| E 18 | Paget ter SE18 |
| X 20 | Pagnell st SE14 |
| M 8 | Pagoda av Rich |
| X 6 | Pagoda gdns SE3 |
| S 19 | Paignton rd N15 |
| C 10 | Paines clo Pinn |
| B 10 | Paines la Pinn |
| S 8 | Painsthorpe rd N 16 |
| L 9 | Painters rd Ilf |
| O 9 | Painters rd Ilf |
| J 4 | Paisley rd N22 |
| F 19 | Paisley rd Carsh |
| C 10 | Pakeman rd N7 |
| Z 17 | Palace av W8 |
| W 7 | Palace ct W2 |
| J 18 | Palace ct Harrow |
| U 9 | Palace Ct gdns N10 |
| B 19 | Palace ga W8 |
| Z 6 | Palace Gates rd N22 |
| A 13 | Palace gdns Enf |
| W 12 | Palace Gdns ms W8 |
| W 14 | Palace Gdns ter W8 |
| M 17 | Palace grn Croy |
| U 18 | Palace gro SE19 |
| G 1 | Palace gro Brom |
| U 7 | Palace ms SW1 |
| B 13 | Palace ms Enf |
| Z 2 | Palace rd N11 |
| Y 15 | Palace rd N8 |
| V 17 | Palace rd SE19 |
| D 2 | Palace rd SW2 |
| G 1 | Palace rd Brom |
| G 10 | Palace rd Kingst |
| A 11 | Palace rd Pinn |
| U 17 | Palace sq SE19 |
| B 2 | Palace st SW1 |
| J 6 | Palace view Brom |
| L 7 | Palace view Croy |
| E 14 | Palace View rd E4 |
| N 3 | Palamos rd E10 |
| T 12 | Palatine av N16 |
| T 12 | Palatine rd N16 |
| H 7 | Palermo rd NW10 |
| F 1 | Palestine gro SW19 |
| Z 12 | Palewell Comm dri SW14 |
| Y 10 | Palewell pk SW14 |
| G 20 | Palgrave av S'hall |
| D 8 | Palgrave rd W12 |
| N 14 | Palissy st E2 |
| E 13 | Pall mall SW1 |
| G 12 | Pall Mall east SW1 |
| C 14 | Pall Mall pl SW1 |
| P 1 | Pallett way SE18 |
| K 10 | Palliser rd W14 |
| W 15 | Palm av Sidcp |
| J 7 | Palm gro W5 |
| L 16 | Palm rd Rom |
| U 8 | Palm st E2 |
| E 6 | Palmar cres Bxly Hth |
| D 6 | Palmar rd Bxly Hth |
| W 7 | Palmeira rd Bxly Hth |
| N 10 | Palmer av Sutton |
| M 9 | Palmer av Sutton |
| F 2 | Palmer clo Hounsl |
| J 5 | Palmer cres Kingst |
| F 16 | Palmer pl N7 |
| W 13 | Palmer rd E13 |
| D 20 | Palmer st SW1 |
| E 1 | Palmer st SW1 |
| O 6 | Palmers la Enf |
| T 8 | Palmers rd E2 |
| G 16 | Palmers rd N11 |
| W 8 | Palmers rd N11 |
| C 3 | Palmers rd SW16 |
| P 17 | Palmerston cres N13 |
| Y 17 | Palmerston cres SE18 |
| Y 18 | Palmerston gro SW19 |
| K 14 | Palmerston rd E17 |
| H 17 | Palmerston rd E7 |
| W 20 | Palmerston rd NW6 |
| P 18 | Palmerston rd N22 |
| C 1 | Palmerston rd SW14 |
| Y 11 | Palmerston rd SW14 |
| Y 17 | Palmerston rd SW19 |
| U 7 | Palmerston rd W3 |
| W 7 | Palmerston rd Buck Hl |
| N 7 | Palmerston rd Carsh |
| V 11 | Palmerston rd Harrow |
| E 10 | Palmerston rd Sutton |
| U 16 | Palmerston rd Twick |

| | | |
|---|---|---|
| 135 | Z6 | Palmiter pl E9 |
| 135 | Y9 | Palmiter st E2 |
| 136 | F6 | Pamber st W10 |
| 156 | K17 | Pampisford rd S Croy |
| 142 | D7 | Pancras la EC4 |
| 132 | F7 | Pancras rd NW1 |
| 45 | X16 | Pandora rd NW6 |
| 80 | B6 | Panfield rd SE2 |
| 136 | D1 | Pangbourne av W10 |
| 11 | X15 | Pangbourne dri Stanm |
| 58 | L19 | Panhard pl Shall |
| 5 | S18 | Pank av Barnt |
| 104 | K20 | Panmuir rd SW20 |
| 110 | A7 | Panmure rd SE26 |
| 127 | R6 | Pantiles the Brom |
| 10 | D4 | Pantiles the Bushey Watf |
| 81 | O20 | Pantiles the E15 |
| 140 | G10 | Panton st WC2 |
| 141 | T8 | Paper bldng EC4 |
| 108 | H3 | Parade ms SW2 |
| 147 | S16 | Parade the SW11 |
| 90 | A4 | Paradise st SW4 |
| 143 | Y19 | Paradise st SE16 |
| 147 | P13 | Paradise wlk SW3 |
| 116 | M14 | Paragon gro Surb |
| 94 | C4 | Paragon pl SE3 |
| 58 | B18 | Paragon rd E9 |
| 150 | D6 | Paragon row SE17 |
| 94 | D4 | Paragon the SE3 |
| 92 | H16 | Parbury rd SE23 |
| 122 | K4 | Parchmore rd Thntn Hth |
| 122 | K3 | Parchmore way Thntn Hth |
| 73 | T5 | Pard Rd north W3 |
| 133 | Y16 | Pardon st EC1 |
| 143 | U4 | Parfett st E1 |
| 151 | Y8 | Parfitt rd SE16 |
| 75 | N12 | Parfitt rd SE16 |
| 144 | E13 | Parfrey st W6 |
| 35 | Y17 | Parham dri Ilf |
| 29 | U8 | Parham way N10 |
| 141 | V13 | Paris gdn SE1 |
| 110 | E17 | Parish la SE20 |
| 97 | P9 | Park appr Welling |
| 51 | Z18 | Park av E15 |
| 66 | S4 | Park av E6 |
| 61 | N8 | Park av NW10 |
| 46 | A4 | Park av NW11 |
| 44 | L18 | Park av N13 |
| 17 | U12 | Park av N13 |
| 18 | J14 | Park av N14 |
| 30 | C6 | Park av N22 |
| 28 | C4 | Park av N3 |
| 85 | Z11 | Park av SW14 |
| 54 | D18 | Park av Bark |
| 112 | F16 | Park av Brom |
| 155 | O13 | Park av Carsh |
| 8 | E20 | Park av Enf |
| 92 | K15 | Park av Hounsl |
| 53 | X5 | Park av Ilf |
| 107 | S18 | Park av Mitch |
| 70 | E4 | Park av S'hall |
| 18 | U3 | Park av W Wkhm |
| 21 | U16 | Park av Wdfd Grn |
| 60 | L7 | Park av Wemb |
| 152 | H15 | Park Av east Epsom |
| 44 | K15 | Park Av north N8 |
| 29 | X13 | Park Av north N8 |
| 29 | W14 | Park Av south N8 |
| 152 | F15 | Park Av west Epsom |
| 32 | A2 | Park Avenue rd N17 |
| 39 | T6 | Park blvd Rom |
| 42 | M12 | Park chase Wemb |
| 43 | N11 | Park chase Wemb |
| 61 | N7 | Park clo NW10 |
| 44 | H10 | Park clo Carsh |
| 155 | N13 | Park clo Carsh |
| 23 | T3 | Park clo Harrow |
| 83 | N13 | Park clo Hounsl |
| 28 | C3 | Park cres N3 |
| 131 | X18 | Park cres W1 |
| 8 | B16 | Park cres Enf |
| 81 | Y17 | Park cres Erith |
| 23 | T4 | Park cres Harrow |
| 39 | V20 | Park cres Hornch |
| 131 | Y18 | Park Cres Ms east W1 |
| 131 | W17 | Park Cres Ms west NW1 |
| 25 | W4 | Park croft Edg |
| 25 | W4 | Park croft Edgw |
| 31 | Y1 | Park ct N15 |
| 117 | Z9 | Park ct New Mald |
| 42 | L14 | Park ct Wemb |
| 45 | Z4 | Park dri NW11 |
| 17 | Y1 | Park dri N21 |
| 7 | Y20 | Park dri N21 |
| 78 | D15 | Park dri SE7 |
| 85 | Z11 | Park dri SW14 |
| 73 | P8 | Park dri W3 |

| | | |
|---|---|---|
| 56 | L10 | Park dri Dgnhm |
| 10 | D20 | Park dri Harrow |
| 22 | F20 | Park dri Harrow |
| 39 | P12 | Park dri Rom |
| 78 | D15 | Park Dri clo SE7 |
| 46 | K12 | Park end NW3 |
| 112 | C20 | Park end Brom |
| 39 | R13 | Park End rd Rom |
| 28 | E11 | Park Farm clo N2 |
| 127 | O1 | Park Farm rd Brom |
| 102 | L17 | Park Farm rd Kingst |
| 28 | H10 | Park ga N2 |
| 17 | O3 | Park ga N21 |
| 60 | F13 | Park ga W5 |
| 103 | T14 | Park Ga clo Kingst |
| 25 | U11 | Park gdns NW9 |
| 81 | Y11 | Park gdns Erith |
| 103 | O14 | Park gdns Kingst |
| 65 | S3 | Park gro E15 |
| 29 | Y2 | Park gro N11 |
| 126 | H1 | Park gro Brom |
| 98 | J11 | Park gro Bxly Hth |
| 12 | A16 | Park gro Edg |
| 51 | Z7 | Park Gro rd E11 |
| 28 | K12 | Park Hall rd N2 |
| 109 | N6 | Park Hall rd SE21 |
| 110 | B3 | Park hill SE23 |
| 89 | Y12 | Park hill SW4 |
| 60 | H15 | Park hill W5 |
| 127 | T9 | Park hill Brom |
| 154 | L13 | Park hill Carsh |
| 84 | M16 | Park hill Rich |
| 125 | Y3 | Park Hill rd Brom |
| 157 | R8 | Park Hill rd Croy |
| 114 | G6 | Park Hill rd Sidcp |
| 155 | S16 | Park Hill rd Wallgtn |
| 157 | T4 | Park Hill ri Croy |
| 17 | O2 | Park ho N21 |
| 84 | D14 | Park Ho gdns Twick |
| 64 | H2 | Park la E15 |
| 32 | A3 | Park la N17 |
| 31 | W3 | Park la N17 |
| 18 | H12 | Park la N9 |
| 139 | T11 | Park la W1 |
| 155 | P9 | Park la Carsh |
| 157 | N4 | Park la Croy |
| 40 | J9 | Park la Harrow |
| 57 | Y17 | Park la Hornch |
| 37 | V19 | Park la Rom |
| 153 | R14 | Park la Sutton |
| 101 | W15 | Park la Tedd |
| 42 | L14 | Park la Wemb |
| 21 | X3 | Park la clo N17 |
| 57 | V2 | Park lane Hornch |
| 40 | K10 | Park mead Harrow |
| 97 | S15 | Park mead Sidcp |
| 62 | E5 | Park pde NW10 |
| 140 | B14 | Park pl SW1 |
| 73 | R9 | Park pl W3 |
| 72 | H3 | Park pl W5 |
| 100 | M15 | Park pl Hampt |
| 43 | N13 | Park pl Wemb |
| 42 | M13 | Park pl Wemb |
| 130 | D20 | Park Pl villa W2 |
| 51 | O4 | Park rd E10 |
| 52 | X3 | Park rd E12 |
| 65 | R3 | Park rd E15 |
| 32 | L16 | Park rd E17 |
| 65 | Y3 | Park rd E6 |
| 131 | O17 | Park rd NW1 |
| 62 | A3 | Park rd NW10 |
| 73 | U4 | Park rd NW3 |
| 26 | K20 | Park rd NW8 |
| 130 | L13 | Park rd NW9 |
| 43 | Y1 | Park rd N11 |
| 29 | Z2 | Park rd N11 |
| 16 | K4 | Park rd N14 |
| 30 | J14 | Park rd N15 |
| 18 | J13 | Park rd N18 |
| 28 | H11 | Park rd N2 |
| 28 | H10 | Park rd N2 |
| 29 | W15 | Park rd N8 |
| 123 | T9 | Park rd SE25 |
| 106 | H17 | Park rd SW19 |
| 90 | B18 | Park rd SW2 |
| 73 | Y16 | Park rd W4 |
| 59 | X19 | Park rd W7 |
| 4 | H13 | Park rd Barnt |
| 5 | X15 | Park rd Barnt |
| 111 | O19 | Park rd Becknhm |
| 110 | M17 | Park rd Becknhm |
| 126 | G2 | Park rd Brom |
| 114 | A14 | Park rd Chisl |
| 100 | L11 | Park rd Hampt |
| 82 | L13 | Park rd Hounsl |
| 83 | N13 | Park rd Hounsl |
| 54 | D9 | Park rd Ilf |
| 84 | A4 | Park rd Islwth |
| 103 | O14 | Park rd Kingst |
| 116 | D1 | Park rd Kingst |
| 117 | Z9 | Park rd N Mald |
| 84 | M15 | Park rd Rich |

| | | |
|---|---|---|
| 117 | N12 | Park rd Surb |
| 153 | S14 | Park rd Sutton |
| 153 | R14 | Park rd Sutton |
| 101 | W15 | Park rd Tedd |
| 84 | E14 | Park rd Twick |
| 155 | R3 | Park rd Wallgtn |
| 155 | T10 | Park rd Wallgtn |
| 42 | K18 | Park rd Wemb |
| 103 | N12 | Park Rd east Kingst |
| 73 | Y15 | Park rd north W4 |
| 103 | N12 | Park Rd west Kingst |
| 23 | T5 | Park ri Harrow |
| 110 | J1 | Park Ri rd SE23 |
| 30 | E10 | Park ridings N8 |
| 76 | J15 | Park row SE10 |
| 61 | S8 | Park royal NW10 |
| 61 | W12 | Park Royal rd NW10 |
| 105 | N9 | Park side SW19 |
| 131 | X17 | Park Sq east NW1 |
| 131 | W17 | Park Sq ms NW1 |
| 131 | W17 | Park Sq west NW1 |
| 142 | B12 | Park st SE1 |
| 139 | S7 | Park st W1 |
| 156 | M4 | Park st Croy |
| 101 | U14 | Park st Tedd |
| 9 | V4 | Park ter Enf |
| 152 | F1 | Park ter Worc Pk |
| 46 | A4 | Park the NW11 |
| 29 | P20 | Park the N6 |
| 109 | T18 | Park the SE19 |
| 110 | B3 | Park the SE23 |
| 72 | G4 | Park the W5 |
| 155 | N12 | Park the Carsh |
| 114 | M11 | Park the Sidcp |
| 17 | P2 | Park view N21 |
| 61 | W14 | Park view W3 |
| 118 | F6 | Park view New Mald |
| 22 | F3 | Park view Pinn |
| 43 | U14 | Park view Wemb |
| 16 | E14 | Park View cres N11 |
| 27 | O17 | Park View gdns NW4 |
| 30 | G4 | Park View gdns N22 |
| 67 | U7 | Park View gdns Bark |
| 35 | T13 | Park View gdns Ilf |
| 44 | E12 | Park View rd NW10 |
| 31 | X10 | Park View rd N17 |
| 28 | B4 | Park View rd N3 |
| 113 | Y3 | Park View rd SE9 |
| 60 | K14 | Park View rd W5 |
| 70 | G1 | Park View rd Shall |
| 97 | U10 | Park View rd Welling |
| 131 | Y9 | Park Village east NW1 |
| 131 | X8 | Park Village west NW1 |
| 78 | L16 | Park vista SE10 |
| 37 | W19 | Park vlls Rom |
| 27 | T16 | Park way NW11 |
| 16 | M7 | Park way N14 |
| 15 | Y14 | Park way N20 |
| 119 | O9 | Park way SW20 |
| 25 | I6 | Park way Edg |
| 7 | S10 | Park way Enf |
| 39 | U19 | Park way Hornch |
| 39 | T7 | Park way Rom |
| 21 | Z16 | Park way Wdfd Grn |
| 29 | P20 | Park wlk N6 |
| 146 | D13 | Park wlk SW10 |
| 128 | L17 | Park wd W10 |
| 94 | B18 | Parkcroft SE12 |
| 79 | U14 | Parkdale rd SE18 |
| 86 | F1 | Parke rd SW13 |
| 74 | E20 | Parke rd SW13 |
| 156 | M8 | Parker Croy |
| 78 | C3 | Parker st E16 |
| 140 | M4 | Parker st WC2 |
| 143 | R19 | Parkers row SE1 |
| 00 | A10 | Parkfield av SW14 |
| 58 | A6 | Parkfield av Grnfd |
| 22 | M7 | Parkfield av Harrow |
| 23 | N8 | Parkfield av Harrow |
| 58 | C5 | Parkfield clo Grnfd |
| 22 | M8 | Parkfield cres Harrow |
| 40 | B8 | Parkfield cres Ruis |
| 58 | A7 | Parkfield dri Grnfd |
| 22 | L10 | Parkfield gdns Harrow |
| 44 | H20 | Parkfield rd NW10 |
| 92 | K1 | Parkfield rd SE14 |
| 58 | B5 | Parkfield rd Grnfd |
| 41 | N9 | Parkfield rd Harrow |
| 133 | U8 | Parkfield st N1 |
| 127 | V13 | Parkfield way Brom |
| 86 | M11 | Parkfields SW15 |
| 124 | L19 | Parkfields Croy |
| 43 | Z3 | Parkfields av NW9 |
| 44 | A3 | Parkfields av NW9 |
| 118 | J1 | Parkfields av SW20 |
| 103 | N13 | Parkfields rd Kingst |
| 94 | D9 | Parkgate SE3 |
| 5 | P5 | Parkgate av Barnt |
| 5 | P7 | Parkgate cres Barnt |
| 85 | X14 | Parkgate gdns SW14 |

S 5 Pennine dri NW2
P 3 Pennine way Bxly Hth
V 11 Pennington st E1
A 20 Pennyfields E14
A 17 Penpoll rd E8
R 9 Penpool la Welling
O 4 Penrhyn av E17
M 6 Penrhyn av E17
P 4 Penrhyn cres E17
W 10 Penrhyn cres SW14
N 5 Penrhyn gro E17
H 8 Penrhyn rd Kingst
X 16 Penrith cres Hornch
H 4 Penrith pl SE27
O 15 Penrith rd N15
Z 8 Penrith rd New Mald
M 2 Penrith rd Thntn Hth
U 14 Penrith st SW16
A 11 Penrose gro SE17
A 12 Penrose rd SE17
L 8 Penry st SE1
R 3 Penrylan pl Edg
E 8 Penryn st NW1
V 4 Pensbury pl SW8
V 4 Pensbury st SW8
R 4 Pensford av Rich
O 15 Penshurst av Sidcp
F 16 Penshurst gdns Edg
C 12 Penshurst grn Brom
T 2 Penshurst rd E9
U 2 Penshurst rd E9
B 1 Penshurst rd Bxly Hth
A 2 Penshurst rd Ilf
H 11 Penshurst rd Thntn Hth
G 12 Pensmead ter E4
W 5 Pentire rd E17
S 8 Pentland clo NW11
C 16 Pentland st SW18
R 6 Pentlands clo Mitch
M 8 Pentlow st SW15
H 5 Pentney rd E4
U 1 Pentney rd SW12
R 19 Pentney rd SW19
S 9 Penton gro N1
X 9 Penton ms SE17
X 8 Penton pl SE17
A 10 Penton pl SE17
P 11 Penton rise WC1
S 9 Penton st N1
N 10 Pentonville rd N1
K 4 Pentrich av Enf
M 19 Pentridge st SE15
B 18 Pentyr av N13
N 20 Penwerris av Islwth
Z 3 Penwith rd SW18
A 3 Penwith rd SW18
T 14 Penwortham rd SW16
V 9 Penywern rd SW5
L 12 Penzance pl W11
L 13 Penzance st W11
O 12 Pepler rd SE15
H 9 Peploe rd NW6
A 16 Pepper st SE1
B 17 Pepys cres Barnt
F 2 Pepys rd SE14
L 19 Pepys rd SW20
M 1 Pepys rd SW20
L 9 Pepys st EC3
H 15 Perceval av NW3
V 13 Perch st E8
V 1 Percival ct N17
U 18 Percival gdns Rom
V 11 Percival rd SW14
H 14 Percival rd Enf
W 15 Percival rd Enf
G 10 Percival st SE2
P 12 Percy cir WC1
17 Percy gdns Enf
P 7 Percy gdns Worc Pk
E 3 Percy ms W1
Z 20 Percy rd E11
N 14 Percy rd E16
U 10 Percy rd NW6
R 16 Percy rd N12
Z 3 Percy rd N21
E 1 Percy rd SE20
W 11 Percy rd SE25
G 6 Percy rd W12
Z 6 Percy rd Bxly Hth
A 6 Percy rd Bxly Hth
O 12 Percy rd Hampt
N 20 Percy rd Ilf
N 20 Percy rd Islwth
O 17 Percy rd Mitch
J 9 Percy rd Rom
H 20 Percy rd Twick
K 3 Percy rd Twick
E 2 Percy st W1
M 1 Percy way Twick

135 N 11 Perham rd W14
144 M 12 Perham rd W14
109 N 1 Perifield SE21
60 E 5 Perimeade rd Grnfd
102 B 8 Peripheral rd Rich
95 N 11 Periton rd SE9
80 A 11 Perivale gdns W13
59 Z 8 Perivale la Grnfd
59 T 10 Perivale park Greenford
42 A 14 Perkin clo Wemb
36 E 16 Perkins rd Ilf
148 F 2 Perkins rents SW1
96 F 17 Perpins rd SE9
108 H 2 Perran rd SW2
47 S 18 Perren st NW5
74 J 9 Perrers rd W6
42 A 12 Perrin rd Wemb
46 E 13 Perrins la NW3
46 D 13 Perrins wlk NW3
79 P 10 Perrott st SE18
20 J 20 Perrott villas E4
61 Z 17 Perry av W3
69 Z 6 Perry clo Rainhm
31 R 18 Perry ct N15
31 R 18 Perry ct N15
18 C 10 Perry gdns N9
110 L 6 Perry hill SE6
118 C 19 Perry how Worc Pk
7 W 7 Perry mead Enf
110 J 8 Perry ri SE23
114 K 15 Perry st Chisl
114 H 16 Perry St gdns Chisl
110 D 4 Perry vale SE23
26 E 20 Perryfield way NW9
102 B 6 Perryfield way Rich
36 D 17 Perrymans Farm rd Ilf
87 X 4 Perrymead st SW6
73 Y 1 Perryn rd W3
61 Z 19 Perryn rd W3
140 E 5 Perrys pl W1
111 Z 5 Persant rd SE6
120 G 14 Pershore clo Carsh
43 Z 2 Perth av NW9
118 F 3 Perth clo SW20
50 K 4 Perth rd E10
65 V 8 Perth rd E13
30 H 5 Perth rd N22
48 F 4 Perth rd N4
57 S 5 Perth rd Bark
125 U 3 Perth rd Becknhm
35 X 18 Perth rd Ilf
54 B 1 Perth rd Ilf
36 A 20 Perth rd Ilf
63 R 16 Perth st E1
54 C 2 Perth ter Ilf
40 E 5 Perwell av Harrow
44 J 20 Peter av NW10
62 J 1 Peter av NW10
140 E 7 Peter st W1
87 X 4 Peterborough ms SW6
33 W 18 Peterborough rd E10
87 X 4 Peterborough rd SW6
120 H 13 Peterborough rd Carsh
41 V 2 Peterborough rd Harrow
41 U 2 Peterborough rd Harrow
88 A 2 Peterborough vlls SW6
88 D 10 Petergate SW11
11 U 18 Peters clo Stanm
141 Z 7 Peters hill EC4
133 X 20 Peters la EC1
17 Y 16 Petersfield clo N18
73 W 5 Petersfield rd W3
86 J 20 Petersfield ri SW15
102 H 3 Petersham clo Rich
153 W 12 Petersham clo Sutton
146 B 2 Petersham la SW7
102 G 1 Petersham lodge Rich
146 B 2 Petersham ms SW7
102 L 2 Petersham park Rich
146 C 1 Petersham pl SW7
102 J 1 Petersham rd Rich
84 J 17 Petersham rd Rich
80 D 7 Peterstone rd SE2
49 N 13 Petherton rd N5
144 E 16 Petley rd W6
131 Y 17 Peto pl NW1
65 O 19 Peto st E16
78 D 10 Pett st SE18
39 R 6 Pettits blvd Rom
39 P 7 Pettits clo Rom
39 P 7 Pettits la Rom
39 N 4 Pettits La north Rom
56 D 16 Pettits pl Dgnhm
56 D 15 Pettits rd Dgnhm

42 E 14 Petts Grove av Wemb
40 K 14 Petts hill Grnfd
140 D 20 Petty france SW1
40 E 20 Petworth clo SW1
15 X 17 Petworth rd N12
98 D 14 Petworth rd Bxly Hth
88 K 2 Petworth st SW11
146 J 15 Petyt pl SW3
146 M 7 Petyward SW3
16 K 17 Pevensey av N11
8 C 8 Pevensey av Enf
52 D 12 Pevensey rd E7
106 G 10 Pevensey rd SW19
100 B 2 Pevensey rd Felt
101 R 12 Peveril dri Tedd
146 L 20 Peveril st SW11
19 Z 17 Pewsy rd E9
76 G 19 Peyton pl SE10
150 E 13 Phelp st SE17
146 L 14 Phene st SW3
145 T 9 Philbeach gdns SW5
143 T 7 Philchurch st E1
57 N 4 Philip av Rom
158 K 2 Philip gdns Croy
31 U 11 Philip la N15
91 Y 7 Philip rd SE15
85 R 12 Philip st E13
95 U 16 Philip path SE9
95 N 12 Philippa gdns SE9
62 L 3 Phillimore gdns NW10
128 B 4 Phillimore gdns NW10
137 S 19 Phillimore gdns W8
137 T 19 Phillimore pl W8
137 U 20 Phillimore wlk W8
134 L 6 Phillipp st N1
142 H 9 Philpot la EC3
143 X 4 Philpot st E1
95 R 7 Phineas Pett rd SE9
134 J 17 Phipp st EC2
106 G 20 Phipps Br rd SW19
120 E 4 Phipps Br rd SW19
7 Z 2 Phipps Hatch la Enf
8 A 3 Phipps Hatch la Enf
147 X 4 Phipps ms SW1
120 F 1 Phipps ter SW1
63 Z 20 Phoebe st E14
93 O 13 Phoebeth rd SE4
133 R 16 Phoenix pl WC1
132 G 10 Phoenix rd NW1
110 C 16 Phoenix rd SE20
140 H 6 Phoenix st WC2
118 K 10 Phyllis av New Mald
81 U 7 Picardy Mnr way Blvdr
81 S 12 Picardy rd Blvdr
81 S 9 Picardy st Blvdr
139 Y 14 Piccadilly W1
140 B 12 Piccadilly W1
140 C 12 Piccadilly arcade SW1
140 E 10 Piccadilly clr W1
140 C 11 Piccadilly pl W1
133 Y 12 Pickard st EC1
66 K 7 Pickering av E6
137 Y 5 Pickering ms W2
133 Z 3 Pickering st N1
10 D 5 Pickets clo Bushey Watf
89 R 18 Pickets st SW12
24 F 5 Pickett croft Stanm
19 U 8 Picketts Lock la N9
97 Y 5 Pickford clo Bxly Hth
97 Z 2 Pickford rd Bxly Hth
97 Y 9 Pickford rd Bxly Hth
126 E 18 Pickhurst grn Brom
126 A 13 Pickhurst la W Wkhm
125 Z 12 Pickhurst la W Wkhm
126 B 17 Pickhurst mead Brom
120 B 13 Pickhurst pk Brom
126 A 18 Pickhurst ri W Wckhm
125 V 19 Pickhurst ri W Wkhm
142 L 14 Pickle Herring st SE1
91 R 17 Pickwick rd SE21
91 R 17 Pickwick st SE1
148 K 19 Pickworth st SW8
139 U 5 Picton pl W1
150 F 15 Picton st SE5
79 T 14 Piedmont rd SE18
78 J 4 Pier parade E16
78 J 4 Pier rd E16
76 H 10 Pier st E14
88 B 10 Pier ter SW18
91 Z 13 Piermont grn SE22
91 Z 13 Piermont rd SE22
61 T 19 Pierrepoint rd W3
133 W 7 Pierrepont row N1
63 Z 18 Piggot st E14

64 A 17 Piggot st E14
108 L 8 Pilgrim hill SE27
141 W 6 Pilgrim st EC4
142 F 19 Pilgrimage st SE1
46 G 13 Pilgrims la NW3
5 X 17 Pilgrims ri Barnt
157 V 12 Pilgrims way S Croy
43 S 4 Pilgrims way Wemb
147 P 14 Pilke st SW3
91 Z 5 Pilkington rd SE15
115 S 17 Pilmans clo Sidcp
147 U 8 Pimlico rd SW1
20 K 8 Pimp Hall park E4
143 T 8 Pinchin st E1
106 B 20 Pincott rd SW19
98 E 11 Pincott rd Bxly Hth
134 K 20 Pindar st EC2
129 Z 18 Pindock ms W9
125 R 19 Pine av W Wkhm
16 H 3 Pine clo N14
158 F 9 Pine coombe Croy
117 X 14 Pine gdns Surb
14 K 5 Pine gro N20
48 B 7 Pine gro N4
45 N 12 Pine rd NW2
16 A 8 Pine rd N11
155 O 19 Pine ridge Carsh
133 T 16 Pine st EC1
117 R 13 Pine wlk Surb
64 A 19 Pinefield clo E14
127 R 3 Pines rd Brom
6 H 15 Pines the N14
21 R 10 Pines the Wdfd Grn
114 J 2 Pinewood Sidcp
158 H 6 Pinewood clo Croy
60 E 17 Pinewood gro W13
80 H 16 Pinewood rd SE2
126 F 8 Pinewood rd Brom
108 A 9 Pinfold rd SW16
16 F 19 Pinkham way N11
68 C 2 Pinley gdns Dgnhm
98 H 11 Pinnacle hill Bxly Hth
95 O 12 Pinnell rd SE9
22 G 13 Pinner ct Pinn
22 B 15 Pinner gro Pinn
22 G 5 Pinner park Pinn
22 L 9 Pinner Pk av Harrow
23 N 8 Pinner Pk av Harrow
23 O 9 Pinner Pk gdns Harrow
22 J 14 Pinner rd Harrow
23 O 19 Pinner rd Harrow
23 N 17 Pinner view Harrow
94 G 10 Pinto way SE3
117 O 5 Piper clo N7
25 W 17 Pipers grn NW9
11 Y 12 Pipers Grn la Edg
120 H 14 Pipewell rd Carsh
124 C 4 Piquet rd SE20
159 V 14 Pitchers croy Croy
87 X 20 Pirbright rd SW18
77 V 3 Pirie st E16
108 M 17 Pitcairn rd Mitch
89 S 6 Pitcairn st SW8
64 L 2 Pitchford st E15
134 H 14 Pitfield st N1
43 V 18 Pitfield way NW10
94 F 17 Pitfold clo SE12
94 E 17 Pitfold rd SE12
156 J 2 Pitlake Croy
63 T 18 Pitsea pk E1
63 T 18 Pitsea st E1
60 D 12 Pitshanger la W5
60 B 9 Pitshanger park Grnfd
105 Z 9 Pitt cres SW19
106 A 10 Pitt cres SW19
122 M 11 Pitt rd Thntn Hth
137 V 3 Pitt st W8
142 K 14 Pitt st SE1
139 V 14 Pitts Head ms W 1
126 E 18 Pittsmead av Brom
123 X 5 Pitville gdns SE25
63 Y 17 Pixley st E14
158 H 20 Pixton way Croy
142 F 18 Plaintain pl SE1
65 O 4 Plaistow gro E15
112 G 18 Plaistow gro Brom
112 G 18 Plaistow la Brom
126 M 2 Plaistow la Brom
65 U 5 Plaistow Pk rd E13
65 R 6 Plaistow rd E15
109 Z 6 Plane st SE26
55 W 2 Plantagenet gdns Rom
55 X 2 Plantagenet pl Rom
5 P 14 Plantagenet rd Barnt
99 V 1 Plantation rd Erith
94 F 5 Plantation the SE3
65 Y 2 Plashet gro E6
66 A 1 Plashet gro E6
53 O 20 Plashet gro E7

93 S 19 Plassy rd SE6
134 G 17 Platina pl EC2
90 A 11 Plato rd SW2
132 F 9 Platt st NW1
87 R 8 Platt the SW15
45 Y 11 Platts la NW3
9 R 7 Platts rd Enf
110 G 20 Plawsfield rd Becknhm
126 L 2 Plaxtol clo Brom
77 T 14 Plaxtol pl SE10
81 T 18 Plaxtol rd Erith
121 N 13 Player rd Mitch
144 E 12 Playfair st W6
38 J 4 Playfield av Rom
91 T 13 Playfield cres SE22
25 W 6 Playfield rd Edg
48 E 7 Playford rd N4
48 E 6 Playford rd N4
48 E 8 Playford rd N4
111 P 9 Playgreen way SE6
141 X 7 Playhouse yd EC4
86 J 12 Pleasance av SW15
86 J 11 Pleasance the SW15
158 L 5 Pleasant gro Croy
133 Y 1 Pleasant pl N1
131 Z 5 Pleasant row NW1
60 F 5 Pleasant way Wemb
20 B 8 Pleasaunce E4
132 B 6 Plender st NW1
47 W 13 Pleshey rd N7
31 S 17 Plevna clo N15
31 S 17 Plevna cres N15
18 L 10 Plevna rd N9
76 F 7 Plevna st E14
66 K 18 Plevna rd E6
109 V 17 Pleydell av SE19
74 E 10 Pleydell av W6
141 U 6 Pleydell st EC4
48 G 8 Plimsoll rd N4
64 D 18 Plimsoll st E14
142 G 8 Plough ct EC3
91 W 17 Plough la SE22
106 C 11 Plough la SW19
156 A 12 Plough la Wallgtn
155 Z 8 Plough la Wallgtn
155 Z 10 Plough La clo Wallgtn
141 T 4 Plough pl EC4
88 G 10 Plough rd SW11
88 G 10 Plough ter SW11
75 W 10 Plough way SE16
134 K 18 Plough yd Brentf
72 F 19 Plough yd Brentf
70 B 9 Pluckington pl Shall
72 H 12 Plum garth Brentf
79 O 18 Plum la SE18
93 T 2 Plumb st SE10
133 U 15 Plumbers pl EC1
143 S 3 Plumbers row E1
120 L 2 Plummer la Mitch
89 X 18 Plummer rd SW4
40 G 17 Plumpton clo Grnfd
78 L 15 Plumstead Comm rd SE18
79 P 16 Plumstead Comm rd SE18
79 W 11 Plumstead High st SE18
79 O 10 Plumstead rd SE18
141 V 3 Plumtree ct EC4
65 S 16 Plymouth rd E16
112 J 20 Plymouth rd Brom
129 N 2 Plympton av NW6
130 K 18 Plympton pl NW8
129 O 1 Plympton rd NW6
130 K 18 Plympton st NW8
80 F 20 Plymstock rd Welling
141 X 17 Pocock st SE1
88 C 11 Podmore rd SW18
49 N 14 Poets rd N5
87 X 11 Point pleasant SW6
28 D 6 Pointalls clo N3
140 C 5 Poland st W1
20 F 3 Pole Hill rd E4
94 L 6 Polebrook rd SE3
110 L 4 Polescroft la SE6
55 X 20 Polesworth rd Dgnhm
68 K 1 Polesworth rd Dgnhm
65 S 19 Pollard clo E16
15 W 9 Pollard rd N20
120 G 12 Pollard rd Mrdn
135 U 13 Pollard row E2
135 U 13 Pollard st E2
122 B 6 Pollards cres SW16
122 C 5 Pollards Hill east SW16
122 C 5 Pollards Hill north SW16

122 B 6 Pollards Hill west SW16
122 A 5 Pollards Wood rd SW16
139 Z 7 Pollen st W1
150 C 5 Pollock rd SE17
92 M 19 Polstead rd SE6
79 R 10 Polthorne gro SE18
108 A 13 Polworth rd SW16
132 D 11 Polygon rd NW1
89 U 9 Polygon the SW4
78 K 11 Polytechnic st SE18
75 P 26 Pomeroy sq SE14
92 C 2 Pomeroy st SE14
75 R 20 Pomeroy st SE14
90 K 7 Pomfret rd SE5
94 E 5 Pond clo SE3
146 J 7 Pond pl SW3
64 M 6 Pond rd E15
94 D 5 Pond rd SE3
47 P 3 Pond sq N6
46 H 14 Pond st NW3
102 D 16 Pond way Tedd
142 A 12 Pond yd SE1
48 C 20 Ponder st N7
126 A 20 Pondfield rd Brom
56 G 14 Pondfield rd Dgnhm
153 R 12 Pondhill gdns Sutton
91 P 15 Pondmead SE21
143 V 7 Ponler st E1
62 J 8 Ponsard rd NW10
50 D 16 Ponsford st E9
148 H 9 Ponsonby pl SW1
86 J 19 Ponsonby rd SW15
148 H 9 Ponsonby ter SW1
147 R 2 Pont st SW1
147 O 2 Pont St ms SW3
112 D 12 Pontefract rd Brom
148 F 15 Ponton rd SW8
141 V 17 Pontypool pl SE1
82 B 4 Poole Ct rd Hounsl
50 E 19 Poole rd E9
134 E 6 Poole st N1
123 R 17 Pooles bldgs WC1
68 M 5 Pooles la Dgnhm
48 E 7 Pooles pk N4
48 E 8 Pooles pk N4
26 B 13 Poolsford rd NW9
127 N 12 Pope rd Brom
142 M 19 Pope st SE1
101 S 3 Popes av Twick
158 L 4 Popes gro Croy
101 V 4 Popes gro Twick
142 F 7 Popes Head all EC3
72 G 9 Popes la W5
90 F 9 Popes rd SW9
134 A 3 Popham rd N1
134 A 4 Popham st N1
133 Y 4 Popham st N1
120 M 1 Poplar av Mitch
70 K 8 Poplar av S'hall
64 K 19 Poplar Bath st E14
105 Y 11 Poplar ct SW19
117 Z 4 Poplar gdns New Mald
136 D 20 Poplar gro W6
117 Z 6 Poplar gro New Mald
43 W 9 Poplar gro Wemb
64 D 20 Poplar High st E14
81 V 10 Poplar mt Blvdr
137 Y 9 Poplar pl W2
119 Y 6 Poplar rd SW19
119 U 20 Poplar rd Sutton
38 K 13 Poplar st Rom
90 L 10 Poplar wlk SE24
156 M 1 Poplar wlk Croy
90 L 9 Poplar wlk SE24
44 M 19 Poplars av NW2
33 R 18 Poplars rd E17
6 F 16 Poplars the N14
141 V 5 Poppins ct EC4
34 A 20 Poppleton rd E11
15 Y 11 Porch way N20
137 Z 7 Porchester Gdns ms W2
138 L 6 Porchester pl W2
137 Y 5 Porchester pl W2
117 T 4 Porchester rd Kingst
137 Y 4 Porchester sq W2
137 Z 5 Porchester Sq ms W2
138 K 4 Porchester st W2
138 B 10 Porchester ter W2
137 Z 3 Porchester Ter north W2
137 Z 7 Porchester terr W2
113 S 4 Porcupine clo SE9
90 D 11 Porden rd SW2
41 N 3 Porlock av Harrow
76 K 7 Porlock rd Enf
142 F 18 Porlock st SE1
108 G 6 Portal clo SE27

63 S 10 Portelet rd E1
144 J 2 Porten rd W14
131 S 20 Porter st W1
55 U 15 Porters av Dgnhm
50 F 5 Portersfield E10
138 E 1 Porteus rd W 2
110 J 10 Porthcawe rd SE26
97 N 9 Porthkerry av Welling
63 Y 13 Portia rd E3
87 U 14 Portinscale rd SW15
49 U 2 Portland av N16
118 E 16 Portland av New Mald
97 O 17 Portland av Sidcp
113 P 4 Portland cres SE9
58 L 13 Portland cres Grnfd
24 J 8 Portland Cres east Stanm
24 G 8 Portland Cres west Stanm
30 K 19 Portland gdns N4
37 X 15 Portland gdns Rom
90 B 1 Portland gro SW8
139 Y 2 Portland ms W1
140 C 7 Portland ms W1
139 Y 1 Portland pl W1
131 Y 19 Portland pl W1
31 T 13 Portland rd W11
123 Y 10 Portland rd SE25
113 R 4 Portland rd SE9
136 M 12 Portland rd Brom
112 L 11 Portland rd Brom
116 K 7 Portland rd Kingst
120 J 3 Portland rd Mitch
70 D 7 Portland rd S'hall
48 K 4 Portland ri N4
48 K 4 Portland Ri est N4
150 E 11 Portland st SE17
84 G 11 Portland ter Rich
85 Y 9 Portman av SW14
139 S 4 Portman clo W1
35 N 7 Portman dri Wdfd Grn
25 X 9 Portman gdns NW9
139 S 6 Portman ms W1
63 R 9 Portman pl E2
117 N 4 Portman rd Kingst
139 S 5 Portman sq W1
139 R 6 Portman st W1
129 O 11 Portnall rd W9
137 T 10 Portobello ms W11
137 T 10 Portobello mws W11
136 M 2 Portobello rd W10
137 S 10 Portobello rd W11
137 T 11 Portobello rd W11
128 K 19 Portobello rd W11
133 S 20 Portpool la EC1
64 K 16 Portree st E14
27 W 19 Portsdown av NW11
138 M 6 Portsea ms W2
138 M 6 Portsea pl W2
89 V 4 Portslade rd SW8
104 J 1 Portsmouth rd SW15
86 L 19 Portsmouth rd SW15
86 L 19 Portsmouth rd SW15
86 L 20 Portsmouth rd SW15
116 F 12 Portsmouth rd Surb & Kingst
141 O 5 Portsmouth st WC2
143 O 8 Portsoken st E1
86 D 17 Portswood pl SW15
100 M 4 Portugal gdns Twick
141 P 5 Portugal st WC2
65 O 2 Portway E15
152 G 20 Portway Epsom
142 F 7 Post Office ct EC3
150 G 2 Potier st SE1
63 N 10 Pott st E2
135 X 14 Pott st E2
87 P 19 Potterne clo SW19
142 L 15 Potters fields SE1
117 W 9 Potters gro New Mald
107 X 14 Potters la SW16
4 L 15 Potters la Barnt
5 O 13 Potters la Barnt
143 V 18 Pottery la SE16
136 L 12 Pottery la W11
101 X 2 Poulet gdns Twick
66 G 5 Poulett rd E6
120 J 13 Poulter park Carsh
154 H 5 Poulton av Sutton
142 D 6 Poultry EC2
116 D 19 Pound clo Surb
44 F 19 Pound la NW10
78 B 12 Pound Pk rd SE7
95 V 15 Pound pl SE9
121 S 4 Pound st Carsh
89 O 7 Pountney rd SW11
82 E 20 Powder Mill la Twick
100 G 1 Powder Mill la Twick
11 Z 18 Powell clo Edg
155 Z 16 Powell clo Wallgtn
56 D 12 Powell gdns Dgnhm

50 A 11 Powell rd E5
21 Z 3 Powell rd Buck H
74 B 17 Powells wlk W4
73 R 12 Power rd W4
50 D 11 Powerscroft rd E5
115 T 17 Powerscroft rd S
145 U 2 Powis gdns NW11
137 P 5 Powis gdns W11
137 R 5 Powis ms W11
132 L 19 Powis pl WC1
64 D 9 Powis rd E3
137 R 6 Powis sq W11
64 L 9 Powis st E15
78 J 9 Powis st SE18
137 R 5 Powis ter W11
47 N 19 Powlett pl NW1
82 L 10 Pownall gdns Hou
135 R 4 Pownall rd E8
82 L 10 Pownall rd Houns
112 G 12 Powster rd Brom
80 K 18 Powys la Bxly H
17 N 14 Powys la N13
16 M 14 Powys la N13
16 M 13 Powys la N14
89 V 18 Poynders gdns SW4
89 W 18 Poynders gdns SW4
47 U 9 Poynings rd N19
14 K 17 Poynings way N1
114 F 20 Poyntell cres Chis
8 J 18 Poynter rd Enf
31 Z 6 Poynton rd N17
88 M 6 Poyntz rd SW11
63 N 7 Poyser st E2
135 X 11 Poyser st E2
138 G 5 Praed ms W2
138 F 6 Praed st W2
65 X 8 Pragel st E13
112 G 3 Pragnell rd SE12
48 G 8 Prah rd N4
89 R 4 Prairie st SW8
132 A 5 Pratt ms NW1
132 B 4 Pratt st NW1
149 O 4 Pratt wlk SE11
45 P 3 Prayle gro NW2
74 D 11 Prebend gdns W4
134 B 5 Prebend st N1
94 A 7 Prendergast rd SE
107 Z 9 Prentis rd SW16
78 A 11 Prentiss ct SE7
118 B 10 Presburg rd New Mald
25 N 5 Prescelly pl Edg
143 O 8 Prescot st E1
127 Y 15 Prescott av Brom
89 X 9 Prescott pl SW4
134 A 13 President st EC1
43 Z 9 Press rd NW10
129 O 19 Prestage st E14
64 H 20 Prestage st E14
52 L 20 Prestbury rd E7
113 T 9 Prestbury sq SE9
88 J 9 Prested rd SW11
20 J 9 Preston av E4
101 S 5 Preston clo Twick
34 K 16 Preston dri E11
97 W 2 Preston dri Bxly Hth
152 C 13 Preston dri Epsom
44 C 18 Preston gdns NW1
9 X 1 Preston gdns Enf
35 N 19 Preston gdns Ilf
24 M 18 Preston hill Harrow
42 K 1 Preston hill Harrow
44 H 18 Preston pl NW2
84 L 13 Preston pl Rich
34 A 20 Preston rd E11
64 G 20 Preston rd E14
64 G 3 Preston rd E15
108 J 15 Preston rd SE19
104 E 18 Preston rd SW20
42 K 2 Preston rd Harrow
42 J 3 Preston waye Harro
76 G 3 Prestons rd E14
70 B 14 Prestwick clo S'hall
24 B 13 Prestwood av Harro
24 C 13 Prestwood clo Harrow
32 G 12 Pretoria av E17
31 U 1 Pretoria clo N17
20 H 6 Pretoria cres E4
51 X 4 Pretoria rd E11
65 O 11 Pretoria rd E16
20 H 5 Pretoria rd E4
31 U 1 Pretoria rd N17
107 T 13 Pretoria rd SW16
53 Y 14 Pretoria rd Ilf
38 J 14 Pretoria rd Rom
18 G 18 Pretoria Rd north N18
16 B 7 Prevost rd N11
106 L 8 Price clo SW17
156 J 10 Price rd Croy
141 Y 14 Prices st SE1
133 O 4 Prices yd N1

| Grid | Name |
|---|---|
| 5 O 19 | Pricklers hill Barnt |
| 3 R 12 | Prideaux pl WC1 |
| 0 A 7 | Prideaux rd SW9 |
| 3 N 10 | Pridham Rd east Thntn Hth |
| 0 J 7 | Priestfield rd SE23 |
| 4 L 7 | Priestlands Pk rd Sidcp |
| 7 P 19 | Priestley gdns Rom |
| 1 V 20 | Priestly clo N16 |
| 1 P 2 | Priestly rd Mitch |
| 0 E 15 | Priestly st E9 |
| 9 N 8 | Priests av N9 |
| 6 B 9 | Priests br SW15 |
| 2 A 5 | Priests ct EC2 |
| 9 T 17 | Prima rd SW9 |
| 8 C 5 | Primrose av Enf |
| 7 P 20 | Primrose av Rom |
| 5 R 1 | Primrose av Rom |
| 4 H 7 | Primrose clo E18 |
| 0 D 11 | Primrose clo Harrow |
| 6 K 17 | Primrose gdns NW3 |
| 1 V 7 | Primrose hill EC4 |
| 6 L 19 | Primrose Hill rd NW3 |
| 1 N 1 | Primrose Hill rd NW3 |
| 1 S 3 | Primrose Hill stds NW1 |
| 1 R 4 | Primrose rd E10 |
| 4 G 7 | Primrose rd E18 |
| 4 K 20 | Primrose st EC2 |
| 0 F 6 | Primrose way Wemb |
| 2 F 18 | Primula st W12 |
| 1 P 6 | Prince Albert rd NW1 |
| 0 K 11 | Prince Albert rd NW1 |
| 6 E 13 | Prince Arthur ms NW3 |
| 6 E 14 | Prince Arthur rd NW3 |
| 4 B 3 | Prince Charles rd SE3 |
| 8 E 20 | Prince Consort rd SW7 |
| 6 A 17 | Prince Edward cres E16 |
| 0 M 17 | Prince Edward rd E9 |
| 6 H 16 | Prince George av N14 |
| 7 N 18 | Prince George av N14 |
| 9 S 12 | Prince George rd N16 |
| 9 N 3 | Prince Georges av SW20 |
| 06 H 20 | Prince Georges rd SW19 |
| 78 B 19 | Prince Henry rd SE7 |
| 78 H 20 | Prince Imperial rd SE7 |
| 95 R 13 | Prince John rd SE9 |
| 47 R 19 | Prince Of Wales cres NW1 |
| 88 L 2 | Prince Of Wales dri SW11 |
| 47 Y 20 | Prince Of Wales dri SW11 |
| 89 O 1 | Prince Of Wales dri SW8 |
| 47 W 20 | Prince Of Wales dri SW8 |
| 65 Y 18 | Prince Of Wales rd E16 |
| 26 L 12 | Prince Of Wales rd NW4 |
| 47 T 18 | Prince Of Wales rd NW5 |
| 94 C 3 | Prince Of Wales rd SE3 |
| 54 G 3 | Prince Of Wales rd Sutton |
| 74 A 13 | Prince Of Wales ter W4 |
| 137 Z 19 | Prince Of Wales ter W8 |
| 23 R 10 | Prince rd SE25 |
| 65 X 12 | Prince Regent la E13 |
| 82 L 7 | Prince Regent rd Hounsl |
| 95 T 8 | Prince Rupert rd SE9 |
| 75 Z 16 | Prince st SE8 |
| 76 A 16 | Prince st SE8 |
| 36 M 14 | Princedale rd W11 |
| 135 P 20 | Princelet st E1 |
| 40 C 12 | Princes arcade SW1 |
| 25 P 13 | Princes av NW9 |
| 29 R 11 | Princes av N10 |
| 17 V 17 | Princes av N13 |
| 29 Y 4 | Princes av N22 |
| 27 Z 4 | Princes av N3 |
| 73 R 7 | Princes av N9 |
| 154 K 18 | Princes av Carsh |
| 58 L 16 | Princes av Grnfd |
| 21 X 14 | Princes av Wdfd Grn |
| 25 P 13 | Princes clo NW9 |
| 12 B 16 | Princes clo Edg |
| 115 V 7 | Princes clo Sidcp |
| 101 P 10 | Princes clo Tedd |
| 42 K 14 | Princes ct Wemb |
| 23 T 11 | Princes dri Harrow |
| 138 G 19 | Princes ga SW7 |
| 146 H 2 | Princes Ga ms SW7 |
| 138 G 19 | Princes gate SW7 |
| 146 H 1 | Princes gdns SW7 |
| 138 H 20 | Princes gdns SW7 |
| 61 R 14 | Princes gdns W3 |
| 60 D 13 | Princes gdns W5 |
| 29 R 11 | Princes la N10 |
| 137 W 9 | Princes ms W2 |
| 27 T 17 | Princes Pk av NW11 |
| 140 C 13 | Princes pl EC4 |
| 136 L 13 | Princes pl W11 |
| 127 T 19 | Princes plain Brom |
| 19 P 13 | Princes rd N18 |
| 110 F 16 | Princes rd SW14 |
| 85 Z 8 | Princes rd SW14 |
| 105 X 15 | Princes rd W13 |
| 21 Y 8 | Princes rd Buck Hl |
| 36 D 13 | Princes rd Ilf |
| 100 P 10 | Princes rd Kingst |
| 84 M 12 | Princes rd Rich |
| 85 N 1 | Princes rd Rich |
| 39 V 18 | Princes rd Rom |
| 101 P 11 | Princes rd Tedd |
| 99 X 17 | Princes Rd north Drtfrd |
| 93 U 5 | Princes ri SE13 |
| 137 W 8 | Princes sq W2 |
| 142 E 5 | Princes st EC2 |
| 18 E 20 | Princes st N17 |
| 140 H 19 | Princes st W1 |
| 139 Z 6 | Princes st W1 |
| 98 A 9 | Princes st Bxly Hth |
| 84 J 11 | Princes st Rich |
| 154 F 8 | Princes st Sutton |
| 65 W 4 | Princes ter E13 |
| 87 P 19 | Princes way SW19 |
| 105 S 2 | Princes way SW19 |
| 21 Y 8 | Princes way Buck Hl |
| 156 D 12 | Princes way Croy |
| 40 B 12 | Princes way Ruis |
| 136 L 14 | Princes yd W11 |
| 42 L 6 | Princess av Wemb |
| 48 K 6 | Princess cres N4 |
| 49 S 13 | Princess May rd N16 |
| 131 U 3 | Princess rd NW1 |
| 129 U 9 | Princess rd NW6 |
| 122 M 14 | Princess rd Croy |
| 123 N 12 | Princess rd Croy |
| 110 E 10 | Princethorpe rd SE26 |
| 141 N 1 | Princeton sq WC1 |
| 107 U 10 | Pringle gdns SW16 |
| 141 X 8 | Printing Hse sq EC4 |
| 57 X 14 | Priolo rd SE7 |
| 154 N 14 | Prior av Sutton |
| 48 K 19 | Prior Bolton st N1 |
| 76 G 20 | Prior st SE10 |
| 32 J 8 | Priors croft E17 |
| 93 U 1 | Priors Point hill SE10 |
| 33 O 15 | Priory av E17 |
| 19 Z 11 | Priory av E4 |
| 20 B 11 | Priory av E4 |
| 29 Y 13 | Priory av N8 |
| 74 B 9 | Priory av W4 |
| 153 P 8 | Priory av Sutton |
| 41 X 12 | Priory av Wemb |
| 34 E 4 | Priory clo E18 |
| 19 Z 11 | Priory clo E4 |
| 6 F 17 | Priory clo N14 |
| 6 F 17 | Priory clo N14 |
| 14 G 3 | Priory clo N20 |
| 124 J 7 | Priory clo Beckhm |
| 127 U 2 | Priory clo Chisl |
| 100 F 19 | Priory clo Hampt |
| 10 J 10 | Priory clo Stanm |
| 41 W 12 | Priory clo Wemb |
| 109 N 18 | Priory cres SE19 |
| 153 P 8 | Priory cres Sutton |
| 41 Y 10 | Priory cres Wemb |
| 32 K 8 | Priory ct E17 |
| 89 Z 1 | Priory ct SW8 |
| 80 J 14 | Priory dri SE2 |
| 10 H 10 | Priory dri Stanm |
| 29 S 18 | Priory gdns N16 |
| 86 C 8 | Priory gdns SW14 |
| 89 Z 1 | Priory gdns SW8 |
| 89 Z 2 | Priory gdns SW8 |
| 74 A 10 | Priory gdns W4 |
| 74 A 10 | Priory gdns W4 |
| 60 K 8 | Priory gdns W5 |
| 100 E 19 | Priory gdns Hampt |
| 41 X 11 | Priory gdns Wemb |
| 89 Z 3 | Priory gro SW8 |
| 41 Y 11 | Priory hill Wemb |
| 86 D 10 | Priory la SW15 |
| 89 Y 2 | Priory ms SW8 |
| 94 C 9 | Priory pk SE3 |
| 129 S 3 | Priory Pk rd NW6 |
| 41 X 12 | Priory Pk rd Wemb |
| 66 A 5 | Priory rd E6 |
| 46 A 19 | Priory rd NW6 |
| 129 X 1 | Priory rd NW6 |
| 29 X 13 | Priory rd N8 |
| 106 F 18 | Priory rd SW19 |
| 73 X 9 | Priory rd W4 |
| 54 E 20 | Priory rd Bark |
| 122 F 17 | Priory rd Croy |
| 100 E 19 | Priory rd Hampt |
| 83 O 13 | Priory rd Hounsl |
| 73 P 18 | Priory rd Rich |
| 153 P 9 | Priory rd Sutton |
| 64 E 8 | Priory st E3 |
| 129 X 4 | Priory ter NW6 |
| 10 E 3 | Priory view Bushey Watf |
| 22 K 12 | Priory way Harrow |
| 146 C 11 | Priory wlk SW10 |
| 64 B 9 | Priscilla rd E3 |
| 135 V 8 | Pritchards rd E2 |
| 151 T 2 | Priter rd SE16 |
| 151 T 3 | Priter way SE16 |
| 18 C 17 | Private rd Enf |
| 90 G 12 | Probert rd SW2 |
| 108 H 4 | Probyn rd SW2 |
| 141 N 2 | Procter st WC1 |
| 30 F 4 | Progress way N22 |
| 156 D 3 | Progress way Croy |
| 8 L 19 | Progress way Enf |
| 74 A 20 | Promenade Appr rd W4 |
| 86 C 2 | Promenade the W4 |
| 93 U 2 | Prospect clo SE16 |
| 81 S 12 | Prospect clo Blvdr |
| 82 F 3 | Prospect clo Hounsl |
| 87 X 11 | Prospect cottages SW18 |
| 83 N 16 | Prospect cres Twick |
| 33 S 12 | Prospect hill E17 |
| 31 S 4 | Prospect pl N17 |
| 28 H 17 | Prospect pl N2 |
| 126 H 7 | Prospect pl Brom |
| 38 K 8 | Prospect pl Rom |
| 116 D 15 | Prospect pl Surb |
| 312 L 20 | Prospect rd E17 |
| 45 W 9 | Prospect rd NW2 |
| 109 Z 9 | Prospect rd SE26 |
| 4 M 15 | Prospect rd Barnt |
| 5 N 14 | Prospect rd Barnt |
| 21 Z 7 | Prospect rd Wdfd Grn |
| 28 H 11 | Prospect ring N2 |
| 133 N 15 | Prospect ter WC1 |
| 132 M 15 | Prospect ter WC1 |
| 78 D 11 | Prospect vale SE18 |
| 63 T 8 | Prospect wk E2 |
| 47 W 4 | Prospero rd N19 |
| 26 K 15 | Prothero gdns NW4 |
| 145 N 17 | Prothero rd SW6 |
| 44 C 13 | Prout gro NW10 |
| 50 A 9 | Prout rd E5 |
| 134 A 8 | Provence st N1 |
| 139 U 8 | Providence ct W1 |
| 133 V 5 | Providence pl N1 |
| 38 B 5 | Providence place Rom |
| 46 M 19 | Provost rd NW3 |
| 134 E 13 | Provost st N1 |
| 10 A 8 | Prowse av Bushey Watf |
| 47 U 20 | Prowse pl NW1 |
| 16 J 9 | Pruden clo N14 |
| 142 D 5 | Prudent pass EC2 |
| 75 O 2 | Prusom st E1 |
| 143 Z 12 | Pryors croft E17 |
| 142 H 10 | Pudding la EC2 |
| 64 E 5 | Pudding Mill la E15 |
| 141 X 9 | Puddle dock EC4 |
| 87 Y 19 | Pulborough rd SW18 |
| 31 P 18 | Pulford rd N15 |
| 28 C 12 | Pulham av N2 |
| 4 E 10 | Puller rd Barnt |
| 66 E 8 | Pulleyns av E6 |
| 86 M 15 | Pullman gdns SW15 |
| 90 C 9 | Pulross rd SW9 |
| 34 G 10 | Pulteney gdns E18 |
| 133 R 5 | Pulteney rd N1 |
| 133 R 5 | Pulteney ter N1 |
| 145 T 19 | Pulton pl SW6 |
| 72 C 10 | Pump all Brentf |
| 141 S 7 | Pump ct EC4 |
| 156 L 7 | Pump pail Croy |
| 74 B 18 | Pumping Station la W4 |
| 74 B 18 | Pumping Station rd W4 |
| 63 N 8 | Pundersons gdns E2 |
| 135 X 12 | Pundersons gdns E2 |
| 118 D 15 | Purbeck av New Mald |
| 118 E 15 | Purbeck av New Mald |
| 45 R 6 | Purbeck dri NW2 |
| 57 X 2 | Purbeck rd Hornch |
| 142 M 20 | Purbrook st SE1 |
| 144 J 17 | Purcell cres SW6 |
| 58 K 13 | Purcell rd Grnfd |
| 134 J 9 | Purcell st N1 |
| 12 B 15 | Purcells av Edg |
| 132 G 9 | Purchese st NW1 |
| 64 C 11 | Purdy st E3 |
| 56 B 4 | Purland clo Dgnhm |
| 79 Z 6 | Purland rd SE18 |
| 45 S 8 | Purley av NW2 |
| 35 X 8 | Purley clo Ilf |
| 48 H 20 | Purley pl N1 |
| 18 C 11 | Purley rd N9 |
| 157 N 18 | Purley rd S Croy |
| 122 D 19 | Purley way Croy |
| 156 E 4 | Purley way Croy |
| 95 N 10 | Purneys rd SE9 |
| 94 M 9 | Purrett rd SE18 |
| 79 X 13 | Purrett rd SE18 |
| 87 W 2 | Purses Cross rd SW6 |
| 26 K 1 | Pursley rd NW7 |
| 120 C 10 | Purves rd NW10 |
| 62 M 7 | Purves rd NW10 |
| 87 S 8 | Putney bridge SW6 |
| 87 S 7 | Putney Bridge app SW6 |
| 87 U 10 | Putney Bridge rd SW15 |
| 86 L 7 | Putney comm SW15 |
| 86 L 11 | Putney heath SW15 |
| 87 O 16 | Putney heath SW15 |
| 104 M 3 | Putney heath SW19 |
| 87 P 17 | Putney Heath la SW15 |
| 87 R 11 | Putney High st SW15 |
| 87 P 14 | Putney hill SW15 |
| 86 H 10 | Putney Pk av SW15 |
| 86 J 10 | Putney Pk la SW15 |
| 14 H 14 | Pyecombe corner N12 |
| 100 L 1 | Pyecroft av Twick |
| 153 Z 6 | Pylbrook rd Sutton |
| 5 U 17 | Pym clo Barnt |
| 109 N 1 | Pymers mead SE21 |
| 17 O 17 | Pymmes clo N13 |
| 18 H 12 | Pymmes Gdns north N9 |
| 18 H 12 | Pymmes Gdns south N9 |
| 16 F 12 | Pymmes Green rd N11 |
| 18 G 13 | Pymmes park N18 |
| 17 O 18 | Pymmes rd N13 |
| 80 R 8 | Pynham clo SE2 |
| 11 O 16 | Pynnacles clo Stanm |
| 49 N 15 | Pyrland rd N5 |
| 85 N 16 | Pyrland rd Rich |
| 108 H 7 | Pyrmont gro SE27 |
| 73 P 16 | Pyrmont rd W4 |
| 54 B 8 | Pyrmont rd Ilf |
| 108 M 16 | Pytchley cres SE19 |
| 91 T 8 | Pytchley rd SE22 |

## Q

| Grid | Name |
|---|---|
| 47 N 16 | Quadrant gro NW5 |
| 84 H 11 | Quadrant rd Rich |
| 122 J 8 | Quadrant rd Thntn Hth |
| 105 S 20 | Quadrant the SW20 |
| 80 K 20 | Quadrant the Bxly Hth |
| 84 J 11 | Quadrant the Rich |
| 94 F 10 | Quaggy wlk SE12 |
| 43 Y 10 | Quainton st NW10 |
| 83 Z 1 | Quaker la Islwth |
| 71 X 19 | Quaker la Islwth |
| 135 N 18 | Quaker st E1 |
| 8 A 19 | Quakers wlk Enf |
| 141 S 3 | Quality ct WC2 |
| 45 O 7 | Quantock gdns NW2 |
| 99 R 3 | Quantock rd Bxly Hth |
| 120 G 14 | Quarr rd Carsh |
| 87 Y 4 | Quarrendon st SW6 |
| 153 U 13 | Quarry Pk rd Sutton |
| 88 E 15 | Quarry rd SW18 |
| 153 U 13 | Quarry ri Sutton |
| 94 E 10 | Quarry wlk SE3 |
| 51 P 12 | Quartermile la E10 |
| 139 P 6 | Quebec ms W1 |
| 36 B 19 | Quebec rd Ilf |
| 54 A 1 | Quebec rd Ilf |

| | | |
|---|---|---|
| 7 O 11 | Ralston st SW3 |
| 0 C 17 | Ram pl E9 |
| 1 T 7 | Rama ct Harrow |
| 0 B 6 | Ramillies av E9 |
| 3 O 9 | Ramillies rd NW7 |
| 3 Y 9 | Ramillies rd W4 |
| 7 P 16 | Ramillies rd Sidcp |
| 0 B 5 | Ramillies rd W1 |
| 5 O 11 | Ramouth rd SE16 |
| 3 W 6 | Rampart st E1 |
| 8 F 9 | Rampayne st SW1 |
| 0 A 10 | Rampton clo E4 |
| 7 Z 12 | Rams gro Rom |
| 2 C 11 | Ramsay rd E7 |
| 3 V 7 | Ramsay rd W3 |
| 9 R 13 | Ramscroft clo N9 |
| 7 R 13 | Ramsdale rd SW17 |
| 8 F 3 | Ramsden dri Rom |
| 5 Z 16 | Ramsden rd N11 |
| 9 P 20 | Ramsden rd E8 |
| 1 Z 20 | Ramsden rd Erith |
| 2 E 13 | Ramsey rd Croy |
| 5 T 16 | Ramsey st E2 |
| 6 H 4 | Ramsey way N14 |
| 9 V 17 | Ramsgate st E8 |
| 6 K 14 | Ramsgil appr Ilf |
| 6 K 14 | Ramsgil dri Ilf |
| 6 F 8 | Rancliffe gdns SE6 |
| 6 F 7 | Rancliffe rd E6 |
| 6 F 7 | Rancliffe rd E6 |
| 4 C 8 | Randall av NW2 |
| 6 F 18 | Randall pl SE10 |
| 9 N 8 | Randall rd SE11 |
| 9 T 18 | Randall rd Rom |
| 9 N 8 | Randall row SE11 |
| 4 L 13 | Randall st E16 |
| 2 L 3 | Randell's rd N1 |
| 2 E 9 | Randle rd Rich |
| 1 R 7 | Randlesdown rd SE6 |
| 3 S 15 | Randolf rd E17 |
| 9 Z 12 | Randolph av W9 |
| 0 C 17 | Randolph av W9 |
| 0 B 17 | Randolph cres W9 |
| 9 X 10 | Randolph gdns NW6 |
| 0 C 19 | Randolph ms W9 |
| 5 Y 18 | Randolph rd E16 |
| 0 C 19 | Randolph rd W9 |
| 0 D 5 | Randolph rd S'hall |
| 2 B 1 | Randolph st NW1 |
| 22 K 7 | Randon clo Harrow |
| 66 G 5 | Ranelagh av SW13 |
| 87 U 7 | Ranelagh av SW6 |
| 12 B 13 | Ranelagh clo Edg |
| 12 B 13 | Ranelagh dri Edg |
| 84 C 12 | Ranelagh dri Twick |
| 34 K 15 | Ranelagh gdns E11 |
| 87 U 8 | Ranelagh gdns SW6 |
| 73 U 18 | Ranelagh gdns W4 |
| 73 U 18 | Ranelagh gdns W4 |
| 53 U 3 | Ranelagh gdns Ilf |
| 47 V 9 | Ranelagh gro SW1 |
| 51 Z 11 | Ranelagh rd E11 |
| 65 O 6 | Ranelagh rd E15 |
| 66 J 4 | Ranelagh rd E6 |
| 62 D 7 | Ranelagh rd NW10 |
| 31 T 10 | Ranelagh rd N17 |
| 30 C 6 | Ranelagh rd N22 |
| 48 C 11 | Ranelagh rd SW1 |
| 72 G 5 | Ranelagh rd W5 |
| 70 A 1 | Ranelagh rd S'hall |
| 42 H 17 | Ranelagh rd Wemb |
| 53 Z 2 | Ranfurly rd Sutton |
| 111 Z 11 | Rangefield rd Brom |
| 112 C 13 | Rangefield rd Brom |
| 31 V 15 | Rangemoor rd N15 |
| 21 R 2 | Rangers rd E4 |
| 93 W 1 | Rangers sq SE10 |
| 142 M 7 | Rangoon st EC3 |
| 81 P 19 | Ranleigh gdns Bxly Hth |
| 89 I 20 | Ranmere st SW12 |
| 23 R 14 | Ranmoor clo Harrow |
| 23 S 13 | Ranmoor gdns Harrow |
| 157 V 7 | Ranmore av Croy |
| 153 O 20 | Ranmore rd Sutton |
| 144 E 16 | Rannoch rd W6 |
| 44 A 1 | Rannock av NW9 |
| 44 A 2 | Rannock av NW9 |
| 77 Y 12 | Ransom rd SE7 |
| 130 K 20 | Ranston st NW1 |
| 45 V 11 | Ranulf rd NW2 |
| 63 X 4 | Ranwell clo E3 |
| 63 X 4 | Ranwell st E3 |
| 99 S 4 | Ranworth clo Erith |
| 19 O 10 | Ranworth rd N9 |
| 39 S 9 | Raphael av Rom |
| 39 T 8 | Raphael park Rom |
| 139 N 19 | Raphael st SW3 |
| 89 T 6 | Rashleigh st SW8 |
| 15 S 9 | Rasper rd N20 |
| 107 X 3 | Rastell av SW2 |
| 52 K 16 | Ratcliff rd E7 |

| | | |
|---|---|---|
| 63 U 18 | Ratcliffe clo E14 |
| 63 T 18 | Ratcliffe cross E1 |
| 63 T 19 | Ratcliffe orchard E1 |
| 63 N 20 | Ratcliffe st E1 |
| 140 E 3 | Rathbone pl W1 |
| 65 O 16 | Rathbone st E16 |
| 140 D 2 | Rathbone st W1 |
| 30 D 15 | Rathcoole av N8 |
| 30 D 15 | Rathcoole gdns N8 |
| 110 M 2 | Rathfern rd SE6 |
| 72 C 4 | Rathgar av W13 |
| 27 V 6 | Rathgar clo N3 |
| 90 J 7 | Rathgar rd SW9 |
| 89 X 16 | Rathmell dri SW4 |
| 77 V 13 | Rathmore rd SE7 |
| 90 F 11 | Rattray rd SW2 |
| 90 F 12 | Rattray rd SW2 |
| 91 X 3 | Raul rd SE15 |
| 47 U 13 | Raveley st NW5 |
| 34 K 6 | Raven rd E18 |
| 143 X 1 | Raven row E1 |
| 63 N 14 | Raven st E1 |
| 106 M 8 | Ravenfield rd SW17 |
| 65 Y 6 | Ravenhill rd E13 |
| 87 P 12 | Ravenna rd SW15 |
| 58 M 9 | Ravenor park Grnfd |
| 59 N 9 | Ravenor Pk rd Grnfd |
| 58 L 9 | Ravenor Pk rd Grnfd |
| 126 C 5 | Ravens clo Brom |
| 8 D 9 | Ravens clo Enf |
| 94 E 12 | Ravens way SE12 |
| 125 Y 1 | Ravensbourne av Brom |
| 111 X 19 | Ravensbourne av Brom |
| 60 A 15 | Ravensbourne gdns W13 |
| 36 A 5 | Ravensbourne gdns Ilf |
| 35 X 4 | Ravensbourne gdns Ilf |
| 93 N 18 | Ravensbourne pk SE6 |
| 92 M 18 | Ravensbourne Pk cres SE6 |
| 92 K 20 | Ravensbourne rd SE6 |
| 126 E 6 | Ravensbourne rd Brom |
| 99 V 7 | Ravensbourne rd Dartford |
| 84 D 14 | Ravensbourne rd Twick |
| 120 D 11 | Ravensbury av Mordn |
| 121 N 4 | Ravensbury clo Mitch |
| 120 F 9 | Ravensbury gro Mitch |
| 120 F 9 | Ravensbury la Mitch |
| 120 F 8 | Ravensbury path Mitch |
| 105 Z 3 | Ravensbury rd SW18 |
| 106 A 3 | Ravensbury rd SW18 |
| 111 Z 10 | Ravenscar rd Brom |
| 74 G 11 | Ravenscourt av W6 |
| 74 F 10 | Ravenscourt gdns W6 |
| 74 G 11 | Ravenscourt pk W6 |
| 74 H 11 | Ravenscourt pl W6 |
| 74 H 11 | Ravenscourt rd W6 |
| 74 F 9 | Ravenscourt sq W6 |
| 16 G 14 | Ravenscraig rd N11 |
| 27 W 20 | Ravenscroft av NW11 |
| 42 L 3 | Ravenscroft av Wemb |
| 45 V 1 | Ravenscroft ave NW11 |
| 65 S 14 | Ravenscroft clo E16 |
| 4 D 13 | Ravenscroft Pk Barnt |
| 4 D 12 | Ravenscroft Pk rd Barnt |
| 65 T 14 | Ravenscroft rd E16 |
| 73 W 11 | Ravenscroft rd W4 |
| 124 F 1 | Ravenscroft rd Becknhm |
| 135 P 10 | Ravenscroft st E2 |
| 15 S 14 | Ravensdale av N12 |
| 31 V 20 | Ravensdale rd N16 |
| 82 B 7 | Ravensdale rd Hounsl |
| 149 U 11 | Ravensdon st SE11 |
| 55 X 12 | Ravensfield clo Dgnhm |
| 152 B 10 | Ravensfield gdns Epsom |
| 45 W 17 | Ravenshaw st NW6 |
| 127 Y 2 | Ravenshill Chisl |
| 26 L 12 | Ravenshurst av NW4 |
| 88 M 19 | Ravenslea rd SW12 |
| 111 X 18 | Ravensmead rd Brom |
| 26 E 19 | Ravenstone rd NW9 |
| 30 E 11 | Ravenstone rd N8 |

| | | |
|---|---|---|
| 107 R 2 | Ravenstone st SW12 |
| 115 Z 1 | Ravenswood Bxly |
| 125 T 20 | Ravenswood av W Wkhm |
| 156 J 6 | Ravenswood clo Croy |
| 40 D 7 | Ravenswood cres Harrow |
| 125 T 19 | Ravenswood cres W Wkhm |
| 103 U 16 | Ravenswood ct Kingst |
| 83 T 1 | Ravenswood gdns Islwth |
| 33 T 14 | Ravenswood rd E17 |
| 89 S 19 | Ravenswood rd SW12 |
| 156 J 6 | Ravenswood rd Croy |
| 62 K 8 | Ravensworth rd NW10 |
| 113 T 8 | Ravensworth rd SE18 |
| 134 J 16 | Ravey st EC2 |
| 79 U 17 | Ravine gro SE18 |
| 87 V 20 | Rawcester clo SW18 |
| 147 N 8 | Rawlings st SW3 |
| 158 K 16 | Rawlins clo S Croy |
| 133 W 12 | Rawstone pl EC1 |
| 133 W 12 | Rawstorne st EC1 |
| 68 A 6 | Ray gdns Bark |
| 11 P 16 | Ray gdns Stanm |
| 21 Z 18 | Ray Lodge rd Wdfd Grn |
| 133 U 18 | Ray st EC1 |
| 4 M 18 | Raydean rd Barnt |
| 47 S 7 | Raydon st N19 |
| 55 S 14 | Raydons gdns Dgnhm |
| 55 Y 15 | Raydons rd Dgnhm |
| 56 A 14 | Raydons rd Dgnhm |
| 127 P 14 | Rayfield clo Brom |
| 94 C 19 | Rayford av SE12 |
| 18 A 10 | Rayleigh clo N13 |
| 117 O 3 | Rayleigh ct Kingst |
| 18 A 10 | Rayleigh rd N13 |
| 17 Z 10 | Rayleigh rd N13 |
| 105 U 20 | Rayleigh rd Wdfd Grn |
| 34 L 1 | Rayleigh rd Wdfd Grn |
| 21 X 20 | Rayleigh rd Wdfd Grn |
| 157 S 14 | Rayleigh ri S Croy |
| 27 N 11 | Raymead NW4 |
| 122 G 11 | Raymead av Thntn Hth |
| 79 T 19 | Raymere gdns SE18 |
| 34 B 9 | Raymond av E18 |
| 71 Z 8 | Raymond av W13 |
| 110 C 11 | Raymond clo SE26 |
| 65 X 2 | Raymond rd E13 |
| 105 T 15 | Raymond rd SW19 |
| 124 H 10 | Raymond rd Becknhm |
| 54 D 2 | Raymond rd Ilf |
| 151 Y 6 | Raymouth rd SE16 |
| 34 C 12 | Rayne ct E18 |
| 40 F 4 | Rayners la Harrow |
| 22 F 20 | Rayners la Pinn |
| 87 R 13 | Rayners rd SW15 |
| 52 L 1 | Raynes av E11 |
| 18 K 18 | Raynham av N18 |
| 18 K 18 | Raynham av N18 |
| 18 K 16 | Raynham av N18 |
| 74 J 10 | Raynham rd W6 |
| 18 K 17 | Raynham terr N18 |
| 70 D 3 | Raynor clo S'hall |
| 40 B 3 | Raynton clo Harrow |
| 19 P 15 | Rays av N18 |
| 19 P 15 | Rays rd N18 |
| 89 T 1 | Rays rd SW8 |
| 50 A 18 | Reading la E8 |
| 49 Z 19 | Reading la E8 |
| 10 L 14 | Reading rd Grnfd |
| 154 D 12 | Reading rd Sutton |
| 75 N 3 | Reardon path E1 |
| 143 X 15 | Reardon path E1 |
| 75 N 2 | Reardon st E1 |
| 143 X 13 | Reardon st E1 |
| 75 R 19 | Reaston st SE14 |
| 75 P 9 | Rebecca ter SE16 |
| 73 Z 14 | Reckitt rd W4 |
| 75 O 15 | Record st SE15 |
| 106 J 12 | Recovery st SW17 |
| 38 L 17 | Recreation av Rom |
| 110 E 9 | Recreation rd SE26 |
| 126 B 3 | Recreation rd Brom |
| 70 A 10 | Recreation rd S'hall |
| 121 Y 8 | Recreation way Mitch |
| 134 A 5 | Rector st N1 |
| 20 B 10 | Rectory clo E4 |
| 27 W 6 | Rectory clo N3 |
| 99 R 11 | Rectory clo Drtfrd |
| 11 O 17 | Rectory clo Stanm |
| 116 C 20 | Rectory clo Surb |

| | | |
|---|---|---|
| 34 K 18 | Rectory cres E11 |
| 77 X 18 | Rectory Field cres SE7 |
| 30 A 12 | Rectory gdns N8 |
| 58 F 2 | Rectory gdns Grnfd |
| 124 N 1 | Rectory grn Becknhm |
| 89 V 7 | Rectory gro SW4 |
| 156 J 4 | Rectory gro Croy |
| 156 J 4 | Rectory gro Croy |
| 100 F 12 | Rectory gro Hampt |
| 107 P 13 | Rectory la SW17 |
| 12 C 17 | Rectory la Edg |
| 115 R 11 | Rectory la Sidcp |
| 115 U 11 | Rectory la Sidcp |
| 11 O 17 | Rectory la Stanm |
| 116 C 20 | Rectory la Surb |
| 155 V 7 | Rectory la Wallgtn |
| 58 B 7 | Rectory park Grnfd |
| 58 D 8 | Rectory Pk av Grnfd |
| 78 J 11 | Rectory pl SE18 |
| 53 U 16 | Rectory rd E12 |
| 33 R 12 | Rectory rd E17 |
| 49 V 9 | Rectory rd N16 |
| 30 A 14 | Rectory rd N8 |
| 86 G 4 | Rectory rd SW13 |
| 73 U 2 | Rectory rd W3 |
| 111 O 20 | Rectory rd Becknhm |
| 124 M 2 | Rectory rd Becknhm |
| 56 F 20 | Rectory rd Dgnhm |
| 70 E 9 | Rectory rd S'hall |
| 153 Z 7 | Rectory rd Sutton |
| 63 T 14 | Rectory sq E1 |
| 75 S 13 | Reculver rd SE16 |
| 142 E 10 | Red Bull yd EC4 |
| 113 Y 13 | Red hill Chisl |
| 121 X 13 | Red Ho rd Croy |
| 97 Y 11 | Red House la Bxly Hth |
| 81 R 17 | Red Leaf clo Blvdr |
| 141 U 5 | Red Lion ct EC4 |
| 28 F 8 | Red Lion hill N2 |
| 78 J 20 | Red Lion la SE18 |
| 95 W 1 | Red Lion la SE18 |
| 95 W 1 | Red Lion pl SE18 |
| 117 O 20 | Red Lion rd Surb |
| 150 D 14 | Red Lion row SE17 |
| 141 N 2 | Red Lion sq WC1 |
| 141 O 2 | Red Lion st WC1 |
| 84 H 13 | Red Lion st Rich |
| 125 V 17 | Red Lodge rd W Wkhm |
| 139 T 8 | Red pl W1 |
| 137 Y 6 | Redan pl W2 |
| 144 G 1 | Redan st W14 |
| 90 K 5 | Redan ter SE5 |
| 140 H 15 | Redanchor clo SW3 |
| 110 C 6 | Redberry gro SE26 |
| 27 Z 4 | Redbourne av N3 |
| 34 L 18 | Redbridge La west E11 |
| 35 N 14 | Redbridge lane S11 |
| 35 S 15 | Redbridge Lane east Ilf |
| 147 N 12 | Redburn st SW3 |
| 40 K 16 | Redcar clo Grnfd |
| 150 A 19 | Redcar st SE5 |
| 53 P 20 | Redcastle clo E1 |
| 135 N 16 | Redchurch st E2 |
| 145 W 14 | Redcliffe clo SW5 |
| 145 Y 10 | Redcliffe gdns SW10 |
| 146 B 14 | Redcliffe gdns SW10 |
| 53 V 3 | Redcliffe gdns Ilf |
| 145 Z 12 | Redcliffe ms SW10 |
| 146 B 15 | Redcliffe pl SW10 |
| 146 C 13 | Redcliffe rd SW10 |
| 145 Z 11 | Redcliffe sq SW10 |
| 145 Z 13 | Redcliffe st SW10 |
| 119 X 12 | Redclose av Mrdn |
| 65 Y 4 | Redclyffe rd E6 |
| 58 M 18 | Redcroft rd S'hall |
| 59 N 18 | Redcroft rd S'hall |
| 142 C 15 | Redcross way SE1 |
| 13 S 12 | Reddings clo NW7 |
| 13 S 11 | Reddings the NW7 |
| 151 R 16 | Reddins rd SE15 |
| 110 G 18 | Reddons rd Becknhm |
| 71 X 19 | Redesdale gdns Islwth |
| 146 M 12 | Redesdale st SW3 |
| 82 G 19 | Redfern av Hounsl |
| 62 B 1 | Redfern rd NW10 |
| 93 U 18 | Redfern rd SE6 |
| 145 W 6 | Redfield la SW5 |
| 122 D 9 | Redford av Thntn Hth |
| 155 Z 14 | Redford av Wallgtn |
| 87 P 9 | Redgrave rd SW15 |
| 25 U 8 | Redhill dri Edg |
| 131 Y 11 | Redhill st NW1 |
| 157 R 20 | Redhill clo S Croy |
| 46 B 11 | Redington gdns NW3 |
| 46 A 10 | Redington rd NW3 |
| 9 N 4 | Redlands rd Enf |

28 M 9 Ringwood av N2
22 B 16 Ringwood av Croy
04 G 3 Ringwood gdns SW15
32 K 18 Ringwood rd E17
17 V 4 Ringwood way N21
00 H 10 Ringwood way Hampt
9 U 15 Ripley clo Croy
85 Z 7 Ripley gdns SW14
54 C 8 Ripley gdns Sutton
65 Y 17 Ripley rd E16
81 P 10 Ripley rd Blvdr
7 Y 4 Ripley rd Enf
00 G 18 Ripley rd Hampt
54 J 8 Ripley rd Ilf
35 P 20 Ripon gdns Ilf
31 O 12 Ripon rd N17
19 N 4 Ripon rd N9
78 L 17 Ripon rd SE18
9 N 3 Rippersley rd Welling
67 P 2 Ripple rd Bark
68 C 4 Ripple rd Bark
69 N 5 Ripple rd Dgnhm
33 R 2 Ripple Vale gro N1
79 X 13 Rippolson rd SE18
40 J 16 Rippon clo Grnfd
81 N 20 Rippoth rd E3
64 A 1 Rippoth rd E3
18 H 17 Risborough dri Worc Pk
41 Z 16 Risborough st SE1
55 P 7 Risdon st SE16
39 U 2 Rise park Rom
39 S 5 Rise Park rd Rom
39 P 7 Rise Park pl Rom
34 D 15 Rise the E11
13 S 20 Rise the NW10
13 S 20 Rise the NW7
17 V 15 Rise the N13
99 U 11 Rise the Drtfrd
12 E 15 Rise the Edg
41 Y 15 Rise the Grnfd
58 C 20 Rise the S Croy
57 T 19 Rise the Sidcp
39 U 6 Risebridge rd Rom
98 J 6 Risedale rd Bxly Hth
50 K 18 Riseholme clo E9
92 H 17 Riseldine rd SE23
41 Y 1 Rising Sun ct EC1
133 R 8 Risinghill st N1
23 T 6 Risingholme clo Harrow
23 T 6 Risingholme rd Harrow
33 X 13 Risings the E17
30 M 5 Risley av N17
31 O 5 Risley av N17
148 M 16 Rita rd SW8
149 N 17 Rita rd SW8
30 L 16 Ritches rd N15
124 A 15 Ritchie rd Croy
133 T 7 Ritchie st N1
32 H 12 Ritchings av E17
107 P 4 Ritherdon rd SW17
49 W 17 Ritson rd E8
50 C 18 Rivaz pl E9
34 B 13 Rivenhall gdns E18
17 V 9 River av N13
17 Y 3 River bank N21
34 L 18 River clo E11
8 C 12 River front Enf
55 O 5 River gdns Carsh
124 M 1 River Gro pk Becknhm
102 H 1 River la Rich
84 H 20 River la Twick
100 J 6 River Meads av Felt
30 D 7 River Park rd N22
111 X 17 River Pk gdns Brom
133 Z 1 River pl N 1
67 Y 14 River rd Bark
68 B 14 River rd Bark
102 E 14 River reach Tedd
133 T 12 River st EC1
74 L 14 River ter W6
34 B 11 River ter W6
101 W 5 River View gdns Twick
77 O 7 River way SE10
152 A 14 River way Epsom
100 J 5 River way Twick
74 H 12 Rivercourt rd W6
84 E 14 Riverdale gdns Twick
79 W 14 Riverdale rd SE18
79 W 13 Riverdale rd SE18
97 Z 17 Riverdale rd Bxly
98 A 17 Riverdale rd Bxly
81 W 14 Riverdale rd Erith
100 C 9 Riverdale rd Twick
84 E 15 Riverdale rd Twick
12 J 12 Riverdene Edg

48 K 10 Riversdale rd N5
38 F 2 Riversdale rd Rom
8 E 11 Riversfield rd Enf
44 J 1 Riverside NW4
77 V 8 Riverside SE7
102 A 1 Riverside Twick
59 U 12 Riverside clo W7
116 G 8 Riverside clo Kingst
155 R 6 Riverside clo Wallgtn
86 B 1 Riverside dri W4
120 J 11 Riverside dri Mitch
102 C 4 Riverside dri Rich
74 J 12 Riverside gdns W6
8 A 10 Riverside gdns Enf
60 K 6 Riverside gdns Wemb
64 H 7 Riverside rd E15
31 Y 18 Riverside rd N15
106 D 8 Riverside rd SW17
115 Z 5 Riverside rd Sidcp
97 W 19 Riverside walk Bxly Hth
14 K 13 Riverside wlk N12
83 U 7 Riverside wlk Islwth
144 A 14 Riverview gdns SW13
74 K 16 Riverview gdns SW19
73 T 18 Riverview gro W4
111 N 3 Riverview pk SE6
73 T 18 Riverview pk W4
17 U 14 Riverway N13
35 N 6 Rivington av Wdfd Grn
134 K 14 Rivington pl EC2
134 L 14 Rivington st EC2
31 N 2 Rivulet rd N17
30 K 2 Rivulet rd N17
39 S 5 Rix Park rd Rom
53 R 15 Rixsen rd E12
64 B 1 Roach rd E3
51 O 20 Roach rd E3
48 B 6 Roads pl N4
76 F 18 Roan st SE10
10 M 19 Robb rd Stanm
125 V 2 Robbins ct Becknhm
139 T 4 Robert Adam st W1
130 D 18 Robert clo W9
78 K 4 Robert st E16
132 A 13 Robert st NW1
131 Y 13 Robert st NW1
79 R 11 Robert st SE18
140 L 11 Robert st WC2
72 G 7 Robert's all W6
133 U 16 Robert's pl EC1
135 T 18 Roberta st E2
126 L 1 Roberton dri Brom
39 Z 4 Roberts clo Rom
147 T 2 Roberts ms SW1
33 R 4 Roberts rd E17
61 T 14 Roberts rd Blvdr
120 E 18 Robertsbridge rd Carsh
64 H 3 Robertson rd E15
80 S 6 Robertson st SW8
38 M 1 Robin clo Rom
38 M 2 Robin clo Rom
142 C 5 Robin ct EC2
47 O 6 Robin gro N6
72 D 17 Robin gro Brentf
26 O 19 Robin gro Harrow
121 V 7 Robin Hood clo Mitch
23 V 3 Robin Hood dri Harrow
64 G 19 Robin Hood la E14
104 A 11 Robin Hood la SW15
97 Z 12 Robin Hood la Bxly Hth
121 W 7 Robin Hood la Mitch
153 Y 11 Robin Hood la Sutton
154 A 11 Robin Hood la Sutton
104 C 11 Robin Hood rd SW15/SW19
104 A 8 Robin Hood way SW15
41 X 17 Robin Hood way Grnfd
141 U 2 Robin Hood yd EC1
97 N 10 Robina clo Bxly Hth
112 K 7 Robins ct SE12
63 P 6 Robinson rd E2
106 K 16 Robinson rd SW17
56 D 11 Robinson rd Dgnhm
147 N 13 Robinson st SW3
90 E 4 Robsart st SW9
62 H 1 Robson av NW10
7 V 9 Robson clo Enf
108 K 7 Robson rd SE27
25 N 6 Roch av Edg
51 N 1 Rochdale rd SE2
80 B 13 Rochdale rd SE2
122 B 1 Roche rd SW16

120 F 15 Roche wlk Carsh
135 N 14 Rochelle st E2
65 X 4 Rochester av E13
126 J 4 Rochester av Brom
94 K 7 Rochester clo SE3
8 F 7 Rochester clo Enf
97 P 15 Rochester clo Sidcp
157 T 5 Rochester gdns Croy
53 T 2 Rochester gdns Ilf
47 V 19 Rochester ms NW1
47 U 19 Rochester pl NW1
47 U 19 Rochester rd NW1
155 N 8 Rochester rd Carsh
148 C 5 Rochester row SW1
47 W 20 Rochester sq NW1
148 E 4 Rochester st SW1
47 U 19 Rochester ter NW1
94 H 1 Rochester way SE3
94 K 6 Rochester way SE3
96 C 9 Rochester way SE9
95 V 8 Rochester way SE9
99 O 19 Rochester way Bxly
37 T 14 Rochford av Rom
121 Z 5 Rochford way Croy
85 Z 8 Rock av SW14
56 G 15 Rock gdns Dgnhm
151 U 4 Rock gro SF16
100 U 10 Rock hill SE26
48 G 7 Rock st N4
110 E 2 Rockburn rd SE23
92 A 17 Rockell's pl SE22
45 O 13 Rockhall rd NW2
108 F 10 Rockhampton clo SE27
108 F 9 Rockhampton rd SE27
157 R 14 Rockhampton rd S Croy
39 Z 20 Rockingham av Hornch
150 B 2 Rockingham st SE1
24 C 8 Rocklands dri Stanm
136 F 18 Rockley rd W14
63 U 3 Rockmead rd E9
79 Y 13 Rockmount rd SE18
86 G 8 Rocks la SW13
59 S 2 Rockware av Grnfd
56 G 15 Rockwell rd Dgnhm
136 C 17 Rockwood pl W12
133 Y 9 Rocliffe st W2
45 W 4 Rodborough rd NW11
123 R 16 Rodenhurst gdns SE26
48 C 11 Roden st N7
53 Y 9 Roden st Ilf
53 X 9 Roden way Ilf
89 Y 14 Rodenhurst rd SW4
46 M 11 Roderick rd NW3
66 M 1 Roding av Bark
34 M 13 Roding la Ilf
35 O 8 Roding la North Wdfd Grn
35 N 14 Roding la South Ilf
35 N 12 Roding lane South Ilf
50 G 13 Roding rd E5
21 Y 19 Rodings the Wdfd Grn
139 R 2 Rodmarton clo W 1
14 H 15 Rodmell slope N12
14 H 15 Rodmell slope N12
77 O 14 Rodmere st SE10
90 A 20 Rodmill la SW2
32 J 7 Rodney pl E17
150 C 5 Rodney pl SE17
106 C 20 Rodney pl SW19
34 G 13 Rodney rd E11
150 F 7 Rodney rd SE17
120 I 15 Rodney rd Mitch
118 A 10 Rodney rd New Mald
133 P 8 Rodney st N1
38 F 6 Rodney way Rom
86 G 18 Rodway rd SW15
112 H 19 Rodway rd Brom
91 V 14 Rodwell rd SE22
25 V 12 Roe end NW9
25 T 12 Roe la NW9
156 B 14 Roe wy Croy
78 J 4 Roebourne way E16
78 J 4 Roebourne way E16
18 H 20 Roebuck clo N17
21 Y 4 Roebuck la Buck Hl
9 O 4 Roedean av Enf
9 O 4 Roedean clo Enf
86 A 14 Roedean cres SW15
86 G 11 Roehampton clo SW15
86 B 15 Roehampton ga SW15
86 H 18 Roehampton High st SW15
86 F 11 Roehampton la SW15

104 C 6 Roehampton vale SW15
76 F 6 Roffey st E14
133 O 18 Roger st WC1
56 F 15 Rogers gdns Dgnhm
65 R 17 Rogers rd E16
106 H 9 Rogers rd SW17
56 F 17 Rogers rd Dgnhm
110 E 1 Rojack rd SE23
34 F 4 Rokeby gdns Wdfd Grn
92 L 3 Rokeby rd SE4
64 L 3 Rokeby st E15
96 F 4 Rokesby clo Welling
30 A 15 Rokesly av N8
146 C 9 Roland gdns SW7
33 W 14 Roland rd E17
146 C 9 Roland way SW7
37 X 12 Roles gro Rom
5 X 15 Rolfe clo Barnt
78 D 11 Rolfe rd SE7
35 W 16 Roll gdns Ilf
127 Z 15 Rolleston av Brom
127 Z 16 Rolleston clo Orp
157 O 17 Rolleston rd S Croy
75 R 16 Rollins st SE15
48 E 14 Rollit st N7
87 H 13 Rollit cres Hounsl
141 S 5 Rolls bldgs EC4
20 C 18 Rolls Park av E4
20 D 17 Rolls Park rd E4
141 S 4 Rolls pas EC4
151 R 9 Rolls rd SE1
90 L 13 Rollscourt av SE24
75 X 15 Rolt st SE8
57 S 2 Rom cres Rom
32 J 10 Roma rd E17
63 U 7 Roman rd E3
66 E 12 Roman rd E6
29 R 2 Roman rd N10
74 C 10 Roman rd W4
54 A 17 Roman rd Ilf
53 Z 17 Roman rd Ilf
109 P 14 Roman ri SE19
48 C 19 Roman way N7
126 A 10 Romanhurst av Brom
125 Z 9 Romanhurst av Brom
125 Y 9 Romanhurst gdns Brom
119 X 18 Romany gdns Sutton
107 O 7 Romberg rd SW17
93 T 13 Romborough gdns SE13
93 U 9 Romer av SE13
108 D 7 Romeyn rd SW16
53 U 11 Romford rd E12
51 Z 19 Romford rd E15
52 K 10 Romford rd E7
37 Z 1 Romford rd Rom
143 U 3 Romford st E1
48 H 8 Romilly rd N4
140 G 7 Romilly st W1
109 N 8 Rommany rd SE27
46 B 4 Romney clo NW11
31 Z 4 Romney clo N17
40 J 1 Romney clo Harrow
40 J 1 Romney dri Harrow
22 H 20 Romney dri Harrow
98 C 1 Romney gdns Bxly Hth
76 J 17 Romney rd SE10
68 J 3 Romney rd Dgnhm
117 Y 15 Romney rd New Mald
148 H 3 Romney st SW1
108 H 1 Romola rd SE21
68 J 2 Romsey gdns Dgnhm
47 N 13 Rona rd NW3
10 K 13 Ronald av E15
124 M 10 Ronald clo Becknhm
63 R 18 Ronald st E1
48 G 15 Ronalds rd N5
112 F 20 Ronalds rd Brom
96 J 15 Ronaldstone rd Sidcp
45 S 14 Rondu rd NW2
57 S 3 Roneo corner Hornch
94 D 20 Ronver st SE12
142 J 9 Rood la EC3
26 D 15 Rookery clo NW9
69 V 1 Rookery cres Dgnhm
127 M 14 Rookery la Brom
89 U 11 Rookery rd SW4
26 C 16 Rookery way NW9
29 U 12 Rookfield av N10
106 L 13 Rookstone rd SW17
118 F 9 Rookwood av New Mald
155 X 8 Rookwood av Wallgtn
21 O 7 Rookwood gdns E4
37 O 1 Rookwood gdns Ilf
31 W 20 Rookwood rd N16

| | | |
|---|---|---|
| 78 L8 | Rope Yd rails SE18 | |
| 142 F1 | Ropemaker st EC2 | |
| 63 X20 | Ropemakers fields E14 | |
| 95 V14 | Roper st SE9 | |
| 121 P2 | Roper way Mitch | |
| 20 G17 | Ropers av E4 | |
| 63 Y12 | Ropery st E3 | |
| 98 F12 | Rosalind cres Bxly Hth | |
| 144 L19 | Rosaline rd SW6 | |
| 109 Z8 | Rosamund st SE26 | |
| 82 B5 | Rosary clo Hounsl | |
| 146 C8 | Rosary gdns SW7 | |
| 145 O19 | Rosaville rd SW6 | |
| 134 C18 | Roscoe st EC1 | |
| 142 B12 | Rose all SE1 | |
| 142 A5 | Rose And Crown ct EC2 | |
| 83 Y2 | Rose And Crown pas Islwth | |
| 140 C13 | Rose And Crown yd SW1 | |
| 34 J7 | Rose av E18 | |
| 34 J7 | Rose av E18 | |
| 120 M1 | Rose av Mitch | |
| 106 M20 | Rose av Mitch | |
| 120 D11 | Rose av Mordn | |
| 32 L11 | Rose Bank gro E17 | |
| 109 Z17 | Rose Bank st SE20 | |
| 72 H8 | Rose gdns W5 | |
| 58 H11 | Rose gdns Shall | |
| 25 X12 | Rose glen NW9 | |
| 57 P4 | Rose glen Rom | |
| 37 W10 | Rose Hatch av Rom | |
| 154 B2 | Rose hill Sutton | |
| 144 B20 | Rose hill Sutton | |
| 37 Z12 | Rose la Rom | |
| 10 A6 | Rose lawn Bushey Watf | |
| 140 J8 | Rose st WC2 | |
| 117 T10 | Rose wlk Surb | |
| 159 W2 | Rose wlk W Wkhm | |
| 60 A13 | Roseacre cl W13 | |
| 97 S9 | Roseacre rd Welling | |
| 41 V13 | Rosebank av Wemb | |
| 33 P19 | Rosebank rd E17 | |
| 63 X6 | Rosebank rd E3 | |
| 71 U6 | Rosebank rd W7 | |
| 33 O14 | Rosebank wlk E17 | |
| 61 X16 | Rosebank way W3 | |
| 133 T14 | Roseberry av EC1 | |
| 53 R18 | Roseberry av E12 | |
| 118 C5 | Roseberry av New Mald | |
| 96 H18 | Roseberry av Sidcp | |
| 30 J18 | Roseberry gdns N4 | |
| 29 U7 | Roseberry rd N10 | |
| 29 U8 | Roseberry rd N10 | |
| 18 K10 | Roseberry rd N9 | |
| 151 W7 | Roseberry rd SE16 | |
| 90 A16 | Roseberry rd SW2 | |
| 89 Z16 | Roseberry rd SW2 | |
| 83 O13 | Roseberry rd Hounsl | |
| 117 S4 | Roseberry rd Kingst | |
| 151 W7 | Roseberry st SE16 | |
| 31 Z7 | Rosebery av N17 | |
| 40 C11 | Rosebery av Harrow | |
| 40 C11 | Rosebery av Harrow | |
| 118 C5 | Rosebery av New Mald | |
| 118 C5 | Rosebery av New Mald | |
| 122 M3 | Rosebery av Thntn Hth | |
| 119 O15 | Rosebery clo Mrdn | |
| 30 A16 | Rosebery gdns N8 | |
| 59 Z19 | Rosebery gdns W13 | |
| 154 B8 | Rosebery gdns Sutton | |
| 49 U19 | Rosebery pl E8 | |
| 18 J10 | Rosebery rd N9 | |
| 153 V14 | Rosebery rd Sutton | |
| 83 R19 | Rosebine av Twick | |
| 88 B6 | Rosebury rd SW6 | |
| 122 C15 | Rosecourt rd Croy | |
| 45 Z10 | Rosecroft gdns NW3 | |
| 44 G10 | Rosecroft gdns NW2 | |
| 83 R20 | Rosecroft gdns Twick | |
| 58 H12 | Rosecroft rd S'hall | |
| 80 C12 | Rosedale clo SE2 | |
| 71 V6 | Rosedale clo W7 | |
| 11 O20 | Rosedale clo Stanm | |
| 68 C1 | Rosedale gdns Dag | |
| 52 L16 | Rosedale rd E7 | |
| 68 C1 | Rosedale rd Daghm | |
| 152 G10 | Rosedale rd Epsom | |
| 84 J9 | Rosedale rd Rich | |
| 38 L10 | Rosedale rd Rom | |
| 74 J9 | Rosedale ter W6 | |
| 108 D7 | Rosedene av SW16 | |
| 122 B17 | Rosedene av SW16 | |
| 58 H8 | Rosedene av Grnfd | |
| 111 Y12 | Rosedene av Mrdn | |
| 35 X12 | Rosedene gdns Ilf | |
| 51 R7 | Rosedene ter E10 | |
| 144 F14 | Rosedew rd W14 | |
| 144 F14 | Rosedew rd W6 | |
| 64 A19 | Rosefield gdns E14 | |
| 11 Y18 | Rosegarden clo Edg | |
| 82 E12 | Roseheath rd Hounsl | |
| 41 W15 | Rosehill gdns Grnfd | |
| 154 C1 | Rosehill gdns Sutton | |
| 154 A1 | Rosehill park Sutton | |
| 154 C1 | Rosehill pk W Sutton | |
| 88 C15 | Rosehill rd SW18 | |
| 120 C19 | Rosehillav Sutton | |
| 48 J13 | Roseleigh av N5 | |
| 84 F17 | Roselieu clo Twick | |
| 28 B8 | Rosemary av N3 | |
| 18 M6 | Rosemary av N9 | |
| 19 N7 | Rosemary av N9 | |
| 8 D5 | Rosemary av Enf | |
| 82 A6 | Rosemary av Hounsl | |
| 39 T10 | Rosemary av Rom | |
| 35 O16 | Rosemary dri Ilf | |
| 56 B4 | Rosemary gdns Dgnhm | |
| 85 W7 | Rosemary la SW14 | |
| 151 O18 | Rosemary rd SE15 | |
| 150 M19 | Rosemary rd SE15 | |
| 96 L2 | Rosemary rd Welling | |
| 134 F4 | Rosemary st N1 | |
| 121 V4 | Rosemead av Mitch | |
| 42 L16 | Rosemead av Wemb | |
| 15 R19 | Rosemont av N12 | |
| 46 C17 | Rosemont rd NW3 | |
| 73 T1 | Rosemont rd W3 | |
| 61 S20 | Rosemont rd W3 | |
| 117 V6 | Rosemont rd New Mald | |
| 84 L16 | Rosemont rd Rich | |
| 147 N6 | Rosemoor st SW3 | |
| 127 U8 | Rosemount dri Brom | |
| 59 Z16 | Rosemount rd W13 | |
| 12 F11 | Rosen's wlk Edg | |
| 88 K1 | Rosenau rd SW11 | |
| 90 K19 | Rosendale rd SE21 | |
| 108 M1 | Rosendale rd SE21 | |
| 17 V5 | Roseneath av N21 | |
| 89 O15 | Roseneath rd SW11 | |
| 8 C14 | Roseneath wlk Enf | |
| 93 S17 | Rosenthal rd SE6 | |
| 92 E13 | Rosenthorpe rd SE15 | |
| 76 G6 | Roserton st E14 | |
| 124 E14 | Rosery the Croy | |
| 148 K18 | Rosetta st SW8 | |
| 112 L9 | Roseveare rd SE12 | |
| 82 G13 | Roseville av Hounsl | |
| 118 M1 | Rosevine rd SW20 | |
| 91 P7 | Roseway SE21 | |
| 91 X2 | Rosewell av SE15 | |
| 41 Y17 | Rosewood av Grnfd | |
| 57 X15 | Rosewood av Hornch | |
| 93 T4 | Rosewood gdns SE13 | |
| 155 U13 | Rosewood gdns Wallgtn | |
| 154 E2 | Rosewood gro Sutton | |
| 50 E16 | Rosina st E9 | |
| 87 O7 | Roskell rd SW15 | |
| 112 F14 | Roslin way Brom | |
| 120 F3 | Roslyn clo Mitch | |
| 39 S7 | Roslyn gdns Rom | |
| 31 P15 | Roslyn rd N15 | |
| 136 M9 | Rosmead rd W11 | |
| 88 K2 | Rosnau rd SW11 | |
| 133 T16 | Rosoman pl EC1 | |
| 133 U15 | Rosoman st EC1 | |
| 56 A5 | Ross av Dgnhm | |
| 23 N1 | Ross clo Harrow | |
| 155 T12 | Ross pde Wallgtn | |
| 64 H5 | Ross rd E15 | |
| 123 S4 | Ross rd SE25 | |
| 99 V17 | Ross rd Drtfrd | |
| 100 L2 | Ross rd Twick | |
| 155 V12 | Ross rd Wallgtn | |
| 95 R7 | Ross way SE9 | |
| 39 W19 | Rossall clo Hornch | |
| 60 M9 | Rossall cres Wemb | |
| 154 K9 | Rossdale Sutton | |
| 19 O2 | Rossdale dr N9 | |
| 43 U14 | Rossdale dri NW9 | |
| 9 O20 | Rossdale dri Enf | |
| 87 N9 | Rossdale rd SW15 | |
| 94 G1 | Rosse ms SE3 | |
| 82 H12 | Rossindel rd Hounsl | |
| 49 Y6 | Rossington st E5 | |
| 107 T1 | Rossiter rd SW12 | |
| 21 O8 | Rosslyn av E4 | |
| 86 C8 | Rosslyn av SW13 | |
| 15 W1 | Rosslyn av Barnt | |
| 56 D2 | Rosslyn av Dgnhm | |
| 23 W14 | Rosslyn cres Harrow | |
| 42 J12 | Rosslyn cres Wemb | |
| 46 H14 | Rosslyn hill NW3 | |
| 33 U14 | Rosslyn rd E17 | |
| 67 S1 | Rosslyn rd Bark | |
| 54 F20 | Rosslyn rd Bark | |
| 84 D16 | Rosslyn rd Twick | |
| 130 L17 | Rossmore rd NW1 | |
| 131 N16 | Rossmore rd NW1 | |
| 106 G10 | Rostella rd SW17 | |
| 31 V19 | Rostrevor av N15 | |
| 70 C14 | Rostrevor gdns S'hall | |
| 105 X13 | Rostrevor rd SW19 | |
| 87 U2 | Rostrevor rd SW6 | |
| 141 X20 | Rotary st SE1 | |
| 71 Z20 | Rothbury gdns Islwth | |
| 50 M20 | Rothbury rd E9 | |
| 9 T1 | Rotherfield rd Carsh | |
| 155 P10 | Rotherfield rd Carsh | |
| 9 T1 | Rotherfield st N1 | |
| 134 B1 | Rotherfield st N1 | |
| 107 Y16 | Rotherhill av Enf | |
| 75 R11 | Rotherhithe New rd SE16 | |
| 151 V11 | Rotherhithe New rd SE16 | |
| 75 S10 | Rotherhithe Old rd SE16 | |
| 75 T2 | Rotherhithe st SE16 | |
| 143 X18 | Rotherhithe st SE16 | |
| 75 S1 | Rotherhithe tunnel E1 | |
| 156 E12 | Rothermere rd Croy | |
| 61 O13 | Rotherwick hill W5 | |
| 45 X2 | Rotherwick rd NW11 | |
| 87 O7 | Rotherwood rd SW15 | |
| 133 X4 | Rothery st N1 | |
| 123 P9 | Rothesay av SE25 | |
| 119 T2 | Rothesay av SW20 | |
| 41 O18 | Rothesay av Grnfd | |
| 85 S9 | Rothesay av Rich | |
| 52 L19 | Rothesay rd E7 | |
| 150 H2 | Rothsay st SE1 | |
| 73 V9 | Rothschild rd W4 | |
| 108 K10 | Rothschild st SE27 | |
| 68 G2 | Rothwell gdns Dgnhm | |
| 68 G3 | Rothwell rd Dgnhm | |
| 131 R3 | Rothwell st NW1 | |
| 89 N1 | Rotten row SW11 | |
| 78 E14 | Rotunda clo SE18 | |
| 151 S5 | Rouel rd SE16 | |
| 119 X15 | Rougemont av Mrdn | |
| 124 G17 | Round gro Croy | |
| 110 B6 | Round hill SE26 | |
| 105 P3 | Roundacre SW19 | |
| 89 U5 | Roundell st SW8 | |
| 110 E5 | Roundhay clo SE23 | |
| 7 P15 | Roundhill dri Enf | |
| 112 D6 | Roundtable rd Brom | |
| 31 P4 | Roundway EN17 | |
| 30 L7 | Roundway WN17 | |
| 35 T6 | Roundway rd Ilf | |
| 62 F2 | Roundwood park NW10 | |
| 62 G3 | Roundwood Pk av NW10 | |
| 44 C19 | Roundwood rd NW10 | |
| 64 B11 | Rounton rd E3 | |
| 90 E20 | Roupell rd SW2 | |
| 108 D1 | Roupell rd SW2 | |
| 141 U15 | Roupell st SE1 | |
| 133 B1 | Rousden st NW1 | |
| 109 R9 | Rouse gdns SE21 | |
| 88 J19 | Routh rd SW18 | |
| 144 K19 | Rowallan rd SW6 | |
| 19 Z19 | Rowan av E4 | |
| 121 V1 | Rowan clo SW16 | |
| 121 V1 | Rowan cres SW16 | |
| 121 V2 | Rowan rd SW16 | |
| 144 F6 | Rowan rd W6 | |
| 72 B20 | Rowan rd Brentf | |
| 97 Z8 | Rowan rd Bxly Hth | |
| 98 A8 | Rowan rd Bxly Hth | |
| 144 F6 | Rowan ter W6 | |
| 37 U11 | Rowan way Rom | |
| 28 E17 | Rowan wlk N2 | |
| 17 X11 | Rowans the N13 | |
| 18 B4 | Rowantree clo N21 | |
| 7 W9 | Rowantree rd N20 | |
| 18 B4 | Rowantree rd N21 | |
| 15 N5 | Rowben clo N20 | |
| 151 O9 | Rowcross st SE1 | |
| 58 H2 | Rowdell rd Grnfd | |
| 20 C20 | Rowden rd E4 | |
| 110 K20 | Rowden rd Becknhm | |
| 89 N4 | Rowditch la SW11 | |
| 44 K20 | Rowdon av NW10 | |
| 159 Z20 | Rowdown cres Croy | |
| 69 O1 | Rowdown rd Dgnhm | |
| 67 Z7 | Rowe gdns Bark | |
| 40 G9 | Rowe wlk Harrow | |
| 88 J5 | Rowena cres SW11 | |
| 107 O2 | Rowfant rd SW17 | |
| 50 H12 | Rowhill rd E5 | |
| 129 X19 | Rowington clo W2 | |
| 24 E11 | Rowland av Harrow | |
| 110 A8 | Rowland gro SE26 | |
| 46 J14 | Rowland Hill st NW | |
| 18 A20 | Rowland hillav N12 | |
| 135 T20 | Rowland st E1 | |
| 56 B8 | Rowlands rd Dgnh | |
| 22 J1 | Rowlands rd Pinn | |
| 97 P19 | Rowley av Sidcp | |
| 43 N20 | Rowley clo Wemb | |
| 61 N1 | Rowley clo Wemb | |
| 48 K1 | Rowley gdns N4 | |
| 30 L16 | Rowley rd N15 | |
| 117 O5 | Rowlls rd Kingst | |
| 55 S18 | Rowney gdns Dgnhm | |
| 55 R18 | Rowney rd Dgnhm | |
| 101 S1 | Rowntree rd Twick | |
| 26 L9 | Rowsley av NW4 | |
| 47 Z16 | Rowstock gdns N7 | |
| 79 P18 | Rowton rd SE18 | |
| 41 S1 | Roxborough av Harrow | |
| 71 W19 | Roxborough av Islwth | |
| 41 T2 | Roxborough pk Harrow | |
| 23 S20 | Roxborough pk Harrow | |
| 40 A4 | Roxbourne park Ro | |
| 108 H11 | Roxburgh rd SE27 | |
| 145 O12 | Roxby pl SW6 | |
| 40 L7 | Roxeth Green av Harrow | |
| 40 L12 | Roxeth gro Harrow | |
| 41 R6 | Roxeth hill Harrow | |
| 93 S16 | Roxley rd SE13 | |
| 159 N12 | Roxton gdns Croy | |
| 74 G5 | Roxwell rd W12 | |
| 68 B7 | Roxwell rd Bark | |
| 34 M1 | Roxwell way Wdfd Grn | |
| 37 S20 | Roxy av Rom | |
| 36 J14 | Roy gdns Ilf | |
| 100 K14 | Roy gro Hampt | |
| 140 B11 | Royal academy W1 | |
| 138 E20 | Royal Albert hall SW7 | |
| 81 U12 | Royal Alfred home Blvdr | |
| 140 A11 | Royal arcade W1 | |
| 147 O10 | Royal av SW3 | |
| 152 B3 | Royal av Worc Pk | |
| 84 K5 | Royal Botanic gardens Rich | |
| 108 H7 | Royal cir SE27 | |
| 132 C3 | Royal College st NW1 | |
| 47 U20 | Royal College st NW1 | |
| 136 J15 | Royal cres W11 | |
| 40 A11 | Royal cres Ruis | |
| 136 H15 | Royal Cres ms W11 | |
| 136 H15 | Royal Cres ms W11 | |
| 142 G6 | Royal Exch bldgs EC2 | |
| 142 G6 | Royal Exchange bldgs EC2 | |
| 141 O14 | Royal Festival hall SE1 | |
| 76 G19 | Royal hill SE10 | |
| 147 P12 | Royal Hospital rd SW3 | |
| 78 F14 | Royal Military repository SE18 | |
| 143 P9 | Royal mint EC3 | |
| 143 P9 | Royal Mint st E1 | |
| 76 H16 | Royal Naval college SE10 | |
| 49 Y18 | Royal Oak rd E8 | |
| 98 C12 | Royal Oak rd Bxly Hth | |
| 76 K19 | Royal observatory SE10 | |
| 140 F13 | Royal Opera arcade SW4 | |
| 94 B5 | Royal pde SE3 | |
| 60 K10 | Royal pde W5 | |
| 114 C19 | Royal pde Chisl | |
| 76 G20 | Royal pl SE10 | |
| 66 A19 | Royal rd E16 | |
| 65 Z18 | Royal rd E16 | |
| 149 N14 | Royal rd SE17 | |
| 115 W6 | Royal rd Sidcp | |
| 101 R11 | Royal rd Tedd | |
| 141 R20 | Royal st SE1 | |
| 63 T6 | Royal Victor pl E3 | |
| 67 X7 | Roycraft av Bark | |
| 67 X6 | Roycraft clo Bark | |
| 67 Y6 | Roycraft gdns Bark | |
| 34 H5 | Roycroft clo E18 | |
| 79 U14 | Roydene rd SE18 | |

| | | | |
|---|---|---|---|
| Y 12 | Royle cres W13 | 50 E 12 | Rushmore cres E5 |
| C 17 | Royston av E4 | 50 C 12 | Rushmore rd E5 |
| G 5 | Royston av Sutton | 56 E 9 | Rusholme av Dgnhm |
| Y 8 | Royston av Wallgtn | 87 R 17 | Rusholme rd SW15 |
| N 19 | Royston gdns Ilf | 24 A 19 | Rushout av Harrow |
| F 5 | Royston park Sutton | 134 G 8 | Rushton st N1 |
| F 1 | Royston rd SE20 | 26 G 11 | Rushworth av NW4 |
| F 20 | Royston rd Becknhm | 141 Y 18 | Rushworth st SE1 |
| S 16 | Royston rd Drtfrd | 53 T 17 | Ruskin av E12 |
| L 14 | Royston rd Rich | 73 R 20 | Ruskin av Rich |
| P 7 | Royston st E2 | 97 N 6 | Ruskin av Welling |
| S 11 | Roystons the Surb | 28 A 18 | Ruskin clo NW11 |
| U 6 | Rozel rd SW4 | 97 N 6 | Ruskin dri Welling |
| M 5 | Rubens st SE6 | 152 L 2 | Ruskin dri Worc Pk |
| Y 11 | Ruberoid rd Enf | 60 F 11 | Ruskin gdns W5 |
| O 10 | Ruby rd E17 | 25 N 13 | Ruskin gdns Harrow |
| W 15 | Ruby st SE15 | 39 Y 4 | Ruskin gdns Rom |
| S 10 | Ruckholt rd E10 | 97 N 6 | Ruskin gro Welling |
| P 12 | Ruckholt rd E10 | 31 U 4 | Ruskin rd N17 |
| E 6 | Rucklidge av NW10 | 81 R 11 | Ruskin rd Blvdr |
| F 12 | Rudall cres NW3 | 155 O 11 | Ruskin rd Carsh |
| N 11 | Rudd st SE18 | 83 V 8 | Ruskin rd Islwth |
| W 19 | Ruddigore rd SE14 | 58 A 20 | Ruskin rd S'hall |
| H 8 | Rudland rd Bxly Hth | 89 T 5 | Ruskin st SW8 |
| U 17 | Rudloe rd SW12 | 18 J 8 | Ruskin wlk N9 |
| W 10 | Rudolf rd NW6 | 90 L 14 | Ruskin wlk SE24 |
| R 7 | Rudolph rd E13 | 127 T 13 | Ruskin wlk Brom |
| H 18 | Rudyard grn NW7 | 23 T 14 | Rusland Pk rd Harrow |
| Z 15 | Ruffetts clo S Croy | 30 L 9 | Rusper rd N22 |
| A 12 | Ruffetts the S Croy | 55 U 18 | Rusper rd Dgnhm |
| L 2 | Rufford st N1 | 26 E 19 | Russel rd NW9 |
| A 10 | Rufus dri Ruis | 30 H 8 | Russell av N22 |
| A 10 | Rufus clo Ruis | 61 V 1 | Russell clo NW10 |
| G 5 | Rugby av N9 | 125 S 5 | Russell clo Becknhm |
| S 17 | Rugby av Grnfd | 98 D 10 | Russell clo Bxly Hth |
| C 14 | Rugby av Wemb | 69 V 3 | Russell clo Dgnhm |
| S 14 | Rugby clo Harrow | 99 W 9 | Russell clo Drtfrd |
| S 19 | Rugby gdns Dgnhm | 140 B 15 | Russell ct SW1 |
| P 20 | Rugby la Sutton | 27 T 19 | Russell gdns NW11 |
| S 12 | Rugby rd NW9 | 15 X 3 | Russell gdns N20 |
| Z 6 | Rugby rd W4 | 144 L 1 | Russell gdns SW14 |
| P 19 | Rugby rd Dgnhm | 102 C 4 | Russell gdns Rich |
| U 15 | Rugby rd Twick | 136 K 20 | Russell Gdns ms W14 |
| N 19 | Rugby rd WC1 | 13 N 14 | Russell gro NW7 |
| K 11 | Ruislip clo Grnfd | 149 U 20 | Russell gro SW9 |
| P 11 | Ruislip rd East Grnfd | 15 X 8 | Russell la N20 |
| L 11 | Ruislip rd Grnfd | 16 X 6 | Russell la N20 |
| M 9 | Ruislip st SW17 | 148 F 9 | Russell pl SW1 |
| Y 19 | Rumbold rd SW6 | 33 R 20 | Russell rd E10 |
| E 7 | Rumsey rd SW9 | 65 U 17 | Russell rd E16 |
| K 9 | Runcorn pl W11 | 32 K 11 | Russell rd E17 |
| J 17 | Rundell cres NW4 | 19 X 14 | Russell rd E4 |
| E 9 | Runham st SE17 | 26 E 19 | Russell rd NW9 |
| T 10 | Runnelfield Harrow | 17 O 18 | Russell rd N13 |
| W 14 | Running Horse yd SE1 | 31 R 16 | Russell rd N15 |
| F 20 | Runnymede SW19 | 15 X 7 | Russell rd N20 |
| L 17 | Runnymede clo Twick | 105 X 19 | Russell rd SW19 |
| Z 20 | Runnymede cres SW16 | 144 M 2 | Russell rd W14 |
| T 6 | Runnymede gdns Grnfd | 21 X 6 | Russell rd Buck Hl |
| K 17 | Runnymede gdns Twick | 123 P 16 | Russell rd Croy |
| L 16 | Runnymede rd Twick | 8 G 3 | Russell rd Enf |
| Y 5 | Runton st N19 | 41 N 13 | Russell rd Grnfd |
| P 6 | Rupack st SE16 | 120 K 6 | Russell rd Mitch |
| K 16 | Rupert av Wemb | 00 V 17 | Russell rd Twick |
| F 9 | Rupert ct W1 | 132 J 19 | Russell sq WC1 |
| P gdns SW9 | Rupert gdns SW9 | 65 U 6 | Russell st E13 |
| R 10 | Rupert rd NW6 | 140 M 8 | Russell st WC2 |
| Y 8 | Rupert rd N19 | 108 C 12 | Russells footpath SW16 |
| B 9 | Rupert rd W4 | | |
| E 8 | Rupert st W1 | 93 T 4 | Russett way SE13 |
| D 3 | Rural pl SE14 | 142 C 5 | Russia ct EC2 |
| I 17 | Rural way SW16 | 63 O 6 | Russia la E2 |
| P 7 | Ruscoe rd E16 | 135 Z 8 | Russia pl E2 |
| L 3 | Rush Green gdns Rom | 142 C 5 | Russia row EC2 |
| K 4 | Rush Green rd Rom | 150 D 17 | Rust sq SE5 |
| H 12 | Rush Gro st SE18 | 73 Y 8 | Rusthall av W4 |
| P 8 | Rush Hill rd SW11 | 107 I 17 | Rustic av SW16 |
| M 17 | Rusham rd SW12 | 119 V 16 | Rustington rd Mrdn |
| R 7 | Rusham rd SW12 | 117 S 17 | Ruston av Surb |
| M 6 | Rushbrook cres E17 | 136 J 6 | Ruston clo W11 |
| A 5 | Rushbrook rd SE9 | 136 K 5 | Ruston ms W11 |
| P 1 | Rushcroft dri E4 | 63 Z 3 | Ruston st E3 |
| R 1 | Rushcroft rd E4 | 108 A 12 | Rutford rd SW16 |
| F 11 | Rushcroft rd SW2 | 154 F 13 | Rutherford clo Sutton |
| A 18 | Rushden gdns NW7 | 148 F 4 | Rutherford st SW1 |
| X 10 | Rushden gdns Ilf | 10 D 5 | Rutherford way Bushey Watf |
| X 3 | Rushdene av Barnt | | |
| G 19 | Rushen wlk Carsh | 79 Z 15 | Rutherglen rd SE2 |
| A 18 | Rushett clo Surb | 152 G 14 | Rutherwyke clo Epsom |
| A 19 | Rushett rd Surb | | |
| S 18 | Rushey grn SE6 | 77 T 16 | Ruthin rd SE3 |
| P 15 | Rushey hill Enf | 97 N 18 | Rutland av Sidcp |
| M 16 | Rushford rd SE4 | 85 U 7 | Rutland clo SW14 |
| D 13 | Rushgrove av NW9 | 106 H 16 | Rutland clo SW19 |
| B 8 | Rushmead Rich | 126 C 9 | Rutland clo Brom |
| U 8 | Rushmead clo Croy | 115 W 3 | Rutland clo Bxly |
| R 7 | Rushmore clo Brom | 119 W 15 | Rutland dri Mrdn |
| | | 138 K 19 | Rutland ga SW7 |
| | | 126 D 9 | Rutland ga Brom |
| | | 138 K 20 | Rutland Ga ms SW7 |
| | | 81 U 14 | Rutland gate Blvdr |

| | | | |
|---|---|---|---|
| 30 J 18 | Rutland gdns N4 | 112 H 4 | Sadstone rd SE12 |
| 138 L 19 | Rutland gdns SW7 | 27 V 17 | Saffron clo NW11 |
| 59 Y 15 | Rutland gdns W13 | 133 U 19 | Saffron hill EC1 |
| 157 T 9 | Rutland gdns Croy | 141 U 1 | Saffron hill EC1 |
| 55 S 14 | Rutland gdns Dgnhm | 38 L 7 | Saffron rd Rom |
| 138 L 19 | Rutland Gdns ms SW7 | 133 U 19 | Saffron st EC1 |
| 74 K 14 | Rutland gro W6 | 149 P 4 | Sail st SW11 |
| 144 A 10 | Rutland rd E9 | 107 N 4 | Sainfoin rd SW17 |
| 146 K 1 | Rutland Ms south SW7 | 109 R 12 | Sainsbury rd SE19 |
| 110 H 5 | Rutland pk SE6 | 97 O 3 | St Abb's st Welling |
| 45 N 18 | Rutland Pk gdns NW2 | 120 L 19 | St Agatha's grn Carsh |
| 34 J 14 | Rutland rd E11 | 149 V 15 | St Agnes pl SE11 |
| 53 N 20 | Rutland rd E12 | 63 P 3 | St Agnes ter E9 |
| 33 O 18 | Rutland rd E17 | 72 C 6 | St Aidan's rd W13 |
| 63 S 3 | Rutland rd E9 | 91 Z 14 | St Aidans rd SE22 |
| 106 J 16 | Rutland rd SW19 | 101 Z 12 | St alban's Gdns Tedd |
| 9 N 18 | Rutland rd Enf | 66 J 9 | St Alban's av E6 |
| 23 N 18 | Rutland rd Harrow | 135 Z 1 | St Alban's gro E9 |
| 54 A 11 | Rutland rd Ilf | 146 A 1 | St Alban's gro W8 |
| 53 Z 11 | Rutland rd Ilf | 133 V 5 | St Alban's pl N1 |
| 58 G 14 | Rutland rd S'hall | 62 A 3 | St Alban's rd NW10 |
| 101 P 4 | Rutland rd Twick | 47 P 9 | St Alban's rd NW5 |
| 146 K 1 | Rutland st SW7 | 54 K 2 | St Alban's rd Ilf |
| 110 M 4 | Rutland wlk SE6 | 144 K 12 | St Alban's ter W6 |
| 106 J 20 | Rutlen rd SW18 | 73 Y 10 | St Albans av W4 |
| 120 E 9 | Rutter gdns Mitch | 30 F 6 | St Albans cres N22 |
| 92 E 4 | Rutts ter SE14 | 34 E 3 | St Albans cres Wdfd Grn |
| 10 D 5 | Rutts the Bushey Watf | 120 K 18 | St Albans gro Carsh |
| 87 P 7 | Ruvigny gdns SW15 | 45 Y 4 | St Albans la NW11 |
| 115 X 15 | Ruxley clo Sidcp | 4 C 4 | St Albans rd Barnt |
| 91 W 18 | Rycott path SE22 | 102 K 16 | St Albans rd Kingst |
| 94 C 4 | Ryculff sq SE3 | 153 U 9 | St Albans rd Sutton |
| 27 R 5 | Rydal clo NW4 | 34 D 3 | St Albans rd Wdfd Grn |
| 60 C 7 | Rydal cres Grnfd | | |
| 98 H 3 | Rydal dri Bxly Hth | 140 F 12 | St Albans st SW1 |
| 26 B 15 | Rydal gdns NW9 | 37 W 15 | St Aldrew's av Hornch |
| 104 A 12 | Rydal gdns SW15 | 76 G 17 | St Alfege pas SE10 |
| 82 K 16 | Rydal gdns Hounsl | 78 B 15 | St Alfege rd SE7 |
| 42 E 3 | Rydal gdns Wemb | 142 C 2 | St Alphage gdn EC2 |
| 107 V 3 | Rydal rd SW16 | 19 O 3 | St Alphage rd N9 |
| 9 R 19 | Rydal way Enf | 25 W 7 | St Alphage wlk Edgw |
| 112 H 13 | Ryder clo Brom | 89 W 11 | St Alphonsus rd SW4 |
| 140 B 13 | Ryder ct SW1 | 8 C 12 | St Andrew rd Enf |
| 66 K 17 | Ryder gdns E6 | 141 V 3 | St Andrew st EC4 |
| 57 U 18 | Ryder gdns Rainhm | 41 Y 12 | St Andrew's av Wemb |
| 140 C 13 | Ryder st SW1 | 44 J 10 | St Andrew's clo NW2 |
| 140 C 12 | Ryder yd SW1 | 15 P 13 | St Andrew's clo N12 |
| 130 A 8 | Ryders ter NW8 | 24 E 7 | St Andrew's clo Stanm |
| 107 T 3 | Rydevale rd SW12 | 41 Y 11 | St Andrew's clo Wemb |
| 95 P 7 | Rydons clo SE9 | | |
| 98 G 15 | Rye clo Bxly | 49 O 4 | St Andrew's gro N16 |
| 92 B 11 | Rye Hill pk SE15 | 141 Y 7 | St Andrew's hill EC4 |
| 91 X 3 | Rye la SE15 | 49 R 3 | St Andrew's ms N16 |
| 92 E 12 | Rye rd SE15 | 131 X 16 | St Andrew's pl NW1 |
| 16 J 2 | Rye the N14 | 32 G 9 | St Andrew's rd E17 |
| 12 A 19 | Rye way Edg | 44 J 19 | St Andrew's rd NW10 |
| 109 S 1 | Ryecotes mead SE21 | | |
| 35 Z 7 | Ryecroft av Ilf | 27 W 19 | St Andrew's rd NW11 |
| 92 L 20 | Ryecroft av Twick | | |
| 100 L 2 | Ryecroft av Twick | 43 X 5 | St Andrew's rd NW9 |
| 93 V 13 | Ryecroft rd SE13 | 19 P 4 | St Andrew's rd N9 |
| 108 G 15 | Ryecroft rd SW16 | 62 B 18 | St Andrew's rd W3 |
| 87 Z 3 | Ryecroft st SW6 | 154 K 4 | St Andrew's rd Carsh |
| 91 Y 18 | Ryedale SE22 | 156 L 8 | St Andrew's rd Croy |
| 108 M 16 | Ryefield rd SE19 | 53 U 1 | St Andrew's rd Ilf |
| 105 X 6 | Ryfold rd SW19 | 116 G 14 | St Andrew's rd Surb |
| 16 F 13 | Ryhope rd N11 | 116 F 14 | St Andrew's rd Surb |
| 47 S 17 | Ryland rd NW5 | 106 C 3 | St Andrew's rd SW18 |
| 44 G 9 | Rylandes rd NW2 | 24 E 5 | St Andrews dri Stanm |
| 80 B 8 | Rylands rd SE16 | | |
| 94 J 16 | Rylands cres SE12 | 33 Z 19 | St Andrews rd E11 |
| 74 D 7 | Rylett cres W12 | 144 M 12 | St Andrews rd W14 |
| 74 D 7 | Rylett rd W12 | 71 S 5 | St Andrews rd W7 |
| 13 O 16 | Rylston rd E1 | 39 O 18 | St Andrews rd Rom |
| 18 A 11 | Rylston rd N13 | 115 X 7 | St Andrews rd Sidcp |
| 145 O 16 | Rylston rd SW6 | 88 D 18 | St Ann's cres SW18 |
| 88 B 12 | Rymer rd SW18 | 47 O 18 | St Ann's gdns NW5 |
| 123 T 17 | Rymer rd Croy | 88 C 17 | St Ann's hill SW18 |
| 90 J 15 | Rymer st SE24 | 88 C 17 | St Ann's Pk rd SW18 |
| 139 O 20 | Rysbrack st SW3 | 30 J 16 | St Ann's rd N15 |
| | | 31 T 18 | St Ann's rd N15 |
| | | 18 G 7 | St Ann's rd N9 |

S

| | | | |
|---|---|---|---|
| 139 W 7 | S Moulton pass W1 | 86 D 3 | St Ann's rd SW13 |
| 65 O 18 | Sabbarton st E16 | 67 P 4 | St Ann's rd Bark |
| 88 M 7 | Sabine rd SW11 | 23 W 18 | St Ann's rd Harrow |
| 89 N 7 | Sabine rd SW8 | 63 Z 18 | St Anne st E18 |
| 118 A 10 | Sable ct New Mald | 63 Z 18 | St Anne's pl E14 |
| 48 J 20 | Sable st N1 | 51 V 5 | St Anne's rd E11 |
| 50 A 6 | Sach rd E5 | 42 H 15 | St Anne's rd Wemb |
| 126 E 19 | Sackville av Brom | 156 K 14 | St Anne's way Croy |
| 41 P 10 | Sackville clo Harrow | 156 K 15 | St Anne's way Croy |
| 53 T 3 | Sackville gdns Ilf | 140 E 6 | St Annes ct W1 |
| 153 X 17 | Sackville rd Sutton | 60 L 8 | St Annes gdns Wemb |
| 140 B 11 | Sackville st W1 | 63 Y 19 | St Annes pass E14 |
| | | 148 G 2 | St Anns la SW1 |

E 17 St Margaret's rd Edg  
A 13 St Margaret's rd Twick  
L 11 St Margaret's sq SE4  
K 19 St Margaret's st SW1  
P 14 St Margaret's ter SE18  
P 7 St Mark st E1  
N 13 St Mark's clo Barnt  
U 4 St Mark's cres NW1  
Y 1 St Mark's ga E9  
Z 16 St Mark's gro E1  
K 13 St Mark's hill Surb  
M 6 St Mark's pl W11  
Y 9 St Mark's rd SE25  
G 2 St Mark's rd W11  
F 20 St Mark's rd W11  
T 5 St Mark's rd W7  
H 19 St Mark's rd Enf  
N 4 St Mark's rd Mitch  
M 4 St Mark's rd Mitch  
B 17 St Mark's rd Tedd  
V 15 St Mark's ri E8  
T 5 St Mark's sq NW1  
V 15 St Marks pl SW19  
G 7 St Marks rd Brom  
A 7 St Martin's av E6  
A 4 St Martin's clo NW1  
M 5 St Martin's clo Enf  
H 9 St Martin's ct WC2  
J 9 St Martin's la WC2  
H 11 St Martin's pl WC2  
M 8 St Martin's rd N9  
C 4 St Martin's rd SW9  
G 11 St Martin's rd WC2  
A 4 St Martins Le grand EC1  
P 3 St Mary Abbot's pl W 8  
P 2 St Mary Abbots ter W14  
J 10 St Mary At hill EC3  
R 6 St Mary av Wallgtn  
K 4 St Mary axe EC3  
Z 18 St Mary Ch st SE16  
P 14 St Mary rd E17  
H 10 St Mary st SE18  
T 15 St Mary's appr E12  
U 7 St Mary's av N3  
Z 6 St Mary's av Brom  
A 7 St Mary's av Brom  
K 11 St Mary's av S'hall  
W 15 St Mary's av Tedd  
E 17 St Mary's av Epsom  
R 19 St Mary's cres Islwth  
K 19 St Mary's gro N1  
J 8 St Mary's gro SW13  
T 17 St Mary's gro W4  
N 11 St Mary's gro Rich  
X 4 St Mary's path N1  
U 8 St Mary's rd E10  
U 6 St Mary's rd E13  
C 2 St Mary's rd NW10  
S 20 St Mary's rd NW11  
B 14 St Mary's rd N8  
O 5 St Mary's rd N9  
C 3 St Mary's rd SE15  
R 7 St Mary's rd SE25  
U 13 St Mary's rd SW19  
G 5 St Mary's rd W5  
P 3 St Mary's rd Bark  
Y 3 St Mary's rd Barnt  
D 8 St Mary's rd Ilf  
E 18 St Mary's rd Surb  
C 3 St Mary's rd Worc Pk  
F 1 St Mary's sq W 2  
P 5 St Marychurch st SE16  
H 20 St Marys av E11  
W 6 St Marys clo N17  
J 11 St Marys cres NW4  
F 5 St Marys ct W5  
U 5 St Marys gdns SE11  
E 1 St Marys ter W2  
U 5 St Marys wlk SE11  
F 2 St Matthew st SW1  
K 19 St Matthew's av Surb  
U 6 St Matthew's dri Brom  
E 12 St Matthew's rd SW2  
S 15 St Matthew's row E2  
K 3 St Matthews rd E6  
V 2 St Maur rd SW6  
S 18 St Merryn clo SE18  
V 16 St Michael clo N12  
P 4 St Michael's av N9  
R 17 St Michael's av Wemb  
Z 9 St Michael's clo SE13  

22 C 18 St Michael's cres Pinn  
126 K 1 St Michael's gdns W10  
44 L 12 St Michael's rd NW2  
90 C 4 St Michael's rd SW9  
122 M 20 St Michael's rd Croy  
156 M 1 St Michael's rd Croy  
155 V 12 St Michael's rd Wallgtn  
97 P 8 St Michael's rd Welling  
39 B 6 St Michael's ter N22  
138 J 3 St Michaels st W2  
142 E 6 St Mildred's ct EC2  
94 C 19 St Mildred's rd SE12  
57 X 11 St Nicholas av Hornch  
127 S 1 St Nicholas la Chisl  
79 Y 12 St Nicholas rd SE18  
154 B 11 St Nicholas rd Sutton  
92 M 3 St Nicholas rd SE14  
92 J 8 St Norbert grn SE4  
92 H 10 St Norbert gro SE4  
92 G 12 St Norbert rd SE4  
135 N 19 St Olaf's rd E1  
144 M 20 St Olaf's rd SW6  
142 D 5 St Olave's ct EC2  
66 J 3 St Olave's rd E6  
121 W 3 St Olave's wlk SW16  
149 O 11 St Oswald's pl SE11  
108 H 20 St Oswald's rd SW16  
148 H 7 St Oswulf st SW1  
132 J 11 St Pancras station NW1  
47 V 20 St Pancras way NW1  
132 E 6 St Pancras way NW1  
134 C 4 St Paul st N1  
44 M 17 St Paul's av NW2  
75 U 2 St Paul's av SE16  
24 M 15 St Paul's av Harrow  
141 Z 6 St Paul's cathedral EC4  
141 Y 6 St Paul's Church yd EC4  
49 N 17 St Paul's pl N1  
48 L 17 St Paul's rd N1  
49 N 18 St Paul's rd N1  
67 P 3 St Paul's rd Bark  
72 G 17 St Paul's rd Brentf  
81 W 19 St Paul's rd Erith  
84 M 8 St Paul's rd Rich  
122 M 6 St Paul's rd Thntn Hth  
49 N 17 St Paul's shrubbery N1  
64 A 14 St Paul's way E14  
28 A 3 St Paul's way N3  
82 C 6 St Pauls clo Hounsl  
114 E 20 St Pauls Cray rd Chisl  
47 Y 19 St Pauls cres NW1  
51 X 19 St Pauls dri E15  
31 Y 3 St Pauls rd N17  
149 Y 13 St Pauls ter SE17  
63 Z 15 St Pauls way E3  
142 H 7 St peter's EC3  
33 Y 12 St Peter's av E17  
18 L 14 St Peter's av N18  
135 U 11 St Peter's clo E2  
36 J 13 St Peter's clo Ilf  
27 N 15 St Peter's ct NW4  
74 F 12 St Peter's gro W6  
8 E 10 St Peter's pl SW11  
19 O 6 St Peter's rd N9  
74 G 13 St Peter's rd W6  
157 O 9 St Peter's rd Croy  
117 O 4 St Peter's rd Kingst  
58 H 15 St Peter's rd S'hall  
84 C 12 St Peter's rd Twick  
74 F 12 St Peter's sq W6  
133 X 5 St Peter's st N1  
157 O 12 St Peter's st S Croy  
60 H 14 St Peter's way W5  
94 D 12 St Peters clo SE3  
145 N 20 St Peters ter SW6  
74 F 12 St Peters villas W6  
137 X 10 St Petersburgh ms W2  
137 X 9 St Petersburgh pl W2  
89 S 6 St Philip st SW8  
49 W 19 St Philip's hill SE18  
116 G 14 St Philip's rd Surb  
138 F 1 St Phillip's rd W2  
152 J 2 St Phillip's av Worc Pk  
96 L 7 St Quentin rd Welling  
136 D 2 St Quintin av W10  
65 V 8 St Quintin rd E13  

5 U 4 St Ronans clo Barnt  
34 E 2 St Ronans cres Wdfd Grn  
89 U 5 St Rule st SW8  
122 L 16 St Saviour's rd Croy  
90 C 14 St Saviours rd SW2  
87 N 14 St Simons av SW15  
60 A 16 St Stephen's av W13  
58 F 16 St Stephen's clo S'hall  
137 V 4 St Stephen's cres W2  
84 D 17 St Stephen's gdns Twick  
137 U 3 St Stephen's ms W2  
84 E 17 St Stephen's pas Twick  
33 S 16 St Stephen's rd E17  
63 X 4 St Stephen's rd E3  
60 C 16 St Stephen's rd W13  
4 B 17 St Stephen's rd Barnt  
9 S 1 St Stephen's rd Enf  
82 H 14 St Stephen's rd Hounsl  
33 T 17 St Stephens av E17  
74 K 4 St Stephens av W12  
33 S 16 St Stephens clo E17  
130 L 6 St Stephens clo NW8  
122 E 6 St Stephens cres Thntn Hth  
137 S 4 St Stephens gdns W2  
93 U 7 St Stephens gro SE13  
65 Z 1 St Stephens rd E6  
142 E 7 St Stephens row EC4  
149 N 20 St Stephens st SW8  
142 F 8 St Swithins la EC4  
93 W 14 St Swithun's rd SE13  
98 D 19 St Thomas ct Bxly  
22 C 5 St Thomas dri Pinn  
54 B 17 St Thomas gdns Ilf  
65 S 17 St Thomas rd E16  
16 L 3 St Thomas rd N14  
142 F 14 St Thomas rd SE1  
73 U 18 St Thomas' rd W4  
81 W 5 St Thomas' rd Blvdr  
47 O 17 St Thomas's gdns NW5  
50 R 20 St Thomas's pl E9  
48 G 9 St Thomas's rd N4  
50 B 20 St Thomas's rd N4  
135 P 17 St Thomas's way E1  
22 A 17 St Ursula gro Pinn  
58 H 16 St Ursula rd S'hall  
82 M 17 St Vincent rd Twick  
139 U 2 St Vincent st W1  
5 V 17 St Wilfreds clo Barnt  
5 V 17 St Wilfrid's clo Barnt  
102 C 14 St Winifred's rd Tedd  
53 U 15 St Winifride's av E12  
149 N 7 Salamanca pl SE1  
148 M 7 Salamanca st SE1&SE11  
149 N 7 Salamanca st SE1&SE11  
119 P 19 Salcombe dri Mrdn  
38 C 20 Salcombe dri Rom  
13 Z 20 Salcombe gdns NW7  
50 M 1 Salcombe rd E17  
49 T 14 Salcombe rd N16  
88 L 13 Salcott rd SW11  
156 B 7 Salcott rd Croy  
138 J 3 Sale pl W2  
24 K 16 Salehurst clo Harrow  
92 L 16 Salehurst rd SE4  
156 K 6 Salem pl Croy  
137 Y 8 Salem rd W2  
107 X 2 Salford rd SW2  
27 U 9 Salisbury av N3  
67 S 1 Salisbury av Bark  
153 U 15 Salisbury av Sutton  
141 V 6 Salisbury ct EC4  
105 T 18 Salisbury gro SW19  
47 V 6 Salisbury ms N19  
145 O 18 Salisbury ms SW6  
131 P 20 Salisbury pl W1  
51 V 7 Salisbury rd E10  
53 O 14 Salisbury rd E12  
33 T 16 Salisbury rd E17  
20 C 11 Salisbury rd E4  
52 E 18 Salisbury rd E7  
30 G 6 Salisbury rd N22  
30 K 17 Salisbury rd N4  
18 J 10 Salisbury rd N9  
123 X 16 Salisbury rd SE25  
105 S 18 Salisbury rd SW19  
72 B 6 Salisbury rd W13  
4 E 12 Salisbury rd Barnt  

127 P 12 Salisbury rd Brom  
98 E 20 Salisbury rd Bxly  
154 M 13 Salisbury rd Carsh  
56 H 19 Salisbury rd Dgnhm  
9 Z 1 Salisbury rd Enf  
23 R 16 Salisbury rd Harrow  
54 H 6 Salisbury rd Ilf  
117 Y 5 Salisbury rd New Mald  
84 K 10 Salisbury rd Rich  
39 Z 16 Salisbury rd Rom  
70 D 11 Salisbury rd S'hall  
152 C 5 Salisbury rd Worc Pk  
150 E 6 Salisbury row SE17  
141 V 6 Salisbury sq EC4  
130 H 18 Salisbury st NW8  
73 W 4 Salisbury st W3  
63 U 1 Salmon la E1  
63 X 17 Salmon la E14  
65 R 7 Salmon rd E13  
81 T 14 Salmon rd Blvdr  
63 Y 11 Salmon st E3  
43 U 3 Salmon st NW9  
18 K 5 Salmons rd N9  
65 X 14 Salomons rd E13  
32 F 18 Salop rd E17  
74 A 6 Salt Coats rd W4  
153 U 9 Saltash clo Sutton  
107 P 14 Saltash rd SW17  
36 D 1 Saltash rd Ilf  
97 U 2 Saltash rd Welling  
63 Z 20 Salter st E14  
142 E 8 Salter's Hall ct EC4  
109 N 13 Salter's hill SE19  
33 X 13 Salter's rd E17  
48 B 10 Salterton rd N7  
90 F 11 Saltoun rd SW2  
129 R 12 Saltram cres W9  
64 B 19 Saltwell st E14  
128 M 4 Salusbury rd NW6  
129 N 8 Salusbury rd NW6  
106 K 11 Salvador pl SW17  
59 Z 4 Salvia gdns Grnfd  
87 O 8 Salvin rd SW15  
34 D 2 Salway clo Wdfd Grn  
34 D 5 Salway hill E18  
51 Y 19 Salway pl E15  
51 X 19 Salway rd E15  
150 L 20 Salwood st SE15  
74 G 14 Samels clo W6  
130 H 18 Samford st NW8  
77 O 19 Samos clo SE3  
124 A 3 Samos rd SE20  
143 U 14 Sampson st E1  
65 X 7 Samson st E13  
76 G 7 Samuda st E14  
78 E 10 Samuel st SE18  
23 X 9 Sancroft rd Harrow  
149 P 8 Sancroft st SE11  
142 B 18 Sanctuary st SE1  
97 V 17 Sanctuary the Bxly  
155 Y 7 Sand hills Wallgtn  
78 C 10 Sand st SE18  
88 B 1 Sand's End la SW6  
10 K 10 Sandal rd N18  
117 Z 10 Sandal rd New Mald  
118 A 10 Sandal rd New Mald  
64 L 3 Sandal st E15  
60 K 1 Sandall clo W5  
47 W 18 Sandall rd NW5  
60 J 1 Sandall rd W5  
119 Z 4 Sandbourne av SW19  
92 H 4 Sandbourne rd SE4  
49 R 10 Sandbrook rd N16  
95 R 8 Sandby grn SE9  
81 Z 12 Sandcliff rd Erith  
141 T 16 Sandell st SE1  
27 N 1 Sanders la NW7  
27 O 1 Sanders la NW7  
26 M 1 Sanders la NW7  
45 S 8 Sanderstead av NW2  
89 V 18 Sanderstead clo SW12  
50 J 3 Sanderstead rd E10  
157 O 18 Sanderstead rd S Croy  
122 K 6 Sandfield gdns Thntn Hth  
122 K 6 Sandfield rd Thntn Hth  
30 L 3 Sandford av N22  
66 F 11 Sandford clo E6  
66 F 9 Sandford rd E6  
66 E 9 Sandford rd E6  
26 G 9 Sandford rd Brom  
97 Z 9 Sandford rd Bxly Hth  
150 F 9 Sandford row SE17  
80 F 18 Sandgate rd Welling  
151 V 13 Sandgate st SE15  
22 L 19 Sandhurst av Harrow  
117 S 17 Sandhurst av Surb  
25 O 10 Sandhurst clo NW9

| | |
|---|---|
| F 10 | Selwood terr SW7 |
| L7 | Selworthy rd SE6 |
| H 19 | Selwyn av E4 |
| J 18 | Selwyn av Ilf |
| L8 | Selwyn av Rich |
| B9 | Selwyn clo Hounsl |
| O9 | Selwyn cres Welling |
| R3 | Selwyn ct Edg |
| U4 | Selwyn rd E13 |
| X7 | Selwyn rd E3 |
| W 11 | Selwyn rd N17 |
| Y 11 | Selwyn rd New Mald |
| W7 | Semley pl SW1 |
| C2 | Semley rd SW16 |
| A 10 | Seneca rd SW4 |
| L9 | Seneca rd Thntn Hth |
| P 20 | Senga rd Wallgtn |
| N6 | Senhouse rd Sutton |
| X 20 | Senior st W2 |
| H2 | Senlac rd SE12 |
| F2 | Sennen rd Enf |
| S 16 | Senrab st E1 |
| G3 | Sequoia clo Bushey Watf |
| P5 | Serle st WC2 |
| Z7 | Sermon la EC4 |
| N5 | Setchell rd SE1 |
| R6 | Seth st SE16 |
| G1 | Seton gdns Dgnhm |
| S6 | Settle rd E13 |
| U4 | Settles st E1 |
| Z6 | Settrington rd SW6 |
| L 19 | Seven Kings park Ilf |
| J6 | Seven Kings rd Ilf |
| P 18 | Seven Sisters rd N15 |
| J5 | Seven Sisters rd N4 |
| B 10 | Seven Sisters rd N7 |
| N 20 | Seven Star all E1 |
| H 11 | Sevenoaks clo Bxly Hth |
| K 15 | Sevenoaks rd SE4 |
| S 19 | Sevenoaks way Sidcp |
| H 12 | Seventh av E12 |
| J 16 | Seventh av Enf |
| Z9 | Severn av Rom |
| L2 | Severn dri Enf |
| C 15 | Severn way NW10 |
| J 10 | Severus rd SW11 |
| R 19 | Seville st SW1 |
| H 19 | Sevington rd NW4 |
| W 18 | Sevington st W9 |
| Y5 | Seward rd W7 |
| R2 | Seward rd Becknhm |
| Y 15 | Seward st EC1 |
| A 14 | Seward st EC1 |
| R5 | Sewardstone rd E2 |
| C1 | Sewardstone rd E4 |
| E 11 | Sewdley st E5 |
| B6 | Sewell rd SE2 |
| T9 | Sewell st E13 |
| U 10 | Seymer rd Rom |
| X7 | Seymour av N17 |
| K 20 | Seymour av Epsom |
| P 17 | Seymour av Mrdn |
| N1 | Seymour bldgs W1 |
| P8 | Seymour ct E4 |
| H7 | Seymour ct NW2 |
| T4 | Seymour gdns Ilf |
| O 12 | Seymour gdns Surb |
| A 19 | Seymour gdns Twick |
| N3 | Seymour mall W1 |
| T5 | Seymour ms W1 |
| Z9 | Seymour pl SE25 |
| N4 | Seymour pl W1 |
| L4 | Seymour rd E10 |
| L4 | Seymour rd E10 |
| D4 | Seymour rd E4 |
| A5 | Seymour rd E6 |
| B2 | Seymour rd N3 |
| H 16 | Seymour rd N8 |
| N8 | Seymour rd N9 |
| W 17 | Seymour rd SW18 |
| P6 | Seymour rd SW19 |
| W9 | Seymour rd W4 |
| O 11 | Seymour rd Carsh |
| N 11 | Seymour rd Hampt |
| F1 | Seymour rd Kingst |
| F 20 | Seymour rd Kingst |
| O 18 | Seymour rd Mitch |
| R6 | Seymour st W1 |
| Z1 | Seymour ter SE20 |
| Z1 | Seymour vlls SE20 |
| O 13 | Seymour wlk SW10 |
| H 11 | Seyssel st E14 |
| Z1 | Shaa rd W3 |
| U 10 | Shacklegate la Tedd |
| B4 | Shackleton clo SE23 |
| F 20 | Shackleton rd S'hall |
| F1 | Shackleton rd Shall |
| V 13 | Shacklewell grn E8 |
| V 13 | Shacklewell la E8 |
| U 12 | Shacklewell rd N16 |

| | |
|---|---|
| U 13 | Shacklewell row E8 |
| P 15 | Shacklewell st E2 |
| P 18 | Shad thames SE1 |
| D3 | Shadbolt clo Worc Pk |
| E7 | Shadwell dri Grnfd |
| O 19 | Shadwell pl E1 |
| A2 | Shadybush clo Bushey Watf |
| Z 17 | Shaef way Tedd |
| J 17 | Shafter rd Dgnhm |
| F9 | Shaftesbury av W1 |
| P 13 | Shaftesbury av Barnt |
| S9 | Shaftesbury av Enf |
| O6 | Shaftesbury av Harrow |
| M3 | Shaftesbury av Harrow |
| J1 | Shaftesbury av Harrow |
| H 19 | Shaftesbury av Harrow |
| H9 | Shaftesbury av S'hall |
| U4 | Shaftesbury ms W8 |
| B2 | Shaftesbury pl EC1 |
| O5 | Shaftesbury rd E10 |
| R 17 | Shaftesbury rd E17 |
| K5 | Shaftesbury rd E4 |
| X1 | Shaftesbury rd E7 |
| M 20 | Shaftesbury rd E7 |
| F 19 | Shaftesbury rd N18 |
| A3 | Shaftesbury rd N4 |
| M4 | Shaftesbury rd Becknhm |
| H 16 | Shaftesbury rd Carsh |
| J9 | Shaftesbury rd Rich |
| U 17 | Shaftesbury rd Rom |
| D9 | Shaftesbury st N1 |
| O5 | Shaftesburys the Bark |
| P3 | Shafto ms SW1 |
| T3 | Shafton rd E9 |
| Y3 | Shakespeare av NW10 |
| H 16 | Shakespeare av N11 |
| T 19 | Shakespeare cres E12 |
| N 20 | Shakespeare dri Harrow |
| M 13 | Shakespeare gdns N2 |
| G8 | Shakespeare rd E17 |
| T 14 | Shakespeare rd NW7 |
| Y3 | Shakespeare rd N3 |
| J 10 | Shakespeare rd SE24 |
| W1 | Shakespeare rd W3 |
| W 19 | Shakespeare rd W7 |
| Y2 | Shakespeare rd Bxly Hth |
| U 10 | Shakespeare rd Rom |
| R 12 | Shakespeare wlk N16 |
| D 15 | Shalcomb st SW10 |
| S 11 | Shaldon dri Mrdn |
| E 14 | Shaldon rd N18 |
| M7 | Shaldon rd Edg |
| M7 | Shaldon rd Edg |
| U 19 | Shalimar rd W3 |
| O 20 | Shalstone rd SW14 |
| G9 | Shalfleet Dri est W10 |
| U 19 | Shallimar gdns W3 |
| Y9 | Shallons rd SE9 |
| L 15 | Shalston vlls Surb |
| C 14 | Shamrock rd Croy |
| W7 | Shamrock rd SW4 |
| H 16 | Shamrock way N14 |
| K 16 | Shand st SE1 |
| V 15 | Shandon rd SW4 |
| T 13 | Shandy st E1 |
| X 13 | Shanklin rd N15 |
| Y 17 | Shanklin rd N8 |
| D 10 | Shannon gro SW9 |
| L8 | Shannon pl NW8 |
| L 15 | Shap cres Carsh |
| N8 | Shap st E2 |
| V 14 | Shard's sq SE1 |
| K 13 | Shardcroft av SE24 |
| K3 | Shardeloes rd SE14 |
| M 10 | Sharman clo Sidcp |
| C 15 | Sharman st E14 |
| E 19 | Sharon clo Surb |
| P2 | Sharon gdns E9 |
| V3 | Sharon rd W4 |
| V8 | Sharon rd Enf |
| R2 | Sharpleshall st NW1 |
| R2 | Sharpleshall st NW1 |
| R 17 | Sharratt st SE15 |
| H 11 | Sharsted st SE17 |
| F 10 | Shaver's pl SW1 |
| L6 | Shaw av Bark |
| L6 | Shaw gdns Bark |

| | |
|---|---|
| B8 | Shaw rd Brom |
| S6 | Shaw rd Enf |
| J5 | Shaw sq E17 |
| Z 15 | Shaw way Wallgtn |
| M 12 | Shawbrooke rd SE9 |
| N 11 | Shawbrooke rd SE9 |
| V 12 | Shawbury rd SE22 |
| O2 | Shawfield pk Brom |
| M 11 | Shawfield st SW3 |
| H 19 | Shawford ct SW15 |
| V 20 | Shaxton cres Croy |
| A 17 | Shearling way N7 |
| B9 | Shearman rd SE3 |
| R 13 | Sheaveshill av NW9 |
| R 12 | Sheen Comm dri Rich |
| R 10 | Sheen Ct rd Rich |
| V 10 | Sheen Ga gdns SW14 |
| R4 | Sheen gro N1 |
| W7 | Sheen la SW14 |
| L 11 | Sheen pk Rich |
| L 11 | Sheen rd Rich |
| P 12 | Sheen rd Rich |
| C 10 | Sheen way Wallgtn |
| V 13 | Sheen wood SW14 |
| M9 | Sheendale rd Rich |
| A 11 | Sheenewood SE26 |
| W5 | Sheep la E8 |
| N5 | Sheepcote la SW11 |
| M5 | Sheepcote la SW11 |
| W 19 | Sheepcote rd Harrow |
| X 13 | Sheepcotes rd Rom |
| Z 18 | Sheephouse way New Mald |
| A 18 | Sheephouse way New Mald |
| O6 | Sheffield st WC2 |
| U 15 | Sheffield ter W8 |
| G1 | Sheila clo Rom |
| G1 | Sheila rd Rom |
| O 11 | Shelbourne clo Pinn |
| Z6 | Shelbourne rd N17 |
| D 12 | Shelburne rd N7 |
| N9 | Shelbury clo Sidcp |
| B 14 | Shelbury rd SE22 |
| K1 | Sheldon av N6 |
| M 17 | Sheldon av N6 |
| Y7 | Sheldon av Ilf |
| P 13 | Sheldon rd NW2 |
| B3 | Sheldon rd Bxly Hth |
| Y 20 | Sheldon rd Dgnhm |
| L6 | Sheldon st Croy |
| S 19 | Sheldrake pl W8 |
| O 10 | Shelford pl N16 |
| A 20 | Shelford rd Barnt |
| T 19 | Shelford ri SE19 |
| L 12 | Shelgate rd SW11 |
| S 15 | Sholl clo Brom |
| P8 | Shell rd SE13 |
| P7 | Shell rd SE13 |
| P 18 | Shelley av E12 |
| P8 | Shelley av Grnfd |
| U6 | Shelley av Hornch |
| B 15 | Shelley clo Edg |
| C 15 | Shelley clo Edg |
| P9 | Shelley clo Grnfd |
| F 18 | Shelley cres S'hall |
| D8 | Shelley gdns Wemb |
| Y4 | Shelley rd NW10 |
| S 15 | Shellgrove rd N16 |
| M6 | Shellwood rd SW11 |
| Y 19 | Shelton rd SW19 |
| J7 | Shelton st WC2 |
| D 15 | Shene st EC1 |
| G1 | Shenfield rd Wdfd Grn |
| G2 | Shenfield rd Wdfd Grn |
| K 10 | Shenfield st N1 |
| S2 | Shenley rd SE5 |
| B2 | Shenley rd Hounsl |
| O9 | Shensley wlk N16 |
| L 11 | Shenstone clo Bxly Hth |
| N5 | Shepard clo Enf |
| V 15 | Shepherd clo Rom |
| X 13 | Shepherd mkt W1 |
| X 14 | Shepherd st W1 |
| T 19 | Shepherd's clo N6 |
| Z 19 | Shepherd's la Drtfrd |
| F 14 | Shepherd's wlk NW3 |
| D 12 | Shepherdess pl N1 |
| B8 | Shepherdess wlk N1 |
| D 17 | Shepherds Bush common W12 |
| F 17 | Shepherds Bush grn W12 |
| C 16 | Shepherds Bush mkt W12 |
| M5 | Shepherds Bush mkt W12 |

| | |
|---|---|
| E 19 | Shepherds Bush rd W6 |
| D5 | Shepherds Bush rd W6 |
| G 18 | Shepherds Bush Shopping centre W12 |
| E 18 | Shepherds grn Chisl |
| S 19 | Shepherds hill N6 |
| E 16 | Shepherds la E9 |
| T8 | Shepherds pl W1 |
| E 17 | Shepherds way S Croy |
| O4 | Shepley clo Carsh |
| P 12 | Sheppard st E1L |
| C3 | Shepperton rd N1 |
| U 20 | Sheppey gdns Dgnhm |
| P 20 | Sheppey rd Dgnhm |
| K 19 | Shepstone st E6 |
| K 17 | Sherard rd E7 |
| S 12 | Sherard rd SE9 |
| D6 | Sheraton st W1 |
| G 10 | Sherborne av S'hall |
| P 10 | Sherborne av NW9 |
| B 15 | Sherborne gdns W13 |
| F8 | Sherborne la EC4 |
| X1 | Sherborne rd Sutton |
| E3 | Sherborne st N1 |
| T 18 | Sherboro rd N15 |
| O8 | Sherbourne av Enf |
| H 17 | Sherbourne cres Carsh |
| B 15 | Sherbourne gdns W13 |
| W3 | Sherbrook gdns N21 |
| H 16 | Sherbrooke gdns E6 |
| L 19 | Sherbrooke rd SW6 |
| X 16 | Shere rd SE8 |
| Y 10 | Shere rd Ilf |
| L7 | Sheredan rd E4 |
| C 16 | Sherfield gdns SW16 |
| F 19 | Sheridan gdns Harrow |
| T 16 | Sheridan rd E12 |
| D 10 | Sheridan rd E7 |
| W1 | Sheridan rd SW19 |
| R9 | Sheridan rd Blvdr |
| Z7 | Sheridan rd Bxly Hth |
| D8 | Sheridan rd Rich |
| L 12 | Sheridan wlk Carsh |
| U 12 | Sheringham av E12 |
| K 18 | Sheringham av N14 |
| L 19 | Sheringham av Rom |
| F2 | Sheringham av Twick |
| L 16 | Sheringham dri Bark |
| E 17 | Sheringham rd E17 |
| B5 | Sheringham rd SE20 |
| H1 | Sherington av Pinn |
| V 17 | Sherington rd SE7 |
| X 20 | Sherland rd Twick |
| X1 | Sherland rd Twick |
| G1 | Sherman rd Brom |
| F8 | Sherman st E3 |
| T 13 | Shernhall st E17 |
| O 16 | Sherrard rd E12 |
| M 19 | Sherrards way Barnt |
| J 15 | Sherrick Green rd NW10 |
| Y 19 | Sherriff rd NW6 |
| X7 | Sherringham av N17 |
| H 12 | Sherrock gdns NW4 |
| F4 | Sherwin rd SE14 |
| H 11 | Sherwood av E18 |
| A 20 | Sherwood av SW16 |
| Y 19 | Sherwood av SW16 |
| L 10 | Sherwood av Grnfd |
| K8 | Sherwood clo SW13 |
| E 20 | Sherwood gdns Bark |
| S 16 | Sherwood Pk av Sidcp |
| V8 | Sherwood Pk rd Mitch |
| Y 12 | Sherwood Pk rd Sutton |
| N9 | Sherwood rd NW4 |
| M 10 | Sherwood rd NW4 |
| V 19 | Sherwood rd SW19 |
| Z 18 | Sherwood rd Croy |
| M 11 | Sherwood rd Hampt |
| N8 | Sherwood rd Harrow |
| M8 | Sherwood rd Harrow |
| D 14 | Sherwood rd Ilf |
| G6 | Sherwood rd Welling |
| S 10 | Sherwood st N20 |
| D9 | Sherwood st W1 |
| T 10 | Sherwood ter N20 |

| | | |
|---|---|---|
| 2 M 16 | Snarsgate st W10 | |
| 5 X 19 | Snead st SE14 | |
| 8 U 20 | Sneath av NW11 | |
| 3 H 18 | Snells pk W18 | |
| M 13 | Sneyd rd NW2 | |
| W 3 | Snow hill EC1 | |
| 3 B 5 | Snowbury rd SW6 | |
| 4 J 19 | Snowden st EC2 | |
| 2 G 17 | Snowsfields SE1 | |
| 1 U 8 | Soames st SE15 | |
| 3 A 1 | Soames wlk New Mald | |
| 1 O 3 | Soan museum WC2 | |
| 6 G 15 | Socket la Brom | |
| 0 F 5 | Soho sq W1 | |
| 0 E 5 | Soho st W1 | |
| 3 V 12 | Solebay pl E1 | |
| 3 X 11 | Solebay st E3 | |
| 6 X 16 | Solent rd NW6 | |
| 6 L 14 | Solna av SW15 | |
| 8 A 3 | Solna rd N21 | |
| 2 A 9 | Solomon's pas SE15 | |
| 0 A 10 | Solon New rd SW4 | |
| 0 A 11 | Solon rd SW4 | |
| 2 C 7 | Solway clo Hounsl | |
| 0 H 4 | Solway rd N22 | |
| 1 X 10 | Solway rd SE22 | |
| 5 U 19 | Somaford gro Barnt | |
| 5 U 14 | Somali rd NW2 | |
| 4 D 20 | Somerby rd Bark | |
| 8 J 7 | Somerfield rd N4 | |
| 9 U 13 | Somerford gro N16 | |
| 1 Y 2 | Somerford gro N17 | |
| 5 X 17 | Somerford st E1 | |
| 7 O 18 | Somerhill av Sidcp | |
| 7 R 4 | Somerhill rd Welling | |
| 0 G 10 | Somerleyton rd SW9 | |
| 3 J 6 | Somers cres W2 | |
| 0 C 17 | Somers pl SW2 | |
| 2 L 14 | Somers rd E17 | |
| 0 C 17 | Somers rd SW2 | |
| 5 T 15 | Somersby gdns Ilf | |
| 0 A 20 | Somerset av SW20 | |
| 6 L 11 | Somerset av Welling | |
| 8 B 13 | Somerset clo New Mald | |
| 3 P 5 | Somerset gdns SE13 | |
| 2 D 6 | Somerset gdns SW16 | |
| 1 T 12 | Somerset gdns Tedd | |
| 1 O 9 | Somerset house WC2 | |
| 3 U 17 | Somerset rd E17 | |
| 6 L 13 | Somerset rd NW4 | |
| 1 V 11 | Somerset rd N17 | |
| 8 F 16 | Somerset rd N18 | |
| 5 R 9 | Somerset rd SW19 | |
| 2 C 3 | Somerset rd W13 | |
| 3 X 7 | Somerset rd W7 | |
| 5 O 16 | Somerset rd Barnt | |
| 2 F 17 | Somerset rd Brentf | |
| 9 Z 17 | Somerset rd Drtfd | |
| 5 R 16 | Somerset rd East Barnt | |
| 2 M 16 | Somerset rd Harrow | |
| 7 N 4 | Somerset rd Kingst | |
| 8 H 15 | Somerset rd S'hall | |
| 70 A 18 | Somerset waye Hounsl | |
| 97 Z 5 | Somersham rd Bxly Hth | |
| 85 S 8 | Somerton av Rich | |
| 45 S 9 | Somerton rd NW2 | |
| 92 A 10 | Somerton rd SE15 | |
| 12 H 5 | Somertrees av SE12 | |
| 40 J 14 | Somervell rd Harrow | |
| 92 E 3 | Somerville rd SE14 | |
| 10 F 17 | Somerville rd SE20 | |
| 37 U 15 | Somerville rd Rom | |
| 48 E 8 | Sonderburg rd N7 | |
| 53 V 20 | Sondes st SE17 | |
| 23 V 20 | Sonia ct Harrow | |
| 44 D 12 | Sonia gdns NW10 | |
| 5 P 14 | Sonia gdns N12 | |
| 70 G 20 | Sonia gdns Hounsl | |
| 23 X 15 | Sonning rd SE25 | |
| 48 D 18 | Sonning st N7 | |
| 51 P 2 | Sophia rd E10 | |
| 65 V 16 | Sophia rd E16 | |
| 64 C 20 | Sophia st E14 | |
| 153 Z 6 | Sorrento rd Sutton | |
| 154 A 6 | Sorrento rd Sutton | |
| 48 K 11 | Sotheby rd N5 | |
| 88 M 3 | Soudan rd SW11 | |
| 144 H 4 | Souldern rd W14 | |
| 32 H 19 | South Access rd E17 | |
| 136 A 10 | South Africa rd W12 | |
| 62 L 20 | South Africa rd W12 | |
| 74 J 1 | South Africa rd W12 | |
| 139 V 12 | South Audley st W1 | |
| 20 E 1 | South av E4 | |
| 155 N 17 | South av Carsh | |

| | | |
|---|---|---|
| 85 O 3 | South av Rich | |
| 58 D 20 | South av S'hall | |
| 58 D 20 | South Av gdns S'hall | |
| 116 K 14 | South bank Surb | |
| 116 K 15 | South Bank ter Surb | |
| 51 X 10 | South Birkbeck rd E11 | |
| 74 F 14 | South Black Lion la W6 | |
| 146 A 10 | South Bolton gdns SW5 | |
| 29 R 17 | South clo N6 | |
| 4 H 12 | South clo Barnt | |
| 97 W 11 | South clo Bxly Hth | |
| 69 S 5 | South clo Dgnhm | |
| 119 X 14 | South clo Mrdn | |
| 40 E 2 | South clo Pinn | |
| 100 H 6 | South clo Twick | |
| 32 K 10 | South Countess rd E17 | |
| 140 F 1 | South cres WC1 | |
| 36 A 15 | South Cross rd Ilf | |
| 109 O 6 | South Croxted rd SE21 | |
| 12 L 12 | South dene NW7 | |
| 153 S 20 | South dri Sutton | |
| 72 G 9 | South Ealing rd W5 | |
| 18 G 11 | South Eastern av N9 | |
| 147 V 6 | South Eaton pl SW1 | |
| 125 R 16 | South Eden Pk rd Becknhm | |
| 145 S 3 | South Edwardes sq W8 | |
| 145 X 1 | South end W 8 | |
| 156 M 8 | South end Croy | |
| 46 K 13 | South End clo NW3 | |
| 46 K 14 | South End grn NW3 | |
| 46 J 11 | South End rd NW3 | |
| 57 Z 14 | South End rd Hornch | |
| 145 Y 1 | South End row W 8 | |
| 52 K 19 | South Esk rd E7 | |
| 106 G 18 | South gdns SW19 | |
| 32 K 16 | South gro E17 | |
| 31 P 16 | South gro N15 | |
| 47 P 4 | South gro N6 | |
| 113 S 16 | South hill Chisl | |
| 41 O 10 | South Hill av Harrow | |
| 41 T 12 | South Hill gro Harrow | |
| 46 K 12 | South Hill pk NW3 | |
| 46 K 11 | South Hill Pk gdns NW3 | |
| 126 A 9 | South Hill rd Brom | |
| 125 Z 8 | South Hill rd Brom | |
| 113 T 17 | South Hill rd Chisl | |
| 149 S 19 | South Island pl SW9 | |
| 116 G 6 | South la Kingst | |
| 117 Z 16 | South la New Mald | |
| 118 A 15 | South la New Mald | |
| 117 X 9 | South La w New Mald | |
| 149 O 19 | South Lambeth est SW8 | |
| 148 L 17 | South Lambeth rd SW8 | |
| 121 Z 8 | South Lodge av Mitch | |
| 122 A 8 | South Lodge av Mitch | |
| 6 K 13 | South Lodge cres Enf | |
| 6 J 14 | South Lodge dr N14 | |
| 7 N 17 | South Lodge dr N14 | |
| 139 W 7 | South Molton la W1 | |
| 65 T 16 | South Molton rd E16 | |
| 139 W 7 | South Molton st W1 | |
| 123 T 10 | South Norwood hill SE25 | |
| 112 B 1 | South Park cres SE6 | |
| 94 A 20 | South Park cres SE6 | |
| 54 F 0 | South Park area Ilf | |
| 54 G 9 | South Park dri Ilf | |
| 157 R 10 | South Park Hill rd S Croy | |
| 106 B 15 | South Park rd SW19 | |
| 105 X 16 | South Park rd SW19 | |
| 54 F 9 | South Park ter Ilf | |
| 54 F 11 | South Park ter Ilf | |
| 146 G 10 | South pde SW3 | |
| 73 Y 10 | South pde W4 | |
| 54 F 9 | South Pk cres Ilf | |
| 117 X 10 | South Pk gro New Mald | |
| 142 G 1 | South pl EC2 | |
| 116 L 16 | South pl Surb | |
| 148 F 1 | South Place mews EC2 | |
| 16 F 17 | South rd N11 | |
| 18 L 5 | South rd N9 | |
| 110 E 4 | South rd SE23 | |
| 106 D 16 | South rd SW19 | |
| 72 G 10 | South rd W5 | |
| 25 U 4 | South rd Edg | |
| 100 A 14 | South rd Felt | |

| | | |
|---|---|---|
| 100 D 16 | South rd Hampt | |
| 37 X 18 | South rd Rom | |
| 70 E 3 | South rd S'hall | |
| 101 R 8 | South rd Twick | |
| 154 K 19 | South ri Carsh | |
| 94 C 4 | South row SE3 | |
| 27 Z 18 | South sq NW11 | |
| 141 R 1 | South sq WC1 | |
| 139 T 12 | South st W1 | |
| 126 F 2 | South st Brom | |
| 9 S 17 | South st Enf | |
| 69 Y 7 | South st Rainhm | |
| 39 R 16 | South st Rom | |
| 143 P 7 | South Tenter st E1 | |
| 146 J 5 | South ter SW7 | |
| 116 K 13 | South ter Surb | |
| 109 R 16 | South vale SE19 | |
| 41 U 12 | South vale Harrow | |
| 126 J 3 | South view Brom | |
| 99 O 13 | South view Drtfrd | |
| 98 B 17 | South View clo Bxly | |
| 35 Y 18 | South View cres Ilf | |
| 34 J 11 | South View dri E18 | |
| 29 Z 11 | South View rd N8 | |
| 47 Y 18 | South vlls NW1 | |
| 14 M 7 | South way N12 | |
| 19 D 9 | South way N9 | |
| 119 O 9 | South way SW20 | |
| 158 K 5 | South way Croy | |
| 22 H 14 | South way Harrow | |
| 43 P 14 | South way Wemb | |
| 83 Z 15 | South Western rd Twick | |
| 84 A 16 | South Western rd Twick | |
| 138 G 4 | South Wharf rd W2 | |
| 159 Z 5 | South wlk W Wkhm | |
| 86 A 8 | South Worple av SW13 | |
| 86 A 8 | South Worple way SW14 | |
| 85 Y 8 | South Worple way SW14 | |
| 142 E 19 | Southall pl SE1 | |
| 128 M 9 | Southam st W10 | |
| 129 O 20 | Southam st W10 | |
| 141 R 3 | Southampton bldgs WC2 | |
| 121 Z 8 | Southampton gdns Mitch | |
| 140 L 2 | Southampton pl WC1 | |
| 46 M 14 | Southampton rd NW5 | |
| 132 K 19 | Southampton row WC1 | |
| 140 L 2 | Southampton st WC2 | |
| 91 T 1 | Southampton way SE5 | |
| 150 G 10 | Southampton way SE5 | |
| 116 A 17 | Southbank Surb | |
| 25 X 8 | Southborne av NW9 | |
| 116 G 19 | Southborough clo Surb | |
| 127 U 12 | Southborough la Brom | |
| 63 S 2 | Southborough rd E9 | |
| 127 S 10 | Southborough rd Brom | |
| 116 J 20 | Southborough rd Surb | |
| 126 F 18 | Southbourne Brom | |
| 22 B 20 | Southbourne clo Pinn | |
| 27 S 13 | Southbourne cres NW4 | |
| 94 H 12 | Southbourne gdns SE12 | |
| 54 B 16 | Southbourne gdns Ilf | |
| 156 K 7 | Southbridge pl Croy | |
| 156 M 8 | Southbridge rd Croy | |
| 94 C 15 | Southbrook rd SE12 | |
| 122 A 1 | Southbrook rd SW16 | |
| 74 K 6 | Southbrook st W12 | |
| 8 K 14 | Southbury av Enf | |
| 8 G 13 | Southbury rd Enf | |
| 66 G 7 | Southchurch rd E6 | |
| 144 L 6 | Southcombe st W14 | |
| 117 S 18 | Southcote av Surb | |
| 32 F 15 | Southcote rd E17 | |
| 47 V 12 | Southcote rd N19 | |
| 124 B 13 | Southcote rd SE25 | |
| 159 U 3 | Southcroft av W Wkhm | |
| 96 H 7 | Southcroft av Welling | |
| 107 N 14 | Southcroft rd SW17 | |
| 105 U 3 | Southdean gdns SW19 | |
| 71 X 9 | Southdown av W7 | |

| | | |
|---|---|---|
| 36 G 15 | Southdown cres Ilf | |
| 105 O 19 | Southdown dri SW20 | |
| 105 R 20 | Southdown rd SW20 | |
| 143 P 1 | Southdown rd SW20 | |
| 155 O 19 | Southdown rd Carsh | |
| 57 X 2 | Southdown rd Hornch | |
| 95 Y 16 | Southend clo SE9 | |
| 95 Y 15 | Southend cres SE9 | |
| 111 O 10 | Southend la SE6&SE26 | |
| 110 L 9 | Southend la SE6&SE26 | |
| 34 H 6 | Southend rd E18 | |
| 53 T 19 | Southend rd E6 | |
| 111 P 17 | Southend rd Becknhm | |
| 35 N 8 | Southend rd Wdfd Grn | |
| 32 G 9 | Southerland rd E17 | |
| 77 T 16 | Southern appr SE10 | |
| 123 V 6 | Southern av SE25 | |
| 63 Y 10 | Southern gro E3 | |
| 142 J 9 | Southern Langbourn champs EC3 | |
| 65 X 6 | Southern rd E13 | |
| 28 L 13 | Southern rd N2 | |
| 128 K 18 | Southern row W10 | |
| 133 N 9 | Southern st N1 | |
| 38 F 19 | Southern way Rom | |
| 144 B 5 | Southerton rd W6 | |
| 74 L 10 | Southesk st SW9 | |
| 90 B 5 | Southesk st SW9 | |
| 31 S 15 | Southey rd N15 | |
| 105 Z 18 | Southey rd SW19 | |
| 90 E 1 | Southey rd SW9 | |
| 110 E 18 | Southey st SE20 | |
| 4 B 20 | Southfield Barnt | |
| 71 W 5 | Southfield cotts W7 | |
| 101 V 8 | Southfield gdns Twick | |
| 22 J 14 | Southfield pk Harrow | |
| 31 T 9 | Southfield rd N17 | |
| 73 X 6 | Southfield rd W4 | |
| 74 H 7 | Southfield rd W4 | |
| 9 P 19 | Southfield rd Enf | |
| 26 H 9 | Southfields NW4 | |
| 87 X 16 | Southfields rd SW18 | |
| 134 G 1 | Southgate gro N1 | |
| 134 G 3 | Southgate rd N1 | |
| 40 P 18 | Southgate rd N1 | |
| 64 E 17 | Southill st E14 | |
| 79 Z 18 | Southland rd SE18 | |
| 83 P 13 | Southland way Hounsl | |
| 127 R 7 | Southlands gro Brom | |
| 126 M 10 | Southlands rd Brom | |
| 127 P 8 | Southlands rd Brom | |
| 152 C 18 | Southmead Epsom | |
| 87 S 20 | Southmead rd SW19 | |
| 42 L 15 | Southmeadows Wemb | |
| 113 V 8 | Southold ri SE9 | |
| 14 K 11 | Southover N12 | |
| 14 L 14 | Southover N12 | |
| 112 F 14 | Southover Brom | |
| 54 F 9 | Southpark cres Ilf | |
| 79 S 11 | Southport rd SE18 | |
| 122 H 20 | Southsea rd Croy | |
| 116 J 8 | Southsea rd Kingst | |
| 74 D 9 | Southside W6 | |
| 105 O 14 | Southside comm SW19 | |
| 96 F 18 | Southspring Sidcp | |
| 94 A 5 | Southvale rd SE3 | |
| 44 D 14 | Southview av NW10 | |
| 155 V 17 | Southview gdns Wallgtn | |
| 111 X 9 | Southview rd Brom | |
| 142 C 11 | Southview rd Brom | |
| 142 B 10 | Southwark Br rd SE1 | |
| 142 A 14 | Southwark gro SE1 | |
| 151 Y 1 | Southwark park SE16 | |
| 151 T 5 | Southwark Pk rd SE16 | |
| 143 X 20 | Southwark Pk rd SE16 | |
| 151 X 2 | Southwark Pk rd SE16 | |
| 142 C 14 | Southwark st SE1 | |
| 63 Y 17 | Southwater clo E14 | |
| 28 B 17 | Southway NW11 | |
| 14 L 9 | Southway N20 | |
| 119 N 10 | Southway SW20 | |
| 126 E 18 | Southway Brom | |
| 155 V 9 | Southway Wallgtn | |
| 74 L 6 | Southway clo W12 | |
| 40 J 16 | Southwell av Grnfd | |
| 146 B 4 | Southwell gdns SW7 | |

| | |
|---|---|
| 90 L7 | Southwell rd SE5 |
| 122 F14 | Southwell rd Croy |
| 24 H18 | Southwell rd Harrow |
| 51 X3 | Southwest rd E11 |
| 138 J5 | Southwick ms W2 |
| 138 J7 | Southwick pl W2 |
| 138 J5 | Southwick st W 2 |
| 55 N15 | Southwold dri Bark |
| 50 A7 | Southwold rd E5 |
| 29 R20 | Southwood av N6 |
| 103 W20 | Southwood av Kingst |
| 117 X18 | Southwood dri Surb |
| 35 Z14 | Southwood gdns Ilf |
| 47 P2 | Southwood la N6 |
| 29 P20 | Southwood la N6 |
| 47 S1 | Southwood Lawn rd N6 |
| 29 S20 | Southwood Lawn rd N6 |
| 47 S1 | Southwood Lawn rd N6 |
| 47 R1 | Southwood pk N6 |
| 113 Y4 | Southwood rd SE9 |
| 114 A3 | Southwood rd SE9 |
| 95 T14 | Sowerby clo SE9 |
| 57 U17 | Sowrey av Rainhm |
| 123 N1 | Spa hill SE19 |
| 109 O19 | Spa hill SE19 |
| 151 O2 | Spa rd SE16 |
| 151 S2 | Spa rd SE16 |
| 133 T15 | Spafield st EC1 |
| 107 S13 | Spalding rd SW17 |
| 64 B12 | Spanby rd E3 |
| 46 E3 | Spaniards clo NW11 |
| 46 F4 | Spaniards end NW3 |
| 46 E6 | Spaniards rd NW3 |
| 139 U3 | Spanish pl W1 |
| 88 E12 | Spanish rd SW18 |
| 123 R2 | Spar clo SE25 |
| 23 T14 | Sparkbridge rd Harrow |
| 152 J9 | Sparrow Farm rd Epsom |
| 56 G8 | Sparrow grn Dgnhm |
| 114 C1 | Sparrows la SE9 |
| 96 B20 | Sparrows la SE9 |
| 10 A4 | Sparrows way Bushey Watf |
| 48 B3 | Sparsholt rd N4 |
| 67 V4 | Sparsholt rd Bark |
| 93 T3 | Sparta st SE10 |
| 145 V7 | Spear ms W8 |
| 78 J17 | Spearman st SE18 |
| 36 L14 | Spearpoint ter Ilf |
| 48 A4 | Spears rd N4 |
| 70 B20 | Speart la Hounsl |
| 149 Y1 | Speech st SE1 |
| 76 A20 | Speedwell st SE8 |
| 132 K14 | Speedy pl WC1 |
| 88 H8 | Speke rd SW11 |
| 123 N3 | Speke rd Thntn Hth |
| 113 U8 | Spekehill SE9 |
| 126 D13 | Speldhurst clo Brom |
| 63 S2 | Speldhurst rd E9 |
| 63 S2 | Speldhurst rd E9 |
| 73 Z7 | Speldhurst rd W4 |
| 135 R20 | Spelman st E1 |
| 143 R1 | Spelman st E1 |
| 17 R19 | Spencer av N13 |
| 61 N7 | Spencer clo NW10 |
| 123 P17 | Spencer clo Croy |
| 21 Y17 | Spencer clo Wdfd Grn |
| 28 D19 | Spencer dri N2 |
| 95 T13 | Spencer gdns SE9 |
| 85 V12 | Spencer gdns SW14 |
| 105 S17 | Spencer hill SW19 |
| 105 T17 | Spencer Hill rd SW14 |
| 88 F13 | Spencer pk SW18 |
| 148 D2 | Spencer pl SW1 |
| 33 U6 | Spencer rd E17 |
| 66 B3 | Spencer rd E6 |
| 16 D14 | Spencer rd N11 |
| 31 X5 | Spencer rd N17 |
| 90 G14 | Spencer rd SE24 |
| 88 G12 | Spencer rd SW18 |
| 118 K1 | Spencer rd SW20 |
| 73 V2 | Spencer rd W3 |
| 73 V20 | Spencer rd W4 |
| 112 B18 | Spencer rd Brom |
| 23 U8 | Spencer rd Harrow |
| 54 L4 | Spencer rd Ilf |
| 83 O3 | Spencer rd Islwth |
| 121 N18 | Spencer rd Mitch |
| 157 S11 | Spencer rd S Croy |
| 101 T5 | Spencer rd Twick |
| 42 C6 | Spencer rd Wemb |
| 47 T11 | Spencer ri NW5 |
| 133 X13 | Spencer st EC1 |
| 87 O10 | Spencer wlk SW15 |
| 49 R13 | Spenser gro N16 |
| 148 C1 | Spenser st SW1 |
| 79 X13 | Speranza st SE18 |
| 31 T9 | Sperling rd N17 |
| 63 V20 | Spert st E14 |
| 6 G20 | Spey side N14 |
| 39 P2 | Spey way Rom |
| 62 G6 | Spezia rd NW10 |
| 118 E13 | Spiers clo New Mald |
| 31 N5 | Spigurnell rd N17 |
| 58 C18 | Spikes Br rd S'hall |
| 79 Y14 | Spindel clo S18 |
| 79 V14 | Spindel st SE18 |
| 40 D4 | Spinnells rd Harrow |
| 56 A14 | Spinney gdns Dgnhm |
| 127 S3 | Spinney oak Brom |
| 17 S2 | Spinney the N21 |
| 107 E7 | Spinney the SW16 |
| 5 O10 | Spinney the Barnt |
| 115 Y12 | Spinney the Sidcp |
| 11 X14 | Spinney the Stanm |
| 152 M9 | Spinney the Sutton |
| 41 X10 | Spinney the Wemb |
| 127 T3 | Spinneys the Brom |
| 134 L20 | Spital sq E1 |
| 135 R19 | Spital st E1 |
| 134 M20 | Spitalfields market E1 |
| 31 W13 | Spondon rd N15 |
| 93 U20 | Sportsbank st SE6 |
| 30 L3 | Spottons gro N17 |
| 159 O11 | Spout hill Croy |
| 34 F18 | Spratt Hall rd E11 |
| 83 R14 | Spray la Islwth |
| 79 N10 | Spray st SE18 |
| 78 M10 | Spray st SE18 |
| 147 N8 | Sprimont pl SW3 |
| 7 P20 | Spring bank N21 |
| 60 G19 | Spring Br rd W5 |
| 153 S12 | Spring Clo la Sutton |
| 7 S3 | Spring Ct rd Enf |
| 140 H13 | Spring gdns SW1 |
| 57 Y13 | Spring gdns Hornch |
| 38 J17 | Spring gdns Rom |
| 155 U11 | Spring gdns Wallgtn |
| 34 J1 | Spring gdns Wdfd Grn |
| 148 L10 | Spring Gdns wlk SE1 |
| 73 O15 | Spring gro W4 |
| 82 M2 | Spring Grove cres Hounsl |
| 82 L3 | Spring Grove rd Hounsl |
| 83 N3 | Spring Grove rd Hounsl |
| 85 N12 | Spring Grove rd Rich |
| 84 M12 | Spring Grove rd Rich |
| 49 X2 | Spring hill E5 |
| 123 Z14 | Spring la SE25 |
| 124 A15 | Spring la SE25 |
| 11 N13 | Spring lake Stanm |
| 139 R1 | Spring ms W1 |
| 159 T7 | Spring park Croy W Wickhm |
| 158 G4 | Spring Pk av Croy |
| 158 F3 | Spring Pk rd Croy |
| 47 R16 | Spring pl NW5 |
| 55 Z15 | Spring Pond rd Dgnhm |
| 138 F7 | Spring st W2 |
| 152 O20 | Spring st Epsom |
| 98 H10 | Spring vale Bxly Hth |
| 25 P1 | Spring Vale rd Edg |
| 144 G2 | Spring Vale ter W14 |
| 151 X19 | Springall st SE15 |
| 75 N20 | Springalls st SE15 |
| 17 P1 | Springbank N14 |
| 93 Z17 | Springbank rd SE13 |
| 111 U20 | Springbourne ct Becknhm |
| 28 L12 | Springcroft av N2 |
| 72 H13 | Springdale av Brentf |
| 49 N12 | Springdale rd N16 |
| 50 A3 | Springfield E5 |
| 49 Y4 | Springfield E5 |
| 10 C4 | Springfield Bushey Watf |
| 29 V11 | Springfield av N22 |
| 119 U5 | Springfield av SW20 |
| 10 L11 | Springfield clo Stanm |
| 36 B17 | Springfield dri Ilf |
| 50 A4 | Springfield gdns E5 |
| 25 Z16 | Springfield gdns NW9 |
| 127 U9 | Springfield gdns Brom |
| 159 T2 | Springfield gdns W Wkhm |
| 34 L2 | Springfield gdns Wdfd Grn |
| 77 Y17 | Springfield gro SE7 |
| 129 W6 | Springfield la NW6 |
| 126 A15 | Springfield mt NW9 |
| 49 Z2 | Springfield park E5 |
| 65 N8 | Springfield rd E15 |
| 32 K19 | Springfield rd E17 |
| 20 L4 | Springfield rd E4 |
| 53 U19 | Springfield rd E6 |
| 130 A5 | Springfield rd NW8 |
| 16 G17 | Springfield rd N11 |
| 31 X12 | Springfield rd N15 |
| 110 B14 | Springfield rd SE26 |
| 105 W13 | Springfield rd SW19 |
| 71 T2 | Springfield rd W7 |
| 127 U9 | Springfield rd Brom |
| 98 G10 | Springfield rd Bxly Hth |
| 23 T18 | Springfield rd Harrow |
| 116 K7 | Springfield rd Kingst |
| 101 Y13 | Springfield rd Tedd |
| 108 L20 | Springfield rd Thntn Hth |
| 122 L1 | Springfield rd Thntn Hth |
| 82 H20 | Springfield rd Twick |
| 155 S11 | Springfield rd Wallgtn |
| 97 P7 | Springfield rd Welling |
| 109 Z8 | Springfield ri SE26 |
| 129 W5 | Springfield wlk NW6 |
| 48 M3 | Springpark dri N4 |
| 125 V5 | Springpark dri Becknhm |
| 93 W16 | Springrice rd SE13 |
| 62 E4 | Springwell av NW10 |
| 108 D10 | Springwell clo SW16 |
| 108 E11 | Springwell rd SW16 |
| 70 A20 | Springwell rd Hounsl |
| 12 G7 | Springwood cres Edg |
| 12 F7 | Springwood cres Edg |
| 52 F16 | Sprowstone ms E7 |
| 52 F16 | Sprowstone rd E7 |
| 33 T9 | Spruce Hills rd E17 |
| 92 H6 | Sprules rd SE4 |
| 31 O13 | Spur rd N15 |
| 67 O9 | Spur rd Bark |
| 11 Y12 | Spur rd Edg |
| 71 Z20 | Spur rd Islwth |
| 109 O19 | Spurgeon av SE19 |
| 109 O19 | Spurgeon rd SE19 |
| 150 E1 | Spurgeon st SE1 |
| 91 V10 | Spurling rd SE22 |
| 56 C17 | Spurling rd Dgnhm |
| 49 Z16 | Spurstowe rd E8 |
| 49 Y16 | Spurstowe ter E8 |
| 155 N10 | Square the Carsh |
| 53 W1 | Square the Ilf |
| 21 R17 | Square the Wdfd Grn |
| 106 E7 | Squarey st SW17 |
| 28 E4 | Squire's la N3 |
| 46 F9 | Squires mt NW3 |
| 15 P13 | Squirrel clo N12 |
| 152 E2 | Squirrels grn Worc Pk |
| 39 Y11 | Squirrels Heath av Rom |
| 22 E11 | Squirrels the Pinn |
| 135 T13 | Squirries st E2 |
| 132 E5 | Stable yd NW1 |
| 140 B16 | Stable yd SW1 |
| 140 B16 | Stable Yd rd SW1 |
| 19 P15 | Stacey av N18 |
| 33 W17 | Stacey clo E10 |
| 140 H6 | Stacey st WC2 |
| 139 P20 | Stackhouse st SW3 |
| 78 E18 | Stadium rd SE18 |
| 95 R1 | Stadium rd SE18 |
| 146 O19 | Stadium st SW10 |
| 43 P13 | Stadium way Wemb |
| 50 G3 | Staffa rd E10 |
| 6 H17 | Stafford clo N14 |
| 153 T13 | Stafford clo Sutton |
| 156 O10 | Stafford clo Croy |
| 129 T12 | Stafford ms NW6 |
| 84 L18 | Stafford ms Rich |
| 140 A20 | Stafford pl SW1 |
| 63 Y7 | Stafford rd E3 |
| 52 M19 | Stafford rd E7 |
| 129 S11 | Stafford rd NW6 |
| 156 D11 | Stafford rd Croy & Wallgtn |
| 23 N3 | Stafford rd Harrow |
| 117 V6 | Stafford rd New Mald |
| 114 H9 | Stafford rd Sidcp |
| 84 B19 | Stafford rd Twick |
| 155 U14 | Stafford rd Wallgtn |
| 156 B12 | Stafford rd Wallgtn |
| 140 A12 | Stafford st W1 |
| 137 U20 | Stafford ter W8 |
| 91 Y1 | Staffordshire st SE15 |
| 25 U7 | Stag clo Edg |
| 25 V10 | Stag la NW9 |
| 104 E5 | Stag la SW15 |
| 21 V7 | Stag la Buck HI |
| 148 A1 | Stag pl SW1 |
| 121 S5 | Stainbank rd Mitc |
| 31 V12 | Stainby rd N15 |
| 142 H15 | Stainer st SE1 |
| 153 P3 | Staines av NW8 |
| 80 E10 | Staines rd Houns |
| 54 D14 | Staines rd Ilf |
| 100 H7 | Staines rd Twick |
| 101 O4 | Staines rd Twick |
| 33 P13 | Stainforth rd E17 |
| 88 K6 | Stainforth rd SW |
| 36 F20 | Stainforth rd SW |
| 142 B4 | Staining la EC2 |
| 114 E20 | Stainmore clo Ch |
| 63 R7 | Stainsbury st E2 |
| 64 A18 | Stainsby rd E14 |
| 93 W18 | Stainton rd SE6 |
| 9 R5 | Stainton rd Enf |
| 130 L20 | Stalbridge st NW |
| 151 Y3 | Stalham st SE16 |
| 109 S19 | Stambourne way SE19 |
| 159 V4 | Stambourne way Wkhm |
| 142 G15 | Stamer st SE1 |
| 74 E10 | Stamford Brook a W6 |
| 74 E9 | Stamford Brook rc W6 |
| 31 X14 | Stamford clo N15 |
| 23 T1 | Stamford clo Harr |
| 70 H1 | Stamford clo S'ha |
| 126 D10 | Stamford dri Brom |
| 68 F2 | Stamford gdns Dgnhm |
| 68 G2 | Stamford gdns Dgnhm |
| 49 W3 | Stamford Grn east N16 |
| 49 W4 | Stamford Grn wes N16 |
| 49 U4 | Stamford hill N16 |
| 66 C3 | Stamford rd E6 |
| 31 W14 | Stamford rd E6 |
| 68 D2 | Stamford rd Dgnhm |
| 141 T13 | Stamford st SE1 |
| 54 F1 | Stamforth rd Ilf |
| 135 O11 | Stamp pl E2 |
| 87 N7 | Stanbridge rd SW |
| 80 C6 | Stanbrook rd SE2 |
| 92 B4 | Stanbury rd SE15 |
| 26 A15 | Stancroft NW9 |
| 61 X10 | Standard rd NW10 |
| 81 R14 | Standard rd Blvdr |
| 98 A11 | Standard rd Bxly H |
| 9 W1 | Standard rd Enf |
| 82 C7 | Standard rd Houns |
| 87 X20 | Standen rd SW18 |
| 74 G12 | Standish rd W6 |
| 65 V10 | Standrew's rd E13 |
| 56 F17 | Stanfield gdns Dgnhm |
| 63 X7 | Stanfield rd E3 |
| 56 F15 | Stanfield rd Dgnhm |
| 38 G18 | Stanford clo Rom |
| 150 J7 | Stanford pl SE17 |
| 16 A16 | Stanford rd N11 |
| 145 Y2 | Stanford rd W 8 |
| 55 U20 | Stanford rd Dgnhm |
| 148 E6 | Stanford st SW1 |
| 121 X3 | Stanford way SW1 |
| 11 O14 | Stangate gdns Stanm |
| 123 X10 | Stanger rd SE25 |
| 27 W10 | Stanhope av N3 |
| 126 E20 | Stanhope av Brom |
| 23 P5 | Stanhope av Harrov |
| 142 C16 | Stanhope bldgs SE |
| 139 U13 | Stanhope ga W1 |
| 13 R17 | Stanhope gdns NW |
| 30 K18 | Stanhope gdns N4 |
| 29 U19 | Stanhope gdns N6 |
| 146 D6 | Stanhope gdns SW |
| 56 A8 | Stanhope gdns Dgnhm |
| 53 T3 | Stanhope gdns Ilf |
| 124 L10 | Stanhope gro Becknhm |
| 146 D5 | Stanhope Ms east SW7 |
| 146 C6 | Stanhope Ms south SW7 |
| 146 C5 | Stanhope Ms west SW7 |
| 59 N10 | Stanhope Pk rd Grnfd |
| 139 N7 | Stanhope pl W2 |
| 33 R16 | Stanhope rd E17 |
| 16 D15 | Stanhope rd N11 |
| 15 S16 | Stanhope rd N12 |
| 47 V1 | Stanhope rd N6 |
| 29 V20 | Stanhope rd N6 |

4 B 19 Stanhope rd Barnt
98 A 4 Stanhope rd Bxly Hth
97 Z 4 Stanhope rd Bxly Hth
55 O 17 Stanhope rd Carsh
57 R 7 Stanhope rd Croy
56 A 8 Stanhope rd Dgnhm
59 N 13 Stanhope rd Grnfd
14 M 8 Stanhope rd Sidcp
39 W 15 Stanhope row W1
32 A 12 Stanhope st NW1
38 G 8 Stanhope ter W2
36 B 15 Stanlake ms W12
74 L 3 Stanlake ms W12
36 A 14 Stanlake rd W12
74 K 2 Stanlake rd W12
36 A 15 Stanlake vlls W12
74 L 3 Stanlake vlls W12
67 X 8 Stanley av Bark
25 U 5 Stanley av Becknhm
56 C 3 Stanley av Dgnhm
58 M 3 Stanley av Grnfd
59 N 3 Stanley av Grnfd
18 F 11 Stanley av New Mald
39 W 14 Stanley av Rom
60 K 1 Stanley av Wemb
149 N 16 Stanley clo SW8
39 X 12 Stanley clo Rom
60 K 1 Stanley clo Wemb
137 O 9 Stanley cres W11
45 N 16 Stanley gdns NW2
107 N 16 Stanley gdns SW17
137 P 9 Stanley gdns W11
74 A 5 Stanley gdns W3
155 U 15 Stanley gdns Wallgtn
101 T 11 Stanley Gdns rd Tedd
89 R 5 Stanley gro SW8
122 F 15 Stanley gro Croy
132 J 9 Stanley pas NW1
60 M 2 Stanley Pk dri Wemb
154 M 16 Stanley Pk rd Carsh
155 S 14 Stanley Pk rd Wallgtn
33 R 19 Stanley rd E10
53 R 16 Stanley rd E12
64 J 4 Stanley rd E15
34 C 6 Stanley rd E18
20 K 4 Stanley rd E4
29 R 2 Stanley rd N10
16 L 17 Stanley rd N11
30 X 13 Stanley rd N15
28 G 12 Stanley rd N2
18 F 7 Stanley rd N9
85 T 10 Stanley rd SW14
105 Y 16 Stanley rd SW19
73 U 8 Stanley rd W3
126 K 8 Stanley rd Brom
155 O 18 Stanley rd Carsh
122 G 15 Stanley rd Croy
8 F 13 Stanley rd Enf
41 N 8 Stanley rd Harrow
140 M 7 Stanley rd Harrow
82 M 8 Stanley rd Hounsl
83 N 9 Stanley rd Hounsl
54 D 8 Stanley rd Ilf
110 Y 8 Stanley rd Mrdn
58 A 20 Stanley rd S'hall
115 O 8 Stanley rd Sidcp
154 A 16 Stanley rd Sutton
153 Z 16 Stanley rd Sutton
101 U 13 Stanley rd Tedd
43 N 17 Stanley rd Wemb
155 N 19 Stanley sq Carsh
66 L 19 Stanley st E6
75 Y 19 Stanley st SE8
48 A 8 Stanley ter N4
83 R 3 Stanleycroft clo Islwth
88 K 4 Stanmer st SW11
85 N 8 Stanmore gdns Rich
154 D 6 Stanmore gdns Sutton
11 O 14 Stanmore hill Stanm
10 L 11 Stanmore hill Stanm
131 Y 4 Stanmore pl NW1
52 C 4 Stanmore rd E11
30 K 12 Stanmore rd N15
81 Y 10 Stanmore rd Blvdr
84 M 7 Stanmore rd Rich
133 N 4 Stanmore st N1
125 P 2 Stanmore ter Becknhm
66 K 17 Stannard cres E6
49 W 17 Stannard rd E8
149 T 12 Stannary pl SE11
149 U 12 Stannary st SE11
90 D 7 Stansfield rd SW9
56 E 9 Stansgate rd Dgnhm
126 C 13 Stanstead clo Brom
57 Z 19 Stanstead clo Hornch
34 H 15 Stanstead rd E11
110 J 1 Stanstead rd SE23
115 W 2 Stansted cres Bxly
107 Z 11 Stanthorpe clo SW16
108 A 11 Stanthorpe rd SW16
107 Z 11 Stanthorpe rd SW16
101 T 14 Stanton av Tedd
153 P 1 Stanton clo Worc Pk
110 K 9 Stanton rd SE26
86 D 4 Stanton rd SW13
119 O 1 Stanton rd SW20
122 L 18 Stanton rd Croy
91 W 1 Stanton st SE15
73 P 1 Stanway gdns W3
12 G 17 Stanway gdns Edg
134 K 9 Stanway st N1
145 O 7 Stanwick rd W14
42 A 9 Stapenhill rd Wemb
141 S 3 Staple inn WC1
141 S 3 Staple Inn bldgs WC1
142 G 19 Staple st SE1
36 H 17 Stapleford av Ilfd
87 R 20 Stapleford clo SW19
108 A 1 Stapleford clo SW2
117 P 5 Stapleford clo Kingst
42 G 20 Stapleford rd Wemb
68 D 8 Stapleford way Bark
93 Y 14 Staplehurst rd SE13
154 J 17 Staplehurst rd Carsh
57 W 19 Stapleton cres Rain
156 F 10 Stapleton gdns Croy
30 F 20 Stapleton Hall rd N4
48 D 3 Stapleton Hall rd N4
107 N 7 Stapleton rd SW17
81 R 14 Stapley rd Blvdr
4 F 12 Stapylton rd Barnt
63 N 20 Star & Garter rd E1
142 K 8 Star all EC 3
84 L 20 Star And Garter hill Rich
99 O 12 Star hill Drtfrd
64 M 12 Star la E16
65 N 13 Star la E16
145 N 12 Star rd W14
83 P 5 Star rd Islwth
138 J 4 Star st W2
141 S 5 Star yd WC2
76 C 8 Starboard way E14
36 E 7 Starch Ho la Ilf
132 C 14 Starcross st NW1
74 G 6 Starfield rd W12
21 U 6 Starling clo Buck Hl
101 W 1 Staten gdns Twick
40 N 11 Statham gro N16
18 D 15 Statham gro N18
16 D 16 Station appr N11
107 Y 12 Station appr SW16
87 U 7 Station appr SW6
98 F 20 Station appr Bxly
127 W 2 Station appr Chisl
152 F 11 Station appr Epsom
100 H 20 Station appr Hampt
23 U 20 Station appr Harrow
117 R 2 Station appr Kingst
22 B 12 Station appr Pinn
85 D 2 Station appr Rich
153 T 16 Station appr Sutton
97 O 5 Station appr Welling
42 C 17 Station appr Wemb
73 V 20 Station Appr rd W4
90 K 7 Station av SW9
152 C 19 Station av Epsom
85 O 3 Station av Rich
27 Z 6 Station clo N3
100 K 20 Station clo Hampt
31 N 14 Station cres N15
77 S 15 Station cres SE3
42 B 17 Station cres Wemb
73 W 20 Station gdns W4
42 J 17 Station gro Wemb
44 N 17 Station pde NW2
45 N 17 Station pde NW2
57 Y 13 Station pde Hornch
85 O 2 Station pde Rich
48 G 7 Station pl N4
51 V 10 Station rd E10
53 O 13 Station rd E12
51 W 18 Station rd E15
32 J 17 Station rd E17
20 K 3 Station rd E4
52 F 13 Station rd E7
26 G 18 Station rd NW4
13 P 18 Station rd NW7
16 E 17 Station rd N11
31 Y 11 Station rd N17
18 G 16 Station rd N18
47 V 10 Station rd N19
17 W 5 Station rd N21
30 A 1 Station rd N22
27 Y 5 Station rd N3
28 A 7 Station rd N3
110 C 15 Station rd SE20
123 V 9 Station rd SE25
86 E 4 Station rd SW13
106 F 20 Station rd SW19
61 N 17 Station rd W5
71 T 2 Station rd W7
81 T 9 Station rd Blvdr
126 A 3 Station rd Brom
98 A 6 Station rd Bxly Hth
97 Z 6 Station rd Bxly Hth
155 N 7 Station rd Carsh
114 A 17 Station rd Chisl
113 Z 19 Station rd Chisl
122 L 20 Station rd Croy
157 P 3 Station rd Croy
99 T 15 Station rd Drtfrd
12 D 18 Station rd Edg
7 Y 12 Station rd Enf
100 H 20 Station rd Hampt
22 K 15 Station rd Harrow
23 V 19 Station rd Harrow
82 K 12 Station rd Hounsl
36 F 11 Station rd Ilf
53 Z 8 Station rd Ilf
117 P 1 Station rd Kingst
118 J 12 Station rd New Mald
81 U 8 Station rd North Blvdr
55 W 1 Station rd Rom
101 X 14 Station rd Tedd
83 W 20 Station rd Twick
125 U 20 Station rd W Wkhm
159 U 1 Station rd W Wkhm
108 J 3 Station rise SE27
64 J 1 Station st E15
51 W 20 Station st E15
78 L 4 Station st E16
90 M 2 Station ter SE5
59 P 2 Station view Grnfd
153 S 15 Station way Sutton
83 X 19 Station yd Twick
141 X 6 Stationers ct EC4
102 L 17 Staunton rd Kingst
75 Y 17 Staunton st SE8
85 Z 1 Staveley gdns W4
92 B 1 Staveley rd SE15
73 X 18 Staveley rd W4
44 M 19 Staverton rd NW2
48 G 13 Stavordale rd N5
120 C 18 Stavordale rd Carsh
63 S 12 Stayners rd E1
153 X 4 Stayton rd Sutton
150 D 7 Stead st SE17
134 C 15 Steadman st EC1
68 B 6 Stebbing way Bark
76 H 10 Stebondale st E14
140 J 3 Stedham pl WC1
149 Z 7 Steedman st SE17
28 M 6 Steeds rd N10
83 Y 11 Steel rd Islwth
46 M 18 Steel's ms NW3
46 M 18 Steel's rd NW3
51 Z 12 Steele rd E11
64 M 5 Steele rd E15
61 W 7 Steele rd NW10
31 T 9 Steele rd N17
73 X 8 Steele rd W4
63 R 18 Steels la El
91 S 12 Steen way SE22
107 Y 8 Steep hill SW16
105 T 11 Steeple clo SW19
87 T 6 Steeple clo SW6
17 Y 17 Steeplestone clo N18
106 C 5 Steerforth st SW18
106 L 20 Steers mead Mitch
120 K 1 Steers mead Mitch
107 N 14 Stella rd SW17
124 A 4 Stembridge rd SE20
123 Z 4 Stembridge rd SE20
57 V 17 Stephen av Rain
140 E 3 Stephen ms W1
98 K 9 Stephen rd Bxly Hth
140 E 3 Stephen st W1
64 M 5 Stephen's rd E15
88 B 6 Stephendale rd SW6
65 O 4 Stephens rd E15
59 W 16 Stephenson rd W7
64 M 15 Stephenson st E16
62 C 8 Stephenson st NW10
132 C 15 Stephensons way NW1
63 T 19 Stepney causeway E1
63 R 13 Stepney grn E1
63 U 16 Stepney High st E1
63 R 15 Stepney way E1
143 W 2 Stepney way E1
12 A 13 Sterling av Edg
11 Z 13 Sterling av Edg
32 G 9 Sterling rd E17
8 A 5 Sterling rd Enf
138 L 20 Sterling st SW7
144 E 2 Sterndale rd W14
136 F 16 Sterne st W12
91 Y 6 Sternhall la SE15
108 A 4 Sternhold av SW2
107 Y 3 Sternhold av SW2
56 D 14 Sterry cres Dgnhm
152 A 8 Sterry dri Epsom
56 E 17 Sterry gdns Dgnhm
67 X 4 Sterry rd Bark
56 D 12 Sterry rd Dgnhm
137 O 1 Stervans rd W10
97 U 5 Stevedale rd Welling
53 V 18 Stevenage rd E6
144 E 20 Stevenage rd SW6
87 O 3 Stevenage rd SW6
50 D 17 Stevens av E9
10 B 6 Stevens grn Bushey Watf
55 R 9 Stevens rd Dgnhm
74 E 1 Steventon rd W12
142 B 9 Stew lane EC4
142 A 9 Stew la EC 4
134 M 20 Steward st E1
142 L 1 Steward st E1
25 W 19 Stewart clo NW9
51 V 13 Stewart rd E15
76 H 6 Stewart st E14
146 J 9 Stewart's gro SW3
89 T 1 Stewart's la SW8
147 Z 20 Stewart's la SW8
148 A 20 Stewart's rd SW8
89 W 3 Stewart's rd SW8
17 X 17 Stewartsby clo N18
73 T 2 Steyne rd W3
113 T 10 Steyning gro SE9
14 K 17 Steynings way N12
115 X 3 Steynton av Bxly
81 S 10 Stickland rd Blvdr
58 K 10 Stickleton clo Grnfd
73 P 14 Stile Hall gdns W4
42 B 11 Stilecroft gdns Wemb
127 U 13 Stiles clo Brom
74 G 18 Stillingfleet rd SW13
148 C 4 Stillington st SW1
92 K 17 Stillness rd SE23
65 V 7 Stirling rd E13
31 X 5 Stirling rd N17
30 H 4 Stirling rd N22
90 A 6 Stirling rd SW9
73 T 8 Stirling rd W3
73 T 8 Stirling rd W3
23 V 9 Stirling rd Harrow
82 H 20 Stirling rd Twick
117 T 14 Stirling wlk Surb
40 E 10 Stiven cres Harrow
48 C 14 Stock Orchard cres N7
48 C 15 Stock Orchard st N7
65 T 8 Stock st E13
56 B 6 Stockdale rd Dgnhm
59 X 9 Stockdove way Grnfd
108 D 6 Stockfield rd SW16
9 X 10 Stockingswater la Enf
38 M 19 Stockland rd Rom
121 X 1 Stockport rd SW16
107 X 20 Stockport rd SW16
33 V 11 Stocksfield E17
12 M 10 Stockton gdns NW7
13 N 10 Stockton gdns NW7
30 L 3 Stockton gdns N17
30 L 3 Stockton rd N17
18 L 18 Stockton rd N18
90 D 8 Stockwell av SW9
90 C 3 Stockwell gdns SW9
90 C 6 Stockwell grn SW9
90 C 6 Stockwell gro SW9
90 C 5 Stockwell la SW9
90 D 4 Stockwell Pk cres SW9
90 D 4 Stockwell Pk rd SW9
90 E 7 Stockwell Pk wlk SW9
90 C 5 Stockwell rd SW9
76 H 18 Stockwell st SE10
90 B 2 Stockwell ter SW8
88 F 9 Stockwood st SW11
110 B 20 Stodart rd SE20
124 B 1 Stodart rd SE20
87 S 20 Stoford clo SW19
49 O 9 Stoke Newington Ch st N16
49 V 8 Stoke Newington comm N16
49 U 9 Stoke Newington High st N16
49 T 13 Stoke Newington rd N16
62 D 9 Stoke pl NW10
103 V 18 Stoke rd Kingst
87 Z 3 Stokenchurch st SW6
66 D 12 Stokes rd E6
124 G 15 Stokes rd Croy
62 E 17 Stokesley st W12

| | | |
|---|---|---|
| 89 P 15 | Sunburgh rd SW12 |
| 12 L 15 | Sunbury av NW7 |
| 85 Z 11 | Sunbury st SW14 |
| 12 L 15 | Sunbury gdns NW7 |
| 63 R 5 | Sunbury rd Sutton |
| 78 H 9 | Sunbury st SE18 |
| 99 U 4 | Suncourt Erith |
| 10 B 7 | Suncroft pl SE26 |
| 10 F 2 | Sunderland rd SE23 |
| 72 G 8 | Sunderland rd SE6 |
| 37 W 5 | Sunderland ter W2 |
| 62 G 19 | Sundew av W12 |
| 74 F 1 | Sundew av W12 |
| 23 V 5 | Sundial av SE25 |
| 77 X 14 | Sundorne rd SE7 |
| 27 N 1 | Sundridge av Brom |
| 13 O 19 | Sundridge av Chisl |
| 96 F 6 | Sundridge av Welling |
| 13 O 15 | Sundridge park Chisl |
| 13 N 17 | Sundridge Park mansion Chisl |
| 23 W 19 | Sundridge rd Croy |
| 77 V 19 | Sunfields pl SE3 |
| 97 Z 11 | Sunland av Bxly Hth |
| 60 K 3 | Sunleigh rd Wemb |
| 59 Y 4 | Sunley gdns Grnfd |
| 62 B 19 | Sunningdale av W3 |
| 67 R 2 | Sunningdale av Bark |
| 00 B 4 | Sunningdale av Felt |
| 10 M 20 | Sunningdale clo Stanm |
| 25 U 17 | Sunningdale gdns NW9 |
| 27 R 10 | Sunningdale rd Brom |
| 53 V 8 | Sunningdale rd Sutton |
| 26 L 9 | Sunningfields cres NW4 |
| 26 L 11 | Sunningfields rd NW4 |
| 93 R 6 | Sunninghill rd SE13 |
| 123 Y 7 | Sunny bank SE25 |
| 61 V 1 | Sunny cres NW4 |
| 26 L 9 | Sunny gdns NW4 |
| 26 J 10 | Sunny hill NW4 |
| 26 J 8 | Sunny Hill park NW7 |
| 157 O 13 | Sunny Nook gdns S Croy |
| 9 U 7 | Sunny Rd the Enf |
| 20 G 3 | Sunny Side dri E4 |
| 25 Y 14 | Sunny view NW9 |
| 28 J 1 | Sunny way N12 |
| 123 V 7 | Sunnycroft rd SE25 |
| 82 K 5 | Sunnycroft rd Hounsl |
| 58 H 13 | Sunnycroft rd S'hall |
| 12 M 18 | Sunnydale gdns NW7 |
| 94 H 12 | Sunnydale rd SE12 |
| 20 J 18 | Sunnydene av E4 |
| 42 E 20 | Sunnydene gdns Wemb |
| 110 G 10 | Sunnydene st SE26 |
| 13 R 12 | Sunnyfield NW7 |
| 108 A 9 | Sunnyhill rd SW16 |
| 153 Y 5 | Sunnyhurst clo Sutton |
| 121 W 5 | Sunnymead av Mitch |
| 25 Y 20 | Sunnymead rd NW9 |
| 86 J 14 | Sunnymead rd SW15 |
| 152 A 18 | Sunnymede av Epsom |
| 35 Z 13 | Sunnymede dri Ilf |
| 105 S 15 | Sunnyside NW2 |
| 51 N 3 | Sunnyside rd E10 |
| 45 W 9 | Sunnyside rd N6 |
| 47 Y 1 | Sunnyside rd N19 |
| 72 F 4 | Sunnyside rd W5 |
| 54 C 9 | Sunnyside rd Ilf |
| 101 R 10 | Sunnyside rd Tedd |
| 18 J 12 | Sunnyside Rd east N9 |
| 18 J 11 | Sunnyside Rd north N9 |
| 18 J 12 | Sunnyside Rd south N9 |
| 21 R 10 | Sunnyvale Wdfd Grn |
| 91 O 10 | Sunray av SE24 |
| 127 T 13 | Sunray av Brom |
| 100 E 7 | Sunrise clo Felt |
| 20 E 4 | Sunset av E4 |
| 91 O 15 | Sunset av Wdfd Grn |
| 123 T 3 | Sunset gdns SE19 |
| 90 M 10 | Sunset rd SE5 |
| 91 N 10 | Sunset rd SE5 |
| 4 F 9 | Sunset view Barnt |
| 120 M 2 | Sunshine way Mitch |
| 92 A 3 | Sunwell st SE15 |
| 116 H 9 | Surbiton cres Kingst |
| 116 F 14 | Surbiton st Surb |

| | | |
|---|---|---|
| 116 M 12 | Surbiton hill Surb |
| 116 M 14 | Surbiton Hill pk Surb |
| 117 P 11 | Surbiton Hill pk Surb |
| 116 J 10 | Surbiton Hill rd Kingst |
| 116 H 8 | Surbiton rd Kingst |
| 78 K 8 | Surgeon st SE18 |
| 48 A 16 | Surr st N7 |
| 129 V 18 | Surrendale pl W9 |
| 154 G 4 | Surrey gro Sutton |
| 88 J 2 | Surrey la SW11 |
| 110 A 1 | Surrey mount SE23 |
| 92 E 12 | Surrey rd SE15 |
| 67 U 2 | Surrey rd Bark |
| 56 J 14 | Surrey rd Dgnhm |
| 22 M 16 | Surrey rd Harrow |
| 125 S 20 | Surrey rd W Wrhm |
| 141 X 17 | Surrey row SE1 |
| 150 K 8 | Surrey sq SE17 |
| 65 X 10 | Surrey st E13 |
| 141 P 8 | Surrey st WC2 |
| 156 L 4 | Surrey st Croy |
| 150 K 8 | Surrey ter SE17 |
| 109 O 16 | Surridge gdns SE19 |
| 38 J 11 | Susan clo Rom |
| 94 J 5 | Susan st SE3 |
| 127 Y 1 | Susan wood Chisl |
| 113 X 20 | Susan wood Chisl |
| 64 F 18 | Susannah st E14 |
| 83 S 8 | Sussex av Islwth |
| 84 B 15 | Sussex clo Twick |
| 40 G 18 | Sussex cres Grnfd |
| 30 K 17 | Sussex gdns N4 |
| 138 H 6 | Sussex gdns W2 |
| 90 H 11 | Sussex gro SW9 |
| 131 N 16 | Sussex ms NW 1 |
| 138 H 8 | Sussex Ms east W2 |
| 138 G 9 | Sussex Ms west W2 |
| 131 O 16 | Sussex pl NW1 |
| 138 H 8 | Sussex pl W2 |
| 144 C 9 | Sussex pl W6 |
| 74 L 13 | Sussex pl W6 |
| 81 V 19 | Sussex pl Erith |
| 118 B 8 | Sussex pl New Mald |
| 66 J 5 | Sussex rd E6 |
| 90 H 10 | Sussex rd SW9 |
| 154 M 15 | Sussex rd Carsh |
| 81 V 19 | Sussex rd Erith |
| 22 M 16 | Sussex rd Harrow |
| 23 N 17 | Sussex rd Harrow |
| 122 A 10 | Sussex rd Mitch |
| 118 B 9 | Sussex rd New Mald |
| 157 P 13 | Sussex rd S Croy |
| 70 A 8 | Sussex rd S'hall |
| 115 R 13 | Sussex rd Sidcp |
| 125 S 20 | Sussex rd W Wrhm |
| 14 L 16 | Sussex ring N12 |
| 14 L 16 | Sussex ring N12 |
| 138 H 8 | Sussex sq W2 |
| 65 W 10 | Sussex st E13 |
| 147 Z 10 | Sussex st SW1 |
| 47 Z 5 | Sussex way N19 |
| 48 A 7 | Sussex way N4 |
| 6 D 16 | Sussex way Barnt |
| 28 B 16 | Sutcliffe clo NW11 |
| 94 J 13 | Sutcliffe park SE9 |
| 79 U 17 | Sutcliffe rd SE18 |
| 97 U 4 | Sutcliffe rd Welling |
| 60 A 18 | Sutherland av W13 |
| 129 V 19 | Sutherland av W9 |
| 130 B 15 | Sutherland av W9 |
| 96 L 12 | Sutherland av Welling |
| 25 S 14 | Sutherland ct NW9 |
| 86 B 9 | Sutherland gdns SW13 |
| 118 J 19 | Sutherland gdns Worc Pk |
| 105 U 1 | Sutherland gro SW18 |
| 87 U 20 | Sutherland gro SW18 |
| 101 U 12 | Sutherland gro Tedd |
| 137 T 5 | Sutherland pl W2 |
| 32 G 9 | Sutherland rd E17 |
| 63 Y 6 | Sutherland rd E3 |
| 31 X 3 | Sutherland rd N17 |
| 18 L 5 | Sutherland rd N9 |
| 59 Z 18 | Sutherland rd W13 |
| 74 A 16 | Sutherland rd W4 |
| 81 S 7 | Sutherland rd Blvdr |
| 122 F 18 | Sutherland rd Croy |
| 9 S 19 | Sutherland rd Enf |
| 58 E 17 | Sutherland rd S'hall |
| 147 Y 9 | Sutherland row W1 |
| 150 A 12 | Sutherland sq SE17 |
| 147 Z 11 | Sutherland st SW1 |
| 150 B 12 | Sutherland wlk SE17 |
| 77 Y 20 | Sutlej rd SE7 |
| 48 B 19 | Sutterton st N7 |
| 154 B 11 | Sutton arc Sutton |

| | | |
|---|---|---|
| 153 Y 2 | Sutton Comm rd Sutton |
| 119 U 18 | Sutton Comm rd Sutton |
| 4 D 16 | Sutton cres Barnt |
| 73 V 17 | Sutton ct W4 |
| 65 Y 9 | Sutton Ct rd E15 |
| 73 W 16 | Sutton Ct rd W4 |
| 154 C 13 | Sutton Ct rd Sutton |
| 82 J 3 | Sutton dene Hounsl |
| 123 V 12 | Sutton gdns SE25 |
| 67 V 5 | Sutton gdns Bark |
| 154 G 10 | Sutton gro Sutton |
| 70 G 20 | Sutton Hall rd Hounsl |
| 73 W 13 | Sutton la W4 |
| 82 E 6 | Sutton la Hounsl |
| 73 U 16 | Sutton La south W4 |
| 154 A 13 | Sutton Pk rd Sutton |
| 50 C 15 | Sutton pl E9 |
| 65 R 12 | Sutton rd E13 |
| 32 F 6 | Sutton rd E17 |
| 29 P 5 | Sutton rd N10 |
| 67 W 4 | Sutton rd Bark |
| 67 U 5 | Sutton rd Bark |
| 82 J 1 | Sutton rd Hounsl |
| 140 G 5 | Sutton row W1 |
| 82 F 2 | Sutton sq Hounsl |
| 63 O 18 | Sutton st E1 |
| 128 B 19 | Sutton way W10 |
| 62 M 13 | Sutton way W10 |
| 82 F 1 | Sutton way Hounsl |
| 106 D 3 | Swaby rd SW18 |
| 88 C 18 | Swaffield rd SW18 |
| 122 M 10 | Swain rd Thntn Hth |
| 47 R 4 | Swain's la N6 |
| 106 L 16 | Swain's rd SW17 |
| 74 C 4 | Swainson rd W3 |
| 99 T 13 | Swaisland dri Drtfrd |
| 99 Z 15 | Swaisland rd Drtfrd |
| 99 V 9 | Swale rd Drtfrd |
| 81 U 14 | Swalecliffe rd Blvdr |
| 111 P 9 | Swallands rd SE6 |
| 139 Z 6 | Swallow pl W1 |
| 140 C 11 | Swallow st W1 |
| 77 W 14 | Swallowfield rd SE7 |
| 100 B 10 | Swan clo Felt |
| 15 R 9 | Swan ct N20 |
| 15 R 9 | Swan ct N29 |
| 142 F 10 | Swan la EC4 |
| 15 R 9 | Swan la N20 |
| 150 J 3 | Swan mead SE1 |
| 75 R 5 | Swan rd SE16 |
| 100 B 11 | Swan rd Felt |
| 58 K 17 | Swan rd S'hall |
| 142 C 19 | Swan st SE1 |
| 84 A 7 | Swan st Islwth |
| 9 S 8 | Swan way Enf |
| 142 F 10 | Swan wharf EC4 |
| 147 O 14 | Swan wlk SW3 |
| 39 R 15 | Swan wlk Rom |
| 48 H 19 | Swan yd N1 |
| 33 U 2 | Swanage rd E4 |
| 88 D 16 | Swanage rd SW18 |
| 98 F 3 | Swanbridge rd Bxly Hth |
| 135 O 15 | Swanfield st E2 |
| 97 U 3 | Swanley rd Welling |
| 136 H 14 | Swanscombe rd W11 |
| 74 B 13 | Swanscombe rd W4 |
| 9 O 14 | Swansea rd Enf |
| 105 R 1 | Swanton gdns SW19 |
| 81 T 19 | Swanton rd Erith |
| 86 D 18 | Swanwick clo SW15 |
| 64 C 11 | Swaton rd E3 |
| 81 S 17 | Swaylands clo Blvdr |
| 143 U 9 | Swedenborg sq E1 |
| 143 V 9 | Swedenborg st E1 |
| 143 O 19 | Swedenborg st E1 |
| 18 G 12 | Sweet Briar grn N9 |
| 18 F 11 | Sweet Briar gro N9 |
| 18 F 14 | Sweet Briar wk N18 |
| 65 T 8 | Swete st E13 |
| 94 G 5 | Sweyn pl SE3 |
| 40 K 7 | Swift clo Harrow |
| 87 U 2 | Swift st SW6 |
| 112 A 15 | Swiftsden way Brom |
| 137 N 1 | Swinbrook rd W10 |
| 124 C 16 | Swinburn cres Croy |
| 86 H 12 | Swinburne rd SW15 |
| 42 H 18 | Swinderby rd Wemb |
| 136 A 14 | Swindon st W12 |
| 74 K 2 | Swindon st W12 |
| 90 H 7 | Swinfield gdns SW9 |
| 79 W 17 | Swingate la SE18 |
| 50 J 16 | Swinnerton st E9 |
| 43 T 5 | Swinton clo Wemb |
| 133 N 13 | Swinton pl WC1 |
| 133 O 12 | Swinton st WC1 |
| 113 V 9 | Swithland gdns SE9 |
| 72 C 12 | Swyncombe av W5 |
| 50 L 2 | Sybourn st E17 |
| 72 G 8 | Sycamore av W5 |

| | | |
|---|---|---|
| 96 L 15 | Sycamore av Sidcp |
| 74 L 7 | Sycamore gdns W12 |
| 136 A 20 | Sycamore gdns W6 |
| 43 W 1 | Sycamore gro NW9 |
| 117 Z 5 | Sycamore gro New Mald |
| 118 A 4 | Sycamore gro New Mald |
| 104 M 15 | Sycamore rd SW19 |
| 134 A 17 | Sycamore st EC1 |
| 122 E 10 | Sycamore way Thntn Hth |
| 110 A 12 | Sydenham av SE26 |
| 109 Y 7 | Sydenham hill SE26 |
| 110 B 8 | Sydenham pk SE26 |
| 110 C 7 | Sydenham Pk rd SE26 |
| 110 G 11 | Sydenham rd SE26 |
| 157 N 1 | Sydenham rd Croy |
| 123 P 15 | Sydenham rd Croy |
| 110 A 3 | Sydenham ri SE23 |
| 109 Z 3 | Sydenham ri SE23 |
| 110 A 2 | Sydenham rise SE23 |
| 49 V 11 | Sydner rd N16 |
| 146 G 8 | Sydney clo SW3 |
| 26 L 16 | Sydney gro NW4 |
| 146 H 8 | Sydney ms SW3 |
| 146 H 7 | Sydney pl SW7 |
| 29 R 5 | Sydney rd N10 |
| 30 F 12 | Sydney rd N8 |
| 80 H 8 | Sydney rd SE2 |
| 119 P 3 | Sydney rd SW20 |
| 74 A 5 | Sydney rd W13 |
| 97 X 10 | Sydney rd Bxly Hth |
| 8 B 14 | Sydney rd Enf |
| 36 B 8 | Sydney rd Ilf |
| 114 J 9 | Sydney rd Sidcp |
| 153 X 9 | Sydney rd Sutton |
| 101 V 13 | Sydney rd Tedd |
| 84 A 16 | Sydney rd Twick |
| 21 S 15 | Sydney rd Wdfd Grn |
| 146 J 8 | Sydney st SW3 |
| 13 P 18 | Sylvan av NW7 |
| 30 E 1 | Sylvan av N22 |
| 27 Z 7 | Sylvan av N3 |
| 38 C 18 | Sylvan av Rom |
| 116 F 19 | Sylvan gdns Surb |
| 75 N 17 | Sylvan gro SE15 |
| 151 Y 16 | Sylvan gro SE15 |
| 109 S 19 | Sylvan hill SE19 |
| 34 E 15 | Sylvan rd E11 |
| 00 N 16 | Sylvan rd E17 |
| 52 G 17 | Sylvan rd E7 |
| 123 V 1 | Sylvan rd SE19 |
| 109 U 20 | Sylvan rd SE19 |
| 54 A 7 | Sylvan rd Ilf |
| 109 V 20 | Sylvan Rd est SE19 |
| 55 P 11 | Sylvan way Dgnhm |
| 159 Z 8 | Sylvan way W Wkhm |
| 113 T 16 | Sylvester av Chisl |
| 50 A 18 | Sylvester path E8 |
| 50 A 17 | Sylvester rd E8 |
| 28 F 7 | Sylvester rd N2 |
| 42 F 14 | Sylvester rd Wemb |
| 43 S 20 | Sylvia gdns Wemb |
| 147 P 7 | Symons st SW3 |
| 84 D 3 | Syon house Islwth |
| 72 A 20 | Syon la Brentf |
| 71 V 16 | Syon la Islwth |
| 84 D 2 | Syon park Islwth |
| 71 V 18 | Syon Pk gdns Islwth |

# T

| | | |
|---|---|---|
| 142 D 18 | Tabard st SE1 |
| 150 E 1 | Tabard st SE1 |
| 65 T 12 | Tabernacle av E13 |
| 134 G 18 | Tabernacle st EC2 |
| 89 W 12 | Tableer av SW4 |
| 47 Z 11 | Tabley rd N7 |
| 153 T 15 | Tabor gdns Sutton |
| 105 U 17 | Tabor gro SW19 |
| 74 K 9 | Tabor rd W6 |
| 148 B 6 | Tachbrook ms SW1 |
| 148 E 9 | Tachbrook st SW1 |
| 146 C 18 | Tadema rd SW10 |
| 136 E 15 | Tadmor st W12 |
| 118 D 10 | Tadworth av New Mald |
| 57 Y 13 | Tadworth pde Hornch |
| 44 G 7 | Tadworth rd NW2 |
| 120 K 5 | Taffeys how Mitch |
| 64 F 8 | Taft st E3 |
| 143 P 2 | Tailworth st E1 |
| 123 R 16 | Tait rd Croy |
| 47 R 18 | Talacre rd NW5 |
| 28 F 11 | Talbot av N2 |
| 31 U 13 | Talbot clo N15 |

| | |
|---|---|
| 26 G 16 | Talbot cres NW4 |
| 54 M 7 | Talbot gdns Ilf |
| 136 L 6 | Talbot gro W11 |
| 136 K 7 | Talbot ms W11 |
| 93 Z 3 | Talbot pl SE13 |
| 94 A 3 | Talbot pl SE13 |
| 94 A 3 | Talbot place SE3 |
| 66 H 4 | Talbot rd E6 |
| 52 E 12 | Talbot rd E7 |
| 44 B 18 | Talbot rd NW10 |
| 31 V 13 | Talbot rd N15 |
| 29 W 6 | Talbot rd N22 |
| 29 O 19 | Talbot rd N6 |
| 137 P 6 | Talbot rd W11 |
| 71 Y 2 | Talbot rd W13 |
| 137 U 4 | Talbot rd W2 |
| 126 H 7 | Talbot rd Brom |
| 155 O 10 | Talbot rd Carsh |
| 56 B 19 | Talbot rd Dgnhm |
| 23 X 9 | Talbot rd Harrow |
| 83 Z 10 | Talbot rd Islwth |
| 70 C 10 | Talbot rd S'hall |
| 123 O 9 | Talbot rd Thntn Hth |
| 83 U 20 | Talbot rd Twick |
| 101 U 1 | Talbot rd Twick |
| 42 G 17 | Talbot rd Wemb |
| 138 G 6 | Talbot sq W2 |
| 142 F 15 | Talbot yd SE1 |
| 91 U 2 | Talfourd pl SE15 |
| 91 T 2 | Talfourd rd SE15 |
| 144 J 9 | Talgarth rd W14 |
| 109 W 9 | Talisman sq SE26 |
| 42 L 9 | Talisman way Wemb |
| 23 U 3 | Tallack clo Harrow |
| 50 M 4 | Tallack rd E10 |
| 77 W 16 | Tallis gro SE7 |
| 141 U 8 | Tallis st EC4 |
| 15 R 17 | Tallyho' corner N12 |
| 83 T 17 | Talma gdns Twick |
| 90 G 12 | Talma rd SW2 |
| 92 D 20 | Talmage clo SE23 |
| 142 H 8 | Talnot ct EC3 |
| 54 E 10 | Talwin st E3 |
| 78 B 10 | Tamar st SE7 |
| 62 E 20 | Tamarisk sq W12 |
| 129 S 16 | Tamplin ms W9 |
| 129 S 16 | Tamplin ms W9 |
| 21 N 18 | Tamworth av Wdfd Grn |
| 121 R 4 | Tamworth la Mitch |
| 121 S 7 | Tamworth pk Mitch |
| 145 T 14 | Tamworth st SW6 |
| 121 T 8 | Tamworth vlls Mitch |
| 30 J 20 | Tancred rd N4 |
| 44 D 11 | Tanfield av NW2 |
| 156 L 8 | Tanfield rd Croy |
| 85 T 9 | Tangier rd Rich |
| 10 F 10 | Tanglewood clo Stanm |
| 86 E 17 | Tangley gro SW15 |
| 57 Z 19 | Tangmere cres Hornch |
| 132 L 13 | Tankerton st WC1 |
| 107 Y 17 | Tankerville rd SW16 |
| 44 K 7 | Tankridge rd NW2 |
| 142 K 18 | Tanner st SE1 |
| 143 O 18 | Tanner st SE1 |
| 54 B 18 | Tanner st Bark |
| 92 M 3 | Tanners hill SE4 |
| 93 N 1 | Tanners hill SE4 |
| 36 C 10 | Tanners la Ilf |
| 56 G 8 | Tannery clo Dgnhm |
| 110 E 12 | Tannsfeld rd SE26 |
| 141 T 18 | Tanswell st SE1 |
| 65 P 16 | Tant av E16 |
| 89 N 20 | Tantallon rd SW12 |
| 37 X 11 | Tantony gro Rom |
| 156 K 3 | Tanworth pl Croy |
| 156 K 3 | Tanworth rd Croy |
| 46 L 11 | Tanza rd NW3 |
| 64 F 17 | Tapley st E14 |
| 135 X 17 | Tapp st E1 |
| 92 B 7 | Tappersfield rd SE15 |
| 4 G 13 | Tapster st Barnt |
| 91 T 12 | Tarbert rd SE22 |
| 18 L 20 | Tariff rd N17 |
| 110 A 3 | Tarleton gdns SE23 |
| 65 R 19 | Tarling rd E16 |
| 143 Y 6 | Tarling st E1 |
| 63 O 18 | Tarling st E1 |
| 7 O 15 | Tarn bank Enf |
| 95 U 20 | Tarnwood pk SE9 |
| 107 X 8 | Tarrington clo SW16 |
| 149 Y 10 | Tarver rd SE17 |
| 76 E 18 | Tarves way SE10 |
| 46 M 16 | Tasker rd NW3 |
| 90 A 8 | Tasman rd SW9 |
| 17 Z 19 | Tasmania ter N18 |
| 144 K 14 | Tasso rd W6 |
| 43 X 19 | Tatam rd NW10 |
| 148 J 7 | Tate gallery SW1 |
| 78 E 3 | Tate rd E16 |
| 153 X 12 | Tate rd Sutton |

| | |
|---|---|
| 92 H 16 | Tatnell rd SE23 |
| 95 R 12 | Tattersall clo SE9 |
| 49 U 1 | Tatton cres N16 |
| 150 G 7 | Tatum st SE17 |
| 118 K 3 | Taunton av SW20 |
| 82 M 4 | Taunton av Hounsl |
| 83 N 3 | Taunton av Hounsl |
| 24 K 9 | Taunton av Stanm |
| 99 O 6 | Taunton clo Bxly Hth |
| 119 X 20 | Taunton clo Sutton |
| 7 T 11 | Taunton dri Enf |
| 131 O 18 | Taunton ms NW1 |
| 131 N 17 | Taunton pl NW1 |
| 94 C 13 | Taunton rd SE12 |
| 58 K 2 | Taunton rd Grnfd |
| 24 K 8 | Taunton way Stanm |
| 32 G 11 | Tavestock av E17 |
| 60 A 6 | Tavistock av Grnfd |
| 59 Z 7 | Tavistock av Grnfd |
| 16 E 2 | Tavistock cres N14 |
| 137 O 2 | Tavistock cres W10 |
| 112 A 9 | Tavistock cres Mitch |
| 121 Z 9 | Tavistock cres Mitch |
| 54 H 13 | Tavistock gdns Ilf |
| 123 N 18 | Tavistock gro Croy |
| 137 N 5 | Tavistock ms W11 |
| 132 H 16 | Tavistock pl WC1 |
| 52 B 19 | Tavistock rd E18 |
| 34 E 11 | Tavistock rd E18 |
| 52 B 11 | Tavistock rd E7 |
| 62 D 5 | Tavistock rd NW10 |
| 31 N 19 | Tavistock rd N4 |
| 137 O 3 | Tavistock rd W11 |
| 120 G 20 | Tavistock rd Carsh |
| 123 N 19 | Tavistock rd Croy |
| 25 O 5 | Tavistock rd Edg |
| 97 T 2 | Tavistock rd Welling |
| 132 G 16 | Tavistock sq WC1 |
| 140 M 9 | Tavistock st WC2 |
| 140 M 9 | Tavistock st WC2 |
| 141 N 7 | Tavistock st WC2 |
| 47 Z 9 | Tavistock ter N19 |
| 120 G 20 | Tavistock wlk Carsh |
| 132 F 16 | Taviton st WC1 |
| 75 T 10 | Tawny way SE16 |
| 39 S 4 | Tay way Rom |
| 83 U 16 | Tayben av Twick |
| 89 P 10 | Taybridge rd SW8 |
| 85 S 4 | Taylor av Rich |
| 101 N 12 | Taylor clo Hampt |
| 38 E 1 | Taylor clo Rom |
| 38 E 1 | Taylor clo Rom |
| 106 K 18 | Taylor rd Mitch |
| 155 R 11 | Taylor rd Wallgtn |
| 78 M 11 | Taylor rd Welling |
| 44 A 20 | Taylor's la NW10 |
| 62 B 16 | Taylors grn W3 |
| 109 Y 10 | Taylors la SE26 |
| 4 G 6 | Taylors la Barnt |
| 110 B 3 | Taymount ri SE23 |
| 58 E 9 | Taywood av Grnfd |
| 135 U 8 | Teale st E2 |
| 31 T 3 | Tebworth rd N17 |
| 66 D 13 | Tedder gdns E6 |
| 158 E 18 | Tedder rd South Croy |
| 101 X 17 | Teddington lodge Tedd |
| 101 W 10 | Teddington pk Tedd |
| 101 W 10 | Teddington Pk rd Tedd |
| 147 N 11 | Tedworth gdns SW3 |
| 147 N 12 | Tedworth sq SW3 |
| 59 V 6 | Tees av Grnfd |
| 83 Z 2 | Teesdale av Islwth |
| 83 Z 2 | Teesdale gdns Islwth |
| 34 B 20 | Teesdale rd E11 |
| 135 V 11 | Teesdale st E2 |
| 135 V 10 | Teesdale yd E2 |
| 123 X 17 | Teevan clo Croy |
| 123 X 18 | Teevan rd Croy |
| 25 N 8 | Teignmouth clo SE9 |
| 89 X 11 | Teignmouth clo SW4 |
| 45 O 16 | Teignmouth gdns NW2 |
| 107 O 17 | Teignmouth rd Mitch |
| 97 T 3 | Teignmouth rd Welling |
| 45 Z 10 | Telegraph hill NW3 |
| 86 K 17 | Telegraph rd SW15 |
| 142 F 4 | Telegraph st EC2 |
| 107 W 1 | Telferscot rd SW12 |
| 108 A 2 | Telford av SW2 |
| 107 Y 2 | Telford av SW2 |
| 26 E 20 | Telford rd NW9 |
| 16 H 18 | Telford rd N11 |
| 114 D 5 | Telford rd SE9 |
| 128 K 20 | Telford rd W10 |
| 58 K 18 | Telford rd S'hall |
| 62 A 15 | Telford way W3 |
| 66 J 7 | Telham rd E6 |
| 91 U 11 | Tell gro SE22 |
| 95 P 1 | Tellson av SE18 |
| 89 P 18 | Temperley rd SW12 |

| | |
|---|---|
| 57 W 18 | Tempest way Rainhm |
| 45 U 17 | Templar ho NW2 |
| 100 H 17 | Templar rd Hampt |
| 50 D 14 | Templar rd E9 |
| 90 J 3 | Templar st SE5 |
| 27 W 19 | Templars av NW11 |
| 27 X 8 | Templars cres N3 |
| 141 U 8 | Temple av EC4 |
| 15 T 3 | Temple av N20 |
| 158 L 4 | Temple av Croy |
| 56 D 3 | Temple av Dgnhm |
| 27 V 8 | Temple clo N3 |
| 27 Y 16 | Temple Fortune hill NW11 |
| 27 X 17 | Temple Fortune la NW11 |
| 27 W 18 | Temple gdns NW11 |
| 55 V 9 | Temple gdns Dgnhm |
| 27 X 18 | Temple gro NW11 |
| 7 W 10 | Temple gro Enf |
| 141 U 7 | Temple la EC4 |
| 51 V 14 | Temple Mills la E15 |
| 51 P 13 | Temple Mills rd E15 |
| 141 P 9 | Temple pl WC2 |
| 66 C 3 | Temple rd E6 |
| 45 N 10 | Temple rd NW2 |
| 44 M 11 | Temple rd NW2 |
| 30 C 13 | Temple rd N8 |
| 73 V 9 | Temple rd W4 |
| 72 F 9 | Temple rd W5 |
| 157 O 9 | Temple rd Croy |
| 82 L 9 | Temple rd Hounsl |
| 85 N 6 | Temple rd Rich |
| 85 U 12 | Temple sheen SW14 |
| 85 T 11 | Temple Sheen rd SW14 |
| 51 Y 10 | Temple st E11 |
| 135 V 9 | Temple st E2 |
| 154 G 6 | Temple way Sutton |
| 135 Z 3 | Templecombe rd E9 |
| 63 O 3 | Templecombe rd E9 |
| 119 R 11 | Templecombe way Mrdn |
| 59 W 15 | Templeman rd W7 |
| 20 C 12 | Templeton av E4 |
| 31 O 19 | Templeton clo N15 |
| 123 P 1 | Templeton clo SE19 |
| 145 U 6 | Templeton pl SW5 |
| 31 O 18 | Templeton rd N15 |
| 60 B 14 | Templewood W13 |
| 46 B 10 | Templewood av NW3 |
| 46 B 10 | Templewood gdns NW3 |
| 22 M 8 | Temsford clo Har |
| 24 B 8 | Tenby av Harrow |
| 89 Z 20 | Tenby clo SW12 |
| 37 Y 19 | Tenby clo Rom |
| 32 G 15 | Tenby rd E17 |
| 25 N 6 | Tenby rd SE3 |
| 9 P 13 | Tenby rd Enf |
| 37 Y 19 | Tenby rd Rom |
| 97 V 1 | Tenby rd Welling |
| 143 W 13 | Tench st E1 |
| 151 V 8 | Tenda rd SE16 |
| 37 T 15 | Tendring way Rom |
| 40 H 18 | Tendy gdns Grnfd |
| 107 X 2 | Tenham av SW2 |
| 140 B 8 | Tenison ct W1 |
| 141 R 14 | Tenison way SE1 |
| 138 A 8 | Tenniel clo W2 |
| 137 Y 8 | Tenniel pl W2 |
| 137 Y 8 | Tenniel pl W2 |
| 142 E 17 | Tennis st SE1 |
| 123 T 10 | Tennison rd SE25 |
| 8 E 7 | Tenniswood rd Enf |
| 52 F 1 | Tennyson av E11 |
| 53 P 20 | Tennyson av E12 |
| 25 V 11 | Tennyson av NW9 |
| 118 K 12 | Tennyson av New Mald |
| 101 W 2 | Tennyson av Twick |
| 51 S 5 | Tennyson rd E 10 |
| 51 Z 19 | Tennyson rd E15 |
| 32 L 18 | Tennyson rd E17 |
| 13 T 15 | Tennyson rd NW1 |
| 129 P 5 | Tennyson rd NW6 |
| 110 F 17 | Tennyson rd SE20 |
| 106 C 14 | Tennyson rd SW19 |
| 59 V 20 | Tennyson rd W7 |
| 82 M 3 | Tennyson rd Hounsl |
| 89 S 5 | Tennyson st SW8 |
| 57 U 6 | Tennyson way Hornch |
| 70 G 8 | Tensing rd S'hall |
| 135 V 17 | Tent st E1 |
| 70 H 12 | Tentelow la S'hall |
| 143 N 2 | Tenter ground E1 |
| 142 E 1 | Tenter st EC2 |
| 56 B 5 | Tenterden av Dgnhm |
| 27 O 10 | Tenterden clo NW4 |

| | |
|---|---|
| 27 R 11 | Tenterden dri NW4 |
| 27 P 11 | Tenterden gdns NW4 |
| 27 O 11 | Tenterden gro NW4 |
| 31 T 2 | Tenterden rd N17 |
| 139 Y 6 | Tenterden st W1 |
| 123 Y 16 | Tenterten rd Croy |
| 123 Y 16 | Tenterton gdns Croy |
| 91 R 13 | Terbach rd Dgnhm |
| 56 D 5 | Terling rd Dgnhm |
| 147 Z 4 | Terminus pl SW1 |
| 86 C 5 | Terrace gdns SW13 |
| 84 K 17 | Terrace la Rich |
| 65 U 4 | Terrace rd E13 |
| 50 D 20 | Terrace rd E9 |
| 129 S 3 | Terrace the NW6 |
| 21 S 18 | Terrace the Wdfd Grn |
| 147 P 16 | Terrace wlk SW11 |
| 56 A 16 | Terrace wlk Dgnhm |
| 55 Z 16 | Terrace wlk Dgnhm |
| 107 S 5 | Terrapin rd SW17 |
| 30 A 6 | Terrick rd N22 |
| 62 K 18 | Terrick st W12 |
| 22 E 10 | Terrilands Pinn |
| 30 L 14 | Terront rd N15 |
| 75 V 11 | Terry La gdns SE8 |
| 133 V 6 | Tetbury pl N1 |
| 146 B 19 | Tetcott rd SW10 |
| 29 P 10 | Tetherdown N10 |
| 126 E 4 | Tetty way Brom |
| 97 R 1 | Teviot rd Welling |
| 64 F 13 | Teviot st E14 |
| 92 A 20 | Tewkesbury av SE23 |
| 22 C 17 | Tewkesbury av Pinn |
| 31 O 19 | Tewkesbury clo N15 |
| 25 U 10 | Tewkesbury gdns SE9 |
| 31 O 19 | Tewkesbury rd N15 |
| 120 F 19 | Tewkesbury rd Carsh |
| 16 H 18 | Tewkesbury ter N11 |
| 79 V 13 | Tewson rd SE18 |
| 8 B 20 | Teynham av Enf |
| 30 M 5 | Teynton ter N17 |
| 31 X 8 | Thackeray av N17 |
| 40 J 4 | Thackeray dri Harrow |
| 55 O 2 | Thackeray dri Rom |
| 66 B 6 | Thackeray rd E6 |
| 89 S 5 | Thackeray rd SW8 |
| 137 Y 20 | Thackeray st W8 |
| 109 Z 11 | Thakeham clo SE26 |
| 69 U 12 | Thames av Grnfd |
| 59 V 6 | Thames av Grnfd |
| 85 W 5 | Thames bank SW14 |
| 75 Z 1 | Thames pl E1 |
| 78 A 4 | Thames rd E16 |
| 73 R 17 | Thames rd W4 |
| 68 A 8 | Thames rd Bark |
| 67 W 9 | Thames rd Bark |
| 99 W 8 | Thames rd Drtfd |
| 102 G 17 | Thames side Kingst |
| 116 G 2 | Thames side Kingst |
| 76 F 16 | Thames st SE10 |
| 38 L 8 | Thameshill av Rom |
| 48 D 9 | Thane vlls N7 |
| 157 T 6 | Thanescroft gdns Croy |
| 156 M 3 | Thanet pl Croy |
| 157 N 7 | Thanet pl Croy |
| 98 E 19 | Thanet rd Bxly |
| 132 J 14 | Thanet st WC1 |
| 155 X 11 | Tharp rd Wallgtn |
| 15 R 3 | Thatcham gdns N20 |
| 37 Y 12 | Thatches gro Rom |
| 141 U 3 | Thavies inn EC4 |
| 114 B 5 | Thaxsted rd SE9 |
| 139 U 4 | Thayer st W1 |
| 124 J 1 | Thayers Farm rd Becknhm |
| 27 O 15 | The approach NW4 |
| 9 N 4 | The approach Enf |
| 16 P 15 | The avenue N11 |
| 154 K 16 | The Beeches av Carsh |
| 146 B 10 | The boltons SW10 |
| 41 X 12 | The boltons Wemb |
| 41 X 12 | The boltons Wemb |
| 20 G 7 | The bracken E4 |
| 18 C 2 | The brackens Enf |
| 18 C 2 | The brackens Enf |
| 20 L 14 | The bramblings E4 |
| 44 G 2 | The broadway NW 9 |
| 60 H 19 | The broadway W5 |
| 60 G 20 | The broadway W5 |
| 22 D 13 | The chase Pinn |
| 143 N 9 | The crescent EC 3 |
| 72 E 16 | The dell Brentf |
| 14 L 20 | The drive N3 |
| 118 F 12 | The grange New Mald |
| 105 O 13 | The green SW19 |
| 119 R 9 | The green Mrdn |
| 159 T 6 | The grove W Wkhm |
| 96 M 20 | The hollies Sidcup |

49 R 15 The liberty Rom
13 S 9 The lincolns NW7
60 D 16 The link Grnfd
32 H 13 The links E17
99 N 11 The marlowes Drtfd
17 Y 19 The mitre E14
18 A 1 The moat New Mald
6 H 15 The pines N14
34 D 10 The priory SE3
25 X 15 The retreat NW9
32 A 17 The tee W3
17 X 20 The tiltwood W3
72 K 3 The vine W5
28 G 9 The walks N2
38 M 8 Theatre st SW11
33 V 4 Theberton st N1
17 T 14 Theed st SE1
95 P 2 Thelma gdns SE3
01 X 14 Thelma gro Tedd
22 L 5 Theobald cres Harrow
56 J 2 Theobald rd Croy
60 E 3 Theobald st SE1
33 O 20 Theobald's rd WC1
15 P 14 Theobalds av N12
30 V 15 Theodore rd SE13
22 A 15 Therapia la Croy
21 X 7 Therapia la Croy
92 C 15 Therapia rd SE22
74 G 12 Theresa rd W6
74 G 12 Theresa st W6
76 E 11 Thermopylae ga E14
10 F 17 Thesiger rd SE20
89 X 3 Thessally rd SW8
48 A 19 Thessaly rd SW8
68 K 2 Thetford gdns Dgnhm
68 K 2 Thetford rd Dgnhm
17 Z 13 Thetford rd New Mald
18 A 12 Thetford rd New Malden
73 O 17 Thetis ter Rich
21 X 19 Theydon gro Wdfd Grn
50 C 5 Theydon rd E5
50 L 9 Theydon st E19
54 E 8 Thicket cres Sutton
52 O 20 Thicket gro SE20
55 U 17 Thicket gro Dgnhm
09 V 18 Thicket rd SE20
10 A 16 Thicket rd SE20
54 E 7 Thicket rd Sutton
53 S 13 Third av E12
65 T 9 Third av E13
33 P 15 Third av E17
28 M 15 Third av W10
74 C 3 Third av W3
69 V 5 Third av Dgnhm
8 G 17 Third av Enf
37 T 17 Third av Rom
42 G 6 Third av Wemb
01 S 4 Third Cross rd Twick
43 U 13 Third way Wemb
25 X 4 Thirleby rd SE18
48 C 3 Thirleby rd SW1
60 C 8 Thirlmere av Grnfd
42 E 4 Thirlmere gdns Wemb
29 T 6 Thirlmere rd N10
07 X 10 Thirlmere rd SW16
98 K 3 Thirlmere rd Bxly Hth
40 J 17 Thirsk clo Grnfd
23 P 8 Thirsk rd SE25
89 N 8 Thirsk rd SW11
07 P 17 Thirsk rd Mitch
63 R 19 Thirza st E1
40 C 10 Thisledene av Harrow
46 C 9 Thistle grn SW5
24 G 6 Thistlecroft gdns Stanm
50 B 10 Thistlewaite rd E5
71 P 18 Thistleworth clo Islwth
41 W 11 Thomas A 'beckett clo W11
88 H 9 Thomas Baines rd SW11
149 X 1 Thomas Doyle st SE1
93 P 19 Thomas la SE6
143 S 11 Thomas More st SE1
63 Z 16 Thomas rd E14
64 A 16 Thomas rd E14
78 K 10 Thomas st SE18
85 S 6 Thompson av Rich
91 V 16 Thompson rd SE22
56 C 10 Thompson rd Dgnhm
150 A 17 Thompsons av SE5
156 F 1 Thomson cres Croy
122 F 19 Thomson cres Croy
23 U 9 Thomson rd Harrow
151 S 7 Thorburn sq SE1

134 B 11 Thoresby st N1
116 A 17 Thorkhill rd Surb
10 A 6 Thorn av Bushey Watf
12 D 20 Thorn bank Edg
127 X 14 Thorn clo Brom
58 E 8 Thorn clo Grnfd
18 L 18 Thornaby gdns N18
71 P 20 Thornbury av Islwth
89 Z 16 Thornbury rd SW2
90 A 17 Thornbury rd SW2
83 R 4 Thornbury rd Islwth
71 R 19 Thornbury rd Islwth
50 L 10 Thornby rd E5
89 Z 17 Thorncliffe rd SW4
70 E 12 Thorncliffe rd S'hall
91 T 12 Thorncombe rd SE22
39 Y 18 Thorncroft Hornch
154 A 9 Thorncroft rd Sutton
153 Z 10 Thorncroft rd Sutton
148 J 19 Thorncroft st SW8
106 C 5 Thorndean st SW18
16 A 7 Thorndene av N11
148 E 8 Thorndike st SW1
152 C 9 Thorndon gdns Epsom
65 R 17 Thorne clo E16
117 V 8 Thorne clo New Mald
86 B 6 Thorne pas SW13
148 L 20 Thorne rd SW8
117 V 8 Thorne rd New Mald
65 R 17 Thorne st E16
86 B 6 Thorne st SW13
156 H 12 Thorneloe gdns Croy
125 T 6 Thornes clo Beckham
125 T 6 Thornes clo Becknhm
127 X 7 Thornet Wood rd Brom
73 T 12 Thorney Hedge rd W4
148 J 6 Thorney st SW1
27 S 3 Thornfield av NW7
74 K 5 Thornfield rd W12
136 A 14 Thornfield rd W12
93 U 14 Thornford rd SE13
65 W 3 Thorngrove rd E13
51 W 16 Thornham gro E15
76 E 18 Thornham st SE10
132 G 18 Thornhaugh ms WC1
132 H 19 Thornhaugh st WC1
79 V 19 Thornhill av SE19
133 O 7 Thornhill bridge N1
133 O 1 Thornhill cres N1
51 S 7 Thornhill gdns E10
54 H 20 Thornhill gdns Bark
116 A 19 Thornhill gdns Surb
133 R 2 Thornhill gro N1
51 R 7 Thornhill rd E10
48 F 20 Thornhill rd N1
133 S 2 Thornhill rd N1
122 M 17 Thornhill rd Croy
133 O 2 Thornhill sq N1
108 J 9 Thornleby rd SE27
40 L 7 Thornley dri Harrow
40 L 7 Thornley dri Harrow
76 L 13 Thornley pl SE10
111 U 3 Thornsbeach rd SE6
125 Z 4 Thornsett pl SE 20
123 Z 4 Thornsett rd SE20
124 A 5 Thornsett rd SE20
106 B 3 Thornsett rd SW18
107 V 2 Thornton av W4
74 B 11 Thornton av W4
122 C 15 Thornton av Croy
125 O 3 Thornton dene Becknhm
107 X 1 Thornton gdns SW12
105 R 18 Thornton hill SW19
51 X 6 Thornton rd E11
89 W 19 Thornton rd SW14
85 X 9 Thornton rd SW14
4 E 13 Thornton rd Barnt
81 T 9 Thornton rd Blvdr
112 F 12 Thornton rd Brom
120 J 18 Thornton rd Carsh
53 Y 13 Thornton rd Ilf
122 E 13 Thornton rd Thntn Hth
105 P 17 Thornton Rd east SW19
90 E 5 Thornton st SW9
28 B 17 Thornton way NW11
56 M 5 Thorntons Farm av
78 B 14 Thorntree rd SE7
93 N 3 Thornville st SE4
94 A 13 Thornwood rd SE13
93 Z 13 Thornwood rd SE13
52 A 16 Thorogood gdns E15
30 B 2 Thorold rd N22

53 Z 7 Thorold rd Ilf
54 C 4 Thorold rd Ilf
148 G 20 Thorparch rd SW8
89 Y 1 Thorparch rd SW8
32 L 6 Thorpe cres E17
33 V 6 Thorpe Hall rd E17
33 T 7 Thorpe rd E17
66 F 4 Thorpe rd E6
52 C 11 Thorpe rd E7
31 T 19 Thorpe rd N15
54 D 20 Thorpe rd Bark
102 K 18 Thorpe rd Kingst
74 G 3 Thorpebank rd W12
35 Y 12 Thorpedale gdns Ilf
48 B 5 Thorpedale rd N4
110 B 5 Thorpewood av SE26
109 R 11 Thorsden way SE19
45 R 10 Thorverton rd NW2
63 V 7 Thoydon rd E3
107 U 13 Thrale rd SW16
142 C 14 Thrale st SE1
143 P 2 Thrawl st E1
142 G 6 Threadneedle st EC2
63 Y 19 Three Colt st E14
135 Y 16 Three Colts la E2
63 N 11 Three Colts la E2
00 J 0 Three corners Bxly Hth
65 W 18 Throckmorten rd E18
142 G 4 Throgmorton av EC2
142 G 5 Throgmorton st EC2
80 E 8 Throwley clo SE2
154 C 11 Throwley rd Sutton
149 Z 9 Thrush st SE17
111 R 12 Thurbarn rd SE6
108 G 9 Thurlby rd SE27
89 P 16 Thurleigh av SW12
88 L 17 Thurleigh rd SW12
89 O 16 Thurleigh rd SW12
119 R 11 Thurleston av Mrdn
15 Y 19 Thurlestone av N12
54 K 14 Thurlestone av Ilf
108 H 9 Thurlestone rd SE27
146 J 5 Thurloe clo SW7
29 S 19 Thurloe gdns Rom
146 H 4 Thurloe pl SW7
146 G 5 Thurloe Pl ms SW7
146 H 5 Thurloe sq SW7
146 G 5 Thurloe sq SW7
42 H 16 Thurlow gdns Wemb
108 K 2 Thurlow hill SE21
108 K 3 Thurlow Pk rd SE21
46 G 14 Thurlow rd NW3
71 Y 6 Thurlow rd NW3
150 H 10 Thurlow st SE17
47 N 17 Thurlow ter NW5
115 Y 14 Thursland rd Sidcp
159 W 16 Thursley cres Croy
105 P 6 Thursley gdns SW19
113 S 8 Thursley rd SE9
106 G 9 Thurso st SW17
93 S 6 Thurston rd SE13
104 J 17 Thurston rd SW20
58 F 18 Thurston rd S'hall
135 O 7 Thurtle rd E2
81 W 16 Thwaite rd Erith
15 O 19 Thyra gro N12
151 S 1 Thyrland rd SE16
42 H 19 Thyrlby rd Wemb
64 D 11 Tibbatt's rd E3
87 O 17 Tibbets ride SW15
105 O 2 Tibbett's clo SW19
110 J 5 Ticehurst rd SE23
131 N 7 Tichfield rd NW8
80 E 5 Tickford clo SE2
65 R 20 Tidal Basin rd E16
87 N 12 Tideswell rd SW15
158 M 5 Tideswell rd Croy
64 B 13 Tidey st E3
96 K 4 Tidford rd Welling
64 A 11 Tidworth rd E3
89 Z 20 Tierney rd SW12
90 A 20 Tierney rd SW2
108 A 1 Tierney rd SW2
75 R 8 Tiger bay SE16
126 H 8 Tiger la Brom
94 M 8 Tilbrook rd SE3
51 T 2 Tilbury rd E10
66 G 7 Tilbury rd E6
86 L 15 Tildesley rd SW15
17 Y 16 Tile Kiln la N13
106 G 2 Tilehurst rd SW18
153 R 11 Tilehurst rd Sutton
46 H 6 Tilekiln la N6
47 Z 20 Tileyard rd N1

159 U 18 Tilford av Croy
105 P 2 Tilford gdns SW19
50 A 13 Tilia rd E5
76 B 8 Tiller rd E14
27 W 11 Tillingbourne gdns N3
27 W 12 Tillingbourne way N3
14 M 13 Tillingham way N12
14 M 13 Tillingham way N12
63 N 18 Tillman st E1
143 X 7 Tillman st E1
133 N 1 Tilloch st N1
18 F 7 Tillotson rd N9
22 K 3 Tillotson rd Harrow
53 W 1 Tillotson rd Ilf
63 S 15 Tillotson st E1
109 U 12 Tilney av SE19
21 U 8 Tilney dri Buch HI
56 B 19 Tilney rd Dgnhm
139 U 13 Tilney st W1
89 Z 18 Tilson gdns SW2
31 X 5 Tilson rd N17
150 M 1 Tilson st E1
144 M 15 Tilton st SW6
95 T 16 Tiltyard appr SE9
127 W 2 Timber clo Chisl
134 A 17 Timber st EC1
162 A U Timbercraft Lssam
79 U 18 Timbercroft la SE18
27 R 7 Timberdene NW4
31 Y 19 Timberwharf rd N16
63 X 14 Timothy rd E3
86 G 20 Timsbury wlk SW15
149 X 20 Tindal st SW9
90 J 1 Tindal st SW9
85 Z 7 Tinderbox all SW14
83 R 14 Tinsley rd E1
91 U 10 Tintagel cres SE22
11 V 15 Tintagel dri Stanm
25 T 10 Tintern av NW9
17 N 2 Tintern gdns N14
30 L 5 Tintern rd N22
120 F 20 Tintern rd Carsh
90 B 10 Tintern st SW4
40 K 4 Tintern way Harrow
65 T 13 Tinto rd E13
65 T 13 Tinto rd E16
148 M 8 Tinworth st SE11
149 N 9 Tinworth st SE11
7 Z 7 Tippetts clo Enf
89 O 7 Tipthorne rd SW11
89 O 7 Tipthorpe rd SW11
157 S 8 Tiptown dri Croy
156 L 15 Tirlemont rd S Croy
122 L 15 Tirrell rd Croy
140 E 8 Tisbury ct W1
121 Z 3 Tisbury rd SW16
150 G 8 Tisdall pl SE17
138 K 6 Titchbourne row W2
141 N 7 Titchfield rd NW1
130 M 7 Titchfield rd NW8
120 F 19 Titchfield rd Carsh
9 U 1 Titchfield st Enf
120 G 18 Titchfield wlk Carsh
88 G 20 Titchwell rd SW18
147 P 13 Tite st SW3
26 F 4 Tithe clo NW7
40 G 9 Tithe Farm av Harrow
40 G 9 Tithe Farm clo Harrow
26 G 3 Tithe wlk NW7
10 E 3 Titian av Bushey Watf
20 B 16 Titley clo E4
35 W 9 Tiverton av Ilf
96 B 20 Tiverton dri SE9
114 B 1 Tiverton dri SE9
128 H 6 Tiverton rd NW10
31 O 18 Tiverton rd N15
18 D 18 Tiverton rd N18
24 M 9 Tiverton rd Edg
82 M 4 Tiverton rd Hounsl
122 F 11 Tiverton rd Thntn Hth
60 K 5 Tiverton rd Wemb
150 A 2 Tiverton st SE1
29 X 16 Tivoli rd N8
108 L 13 Tivoli rd SE27
82 B 11 Tivoli rd Hounsl
35 W 9 Tivoton rd Ilt
76 A 5 Tobago st E14
46 K 19 Tobin clo NW3
20 A 14 Tofton rd E4
142 F 5 Tokenhouse yd EC2
43 P 18 Tokyngton av Wemb
86 G 14 Toland sq SW15
42 K 2 Toley av Wemb
36 D 9 Tollesbury gdns Ilf
63 S 11 Tollet st E1
109 T 5 Tollgate dri SE21
47 V 6 Tollhouse way N19
48 D 5 Tollington pk N4
48 C 6 Tollington pl N4

7 N9 Tryon st SW3
9 R17 Tuam rd SE18
2 E7 Tubbs rd NW10
7 W18 Tuck rd Rainhm
6 E18 Tuckton wlk SW15
0 H17 Tudor av Hampt
9 W11 Tudor av Rom
2 L9 Tudor av Worc Pk
6 J16 Tudor clo NW3
7 V20 Tudor clo NW7
3 W6 Tudor clo NW9
7 V1 Tudor clo Chisl
3 V20 Tudor clo Chisl
9 Y16 Tudor clo Drtfrd
3 P12 Tudor clo Sutton
5 W17 Tudor clo Wallgtn
1 V16 Tudor clo Wdfd Grn
7 X4 Tudor cres Enf
2 K20 Tudor ct E17
R16 Tudor Ct north Wemb
3 R17 Tudor Ct south Wemb
3 N14 Tudor dri Kingst
2 H11 Tudor dri Kingst
3 T17 Tudor dri Mrdn
9 V12 Tudor dri Rom
3 W7 Tudor gdns NW9
6 C8 Tudor gdns SW13
1 R15 Tudor gdns W3
9 W12 Tudor gdns Rom
9 T6 Tudor gdns W Wkhm
5 Z2 Tudor gro E9
3 O1 Tudor gro E9
0 F3 Tudor pl W1
6 K19 Tudor pl Mitch
0 E19 Tudor rd E4
5 Z4 Tudor rd E6
5 Y3 Tudor rd E9
3 O2 Tudor rd E9
9 O4 Tudor rd N9
9 U18 Tudor rd SE19
4 B13 Tudor rd SE25
7 X3 Tudor rd Bark
5 N11 Tudor rd Barnt
4 M11 Tudor rd Barnt
5 S6 Tudor rd Becknhm
0 H18 Tudor rd Hampt
2 P8 Tudor rd Harrow
3 P10 Tudor rd Hounsl
8 B20 Tudor rd S'hall
1 U8 Tudor st EC4
6 K5 Tudor way N14
3 O6 Tudor way W3
A11 Tufnell Park rd N7
7 V11 Tufnell Pk rd N19
0 A14 Tufton rd SE0
H2 Tufton st SW1
3 O14 Tugela rd Croy
0 M4 Tuilerie st SE0
5 S9 Tuilerie st E2
5 U6 Tulse clo Becknhm
8 G1 Tulse hill SW2
0 F18 Tulse hill SW2
8 M4 Tulsemere rd SE27
9 X7 Tunbridge ct SE26
8 D12 Tuncombe rd N18
4 L3 Tunis rd W12
A14 Tunis rd W12
2 B2 Tunley rd NW10
7 N3 Tunley rd SW17
5 X10 Tunmarsh la E13
3 T19 Tunnel appr E1
4 G17 Tunnel appr E14
6 L6 Tunnel appr SE10
7 P12 Tunnel av SE10
0 L6 Tunnel av SE10
5 P6 Tunnel entrance SE16
9 V2 Tunnel gdns N11
0 D10 Tunstall rd SW19
7 T1 Tunstall rd Croy
3 T20 Tunstall rd Croy
5 V19 Tunworth clo NW9
6 C17 Tunworth cres SW15
0 L20 Turdinghall la Felt
9 P4 Turin rd N9
5 S14 Turin st E2
3 W19 Turks Head yd EC1
7 R9 Turks row SW3
8 C5 Turle rd N4
8 C5 Turle rd N4
1 Z2 Turle rd SW16
5 N4 Turley clo E15
1 W14 Turnagain la EC4
5 Y5 Turnage rd Dgnhm
1 R14 Turner av N15
6 L20 Turner av Mitch
1 O6 Turner av Twick
8 A19 Turner clo NW11
8 A19 Turner dri NW11
3 U11 Turner rd E17

24 L8 Turner rd Edg
117 Z16 Turner rd New Mald
143 W4 Turner st E1
65 P17 Turner st E16
142 J9 Turners all EC3
63 Y15 Turners rd E3
134 K9 Turners st N1
46 D2 Turners wood NW11
35 O13 Turneville rd E2
145 O13 Turneville rd W14
90 M19 Turney rd SE21
91 O18 Turney rd SE21
74 A11 Turnham Green ter W4
92 H12 Turnham rd SE4
133 V19 Turnmill st EC1
30 F12 Turnpike la N8
157 S4 Turnpike link Croy
147 X11 Turpentine la SW1
38 E1 Turpin av Rom
127 T16 Turpington la Brom
127 R15 Turpington la Brom
150 C8 Turquand st SE17
89 U6 Turret gro SW4
106 C7 Turtle rd SW17
42 J16 Turton rd Wemb
79 T14 Tuscan rd SE18
76 M15 Tuskar st SE10
75 O18 Tustin st SE15
151 Z16 Tustin st SE15
21 U8 Tuttlebee la Buck HI
39 O2 Tweed way Rom
39 O3 Tweed way Rom
120 F19 Tweeddale rd Carsh
65 V7 Tweedmouth rd E13
126 F2 Tweedy rd Brom
141 R8 Tweezer's all WC2
84 D13 Twickenham br Twick
41 X15 Twickenham gdns Grnfd
23 T2 Twickenham gdns Harrow
51 V6 Twickenham rd E11
100 C9 Twickenham rd Felt
84 A1 Twickenham rd Islwth
83 X10 Twickenham rd Islwth
84 A1 Twickenham rd Iswth
84 F11 Twickenham rd Rich
101 Y9 Twickenham rd Tedd
00 A10 Twilley st SW18
14 M13 Twineham green N12
14 M13 Twineham green N12
101 O6 Twining av Twick
47 S11 Twisden rd NW5
61 W1 Twybridge way NW10
60 M9 Twyford Abbey rd Wemb
29 N10 Twyford av N2
28 L11 Twyford av N2
61 P19 Twyford av W3
73 P1 Twyford av W3
73 R2 Twyford cres W3
141 N4 Twyford pl WC2
120 F19 Twyford rd Carsh
40 J2 Twyford rd Harrow
54 R14 Twyford rd Ilf
78 B4 Twyford st E16
133 N4 Twyford st N1
65 O13 Tyas rd E16
119 X5 Tybenham rd SW19
9 O10 Tyberry rd Enf
41 U1 Tyburn la Harrow
63 X17 Tye st E14
142 J18 Tyers gate SE1
149 O8 Tyers st SE11
149 O10 Tyers ter SE11
81 O14 Tyeshurst clo SE2
121 Z3 Tylecroft rd SW16
122 C3 Tylecroft rd SW16
54 B14 Tylehurst gdns Ilf
111 R20 Tyler rd Becknhm
77 N14 Tyler st SE10
24 L19 Tylers ga Harrow
52 K11 Tylney rd E7
127 N3 Tylney rd Brom
48 J20 Tyndale ter N1
51 T7 Tyndall rd E10
96 L8 Tyndall rd Welling
143 O4 Tyne st E1
89 O6 Tyneham rd SW11
8 L3 Tynemouth dri Enf
31 W13 Tynemouth rd N15
107 O17 Tynemouth rd Mitch
88 C4 Tynemouth st SW6
126 D11 Tynham grn Brom
87 Z1 Tyrawley rd SW6

154 M8 Tyrell ct Carsh
114 J11 Tyron way Sidcp
66 H7 Tyrone rd E6
97 P13 Tyrrell av Welling
91 X11 Tyrrell st EC3
93 O6 Tyrwhitt rd SE4
133 T15 Tysoe st EC1
92 D19 Tyson rd SE23
49 U17 Tyssen pas E8
49 S8 Tyssen st E8
47 X10 Tytherton rd N19

# U

64 E14 Uamvar st E14
107 V19 Uckfield gro Mitch
9 U1 Uckfield rd Enf
148 D6 Udall st SW1
101 Z13 Udney Pk rd Tedd
62 H13 Uffington rd NW10
108 G9 Uffington rd SE27
22 L2 Ufford clo Harrow
22 L2 Ufford rd Harrow
141 V17 Ufford st SE1
49 P20 Ufton gro N1
49 R20 Ufton rd N1
134 H2 Ufton rd N1
107 V10 Ullathorne rd SW16
17 P11 Ulleswater rd N13
64 F15 Ullin st E14
103 Y10 Ullswater clo SW15
103 Y9 Ullswater cres SW15
104 A10 Ullswater cres SW15
108 J5 Ullswater rd SE27
74 G20 Ullswater rd SW13
57 W14 Ullswater way Hornch
17 X13 Ulster gdns N13
48 C12 Ulster ms N7
131 W18 Ulster ter W1
77 N16 Ulundi rd SE3
87 P12 Ulva rd SW15
91 W13 Ulverscroft rd SE22
33 X7 Ulverston rd E17
108 J5 Ulverstone rd SE27
45 W14 Ulysses rd NW6
86 G17 Umbria st SW15
30 H19 Umfreville rd N4
9 W10 Under Bridge way Enf
93 P6 Undercliff rd SE13
4 K16 Underhill Barnt
131 Z5 Underhill pas NW1
91 Z19 Underhill rd SE22
131 Z5 Underhill st NW1
16 F9 Underne av N14
77 V20 Underpass SE3
112 B8 Undershaw rd Brom
159 U12 Underwood Croy
138 S19 Underwood rd E1
20 E15 Underwood rd E4
134 D11 Underwood rd E4
113 V5 Underwood the SE9
106 L12 Undine st SW17
59 R3 Uneeda dri Grnfd
142 L15 Unicorn pas SE1
142 H4 Union ct EC2
89 X4 Union gro SW8
32 L19 Union rd E17
16 L18 Union rd N11
89 X4 Union rd SW8
127 O11 Union rd Brom
123 N16 Union rd Croy
122 M16 Union rd Croy
42 J18 Union rd Wemb
18 H20 Union row N17
134 B6 Union sq N1
64 H4 Union st E15
142 A15 Union st SE1
141 X16 Union st SE1
4 F13 Union st Barnt
116 H3 Union st Kingst
134 M11 Union wlk E2
132 E17 University college WC1
132 H20 University Of london WC1
106 G15 University rd SW19
132 C18 University st WC1
151 R16 Unwin rd SE15
83 U7 Unwin rd Islwth
81 R10 Up Abbey rd Blvdr
136 J17 Up Addison gdns W14
109 R20 Up Beaulah hill SE19
147 V2 Up Belgrave st SW1
139 P5 Up Berkeley st W1
92 L4 Up Brockley rd SE4
139 S9 Up Brook st W1
146 K14 Up Cheyne row SW3

50 A8 Up Clapton rd E5
49 Y4 Up Clapton rd E5
124 J10 Up Elmers end Becknhm
125 P13 Up Elmers End rd Becknhm
139 T10 Up Grosvenor st W1
101 V4 Up Grotto rd Twick
141 S13 Up ground SE1
141 V12 Up ground SE1
123 T9 Up grove SE25
81 O16 Up Grove rd Blvdr
102 G8 Up Ham rd Rich
131 V17 Up Harley st NW1
81 V13 Up Holly Hill rd Blvdr
140 C8 Up James st W1
140 D9 Up John st W1
74 H14 Up mall W6
141 P20 Up marsh SE1
139 O1 Up Montagu st W1
153 T16 Up Mulgrave rd Sutton
64 B15 Up North st E14
46 L17 Up Park rd NW3
16 G17 Up Park rd N11
81 U12 Up Park rd Blvdr
112 K20 Up Park rd Brom
103 O16 Up Park rd Kingst
137 T19 Up Phillimore gdns W8
57 T11 Up Rainham rd Hornch
85 T10 Up Richmond Rd w SW14
157 T17 Up Selsdon rd S Croy
81 R10 Up Sheridan rd Blvdr
158 D4 Up Shirley rd Croy
82 G2 Up Sutton la Hounsl
102 D19 Up Teddington rd Kingst
142 D0 Up Thames st EC1
141 Z8 Up Thames st EC4
48 F4 Up Tollington pk N4
107 N4 Up Tooting pk SW17
106 M4 Up Tooting rd SW17
106 L9 Up Tooting rd SW17
107 N6 Up Tooting rd SW17
58 J12 Up Town rd Grnfd
90 C18 Up Tulse hill SW2
154 F10 Up Vernon rd Sutton
123 W11 Up Walthamstow rd E17
97 P4 Up Wickham la Welling
131 V20 Up Wimpole st W1
139 V2 Up Wimpole st W1
138 D7 Upbrook ms W2
146 B19 Upcerne rd SW10
75 R17 Upcot st SE15
12 H14 Upcroft av Edg
159 A3 Upfield Croy
157 Z5 Upfield Croy
59 V13 Upfield rd W7
53 X11 Uphall av Ilf
53 X10 Uphall rd Ilf
53 Y12 Uphall rd Ilf
74 B11 Upham Pk rd W4
13 O15 Uphill dri NW7
25 W16 Uphill dri NW9
13 P13 Uphill gro NW7
13 P14 Uphill rd NW7
65 R12 Upland rd E13
91 X12 Upland rd SE22
91 X18 Upland rd SE22
98 B8 Upland rd Bxly Hth
157 O12 Upland rd S Croy
154 G14 Upland rd Sutton
125 N4 Uplands Becknhm
32 F9 Uplands av E17
85 T13 Uplands clo SW14
35 P2 Uplands end Wdfd Grn
7 U9 Uplands Pk rd Enf
30 E17 Uplands rd N8
16 B6 Uplands rd Barnt
37 U11 Uplands rd Rom
35 P2 Uplands rd Wdfd Grn
7 T16 Uplands way N21
54 L20 Upney la Bark
67 Y1 Upney la Bark
36 C18 Uppark dri Ilf
6 G16 Upper Brighton rd Surb
72 F17 Upper butts Brentf
27 X9 Upper Cavendish av N3
18 J17 Upper Fore st N18
120 L4 Upper green Mitch
65 R9 Upper rd E13
155 Z11 Upper rd Wallgtn

| | | | |
|---|---|---|---|
| 87 N 11 Upper Richmond rd SW15 | 56 A 9 Valence Wood rd Dgnhm | 148 J 10 Vauxhall br SW1&SE11 | 137 W 15 Vicarage gdns W8 |
| 83 Z 7 Upper sq Islwth | 11 S 14 Valencia rd Stanm | 148 C 6 Vauxhall Br rd SW1 | 120 J 7 Vicarage gdns Mit |
| 48 H 20 Upper st N1 | 115 Y 2 Valentine av Bxly | 156 M 15 Vauxhall gdns S Croy | 91 P 1 Vicarage gro SE5 |
| 133 W 2 Upper st N1 | 110 E 5 Valentine ct SE23 | 148 M 13 Vauxhall gro SW8 | 52 B 19 Vicarage la E15 |
| 133 V 8 Upper street N1 | 141 V 18 Valentine pl SE1 | 149 N 13 Vauxhall gro SW8 | 65 O 2 Vicarage la E15 |
| 46 D 10 Upper ter NW3 | 50 E 19 Valentine rd E9 | 149 P 8 Vauxhall st SE11 | 66 K 8 Vicarage la E6 |
| 132 G 15 Upper Woburn pl WC1 | 40 L 10 Valentine rd Harrow | 148 M 10 Vauxhall wlk SE11 | 152 G 19 Vicarage la Epsom |
| 114 M 12 Upperton rd Sidcp | 141 W 18 Valentine row SE1 | 107 R 16 Vectis gdns SW17 | 54 D 5 Vicarage la Ilf |
| 65 X 9 Upperton Rd west E13 | 53 Y 4 Valentine's rd Ilf | 93 P 11 Veda rd SE13 | 47 Z 1 Vicarage path N15 |
| 65 Y 8 Upperton Rd west E13 | 57 P 8 Valentine's way Rom | 10 A 3 Vega rd Bushey Watf | 79 P 14 Vicarage pk SE18 |
| 24 E 9 Uppingham av Stanm | 53 Y 2 Valentines park Ilf | 91 S 12 Velde way SE22 | 51 O 1 Vicarage rd E10 |
| 17 S 19 Upsdell av N13 | 112 B 13 Valeswood rd Brom | 130 H 19 Venables st NW8 | 52 B 20 Vicarage rd E15 |
| 90 L 3 Upstall st SE5 | 65 R 5 Valetta gro E13 | 74 G 12 Vencourt pl W6 | 44 B 17 Vicarage rd NW10 |
| 52 G 20 Upton av E7 | 74 C 4 Valetta rd W3 | 30 J 20 Venetia rd N4 | 26 G 20 Vicarage rd NW4 |
| 98 B 15 Upton clo Bxly | 50 B 18 Valette st E9 | 72 F 7 Venetia rd W5 | 31 X 3 Vicarage rd N17 |
| 153 Z 16 Upton dene Sutton | 38 F 7 Valiant clo Rom | 90 M 5 Venetian rd SE5 | 85 Y 12 Vicarage rd SW14 |
| 24 C 17 Upton gdns Harrow | 143 U 1 Vallance rd E1 | 89 W 9 Venn st SW4 | 156 G 4 Vicarage rd Croy |
| 65 T 1 Upton la E7 | 135 U 14 Vallance rd E2 | 110 D 14 Venner rd SE26 | 56 F 20 Vicarage rd Dgnhm |
| 52 G 19 Upton la E7 | 29 V 6 Vallance rd N22 | 99 P 4 Venners clo Bxly Hth | 57 X 4 Vicarage rd Hornc |
| -65 V 1 Upton Park rd E7 | 33 U 12 Vallentin rd E17 | 63 W 11 Venour rd E3 | 116 G 2 Vicarage rd Kingst |
| 52 H 20 Upton Pk rd E7 | 15 U 14 Valley av N12 | 24 C 6 Ventnor av Stanm | 153 Z 7 Vicarage rd Sutton |
| 18 L 16 Upton rd N18 | 99 U 15 Valley clo Drtfd | 15 N 9 Ventnor dri N20 | 101 X 12 Vicarage rd Tedd |
| 79 P 18 Upton rd SE18 | 25 R 18 Valley dri NW9 | 54 G 17 Ventnor gdns Bark | 101 T 4 Vicarage rd Twick |
| 98 A 14 Upton rd Bxly Hth | 106 G 17 Valley gdns SW19 | 75 T 19 Ventnor rd SE14 | 35 S 2 Vicarage rd Wdfd Grn |
| 97 Y 10 Upton rd Bxly Hth | 42 L 20 Valley gdns Wemb | 154 B 17 Ventnor rd Sutton | 43 Z 10 Vicarage way NW1 |
| 82 H 9 Upton rd Hounsl | 77 Y 13 Valley gro SE7 | 97 Y 18 Venture clo Bxly | 40 G 1 Vicarage way Harr |
| 123 N 2 Upton rd Thntn Hth | 101 X 3 Valley ms Twick | 7 U 18 Vera av N21 | 65 S 3 Vicars clo E15 |
| 15 V 20 Upway N12 | 108 D 10 Valley rd SW16 | 87 T 2 Vera rd SW6 | 8 F 10 Vicars clo Enf |
| 94 D 16 Upwood rd SE12 | 81 X 11 Valley rd Blvdr | 74 F 14 Verbena gdns W6 | 93 P 9 Vicars hill SE13 |
| 122 A 1 Upwood rd SW16 | 126 A 4 Valley rd Brom | 112 A 2 Verdant la SE6 | 17 U 3 Vicars Moor la N21 |
| 150 B 16 Urlwin st SE5 | 99 U 15 Valley rd Dartfd | 158 F 2 Verdayne av Croy | 146 D 18 Vicat st SW10 |
| 105 T 1 Urmston dri SW19 | 115 R 20 Valley rd Orp | 80 A 14 Verdun rd SE2 | 90 A 1 Viceroy rd SW8 |
| 88 J 3 Ursula st SW11 | 20 B 5 Valley side E4 | 74 F 19 Verdun rd SW13 | 42 L 20 Victor gro Wemb |
| 68 K 1 Urswick gdns Dgnhm | 4 F 19 Valley view Barnt | 139 X 6 Vere st W1 | 62 K 7 Victor rd NW10 |
| 50 C 15 Urswick rd E5 | 158 C 2 Valley wlk Croy | 145 N 12 Vereker rd W14 | 48 D 7 Victor rd N7 |
| 68 K 1 Urswick rd Dgnhm | 108 D 11 Valleyfield rd SW16 | 109 P 16 Vermont rd SE19 | 110 F 17 Victor rd SE20 |
| 63 Z 4 Usher rd E3 | 7 T 9 Valleyfields cres Enf | 88 B 16 Vermont rd SW18 | 23 O 11 Victor rd Harrow |
| 88 F 11 Usk rd SW11 | 20 A 7 Valleyside parade E4 | 154 A 4 Vermont rd Sutton | 101 T 11 Victor rd Tedd |
| 65 P 20 Usk st E16 | 62 H 8 Valliere rd NW10 | 55 Y 13 Verney gdns Dgnhm | 18 C 10 Victor villas N9 |
| 63 S 8 Usk st E2 | 114 G 2 Valliers Wood rd Sidcp | 75 O 14 Verney rd SE16 | 18 C 10 Victor villas N9 |
| 56 E 9 Uvedale rd Dgnhm | 59 Y 13 Vallis way W13 | 151 V 12 Verney rd SE16 | 146 H 3 Victoria And Albert museum SW7 |
| 8 B 17 Uvedale rd Enf | 90 M 3 Valmar rd SE5 | 55 Y 12 Verney rd Dgnhm | 142 K 2 Victoria av EC2 |
| 146 B 18 Uverdale rd SW10 | 91 N 2 Valmar rd SE5 | 43 V 10 Verney st NW10 | 66 A 3 Victoria av E6 |
| 74 G 3 Uxbridge rd W12 | 106 M 12 Valnay st SW17 | 151 V 11 Verney way SE16 | 27 W 5 Victoria av N3 |
| 136 B 16 Uxbridge rd W12 | 32 H 4 Valognes av E17 | 79 O 16 Vernham rd SE18 | 5 U 15 Victoria av Barnt |
| 72 C 1 Uxbridge rd W13 | 87 V 15 Valonia gdns SW18 | 53 T 13 Vernon av E12 | 82 G 12 Victoria av Hounsl |
| 73 O 2 Uxbridge rd W5 | 79 O 16 Vamberry rd SE18 | 119 O 3 Vernon av SW20 | 116 F 16 Victoria av Surb |
| 60 K 20 Uxbridge rd W5 | 117 Z 17 Van Dyck av New Mald | 34 G 1 Vernon av Wdfd Grn | 155 P 5 Victoria av Wllgtn |
| 100 L 13 Uxbridge rd Hampt | 94 C 1 Vanborough ter SE3 | 6 B 18 Vernon cres Barnt | 5 V 15 Victoria clo Barnt |
| 22 L 1 Uxbridge rd Harrow | 77 O 18 Vanbrugh fields SE3 | 24 A 4 Vernon ct Stanm | 85 O 3 Victoria cotts SE1 |
| 23 O 1 Uxbridge rd Harrow | 77 O 17 Vanbrugh hill SE3 | 23 Z 4 Vernon dri Stanm | 31 R 16 Victoria cres N15 |
| 116 G 10 Uxbridge rd Kingst | 77 P 19 Vanbrugh pk SE3 | 24 A 4 Vernon dri Stanm | 109 R 14 Victoria cres SE19 |
| 70 L 2 Uxbridge rd S Hall | 77 P 20 Vanbrugh Pk rd SE3 | 144 L 6 Vernon ms W14 | 105 W 17 Victoria cres SW19 |
| 10 K 18 Uxbridge rd Stanm | 77 O 18 Vanbrugh Pk Rd west SE3 | 140 L 2 Vernon pl WC1 | 43 P 17 Victoria ct Wemb |
| 11 O 17 Uxbridge rd Stanm | 73 Z 8 Vanbrugh rd W4 | 51 Z 4 Vernon rd E11 | 65 T 19 Victoria Dock rd E1 |
| 137 S 13 Uxbridge st W8 | 94 C 1 Vanbrugh ter SE3 | 52 A 5 Vernon rd E11 | 65 N 17 Victoria Dock rd E1 |
| 42 K 4 Uxendon cres Wemb | 75 W 19 Vance st SE14 | 51 Z 19 Vernon rd E15 | 105 R 3 Victoria dri SW19 |
| 43 N 2 Uxendon hill Wemb | 110 L 3 Vancouver rd SE23 | 32 L 14 Vernon rd E17 | 105 S 4 Victoria dri SW19 |
| 42 M 3 Uxendon hill Wemb | 25 T 5 Vancouver rd Edg | 63 Z 6 Vernon rd E3 | 141 S 9 Victoria emb EC4/WC2/SW1 |
| | 88 C 20 Vanderbilt rd SW18 | 30 G 11 Vernon rd N8 | 140 L 16 Victoria emb EC4/WC2/SW1 |
| | 140 D 20 Vandon pas SW1 | 85 Y 8 Vernon rd N8 | 137 S 12 Victoria gdns W11 |
| **V** | 148 D 1 Vandon st SW 1 | 54 K 5 Vernon rd Ilf | 82 A 1 Victoria gdns Hounsl |
| | 87 P 17 Vandyke clo SW15 | 154 E 10 Vernon rd Sutton | 15 T 15 Victoria gro N12 |
| 21 O 6 Valance av E4 | 95 P 14 Vandyke cross SE9 | 41 P 16 Vernon ri Grnfd | 146 A 1 Victoria gro W8 |
| 130 B 13 Vale clo W9 | 24 M 19 Vane clo Harrow | 133 P 12 Vernon rise WC1 | 137 V 10 Victoria Gro ms W2 |
| 104 B 8 Vale cres SW15 | 148 D 5 Vane st SW1 | 133 O 11 Vernon sq WC1 | 129 S 4 Victoria ms NW6 |
| 22 A 15 Vale croft Pinn | 81 S 13 Vanessa clo Blvdr | 144 L 6 Vernon st W14 | 63 W 2 Victoria park E9 |
| 4 K 16 Vale dri Barnt | 38 E 8 Vanguard clo Rom | 97 Y 5 Veroan rd Bxly Hth | 135 Y 5 Victoria Pk rd E9 |
| 30 L 20 Vale gro N4 | 93 O 2 Vanguard st SE4 | 52 F 20 Verona rd E7 | 63 P 3 Victoria Pk rd E9 |
| 73 Y 4 Vale gro W3 | 156 A 16 Vanguard way Wallgtn | 107 S 5 Veronica rd SW17 | 135 Z 11 Victoria Pk sq E2 |
| 61 P 15 Vale lane W3 | 112 E 8 Vanoc gdns Brom | 36 A 15 Veronique gdns Ilf | 63 O 8 Victoria Pk sq E2 |
| 52 H 17 Vale rd E7 | 52 D 12 Vansittart rd E7 | 89 R 19 Verran rd SW12 | 84 H 13 Victoria pl Rich |
| 30 M 20 Vale rd N4 | 145 U 18 Vanston pl SW6 | 109 X 19 Versailles rd SE20 | 51 Y 12 Victoria rd E11 |
| 31 N 19 Vale rd N4 | 135 P 17 Vanstone pl E1 | 32 K 20 Verulam av E17 | 65 S 7 Victoria rd E13 |
| 127 V 2 Vale rd Brom | 145 U 18 Vanstone pl SW6 | 58 J 11 Verulam rd Grnfd | 33 T 7 Victoria rd E17 |
| 152 E 8 Vale rd Epsom | 107 N 13 Vant rd SW17 | 133 S 20 Verulam st EC1 | 34 H 8 Victoria rd E18 |
| 121 W 8 Vale rd Mitch | 106 M 13 Vant rd SW17 | 22 M 8 Verwood rd Harrow | 21 N 4 Victoria rd E4 |
| 153 Z 8 Vale rd Sutton | 75 O 15 Varcoe rd SE16 | 74 F 4 Vespan rd W12 | 20 M 5 Victoria rd E4 |
| 152 F 5 Vale rd Worc Pk | 151 Z 12 Varcoe rd SE16 | 92 J 5 Vesta rd SE4 | 62 A 12 Victoria rd NW10 |
| 45 V 4 Vale ri NW11 | 143 W 3 Varden st E1 | 110 G 4 Vestris rd SE23 | 27 N 13 Victoria rd NW4 |
| 48 J 10 Vale row N5 | 88 G 12 Vardens rd SW11 | 33 R 14 Vestry rd E17 | 129 T 4 Victoria rd NW6 |
| 132 J 1 Vale royal N1 | 65 W 16 Varley rd E16 | 91 S 2 Vestry rd SE5 | 13 R 15 Victoria rd NW7 |
| 30 L 20 Vale ter N4 | 135 N 19 Varna rd SW6 | 134 F 12 Vestry st N1 | 31 W 14 Victoria rd N15 |
| 45 T 6 Vale the NW11 | 132 A 12 Varndell st NW1 | 110 K 5 Vevey st SE6 | 29 W 5 Victoria rd N22 |
| 29 O 4 Vale the N10 | 31 P 19 Vartry rd N15 | 56 D 9 Veysey gdns Dgnhm | 48 E 3 Victoria rd N4 |
| 17 N 1 Vale the N14 | 149 V 20 Vassall rd SW9 | 141 V 2 Viaduct bldgs EC1 | 18 J 9 Victoria rd N9 |
| 16 L 3 Vale the N20 | 151 P 3 Vauban st SE16 | 135 W 14 Viaduct pl E2 | 85 X 7 Victoria rd SW14 |
| 74 C 3 Vale the N3 | 63 O 13 Vaudrey clo W1 | 135 W 14 Viaduct rd E2 | 61 Y 13 Victoria rd W3 |
| 146 G 14 Vale the SW3 | 26 C 16 Vaughan av NW4 | 34 G 8 Viaduct the E18 | 60 C 14 Victoria rd W5 |
| 158 G 3 Vale the Croy | 74 E 10 Vaughan av W6 | 93 S 8 Vian st SE13 | 138 A 19 Victoria rd W8 |
| 70 B 17 Vale the Hounsl | 53 T 1 Vaughan gdns Ilf | 90 D 20 Vibart gdns SW2 | 54 A 18 Victoria rd Bark |
| 34 F 3 Vale the Wdfd Grn | 151 X 13 Vaughan pl SE15 | 47 O 14 Vicar's rd NW5 | 53 Z 18 Victoria rd Bark |
| 55 W 3 Valence av Dgnhm | 52 C 19 Vaughan rd E15 | 77 T 20 Vicarage av SE3 | 5 U 15 Victoria rd Barnt |
| 55 X 10 Valence cir Dgnhm | 90 L 6 Vaughan rd SE5 | 88 G 3 Vicarage cres SW11 | 127 P 12 Victoria rd Brom |
| 55 Y 8 Valence park Dgnhm | 22 M 19 Vaughan rd Harrow | 85 X 12 Vicarage dri SW14 | 98 D 12 Victoria rd Bxly Hth |
| | 23 R 20 Vaughan rd Harrow | 67 R 2 Vicarage dri Bark | 113 X 12 Victoria rd Chisl |
| | 116 A 17 Vaughan rd Surb | 82 C 3 Vicarage Farm rd Hounsl | 56 J 14 Victoria rd Dgnhm |
| | 96 L 5 Vaughan rd Welling | 70 C 20 Vicarage Farm rd Hounsl | 36 A 15 Victoria rd Ilf |
| | | 137 W 16 Vicarage ga W8 | 35 Z 15 Victoria rd Ilf |
| | | 79 P 14 Vicarage gdns SE18 | |

17 N3 Victoria rd Kingst
106 K19 Victoria rd Mitch
39 S18 Victoria rd Rom
40 A13 Victoria rd Ruis
70 D9 Victoria rd S'hall
14 M8 Victoria rd Sidcp
16 G15 Victoria rd Surb
154 F12 Victoria rd Sutton
101 X15 Victoria rd Tedd
84 A18 Victoria rd Twick
89 S10 Victoria ri SW4
129 T4 Victoria sq NW6
147 Y2 Victoria sq SW1
147 Y1 Victoria sq SW1
51 Y20 Victoria st E15
140 G20 Victoria st SW1
148 D2 Victoria st SW1
81 P14 Victoria st Blvdr
147 Y5 Victoria station SW1
48 F4 Victoria ter N4
41 S4 Victoria ter Harrow
129 T5 Victoria vlls NW6
85 N10 Victoria vlls Rich
77 W15 Victoria way SE7
49 T10 Victorian gro N16
49 T11 Victorian rd N16
120 D11 Victory av Mrdn
150 D5 Victory pl SE17
109 T16 Victory pl SE19
106 B18 Victory rd SW19
150 G17 Victory sq SE5
38 F7 Victory way Rom
23 P12 View clo Harrow
29 N19 View rd N6
28 M20 View rd N6
81 N13 View the SE2
87 V16 Viewfield rd SW18
97 T20 Viewfield rd Sidcp
79 W14 Viewland rd SE18
7 U19 Viga rd N21
109 X9 Vigilant clo SE26
140 B10 Vigo st W1
58 C19 Viking st S'hall
90 F7 Villa rd SW9
150 G12 Villa st SE17
80 A18 Villacourt rd SE18
20 H16 Village clo E4
99 U11 Village Green rd Drtfrd
27 S7 Village rd N3
8 D19 Village rd Enf
77 Z16 Village the SE7
78 A16 Village the SE7
43 Z12 Village way NW10
44 A12 Village way NW10
91 O15 Village way SE21
125 N3 Village way Becknhm
40 F1 Village way E Harrow
40 D1 Village way Pinn
79 P12 Villas rd SE18
116 L11 Villiers av Surb
100 F2 Villiers av Twick
51 O6 Villiers clo E10
117 N9 Villiers clo Surb
116 L11 Villiers path Surb
44 G17 Villiers rd NW10
124 F4 Villiers rd Becknhm
83 S4 Villiers rd Islwth
116 M6 Villiers rd Kingst
140 K12 Villiers st WC2
70 F4 Villiers st S'hall
82 H18 Vincam clo Twick
134 G14 Vince st EC1
126 J9 Vincent clo Brom
44 E10 Vincent gdns NW2
20 K20 Vincent rd E4
30 L13 Vincent rd N15
30 F7 Vincent rd N22
79 N11 Vincent rd SE18
73 U8 Vincent rd W3
123 S18 Vincent rd Croy
68 L2 Vincent rd Dgnhm
83 P3 Vincent rd Islwth
117 P5 Vincent rd Kingst
61 D1 Vincent rd Wemb
100 M14 Vincent row Hampt
148 E5 Vincent sq SW1
65 P16 Vincent st E16
148 F6 Vincent st SW1
133 X9 Vincent ter N1
24 K17 Vine ct Harrow
54 B15 Vine gdns Ilf
133 S18 Vine la EC1
142 L15 Vine la SE1
82 J10 Vine pl Hounsl
86 D9 Vine rd SW13
143 N7 Vine st EC3
38 L14 Vine st Rom
133 U18 Vine St br EC1
142 B18 Vine yd SE1
33 T13 Vinegar all E17
6 H18 Vineries the N14
8 E11 Vineries the Enf

130 K14 Vinery vlls NW8
28 A5 Vines av N3
93 S8 Viney st SE13
27 S2 Vineyard av NW7
105 X9 Vineyard Hill rd SW19
84 J13 Vineyard pas Rich
85 X7 Vineyard path SW14
84 K14 Vineyard the Rich
133 T16 Vineyard wlk EC1
90 F10 Vining st SW9
142 C9 Vintners pl EC4
80 C12 Viola av SE2
62 E20 Viola sq W12
62 E20 Viola sq W12
8 B3 Violet av Enf
156 K17 Violet gdns Croy
130 B10 Violet hill NW8
156 J9 Violet la Croy
33 P19 Violet rd E17
34 H7 Violet rd E18
64 C12 Violet rd E3
139 N1 Virgil pl W1
149 R1 Virgil st SE1
36 D8 Virginia gdns Ilf
134 M14 Virginia rd E2
100 J20 Virginia rd Mitch
143 T10 Virginia st E1
134 B19 Viscount st EC1
9 T9 Vista av Enf
35 O16 Vista dri Ilf
95 P19 Vista the SE9
24 J19 Vista way Harrow
26 J17 Vivian av NW4
43 S17 Vivian av Wemb
43 O15 Vivian gdns Wemb
91 Z7 Vivian gro SE15
63 V6 Vivian rd E3
28 G15 Vivian way N2
84 F17 Vivienne clo Twick
79 T20 Voce rd SE18
118 D14 Voewood clo New Mald
89 X8 Voltaire rd SW4
34 E18 Voluntary pl E11
47 V7 Vorley rd N19
108 B16 Voss ct SW10
135 U14 Voss st E2
150 A6 Vowler st SE17
156 C15 Vulcan clo Croy
92 K5 Vulcan rd SE4
92 L4 Vulcan st SE4
98 H8 Vyne the Bxly Hth
61 Z20 Vyner rd W3
63 N4 Vyner st E2

# W

97 Z20 W woodside Bxly
65 Y19 Wada rd E11
150 D7 Wadding st SE17
51 X16 Waddington rd E15
51 X17 Waddington st E15
108 M19 Waddington way SE19
109 N20 Waddington way SE19
156 G4 Waddon clo Croydon
156 E6 Waddon Ct rd Croy
122 C20 Waddon Marsh way Croy
156 K2 Waddon New rd Croy
156 F7 Waddon Pk av Croydon
156 H5 Waddon rd Croydon
156 F14 Waddon way Croydon
64 C19 Wade rd E14
64 C19 Wade's pl E14
17 T3 Wades gro N21
17 U3 Wades hill N21
7 T19 Wades hill N21
135 Y7 Wadeson st E2
63 O5 Wadeson st E2
38 A20 Wadeville av Rom
33 S3 Wadham av E17
130 J2 Wadham gdns NW3
41 P17 Wadham gdns Grnfd
33 T3 Wadham rd E17
87 T11 Wadham rd SW15
73 Y9 Wadhurst rd W4
33 Z20 Wadley rd E11
60 C6 Wadsworth rd Grnfd
65 T15 Waford rd E16
63 Y13 Wager st E3
5 P3 Waggon rd Barnt
65 X4 Waghorn rd E13
24 H11 Waghorn rd Harrow
91 X7 Waghorn st SE15

75 P18 Wagner st SE15
18 J20 Wagon la N17
38 K8 Wainfleet av Rom
87 P20 Wainford cl SW19
94 C19 Waite Davies rd SE12
151 O13 Waite st SE15
149 P6 Wake st SE11
109 S18 Wakefield gdns SE19
35 P20 Wakefield gdns Ilf
16 L17 Wakefield rd N11
31 U15 Wakefield rd N15
84 H13 Wakefield rd Rich
66 E3 Wakefield st E6
18 K17 Wakefield st N18
132 L15 Wakefield st WC1
49 O18 Wakeham st N1
22 E11 Wakehams hill Pinn
88 L13 Wakehurst rd SW11
89 N12 Wakehurst rd SW11
64 M6 Wakelin rd E15
59 W15 Wakeling rd W7
63 U18 Wakeling st E14
128 D13 Wakeman rd NW10
25 Y14 Wakemans Hill av NW9
54 B19 Wakering rd Bark
133 X11 Wakley st EC1
148 M19 Walberswick st SW8
142 E7 Walbrook EC4
150 C8 Walcorde av SE17
149 U4 Walcot sq SE11
148 D5 Walcott st SW1
108 H7 Waldeck gro SE27
30 J12 Waldeck rd N15
85 W7 Waldeck rd SW14
60 C18 Waldeck rd W13
73 P15 Waldeck rd W4
101 V5 Waldegrave gdns Twick
101 W9 Waldegrave nk Twick
30 G10 Waldegrave rd N8
109 V18 Waldegrave rd SE19
60 M18 Waldegrave rd W5
127 S10 Waldegrave rd Brom
55 T6 Waldegrave rd Dgnhm
101 V8 Waldegrave rd Twick
157 U7 Waldegrove rd Croy
87 T3 Waldemar av SW6
72 D4 Waldemar av W13
105 X11 Waldemar rd SW19
17 Z13 Walden av N13
113 V10 Walden av Chisl
69 Z7 Walden av Rnham
81 O13 Walden clo Blvdr
122 D7 Walden gdns Thntn Hth
113 U14 Walden rd Chisl
143 W3 Walden st E1
63 N10 Walden st E1
36 H1 Walden way Ilf
110 C2 Waldenshaw rd SE23
106 K19 Waldo pl Mitch
62 J9 Waldo rd NW10
126 M7 Waldo rd Brom
110 D2 Waldram cres SE23
110 E2 Waldram Pk rd SE23
110 D2 Waldram pl SE23
125 W6 Waldron gdns Brom
106 D5 Waldron rd SW18
41 S4 Waldron rd Harrow
41 P7 Waldron's yd Harrow
156 K9 Waldronhyrst Croy
156 K8 Waldrons the Croy
93 W6 Walerand rd SE13
104 K12 Wales av Carsh
61 Y15 Wales Farm rd W3
63 U14 Waley st E1
15 O1 Walfield av N20
49 T12 Walford rd N16
93 Y12 Walfram clo SE13
56 A20 Walfrey gdns Dgnhm
145 T17 Walham gro SW6
145 T16 Walham yd SW6
113 X11 Walkden rd Chisl
140 E8 Walker's ct W1
109 N2 Walkerscroft mead SE21
108 M1 Walkerscroft mead SE21
99 Y14 Walkley rd Drtfrd
28 G9 Walks the N2
66 H2 Wall End rd E6
64 E14 Wall End rd E14
49 P19 Wall st N1
137 T4 Wallace collection W2
154 L11 Wallace cres Carsh
65 N9 Wallace rd E15

64 M9 Wallace rd E15
48 M17 Wallace rd N1
92 H6 Wallbutton rd SE4
45 P3 Wallcote av NW2
39 Z11 Wallenger av Rom
92 E3 Waller rd SE14
74 E1 Wallflower st W12
145 W6 Wallgrave rd SW5
145 V5 Wallgrave ter SW5
136 E4 Wallingford av W10
36 L20 Wallington rd Ilf
51 N18 Wallis rd E9
50 M19 Wallis rd E9
58 K17 Wallis rd S'hall
85 Z10 Wallorton gdns SW14
51 X2 Wallwood rd E11
63 Z15 Wallwood st E14
45 R15 Walm la NW2
38 H8 Walmer clo Rom
71 Z7 Walmer gdns W13
139 N1 Walmer pl W1
136 J7 Walmer rd W11
139 N1 Walmer st W1
79 R11 Walmer ter SE18
60 B4 Walmgate rd Grnfd
14 K18 Walmington feld N12
154 K11 Walnut clo Carsh
8 B18 Walnut gro Enf
114 D20 Walnut Tree clo Chisl
77 O15 Walnut Tree rd SE10
72 K17 Walnut Tree rd Brentf
55 X7 Walnut Tree rd Dgnhm
70 F17 Walnut Tree rd Hounsl
149 S4 Walnut Tree wlk SE11
84 M5 Walpole av Rich
85 N5 Walpole av Rich
72 D4 Walpole clo W13
101 V13 Walpole cres Tedd
73 V13 Walpole gdns W4
101 U6 Walpole gdns Twick
101 V13 Walpole pl Tedd
32 J12 Walpole rd E17
34 B6 Walpole rd E18
65 Y2 Walpole rd E6
30 M7 Walpole rd N17
106 G15 Walpole rd SW19
127 N11 Walpole rd Brom
157 N2 Walpole rd Croy
116 H16 Walpole rd Surb
101 V13 Walpole rd Tedd
101 T4 Walpole rd Twick
75 X20 Walpole st SE14
147 O9 Walpole st SW3
42 L17 Walrond av Wemb
92 E4 Walsham rd SE14
152 C10 Walsingham gdns Epsom
49 Y10 Walsingham rd E5
8 B16 Walsingham rd Enf
120 M10 Walsingham rd Mitch
83 T9 Walter st W2
116 J1 Walter st Kingst
63 T16 Walter ter E1
12 J20 Walter wlk Edg
123 S10 Walters rd SE25
9 R16 Walters rd Enf
126 E2 Walters yd Brom
129 R17 Walterton rd W9
25 R18 Waltham av NW9
99 V15 Waltham clo Drtfrd
25 P9 Waltham dri Edg
120 G19 Waltham rd Carsh
70 B8 Waltham rd S'hall
10 Z12 Waltham way E4
20 B5 Waltham way E4
33 N2 Walthamstow av E4
33 X11 Walthamstow rd E17
31 N5 Waltheof av N17
31 N4 Waltheof gdns N17
40 E12 Walton av Harrow
118 D10 Walton av New Mald
153 U5 Walton av Sutton
44 K7 Walton clo NW2
23 R12 Walton clo Harrow
40 E12 Walton cres Harrow
23 R13 Walton dri Harrow
61 T15 Walton gdns W3
42 J7 Walton gdns Wemb
159 U17 Walton grn Croy
147 O2 Walton pl SW3
53 W12 Walton rd E12
53 W13 Walton rd E12
65 X6 Walton rd E13
31 V14 Walton rd N15
23 R12 Walton rd Harrow
38 C2 Walton rd Rom
115 S8 Walton rd Sidcp

| Ref | Name |
|---|---|
| 00 G 1 | Waverley av Twick |
| 82 E 20 | Waverley av Twick |
| 43 N 16 | Waverley av Wemb |
| 34 K 6 | Waverley clo E18 |
| 27 N 12 | Waverley clo N12 |
| 79 R 15 | Waverley cres SE18 |
| 61 N 7 | Waverley gdns NW 10 |
| 67 U 7 | Waverley gdns Bark |
| 36 D 8 | Waverley gdns Ilf |
| 27 S 10 | Waverley gro N3 |
| 30 F 8 | Waverley pl NW8 |
| 33 V 10 | Waverley rd E17 |
| 34 K 6 | Waverley rd E18 |
| 31 Y 2 | Waverley rd N17 |
| 29 Z 20 | Waverley rd N8 |
| 79 R 14 | Waverley rd SE18 |
| 124 A 8 | Waverley rd SE25 |
| 123 Z 8 | Waverley rd SE25 |
| 7 X 12 | Waverley rd Enf |
| 152 J 11 | Waverley rd Epsom |
| 40 C 4 | Waverley rd Harrow |
| 58 H 19 | Waverley rd S'hall |
| 154 K 14 | Waverley way Carsh |
| 31 V 8 | Waverly vlls N17 |
| 139 W 12 | Waverton st W1 |
| 34 F 7 | Wavertree rd E18 |
| 108 B 2 | Wavertree rd SW2 |
| 58 G 17 | Waxlow cres S'hall |
| 61 X 6 | Waxlow rd NW10 |
| 22 A 8 | Waxwell clo Pinn |
| 22 A 9 | Waxwell la Pinn |
| 58 A 9 | Wayfarer rd Grnfd |
| 136 G 9 | Wayflete st W10 |
| 88 K 6 | Wayford st SW11 |
| 49 X 15 | Wayland av E8 |
| 88 F 9 | Wayland rd SW11 |
| 108 J 6 | Waylett pl SE27 |
| 136 G 8 | Waynfere St est W10 |
| 156 J 7 | Waynflete av Croy |
| 106 D 4 | Waynflete st SW18 |
| 45 T 4 | Wayside NW11 |
| 85 W 12 | Wayside SW14 |
| 159 S 14 | Wayside Croy |
| 10 C 1 | Wayside av Bushey Watf |
| 6 J 19 | Wayside clo N14 |
| 39 S 10 | Wayside clo Rom |
| 56 D 14 | Wayside gdns Dgnhm |
| 113 T 10 | Wayside gro SE9 |
| 23 S 5 | Weald la Harrow |
| 23 V 3 | Weald ri Harrow |
| 49 Y 6 | Weald sq E5 |
| 113 U 15 | Weald the Chisl |
| 38 G 19 | Weald way Rom |
| 153 V 3 | Wealdstone rd Sutton |
| 20 K 10 | Weale rd E4 |
| 99 Z 20 | Weardale av Drtfrd |
| 8 C 6 | Weardale gdns Enf |
| 93 X 11 | Weardale rd SE13 |
| 135 S 18 | Weaver st E1 |
| 108 K 10 | Weaver wlk SE27 |
| 142 L 15 | Weavers la SE1 |
| 150 J 3 | Webb st SE1 |
| 141 U 19 | Webber row SE1 |
| 141 X 18 | Webber st SE1 |
| 88 L 12 | Webbs rd SW11 |
| 72 G 3 | Webster gdns W5 |
| 51 V 11 | Webster rd E11 |
| 151 U 2 | Webster rd SE16 |
| 46 G 15 | Wedderburn rd NW3 |
| 67 T 4 | Wedderburn rd Bark |
| 128 M 17 | Wedlake st W10 |
| 35 W 4 | Wedmore av Ilf |
| 47 X 8 | Wedmore gdns N19 |
| 59 R 10 | Wedmore rd Grnfd |
| 47 Y 9 | Wedmore st N19 |
| 45 X 13 | Weech rd NW6 |
| 47 P 15 | Weedington rd NW5 |
| 76 L 8 | Weetman st SE10 |
| 94 F 12 | Weigall rd SE12 |
| 139 V 7 | Weighhouse st W1 |
| 123 Z 3 | Weighton rd SE20 |
| 23 R 4 | Weighton rd Harrow |
| 154 G 11 | Weihurst gdns Sutton |
| 87 R 9 | Weimar st SW15 |
| 18 B 19 | Weir Hall av N18 |
| 18 A 15 | Weir Hall gdns N15 |
| 31 P 1 | Weir Hall rd N17 |
| 18 C 17 | Weir Hall rd N18 |
| 89 V 19 | Weir rd SW12 |
| 98 G 19 | Weir rd Bxly |
| 132 G 13 | Weir's pas NW1 |
| 15 Z 8 | Weirdale av N20 |
| 15 Z 7 | Weirdale ave N11 |
| 87 P 8 | Weiss rd SW15 |
| 112 G 10 | Welbeck av Brom |
| 115 N 2 | Welbeck av Sidcp |
| 15 T 15 | Welbeck clo N12 |

| Ref | Name |
|---|---|
| 15 T 15 | Welbeck clo N12 |
| 152 F 17 | Welbeck clo Epsom |
| 118 C 11 | Welbeck clo New Mald |
| 66 A 8 | Welbeck rd E6 |
| 5 V 19 | Welbeck rd Barnt |
| 120 H 20 | Welbeck rd Carsh |
| 40 K 3 | Welbeck rd Harrow |
| 154 G 2 | Welbeck rd Sutton |
| 139 W 5 | Welbeck st W1 |
| 139 W 4 | Welbeck way W1 |
| 311 V 1 | Welbourne rd N17 |
| 49 U 20 | Welbury st E8 |
| 90 K 3 | Welby st SE5 |
| 107 R 13 | Welham rd SW17 |
| 154 H 1 | Welhouse rd Carsh |
| 4 A 16 | Well appr Barnt |
| 40 B 10 | Well clo Ruis |
| 142 C 7 | Well ct EC4 |
| 95 S 10 | Well Hall rd SE9 |
| 85 V 12 | Well la SW14 |
| 46 G 10 | Well pl NW3 |
| 46 G 10 | Well rd NW3 |
| 4 A 17 | Well rd Barnt |
| 51 Y 17 | Well st E15 |
| 63 P 1 | Well st W1 |
| 135 Z 1 | Well st E9 |
| 50 D 20 | Well st E9 |
| 76 G 17 | Well st SE10 |
| 46 G 10 | Well wlk NW3 |
| 24 C 18 | Wellacre rd Harrow |
| 59 V 7 | Welland gdns Grnfd |
| 143 T 8 | Wellclose sq E1 |
| 143 T 10 | Wellclose st E1 |
| 23 T 17 | Welldon cres Harrow |
| 142 A 17 | Weller st SE1 |
| 132 J 10 | Wellers ct NW1 |
| 74 H 8 | Wellesley av W6 |
| 101 S 5 | Wellesley cres Twick |
| 157 N 3 | Wellesley Ct rd Croy |
| 119 T 19 | Wellesley fount Sutton |
| 157 O 3 | Wellesley gro Croy |
| 47 O 15 | Wellesley pl NW5 |
| 34 F 16 | Wellesley rd E11 |
| 33 O 18 | Wellesley rd E17 |
| 47 O 15 | Wellesley rd NW5 |
| 30 F 7 | Wellesley rd N22 |
| 73 P 14 | Wellesley rd W4 |
| 122 M 20 | Wellesley rd Croy |
| 156 M 2 | Wellesley rd Croy |
| 157 N 3 | Wellesley rd Croy |
| 23 T 17 | Wellesley rd Harrow |
| 53 Y 6 | Wellesley rd Ilf |
| 54 B 4 | Wellesley rd Ilf |
| 154 D 13 | Wellesley rd Sutton |
| 101 S 6 | Wellesley rd Twick |
| 134 C 11 | Wellesley ter N1 |
| 29 S 9 | Wellfield av N10 |
| 108 B 10 | Wellfield rd SW16 |
| 108 D 11 | Wellfield wlk SW16 |
| 42 A 18 | Wellgarth Grnfd |
| 40 A 4 | Wellgarth rd NW11 |
| 4 B 14 | Wellhouse la Barnt |
| 125 N 9 | Wellhouse rd Becknhm |
| 97 R 8 | Welling High st Welling |
| 96 D 7 | Welling way SE9 |
| 20 C 9 | Wellington av E4 |
| 31 W 18 | Wellington av N15 |
| 19 N 10 | Wellington av N9 |
| 82 G 13 | Wellington av Hounsl |
| 22 E 4 | Wellington av Pinn |
| 97 N 15 | Wellington av Sidcp |
| 152 M 6 | Wellington av Worc Pk |
| 137 S 6 | Wellington clo W11 |
| 69 X 1 | Wellington clo Dgnhm |
| 117 W 7 | Wellington cres New Mald |
| 69 Y 1 | Wellington drl Dgnhm |
| 77 X 14 | Wellington gdns SE7 |
| 101 P 9 | Wellington gdns Hampt |
| 130 H 12 | Wellington pl NW8 |
| 50 M 3 | Wellington rd E10 |
| 34 G 14 | Wellington rd E11 |
| 32 J 12 | Wellington rd E17 |
| 66 G 5 | Wellington rd E6 |
| 52 D 14 | Wellington rd E7 |
| 128 G 14 | Wellington rd NW10 |
| 130 G 10 | Wellington rd NW8 |
| 105 Z 5 | Wellington rd SW19 |
| 72 D 9 | Wellington rd W5 |
| 81 P 12 | Wellington rd Blvdr |
| 126 L 9 | Wellington rd Brom |
| 97 V 14 | Wellington rd Bxly |
| 122 J 17 | Wellington rd Croy |
| 18 E 4 | Wellington rd Enf |
| 8 E 18 | Wellington rd Enf |

| Ref | Name |
|---|---|
| 101 P 10 | Wellington rd Hampt |
| 23 T 9 | Wellington rd Harrow |
| 82 E 10 | Wellington rd North Hounsl |
| 22 D 4 | Wellington rd Pinn |
| 85 N 15 | Wellington rd Rick |
| 82 G 14 | Wellington rd South Hounsl |
| 135 R 12 | Wellington row E2 |
| 147 N 10 | Wellington sq SW3 |
| 64 L 14 | Wellington st E16 |
| 78 K 11 | Wellington st SE18 |
| 140 M 8 | Wellington st WC2 |
| 141 N 8 | Wellington st WC2 |
| 67 O 2 | Wellington st Bark |
| 41 R 4 | Wellington ter Harrow |
| 64 A 11 | Wellington way E3 |
| 93 Z 18 | Wellmeadow rd SE13 |
| 111 Z 3 | Wellmeadow rd SE6 |
| 71 Y 10 | Wellmeadow rd W7 |
| 120 G 20 | Wellow wlk Carsh |
| 140 B 2 | Wells bldgs W1 |
| 150 K 20 | Wells cres SE5 |
| 56 G 16 | Wells gdns Dgnhm |
| 53 R 1 | Wells gdns Ilf |
| 57 U 18 | Wells gdns Rainhm |
| 62 B 13 | Wells house rd NW10 |
| 70 J 1 | Wells la S'hall |
| 140 B 3 | Wells ms W1 |
| 110 A 8 | Wells Park gro SE26 |
| 109 X 8 | Wells Park rd SE26 |
| 74 M 7 | Wells rd W12 |
| 136 C 19 | Wells rd W12 |
| 127 U 3 | Wells rd Brom |
| 131 O 6 | Wells ri NW8 |
| 140 B 3 | Wells st W1 |
| 48 F 6 | Wells ter N4 |
| 16 L 4 | Wells the N14 |
| 150 H 16 | Wells way SE5 |
| 150 G 15 | Wells Way bridge SE5 |
| 48 E 15 | Wells yd N7 |
| 4 A 15 | Wellside clo Brentf |
| 85 V 12 | Wellside gdns SW14 |
| 127 W 5 | Wellsmoor gdns Brom |
| 19 R 4 | Wellstead av N9 |
| 66 J 7 | Wellstead rd E6 |
| 55 N 2 | Wellwood rd Ilf |
| 88 D 13 | Wellwood rd SW18 |
| 151 S 8 | Welsford st SE1 |
| 135 U 4 | Welshpool st E8 |
| 74 G 13 | Weltje rd W6 |
| 79 U 20 | Welton rd SE18 |
| 42 L 10 | Wembley Hill rd Wemb |
| 43 N 13 | Wembley Hill rd Wemb |
| 43 O 10 | Wembley Pk dri Wemb |
| 42 M 12 | Wembley Pk dri Wemb |
| 100 G 19 | Wembley rd Hampt |
| 43 U 17 | Wembley way Wemb |
| 47 U 1 | Wembury rd N6 |
| 94 C 5 | Wemyss rd SE3 |
| 41 S 8 | Wendela ct Harrow |
| 74 C 7 | Wendell rd W12 |
| 154 F 1 | Wendling rd Sutton |
| 63 Z 3 | Wendon st E3 |
| 118 E 14 | Wendover dri New Mald |
| 62 D 6 | Wendover rd NW10 |
| 95 O 7 | Wendover rd SE9 |
| 126 H 7 | Wendover rd Brom |
| 97 O 11 | Wendover way Welling |
| 8 G 19 | Wendy clo Enf |
| 60 K 4 | Wendy way Wemb |
| 134 B 10 | Wenlock rd N1 |
| 12 G 20 | Wenlock rd Edg |
| 134 D 10 | Wenlock st N1 |
| 63 T 6 | Wennington rd E3 |
| 34 D 1 | Wensley av Wdfd Grn |
| 18 M 19 | Wensley rd N18 |
| 35 S 5 | Wensleydale av Ilf |
| 100 K 18 | Wensleydale gdns Hampt |
| 100 J 17 | Wensleydale rd Hampt |
| 111 Y 4 | Wentland clo SE6 |
| 111 Y 5 | Wentland rd SE6 |
| 27 Z 1 | Wentworth av N3 |
| 14 M 20 | Wentworth av N3 |
| 119 W 17 | Wentworth clo Mrdn |
| 99 V 17 | Wentworth dri Drtfrd |

| Ref | Name |
|---|---|
| 42 M 3 | Wentworth hill Wemb |
| 43 N 3 | Wentworth hill Wemb |
| 27 Z 2 | Wentworth pk N3 |
| 53 N 14 | Wentworth rd E12 |
| 27 V 19 | Wentworth rd NW11 |
| 4 D 11 | Wentworth rd Brentf |
| 122 F 18 | Wentworth rd Croy |
| 143 P 3 | Wentworth st E1 |
| 22 A 13 | Wentworth way Pinn |
| 98 F 4 | Wenvoe av Bxly Hth |
| 63 X 11 | Wenwith pl E3 |
| 144 M 17 | Werley av SW6 |
| 24 E 3 | Wernborough rd Stanm |
| 79 P 15 | Wernbrook st SE18 |
| 123 X 10 | Werndee rd SE25 |
| 35 V 10 | Werneth Hall rd Ilf |
| 132 D 10 | Werrington st NW1 |
| 87 R 11 | Werter rd SW15 |
| 61 X 8 | Wesley av NW10 |
| 82 D 4 | Wesley av Hounsl |
| 41 N 6 | Wesley clo Harrow |
| 51 U 2 | Wesley rd E10 |
| 61 X 3 | Wesley rd NW10 |
| 100 V 1 | Wesley st W1 |
| 47 R 12 | Wesleyan pl NW5 |
| 119 Z 5 | Wessex av SW19 |
| 99 S 3 | Wessex dri Erith |
| 45 S 3 | Wessex gdns NW11 |
| 63 P 10 | Wessex st E2 |
| 45 S 2 | Wessex way NW11 |
| 63 R 17 | West Arbour st E1 |
| 33 R 15 | West av E17 |
| 27 O 15 | West av NW4 |
| 14 L 19 | West av N3 |
| 22 D 19 | West av Pinn |
| 58 D 19 | West av S'hall |
| 56 B 12 | West av Wallgtn |
| 33 P 14 | West Avenue rd E17 |
| 49 S 2 | West bank N16 |
| 66 M 3 | West bank Bark |
| 118 L 9 | West Barnes la New Mald |
| 30 G 9 | West Beech rd N22 |
| 140 K 4 | West Central st WC1 |
| 22 A 4 | West chantry Harrow |
| 18 H 11 | West clo N9 |
| 5 B 16 | West clo Barnt |
| 59 N 6 | West clo Grnfd |
| 43 N 4 | West clo Wemb |
| 45 Y 15 | West cotts NW6 |
| 145 T 6 | West Cromwell rd SW5 |
| 14 L 20 | West ct N3 |
| 42 D 8 | West ct Wemb |
| 42 M 4 | West ct Wemb |
| 107 U 9 | West drive SW16 |
| 10 C 19 | West drive Harrow |
| 153 P 19 | West drive Sutton |
| 10 C 20 | West Drive gdns Harrow |
| 147 S 4 | West Eaton pl SW1 |
| 62 A 1 | West Ella rd NW10 |
| 33 W 16 | West End av E10 |
| 22 A 13 | West End av Pinn |
| 45 Z 15 | West End la NW6 |
| 129 V 4 | West End la NW6 |
| 45 Z 20 | West End la NW6 |
| 4 C 14 | West End la Barnt |
| 22 A 15 | West End la Pinn |
| 70 B 2 | West End rd S'hall |
| 76 D 12 | West Ferry rd E14 |
| 143 Z 10 | West gdns E1 |
| 68 N 20 | West gdns E1 |
| 106 J 15 | West gdns SW17 |
| 31 P 14 | West Green rd N15 |
| 30 K 13 | West Green rd N15 |
| 21 Z 17 | West gro Wdfd Grn |
| 147 S 1 | West Halkin st SW1 |
| 85 S 3 | West Hall rd Rich |
| 113 P 1 | West hallowes SE9 |
| 64 M 2 | West Ham la E15 |
| 65 R 1 | West Ham park E15 |
| 45 Z 19 | West Hampstead ms NW6 |
| 141 T 5 | West Harding st EC4 |
| 45 Y 5 | West Heath av NW11 |
| 45 Y 9 | West Heath clo NW3 |
| 99 U 16 | West Heath clo Drtfrd |
| 45 Y 4 | West Heath dri NW11 |
| 45 Y 8 | West Heath gdns NW3 |
| 45 Y 7 | West Heath rd NW3 |
| 46 B 9 | West Heath rd NW3 |
| 80 H 17 | West Heath rd SE2 |
| 99 U 16 | West Heath rd Drtfrd |

| | | |
|---|---|---|
| 87 P 18 | West hill SW15 |
| 41 S 6 | West hill Harrow |
| 157 S 19 | West hill S Croy |
| 43 O 4 | West hill Wemb |
| 42 M 4 | West hill Wemb |
| 87 W 16 | West Hill rd SW18 |
| 15 N 6 | West Hill way N20 |
| 98 L 1 | West holme Erith |
| 64 A 20 | West India Dock rd E14 |
| 143 W 19 | West la SE16 |
| 73 P 3 | West Lodge av W3 |
| 137 V 12 | West mall W8 |
| 152 B 14 | West mead Epsom |
| 111 U 18 | West Moat clo Beckhm |
| 147 Z 8 | West ms SW1 |
| 111 W 20 | West oak Beckhm |
| 113 R 2 | West park SE9 |
| 85 R 2 | West Park av Rich |
| 37 X 16 | West Park clo Rom |
| 85 R 1 | West Park gdns Rich |
| 85 P 3 | West Park rd Rich |
| 104 L 12 | West pl SW19 |
| 141 W 2 | West Poultry av EC1 |
| 65 R 3 | West rd E15 |
| 31 Z 1 | West rd N17 |
| 18 M 20 | West rd N17 |
| 85 W 6 | West rd SW14 |
| 147 R 12 | West rd SW3 |
| 89 Z 12 | West rd SW4 |
| 60 J 14 | West rd W5 |
| 16 B 5 | West rd Barnt |
| 103 W 20 | West rd Kingst |
| 37 X 17 | West rd Rom |
| 56 M 3 | West rd Rom |
| 58 M 6 | West Ridge gdns Grnfd |
| 128 J 17 | West row W10 |
| 84 L 10 | West Sheen vale Rich |
| 105 N 15 | West Side comm SW19 |
| 104 M 13 | West Side comm SW19 |
| 141 X 2 | West smithfield EC1 |
| 149 W 3 | West sq SE11 |
| 51 Z 8 | West st E11 |
| 33 R 16 | West st E17 |
| 140 H 7 | West st WC2 |
| 72 D 18 | West st Brentf |
| 126 E 2 | West st Brom |
| 98 A 9 | West st Bxly Hth |
| 154 L 9 | West st Carsh |
| 156 M 7 | West st Croy |
| 41 S 4 | West st Harrow |
| 154 A 11 | West st Sutton |
| 154 M 8 | West St la Carsh |
| 85 T 12 | West Temple sheen SW14 |
| 143 O 7 | West Tenter st E1 |
| 26 M 15 | West view NW4 |
| 18 D 3 | West View cres N9 |
| 147 Z 8 | West Warwick pl SW1 |
| 43 Z 10 | West way NW10 |
| 62 G 19 | West way W12 |
| 12 G 19 | West way Edg |
| 82 D 1 | West way Hounsl |
| 125 Y 15 | West way W Wkhm |
| 158 G 2 | West Way gdns Croy |
| 60 J 15 | West wlk W5 |
| 16 B 4 | West wlk Barnt |
| 100 M 15 | Westbank rd Hampt |
| 11 U 15 | Westbere dri Stanm |
| 45 T 14 | Westbere rd NW2 |
| 61 X 18 | Westbourne av W3 |
| 153 S 1 | Westbourne av Sutton |
| 138 E 8 | Westbourne cres W2 |
| 110 E 3 | Westbourne dri SE23 |
| 137 X 4 | Westbourne gdns W2 |
| 137 W 6 | Westbourne gro W2 |
| 98 G 11 | Westbourne gro Bxly Hth |
| 137 T 7 | Westbourne Gro ms W11 |
| 137 X 5 | Westbourne Gro ter W2 |
| 137 X 5 | Westbourne Pk ms W2 |
| 137 R 4 | Westbourne Pk rd W11 |
| 137 X 4 | Westbourne Pk rd W2 |
| 137 W 3 | Westbourne Pk vlls W2 |
| 19 N 11 | Westbourne pl N9 |
| 48 D 17 | Westbourne rd N7 |
| 110 E 14 | Westbourne rd SE26 |
| 123 V 15 | Westbourne rd Croy |
| 138 G 9 | Westbourne st W2 |
| 138 A 3 | Westbourne ter W2 |
| 138 A 1 | Westbourne ter W2 |
| 138 C 5 | Westbourne Ter ms W2 |
| 88 H 2 | Westbridge rd SW11 |
| 146 J 20 | Westbridge rd SW11 |
| 100 E 17 | Westbrook av Hampt |
| 5 U 11 | Westbrook clo Barnt |
| 5 T 12 | Westbrook cres Barnt |
| 94 H 2 | Westbrook rd SE3 |
| 70 E 19 | Westbrook rd Hounsl |
| 123 O 2 | Westbrook rd Thntn Hth |
| 5 T 11 | Westbrook sq Barnt |
| 97 T 6 | Westbrooke cres Welling |
| 114 F 5 | Westbrooke rd Sidcp |
| 97 T 7 | Westbrooke rd Welling |
| 32 M 12 | Westbury E17 |
| 30 L 6 | Westbury av N22 |
| 30 H 10 | Westbury av N22 |
| 58 G 12 | Westbury av S'hall |
| 42 K 20 | Westbury av Wemb |
| 14 L 18 | Westbury gro N3 |
| 21 Y 7 | Westbury la Buck Hl |
| 72 G 15 | Westbury pl Brentf |
| 33 N 13 | Westbury rd E17 |
| 52 J 16 | Westbury rd E7 |
| 44 A 20 | Westbury rd NW10 |
| 17 N 19 | Westbury rd N11 |
| 14 M 17 | Westbury rd N12 |
| 124 E 1 | Westbury rd SE20 |
| 60 J 18 | Westbury rd W5 |
| 67 S 3 | Westbury rd Bark |
| 124 J 6 | Westbury rd Becknhm |
| 127 O 1 | Westbury rd Brom |
| 21 Y 6 | Westbury rd Buck Hl |
| 113 O 20 | Westbury rd Chisl |
| 123 O 15 | Westbury rd Croy |
| 100 A 2 | Westbury rd Felt |
| 53 V 7 | Westbury rd Ilf |
| 117 Z 11 | Westbury rd New Mald |
| 42 K 20 | Westbury rd Wemb |
| 89 V 4 | Westbury st SW8 |
| 52 J 17 | Westbury ter E7 |
| 27 O 10 | Westchester dri NW4 |
| 118 E 1 | Westcombe av SW20 |
| 122 B 16 | Westcombe av Croy |
| 4 L 17 | Westcombe dri Barnt |
| 77 T 18 | Westcombe hill SE3 |
| 77 T 14 | Westcombe hill SE7 |
| 77 N 15 | Westcombe Pk rd SE10 |
| 77 R 18 | Westcombe Pk rd SE3 |
| 107 V 13 | Westcote rd SW16 |
| 159 T 19 | Westcott clo Croy |
| 59 U 16 | Westcott cres W7 |
| 149 X 12 | Westcott rd SE17 |
| 45 S 12 | Westcroft clo NW2 |
| 119 U 8 | Westcroft gdns Mrdn |
| 155 P 8 | Westcroft rd Carsh |
| 74 F 11 | Westcroft sq W6 |
| 45 S 12 | Westcroft way NW2 |
| 58 M 17 | Westdale pas SE18 |
| 78 M 16 | Westdale rd SE18 |
| 112 K 2 | Westdean av SE12 |
| 51 U 12 | Westdown rd E15 |
| 93 N 19 | Westdown rd SE6 |
| 77 S 14 | Westerdale rd SE10 |
| 31 T 15 | Westerfield rd N15 |
| 18 D 11 | Westerham av N9 |
| 97 S 15 | Westerham dri Sidcp |
| 33 S 20 | Westerham rd E10 |
| 110 L 11 | Westerly cres SE26 |
| 27 R 19 | Western av NW11 |
| 62 B 19 | Western av N3 |
| 61 U 13 | Western av W3 |
| 60 F 8 | Western av W5 |
| 56 L 17 | Western av Dgnhm |
| 57 N 17 | Western av Dgnhm |
| 58 F 3 | Western av Grnfd |
| 59 S 7 | Western av Grnfd |
| 60 F 8 | Western av Grnfd |
| 70 D 1 | Western av Shall |
| 137 V 2 | Western Av extension W2 |
| 14 M 20 | Western ct N3 |
| 14 M 20 | Western ct N3 |
| 61 O 19 | Western gdns W5 |
| 129 R 19 | Western ms W9 |
| 65 X 5 | Western rd E13 |
| 33 U 16 | Western rd E17 |
| 28 L 12 | Western rd N2 |
| 27 L 12 | Western rd N2 |
| 30 C 9 | Western rd N22 |
| 90 G 8 | Western rd SW9 |
| 72 H 1 | Western rd W5 |
| 60 H 20 | Western rd W5 |
| 120 J 2 | Western rd Mitch |
| 39 S 15 | Western rd Rom |
| 70 B 8 | Western rd S'hall |
| 153 X 12 | Western rd Sutton |
| 51 W 19 | Western st E15 |
| 74 E 14 | Western ter W6 |
| 14 M 1 | Western way N20 |
| 36 B 20 | Westernville gdns Ilf |
| 9 V 11 | Westfield clo Enf |
| 153 U 8 | Westfield clo Sutton |
| 24 H 14 | Westfield dri Harrow |
| 24 G 13 | Westfield gdns Harrow |
| 24 G 13 | Westfield la Harrow |
| 22 E 1 | Westfield pk Pinn |
| 12 M 11 | Westfield rd NW7 |
| 30 B 14 | Westfield rd N8 |
| 71 Z 3 | Westfield rd W13 |
| 72 A 4 | Westfield rd W13 |
| 124 L 3 | Westfield rd Becknhm |
| 98 L 7 | Westfield rd Bxly Hth |
| 156 J 3 | Westfield rd Croy |
| 123 A 12 | Westfield rd Dgnhm |
| 120 K 4 | Westfield rd Mitch |
| 116 F 13 | Westfield rd Surb |
| 153 U 8 | Westfield rd Sutton |
| 78 B 9 | Westfield st SE18 |
| 86 D 7 | Westfields SW13 |
| 86 C 7 | Westfields av SW13 |
| 61 U 15 | Westfields rd W3 |
| 128 J 17 | Westgate ms SW1 |
| 80 L 15 | Westgate rd SE2 |
| 123 Z 9 | Westgate rd SE25 |
| 124 A 9 | Westgate rd SE25 |
| 111 T 19 | Westgate rd Becknhm |
| 125 S 2 | Westgate rd Becknhm |
| 135 X 3 | Westgate st E8 |
| 145 Y 12 | Westgate ter SW10 |
| 93 W 2 | Westgrove la SE10 |
| 149 Z 19 | Westhall rd SE5 |
| 85 U 12 | Westhay gdns SW14 |
| 28 A 14 | Westholm NW11 |
| 94 G 17 | Westhorne av SE12 |
| 95 P 12 | Westhorne av SE9 |
| 87 N 8 | Westhorpe rd SW15 |
| 105 S 1 | Westhouse clo SW20 |
| 114 A 12 | Westhurst dri Chisl |
| 17 T 11 | Westlake clo N13 |
| 72 R 12 | Westlake rd SE16 |
| 134 D 12 | Westland pl N1 |
| 89 U 17 | Westlands ter SW12 |
| 71 X 8 | Westlea rd W7 |
| 86 L 14 | Westleigh av SW15 |
| 85 O 15 | Westleigh av SW15 |
| 127 R 2 | Westleigh dri Brom |
| 25 P 6 | Westleigh gdns Edg |
| 86 J 17 | Westmead SW15 |
| 154 H 9 | Westmead rd Sutton |
| 12 K 10 | Westmere dri NW7 |
| 140 J 20 | Westminster abbey SW1 |
| 122 H 2 | Westminster av Thntn Hth |
| 140 L 18 | Westminster br SW1 |
| 141 P 19 | Westminster Br rd SE1 |
| 148 B 3 | Westminster cathedral SW1 |
| 101 X 12 | Westminster clo Tedd |
| 17 N 17 | Westminster dri N13 |
| 67 U 7 | Westminster gdns Bark |
| 36 D 8 | Westminster gdns Ilf |
| 19 N 6 | Westminster rd N9 |
| 71 U 4 | Westminster rd W7 |
| 154 E 1 | Westminster rd Sutton |
| 9 T 8 | Westmoor gdns Enf |
| 9 S 9 | Westmoor rd Enf |
| 78 A 10 | Westmoor st SE7 |
| 96 H 9 | Westmoreland av Welling |
| 84 B 15 | Westmoreland clo Twick |
| 137 S 4 | Westmoreland ms W2 |
| 147 Y 11 | Westmoreland pl SW1 |
| 33 O 19 | Westmoreland rd E17 |
| 25 N 11 | Westmoreland rd NW9 |
| 86 F 2 | Westmoreland rd SW13 |
| 126 B 10 | Westmoreland rd Brom |
| 139 W 1 | Westmoreland st W W1 |
| 147 Y 11 | Westmoreland ter SW 1 |
| 22 L 16 | Westmorland rd Harrow |
| 121 Z 10 | Westmorland way Mitch |
| 95 W 10 | Westmount rd SE9 |
| 19 N 10 | Westoe rd N9 |
| 55 N 15 | Weston dri Bark |
| 24 C 5 | Weston dri Stanm |
| 83 R 3 | Weston gdns Islwth |
| 56 A 11 | Weston grn Dgnhm |
| 112 D 19 | Weston gro Brom |
| 89 O 18 | Weston la SW2 |
| 30 C 17 | Weston pk N8 |
| 73 U 9 | Weston rd W4 |
| 112 D 19 | Weston rd Brom |
| 55 Z 11 | Weston rd Dgnhm |
| 8 C 8 | Weston rd Enf |
| 133 O 11 | Weston rise WC1 |
| 150 G 3 | Weston st SE1 |
| 142 H 17 | Weston st SE1 |
| 142 H 15 | Weston st SE1 |
| 135 Z 1 | Weston wlk E9 |
| 88 E 17 | Westover rd SW18 |
| 109 T 15 | Westow hill SE19 |
| 109 T 17 | Westow st SE19 |
| 6 F 15 | Westpole av Barnt |
| 63 T 17 | Westport rd E1 |
| 65 V 13 | Westport rd E1 |
| 63 T 17 | Westport rd E1 |
| 65 V 13 | Westport rd E13 |
| 54 M 14 | Westrow dri Bark |
| 54 K 19 | Westrow dri Bark |
| 54 L 9 | Westrow gdns Ilf |
| 26 H 6 | Westside NW4 |
| 44 C 14 | Westview clo NW10 |
| 35 N 6 | Westview dri Wdfd Grn |
| 74 G 6 | Westville rd W12 |
| 20 A 18 | Westward rd E4 |
| 19 Y 18 | Westward rd E4 |
| 24 K 19 | Westward way Harrow |
| 118 K 7 | Westway SW20 |
| 136 B 7 | Westway W12 |
| 118 K 6 | Westway clo SW20 |
| 152 E 8 | Westways Epsom |
| 107 Z 15 | Westwell rd SW16 |
| 136 E 19 | Westwick gdns W14 |
| 109 N 19 | Westwood av SW19 |
| 40 L 12 | Westwood av Harrow |
| 86 D 8 | Westwood gdns SW13 |
| 110 B 10 | Westwood hill SE26 |
| 96 L 10 | Westwood la Welling |
| 97 N 13 | Westwood la Welling |
| 110 B 1 | Westwood pk SE23 |
| 92 A 19 | Westwood pk SE23 |
| 77 V 3 | Westwood rd E16 |
| 86 D 8 | Westwood rd SW13 |
| 54 L 4 | Westwood rd Ilf |
| 24 D 6 | Wetheral dri Stanm |
| 40 J 17 | Wetherby clo Grnfd |
| 146 A 8 | Wetherby gdns SW5 |
| 145 Y 9 | Wetherby ms SW5 |
| 146 B 7 | Wetherby pl SW7 |
| 7 Z 14 | Wetherby rd Enf |
| 50 L 1 | Wetherden st E17 |
| 63 T 3 | Wetherill rd E9 |
| 29 P 4 | Wetherill rd N10 |
| 88 L 19 | Wexford rd SW12 |
| 106 C 6 | Weybourne st SW18 |
| 122 G 10 | Weybridge rd Thntn Hth |
| 105 S 2 | Weydown clo SW19 |
| 56 B 10 | Weylond rd Dgnhm |
| 94 M 2 | Weyman rd SE3 |
| 13 O 15 | Weymouth av NW7 |
| 72 E 8 | Weymouth av W5 |
| 153 Z 16 | Weymouth ct Sutton |
| 139 X 1 | Weymouth ms W1 |
| 135 O 8 | Weymouth pl E2 |
| 139 W 1 | Weymouth st W1 |
| 131 X 20 | Weymouth st W1 |
| 135 O 9 | Weymouth ter E2 |
| 10 L 20 | Weymouth wlk Stanm |
| 48 F 7 | Whadcoat st N4 |
| 38 A 18 | Whalebone av Rom |
| 142 F 4 | Whalebone ct EC2 |
| 38 A 18 | Whalebone gro Rom |
| 64 M 1 | Whalebone la E15 |
| 37 Y 3 | Whalebone la N Rom |
| 38 A 7 | Whalebone la N Rom |
| 56 B 3 | Whalebone la S Dgnhm |
| 38 A 17 | Whalebone la S Rom |

01 Y2 Wharf la Twick
35 U7 Wharf pl E2
64 J3 Wharf rd E15
34 A9 Wharf rd N1
34 B11 Wharf rd N1
19 V1 Wharf rd N9
9 W18 Wharf rd Enf
64 L15 Wharf st E16
32 L8 Wharfdale rd N1
22 P13 Wharfedale gdns Thntn Hth
45 X11 Wharfedale st SW10
71 P2 Wharncliffe dri S'hall
23 R4 Wharncliffe gdns SE25
23 R4 Wharncliffe rd SE25
63 R8 Wharncliffe st E2
26 H1 Wharton rd Brom
33 P13 Wharton st WC1
10 F17 Whateley rd SE20
91 U13 Whateley rd SE22
19 R5 Whatley av SW20
92 G19 Whatman rd SE23
9 U7 Wheatfields Enf
9 U8 Wheatfields Enf
23 Z5 Wheathill rd SE20
24 A6 Wheathill rd SE20
90 H17 Wheatlands Hounsl
107 O7 Wheatlands SW17
18 C9 Wheatley gdns N9
83 V7 Wheatley rd Islwth
23 V1 Wheatley st W1
148 K17 Wheatsheaf la SW8
39 T18 Wheatsheaf rd Rom
39 T19 Wheatsheaf rd Rom
145 R20 Wheatsheaf ter SW6
28 L20 Wheatstone rd W10
56 K9 Wheel Farm dri Dgnhm
48 C20 Wheelwright st N7
135 N18 Wheler st E1
74 A7 Whellock rd W4
15 S8 Whetstone clo N20
141 O3 Whetstone pk WC2
94 L4 Whetstone rd SE3
48 A7 Whewell rd W4
132 K13 Whidborne st WC1
107 X11 Whinfell clo SW16
95 R8 Whinyates rd SE9
33 W15 Whipps cross E17
34 B18 Whipps Cross rd E11
33 X10 Whipps Cross rd E11
133 U14 Whiskin st EC1
25 N7 Whistler gdns Edg
48 H14 Whistler st N5
135 S8 Whiston rd E2
134 M7 Whiston rd N1
92 K11 Whitbread rd SE4
93 S11 Whitburn rd SE13
81 S8 Whitby av NW10
25 R10 Whitby gdns NW9
154 F1 Whitby gdns Sutton
40 M10 Whitby rd Harrow
41 N10 Whitby rd Harrow
134 F2 Whitby rd Sutton
135 N18 Whitby st E1
47 V19 Whitcher pl NW1
24 M2 Whitchurch av Edg
11 Z19 Whitchurch clo Edg
11 Z20 Whitchurch gdns Edg
24 K2 Whitchurch la Edg
12 B20 Whitchurch la Edg
140 G11 Whitcomb st WC2
103 P5 White Ash lodge Rich
133 T19 White Bear yd EC1
143 S4 White City la E1
62 L19 White City rd W12
136 A9 White City rd W12
136 B9 White City stadium W10
133 T7 White Conduit st N1
23 V2 White Ga gdns Harrow
56 D17 White gdns Dgnhm
142 J3 White Hart ct EC2
31 S1 White Hart la N17
30 J2 White Hart la N22
86 B6 White Hart la SW14
38 E4 White Hart la Rom
79 V11 White Hart rd SE18
142 F15 White Hart yd SE1
11 S14 White Ho dri Stanm
7 Z5 White Ho la Enf
113 V10 White Horse hill Chisl
63 T13 White Horse la E1
63 U17 White Horse rd E1
66 G8 White Horse rd E6
139 Y14 White Horse st W1
142 D3 White Horse yd EC2

142 M4 White Kennett st E1
142 H6 White Lion ct EC2
133 S9 White Lion st N1
139 Y8 White Lion yd W1
108 K17 White lodge SE19
103 V1 White lodge Rich
28 H19 White Lodge clo N2
123 V3 White Oak dri Becknhm
50 M19 White Post la E9
51 N19 White Post la E9
75 P19 White Post la SE15
52 A20 White rd E15
143 N2 White's row E1
89 Y10 White's sq SW4
69 S3 Whitebarn la Dgnhm
127 W15 Whitebeam av Brom
143 R3 Whitechapel High st E1
135 X20 Whitechapel rd E1
143 U2 Whitechapel rd E1
125 W8 Whitecote rd S'hall
125 W8 Whitecroft clo Becknhm
125 V9 Whitecroft way Becknhm
134 H20 Whitecross pl EC2
45 N2 Whitefield av NW2
112 A7 Whitefoot la Brom
112 B7 Whitefoot ter Brom
23 S8 Whitefriars av Harrow
23 S7 Whitefriars dri Harrow
141 U6 Whitefriars st EC4
140 J15 Whitehall SW1
140 K14 Whitehall ct SW1
20 L6 Whitehall gdns E4
140 K15 Whitehall gdns SW1
73 R3 Whitehall gdns W3
73 T16 Whitehall gdns W4
21 U8 Whitehall la Buck Hl
99 Y3 Whitehall la Erith
47 V3 Whitehall pk N19
73 T16 Whitehall Pk rd W4
140 K13 Whitehall pl SW1
155 R9 Whitehall pl Wallgtn
71 Y7 Whitehall rd W7
127 O10 Whitehall rd Brom
23 S20 Whitehall rd Harrow
122 F13 Whitehall rd Thntn Hth
21 O7 Whitehall rd Wdfd Grn
31 U2 Whitehall st N17
126 F3 Whitehart slip Brom
130 J19 Whitehaven st NW8
146 M8 Whitehead's gro SW3
99 W14 Whitehorse la SE25
123 P8 Whitehorse rd Croy
123 N13 Whitehorse rd Croy
16 E10 Whitehouse way N14
60 D17 Whiteledges W13
109 P12 Whiteley rd SE19
100 H7 Whiteley's way Felt
51 X17 Whiter wlk E15
36 G17 Whites av Ilf
142 L17 Whites grounds SE1
89 Y10 Whites sq SW4
72 E13 Whitestile rd Brentf
46 E9 Whitestone la NW3
158 A1 Whitethorn gdns Croy
8 A16 Whitethorn gdns Enf
64 B13 Whitethorn st E3
66 Z2 Whitfield rd E6
93 X3 Whitfield rd SE3
81 N18 Whitfield rd Bxly Hth
132 B18 Whitfield st W1
132 B18 Whitfield st W1
140 D1 Whitfield st W1
120 L6 Whitford gdns Mitch
156 L11 Whitgift av S Croy
156 M2 Whitgift sq Croy
149 N6 Whitgift st SE11
156 L5 Whitgift st Croy
67 N1 Whiting av Bark
4 A18 Whitings rd Barnt
154 G1 Whitland rd Carsh
31 T7 Whitley rd N17
47 W7 Whitley st N19
87 T20 Whitlock dri SW19
63 V10 Whitman rd E3
62 M6 Whitmore gdns NW10
128 C8 Whitmore gdns NW10
134 J8 Whitmore rd N1

40 M3 Whitmore rd Harrow
41 O2 Whitmore rd Harrow
87 O14 Whitnell way SW15
35 N12 Whitney av Ilf
51 P1 Whitney rd E10
53 O12 Whitta rd E12
34 G14 Whittaker av Rich
65 Z2 Whittaker rd E6
153 V5 Whittaker rd Sutton
147 S7 Whittaker st SW1
110 C8 Whittall gdns SE26
40 L15 Whittan av Grnfd
87 V2 Whittingstall rd SW6
142 J7 Whittington av EC3
17 O20 Whittington rd N22
30 A1 Whittington rd N22
92 B1 Whittington rd SE15
22 C16 Whittington way Pinn
58 K17 Whittle clo S'hall
155 N17 Whittlebury clo Carsh
22 M3 Whittlesea clo Harrow
22 M4 Whittlesea path Harrow
22 M3 Whittlesea rd Har
23 N4 Whittlesea rd Harrow
23 N3 Whittlesea rd Harrow
141 T15 Whittlesea rd SE1
41 W16 Whitton av East Grnfd
41 P16 Whitton av West Grnfd
42 B19 Whitton clo Grnfd
82 M14 Whitton dene Hounsl
83 T13 Whitton dene Islwth
41 Z17 Whitton dri Grnfd
83 O14 Whitton Manor rd Islwth
82 L12 Whitton rd Hounsl
83 T16 Whitton rd Twick
82 H18 Whitton ways Hounsl
65 S10 Whitwell rd E13
79 N11 Whitworth pl SE18
78 K18 Whitworth rd SE18
123 U8 Whitworth rd SE25
77 N13 Whitworth rd SE18
91 Y8 Whorlton rd SE15
30 G10 Whymark av N22
52 H18 Whyteville rd E7
50 E18 Wick rd E9
102 C19 Wick rd Tedd
143 V7 Wicker st E1
89 P7 Wickersley rd SW11
159 O11 Wicket the Croy
135 Z17 Wickford st E1
83 O11 Wickford st E1
158 H1 Wickham av Croy
153 O11 Wickham av Sutton
152 M10 Wickham av Sutton
125 X18 Wickham chase W Wkhm
126 A16 Wickham chase W Wkhm
9 O11 Wickham clo Enf
159 Y9 Wickham court W Wkhm
159 V2 Wickham cres W Wkhm
159 V2 Wickham Ct rd W Wkhm
92 L8 Wickham gdns SE4
80 B18 Wickham la SE2
79 Z15 Wickham la SE2
33 U1 Wickham rd E4
92 M6 Wickham rd SE4
93 N4 Wickham rd SE4
125 S5 Wickham rd Becknhm
158 F3 Wickham rd Croy
159 N1 Wickham rd Croy
23 R8 Wickham rd Harrow
149 O9 Wickham st SE11
96 M3 Wickham st Welling
97 P1 Wickham st Welling
125 T9 Wickham way Becknhm
27 T9 Wickliffe av N3
43 R6 Wickliffe gdns Wemb
132 M12 Wicklow st WC1
133 N12 Wicklow st WC1
90 K6 Wickwood st SE5
40 B7 Widdecombe av Harrow
48 C13 Widdenham rd N9
64 L1 Widdin st E15
121 X6 Wide way Mitch
35 R12 Widecombe gdns Ilf
113 S7 Widecombe rd SE9
28 F15 Widecombe way N2
142 L2 Widegate st E1

129 V15 Widley rd W9
127 O4 Widmore Lodge rd Brom
127 O3 Widmore rd Brom
127 O3 Widmore rd Brom
126 K2 Widmore rd Brom
43 R19 Wiggington av Wemb
30 G19 Wightman rd N4
100 A2 Wigley rd Felt
139 X4 Wigmore pl W1
154 H1 Wigmore rd Carsh
139 X4 Wigmore st W1
154 G2 Wigmore wlk Carsh
34 K18 Wigram rd E11
33 V9 Wigram sq E17
65 W11 Wigston rd E13
24 J5 Wigton gdns Stanm
149 T11 Wigton pl SE11
32 L5 Wigton rd E17
26 F19 Wilberforce rd NW9
48 H6 Wilberforce rd N4
105 O15 Wilberforce way SW19
147 R5 Wilbraham pl SW1
18 B17 Wilbury way N18
137 P12 Wilby ms W11
142 J16 Wilcox clo SW8
153 Z9 Wilcox rd Sutton
154 A8 Wilcox rd Sutton
101 R9 Wilcox rd Tedd
140 M5 Wild ct WC2
27 Z20 Wild hatch NW11
140 M6 Wild st WC2
150 H1 Wild's rents SE1
11 U20 Wildcroft gdns Edg
87 O17 Wildcroft rd SW15
87 N17 Wildcroft rd SW15
86 M20 Wildcroft rd SW15
113 Z18 Wilderness rd Chisl
100 K10 Wilderness the Hampt
48 T2 Wilderton rd N16
93 R18 Wildfell rd SE6
142 H20 Wilds rents SE1
46 C5 Wildwood gro NW3
46 C2 Wildwood rd NW11
28 C19 Wildwood rd NW11
46 E3 Wildwood ri NW11
122 M15 Wilford rd Croy
148 B1 Wilfred st SW1
61 V13 Wilfrid gdns W3
135 O19 Wilkes st E1
47 R17 Wilkin st NW5
106 E9 Wilkinson rd SW17
116 N20 Wilkinson st SW8
134 K9 Wilks pl N1
06 N10 Will Crooks gdns SE9
94 M10 Will Crooks gdns SE9
31 P8 Willan rd N17
89 S7 Willard st SW8
73 R3 Willcott rd W3
5 P20 Willenhall av Barnt
78 L15 Willenhall rd SE18
96 L19 Willersley av Sidcp
114 K2 Willersley av Sidcp
114 K1 Willersley clo Sidcp
45 O19 Willesden la NW6
128 M1 Willesden la NW6&NW2
129 R2 Willesden la NW6&NW2
122 F11 Willett pl Thntn Hth
122 F11 Willett rd Thntn Hth
47 S17 Willey's rd NW5
113 X5 William Barefoot dri SE9
38 L6 William clo Rom
140 J11 William lv st WC2
132 K10 William Morris clo E17
139 R18 William ms SW1
132 A15 William rd NW1
131 Z14 William rd NW1
105 T18 William rd SW19
154 E10 William rd Sutton
33 T19 William st E10
51 W19 William st E15
15 R15 William st N12
31 U1 William st N17
139 R18 William st SW1
54 A20 William st Bark
154 L5 William st Carsh
150 H9 William's gro SE17
71 Z1 William's rd W13
32 K5 Williams av E17
30 F5 Williams gro N22
85 V6 Williams la SW14
120 D12 Williams la Mrdn
70 B12 Williams rd S'hall
156 F13 Williams ter Croy

9 O 5 Wythburn pl W1
5 Y 15 Wythens wlk SE9
6 F 10 Wythenshawe rd Dgnhm
7 T 3 Wythes clo Brom
8 C 3 Wythes rd E16
5 T 15 Wythfield rd SE9
5 S 16 Wythfield rd SE9
0 M 11 Wyvenhoe rd Harrow
8 J 17 Wyvil est SW8
8 K 16 Wyvil rd SW8
4 E 14 Wyvis st E14

# Y

6 H 2 Yabsley st E14
1 R 5 Yainton way Blvdr
1 R 5 Yalding rd SE16
0 E 1 Yarborough rd SW19
3 W 3 Yarden st E1
3 W 4 Yarden st E1
3 S 14 Yardley st WC1
9 X 14 Yarmouth ms W1
0 II 0 Yarnton way Belvdr
0 B 5 Yeading av Harrow
2 G 16 Yeading wlk Har
9 N 19 Yeatman rd N6
4 E 10 Yeldham rd W6
8 G 5 Yelverton rd SW11
4 C 14 Yeo st E3
6 V 11 Yeoman st SE8
3 S 14 Yeomans ms Islwth
3 P 8 Yeomans yd E1
6 L 3 Yeomans' row SW3
7 Y 9 Yerbury rd N19
3 S 19 Yester dri Chisl
3 U 16 Yester pk Chisl
3 U 17 Yester rd Chisl
5 R 13 Yew gro NW2
7 T 4 Yew Tree clo N21
7 N 3 Yew Tree clo Welling
8 B 19 Yew Tree clo Worc Pk
47 Z 15 Yew Tree gdns Rom
2 F 20 Yew Tree rd W12
8 K 20 Yew Tree way Croy
2 E 13 Yew Tree wlk Hounsl
1 S 3 Yew wlk Harrow
2 A 16 Yewdale clo Brom
4 D 19 Yewfield rd NW10
4 K 5 Yewtree rd Becknhm
9 P 6 Yoakley rd N16
5 R 13 Yolande gdns SE9
8 F 8 Yong pk N4
5 W 12 York av SW14
1 U 2 York av W7
4 J 4 York av Sidcp
4 B 6 York av Stanm
0 L 11 York bldgs WC2
1 U 2 York clo W7
9 Z 9 York clo Mrdn
1 U 10 York ga NW1
6 M 2 York gate N14
2 C 2 York gro SE15
8 J 5 York Hill se27 SE27
7 X 17 York Ho pl W8
7 T 15 York ms NW5
8 E 7 York pl SW11
0 K 11 York pl WC2
1 T 2 York pl W7
1 T 9 York rd E10
2 F 17 York rd E17
9 Z 18 York rd E4
2 E 19 York rd E7
6 E 20 York rd NW9
6 L 19 York rd N11
6 M 2 York rd N14
8 M 17 York rd N18
8 B 3 York rd N21
1 F 16 York rd SE1
8 E 8 York rd SW11
6 B 15 York rd SW19
1 X 16 York rd W3
2 E 9 York rd W5
5 S 16 York rd Barnt
2 G 15 York rd Brentf
2 F 16 York rd Croy
2 K 8 York rd Hounsl
3 X 8 York rd Ilf
3 N 19 York rd Kingst
4 M 13 York rd Rich
3 X 16 York rd Sutton
1 T 10 York rd Tedd
7 S 10 York ri NW5
4 M 8 York row E2
3 V 18 York sq E14
3 Z 20 York st Twick
9 R 1 York st W1
7 N 4 York st Bark

121 O 18 York st Mitch
131 T 18 York ter NW1
7 Z 3 York ter Enf
98 J 1 York ter Erith
131 T 17 York Ter east NW1
131 T 17 York Ter west NW1
132 K 4 York way N1
15 Y 10 York way N20
47 Z 19 York way N7
100 D 7 York way Felt
96 J 8 Yorkland av Welling
18 M 17 Yorkshire gdns N18
49 T 10 Yorkshire gro N16
63 V 17 Yorkshire rd E14
112 A 9 Yorkshire rd Mitch
122 A 9 Yorkshire rd Mitch
121 Z 10 Yorkshire rd Mitch
135 R 9 Yorkton st E2
137 Y 19 Young st W8
7 Z 6 Youngmans clo Enf
36 D 17 Youngs rd Ilf
36 B 18 Yoxley appr Ilf
36 B 18 Yoxley dri Ilf
89 S 18 Yukon rd SW12
44 A 19 Yuletide rd NW10

# Z

75 P 14 Zampa rd SE16
95 P 2 Zangwill rd SE3
63 V 6 Zealand rd E3
89 T 20 Zennor rd SW12
91 U 10 Zenoria st SE22
122 L 10 Zermatt rd Thntn Hth
64 F 14 Zetland st E14
123 O 10 Zion pl Thntn Hth
123 O 10 Zion rd Thntn Hth
141 Z 13 Zoar st SE1
47 Y 6 Zoffany st N19

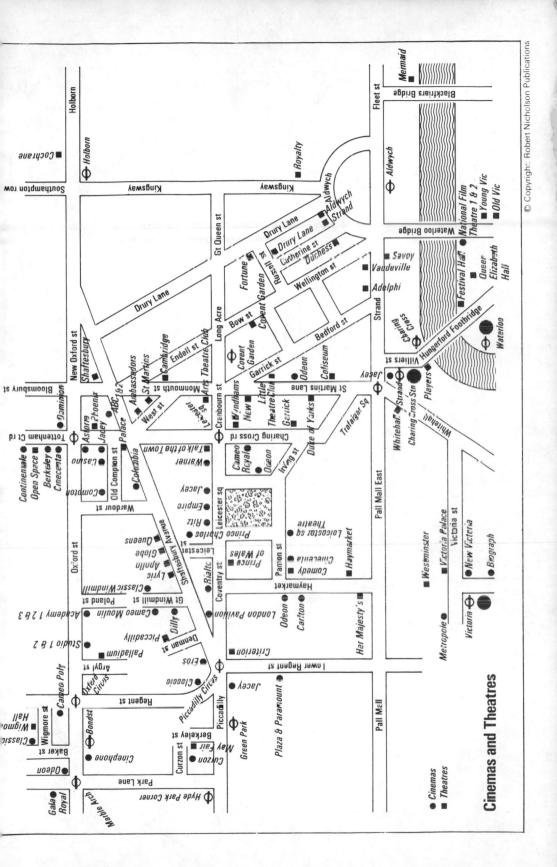

**Cinemas and Theatres**

● Cinemas
■ Theatres

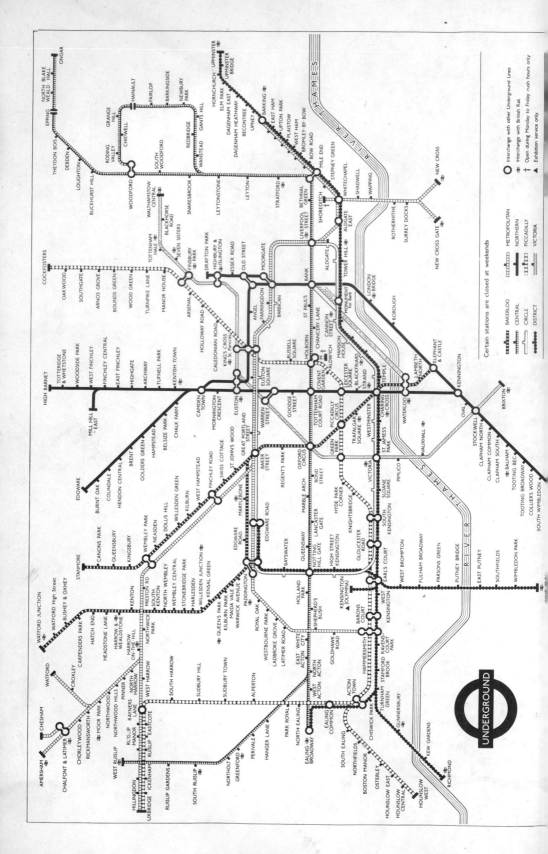